D0554821

LONELY PLANET'S

BEST PLACES TO EAT IN EVERY COUNTRY

Over 2000 Recommendations from the World's Leading Travel Authority

CONTENTS

ASIA

OCEANIA

3

INTRODUCTION

This book is the result of hundreds of thousands of mediocre meals, eaten the world over in the name of research. You'll be pleased to hear that none of these has made it into these pages, however. Instead this is a collection of the sublime – a distillation of notes taken, streets pounded, blogs scoured, locals interrogated, and, yes, bad meals eaten, by Lonely Planet travel writers in search of what they know and recognise to be a trip-defining food experience. We're talking that blink-and-you'll-miss-it wine bar in Paris serving the most exquisite charcuterie, the beach taco joint in Baja California dishing up the freshest and tangiest ceviche, or indeed the Michelin-starred restaurant in Thailand pushing new and delicious boundaries of texture and flavour. These are the types of places we enthusiastically tell our friends about when we get home, and last in our memories as moments of quiet joy.

It was moments like these that inspired us to create this book. We know that amazing food can make us fall for a place and culture as much as any great sunset, but that the risk of not eating well is high, pretty much everywhere. We have created this book, therefore, as a comprehensive resource and insurance for fabulous dining the world over. In it you will find our travel writers' top choices for eating in every country in the world – from Azerbaijan to Zimbabwe, and literally everywhere in between.

Our book is a little different to other Best Restaurants lists. We find that great food does not always mean fine dining, and also that the atmosphere of a place is integral to the experience. Our picks therefore run the gamut from Michelin-starred restaurants and neighbourhood favourites, to buzzing cafes, canteens, food trucks, ice cream parlours, bakeries and more. You'll find inspiration here whatever your budget and preferred style of dining.

Within the listings we have been sure to feature cuisine that is authentic and native to that country; after all, homegrown produce and dishes teach us so much about the history, climate and culture of a place. For each country profile we have given an introduction to the food scene and, in the What to Eat section, some advice on dishes you might like to order at least once. This doesn't mean we have forgotten a country's delectable imports, however. We have listed Japanese restaurants in Melbourne and French restaurants in Gabon.

Above all we hope this book works as a window to the world's cuisine. While you may not be booking a trip to Mongolia right now, we hope that discovering where locals in Ulaanbaatur like to dine on special occasions, or the best market booth to sit at if you're ever in Vanuatu is inspiring nonetheless. And maybe it will be the spark that leads to that dream trip in years to come.

'Each dish and drink has a story to tell, promising you an exciting journey on a plate (and in a glass)!'
The Bombay Canteen, Mumbai

AM

ERICAS

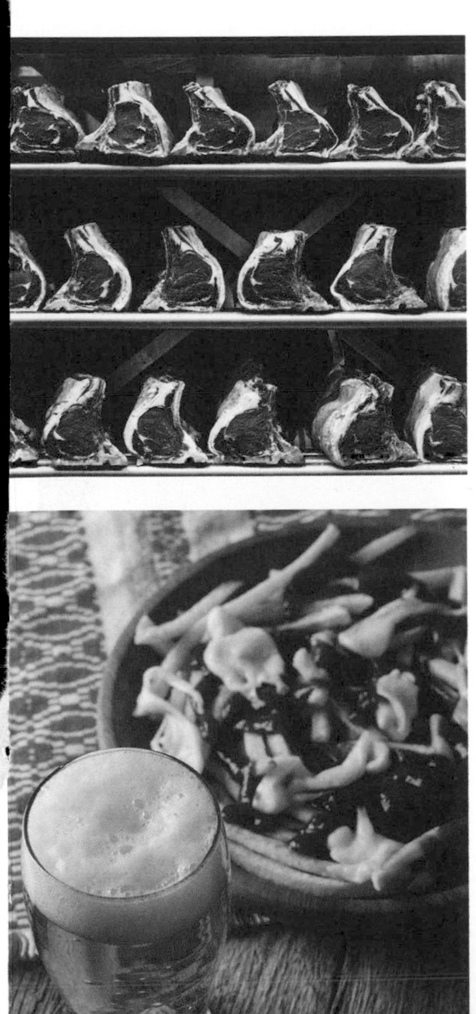

CANADA

Canadian cuisine is nothing if not eclectic, a casserole of food cultures blended through centuries of immigration. You'll find discernable French flavours in Québec, chopstick-friendly Asian bowls in Vancouver, Ukrainian-style perogies on the Prairies and crustaceans in the Maritimes. Backing it up is a multifarious coast-to-coast larder of unique ingredients grown, foraged and produced within shouting distance of Canadian kitchens.

WHAT TO EAT

Poutine
Canada's artery-clogging national dish hails from Québec and consists of French fries topped with cheese curds and gravy.

Maple syrup
A super-sweet flavoring of choice that's found on everything from beavertails (fried, sugared dough), breakfast pancakes the size of Frisbees, and sweetened cuts of BC salmon.

Alberta steak
Charred on the outside, pink and succulent in the middle.

Nanaimo bars
A small three-layered slab of wafer topped with cream and icing that's intensely sweet and heavy on calories.

Lobster
The main dish of the Maritime provinces is usually boiled in a pot and served with a little butter.

PRICE RANGES
$ less than $15
$$ $15–25
$$$ $25 or more

Tipping: 15–20%

JAM CAFÉ

VICTORIA | $$ | BREAKFAST
542 Herald St; 778-440-4489; www.jamcafes.com; breakfast $13-17

No need to conduct an opinion poll: the perennial lines in the street outside Jam suggest that this is the best breakfast spot in Victoria. The reasons? Tasteful vintage decor (if you'll excuse them the moose's head); fast, discreet service; and the kind of creative breakfast dishes that you'd never have the energy or ingenuity to cook yourself. Jam classics include the 'cracker jack' (a banana-and-nutella brioche sandwich), the 'three pigs' (sausages fried in pancake batter).

PUREBREAD

WHISTLER | $ | BAKERY
4338 Main St; 604-962-1182; www.purebread-ca; baked goods $3-8

Imagine the best bakery you've ever visited, elevate the quality by the power of 10 and you might just get Purebread. It's hard to overstate the ambrosial perfection of this small but crowded café's melt-in-your-mouth scones, wonderfully stodgy cakes and doorstep-sized sandwiches. Rather like a Whistler 'black diamond,' it will remain etched in your memory long after you leave.

VIJ'S

VANCOUVER | $$$ | INDIAN
3106 Cambie St, Cambie Village; 604-736-6664; www.vijs.ca; mains $23-36

Spicy aromas scent the air as you enter this warmly intimate dining space for Vancouver's finest Indian cuisine. Exemplary servers happily answer menu questions, while bringing over snacks and chai tea. There's a one-page array of tempting dishes but the trick is to order three or four to share (orders come with rice and naan). Alongside popular meat dishes (including near-legendary lamb popsicles), there's an excellent array of vegetarian options.

KLONDIKE RIB & SALMON

WHITEHORSE | $$ | CANADIAN
2116 2nd Ave; 867-667-7554; www.klondikerib.com; mains from $14

The food is superb at this sprawling casual half-tent restaurant in a place originally opened as a tent-frame bakery in 1900. Besides the namesakes (the salmon skewers and smoked pork ribs are tops), there are other local faves. Great place to try bison steak or Yukon Arctic char. It's half-tent, so closed when winter temperatures turn up.

DUCHESS BAKE SHOP

EDMONTON | $ | BAKERY/CAFÉ
10720 124th St; 780-488-4999; www.duchessbakeshop.com; baked goods from $2, breakfast & lunch $8-13

Duchess is a destination. You'd cross town to eat here – barefoot in snow if necessary. Feeling like it dropped straight from France, complete with Louis XV–style chairs, the Duchess' French-press coffee and huge array of fresh baking leave you spoiled for choice. Mocha meringues, cream-cheese-and-leek croissants, and cherry basil eclairs are just the tip of the iceberg. It's also famous for its macarons. Try the salted caramel and you'll know why.

'Balancing the epicurean traditions of China with the classical techniques of French cuisine, Chef Susur Lee improvises a daring and original culinary aesthetic.'
Lee

MARKET

CALGARY | $$$ | CANADIAN
718 17th Ave SW; 403-474-4414; www.marketcalgary.ca; mains $18-42

With an earthy yet futuristic feel, award-winning Market has gone a step further in the fresh-local trend. Not only does it bake its own bread, it butchers and cures meat, makes cheese and grows 16 varieties of heirloom seeds year-round. As if that weren't enough, it's then all whipped into meals that are scrumptious and entirely satisfying. Look for dishes like truffle buttermilk chicken wings, hand-rolled pasta or duck waffles.

RUSTY OWL

PRINCE ALBERT | $ | CAFÉ
21 River St W; 306-970-8022; www.the-rusty-owl.com; lunch mains from $8

This place describes itself as a cafe and restaurant steeped in steampunk fantasy and drawing from worldwide culinary cultures. In a historic building down by the North Saskatchewan River, it's a gem of a place with maps on the ceiling and a metallic bar that looks like it sprung from a Jules Verne novel. Savoury crepes, artisan pizzas and steak dinner mains transport you back to the 21st century.

9

CLOSE COMPANY

WINNIPEG | $$ | FUSION

256 Stafford St; 204-691-7788; www.close.company; dishes $16-20

With only 12 seats, this on-trend little restaurant is aptly named. The ten small-plate dishes change at the chef's whim, but you might be treated to tuna with black garlic or scallop ceviche singing with the high notes of passion fruit. The short and sweet cocktail menu also mostly changes with the seasons, though Oui Chef is a keeper.

TOMLIN

THUNDER BAY | $$ | CANADIAN

202 Red River Rd; 807-346-4447; www.tomlinrestaurant.com; mains $16-28

Locally lauded chef Steve Simpson's elevated comfort food uses seasonal local ingredients, with the regularly changing menu split between small plates (eg beef tartare and smoked cauliflower) and large (crab and scallop linguine). The wine list is 100% Ontario and includes ice wine, while creative cocktails such as the smoked port Manhattan also incorporate local ingredients. The restaurant's long bar is a suave hangout amid an industrial aesthetic of exposed brick and cage lamps.

BECKTA DINING & WINE BAR

OTTAWA | $$$ | CANADIAN

150 Elgin St; 613-238-7063; www.beckta.com; mains $32-45

Book in advance for one of the hottest tables in the Canadian capital, if not the whole country. Beckta offers an upmarket dining experience with an original spin on regional cuisine. You can choose between à la carte dining or a five-course pairing with wine that juxtaposes scallop ceviche with bison rib-eye steak.

TACOFINO

TOFINO | $ | MEXICAN

1184 Pacific Rim Hwy; 250-726-8288; www.tacofino.com; mains $11-12

One of BC's most celebrated food trucks, Tacofino serves the best fish

PASHA TU STUDIO/SHUTTERSTOCK ©

Opening spread, anti-clockwise from top left: Clam chowder; Broka Bistrot; Aged steaks; Poutine; Churning butter. This page: Vancouver, BC. Opposite page: Fish taco from Tacofino.

OPENING SPREAD CREDITS JUAN MONINO/GETTY IMAGES ©; COURTESY BROKE BISTROT, ANDREW MONTGOMERY/LONELY PLANET ©; ALLEKO/GETTY IMAGES ©; ANDREW MONTGOMERY/LONELY PLANET ©

COURTESY TACOFINO

tacos in the region from a dishevelled metallic machine with the Virgin of Guadalupe emblazoned on the side. The specialities are Baja-style fish tacos, *gringas* (grilled cheese tortillas) and larger burritos. The lines of hungry Tofino surfers can be long in summer; consider calling ahead to place your order.

BUCA

TORONTO | $$$ | ITALIAN

604 King St W; 416-865-1600; www.buca.ca; mains $17-55

A breathtaking basement-level restaurant with exposed-brick walls and a soaring ceiling, Buca serves artisanal Italian fare such as homemade pasta and nose-to-tail-style dishes such as orecchio di maiale (crispy pig's ears) and *cervello* (lamb's brains wrapped in prosciutto and sage). Ease into the experience with a charcuterie board of house-cured meats, flavorful cheeses and bread knots.

SEVEN LIVES

TORONTO | $ | TACOS

69 Kensington Ave; 416-803-1086; tacos from $6

What started as a pop-up taqueria is now a hole-in-the-wall place with lines of people snaking out the door, waiting to order Baja-style fish tacos: light and flaky *mahi-mahi* with *pico de gallo*, cabbage and a creamy sauce. Other seafood and veggie combos are offered, too. Most diners eat standing or take their meal to nearby Bellevue Sq.

WHERE TO DRINK...

MICROBREWS

Griendel Brasserie Artisanale, Québec City
Among the two-dozen broues (brews) on offer, you'll find burgers, poutine and the best fish 'n' chips in town.

Persephone Brewing Company, Gibsons, BC
Grows it own hops for beer and its own vegetables for food snacks such as crispy pizzas and well-stuffed tacos.

Torque Brewing, Winnipeg
The winner of the 2019 Canadian Brewing Awards, this offbeat brewery has a great food truck parked outside on summer evenings.

Brassneck Brewery, Vancouver
A beloved West Coast microbrewery with a small, wood-lined tasting room where you can couple your libations with cured sausages from the counter.

PAN CHANCHO

KINGSTON | $$ | FUSION
44 Princess St; 613-544-7790; www.panchancho.com; mains $17

This phenomenal bakery and cafe fuses unlikely ingredients into palate-pleasing dishes such as Vietnamese spring rolls and sesame tuna meatballs. The Moroccan-style, cumin-spiced lamb pita wrap with chickpeas is heartily recommended. The all-day breakfast menu features dishes such as curried eggs. Kingstonians crowd the rear courtyard on summer days.

LIVERPOOL HOUSE

MONTREAL | $$$ | QUÉBÉCOIS
2501 Rue Notre-Dame Ouest; 514-313-6049; www.joebeef.ca; mains $24-50

Liverpool House sets the standard so many Québec restaurants are racing for: an ambience that feels laid-back, like a friend's dinner party, where the food is sent from angels on high. Expect oysters, smoked trout, braised rabbit, lobster spaghetti and various other iterations of regional excellence. There is usually a vegetarian main, but sometimes just one choice.

OLIVE & GOURMANDO

MONTREAL | $$ | CAFÉ
351 Rue St-Paul Ouest; 514-350-1083; www.oliveetgourmando.com; mains $11-18

Named after the owners' two cats, this bakery-cafe is legendary in town for its hot panini, generous salads and flaky baked goods. Excellent choices include the melted goat's-cheese panini with caramelised onions, decadent mac 'n' cheese, and 'the Cubain' (a ham, roast pork and Gruyère sandwich). You'll also find decent morning choices (poached eggs, granola, house-made ricotta and toast) and fresh loaves for takeout, including olive and rosemary bread.

'We combine seaside cottage charm, a bustling oyster counter, sexy Old World wines, and crazy fresh market food.'
Liverpool House

L'EXPRESS

MONTREAL | $$ | FRENCH
3927 Rue St-Denis; 514-845-5333; www.restaurantlexpress.com; mains $19-29

L'Express, in Montreal's trendy Plateau neighbourhood, has all the hallmarks of a Parisian bistro – black-and-white chequered floor, art-deco globe lights, papered tables and mirrored walls. High-end bistro fare completes the picture, with excellent dishes such as grilled salmon, bone marrow with sea salt, roast duck with salad and beef tartare. The waiters can advise on the extensive wine list.

DAMAS RESTAURANT

MONTREAL | $$$ | SYRIAN
1201 Ave Van Horne; 514-439-5435; www.restaurant-damas.com; mains $34-62

Unique Syrian-inspired cuisine just a few minutes from Mile End and Little Italy, Damas is consistently rated as one of the top restaurants in Montreal.

A warm and welcoming ambience, along with an eclectic menu of Syrian classics (Damascus marinated chicken, tahini seabass), and inspiring new flavors (herbed dumplings, sumac fries), all come together for a complete fine-dining experience.

BUVETTE SCOTT

QUÉBEC CITY | $$ | FRENCH
821 Rue Scott, St-Jean Baptiste; 581-741-4464; www.buvettescott.com; mains $12-18

At this tiny wine bistro with just eight tables and seating at the bar, enlightened French classics like breaded calf's brains, bone marrow and brandade de morue (Provençal puree of cod mixed with milk, olive oil and garlic and served with croutons) dominate the menu. The chalkboard wine list is exceptional, with six reds and six whites.

FRESCO

BATHURST | $$$ | CANADIAN
224 King St; 506-546-1061; mains $25-40

Following on from a successful food truck and an appearance on Canada's Top Chef, Joel Aubie is working his culinary magic in his own open-kitchen restaurant. The well-honed menu uses local ingredients, and everything is made from scratch, from hand-rolled pasta to pâté and stocks. These gourmet dishes are so good, you'll want to lick your plate especially after polishing off the lemon meringue desert.

11TH MILE

FREDERICTON | $$ | CANADIAN
79 York St; 506-443-1187; www.11thmile.ca; small plates $12-18

All class, the muted colours of this new-to-the-scene, chef-owned restaurant belie the bright flavors of its food. An ever-changing menu of small plates goes the distance with dishes like roasted broccoli with walnut crema, seared coulotte steak and salmon with salsa verde. Bespoke cocktails are exceptional. This Fredericton secret is well and truly out; book ahead.

EDNA

HALIFAX | $$ | CANADIAN
2053 Gottingen St; 902-431-5683; www.ednarestaurant.com; mains $24-36

At the edge of Halifax's North End, this hipster diner has strong competition but is still many people's first choice in town. It's bare bones as far as decor goes: a long wooden table for communal dining, a tiled bar, metal stools and tables for two. Food is modern bistro: risotto, seared scallops, classic steaks, all lovingly prepared. Edna equals excellence.

CHEZ BOULAY

QUÉBEC CITY | $$$ | QUÉBÉCOIS
1110 Rue St-Jean, Old Upper Town; 418-380-8166; www.chezboulay.com; dinner mains $26-35

WHERE TO EAT...

VEGETARIAN FOOD

Acorn, Vancouver
Ideal for those craving something more inventive than mung-bean soup – try the beer-battered haloumi or vanilla-almond-beet cake.

enVie: A Vegan Kitchen, Halifax
Delicious homemade soups, crunchy pear and arugula salads, loaded flatbreads, and imaginative non-meat versions of cheeseburgers, wings, tacos and pad thai.

Calactus, Moncton, NB
Busy, bright and welcoming with a bit of a hippy vibe, this vegetarian restaurant excels with unexpected dishes like lasagna and burgers.

Café Mosaics, Edmonton
A city institution, this artsy vegetarian-vegan haunt is a meat-free zone that makes vegetable dishes both interesting and tasty.

Renowned chef Jean-Luc Boulay's flagship restaurant serves an ever-evolving menu inspired by seasonal Québécois staples such as venison, goose, blood pudding, wild mushrooms and Gaspé Peninsula seafood. Lunch specials and charcuterie platters for two offer an affordable afternoon pick-me-up, while the sleek, low-lit dining area with views of the open kitchen makes a romantic dinner setting.

LEE

TORONTO | $$$ | ASIAN

601 King St W; 416-504-7867; www.susur.com/lee; mains $16-38

Truly a feast for the senses, dinner at acclaimed *cuisinier* Susur Lee's self-titled flagship is an experience best shared. Slick servers assist in navigating the artisan selection of East-meets-West delights: you really want to get the pairings right. It's impossible to adequately convey the dance of flavors, textures and aromas one experiences in the signature Singaporean slaw, with...how many ingredients?!

COURTESY LEE

This page: Dishes from Lee. Opposite page: Forage. Next spread: San Francisco; hamburger.

FIREWORKS

SOURIS | $$$ | CANADIAN

758 Rte 310, Bay Fortune; 902-687-3745; https://innatbayfortune.com/fireworks; per person $155

Since taking over the Inn at Bay Fortune in 2015, Food Network star Michael Smith has created one of PEI's most unique dining experiences: the 'FireWorks feast,' based around a monstrous 7.5m brick-lined, wood-burning oven. It features a smorgasbord of oysters, hot-smoked fish, flame-grilled steaks, seafood chowder and fire-oven bread, served at long butcher-block tables: a truly epic barbecue banquet.

BOREAL DINER

BONAVISTA | $$ | CANADIAN

61 Church St; 709-476-2330; www.theborealdiner.com; mains $13-19

In a bright-red colonial house, this innovative restaurant manages what many others aspire to: creative, international takes on local Newfoundland ingredients. Thus: Crab pot stickers, cod in tarragon sauce, and polenta with wild mushroom stew are all

COURTESY FORAGE

potential options on the ever-shifting menu. It also does vegan and gluten free. Real espresso drinks keep you wired.

FORAGE

VANCOUVER | $$ | CANADIAN
1300 Robson St, West End; 604-661-1400; www.foragevancouver.com; mains $16-35

A popular farm-to-table eatery, this sustainability-focused restaurant is the perfect way to sample regional BC flavors. Brunch has become a firm local favourite (halibut eggs Benny recommended), and for dinner there's everything from bison steaks to slow-cooked salmon. Add a flight of BC craft beers, with top choices from the likes of Four Winds, Strange Fellows and more. Reservations recommended.

'Boreal Diner manages what many others aspire to: creative, international takes on local Newfoundland ingredients.'
Boreal Diner

WHAT TO EAT

Hamburger
Invented in the USA (though it's a matter of some dispute), the ground beef patty is the unofficial symbol of American cuisine, enriching buns nationwide.

Pie
The South prefers pecan, the Midwest likes sugar cream, and the Northeast and West bake fruit between the crusts; pie is America's classic sweet treat.

Barbecue
Slow-cooked, wood-smoked meat dates back to colonial times. These days it's often doused in sweet, spicy or vinegary sauce; regional variations abound.

Clam chowder
A potato-based soup full of clams, vegetables and sometimes bacon, typically thickened with milk; popular on the East coast.

PRICE RANGES
$ less than $15
$$ $15–25
$$$ $25 or more

Tipping: 15–20%, unless a gratuity is already included.

USA

From Korean tacos in Los Angeles to vegan mac 'n' cheese in Wyoming to lobster rolls at a seaside shack in Maine, the USA's dining scene is infinite, freewheeling and a proud testament to its kaleidoscope of citizens. Good food is democratic here, with masterful dishes often hitting the table at very reasonable prices.

SUPER J'S

HAWAII'I, THE BIG ISLAND, HI | $ | HAWAIIAN

83-5409 Mamalahoa Hwy, South Kona Coast; 808-328-9566; www.facebook.com/SuperJsLaulau; plates $8-12

The full title of this place is 'Ka'aloa's Super J's Hawaiian Food,' but everyone calls it Super J's. They also call it freakin' delicious. The laulau (pork, chicken or fish wrapped inside *taro* or *ti* leaves) is steamed until it's so tender it melts under your fork, the *lomilomi* salmon is perfectly salty. Best of all is the setting: you're basically eating in a welcoming Hawaiian family's kitchen.

MANEKI

SEATTLE, WA | $$ | JAPANESE

206-622-2631; www.manekirestaurant.com; 304 6th Ave S; mains $14-26

For an unforgettable experience reserve one of Maneki's tatami mat dining rooms (paper and wood lattice private chambers with seating on the floor) and feast on a meal of traditional Japanese cuisine and sake. The fish is legendarily fresh, and the crispy *takoyaki* (dough balls stuffed with octopus) and *saba ichiya boshi* (salted mackerel) are authentic bites of glory.

COWBOY DINNER TREE

SILVER LAKE, OR | $$ | AMERICAN

50836 E Bay Rd; 541-576-2426; www.cowboydinnertree.net; meals adult/child $33/11

This wonderfully bizarre place in the middle of nowhere is one of the most real and unique Wild West eating experiences you'll find. Order a whole spit-roasted chicken or a 30oz grilled steak; you'll see it being cooked over a flame as you arrive. Accompanying bowls of soup, salad and baked potatoes are served family style in a wood shack setting you share with hunters and fisherfolk. Cash only. Reservations essential.

ARSICAULT BAKERY

SAN FRANCISCO, CA | $ | BAKERY
397 Arguello Blvd; 415-750-9460; www.facebook.com/arsicaultbakery; pastries $3-7

Armando Lacayo left his job in finance because he, like his Parisian grandparents, was obsessed with making croissants. After perfecting his technique, Lacayo opened this modest bakery with a smattering of rustic wood tables in 2015. Within a year, Bon Appétit magazine had declared it the best new bakery in America, and the golden, flaky, buttery croissants regularly sell out.

MISTER JIU'S

SAN FRANCISCO, CA | $$ | CHINESE
28 Waverly Pl; 415-857-9688; www.misterjius.com; mains $14-45

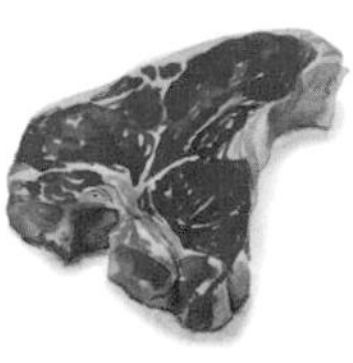

'Eating out should remind you of the good times you share with family while introducing you to new tastes in the company of friends.'
Evan Rich, Rich Table

ANDREW MONTGOMERY/LONELY PLANET ©

Success has been celebrated in this historic Chinatown banquet hall since the 1880s. Build a memorable feast from chef Brandon Jew's ingenious Chinese/Californian signatures: quail and Mission-fig sticky rice, hot and sour Dungeness crab soup, Wagyu sirloin and tuna heart fried rice. Don't skip dessert – the salted plum sesame balls are flavor bombs. Auspicious lotus-flower chandeliers overhead set a party mood, as do the seductive cocktails.

1760

SAN FRANCISCO, CA | $$ | CALIFORNIAN
1760 Polk St; 415-359-1212; www.1760sf.com; mains $15-22

Every night is a culinary throw-down at 1760: chef Carl Foronda must find the right techniques and inspirations to highlight today's star ingredients. No single cuisine dominates and unexpected strengths shine – shiitake add depth to Korean-style short rib, while tomato confit makes papardelle with ragu sing. It's all equally inspired and exquisitely presented in a sleek but unpretentious ambience.

GRAND CENTRAL MARKET

LOS ANGELES, CA | $ | MARKET
317 S Broadway; www.grandcentralmarket.com; dishes & sandwiches $7-19

LA's beaux arts market hall has been satisfying appetites since 1917 and today is downtown's gourmet mecca. Lose yourself in its bustle of neon signs, stalls and counters, peddling everything from fresh produce and nuts to sizzling Thai street food, hipster breakfasts, modern deli classics, artisanal pasta and speciality coffee.

RICH TABLE

SAN FRANCISCO, CA | $$ | CALIFORNIAN
199 Gough St; 415-355-9085; www.richtablesf.com; mains $17-37

Impossible cravings begin at Rich Table, where mind-bending dishes like porcini doughnuts, sardine chips, and burrata funnel cake blow up Instagram feeds nightly. Married co-chefs and owners Sarah and Evan Rich riff on seasonal San Francisco cuisine with soul and ingenuity in the relaxed space filled with salvaged barn-wood decor. Book two to four weeks ahead.

'Kogi is the crazy little taco truck that used Twitter and started a food revolution in 2008 with an addictive harmony known as the Korean Short Rib Taco.'
Kogi BBQ

JOSS CUISINE

LOS ANGELES, CA | $$ | CHINESE
9919 S Santa Monica Blvd; 310-277-3888; www.josscuisine.com; dishes $15-30

With fans including Barbra Streisand, Gwyneth Paltrow and Jackie Chan, this intimate nosh spot in Beverly Hills serves up superlative, MSG-free Chinese cuisine at non-celebrity prices. Premium produce drives a menu of exceptional dishes, from flawless dim sum to crispy mustard prawns and one of the finest Peking ducks you'll encounter this side of East Asia.

KOGI BBQ

LOS ANGELES, CA | $ | FOOD TRUCK
www.kogibbq.com; mains $2.50-9

Chef Roy Choi is a founding dude of the LA food-truck scene and his four trucks peddle standout Korean-Mexican fusion fare. Sink your teeth into the signature short-rib taco, an expert balancing act of double-caramelised Korean BBQ, salsa roja and chilli-soy slaw on griddled corn tortillas. The tofu tacos and kimchi quesadillas are other classics.

KAI RESTAURANT

PHOENIX, AZ | $$$ | AMERICAN INDIAN
5594 W Wild Horse Pass Blvd; 602-225-0100; mains $46-62, tasting menus $145-$245

American Indian cuisine – based on traditional crops grown along the Gila River – soars to new heights at Kai ('seed'). Expect creations such as grilled buffalo tenderloin with smoked corn puree and cholla buds, or wild scallops with mesquite-smoked caviar and tepary-bean crackling. It's located in a resort on the Gila River Indian Reservation at Phoenix's southern edge. Book ahead and dress nicely.

CAFE PASQUAL'S

SANTA FE, NM | $$$ | NEW MEXICAN

121 Don Gaspar Ave; 505-983-9340; www.pasquals.com; mains $18-39

The organic food at this exuberantly colourful, utterly unpretentious place has a definite south-of-the-border flavor. The breakfast menu is famous for dishes such as huevos *motuleños*, made with eggs, sautéed bananas, feta cheese and more. Meat and fish mains hit the tables for lunch and dinner, while the chef's renowned red chilli and green chilli sauces spice up plates all day long.

LA CHOZA

SANTA FE, NM | $ | NEW MEXICAN

905 Alarid St; 505-982-0909; www.lachozasf.com; mains $10-20

Blue-corn burritos, stuffed *sopapillas* (puffy dough pillows plumped with beans, cheese and chillis) and an extensive margarita list make La Choza a perennial favourite among Santa Fe's discerning diners. The brightly painted pink, orange and blue interior stokes a festive scene as locals hobnob at the tables. Arrive early or make a reservation.

GOLDEN CROWN PANADERIA

ALBUQUERQUE, NM | $ | BAKERY

1103 Mountain Rd NW; 505-243-2424; www.goldencrown.biz; pastries $1-3, pizzas from $11

Who doesn't love a friendly neighbourhood cafe-bakery? Especially one in a cosy old adobe, with gracious staff, oven-fresh bread and pizza (with green chilli or blue-corn crusts), fruity empanadas, smooth espresso coffees and cookies all round. Call ahead to reserve a loaf of quick-selling green-chilli bread – then eat it hot, out on the patio.

HELL'S BACKBONE GRILL

BOULDER, UT | $$$ | AMERICAN

20 N Hwy 12; Boulder Mountain Lodge; 435-335-7464; www.hellsbackbonegrill.com, mains $23-37

Hell's Backbone, a trailblazer in sustainable eating and mindfulness, operates following Buddhist principles. Earthy dishes include gorgeous salads made from produce from the owners' organic farm, pumpkin apple soup with sage, and braised beef with green chilli polenta. While the restaurant sits far off the beaten path, amid the wild cliffs of southern Utah, dinner reservations are a must.

WHERE TO EAT...

FRIED CHICKEN

Willie Mae's Scotch House, New Orleans, LA
Willie Mae's secret recipe brings forth a deep-fried bird with a crunch and juiciness like no other.

Gus's World Famous Fried Chicken, Memphis, TN
Connoisseurs twitch in their sleep as they dream about the gossamer-light chicken and fried okra at this neon-lit bunker.

Beasley's Chicken & Honey, Raleigh, NC
Bite into gorgeous fried bird on a biscuit, with waffles or in a potpie from a James Beard Award–winning chef.

Howlin' Ray's, Los Angeles, CA
Crowds amass at Ray's noisy takeout counter for spicy fried chicken, vinegar slaw and peach tea.

RED IGUANA

SALT LAKE CITY, UT | $$ | MEXICAN
736 W North Temple St; 801-322-1489, www.rediguana.com; mains $11-18

The Red Iguana wafts Mexican food at its most authentic and aromatic – no wonder the line is usually snaking out the door at the relaxed, family-run restaurant. Ask for samples of the mole to decide on one of six chilli- and chocolate-based sauces. The incredibly tender cochinita pibil (shredded roast pork) tastes like it's been roasting for days.

DENVER CENTRAL MARKET

DENVER, CO | $ | FOOD HALL
2669 Larimer St; www.denvercentralmarket.com; mains $7-16

This stylish marketplace in a repurposed warehouse wows with its breadth of options. Eat a bowl of handmade pasta or an artisanal sandwich; consider a wood-fired pizza or street tacos. Or just grab a cocktail at the bar and wander between the fruit stand and chocolatier. Patrons eat at communal tables or on the street-side patio.

FOLLOW YER' NOSE BBQ

EMIGRANT, MT | $ | BARBECUE
4 Overlook Rd; 406-224-2847; www.followyernosebbq.com; mains $10-20

What started as a portable smoker in a gravel parking lot is now Montana's liveliest barbecue joint. Locals flock to the covered patio with sweeping views of the surrounding valley and mountains to wash down plates of tender brisket and juicy chicken with one (or several) of 40 craft beers. The home-smoked pulled pork is magnificent.

***This page:* Sausages and brisket over a barbecue pit. *Opposite page:* Chargrilled oysters from Ulele.**

COURTESY ULELE

ner art-deco flower shop is
ıpscale cafe with excellent
ı- and Mexican-influenced fare
:ally sourced. The ice-cream-
;ert is the stuff of dreams. The
fried steak – an Oklahoma
y of tenderised beef that's
and fried – is considered the
he state; thank the jalapeño
ravy for the honor.

KLIN BBQ

TX | $ | BARBECUE

th St; 512-653-1187; www.
ɔbq.com; sandwiches $7-
ɔs/brisket per lb $19/25

ous BBQ joint only serves
nd only till it runs out – usually
ɔre 2pm. To avoid missing out,
line – and there will be a line
m (9am on weekends). Treat

WHERE TO DRINK...

MICROBREWS

Tree House Brewing Co, Charlton, MA
Make a pilgrimage to central Massachusetts to down the ballyhooed Julius, a New England–style IPA.

Jester King, Austin, TX
This barn-style brewery under shady oaks in the Hill Country pours a long menu of acclaimed sour brews.

3 Floyds Brewing Co, Munster, IN
Set in a remote industrial park with death metal blaring, 3 Floyds has earned a cult following by brewing with tons of unusual hops.

Breakside Brewery, Portland, OR
Settle in for experimental brews spiked with fruits, vegetables and spices, plus an award-winning IPA.

it as a tailgating party: bring beer or mimosas to share and make friends. And yes, you do want the fatty brisket.

PIEOUS

DRIPPING SPRINGS, TX | $ | PIZZA
166 Hargraves Dr, Belterra Village mall; 512-394-7041; www.facebook.com/pieous; pizzas $11-16

Holy moly, this casual, wood-fired pizza joint in a strip mall 7 miles east of Dripping Springs – on the outskirts of Austin – serves good pie. Its motto, 'food is our religion,' gives a nod to its name, and to its focus on using fresh and homemade ingredients. The beloved pastrami, which graces pizzas, sandwiches and stand-alone plates, is cooked in-house in a BBQ smoker.

KEG & CASE

ST PAUL, MN | $ | FOOD HALL
928 7th St W; 651-443-6060; www.kegandcase.com; sandwiches $12-15

National newspaper USA Today crowned Keg & Case the nation's best new food hall in 2019, and who's to argue? Some two dozen vendors serve locally sourced sandwiches, pizza, ice cream and craft beer in the spiffy, remodelled 1855 Schmidt Brewery. Stalls selling switchel (an apple cider vinegar-based drink), freshly foraged mushrooms and organic cotton candy are also among the wares.

OLD FASHIONED

MADISON, WI | $$ | AMERICAN
23 N Pinckney St; 608-310-4545; www.theoldfashioned.com; mains $12-25

With its dark, woodsy decor, the Old Fashioned evokes a supper club, a type of retro eatery common in the USA's Upper Midwestern states. The menu is all local specialities, including walleye (a freshwater fish), cheese soup and sausages. It's hard to choose from among the 150 types of Wisconsin-brewed ales in bottles, so opt for a sampler (four or eight little glasses) from the 50 Wisconsin tap beers.

HOPLEAF

CHICAGO, IL | $$ | EUROPEAN
5148 N Clark St; 773-334-9851; www.hopleaf.com; mains $14-27

A cosy, European-like tavern, Hopleaf draws crowds for its Montreal-style smoked brisket, cashew-butter-and-fig-jam sandwich, and the house-speciality *frites* (fries) and beer-broth-soaked mussels. It also pours 200 types of brew (with around 60 on tap), emphasising craft and Belgian suds. In winter, a fireplace warms the tables full of convivial locals. In summer, everyone heads to the umbrella-shaded patio.

MONTEVERDE

CHICAGO, IL | $$ | ITALIAN

1020 W Madison St; 312-888-3041; www.monteverdechicago.com; mains $18-24

House-made pastas are Monteverde's speciality, as you can see from staff rolling and shaping dough in the open kitchen. The dishes seem simple in concept, such as the *cacio whey pepe* (small tube pasta with pecorino Romano, ricotta whey and four-peppercorn blend), but the flavors are lusciously complex. That's why the light-wood tables in the lively room are always packed. Reserve ahead, or try the bar for walk-in seats.

GIORDANO'S

CHICAGO, IL | $$ | PIZZA

730 N Rush St; 312-951-0747; www.giordanos.com; small pizzas from $18

Giordano's makes 'stuffed' pizza, a bigger, gooier version of Chicago's famed deep dish. It's dough, with cheese on top, then another layer of dough atop that, plus toppings. Each pie takes 45 minutes to rise to thick-crusted perfection. Giordano's has loads of branches around town, but this huge, open, industrial one in the thick of downtown's commercial hub is particularly festive.

MILKTOOTH

INDIANAPOLIS, IN | $$ | BREAKFAST

534 Virginia Ave; 317-986-5131; www.milktoothindy.com; mains $4-17

Breakfast lovers of the world unite at artsy Milktooth, a can't-miss morning hot spot set in a *tchotchke*-peppered garage. Wondrous farm-to-fork stunners include the sourdough pearl sugar waffle (with burnt honeycomb candy, parmesan, whipped citrus honey butter and raw honey) and the spiced fried potatoes (with egg, cream cheese and chive aioli, shallot, caper and dill pickle).

SISTER PIE

DETROIT, MI | $ | BAKERY

8066 Kercheval Ave; 313-447-5550; www.sisterpie.com; baked goods $1-5

Owner Lisa Ludwinski (a 2019 James Beard Award finalist) and her army of female bakers create amazing treats at this corner storefront in Detroit's leafy West Village neighbourhood. The milk chocolate chess, salted maple, marshmallow butterscotch and other flaky-crust pies are fabulous, and the perfectly soft peanut-butter paprika cookies will spoil your taste buds for evermore. Everything is made with seasonal ingredients purchased from local farmers.

FARMHOUSE DELI

DOUGLAS, MI | $ | DELI

100 Blue Star Hwy; 269-455-5274; www.thefarmhousedeli.com; mains $8-12

While it could coast on its looks – the shabby-chic farmhouse decor is cute as a button – the deli ups the ante with seriously top-notch food. The Cubano sandwich (pulled pork, porchetta and Gruyère), tarragon-tinged chicken salad, tangy goat cheeses, cleansing juices and house-baked croissants,

WHERE TO EAT...

ICE CREAM

Ample Hills Creamery, NY, NY
It churns organic, imaginative flavors like honey-cinnamon with baklava, salted crack caramel and gooey butter cake.

Ted Drewes, St Louis, MO
Lick yourself silly on the super-creamy, ice-cream-like frozen custard at this historic spot on old Route 66.

Mount Desert Island Ice Cream, Bar Harbor, ME
Small-batch, butterfat-rich concoctions from blueberry to basil to butterscotch miso grace cones and cups.

Amy's Ice Creams, Austin, TX
Choose your toppings and staff smash them into your scoops, say Mexican vanilla bean with fresh strawberries or dark chocolate with peanut butter cups.

cakes and cookies (try the triple ginger molasses one) dazzle. Everything is made with local, organic ingredients.

TUCKER'S

CINCINNATI, OH | $ | DINER

1637 Vine St; 513-954-8920; www.facebook.com/TuckersRestaurantOTR; mains $5-9

Located in a tough zone fringing downtown Cincinnati, family-run Tucker's has been feeding locals – African American, white, foodies, penniless, friars, drug dealers – since 1946. It's an archetypal diner, serving six-cheese omelettes, biscuits and gravy, potatoes with bacon jam and other hulking breakfast dishes. Joe Tucker does the cookin'. Wife Carla does everything else. Try the *goetta* (pronounced get-uh), a local herb-spiced, pork-and-oats breakfast sausage.

SAMYSTCLAIR/GETTY IMAGES ©

This page: French Quarter, New Orleans. Opposite page: Dishes from Marjie's Grill.

HATTIE B'S

NASHVILLE, TN | $ | CHICKEN

112 19th Ave S; 615-678-4794; www.hattieb.com; plates $8.50-13.50

When it comes to hot chicken – Nashville's beloved speciality – Hattie B's reigns supreme. The industrial-vibed, picnic-table-dotted fried chicken spot serves up moist birds that come devilishly fried to levels that top out at 'Shut the Cluck Up!' hot, and it means nose-runnin' business. The eatery is ultra popular, so expect a line.

BALTER BEERWORKS

KNOXVILLE, TN | $ | GASTROPUB

100 S Broadway; 865-999-5015; www.balterbeerworks.com; mains $12-17

From the communal tables on the patio to the standing-room-only bar to the buzzing dining room, this convivial joint – a former gas station – exudes a welcoming vibe. The pub fare is dreamy, and options range from the Gouda-topped burger with sriracha sauce to cheesy shrimp and grits with andouille sausage. The easy-drinking house beer is brewed on-site.

MARJIE'S GRILL

NEW ORLEANS, LA | $$ | ASIAN

320 S Broad St; 504-603-2234; www.marjiesgrill.com; mains $9-26

Marjie's is run by chefs who were inspired by Southeast Asian street food, but rather than coming home and doing pale imitations of the real thing,

COURTESY MARJIE'S GRILL

they've turned an old house in the colourful, quirky Mid-City neighbourhood into a corner in Hanoi, Luang Prabang or Chiang Mai. Coal-roasted fish has a flaky, wonderfully charred skin, while cornmeal-battered chicken goes down a treat with *sambal* and cane syrup.

BACCHANAL

NEW ORLEANS, LA | $$ | AMERICAN
600 Poland Ave; 504-948-9111; www.bacchanalwine.com; mains $9-24

From the outside, Bacchanal looks like a leaning shack that has seen better days; inside are racks of wine and stinky-but-sexy cheese. Musicians play in the garden, while cooks dispense delicious meals on paper plates from the kitchen in the back; on any given day you may try chorizo-stuffed dates or seared diver scallops that will blow your gastronomic mind.

'Rather than coming home and doing pale imitations of the real thing, they've turned an old house in the colourful, quirky Mid-City neighbourhood into a corner in Hanoi, Luang Prabang or Chiang Mai.'
Marjie's Grill

BOUCHERIE

NEW ORLEANS, LA | $$ | SOUTHERN
8115 Jeannette St; 504-862-5514; www.boucherie-nola.com; mains $18-26

Boucherie is the Cajun word for a celebratory community pig-pickin'. The food served in this little purple cottage captures that down-home exuberance. Chef Nathanial Zimet's house-cured meats and succulent Southern dishes are lauded throughout New Orleans. Savour boudin (Cajun sausage) balls with garlic aioli, blackened shrimp in bacon vinaigrette, and smoked Wagyu-style brisket. The Krispy Kreme bread pudding with rum syrup is a wonder.

SAW'S SOUL KITCHEN

BIRMINGHAM, AL | $$ | BARBECUE
215 41st St S; 205-591-1409; www.sawsbbq.com; mains $9-17

Never mind the ramshackle exterior. Inside this teeny joint offers some of the most mouthwatering smoked meat in the South, served in a no-fuss, memorabilia-laden atmosphere. Stuffed potatoes make a nice addition to your meal, and the smoked chicken with a tangy local white sauce is divine – although with that said, bring on the ribs!

DISH DIVE

ATLANTA, GA | $$ | AMERICAN
2233 College Ave NE; 404-957-7918; www.dishdivekitchen.com; mains $10-18

Located in a teeny house near some railroad tracks, Dish Dive is cooler than you and it doesn't care. Anyone is welcome here, and the food – fresh, seasonal cuisine such as turmeric and black-pepper pappardelle, fried spaghetti squash with poblano-chocolate sauce and the never-off-the-menu masterpiece, braised pork-belly French toast – is high-value, easy-on-the-wallet eating. Make reservations and BYOB.

FRESH AIR

JACKSON, GA | $ | BARBECUE
1164 Hwy 42; 770-775-3182; www.freshairbarbecue.com; mains $3-7.50

'Barbecue doesn't have to be complicated and it doesn't take a lot of specialised equipment.'
Aaron Franklin, Franklin BBQ

Fresh Air is swine nirvana, a glorious warm and friendly pioneer-style wooden roadside shack with outdoor seating and sawdust out front. Only three things are served here: chopped pork, Brunswick stew and coleslaw. No ribs. No shoulder. The result is transcendent, vinegary BBQ. The pork spends a full 24 hours in the smoker to stoke its flavour. The famous tangy sauce will haunt your dreams.

KYU

MIAMI, FL | $$ | FUSION
251 NW 25th St; 786-577-0150; www.kyurestaurants.com; shared plates $17-38

Kyu has been dazzling locals and food critics alike with its creative Asian-inspired dishes, most of which are cooked over the open flames of a wood-fired grill. The open, rustic-industrial room buzzes with stylish Miamians sharing plates of the Florida red snapper, beef tenderloin, soft-shell-crab steamed buns and a magnificent head of cauliflower. Book well ahead.

ULELE

TAMPA, FL | $$$ | AMERICAN
1810 N Highland Ave; 813-999-4952; www.ulele.com; mains $19-42

This former water-pumping station has been transformed into an enchanting restaurant and brewery whose menu harkens back to Florida's native staples made over for modern times. That means liberal use of datil peppers, sides like alligator beans and okra 'fries', mains like local pompano fish and desserts like guava pie. The flavors here are a rare treat.

COLUMBIA RESTAURANT

TAMPA, FL | $$ | SPANISH & CUBAN
2117 E 7th Ave; 813-248-4961; www.columbiarestaurant.com; mains $18-32

Columbia is the oldest restaurant in Florida, in business since 1905. Occupying an entire block, it consists of 15 elegant dining rooms and romantic, fountain-centered courtyards. Many of the gloved waiters have been here a lifetime delivering plates of juicy Cuban roasted pork, hulking Cuban sandwiches and silky flan. They make the smashing mojitos right at your table.

DIXIE CROSSROADS

TITUSVILLE, FL | $$ | SEAFOOD
1475 Garden St; 321-268-5000; www.dixiecrossroads.com; mains $13-30, rock shrimp $16/dozen

This landmark spot serves up seasonal shrimp from local waters, including sweet, blush-coloured royal reds, succulent white shrimp and melt-in-your-mouth broiled rock shrimp. Order rock shrimp by the dozen, and they arrive sliced open by a wondrous machine that the restaurant's owners invented. Despite generous seating in the funky wooden chalet, there's often a queue, so head to the gazebo bar to wait with a drink.

167 RAW

CHARLESTON, SC | $$ | SEAFOOD
289 E Bay St; 843-579-4997; www.167raw.com/charleston; oysters each $3, mains $14-27

There are no reservations at this tiny hole-in-the-wall that unassumingly serves up stupendous seafood. People wait in lines down the block for the delicious lobster roll, and the tuna burger and sea-scallop po'boy are also off-the-charts toothsome. Oysters arrive fresh daily from Nantucket (where the restaurant runs its very own oyster farm), and the service is truly on point.

CÚRATE

ASHEVILLE, NC | $$ | TAPAS
13 Biltmore Ave, 828-239-2946; www.katiebuttonrestaurants.com/curate; small plates $6-18

Owned by hip Ashevillian chef Katie Button and her Catalan husband Félix, this convivial hangout celebrates the simple charms and sensual flavors of Spanish tapas, while adding an occasional Southern twist. Standout dishes run long and wide: *pan con tomate* (grilled bread with tomato), lightly fried aubergine drizzled with honey and rosemary, and a knockout squid-ink 'paella' with vermicelli.

THE SHACK

STAUNTON VA | $$ | AMERICAN
105 S Coalter St; 540-490-1961; www.theshackva.com; mains $13-30, 3-course prix fixe $50

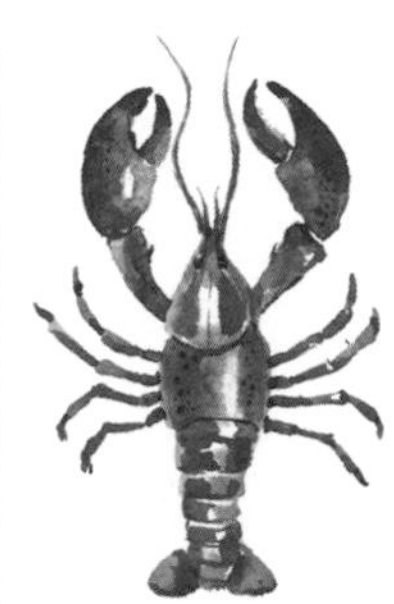

Tucked in a remote hamlet in Virginia's Shenandoah Valley, the Shack is a wee, unadorned space (hence the name) that cooks Appalachian- and Southern-inspired dishes that rock the palate. Chef Ian Boden, a two-time James Beard semi-finalist, makes the most of seasonal ingredients from local farms. The menu changes regularly, but might include mains like the pork sausage and clam stew with okra.

TAIL UP GOAT

WASHINGTON, DC | $$ | MEDITERRANEAN
1827 Adams Mill Rd NW; 202-986-9600; www.tailupgoat.com; mains $18-27

With its pale blue walls, light wood decor and dangling lantern-like lights, Tail Up Goat exudes a warm, island-y vibe. The lamb ribs are the speciality – crispy and lusciously fatty, served with date-molasses juice. House-made breads and spreads are outstanding too – flaxseed sourdough with beets. No wonder Michelin gave it a star.

CHEZ PANISSE

BERKELEY, CA | $$$ | CALIFORNIAN
1517 Shattuck Ave; 510-548-5525; www.chezpanisse.com; cafe mains $21-35, restaurant prix-fixe dinner $75-125

Foodies come to worship here at the church of Alice Waters, inventor of California cuisine, who pioneered the focus on local, sustainable ingredients when she opened Panisse in 1971. The ever-changing menu showcases California's bounty in creative ways, from sea scallops with watermelon radishes to wild nettle soup and trout rillettes. It's is located in a lovely arts-and-crafts house amid other chowhound hot spots.

BEN'S CHILI BOWL

WASHINGTON, DC | $ | AMERICAN
1213 U St NW; 202-667-0058; www.benschilibowl.com; mains $6-10

Ben's is a DC institution. The main stock in trade is half-smokes, DC's meatier, smokier version of the hot dog, usually slathered with mustard, onions and the namesake chili. For 60-plus years presidents, rock stars and Supreme Court justices have come to indulge in the humble diner, but despite the hype, Ben's remains a true neighbourhood establishment where locals hang out and gossip over sweet iced tea.

BLACKSMITH BAR & RESTAURANT

BERLIN, MD | $$ | AMERICAN
104 Pitts St; 410-973-2102; www.blacksmithberlin.com; mains $19-29

This page: Chez Panisse. Opposite page: Burger from Edmund's Oast.

COURTESY EDMUND'S OAST

Folks across Maryland's Eastern Shore recommend this cosy and congenial spot, which began life as a blacksmith shop and now serves hearty portions of farm-to-table comfort food. Servers soon feel like friends, while the low ceiling and thick walls evoke a warm roadside tavern. The jumbo lump crab cakes with herbed potatoes are divine.

THAMES STREET OYSTER HOUSE

BALTIMORE, MD | $$ | SEAFOOD

1728 Thames St, Fells Point; 443-449-7726; www.thamesstreetoysterhouse.com; mains $18-31

A waterfront Baltimore icon, this vintage dining and drinking hall serves some of the East Coast's best seafood. Eat in the polished upstairs room with harbour views, take a seat in the backyard, or plunk down at the bar in front and watch the drink-makers and oyster-shuckers in action. The lobster rolls melt in your mouth.

GRAN CAFFÈ L'AQUILA

PHILADELPHIA, PA | $$ | ITALIAN

1716 Chestnut St; 215-568-5600; www.grancaffelaquila.com; mains $16-35

This is impressive Italian food. The chefs hail straight from the motherland, and one of them is Italy's gelato-making champion. Indulge in his creations at the gelato counter or via some of the main courses that incorporate savoury gelato, (like the spaghetti carbonara with Italian bacon gelato). Dapper wait-staff are eager to please, and the warm, elegant space invites lingering.

COURTESY CHEZ PANISSE

WHERE TO EAT...

DINER FOOD

Clayton's Coffee Shop, San Diego, CA
The real deal from the 1940s, with red swivel stools, booths with mini-jukeboxes, and plates of pancakes, eggs, meatloaf and mile-high pie.

Liuzza's By The Track, New Orleans, LA
The gumbo, barbecue shrimp po'boy and deep-fried garlic oysters reign supreme at this neighbourhood joint.

Lou Mitchell's, Chicago, IL
Old-school waitresses deliver fluffy omelettes and thick-cut French toast, while calling you 'honey' and filling your coffee cup endlessly.

Bubba's Cooks Country, Dallas, TX
Portions of fried chicken, mashed potatoes and black-eyed peas are huge, and the ice teas never stop coming.

EDMUND'S OAST

CHARLESTON, SC | $$ | PUB FOOD
1081 Morrison Dr; 843-727-1145; www.edmundsoast.com; mains $14-30

Occupying a gutted former hardware store, Charleston's highest-brow brewpub cooks cheffy takes on Southern favourites, such as salt chicken with green curry, hanger steaks with potato pancakes and tempura catfish with white grits and red curry. For drinks, 64 taps flow with goodness, including a dozen house-made beers.

CHEFS CLUB

NEW YORK, NY | $$$ | FUSION
275 Mulberry St; 212-941-1100; www.chefsclub.com; prix-fixe $85-125

Acclaimed visiting chefs have residencies at Chefs Club for anywhere from three weeks to three months, offering their finest selections in menus that span the flavors of the globe. You might feast on anything from Michelin-lauded Spanish tapas to Portuguese dumplings to French gastronomy in the cool industrial warehouse digs. It's set in the historic Puck Building, star of many a film and TV show, in Manhattan's Nolita district.

UNCLE BOONS

NEW YORK, NY | $$ | THAI
7 Spring St, btwn Elizabeth St & Bowery; 646-370-6650; www.uncleboons.com; small plates $15-18, large plates $25-31

Michelin-star Thai food is served up in a fun, tongue-in-cheek combo of retro wood-panelled dining room with Thai film posters and old family snaps. Spanning the old and the new, dishes are tangy, rich and creative. Standouts include the *kob woonsen* (garlic and soy marinated frogs legs), *koong* (grilled head-on prawns) and *kaduuk* (roasted bone marrow satay).

CHELSEA MARKET

NEW YORK, NY | $ | MARKET
75 Ninth Ave, btwn W 15th & W 16 Sts; www.chelseamarket.com; mains $10-15

In a shining example of redevelopment, Chelsea Market has taken a 19th-century Nabisco cookie factory and turned it into an 800ft-long food court of mouthwatering diversity. On the site where the beloved Oreo was first conceived, now more than 35 vendors sell everything from tongue-tingling hand-pulled dan dan noodles to Jamaican jerk, fine cheese and whole lobsters.

ROBERTA'S

BROOKLYN, NY | $$ | PIZZA
261 Moore St; 718-417-1118; www.robertaspizza.com; pizzas $17-21

This hiply renovated warehouse restaurant in Williamsburg, one of Brooklyn's booming food enclaves, makes some of the best pizza in New York City. Service is relaxed, but the brick-oven pies are serious: chewy, fresh and topped with knowing combinations of outstanding ingredients. The classic margherita is sublime; more adventurous palates can opt for near-legendary options like 'beastmaster' (gorgonzola, pork sausage and jalapeño).

TJ BUCKLEY'S

BRATTLEBORO, VT | $$$ | AMERICAN
132 Elliot St; 802-257-4922; www.tjbuckleysuptowndining.com; mains $45

Chef-owner Michael Fuller founded this exceptional, upscale little eatery in an authentic 1925 Worcester dining car more than 30 years ago. Ever since, he's been offering a verbal menu of four seasonally changing items – say, rabbit loin wrapped in Spanish ham, or seared salmon with wild rice risotto – sourced largely from local farms. The intimate space seats just 18 souls, so reserve ahead.

SALTIE GIRL

BOSTON, MA | $$$ | SEAFOOD
281 Dartmouth St; 617-267-0691; www.saltiegirl.com; small plates $12-20, mains $26-40

Squeeze into a seat at delightfully snug Saltie Girl to feast on dishes that blow away all preconceived notions about seafood. From your traditional Gloucester lobster roll to tinned fish on toast to the irresistible torched salmon belly, the tiny space is full of tantalizing surprises. Reservations are not accepted, so expect to wait. (It's worth it.)

'I wanted to open a good-food/do-good kind of place that emphasised the importance of happy employees and sustainable food-business practice.'
Lisa Ludwinski, Sister Pie

CHATHAM PIER FISH MARKET

CAPE COD, MA | $$ | SEAFOOD
45 Barcliff Ave, Chatham; 508-945-3474; www.chathampierfishmarket.com; mains $12-24

If you like food that's fresh and hyper-local, this salt-sprayed fish shack with its own sushi chef and day-boats is for you. The chowder's incredible, the fish so fresh it was swimming earlier in the day. It's all takeout, but there are shady picnic tables where you can watch fishers unloading their catch and seals frolicking as you savour dinner.

THURSTON'S LOBSTER POUND

MOUNT DESERT ISLAND, ME | $$ | SEAFOOD
9 Thurston Rd, Bernard; 207-244-7600; www.thurstonforlobster.com; mains $12-30

Super-fresh lobster and crab are the headliners at yellow-roofed Thurston's, overlooking Bass Harbor in the fishing village of Bernard. Tie on a bib and crack into a steamy, butter-dripping lobster, or a seafood-filled roll. As the menu declares, 'these guys were in the ocean when you woke up this morning'. The casual spot is often cited as one of Maine's best seafood shacks.

MEXICO

Eating your way around Mexico is a real treat, whether you're grazing at late-night taco stands or digging into multi-course extravaganzas. One of the world's most vibrant cuisines, Mexican food delights with its variety, its abundant use of herbs and chillies, and ingredients as diverse as fresh coastal seafood and the dried beef of the desert-like northern states.

WHAT TO EAT

Tacos
The quintessential Mexican food can be made of any cooked meat, fish or vegetable wrapped in a soft corn or flour tortilla, with a dash of salsa and an onion and coriander garnish. Every region has its own take.

Quesadillas
Fold a tortilla with cheese, heat it on a griddle and you have a quesadilla. They can be stuffed with chorizo and cheese, squash blossoms, mushrooms with garlic, chicharrón (fried pork fat), beans, stewed chicken or meat.

Mole
A complex sauce made with nuts, chilies and spices, mole defines Mexican cuisine.

PRICE RANGES
For a main course:
$ less than M$100
$$ M$100–200
$$$ M$200 or more

Tipping: 10–15%

EL HIDALGUENSE

MEXICO CITY | $$ | MEXICAN
Campeche 155; 55-5564-0538; mains M$90-250

Slow-cooked over aged oak wood in an underground pit, the Hidalgo-style *barbacoa* at this family-run eatery is off-the-charts delicious. Get things started with a rich consommé or *queso asado* (grilled cheese with herbs), then move on to the tacos. Top it off on a warm and fuzzy note, sampling the flavored *pulques* (mildly alcoholic fermented agave juice).

PUJOL

MEXICO CITY | $$$ | MEXICAN
Tennyson 133; 55-5545-4111; www.pujol.com.mx; menú degustación M$$2227-3332

Arguably Mexico's best gourmet restaurant, Pujol offers a contemporary take on classic Mexican dishes in a stylish and modern setting. Its multiple-course tasting extravaganzas might include *huitlacoche* (a fungus that grows on corn) with black truffle or octopus with *chintextle* sauce and pickled carrot. Menus can be either corn- or seafood-

focused. It might take up to several weeks to get a table here, though seats at the taco bar are easier to book at short notice and come as 10-courses of Asian-inspired bites with drinks, all decided by the chef and your host.

POR SIEMPRE VEGANA TAQUERÍA

MEXICO CITY | $ | VEGAN
Cnr Manzanillo & Chiapas; 55-3923-7976; www.facebook.com/porsiempreveganataqueria; tacos M$10-20, tortas M$50

Vegans can join in the street-food action with delicious soy taco versions of al pastor, loganiza and chorizo. The late-night experience is complete with self-serve tubs of toppings – potato, *nopales* (cactus paddles), beans and salsas. There are also dairy-free cakes and Oaxacan ice cream at this street stall. Another branch with seating and the same hours is around the corner at Coahuila 169.

LA GUERRERENSE

BAJA CALIFORNIA | $ | SEAFOOD
Cnr Avs Alvarado & López Mateos, Ensenada; www.laguerrerense.com; tostadas from M$27

Sabina Bandera's award-winning seafood stand dates from the 1960s and attracts long lines with its outstanding juicy *ceviche* and tostadas (deep-fried tortillas). Anthony Bourdain gave his approval in 2018 and shortly thereafter, Bandera opened the equally delicious restaurant Sabina right next door.

FINCA ALTOZANO

BAJA CALIFORNIA | $$$ | CALIFORNIAN
Carretera Tecate–Ensenada Km 83, Valle de Guadalupe; 646-156-80-45; www.fincaltozano.com; mains M$135-700

Our favourite of celebrity Mexican chef Javier Placensia's restaurants, this laid-back place looking out over the vineyards of Baja wine country has a cracking oyster bar and not-to-miss starters like grilled squid and roasted corn. Mains include everything from risotto and confit duck in *mole* (chilli sauce) to locally sourced beef brisket or wood-fired tacos.

TACO FISH LA PAZ

BAJA CALIFORNIA | $ | TAPAS
Cnr Avs Márques de León & Héroes de la Independencia, La Paz; tacos M$24-30

It remains largely undiscovered by tourists, but locals have been coming here in droves since 1992. Expect pristine stainless-steel surfaces and what might just be the best fish tacos in the whole of Baja. The extra battered, crispy fish style is reminiscent of an outstanding British fish and chips. The ceviche is off the charts as well.

PANCHO'S TAKOS

CENTRAL PACIFIC COAST | $ | TACOS
Badillo 162, Puerto Vallarta; 322-222-16-93; tacos M$13-64

WHERE TO DRINK...

MEZCAL

Bósforo, Mexico City
Blink and you might walk right past the coolest neighbourhood *mezcalería* in town. Behind a nondescript curtain await top-notch mezcals, eclectic music and surprisingly good bar grub.

El Rey de Matatlán, Valle de Tlacolula
This handsome Oaxacan hacienda sits amid agave fields and offers tours, tastings and plenty of excuses to get tipsy.

In Situ, Oaxaca City
Find some of Oaxaca's most unusual artisanal mezcals at this bar, with the help of its super-knowledgeable owner.

La Clandestina, Mexico City
This joint's detailed menu describes the distillation process of its delicious drops.

Set near the beach in Puerto Vallarta's appealing, cobblestoned Zona Romántica, Pancho's has queues forming right from when its door open at 6pm. It serves delicious *tacos al pastor* (spit-cooked pork with diced onions, coriander and pineapple), plus stuffed avocado, beef, chorizo and other options, after many neighbourhood restaurants have closed. You can sip a beer while you wait for your table.

TACOS DOÑA MARY

CENTRAL HIGHLANDS | $ | TACOS
5 de Mayo 144, Comala; dishes M$45

Locals in the glorious white-walled town of Comala will tell you this simple stall with a few outside seats has the some of the best tacos you'll ever taste. And the half dozen or so on offer here are blissfully tasty. The *asado de res* – roast beef – are perhaps the finest, closely followed by the moreish chorizo tacos.

NOMADA

CENTRAL HIGHLANDS | $$$ | MEXICAN
Macias 88, San Miguel de Allende; 415-121-61-65; www.facebook.com/nomadacocinadeinterpretacion; mains M$70-180, tasting menu M$550

This gorgeous place with friendly English-speaking staff serves up some great contemporary Mexican cuisine. Try its sublime pork-belly tacos, avocado with shrimp and pickled carrot puree or risotto with *huitlacoche* (corn fungus), serrano chilli and locally sourced cheese.

BROKA BISTROT

MEXICO CITY | $$ | FUSION
Zacatecas 126; 55-4437-4285; www.brokabistrot.com; set lunch M$165, mains M$155-255

Set in a stylish hidden patio in hip Roma, Broka serves delectable Euro–Mexican fusion dishes such as a fish and *nopal* stack with blue-corn tortillas. The restaurant's photogenic lunches – from cream of cauliflower soup to watercress tacos with bacon and strawberry – are regularly tweeted @brokabistrot.

LULA BISTRO

GUADALAJARA | $$$ | FUSION
San Gabriel 3030; 33-3647-64-32; www.lulabistro.com; mains M$190-310, 8-/12-course menu M$1200/160

This super-chic eatery west of the centre is Guadalajara's most inventive restaurant. Sleek and industrial though the setting is, it's the food people come for. The menus fuse French

***Previous page:* Restaurant in Oaxaca.**
***This page:* Stuffed poblano pepper in walnut sauce.**
***Opposite page:* Dishes from Broka Bistrot.**

COURTESY BROKA BISTROT

preparation with Mexican flavours in dishes such as confit of suckling pig with orange mole or grilled octopus with peanut and chili – the seafood dishes are particularly strong. Wine pairings are also available.

EL CIRUELO

AROUND MEXICO CITY | $$ | MEXICAN

Zaragoza 17, Tepoztlán; 777-219-37-20; www.elciruelo.com.mx; mains M$200-340

Eighty kilometres south of Mexico City, Tepoztlán is revered as the mythical birthplace of the great serpent god Quetzalcóatl. You can ponder his splendour this courtyard restaurant, which has impressive views of Tepoztlán's cliffs and pyramid. It's a long-standing favourite with an upmarket menu of dishes from *pechuga con plátano macho* (chicken with plantain in mole) and *salmón chileno a la mantequilla* (Chilean salmon in butter sauce) to good salads and soups, though prices are inflated by the scenery. There's a good wine selection, and on Saturday and Sunday there are play areas for kids.

WHERE TO EAT...

MOLE

Los Pacos, Oaxaca City
Order a sample dish of Oaxaca's seven *moles* with dipping tortillas before you make your dinner choice.

Augurio, Puebla
The creation of a Puebla celebrity chef, Augurio's ten types of *mole* are intriguing enough to even convert non-*mole* fans.

Azul Historico, Mexico City
Try the traditional house *mole* or the sweet *mole* with duck in a beautifully restored historical building in busy Cuauhtémoc.

El Mural de los Poblanos, Puebla
This lovely courtyard restaurant offers an array of excellent *moles*, alongside other traditional dishes.

PAITITI DEL MAR

ACAPULCO | $$ | SEAFOOD
Zaragoza 6, La Poza; 744-480-00-31; www.facebook.com/paititidelmar; mains M$140-220

Set in a tropical garden under a *palapa*, this inland seafood restaurant prepares dishes that put most of Acapulco's beachside eateries to shame. The *ceviche paraiso* is a flavour explosion of fresh tuna, mango, ginger, strawberry and habanero; order it with a refreshing cucumber-lime water. For the main course, the grilled or *ajillo*-style octopus draws high praise.

ALESSANDRO

OAXACA | $$ | ITALIAN
Rinconcito, Mazunte; 958-173-66-45; mains M$95-200

On Oaxaca's coast you're never far from an expat Italian chef, but few are as good as Alessandro. His small but brilliant place has just eight tables in a corner of the Posada del Arquitecto in the laid-back beach village of Mazunte. It serves up wonderful homemade pasta such as in arugula-and-avocado pesto, plus fresh fish (which might be served in *guajillo* chili and tomatillo sauce), *filet miñón* (beef tenderloin in white wine and olive oil) and desserts (don't miss the Oaxacan chocolate mousse with orange-and-rum perfume). Good drinks include Argentine wine, Oaxacan mezcal and thirst-quenching aguas de frutas (fruit cordials). Go early to avoid waiting.

EL MURAL DE LOS POBLANOS

PUEBLA | $$$ | MEXICAN
Av 16 de Septiembre 506; 222-225-06-50; www.elmuraldelospoblanos.com; mains M$175-350

Set back from the street in a gorgeous, plant-filled colonial courtyard, El Mural de los Poblanos serves excellent, traditional *poblano* dishes in an elegant setting. The house speciality is an array of mole sauces, and other favourites include a smokey goat's-cheese-stuffed *chilli relleno* and a trilogy of *cemitas* (a burger unique to Puebla). Cocktails and other drinks are also excellent, and the service exceptional. At different times of the year you can try local insect dishes such as *escamoles* (ant larvae).

CASA OAXACA

OAXACA CITY | $$$ | MEXICAN
Constitución 104A; 951-516-85-31; www.casaoaxacaelrestaurante.com; mains M$400-600

It's not easy living up to the mantle of Oaxaca's best restaurant, but this place consistently achieves. A glamorous rooftop terrace, theatrical tableside preparation, a posh cocktail scene, and an array of ravishing dishes – seared tuna, heirloom pepper stuffed with *ceviche*, duck in black *mole* sauce, and grilled octopus among them. Iron your shirt and make a reservation.

LOS PACOS

OAXACA CITY | $$$ | MEXICAN

Abasolo 121, 951-516-17-04; www.lospacosrestaurante.mx; mains M$70-260, mole tasting menu M$280

Moles are the prize here and, to make things easier, a tasting menu allows you to sample all seven of the revered sauces along with tortillas for dipping. They're all great, but the *mole negro* with chicken might just be the best. Los Pacos also offers *tasajo* (thinly sliced grilled beef) done 15 different ways. Grab a table on the rooftop terrace. There's another Los Pacos – older, more local and more family-oriented – in the Colonia Reforma neighbourhood in the northern suburbs.

LA PROVIDENCIA

OAXACA | $$ | MEXICAN

On the road behind the beach, Zipolite; 958-100-92-34; www.laprovidenciazipolite.com; mains M$130-225

The likeably bohemian costal village of Zipolite has a suitably laid-back stand-out restaurant, the outstanding La Providencia. It combines exquisite flavours with artful presentation and a relaxed ambience. You can sip a cocktail in the open-air lounge while you peruse the menu. It's a contemporary Mexican treat, from amaranth-encrusted aubergine to beef medallions with red-wine reduction or coconut-crusted prawns with mango sauce. Save room for the chocolate mousse!

'Our cooking is always changing, it draws ideas from everywhere, always reinterpreting and evolving, but with the roots in Mexican ingredients and techniques.'
Pujol

DOS

VERACRUZ CITY | $$$ | MEXICAN

Navegantes 96, Fraccionamiento Virginia; 229-935-47-84; http://dosboca.mx; mains M$290-395, set menu $785

At the best restaurant in the Veracruz City, if not the whole state, the six-course tasting menu is the way to go, each small dish supremely satisfying and bringing a new taste angle to simple things such as a taco or enchilada. Chef Erik Guerrero sources the produce for his inspired contemporary Mexican cuisine from across Veracruz, with a focus on sustainable fish (the soft-shelled crab taco is a favourite).

LA CEVICHERÍA TABASCO

TABASCO | $$ | SEAFOOD

Francisco José Hernández Mandujano 114, Villahermosa; 993-345-00-35; www.lacevicheriatabasco.com; mains M$130-250

This stellar seafood restaurant is just over the river from Tabasco's buzzing centre. With bright murals inside and out and a friendly neighbourhood vibe, it's a busy, and slightly chaotic place that serves seafood dishes that are so arty you can happily gaze in wonder at your meal before settling down to eat it. The tacos stuffed with marlin are especially impressive, and freshwater gar, grilled octopus and *ceviche* are also on offer.

EL SECRETO

CHIAPAS | $$ | INTERNATIONAL

Av 16 de Septiembre 24, San Cristóbal de las Casas; 967-674-91-21; http://www.casadelalma.mx; mains M$185-240

One of the best places to eat in Chiapas province – and one of the best value places this side of the equator. This excellent restaurant in the colonial highland city of San Cristóbal offers high-end gourmet cuisine, carefully plated and presented in a colour palette that would make Frida Kahlo blush. Get your eyes and tastebuds around everything from mushroom *ceviche* to suckling pig tacos to bass. There are good Mexican breakfasts, too.

KU'UK

MÉRIDA | $$$ | INTERNATIONAL

Av Rómulo Rozo No 488, cnr Calle 27; 999-944-33-77; www.kuukrestaurant.com; mains M$290-550, tasting menu M$1700, with wine pairing M$2600

The stunning historic home sets the scene for what's to come: a high-end, gourmet meal that ranks among the very best of Mexican cuisine. You can dine in a number of elegant, if slightly bare, rooms. The cuisine gives a nod to Yucatecan cuisine with contemporary preparation and flavour twists, such as suckling-pig cured ham stuffed with corn, barley and nuts or amberjack *ceviche* in black recado paste.

This page: Merida. Opposite page: Merida.

EL MIRADOR

YUCATÁN PENINSULA | $ | MEXICAN
Off Calle 42,Ticul; 997-972-13-43; mains M$80-90

El Mirador means lookout in Spanish and, yes, you get an awesome view of Ticul and beyond from this large *palapa* (thatched hut) restaurant. But it's the tasty Yucatecan comfort food that makes this place truly special. Try the *relleno blanco*, a hearty turkey stew, or go with a local favourite, *frijol con puerco* (beans and pork). Also has excellent *jugos naturales* (juices). It's best reached by taxi from Ticul.

'We make Mexican cuisine inspired by the flavors of Veracruz with fresh and local products. We look for each dish to evoke a memory or transport you somewhere.'
Dos

MANGO Y CHILE

YUCATÁN PENINSULA | $$ | VEGAN
Av 3 s/n, btwn Calles 22 & 24, Laguna Bacalar; 983-688-20-00; www.facebook.com/mangoychile; mains M$100-150

Set a block back from the crystal-clear waters of Laguna Bacalar, Mango y Chile has a large and beautiful deck overlooking the fort and the lagoon, and friendly service. The vegan food includes salads and (very tasty) plant-based burgers, doughnuts and cookies, and there are coffee and shakes to sip as you enjoy the views.

TERESITA'S

NORTHWEST MEXICO | $$ | BISTRO
Allende 46B, Álamos; 647-428-01-42; www.teresitasalamos.com; mains M$110-300

Nestled in the forested foothills of the Sierra Madre Occidental, the small town of Álamos is home to silver-mining heritage, jumping beans (they hop because of a larva inside) and this simply outstanding bakery-cum-bistro. There's an open kitchen and a changing menu that features mouthwatering salads, pastas, steaks and paninis, as well as offerings less usual in rural Mexico: spicy chicken wings, gazpacho and Middle Eastern veggie bowls. Desserts are fully catered for with sublime cakes and pastries. Either eat in the fountain-flanked garden or enjoy the comfort of a royal-blue banquette inside.

THE BAHAMAS

Food in the Bahamas is about the bounty of the seas. Conch (sea snail) and spiny Caribbean lobster star in a seafood-rich line-up. These seafoods are centrifugal forces, too, in that most intrinsically Bahamian tradition of all: fish fry, where locals gather beachside to munch fried-up fresh catch, drink beer and chat.

WHAT TO EAT

Boil fish
This Bahamas breakfast dish consists of grouper stewed with lime juice, onions and potatoes. It's usually served with johnnycake, a sweetish flat cornbread.

Conch
Whether roasted, cracked (fried), chopped into salads or fried into fritters, this chewy pink-shelled sea snail is ubiquitous.

Spiny Caribbean lobster
The islands' native lobster, often served sautéed with onions and pepper, minced or curried, bobs up a lot on menus.

Souse
Souse is a thick stew of chicken, sheep's head, pig's trotter or other 'leftover' meats.

PRICE RANGES
$ less than BS$20
$$ BS$20–30
$$$ BS$30 or more

Tipping: 15%

FISH FRY

NEW PROVIDENCE | $ | BAHAMIAN
Arawak Cay, off West Bay St, Nassau; 242-425-7275; mains BS$12-25

This colourful collection of conch stands, bars, jerk joints and seafood restaurants, known collectively as the 'Fish Fry', ranks among Nassau's greatest experiences. Come for conch salad, fried chicken wings, fritters, blackened snapper, 'sky juice' (a high-octane libation of coconut water and gin), reggae DJs, Junkanoo dances and friendly chatter. Open most days, it's Friday to Sunday evenings that are most popular here. Sunday is the big locals night, when crowds gather after spending the day with family.

GRAYCLIFF RESTAURANT

NEW PROVIDENCE | $$$ | INTERNATIONAL
Graycliff Hotel, West Hill St, Nassau; 242-302-9150; www.graycliff.com; mains BS$45-72

Colonial elegance hangs heavily at this atmospheric fine-diner in the 18th-century Graycliff Hotel. The predominantly European menu deploys a lot of imported ingredients but also uses Bahamian lobster and other local treasures. The wine cellar is legendary, with precious vintages like an 1865 Château Lafite among its 250,000 bottles. Dress code is elegant, especially in the evenings: no shorts or sandals.

DUNE

NEW PROVIDENCE | $$$ | FUSION
Ocean Club, 1 Casino Dr, Paradise Island; 242-363-2501; www.fourseasons.com/oceanclub/dining/restaurants/dune; mains BS$20-55

French–American celebrity chef Jean-Georges Vongerichten created the menu at this ultra-popular (and ultra-pricey!) fusion restaurant, floating atop a dune in front of the genteel Ocean Club hotel on Paradise Island, north of downtown Nassau. The menu globe-hops with agility: Asian fish dishes, Australian lamb, Bahamian lobster and truffle pizza.

SMITH'S POINT FISH FRY

GRAND BAHAMA | $ | BAHAMIAN
Taino Beach, Freeport; mains BS$12-15

Wednesday night is *the* night at Smith's Point Fish Fry, with an atmosphere like a giant neighbourhood party. Beachfront shacks fire up oil-drum cookers and fry turbot, lobster and conch fritters for crowds of locals, who gossip the night away eating and drinking cold Kalik beers and rum punch. The scene heats up after 9pm, when live music gets rolling. The party happens Saturday nights too, to a lesser extent.

COLORS BY THE SEA

THE ABACOS | $ | BAHAMIAN
East Bay St, Marsh Harbour; 242-699-3294; mains BS$11-20

This brightly painted open-sided shack over the water is a contender for the most atmospheric restaurant-bar in Marsh Harbour, third-largest settlement in the Bahamas. Some come to argue good-naturedly over football and a few beers, but most take advantage of the deft hands in the kitchen, savouring blackened grouper, excellent conch and lobster (in season).

'The menu globe-hops with agility: Asian fish dishes, Australian lamb, Bahamian lobster and truffle pizza.'
Dune

SIP SIP

ELEUTHRA | $$ | INTERNATIONAL
Court St, Harbour Island; 242-333-3316; www.sipsiprestaurant.com; mains BS$16-26

The 'sip sip' at this uber-popular and convivial lime-green lunchtime-only cafe refers not to drinking but to the local term for gossip, which you can partake of along with the blissful pink-sand beach views from the terrace whilst wondering what to select from a cosmopolitan Bahamian menu ranging from lobster quesadillas to curried chicken salad. No reservations: first come, first served.

TIPPY'S BAR & BEACH RESTAURANT

ELEUTHRA | $$ | INTERNATIONAL
North Palmetto Point Beach, near Banks Rd, Governor's Harbour; 242-332-3331; www.pineapplefields.com/tippys-restaurant-eleuthera.html; mains BS$20-38

This beach bar has a delightful ocean-facing deck and eclectic, welcoming timber decor inside its individual huts. The restaurant specialises in globally influenced seafood dishes – coconut shrimp, Bahamian bouillabaisse – presented on a huge chalkboard menu. Jam-packed even in low season, it gets wild on busy weekend nights. Book ahead.

WHAT TO EAT
Ropa vieja
With a name that translates as 'old clothes' Cuba's national dish consists of spicy shredded beef cooked in a tomato-based sauce.
Lechon asado
Whole spit-roasted pork is a favourite feast at festivals and on public holidays.
Moros y cristianos
White rice and black beans blended together and doused with a fragrant *sofrito* (sauce) made from onions, garlic and peppers.
Lobster
Popular and relatively cheap shellfish that's usually cooked whole on a grill and served with butter.
Picadillo
Minced beef flavoured with peppers, herbs and capers, and usually served with rice.

PRICE RANGES
For a main course:
$ less than CUC$7
$$ CUC$7–15
$$$ CUC$15 or more

Tipping: 10–15%

CUBA

Good food in Cuba has a short history. Until recently, economic challenges coupled with stringent government restrictions meant that basic ingredients were thin on the ground. But, in the past decade with private restaurants proliferating, local chefs have sharpened their creative knives and Cuba has injected some much-needed spice into its Spanish meets African meets Indigenous flavoured food.

TRES JOTAS

VIÑALES | $$ | TAPAS
Salvador Cisneros No 45; 5331-1658; tapas CU C$2-6

One of the best restaurants in Cuba outside Havana, Tres Jotas is Viñales' original tapas bar that has since been copied by all and sundry. Its inviting polished-wood interior is the perfect place to unwind after a day in the countryside with classy cocktails, taste-exploding tapas, and deli-boards overflowing with cured ham and manchego cheese. For something more dinner-worthy, taste the lamb slow-cooked in red wine – not a tapa this one, but a real feast.

LA REDACCIÓN

TRINIDAD | $$ | INTERNATIONAL
Antonio Maceo No 463; 4199-4593; www.laredaccioncuba.com; mains CUC $8-10

Contrasting its colonial style with a cleverly titled menu and excellent service, this French-run eatery provides a dose of comfort for travelers with culinary homesickness. Think huge lamb burgers with sweet

potato fries, pasta tossed with lobster, and appealing vegetarian options. For solo travelers, there's a huge shared table in the center conducive to making friends. The 19th century furnishings, including chessboard floor-tiles and elegant mirrors, are as attractive as the food.

EL GALEON

NUEVA GERONA | $ | CUBAN

Calle 24, btwn Calles 45 & 47; 4650-9128; mains CU C$4-7

A superb rooftop restaurant above a casa particular (homestay) on the little-visited Isla de la Juventud, El Galeon serves Havana-worthy Cuban classics off a smoking charcoal grill. Service is friendly and fast, the decor is nautical, traditional live music adds to the ambience, and mojitos cost just CUC$1.50 – and they come around at least once with a top-up of rum! You'll end the night surprised, satisfied and slightly sloshed.

COURTESY ROY'S TERRACE INN

'Situated in a beautiful early-20th-century mansion, La Guarida is a place that's full of magic'.
La Guardia

ROY'S TERRACE INN ROOF GARDEN RESTAURANT

SANTIAGO DE CUBA | $$ | CUBAN

Diego Palacios No 177, btwn Padre Pico & Mariano Corona; 2262-0522; meals CUC $10-15

If only the rest of Cuba could harness this formula: quality homemade food, caring service and excellent atmosphere. Reserve one day ahead for one of only six rooftop tables surrounded by tumbling flowers in candlelight at this pioneering homestay cum restaurant. Tongue-loosening cocktails and family-style servings arrive brimming. Fish, chicken or pork are accompanied with sides such as crispy tamales or sautéed aubergine. Vegans and vegetarians won't go hungry.

LA GUARIDA

HAVANA | $$$ | INTERNATIONAL

Concordia No 418, btwn Gervasio & Escobar; 7-866-9047; www.laguarida.com; mains CUC $15-22

The entrance to Havana's most legendary private restaurant greets you like a scene out of a 1940s film noir.

COURTESY LA REDACCION

A decapitated statue stands at the bottom of a grand but dilapidated staircase that leads past lines of drying clothes to a wooden door, beyond which lie multiple culinary surprises. Dishes sway between classic (*ropa vieja;* shredded beef) and those that are unusual for Cuba (lamb tikka masala).

DONA EUTIMIA

HAVANA | $$ | CUBAN
Callejón del Chorro 60c; 7-861-1332; mains CUC $8-12

The secret at Doña Eutimia is that there is no secret: just serve decent-size portions of the best Cuban food. Expect punchy *ropa vieja* (shredded beef), epic *picadillo a la habanera* (spicy beef), glorious *lechon asado* (roast pork) and beautifully rustic roast chicken, all served with ample rice, beans and fried plantains. This is trip-defining food of the highest order, and proof traditional Cuban cuisine can still be pretty spectacular.

LAMPARILLA 361 TAPAS Y CERVEZAS

HAVANA | $$ | TAPAS
Lamparilla No 361, btwn Aguacate & Villegas; 5289-5324; tapas CU C $5-12

Havana's best tapas bar might also be the city's finest all-round eating establishment getting its food, presentation and service down to a fine art. Nestled in the loungy, romantically lit interior there's plenty to look at as you enjoy ice-cold beer, fabulous cocktails, and creative but interestingly presented tapas (on plates, slates, pans and mini-shopping trolleys). But, best of all is the sharp, discreet and multilingual service that ought to be bottled and exported all around Cuba.

AJIACO CAFÉ - HAVANA

HAVANA | $$ | CUBAN
Calle 92 No 267, btwn Av 3E & 5, Cojímar; 7-765-0514; mains CUC $4-12

There are, arguably, two reasons to come to the Havana suburb of Cojímar: 1) to pursue the ghost of Ernest Hemingway and 2) to visit this farm-to-table restaurant named for a quintessential Cuban stew that headlines a menu of Cuban classics, all executed with rustic creativity. Here you can order fried chickpeas, pork ribs in a barbecue-and-honey sauce, or a unique shredded-beef and plantain pizza. Round it all off with the smoothest and best coffee in Cuba.

EL RUM RUM DE LA HABANA

HAVANA | $$ | SEAFOOD
Empedrado No 256, btwn Cuba & Aguiar; 7-861-0806; mains CU C$7-18

Not every restaurant has a wine sommelier *and* a cigar sommelier, but this is Havana, and El Rum Rum (Cuban slang for 'gossip') can put you straight on every area of consumption. Be serenaded by concert-worthy musical entertainment as you navigate through a menu of subtle scents and sauces

Previous spread: Cocktails in La Redacción, Roy's Terrace Inn. P46-7: Jerk chicken, Port Antonio. P49: Fried fish.

including *caldereta de mariscos* (a rich seafood stew), steak with three toppings and about 10 ways of imbibing your mojito.

LO DE MONIK

HAVANA | $$ | TAPAS

Compostela No 201, cnr Chacón; 7-864-4029; mains CUC $10-15

Eschewing colonial splendor for a French bistro feel, the Monik blends seamlessly into Habana Vieja's increasingly chic Loma del Ángel quarter, with a bright-white interior and arguably the city's friendliest and chattiest staff. Search the ever-changing blackboard menu for brunch or tapas ideas (fish tacos, well-stuffed Cuban baguettes, creamy cheesecake) and come back later for spectacular cocktails.

RESTAURANTE FLORIDA TERRACE

SANTA CLARA | $$ | CUBAN

Maestra Nicolasa No 56, btwn Colón & Maceo; 4220-8161; mains CUC $10-15

The Florida has been Santa Clara's best restaurant for at least a decade. The food is as good as the experience. Diners feast in a colonial, plant-festooned, candlelit courtyard full of interesting antiques. Ever-present owner Ángel is the perfect host, advising on the nuances of the dishes in French, English, Italian and Spanish. The menu is simple but classic Cuban. The highlight: lobster with prawns in a 'secret' tomato sauce.

RESTAURANTE MAITE LA QBANA

MORÓN | $$ | INTERNATIONAL

Luz Caballero No 40b, btwn Libertad & Agramonte; 3350-4181; mains CUC $10-15

Owner-chef, Maité is a highly creative cook whose international dishes, prepared with *mucho amor*, will leave you wondering why insipid all-inclusive buffets ever got so popular. Prepare for abundant appetisers, fine wines and cocktails, homemade cakes and paella that has visiting *valencianos* reminiscing about their homeland. In the journeyman, little visited town of Morón, this place, affiliated to an equally congenial homestay, is a godsend.

EL BUEN SABOR

BARACOA | $$ | CUBAN

Calixto García No 134 altos; 2164-1400; meals CUC $6-15

Served on a spotless upstairs terrace, meals at this breeze-licked private restaurant come with salad, soup and side included. Get ready for the best of Baracoa's unique cuisine, including swordfish in a coconut sauce, *bacán* (raw green plantain melded with crabmeat and wrapped in a banana leaf) and chocolate-y desserts. Table-hopping troubadours enhance the typically Cuban ambience.

WHERE TO DRINK...

MOJITOS

El Chanchullero, Havana
Appetite-quenching tapas; cheap, potent mojitos; and cool people.

Hotel Nacional, Havana
As much about setting as booze, a minty mojito in Havana's most emblematic hotel with its elegant garden-terrace is practically de rigueur.

O'Reilly 304, Havana
Small bar-restaurant filled nightly with a buoyant crowd all happy to be enjoying delectable food and the best fruity alcoholic beverages in Havana.

Bodeguita del Medio, Santa Clara
Bodyswerve the tourist-heavy original bar in Havana and hit this provincial branch where the signature mojitos are just as good but a lot cheaper.

JAMAICA

Jamaica is rightly famous for its succulent, spicy jerk, but there's a whole lot more to the island's cuisine. Only the adventurous wander into the surprisingly delicious territory of mannish water (aka goat-head soup), but the day-to-day staples, from fresh seafood to ackee and saltfish, are utterly addictive.

WHAT TO EAT

Jerk
Named for its fiery local-spice marinade, jerk meat (usually pork or chicken) cooked long and slow on a covered pimento-wood firepit. Served with roast yam/breadfruit or 'festival' (fried dumplings).

Ackee and saltfish
Ackee fruit, similar in taste to avocado and in looks to scrambled eggs, sautéed with flaked salt cod.

Curry goat
Tender goat in a rich curry sauce.

Escoveich fish
Well-seasoned fish, fried then slathered with a tangy sauce of vinegar, scotch bonnet peppers, onion and carrot.

Calalloo
Spinach-like leafy green, sautéed with onion, garlic and tomato.

Rice and peas
Kidney beans and rice, cooked in coconut milk.

PRICE RANGES

$ less than J$1900
$$ J$1900–3200
$$$ J$3200 or more

Tipping: 10–15%

LITTLE OCHIE

ST ELIZABETH | $$ | SEAFOOD

Alligator Pond Beach, Treasure Beach; 852-6430; mains per lb J$880-2365

Little Ochie is a culinary phenomenon that, despite a cult following, refuses to sell out. Set on a slice of black-sand beach, it uses the same charcoal-blackened kitchen and scribbled chalk-board menu it has for eons. The secret? Pay-by-weight fish and seafood straight from the sea, served steamed, jerked, curried or grilled, with dining tables in boats on stilts under thatched awnings. The jerk is always a good bet; grilled lobster and jerk snapper also have a dedicated following. And 'dedicated' is the word – this is one of Jamaica's few bona fide destination restaurants.

PEPPER'S JERK

FALMOUTH | $ | JERK

20 Duke St; 617-3427; www.peppersjerkcenter.com; quarter pork/chicken J$600/500

A little tourist-centred, but still the epitome of a great jerk spot: thatched-roof, casual outdoor seating, mellow reggae and an awful lot of flavour packed into the meat, slow-cooked over pimento wood. There's the chicken with the crisp, blistered skin, liberally seasoned with allspice, and the spicy hit of jerk pork that bounces pleasingly between the teeth. Fish, oxtail, seafood and all the jerk sides, too, from roast breadfruit or yam to 'festival'.

STUSH IN THE BUSH

OCHO RIOS | $$$ | GASTRONOMY
Bamboo, Priory; 562-9760; www.stushinthebush.com; meals US$70-95

This farm-to-table dining experience embraces seasonality and sustainability, and offers some of the best food anywhere in Jamaica. After a welcome platter of yam and pineapple croquettes, plantain or jerked pumpkin chips and zingy dipping sauces, you take a walking tour to learn about the farm, then eat in a gorgeous rustic cabin with tremendous views. There's a four-course gourmet pizza menu, or a seven-course 'sexy vegetarian' (or vegan) spread which showcases the home-grown produce, from gorgeous greens and coconut-based soups to chocolate cake and beignets. Reservations are essential.

MI HUNGRY

KINGSTON | $ | VEGETARIAN
Market Place, 67 Constant Spring Rd; www.facebook.com/MihungryWholSomeFood; mains J$550/1150

Mi Hungry serves up fresh juices and raw or sun-cooked I-tal (natural) food that you wouldn't believe. The 'pleaza' comes with a base of seeds and grains, topped with sun-dried tomatoes and crunchy veg (try ackee with a few chillies) and is delicious in a way that the phrase 'raw vegan pizza' can't convey – you'll definitely want to come back for more. The nyamburgers with ackee and plantain are equally moreish. Made with love.

BRENT HOFACKER/SHUTTERSTOCK ©

'At Pepper's you can indulge in authentic Jamaican dishes in a historic setting that offers a true feel of life in Jamaica.'
Pepper's Jerk

WESTEND61/GETTY IMAGES ©

WILKES SEAFOOD

PORT ANTONIO | $$ | SEAFOOD
Allen Ave; 378-5970; mains J$2600 3800

Wilkes is a thoroughly unassuming beach bar from the outside, but a delightful small restaurant within. Overlooking the sea, there is a semi-open kitchen that lets the cooking aromas make you hungry as you watch the sun go down. Nothing you order will disappoint, though the coconut curried fish is a particular winner. Dining here is a real Jamaican highlight. On Sundays, visit early for filling Jamaican breakfasts: ackee, saltfish and the works.

WHAT TO EAT

Mofongos
One of the DR's most interesting local specialities: plantains mashed with pork rinds and loaded with meat or seafood.

Chivo guisado
Goat stewed in tomato sauce – well worth seeking out in the highlands.

***Mero* (grouper) or *chillo* (red snapper)**
Fresh fish served *al ajillo* (with garlic), *al coco* (in coconut sauce), *al criolla* (mild tomato sauce) or *a la diabla* (spicy tomato sauce) is ubiquitous.

Mangú
Boiled plantains mashed with butter and topped with vinegary onions, often served alongside fried cheese, Dominican salami and eggs in a dish called Los Tres Golpes (The Three Strikes).

PRICE RANGES
For a main course:
$ less than RD$350
$$ RD$350–700
$$$ RD$700 or more

Tipping: 10%

DOMINICAN REPUBLIC

The Dominican Republic's creole-style cuisine owes debts to Taíno, European and African origins. Lobster, shrimp, conch (and other Caribbean seafood) as well as goat fuel the domestic gastronomic culture alongside droves of international options with dreamy sea views on the side.

RANCHO TIPICO

PENÍNSULA DE PEDERNALES | $$ | SEAFOOD
Playa Las Cuevas, Bahía de Las Águilas; 809-753-8058; mains RD$350-750

Rancho Tipico does some of the best *mofongos* (mashed plantains with meat or seafood) you will ever eat in one of the most stunning settings in the DR. Stop en route to/from cinematic Bahía de Las Águilas.

AROMA DE LA MONTAÑA

CENTRAL HIGHLANDS | $$$ | DOMINICAN
Carretera Palo Blanco, Jarabacoa; 829-452-6879; www.aromadelamontana.com; mains RD$600-1500

Sweeping, practically aerial views of the Jarabacoa countryside are available from the terrace of this mountaintop restaurant – the only rotating restaurant in the Caribbean. Upscale takes on Dominican classics like *mero* (grouper) *al coco* (coconut sauce) complement the vista.

TIPICO BONAO

CENTRAL HIGHLANDS | $$ | DOMINICAN
Autopista Duarte, Km90, Bonao; 809-525-3941; mains RD$190-890

The DR's most Dominican restaurant, located smack in the middle of the country. All manner of creole-style meat and seafood (stews of rabbit, wild guinea hen, conch or crab tails and garlic) are prettily plated under a colossal thatched roof.

MARES RESTAURANT

NORTH COAST | $$$ | DOMINICAN
Francisco Peynado 6, Puerto Plata; 809-261-3330; www.maresrestaurant.com; mains RD$700

Distinguished chef Rafael Vasquez-Heinsen has converted his elegant home into a candlelit dining destination, turning out dishes that creatively combine Dominican ingredients with tried and true culinary traditions. The Dominican goat marinated with rum is a favourite.

MICHAEL'S STONE BAR

NORTH COAST | $ | SEAFOOD
Julio Arzeno, Sosúa; 809-804-3666; mains RD$330

Perched on a cliff at the very southern end of Playa Sosúa, this simple, traditional beach shack combines million-dollar views with freshly prepared crab, fish and lobster.

BARRA PAYÁN

SANTO DOMINGO | $ | SANDWICHES
Av Tiradentes 16; 809-565-1555; sandwiches RD$110-240

Capitaleños have been lining up for this fast food joint's signature delicious pork sandwich before and after late nights out since the 1950s. Freshly made juices make for a perfect pairing.

MAISON KREYOL RESTAURANT

SANTO DOMINGO | $$ | HAITIAN
Las Mercedes 321; 809-221-0459; www.maisonkreyol.com; mains RD$325-600

The bare bones dining room belies the quality of Haitian cooking in delicious dishes like grilled spicy goat, whole snapper and okra fritters. Wash it all down with a bottle of Haitian beer or unusual fruit juice flavors.

'Our creative Dominican kitchen loves to break the rules – try the shrimp and fried plantains with creole, chipotle and tarragon sauce.'
Rafael Vasquez, Mares Restaurant

MATT MUNRO/LONELY PLANET ©

EL CABITO

PENÍNSULA DE SAMANÁ | $$$ | SEAFOOD
Calle La Bahia 1, Las Galeras; 809-820-2263; mains RD850

Sure, the rough road might take out the axel on an ordinary car. And the paved and messy parking area doesn't inspire confidence. And service can be lacklustre. But trust us! Enjoy heaped plates of fresh seafood perched over a commanding cliffside on the edge of the DR with hawks soaring overhead and whales in the distance. Perfection.

PUERTO RICO

Puerto Rico might be better-known for phenomenal drinks – Bacardi, piña colada – but eating is big too: quality-wise and quantity-wise. First-choice chow is pork (islanders adore it) although seafood is also sublime. Sample this simple-but-sensational cuisine spearheaded as much by hipster-frequented food trucks and beach bars as by Michelin star–winning chefs.

MARMALADE

SAN JUAN | $$$ | FUSION
317 Fortaleza, Old San Juan; 787-724-3969; www.marmaladepr.com; mains US$18-45, tasting menu US$75-95

The vision of James Beard Award–winning chef Peter Schintler, suavely minimalist Marmalade was among the first restaurants to bring real foodie recognition to Old San Juan. The menu utilises top-notch local produce – yellowtail, pork belly, avocados – to create delicious food art and the wine list is excellent.

SEÑOR PALETA

SAN JUAN | $ | ICE CREAM
153 Tetúan, Old San Juan; 787-724-5588; www.facebook.com/srpaletapr; paletas US$3.50-5

This hole-in-the-wall institution sells artisanal *paletas* (popsicles) made from fresh fruit and other tasty treats. Flavours range from passion fruit and *guanabana* (soursop) to carrot cake, chocolate and coconut. Queues lengthen as the city starts sizzling.

1919 RESTAURANT

SAN JUAN | $$$ | PUERTO RICAN
1055 Av Ashford, Condado; 787-721-5500; www.condadovanderbilt.com/condado-1919-restaurant; mains US$45-55, tasting menu US$95

Juan José Cuevas is the Puerto Rican, Michelin-starred executive chef at the classy Condado Vanderbilt hotel's fine-dining flagship restaurant. He champions local farmers and spent months sourcing the island's finest ingredients for dishes like tuna-*hiramasa* crudo with local radish, lobster and salami risotto and his speciality *cochinillo*, or pig cheek. The elegant, colonnaded surroundings make dinner here extra special.

CAFÉ COMUNIÓN

SAN JUAN | $ | COFFEE

WHAT TO EAT

Mofongo
Puerto Rico's palate-stimulating staple is smashed plantains cooked with garlic, spices, broth and pork chunks. Other flavourings include shrimps and chicken.

Lechón asado
The heavenly smell of whole roast pig wafts from countless stalls island-wide. This succulent, lavishly seasoned treat is best enjoyed at Guavate, where numerous roadside outlets vend it.

Chuletas Can Can
Puerto Rico's pork fetish is also showcased by this popular pork chop cooked so meat looks fringed like a showgirl's skirt.

Alcapurrias
Torpedo-shaped fritters stuffed with ground beef or conch (pink-shelled sea snail) make perfect beachside hunger-busters.

PRICE RANGES

For a one- to two-course meal:
$ less than US$18
$$ US$18–30
$$$ US$30 or more

Tipping: 15–20%

1616 Avenida Ponce de León; Santurce; www.facebook.com/cafecomunion; coffees and cakes US$2-6

Award-winning barista Abner Roldan's cafe wouldn't look out-of-place in New York or London. It supports the island's highly regarded home-grown beans, as well as showcasing coffee from the likes of Colombia and Ethiopia. The coffee is San Juan's best; locally baked sweet treats are pretty good too.

VIANDA

SAN JUAN | $$ | PUERTO RICAN
1413 Av Ponce de León, Santurce; 939-475-1578; www.viandapr.com; mains US$19-34

This stylish farm-to-fork restaurant from husband-and-wife team Francis Guzmán and Amelia Dill has become a favourite fixture in the city's vibrant food scene. Its super-seasonal menu reinvents Puerto Rican staples, like the 'Tom Kha' Bacalo, coconut-rich broth with mushrooms and crispy rice, or *mofongo* with garlic shrimps and rouille salsa.

BISTRO DEL MAR

LUQUILLO | $ | FOOD TRUCK
Herminio Díaz Navarro, Playa la Pared; 939-269-1978; meals US$3-19

Bistro del Mar is a crown jewel in the island's booming food truck business, with enticing takes on Puerto Rican and pan-Latin eats. Order *mofongos*, seafood ceviches, stuffed avocado, quesadillas and more. The perfect pit stop in Luquillo, renowned for its fabulous beaches, its surfing – and its food kiosks.

'An oh-so-Rincón mix of vacationing surfers, alternative lifestylers and stalwart expats tuck into uncomplicated but sensational food.'
La Copa Llena

EL QUENEPO

VIEQUES | $$$ | SEAFOOD
148 Flamboyan, Esparanza; 787-741-1215, www.elquenepovieques.com; mains US$25-35

On sandy island paradise Vieques, upscale El Quenepo has a lovely interior and an equally delectable menu. The food is catch-of-the-day fresh, including whole Caribbean lobsters, *mofongo* made with backyard-grown breadfruit and delicately pan-seared scallops with coconut crème fraîche and caviar. Good craft beers, cocktails and even pretty guestrooms for those who have over-indulged await. Book ahead.

LA COPA LLENA

RINCÓN | $$ | INTERNATIONAL
Black Eagle Marina; 787-823-0896; http://attheblackeagle.com; mains US$17-36

This numbers among Rincón's best restaurants but is also almost certainly its liveliest. An oh-so-Rincón mix of vacationing surfers, alternative lifestylers and stalwart expats tuck into uncomplicated but sensational food, such as shredded papaya, peanut and shrimp salad or lip-smacking cashew nut and catch-of-the-day fish curry, whilst the ocean looms huge alongside the picturesquely positioned patio.

ST KITTS & NEVIS

The twin islands of St Kitts & Nevis offer superb dining opportunities, inspired by the surrounding waters of the Caribbean and also drawing on the islands' long culinary traditions which marry influences from Europe and Africa.

WHAT TO EAT

Stewed saltfish
The national dish of St Kitts & Nevis is normally served with spicy plantains, coconut dumplings and seasoned breadfruit.

Tannia fritters
These gorgeous root vegetable fritters are a much-loved accompaniment to any Kittitian meal.

Conch
This Caribbean favourite is served in various forms locally: curried, marinated or soused (boiled).

Pelau
Also known as 'cook-up,' this is the Kittitian version of paella: a tasty, messy blend of rice, meat, saltfish, vegetables and pigeon peas.

Goat water
This rich, brown soup is said to be an aphrodisiac and containsherbs, spices and virtually every part of its namesake goat.

PRICE RANGES

For a main course:
$ less than US$10
$$ US$10–20
$$$ US$20 or more

Tipping: 10–15%

EL FREDO'S

ST KITTS | $$ | CARIBBEAN

cnr Bay & Sanddown Rds, Basseterre;. 869-466-8871; mains EC$30-50

This charming spot on Basseterre's busy seafront is massively popular with locals and cruise-ship escapees alike. Try its creole snapper, garlic shrimp, oxtail soup or goat stew, all paired with a potpourri of provisions (starchy sides), including delicious dumplings. The setting is classic Caribbean cool but the homemade sauce is famously hot – proceed with caution.

BANANAS RESTAURANT

NEVIS | $$$ | INTERNATIONAL

Upper Hamilton Estate; 869-469-1891; www.bananasnevis.com; mains US$18-45

A torchlit walkway leads to this enchanting two-storey garden hideaway hand-built by British transplant, former dancer Gillian Smith. Come for a cocktail and the exceptional sunsets upstairs before heading to the animated veranda downstairs and tucking into food inspired by Gillian's travels. Local flavours such as conch gratin, curried goat, salt fish and tannia fritters stuff the menu and the desserts are just as varied and ambitious.

GIN TRAP BAR & RESTAURANT

NEVIS | $$$ | CARIBBEAN

Main Island Rd, Jones Bay; 869-469-8230; www.thegintrapnevis.com; mains US$18-40

Sunset views out to St Kitts are positively dreamy at this worldly traveller outpost with a kitchen showcasing the very best of Caribbean cooking including dishes such as conch chowder with coconut dumplings, island spiced scallops, and shrimp curry. Kick things off in the stylish bar with a jalapeño-laced Gin Trap cocktail.

ANTIGUA & BARBUDA

Antigua and Barbuda are two very different slices of the Caribbean, with glitzy yachtie favourite Antigua heaving with sophisticated international restaurants catering to well-heeled customers, while sleepy Barbuda offers a more unadulterated, traditional Caribbean experience.

WHAT TO EAT

Pepperpot
Antigua's national dish is a hearty stew blending meat and locally grown crops such as okra, spinach, aubergine, squash and potatoes.

Fungi
The traditional accompaniment to pepperpot, fungi are actually traditional cornmeal patties – nothing to do with mushrooms at all.

Rock lobster
This hulking crustacean has a succulent tail but no claws and is often served grilled.

Black pineapple
Known as 'black' because it's eaten when dark green and at its sweetest, this small Antiguan pineapple is found on sale along the roadside particularly in the island's southwest corner, where it's often used to make jam.

PRICE RANGES

For a main course:
$ less than US$10
$$ US$10–25
$$$ US$25 or more

Tipping: 10–15%

PAPA ZOUK

ST JOHN'S | $$ | SEAFOOD

Hilda Davis Dr; 268-464-6044; www.facebook.com/Papazouk; mains EC$50-100

This high-energy joint is a local institution, famous for its Antiguan-style bouillabaisse and superb fresh fish – *mahimahi*, lionfish, red snapper, butterfish. With zouk on the sound system, crazy murals, Christmas lights and a nautical decor, it's the kind of place that's downright trippy even before you've started sampling the vast rum selection. Booking is essential.

CECILIA'S HIGH POINT CAFE

DUTCHMAN'S BAY | $$$ | MEDITERRANEAN

Texaco Dock Rd; 268-562-7070; www.highpointantigua.com; mains EC$55-110

With gorgeous views of the surf crashing onto the beach below, Cecilia's is presided over by a former Swedish model and her host of animal friends. It's beloved by an international crowd of regulars who pack the place out for lunch. Top menu picks include the lobster ravioli and the beef tenderloin, although the regularly changing blackboard specials are also top-notch.

COLIBRI

ENGLISH HARBOUR | $$$ | FRENCH CARIBBEAN

Dockyard Dr; 268-460-3434; www.colibri-antigua.com; mains EC$70-85

The most talked-about recent addition to English Harbour's fine slew of dining options, Colibri is the brainchild of French transplant Didier, who works hard to deliver a superlative Gallic–Caribbean dining experience. Don't miss the accras and *boudin noir creole* starters, or the excellent lobster risotto.

DOMINICA

Rainforest-swathed Dominica has generally lagged behinds its more developed Caribbean neighbours when it comes to sophisticated dining experiences, but as ecotourism here booms, the island is slowly beginning to explore its unique flavours, varied local ingredients and rich creole cookery traditions.

WHAT TO EAT

Callaloo
This thick and creamy soup blends a variety of locally grown crops such as dasheen (taro root), spinach, aubergine or okra with coconut milk and crabmeat.

Oxtail stew
This much-loved local stew heaves with spices in its signature thick sauce.

Braf
A very simple Dominican staple, in which essentially a range of provisions (vegetables, roots and other crops) are mixed with whatever herbs, spices and meat or fish can be found in the kitchen.

Mountain chicken
This unusually named dish is made from the legs of the crapaud, a huge frog found only in Dominica and neighbouring Montserrat.

PRICE RANGES
For a main course:
$ less than US$10
$$ US$10–20
$$$ US$20 or more

Tipping: 10–15%

PEARL'S CUISINE

ROSEAU | $$ | CARIBBEAN
Great Marlborough St; 767-448-8707; mains EC$25-50

This 25-year-old Roseau institution may keep changing location, but its much-loved creole food stays the same, making it the ideal place to try some authentic Dominican dishes such as bullfoot soup, chicken callaloo or stewed *agouti* (a local rodent). It's a simple and unpretentious place (think: plastic tables and bright lighting) and gets busiest on Saturdays when all dishes cost just EC$25. Soursop ice cream makes for a delicious dessert.

C&D BEACH BAR & GRILL

PORTSMOUTH | $$$ | CARIBBEAN
Picard; 767-315-6291; mains EC$50-75

The most interesting menu in Dominica's second town of Portsmouth can be found at Candy and David's charming restaurant right on the beach, where music and lighting are at just the right level, service is friendly and the chalkboard menu includes dishes such as panko-crusted pork chop with sweet-chili tomato sauce, and garlic mussels simmered in locally-brewed Kubuli beer. Do not miss the Hurricane shrimp appetiser!

POZ RESTAURANT & BAR

CALIBISHIE | $$ | CARIBBEAN
off Main Rd; 767-612-5176; mains EC$40-60

'Poz' is the nickname of Troy, a warm-hearted dreamer from Toronto whose magical restaurant has evolved into a community hangout for expats, visitors and villagers on Dominica's enchanting northern coast. From bacon-wrapped plantain to oxtail stew, and lobster in garlic butter to curried goat, the tastes are superb and totally authentic. The poolside dining area built entirely from local wood is a cosy delight, and you're guaranteed to meet your fair share of local characters.

ST VINCENT & THE GRENADINES

The main island of St Vincent has some interesting traditional Caribbean dishes on offer, but the best eats in the country are found further south in the Grenadines, especially on delightful Bequia, where the seafood is fresh and the flavours bold.

WHAT TO EAT

Lobster
SVG lobster is harvested in the Grenadines and is so good it's exported throughout the region but it's better fresh from the boat right here.

Rotis
Curried vegetables, potatoes and meat or seafood wrapped in a flour tortilla are a national passion.

Saltfish
Salted cod if a key ingredients in many Vincentian dishes but its at it's tastiest when made into fish cakes.

Callalloo
A green leafy vegetable somewhat similar to spinach that is prepared in soup or as a side dish.

Pumpkin Soup
Thick, rich and delicious, this Vincentian soup made is a meal on its own.

PRICE RANGES

$ less than EC$35
$$ EC$35–70
$$$ EC$70 or more

Tipping: 10–15%

THE LOCAL

UNION ISLAND | $$ | CARIBBEAN
Front St; Clifton; mains EC$10-50

A modern and welcoming spot on the 2nd floor overlooking the comings and goings on Clifton's main road, the Local serves up quality burgers, wraps and fish plates. It's especially worthwhile at lunch when it offers affordable portions of typical local dishes including outstanding salt fish with coconut dumplings.

BASIL'S BAR & RESTAURANT

KINGSTOWN | $$ | CARIBBEAN
Upper Bay St; 457-2713; mains EC$35-87

If the food wasn't so good, you might think you'd entered a pirate's dungeon, given the moody lighting and stone walls. Food spans American and Caribbean favourites; the lunch buffet is the best place to fill up in the capital. Bonus: it has Kingstown's classiest bar.

FIG TREE

BEQUIA | $$ | CARIBBEAN
Belmont Walkway; Port Elizabeth; 457-3008; mains EC$40-70

A 300m stroll along the waterfront west of the docks, this open-air restaurant has views to match both the great food and hospitality of the owner, Cheryl Johnson. During the day its light meals with rotis the main attraction while in the evening full-flavoured creole dishes are offered.

GREEN BOLEY

BEQUIA | $ | CARIBBEAN
Belmont Walkway; Port Elizabeth; rotis EC$10-18

This simple green wooden bar sells cheap and delicious rotis; take your pick of chicken, conch or beef all perfectly spiced and full until bursting. Best accompanied with a glass of the famous Green Boley rum punch at one of the breezy picnic tables outside.

ST LUCIA

With pan-Caribbean and French-Creole origins, St Lucian cuisine is one of the most interesting of the Windward Islands; visitors can get a taste everywhere from bustling market stalls to homely creole kitchens and fine dining restaurants with exhilarating views.

WHAT TO EAT

Green fig & salt fish
National dish of seasoned salted cod mixed with boiled green banana, which are called 'green figs' locally.

Lambi
On the island conch is referred to as Lambi and is usually served grilled, smothered in sauce or in soup.

Fried bakes
Fried, salted bread. Eaten on their own or filled with cheese or salt fish.

Bouillon
A filling soup made with salted pig tails, red beans, dumplings and green plantains.

Accras
Deep fried fish cakes made from salted cod, parsley and spices.

Souse
Cow heel or pig's feet broth served with cucumber salad.

PRICE RANGES
$ less than EC$35
$$ EC$35–70
$$$ EC$70 or more

Tipping: 10–15%

BOUCAN RESTAURANT & BAR

SOUFRIÈRE | $$$ | FUSION
Rabot Estate, Vieux Fort Rd; 459-7966; www.hotelchocolat.com/uk/boucan; mains EC$51-123

Succulent cocoa-inspired cuisine in relaxed, contemporary surrounds. You'll find cocoa from the plantation in many plates over all three courses. The dessert menu alone is reason enough to come here – try the Rabot Marquise, house dark chocolate with cream marquise served atop a crunchy cocoa base.

COAL POT

CASTRIES | $$ | CARIBBEAN
Vigie Cove; 452-5566; mains EC$47-96

Follow the road around the harbour to find this little hidden open-air hideaway It's right on the water and far enough from town that the tranquility of the sea lulls you into a diner's dream. The cooking is modern French–Creole, with fresh produce and local spices combining in dishes bursting with flavour. The changing menu always has half a dozen fish options in a choice of sauces. The pick: dorado in coconut curry.

CASTRIES CENTRAL MARKET

CASTRIES | $ | CARIBBEAN
Jeremie St; meals EC$15

The narrow corridor on the eastern side of the bustling central market in Castries is the best place on the island for cheap traditional eats. More than a dozen stalls churn out an astounding variety of dishes from tiny kitchens. Among the many dishes there's a variety of filling soups, creole fish and richly spiced goat curry. Tables are communal so its a good chance to get to know Castries' characters.

FLAVOURS OF THE GRILL

RODNEY BAY | $$ | CARIBBEAN
Castries-Gros Islet Highway, Bois d'Orange; 450-9722; mains EC$30-55

This popular eatery on the Castries highway is not in the most romantic location but serves fantastic fresh seafood and outrageously good traditional St Lucian dishes. The buffet at lunch is a great option to try a variety of local plates just how they're supposed to be cooked.

JAMBE DE BOIS

PIGEON ISLAND | $$ | CARIBBEAN
450-8166; mains EC$37.50-47.50

Named after St Lucia's first French settler, pirate Jambe de Bois, this wonderful cafe in a historic building inside the Pigeon Island reserve is popular with locals, yachties and visitors alike who come for delicious meals with a wonderful view of the bay. The menu is fairly small but varied, with local specialities lining up with Mediterranean plates.

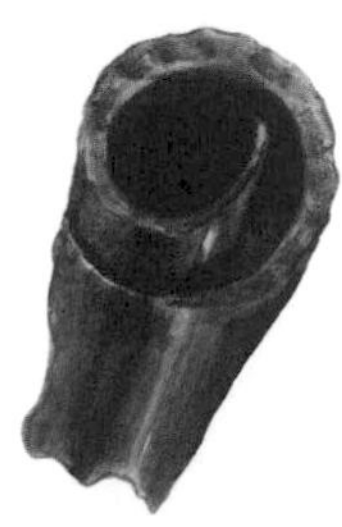

'Our exclusive menu uses cocoa sometimes as a light and subtle spice, sometimes as a delicate infusion, but always in a natural, healthy and exciting harmony.' *Boucan Restaurant & Bar*

GROS ISLET FISH FRY

GROS ISLET | $ | SEAFOOD
Bay St; meals EC$20-25

A couple of open-air joints across from the water serve up excellent seafood grills a few nights a week at the Gros Islet Fish Fry. They are ultracasual: wait for a plate of barbecued fresh fish or grilled conch, get a few sides, then find a spot in the dark at a picnic table. Wash it all down with a bottle of sea moss punch.

COURTESY BOUCAN RESTAURANT & BAR

WHAT TO EAT

Flying fish
Barbados' national dish is served fried in sandwiches or sautéed in sauce with cornmeal and okra mash.

Conkies
A mixture of cornmeal, coconut, pumpkin, sweet potato, raisins and spices, steamed in a plantain leaf.

Fish cakes
There are myriad Bajan recipes, made from salted cod and deep-fried.

Rotis
While traditionally from neighbouring Trinidad & Tobago these flat breads filled with curry are now a Bajan favourite.

Hot sauce
Radioactive yellow in colour and packing a nuclear punch, Bajan hot sauce is a mustard based flavour bomb.

Jug-jug
A mix of cornmeal, green peas and salted meat.

PRICE RANGES
For a main course:
$ less than B$30
$$ B$30–60
$$$ B$60 or more

Tipping: 10–15%

BARBADOS

Despite being a fairly small island, dining out in Barbados never gets dull. Options range from elegant waterside fine dining to fantastic neighbourhood food vans and everything in between many of which specialise in the island's own tangy, spicy cuisine.

PRC BAKERY

SPEIGHTSTOWN | $ | BAKERY
Sand St; rolls from B$2.50

One of the best traditional bakeries in the Eastern Caribbean, this place if worth crossing the island for. Take your pick from sweet and savoury delights. The highlight is the unadvertised currant rolls – delicious layers of buttery pastry filled with sweet currants – but everything is good. Best time to come is between 2pm and 4pm when most things come out hot from the ovens.

FISHERMAN'S PUB

SPEIGHTSTOWN | $ | CARIBBEAN
Queen St; 422-2703; mains from B$15

This waterfront cafe is a local institution that serves up fish from the boats floating off the side deck. Some of the island's freshest and tastiest plates.

CIN CIN BY THE SEA

PROSPECT | $$$ | INTERNATIONAL
Prospect Main Rd; www.cincinbythesea.com; mains B$48-125

The location alone overlooking the gorgeous west coast is enough reason to choose Cin Cin for a special meal, fortunately the dishes are every bit os spectacular. It stands out from the fine-dining pack with a varied menu of exquisitely prepared international dishes including plenty of inventive seafood options.

MUSTOR'S RESTAURANT

BRIDGETOWN | $ | CARIBBEAN
McGregor St; meals B$14-20

While it's not fancy, this downtown institution is one of the best places on the island to sample skillfully prepared traditional plates. Climb the stairs to a large, plain dining room. Choose from staples such as baked pork chops and flying fish. Then select the sides – we love the macaroni pie. Finally, hope for an open-balcony table.

BROWN SUGAR

GREATER BRIDGETOWN | $$ | CARIBBEAN
Aquatic Gap; 426-7684; www.brownsugarbarbados.net; mains B$42-95

The much-loved Brown Sugar at Aquatic Gap is a lush paradise inside and out. The decadent West Indian buffet includes a variety of starters, half a dozen mains, salads and sweet delights. Dinner is off a menu that includes shrimp creole, lobster, flying fish and much more. The Bajan bread pudding is a rummy delight.

CUZ'S FISH SHACK

GREATER BRIDGETOWN | $ | SEAFOOD
Pebbles Beach; sandwiches B$9-10

Doles out stupendously juicy fish cutters (sandwiches) from a beachside food truck. Add cheese and hot sauce and you have some of the Caribbean's best fast food.

INDIA GRILL

GREATER BRIDGETOWN | $ | CARIBBEAN
Bay St; 436-2361; roti B$14-25

Ask serious roti connoisseurs the best place on the island to indulge and they'll point you to this simple hole-in-the-wall restaurant at the entrance to Aquatic Gap. It also does curry and rice, but the rotis are where it's at. Go for the shrimp and potato option.

OISTINS FISH FRY

OISTINS | $ | SEAFOOD
Oistins Main Rd; mains B$25-40

This legendary spot for fresh fish meals attracts masses on Friday night which turns into a full party once the plates are cleared. Around 30 stalls serve similar menus: grilled fish and shellfish, pork chops, ribs and chicken. Sides include macaroni pie, chips, plantain, grilled breadfruit, garlic bread and more. Buy a cheap and icy bottle of Banks and plunge in.

'Our internationally inspired island menu emphasises fresh, locally sourced ingredients directly from the garden, farm and the sea to the table.'
Elise Manley, Roundhouse

GOLDEN SANDS

OISTINS | $$ | CARIBBEAN
Maxwell Main Rd; 428-8051; mains B$20-45

This unassuming restaurant out the back of a hotel is a great place to try some traditional Bajan dishes, especially on Saturday when it serves souse – pickled pieces of pork served cold with steamed potato and blood pudding. It includes all parts (ears and feet are highly prized), but if you're feeling squeamish you can order 'steam and lean', the all-meat version.

ROUNDHOUSE

BATHSHEBA | $$ | CARIBBEAN
www.roundhousebarbados.com; Hillswick Rd; 433-9678; mains B$34-74

Set in a dramatic stone building up on the hillside at the northern end of town, this excellent restaurant has customers throughout the day who sit around, sip cocktails and savour the fresh breeze and fine views south over the crashing waves below. The diverse menu goes big on traditional flavours: the citrusy flying fish paté and the pumpkin fritters with cane sugar and cinnamon are among the standouts.

BAY TAVERN

MARTIN'S BAY | $ | SEAFOOD
Main Rd; mains B$25-40

Surrounded by wilderness in the tiny fishing village of Martin's Bay this is the home of the east coast's tranquil fish fry. The tavern has been redeveloped from a simple shack into a three-floor modern structure but is still a fine place to dig into plates of fresh-from-the-boat marlin or snapper and macaroni pie. Take it to go and cross the road to one of the picnic tables on the water's edge for the old-school experience.

P56-7: Green figs and salt fish; cocoa pods. This page from top: Beach bar on Mullet Bay Beach; Silver Sands.

GRENADA

As you'd expect from the Spice Isle, Grenadian cuisine is absolutely delicious and – yes – wonderfully spiced. From roadside vans and beachside shacks to fine waterside restaurants it's hard to go wrong ordering traditional dishes which are among the best in the Caribbean.

WHAT TO EAT

Oil down
Grenada's national dish is a hearty concoction of beef and salt pork stewed with coconut milk.

Salt fish and bake
Seasoned salt fish with onion and veg, and a side of baked or fried bread. Generally served for breakfast but great anytime.

Lambi
Local conch is tender and delicious hot of the grill. It's especially good on the island of Carriacou.

Goat
Soup This spicy soup is made with various parts of the goat and is said to revitalise marriages. The best are found in the soup houses in the interior.

PRICE RANGES

$ less than EC$35
$$ EC$35–EC$70
$$$ EC$70 or more

Tipping: 10%

BB'S CRABBACK

ST GEORGE'S | $$ | CARIBBEAN
Carenage; 435-7058; www.bbscrabbackrestaurant.com; mains EC$58-79

The namesake waterfront restaurant of celebrity chef and local *bon vivant* Brian Benjamin is on the water at the end of the Carenage. Local faves like callaloo soup (a rich stew) and fresh seafood are popular, as is the signature goat curry.

ANDY'S SOUP HOUSE

GRANDE ANSE REGION | $ | CARIBBEAN
Grand Anse Valley Rd; Woodlands; 406-1600; soups EC$15, mains EC$15-25

This humble roadside diner is our favourite place on the whole island for fantastic local eats. It serves a variety of traditional dishes and snacks including great rotis, but the main reason to come here is for the 'waters' (soups). There are usually at least five different varieties on offer; they're all delicious but among the best is the 'mannish water,' the house special goat soup.

GOUYAVE FISH FRY

GOUYAVE | $ | CARIBBEAN
Edward St; mains from EC$20

Gouyave is Grenada's fishing capital, a fact that is celebrated in style with the festive Friday Fish Fry. Local vendors grill and fry fresh fish right off the boat. Most locals stick around for a few drinks well after their meal is done.

BOGLE'S ROUND HOUSE

CARRIACOU | $$ | CARIBBEAN
Bogles; 443-7841; mains from EC$52-85

It's a bit of a hike from town but it's worth the effort to visit this inventive cottage restaurant that features gourmet European dishes infused with Caribbean touches.

TRINIDAD & TOBAGO

An intoxicating blend of Indian-inspired cooking and the fresh seafood and hearty sides of creole fare, the cuisine of Trinidad and Tobago is as varied as it is delicious. The roti is the best-known Trinbago export, but this is also a place to sample a huge array of tempting street food, and settle in for some of the most succulent fish and seafood in the Caribbean.

WHAT TO EAT

Roti
Stretchy flatbread 'skins' wrapped around curried meat and vegetables; ask for sweet curried mango topping and 'slight pepper' only.

Crab and dumplings
Small whole crabs in a rich curry sauce, served over thin flour dumplings.

Doubles
Curried *channa* (chickpeas) on a soft fried bara bread; dressed with spicy sauces.

Pelau
Marinated chicken and pigeon peas, browned in burnt sugar and cooked with rice, pumpkin and coconut milk.

Bake and shark
Seasoned fish, topped with salad and piquant tamarind or cilantro-like chadon beni sauce, sandwiched into a light fried bread; go for kingfish rather than unsustainable shark.

PRICE RANGES
$ less than TT$60
$$ TT$60–160
$$$ TT$160 or more

Tipping: 10–15%

DOPSON'S ROTI SHOP

PORT OF SPAIN | $ | INDIAN
28 Maraval Rd, Newtown; 628-6141; rotis from TT$30

This tiny place is a favourite locals' spot – many Trinis claim it makes the best rotis in Port of Spain. Fillings are fresh, succulent and generous: try the curried duck. There are lots of veggie choices and fabulous traditional breakfasts like sada roti with choka (sautéed aubergine or tomato, laced with garlic).

VENI MANGÉ

PORT OF SPAIN | $$ | CARIBBEAN
67a Ariapita Ave, Woodbrook; 624-4597; www.facebook.com/venimangett; mains TT$120-140

West Indian flavour, art and enthusiasm infuse this vibrant restaurant. Serving classic Caribbean cuisine cooked with what Trinis call a 'sweet hand', it's one of the capital's best spots for authentic local food. Try the oxtail with dumplings, the grilled fresh fish with tamarind sauce or the excellent veggie options. From coconut ice cream to rum-laced trifle, the desserts are equally delicious. Don't leave without a glass or two of the excellent homemade rum punch.

SAVANNAH FOOD STALLS

PORT OF SPAIN | $ | STREET FOOD
Queen's Park West; corn soup from TT$25, roti from TT$30

The southern Savannah has taken off as a cool spot to enjoy classic

Trinbago street food. Hunkered under white tents, stalls sell fresh fruit juices, roti, *pholourie* (chickpea-flour doughballs with tamarind dipping sauce), bake-and-fish or corn soup, plus barbecued meats, Lebanese-style gyro wraps and Jamaican jerk chicken. Prices are low, but queues can be long. There's no seating, so bag one of the benches on the Savannah's perimeter path, and chase your meal with a fresh coconut water.

CHAUD

PORT OF SPAIN | $$$ | INTERNATIONAL
6 Nook Ave, St Ann's; 621-2002; www.creole.com/chaud/restaurant/trinidad/dining; prixe fixe 3-course lunch TT$250, mains TT$195-$350

Set in secluded St Ann's, this is Trini fine-dining at its best. The gourmet creations of local superchef Khalid Mohammed might include pepper-jelly glazed pork with sweet potato hash, pineapple chow and tamarin jus; or guava-barbecue kingfish with garlic yams, callaloo fondue and pumpkin essence. Prices reflect the high quality, but the set lunch menu is a great deal.

TOBAGO PARADISE TRAVEL & GRILL

CROWN POINT | $$$ | SEAFOOD
Pigeon Point Rd; 344-1703; lobster from TT$200

With tables on a rustic deck just steps from the sea, beachfront dining doesn't get better than this. The speciality is lobster, grilled in garlic butter, but you can also get fresh shrimp and fish served with local sauces and sides. It's tiny and very popular, so book ahead. Bring your own booze, and get there in time to watch the sunset.

'Veni Mangé is not just a restaurant, it's our passion, where we share our pride and love of our islands.'
Roses Hezekiah, owner, Veni Mangé

KARIWAK VILLAGE

CROWN POINT | $$ | CARIBBEAN
Store Bay Local Rd; 639-8442; www.kariwak.com; mains TT$100-230

Beneath the thatched roof and coral-stone walls of this open-air restaurant, enjoy masterpieces of Caribbean cuisine made with fresh organic herbs and vegetables from the kitchen garden. The imaginative set dinner menus feature grilled fish, meat and seafood (plus a vegetarian option), and are cooked with plenty of love.

FISH POT

LEEWARD COAST | $$ | SEAFOOD
Pleasant Prospect; 635-1728; dinner mains TT$160-275

With tables on a fairy-lit open-air patio overlooking lively Pleasant Prospect, this laid-back restaurant specialises in super-fresh, simply prepared seafood (with some chicken and steak dishes), served in subtle sauces and with flavoursome sides. Excellent homemade bread, and great starters too, from fish chowder to crab cakes. Don't miss it – but do book ahead.

BELIZE

Being a proudly Caribbean nation, Belize's flavours are often more aligned with its island buddies than its Latin neighbours. Seafood is the star of the show but diverse immigration has bought a wonderful mix of tastes to the table.

WHAT TO EAT

Gibnut
Belize's top bush meat, Gibnut is a small native rodent that's best barbecued.

Chirmole
With ancient Mayan origins, this rich chicken concoction in a dark chili sauce is also known as 'black dinner'.

Habanero sauce
Belize has some fantastic hot sauces with the most renowned being Marie Sharp's many varieties

Cow foot soup
Thick and gelatinous with a full cow's heel submerged, this is Belize's number one comfort food and hangover buster.

Fry-jacks
Belize's favourite breakfast is a deep fried wheat dough filled with anything from beans to fish.

PRICE RANGES

For a main course:
$ less than BZ$15
$$ BZ$15–35
$$$ BZ$35 or more

Tipping: 10–15%

HIDDEN TREASURE

SAN PEDRO | $$$ | CARIBBEAN
4088 Sarstoon St; 226-4111; www.hiddentreasurebelize.com; mains BZ$29-68

Living up to its name, Hidden Treasure is a gorgeous open-air restaurant in an out-of-the-way residential neighbourhood on the south side of the island. Lit by candles, the beautiful bamboo and hardwood dining room is the perfect setting for a romantic dinner, which might feature almond-crusted grouper, blackened snapper with bacon-wrapped shrimp, or pork ribs with a ginger-pineapple BBQ glaze.

ROBIN'S KITCHEN

SAN PEDRO | $$ | JAMAICAN
Sea Grape Dr; 651-3583; mains BZ$14-25

He works as a pastor, a handyman and a host of other trades but what Jamaican born Robin is best known for among many on San Pedro is the amazing jerk barbecue served at this simple, small roadside restaurant south of town. Enjoy the best jerk chicken and fish this side of Kingston. Dishes are spicy but with subtle flavours.

WILD MANGO'S

SAN PEDRO | $$$ | INTERNATIONAL
42 Barrier Reef Dr; 226-2859; mains BZ$20-48

Exuding a carefree, casual ambience (as a beachfront restaurant should), this open-air restaurant manages to serve up some of the island's most consistent and creative cuisine. With a hint of the Caribbean and a hint of Mexico, the dishes showcase fresh seafood, Cajun spices and local fruits and vegetables.

ERROLYN'S HOUSE OF FRYJACKS

CAYE CAULKER | $ | BELIZEAN
Middle St; fry-jacks BZ$1.50-6

Chow down on the island's best-value breakfast at this neat takeout hut – delicious golden fry-jacks (deep-fried dough) filled with any combination of beans, cheese, egg, beef or chicken. Cheap, filling and delicious.

HIBISCA BY HABANEROS

CAYE CAULKER | $$$ | INTERNATIONAL
cnr Front St & Calle al Sol; 626-4911; mains BZ$32-58

In a brightly painted clapboard house in the center of town, Hibisca's chefs prepare gourmet international plates with a Belizean bent including outrageously good seafood. Go for the coconut encrusted snapper or Caye-fresh lobster.

'The beauty of our location in Belize is you can enjoy locally grown food prepared with global flair just steps away from the Caribbean Sea.'
Rob Pronk, Chef Rob's

CHEF ROB'S

STANN CREEK DISTRICT | $$$ | SEAFOOD
Sittee River Rd; 523-7225; www.chefrobbelize.com; mains BZ$37-59

Well-known locally for his sublime seafood creations and steaks cooked over hot rocks, Chef Rob's changing menu might include sautéed red snapper, grilled jumbo shrimp kebabs or rib eye in rum sauce. The waterfront dining area at Parrot Cove is suitably romantic.

NERIE'S II RESTAURANT

BELIZE CITY | $ | BELIZEAN
cnr Queen & Daly Sts; 223-4028; mains BZ$10-18

Nerie's offers most accompaniments imaginable to rice and beans, including curried lamb, stewed cow foot, lobster and deer. Begin with a choice of soups, including chicken, escabeche (with chicken, lime and onions), *chirmole* or cow foot, and finish with cassava pudding.

CENAIDA'S

SAN IGNACIO | $ | BELIZEAN
Far West St; 631-2526; mains BZ$7-12

An unassuming local diner with a fly-screen door, Cenaida's is one of the best places in Cayo District authentic traditional Belizean food. It serves rice and beans, stew chicken and cow-foot soup, along with super tasty Belizean-style burritos and fajitas.

GUATEMALA

Guatemalan cooking is heavily influenced by pre-Hispanic flavours and local markets are full of ingredients that were also staples on ancien-Mayan tables. Dishes here are generally delicately spiced rather than exploding with flavour but the sheer variety of traditional plates and unusual snacks make it a fertile land for culinary exploration while several fine international restaurants offer diversity.

WHAT TO EAT

Pepián
One of Guatemala's favourite filling meals consists of beef or chicken seasoned with squash seeds and tomatoes.

Jocón
Chicken in a lightly spiced husk tomato sauce with a distinctive green colour; it's a speciality of the Antigua area.

Platanos en mole
A traditional dessert of bananas cooked in a thick cinnamon, chocolate and sesame sauce.

Jocotes
This slightly bitter small fruit is eaten with lime, salt and nutmeg and is sold everywhere – even on buses – for a healthy snack on the go.

Chuchitos
A traditional maize-based snack similar to a small tamal.

PRICE RANGES
For a main course:
$ less than Q50
$$ Q50–150
$$$ Q150 or more

Tipping: 10%

LA TINAJA

HUEHUETENANGO | $ | GUATEMALAN
4a Calle 6-51; 7764-1513; www.facebook.com/LaTinajaHuehuetenango; mains Q25

As much a cultural center as a cafe, the home of historian-gourmet Rolando Gutiérrez has an interesting library and a collection of old clocks, radios and namesake *tinajas* (urns), all displayed in a series of inviting salons. Aside from quesadillas and tamales, you'll find a variety of delicious local snacks including *sangüichitos* (Huehue-style sandwiches) and *rellenitos* (fried stuffed plantain balls).

SL PHOTOGRAPHY/GETTY IMAGES ©

CAFE EL ARTESANO

LAGO DE ATITLÁN | $$ | CHEESE
La salida a Guatemala, San Juan La Laguna; 4555-4773; Cheese or smoked meat platter Q125

El Artesano offers one of Guatemala's best dining experiences. Let the staff guide you around the platter of two dozen cheeses (all produced in Guatemala and aged in-house), from creamy goat through blue to hard pecorino, served with fruits, nuts, jams, pickles and artisanal breads. The same is on offer for some extraordinary home-smoked meats. Everything is served under a delightful rustic arbour, with perfectly matched wines.

COMEDOR KONOJEL

LAGO DE ATITLÁN | $ | GUATEMALAN
San Marcos La Laguna; 3326-5510; mains Q30

This cheerily painted clapboard canteen serves up big healthy portions of traditional Guatemalan food according to a changing daily menu to help support a wider feeding programme and other community projects. They prepare traditional dishes from all over the country including Pulique – a Mayan chili chickpea soup. The pupusas are excellent too. It's near the top of the path from the dock.

CAFE SABOR CRUCEÑO

LAGO ATITLÁN | $ | GUATEMALAN
Santa Cruz de La Laguna; www.amigosdesantacruz.org; mains Q32-50

Perched in the village of Santa Cruz de la Laguna, this brilliant community project comedor is run by local students who are learning to make traditional Guatemalan dishes to global tourism standards. Such Kaqchiquel fare as *subanik* (a tomato sauce of ground seeds and chilies accompanied by tamalitos) is prepared with locally grown herbs and veggies and served in the terrace restaurant with obligatory stunning lake views.

'At Sabor Cruceño our young chef graduates pride themselves on elevating traditional Guatemalan dishes through beautiful presentation and choice ingredients.'
Alex MacFarlan, Cafe Sabor Cruceño

CASA TROCCOLI

ANTIGUA | $$$ | INTERNATIONAL
cnr 3a Calle Poniente & 5a Av Norte; 7832-0516; mains Q90-175

Front of house at this restaurant looks just like the early-20th-century general store it once was, but with the walls racked with a rather more impressive collection of wine bottles. Amid the period photos and bistro furniture, enjoy superior seafood and meat dishes, including good racks of lamb and local rabbit stew, washed down with a good glass, of course.

DANIEL LÓPEZ PÉREZ PHOTOGRAPHY, COURTESY CAFE SABOR CRUCEÑO

RINCON TIPICO

ANTIGUA | $$ | GUATEMALAN
3a Av Sur 3; mains Q30

This courtyard restaurant is always packed with locals who know a good thing when they see it. If you don't come for the huge Guatemalan breakfast, make it for the chicken cooked over coals with garlicky potatoes or pork *adobado* (pork marinated with paprika and pepper), served up at simple bench tables.

MESÓN PANZA VERDE

ANTIGUA | $$$ | FUSION
5a Av Sur 19; 7832-2925; www.panzaverde.com; mains Q150-200

The restaurant attached to an exclusive B&B serves up divine continental cuisine in an appealing Antiguan atmosphere. The menu features an eclectic global line-up, with the French-trained chef putting an emphasis on fresh seafood and organic ingredients. Regular live music (jazz, Cuban) enhances the ambience.

RESTAURANTE CERRO SAN CRISTOBAL

SAN CRISTOBAL EL ALTO | $$ | INTERNATIONAL
Calle Principal 5; 5941-8145; www.restcerrosancristobal.com; mains Q50-110

The slow-food star of the Antigua area, this restaurant puts its own organically grown produce on the table. Giant salads are loaded with avocados, nasturtiums, greens and herbs from the surrounding gardens. It also serves tilapia from its own fish pond. Dine on a terrace with stupendous views of the Panchoy valley.

AMBIA

GUATEMALA CITY | $$$ | FUSION
10a Av 5-49, Zona 14; 2312-4666; ambia.com.gt; mains Q115-510

This is some of Guatemala City's finest dining, with a wide-ranging menu offering some flavourful fusion dishes, leaning heavily on influences as far ranging as Asia and Peru. The presentation is fantastic and the ambience superb. On balmy nights, the outdoor courtyard-lounge area is the place to be. Cocktail lovers, you're in for a treat, as many of the specialities include a bit of dry ice, making your beverage bubble like a witch's potion.

LA COÇINA DE SEÑORA PU

GUATEMALA CITY | $$ | GUATEMALAN
6a Av A 10-16, Zona 1; 5055-6480; www.senorapu.com; mains Q75-125

This tiny hole-in-the-wall eatery serves up excellent 'modernised' versions of classic Maya dishes. The menu is impressively wide – featuring beef, chicken, pork, duck, turkey, pigeon, rabbit, fish and shrimp – considering it's all done on a four-burner stove in front of your eyes. The flavours are delicious and sometimes surprising.

P64: Cocktail at Chef Rob's. Previous spread: Antigua with Agua Volcano in the background; Cafe Sabor Cruceño; cooking class at Cafe Sabor Cruceño.

KACAO

GUATEMALA CITY | $$ | GUATEMALAN
2a Av 13-44, Zona 10; 2337-4188; kacao.gt; mains Q90-160

Set under a thatched palapa roof with a soft marimba soundtrack, this is Zona 10's best comida *típica* (regional food) restaurant. The atmosphere and food are both outstanding. There is a selection of traditional snacks to begin with while among the house specialities are Jocón – chicken breast served in a spiced husk tomato sauce – and Pepián. The traditional desserts are amazing too.

XKAPE KOBA'N

COBÁN | $ | GUATEMALAN
2a Calle 5-13, Zona 2; 7951-4152; mains Q50-90

The perfect place to take a breather or while away a whole afternoon, this beautiful, artsy little cafe has a lush garden out back. Some interesting indigenous-inspired dishes are on the small menu including delicious tamales with heart of palm and amaranth. The cakes are homemade, the coffee is delectable and there are some handicrafts for sale.

ANTOJITOS MEXICANOS

FLORES | $$ | STEAK
Calle Playa Sur; 3130-5702; mains Q60-70

Every evening at the foot of the causeway these characters fire up the grill and char steak, chicken and pork ribs of exceptional quality. Their speciality is *puyazo* (sirloin) swathed with garlic sauce. Sit outside facing the twinkly lights on the lake or, if it's raining, inside under a tin roof. While it's a very local experience, staff behave with all the formality of an elegant restaurant.

LAS ORQUIDEAS

EL REMATE, PETÉN | $$ | ITALIAN
Calle Jobompiche; 5701-9022; pastas Q55-120

Almost hidden in the forest, a 10-minute walk along the north shore from the Tikal junction, is this marvelous open-air dining hall. The genial Italian owner-chef blends chaya, a local herb used in traditional Mayan cooking, into his own tagliatelle and panzarotti. There are tempting desserts too.

RESTAURANTE BUGA MAMA

LIVINGSTON | $$ | SEAFOOD
Calle Marcos Sanchez Diaz; 7947-0198; mains Q70-120

This place enjoys the best location of any restaurant in Livingston – jutting out right over the water – and profits go to the Asociación Ak' Tenamit, an NGO with several projects in the area. There's a wide range of seafood, homemade pasta, curries and other dishes on the menu, including a very good *tapado*.

WHERE TO DRINK...

REAL COFFEE

Crossroads Café, Panajachel
Hip cafe specialising in local small estate coffees including the tangy Acatenango Eighth Wonder and smooth Huehue Organic.

Las Cristalinas Café, San Pedro La Laguna
A thatched-roof cafe that offers a variety of coffees grown on the surrounding slopes and roasted in house.

Cafe La Luna, Quetzaltenango
Local cocoa and coffee beans are used to make the flavourful chocolate cappuccino at this fine café littered with vintage bric-a-brac.

Café Leon, Guatemala City
A capital classic with old images of the city on the walls and excellent locally grown coffee.

HONDURAS

Honduras boasts a surprising number of local delights you won't find elsewhere in Central America. Between the glitzy international restaurants of the Bay Islands and the more down-to-earth cooking on the mainland, you'll discover two very distinct sides to this country.

WHAT TO EAT

Baleada
This most adored Honduran street food is a flour tortilla folded in half and filled with refried beans and other ingredients, such as cheese, scrambled egg, avocado and beef.

Sopa de Caracol
This conch soup is a superb treat and is prepared with coconut milk mixed with the conch's only broth, spices and green bananas.

Tapado
This popular Garifuna fish soup prepared with coconut and spices can be found along the country's North coast.

Pan de coco
Also on the North coast, try this delicious Garifuna coconut bread.

Pinchos
These small Honduran kebabs are another tasty street food snack.

PRICE RANGES
For a main course:
$ less than L100
$$ L100–200
$$$ L200 or more

Tipping: 10% in smarter restaurants

MERCARDO LOS DOLORES

TEGUCIGALPA | $ | HONDURAN
Av Paulino Valladares; snacks L20-70

At the side of Iglesia Los Dolores in the heart of Tegucigalpa's old town, these stands inside a covered market offer some of the best value lunchtime street-food dishes in the Honduran capital, including *pupusas* (cornmeal stuffed with cheese or refried beans, *tapado* (Caribbean seafood soup) and *baleadas* (flour tortillas filled with various ingredients). For the latter, head straight to Baleadas Dolores, which has been a Tegus favourite since 1980.

ROATÁN OASIS

ROATÁN | $$$ | INTERNATIONAL
Main Rd, West End; 9484-6659; www.roatanoasis.com; mains L395-715

The best restaurant on the island of Roatán, and as such, probably in the entire country, gorgeous Oasis uses seasonal and locally sourced produce to create delectable creations such as duck confit risotto, chipotle-glazed baby-back ribs or scallop and shrimp ravioli. The setting alone is reason to come – a charmingly restored old house with both indoor and outdoor seating and cocktails that are out of this world.

GALEANO CAFÉ

TEGUCIGALPA | $$ | INTERNATIONAL
Plaza San Martín, Colonia Palmira; 3356-5140; www.facebook.com/galeanocoffee; mains L160-200

This very hip cafe rocks both an industrial and upcycling look, with brushed concrete fittings, salvaged wood furniture and an extremely friendly team greeting you behind the counter. It's an absolute lifeline, as it does great coffee, enormous smoothies served up in glass jars, tasty crepes and various filling panini – try the delicious *pero aguacatero* – as well as breakfasts and pastries, things that are essentially traveller gold dust in Honduras.

PISCO

TEGUCIGALPA | $$$ | PERUVIAN
5 Calle, 2143 Paseo Republica de Argentina; 9697-1962; www.pisco.rest; mains L165-330

In a city where fine dining hasn't really yet taken off outside a few select locales, you can't beat this classy and delicious Peruvian fusion restaurant in Palmira for a special night out. The voluminous 72-page photo menu here is divided by ingredients such as lemon, octopus or shallot, with obvious standout dishes including the seafood and fish ceviche and the shrimp in garlic sauce.

CÉSAR MARISCOS RESTAURANTE

TELA| $$$ | SEAFOOD
Calle Peatonal frente al mar; 2448-2083; mains L300-450

Combine grilled lobster sold by weight and dripping with garlic butter with a perfect people-watching spot right on the beach and you'll understand why this place is the reason many city

'Our aim is a consistently changing, globally inspired menu utilising the freshest ingredients available on the island at any given time.'
Loren Welbourn, Head Chef & Owner, Roatán Oasis.

COURTESY ROATÁN OASIS

folk come to the unassuming seaside town of Tela. Other house specialities include conch soup and coconut breaded shrimp and dishes come with homemade, hot and crispy coconut bread and an outrageously chunky hot sauce.

MANGO TANGO

UTILA | $$$ | INTERNATIONAL
Utila Dock; 3211-9469; mains L275-390

Housed in an over-the-water building that takes in views from three sides, Mango Tango has some of the best food in town. Try the Galician-style octopus, homemade shrimp and ricotta ravioli or *filet mignon* with *chimichurri* from the interesting international menu while enjoying the sea breezes.

EL SALVADOR

Salvadoran cuisine has notable pre-Columbian influences and indigenous traditions continue in many of the nation's most popular dishes. Maize is omnipresent but rice and beans also important staples with fresh seafood and tropical fruits adding colour and flavour.

WHAT TO EAT

Pupusas
El Salvador's best loved plate, the *pupusa* is a round cornmeal tortilla stuffed with cheese, refried beans, *ayote* (sweet potato) and *mora* (a local herb), *chicharrón* (pork rinds), or *revuelta* (mixed filling), then grilled.

Nuégados
Fried yucca dumplings with sugarcane syrup.

Riguas
Sweet cornmeal cakes wrapped in a leaf and grilled.

Tamales
Maize meal steamed in banana leaves often filled with chicken and vegetables.

Sopa de pata
Hearty soup of cow foot and tripe seasoned with onions and coriander.

Yuca
Fried cassava is served with pork rinds or fish and pickles.

PRICE RANGES
For a main course:
$ less than US$5
$$ US$5–15
$$$ US$15 or more

Tipping: 10%

R&R

JUAYÚA | $$ | INTERNATIONAL
Calle Mercedes Caceres Poniente; 2452-2083; facebook.com/restauranterr; mains US$7-12

The finest restaurant in Juayúa, and possibly in the whole Ruta de las Flores, R&R is lovingly run by Chef Carlos who puts a twist on steaks, salads and Mexican food which is served in the small, brightly painted corner building.

BETO'S

SAN SALVADOR | $$$ | SEAFOOD
cnr 85a Av Norte & Pasaje Dordely; 2263-7304; www.betosrestaurants.com; mains US$7-21

Colonia Escalón is the place in the capital to be seen lingering over crustaceans and the airy porch at Beto's is a choice to sample some great Salvadoran seafood dishes. It'll take a while to decide from the 14-page menu; there are dozens of types of ceviche but it's hard to beat the classic *conchas* (black ark clams) served raw with lime.

EL SOPÓN TÍPICO

SAN SALVADOR | $$ | SALVADORAN
Paseo General Escalón; mains US$5-15

Simple, fresh and delicious local food is the order of the day at this famous típico restaurant on a busy corner beside Galerías Escalón. Winning dishes include *marisco en crema* (seafood with cream) and *sopa de chorizo* (soup with sausage). Also a good place to sit down for *pupusas*.

POLLO BONANZA

SAN SALVADOR | $ | SALVADORAN
Calle Arce 525; mains $2.75

Locals claim the broiled chicken at this simple downtown diner is the best in the country: generous portions of pollo cooked in a wood-fired oven, served with *escabeche* (pickled cabbage) and fries.

NICARAGUA

Nicaragua's culinary scene is almost as varied as its majestic scenery: fish and seafood is superb on the country's two coastlines and along its vast rivers, meat is king inland and international influences predominate in traveller favourites such as Grenada and the Corn Islands.

WHAT TO EAT

Gallo pinto Nicaragua's workaday staple can be found on nearly all menus and is composed of red beans boiled with garlic, mixed with rice fried with onion and red pepper.

Quesillo Tortilla A much-loved Nica street snack, these maize tortillas are stuffed with cheese and topped with pickled onions and sour cream.

Nacatamal Similar to the Mexican tamale, with spiced chicken and vegetables cooked inside ground corn dough, wrapped in a banana leaf.

Indio Viejo This thick pre-Columbian soup is made from maize dough, onion and shredded beef, then flavoured with mint and bitter orange and served with *tostones* (fried green plantains).

PRICE RANGES

For a main course:
$ less than US$5
$$ US$5–100
$$$ US$10 or more

Tipping: 10% in smarter places.

MERCADO LA ESTACIÓN

LÉON | $ | NICARAGUAN
Parque San Juan, 1c E, 1c N; mains US$1.50

Head here in the evenings for your fill of the BX (bajón extremo), León's most famous dish. Created by local students in the 1990s; it's the local take on the *fritanga*, consisting of gallo pinto, slaw and marinated grilled beef, topped with a tortilla and a piece of omelette, and served on *bijagua* leaves. The Mama Tere's stall is the best, but half the fun is just enjoying the atmosphere.

ASADOS DOÑA TANIA

MANAGUA | $ | NICARAGUAN
Hotel Colón, 1c S, ½c O, Los Robles; 2270-0747; www.facebook.com/asadosdonatania; mains US$3-5

Come evening, Managuans make their way to this great value meat temple where Doña Tania has perfected her grilling craft over more than 20 years. There is only one thing to order: strips of marinated meat, smokey and seared and bursting with flavour, plus sides of *gallo pinto, ensalada criolla* (salad of onions, peppers and tomatoes), fried plantain and fried cheese. Portions are large enough to get you through a siege.

TERRAZA PERUANA

MANAGUA | $$ | PERUVIAN
de la Pastelería Sampson, 100m N; 2278-0013; www.laterrazaperuana.com; mains US$5-12

Set on a cool front balcony overlooking a leafy side street, refined Terraza's authentic Peruvian menu takes you from coastal ceviches and *tiraditos* (Japanese-Peruvian raw fish), to high Andean cuisine with great flair and commitment to top quality ingredients. Classics such as *anticuchos de corazón* (ox-heart skewers) and *suspiro limeño* (a dulce de leche and meringue-based dessert) are also present and correct, and you shouldn't miss having cocktail from the excellent pisco list.

DON CÁNDIDO

MANAGUA | $$$ | STEAK
de donde fue el Chaman 75 vrs al Sur, 15 Av Sureste, Los Robles; 2277-2485; steaks US$18-35

In a sleek space of wooden beams and exposed brick walls covered in contemporary art, this smart Managua steakhouse takes its atmosphere almost as seriously as it takes its meats. Choose from a sizeable list of cuts – from the beautifully grilled sirloin with crisped ribbons of fat, the T-bone and New York steak to short ribs and baby back ribs. The wine list spans the world, but is particularly strong on Spanish producers.

MISS DELL'S KITCHEN

GRANADA | $$$ | FUSION
cnr Calle Cervantes & Calle El Arsenal; 2552-2815 mains US$10-14

Mellow jazz plays in the background at this candlelit spot, with a mural of a rooster, Mr Beautiful, gracing the back wall. The rooster belonged to Miss Dell, a Haitian cook, whose recipes have been adapted by the chef for the short and sweet menu. The *piri piri pescado* (fish in a chilli sauce) is the establishment's absolutely unmissable dish, however.

BOCADILLOS TAPAS KITCHEN & BAR

GRANADA | $$ | INTERNATIONAL
frente Convento San Francisco; 2552-5089; www.bocadillosgranada.com mains US$4-8

The interior leafy courtyard of this stylish yet casual restaurant is an ideal setting for a cocktail (including some original ones created here), a local craft beer or two, and imaginative tapas that span the globe, from spicy samosas and pulled pork sliders to

P70-1: Dishes at Roatán Oasis. This page: Leon. Opposite page: Dish from Asados Doña Tania.

COURTESY ASADOS DOÑA TANIA

Thai noodle salad and roasted garlic hummus. There's a handful of substantial dishes too, including the drunken gnocchi, which come cooked in a creamy vodka and tomato sauce.

COMEDOR BRIDGET

LITTLE CORN ISLAND | $$ | CARIBBEAN

Village; 8437-7295; mains US$7-10

Pull up a chair on the porch of this converted family home and order the superb salt-dusted, lightly fried fish and a cold beer. Alternatively, try its mind-bogglingly good shrimp coconut curry or the great-value lobster. Bridget pioneered tourism on the remote and car-free island of Little Corn and her homey place is still your number-one choice for no-nonsense authentic local dining.

'Bridget's homey place is still your number-one choice for no-nonsense authentic local dining.'
Comedor Bridget

DARINIA'S KITCHEN

LITTLE CORN ISLAND | $$$ | INTERNATIONAL

Village; 8744-3419; per person US$25

For a truly local experience on the island of Little Corn, reserve an evening meal at this ambitious and eclectic supper club. Self-taught Managua transplant Darinia cooks up a four-course feast at her simple alfresco dining table. Food is superb, featuring fresh vegetable, fish and seafood dishes skewing Thai and excellent desserts. You'll be dining at one large table, often with several other people, which makes this a very sociable night out.

DESIDERI

LITTLE CORN ISLAND | $$$ | INTERNATIONAL

Village; 8412-6341; mains US$9-15

This fabulous and sophisticated terrace restaurant overlooking the water boasts the most interesting menu in the Village, tempting hungry travellers with authentic Italian pastas, tasty burritos and the house speciality, lobster thermidor. There's also a good selection of desserts and excellent coffee. The spacious deck is a superb spot place for a drink after the plates have been cleared away, and there's always something of a party atmosphere here.

COSTA RICA

With a privileged geographic position providing bountiful fresh ingredients, Costa Rica is a foodie's delight, both in terms of local flavours and international plates. The large expat population has expanded the country's horizons beyond rice and beans and across the country small sodas serving typical hearty platters jostle for attention alongside superb sushi joints, hip taquerias and fine Italian pastry shops.

WHAT TO EAT

Gallo pinto
For Costa Rican's this staple is more than just a simple mix of rice and beans, it's a source of national pride. Lightly spiced, it's most often served for breakfast with eggs, cheese and sour cream on one high-energy plate.

Pejivalle
The roasted peach-palm fruit is a roadside standard, delicious warm and salted, although locals like to add a dab of mayonnaise.

Patí
A flaky, Caribbean-style turnover filled with meat, onions, garlic and spicy goodness.

Chifrijo
Costa Rica's favourite bar snack mixes beans, pork rinds, tortilla chips and tomatoes in one salty fatty delight.

PRICE RANGES
$ less than US$10
$$ US$10–20
$$$ US$20 or more

Tipping: 10%

CAFE LIBERIA

LIBERIA | $$ | FUSION
Calle Real btwn Avs 2 & 4; 2665-1660; mains US$9-14

This beautifully restored colonial-era building has heavy wooden furniture and frescoed ceilings, creating a romantic ambience for enjoying rich coffee and gourmet fare. French chef Sebastien and his Tica wife Ligia have taken staple foods to new levels: super-fresh ceviche is served with fresh-baked tortilla chips, and the lasagna and crepes are top-notch.

LOCOS COCOS

CENTRAL NICOYA PENINSULA | $$ | CEVICHE
Playa San Miguel; www.locoscocos.com; mains US$5-12

Best. Beach. Bar. And that's saying something in Costa Rica. On an amazing, nearly deserted stretch of beach, Henner serves up his secret-family-recipe ceviche out of an old shipping container. Ice cold beers cap off this near-perfect experience.

KOJI'S

SANTA TERESA | $$$ | JAPANESE
Calle Buenos Aires; 2640-0815; kojisrestaurant.com; sushi US$5-10

Koji Hyodo's outdoor patio is a twinkling beacon of fresh, raw excellence. The atmosphere and service are superior, of course, but his food is a higher truth. The grilled octopus is barely fried and sprinkled with sea salt, and there's a sweet crunch to his lobster sashimi, sliced tracing-paper thin and sprinkled with fresh ginger.

CLANDESTINA

MONTEZUMA | $$ | LATIN AMERICAN
Butterfly Gardens; 8315-8003; mains US$8-12

The secret is out. The hottest restaurant in Montezuma is this awesome, artistic place in the trees at the butterfly gardens. Look for innovative takes on Central American standards, such as daily changing taco specials and delectable chicken mole enchiladas. Vegetarians are joyfully accommodated with yam and lentil cakes or *chilles rellenos* (stuffed peppers). Try the Butterfly Beer, brewed on-site.

GINGERBREAD RESTAURANT

ARENAL | $$$ | INTERNATIONAL
Ruta 142; 2694-0039; www.gingerbreadarenal.com; mains US$25-40

Perched right on the edge of the Laguna de Arenal, this fine restaurant is run by larger-than-life chef Eyal turns out transcendent meals from the freshest local ingredients (some from the gardens outside). Favourites include mushrooms smothered in cream sauce, tuna *poke* and (occasionally) local lamb and duck. Enormous, juicy burgers. It's big food that goes down well.

LA VENTANITA

ARENAL | $ | CAFE
Carretera El Castillo–La Fortuna; 2479-1735; mains US$4-6

La Ventanita is the 'little window' where you place your order. Soon, you'll be devouring the best *chifrijo* (rice and pinto beans with fried pork, capped with fresh salsa and corn chips) that you've ever had, along with a nutritious/delicious *batido*. It's typical food with a twist – pulled pork and bacon burritos, for example.

'We give special attention to quality and details using only the freshest locally sourced ingredients including fruits and vegetables from our own greenhouse.'
Koji Hyodo, Koji's

RESTAURANT DON RUFINO

LA FORTUNA | $$$ | INTERNATIONAL
cnr Via 142 & Calle 466; 2479-9997; www.donrufino.com; mains US$16-40

The vibe is trendy at this indoor-outdoor grill. The highlight is the perfectly prepared grilled meats: the New York Steak with mushrooms is out of this world. If you're cutting back, go for Grandma's BBQ chicken (with chocolate, wrapped in a banana leaf) or a house favourite, the *kobocha* squash risotto with grilled chicken breast and *chimchurri*-glazed shrimp.

LOS ALMENDROS

PLAYA ESTERILLOS | $$ | INTERNATIONAL
Esterillos Oeste; 2778-7322; mains from US$8

Just west of the soccer field in Esterillos Oeste, an expat has decided to take a global theme and bring it to this tiny beachside town. The results? Delectable Jamaican jerk, Caribbean-style curry, whole red snapper with homemade salsa, pad thai, black-bean soup and more. The dishes are beautifully executed, the atmosphere convivial and the service sweet. Worth travelling for.

GABRIELLA'S

QUEPOS | $$$ | SEAFOOD
Marina Pez Vela; 2519-9300; www.gabriellassteakhouse.com; mains US$25-35

Perched right by the water's edge on the outskirts of this fishing town, you can be sure Gabriella's seafood arrives super fresh. The veranda catches the sunset and the service is attentive, but the food is the real star, with a great emphasis on fresh fish and mouthwatering steak. Best in show: the seared tuna with chipotle sauce and the spicy sausage and shrimp pasta

PARK CAFE

SAN JOSÉ | $$$ | EUROPEAN
Calle 48; 2290-6324; www.parkcafecostarica.blogspot.com; mains US$17-35

At this felicitous fusion of antique shop and French restaurant, Michelin-starred chef Richard Neat offers an exquisite menu of smaller sampling plates (Spanish tapas-style), normal-sized mains, and a thoughtful wine list. The romantic candlelit courtyard is eclectically decorated with imported Asian antiques.

CAFE DE LOS DESEOS

SAN JOSE | $ | CAFE
Calle 15 btwn Avs 9 & 11; 2222-0496; mains US$5-12

Abuzz with artsy young bohemians, this colourful Barrio Otoya cafe makes a romantic spot for drinks (from wine to cocktails to smoothies), *bocas* (handmade tortillas with Turrialba cheese), salads, teriyaki chicken, individual pizzas and tempting desserts. Walls are hung with interesting works by local artists.

ANTOJOS DE MAIZ

SAN GERADO DE RIVAS | $ | COSTA RICAN
Carretera Parque Nacional Chirripó; 2772-4381; chorreadas US$3

For all things made of maize, stop at this traditional roadside restaurant on the highway to Parque Nacional Chirripó. Make sure to try the *chorreada*, a traditional sweet pancake made with fresh white or yellow corn and served with sour cream. Pairs very well with strong, organic coffee.

EXOTICA

OJOCHAL | $$ | INTERNATIONAL
Av Principal de Ojochal; 2786-5050; mains US$10-23

This phenomenal gourmet restaurant is worth planning your evening around. In a sultry, jungle ambience with orchids everywhere, the nouveau-French dishes each emphasise a breadth of ingredients brought together in masterful combinations. Some of the highlights include Tahitian fish carpaccio,

Opposite page: Koji's.

wild-duck breast with port-pineapple reduction and its signature dessert – the chilli-tinged chocolate Devil's Fork.

TAYLOR'S PLACE

TORTUGUERO VILLAGE | $ | CARIBBEAN
8319-5627; mains US$7-14

Low-key atmosphere and high-quality cooking come together beautifully at this backstreet eatery southwest of the soccer field. The inviting garden setting, with chirping insects and picnic benches spread under colourful paper lanterns, is rivalled only by friendly chef Ray Taylor's culinary artistry. House specialities include beef in tamarind sauce and delectable grilled fish in garlic sauce.

SODA EL PATTY

PUERTO LIMÓN | $ | CARIBBEAN
cnr Av 5 & Calle 7; 2798-3407; patí US$1.50, mains US$2-5

This beloved nine-table Caribbean eatery, with soccer memorabilia on the walls, serves up delicious *patí*, along with sweet plantain tarts and heaping plates of rice-and-beans (the spicier, more flavourful version of the country's traditional *casado*).

WHERE TO BUY...

COSTA RICAN COFFEE

Coopedota, Santa Maria de Dota
A local cooperative producing some of Costa Rica's best arabica, it offers tours and tastings and has a well stocked shop.

Coopeldos RL, Monteverde
Coopeldós is a cooperative of 450 small- and medium-sized organic farmers from the Monteverde mountains with a selling a variety of local coffees.

Feria Verde de Aranjuez, San José
This fabulous Saturday farmers market has bags of quality organic beans and plenty of other fresh produce.

Cafe Britt, Barva
Costa Rica's most famous coffee roaster offers a 90-minute bilingual tour of its plantation that includes coffee tasting.

PANAMA

Long a crossroads for the Americas and the Caribbean, Panamanian cooking has influences from Europe, Africa and indigenous America. While it's possible to find restaurants of all kinds in the modern capital, in the countryside traditional dishes still dominate tables.

WHAT TO EAT

Sancocho
Panama's favourite meal is a slow-cooked chicken and vegetable soup seasoned with coriander. Purists demand it's cooked with free-range hen rather than commercial chicken.

Ropa vieja
Literally 'old clothes', this traditional Caribbean dish consists of spiced shredded beef served over rice.

Carimañola
Yucca flour rolls filled with chopped meat and then deep-fried.

Patacones
Fried green plantains; served as an accompaniment to many dishes.

Hojaldras
Deep-fried dough served hot and covered with sugar; often served at breakfast.

Raspados
Crushed ice topped with fruit syrup and sweetened condensed milk.

PRICE RANGES
For a main course:
$ less than US$12
$$ US$12–18
$$$ US$18 or more

Tipping: 10%

CERRO BRUJO

CHIRIQUI PROVINCE | $$ | MEDITERRANEAN

Brisas del Norte, Volcan; mains US$9-18

A gourmet restaurant in a funky country house with garden seating. The chalkboard menu offers just three or four daily options. Gregarious owner-chef Patti Miranda's mouthwatering creations use organic and local ingredients only and combine flavours not found elsewhere.

LEAF EATERS CAFE

BOCAS DEL TORO | $ | INTERNATIONAL

Contiguo Muelle de Gasolina; Isla Carenero; 6675-1354; www.leafeaterscafe.com; mains US$8-12

For excellent pescatarian, vegetarian and vegan lunches, head to this over-the-water restaurant on Isla Carenero. Start with a cool cucumber-mint-coconut-watermelon shake. Quirky and flavorful offerings include 'hippie bowls' (brown rice with vegetables and dressing), grilled fish sandwiches with caramelised onions, blackened fish tacos and scrumptious *shiitake* burgers.

CHILINGUITO

VERAGUAS PROVINCE | $$ | SEAFOOD

Via Playa Estero; Santa Catalina; 6687-2992; mains US$8-15

This thatched restaurant does seafood in slightly different, scrumptious preparations. Try the shrimp in garlic sauce with crunchy sautéed vegetables, abundant green salads or fried clam ceviche with yucca. There's also fresh fruit drinks, organic kombucha and cocktails. Its signature drink, Tropical Dream, combines gin with frosty watermelon and mint.

PANGA

PENINSULA DE AZUERO | $$ | PANAMANIAN

Playa Venao; 6787-2146; www.facebook.com/restaurantepanga; mains US$10-18

When chef Andres Morataya left award-winning Manolo Caracol and the hubbub of Panama City for hip Playa Venao, he opened this most inventive restaurant. The idea is to use products often discarded – deep-fried snapper gills, anyone? – or to prepare them in unique ways as in 'Prawns that Want to be Pork' cooked in a sauce usually served with suckling pig. It's excellent for cocktails too.

PIPA'S BEACH RESTAURANT

COCLÉ PROVINCE | $$ | SEAFOOD
Via Farallón-Playa Blanca; pipasbeach.com; 6844-0373; mains US$10-25

Utterly tranquil, this mostly outdoor bar and restaurant right by the beach serves fresh seafood with gourmet touches (such as Thai mussels and crab claws in three sauces). One of the delights of dining here is enjoying a cold beer or tropical cocktail while looking out to sea, feet buried in the sand.

LO QUE HAY

PANAMA CITY | $$ | PANAMANIAN
Calle 12 Este; mains US$12-20

Neighbourhood *fondas* (cheap restaurants) serve cheap Panamanian classics, but this one – by one of Panama's top chefs – delivers a massive twist. Sexy rice (*concolón*) has a crust of crisp perfection, served with smoked tomatoes or fragrant clams. There's also tender whole fish, yucca tostadas with carpaccio and mango kimchee served as streetside *encurtido*.

'Being surrounded by jungle and beaches we are inspired by what is produced around us and are committed to good honest cuisine.' *Andres Morataya, Panga*

MERCADO DE MARISCOS

PANAMA CITY | $ | SEAFOOD
Av Balboa, Casco Viejo; 506-5741; mains US$3-14

Get your seafood fix above a bustling fish market. Come early, as service at peak time is painfully slow. Gems include whole fried fish and cavernous bowls of 'Get Up Lazarus' soup (a sure hangover cure). Outside, stands ladle out delicious plastic cups of *ceviche*, including classic concoctions, Mediterranean style (with olives) and curry.

DONDE JOSÉ

PANAMA CITY | $$$ | PANAMANIAN
Av Central s/n, Casco Viejo; 262-1682; www.dondejose.com; 8-course meal US$80

Elevating humble Panamanian staples to haute cuisine, this 16-seat eatery is Panama's hottest reservation. Chef Jose prepares *ñandu* beans (native black beans), crisp, tender pork and *ñame* (an indigenous tuber) in playful, revelatory fashion. Servers have an intimate, casual rapport through a cascade of eight courses.

COLOMBIA

Colombia's blessed fertile landscapes dictate its culinary inspiration: fish and plantains pack its coastlines; incredible tropical fruits, chocolate, coffee and dairy shroud the Andes; the expansive plains of Los Llanos harbour hearty and succulent meats; and the Amazon provides an exotic bounty of unique ingredients. Converging in its collective *comida criolla* (creole food), Colombia comforts epicureans from Bogotá and beyond.

WHAT TO EAT

Bandeja paisa
The 'paisa platter', a gut-busting mound of sausage, beans, rice, egg and arepas (corn cakes) – Colombia's de facto national dish.

Ajiaco
A soul-soothing Andean chicken soup with corn, potato, cream and capers.

Arepas
A street food staple, especially at breakfast: griddle-fried ground maize dough stuffed with eggs, ham and cheese.

Obleas con arequipe
Thin wafers doused in milk caramel, usually whipped up street-side.

Sancocho
A hearty stew of meat, plantains, potatoes, corn, and yucca, served with sliced avocado and white rice.

PRICE RANGES
$ less than COP$15,000
$$ COP$15,000–30,000
$$$ COP$30,000 or more

Tipping: 10%

CAFÉ STUDIO

PROVIDENCIA | $$ | SEAFOOD
Bahía Suroeste; 8-514-9076; mains COP$30,000-60,000

A Canadian–Raizal couple dish up delightful and memorable seafood at Providencia's most popular restaurant, including lobster tails in garlic sauce, creole fish balls, and Wellington's conch (cooked in a house-made creole sauce made with wild basil from the garden).

DONDE FRANCESCA

SAN ANDRÉS | $$$ | SEAFOOD
San Luis; 8-513-0163; mains COP$30,000-60,000

Right on the beach, this breezy place may be little more than a shack, but it serves up absolutely delicious traditional Caribbean food, such as *langostinos al coco* (breaded crayfish deep-fried with coconut), *pulpo al ajillo* (octopus cooked in garlic) and tempura calamari.

SUÁ

CARIBBEAN COAST | $$ | COLOMBIAN
Palomino; 310-251-5738; mains COP$18,000-35,000

Set in a lovely garden, Suá is a collectively run project with impeccable environmental and sustainability credentials, including a great vegetarian selection. Ironically, it also does one of the best steaks on the Caribbean

coast. Altogether the fare is rather inventive, including specialities such as prawns marinated in garlic, sea salt and butter.

EL BOLICHE

CARIBBEAN COAST | $$$ | CEVICHE
Cochera del Hobo No 38-17, Cartagena; 310-368-7908; mains COP$48,000-60,000

Small, delightful and not so well known that it's inundated, El Boliche basks in its relative obscurity. If you're reticent about raw fish, Boliche offers hot and cold ceviche daubed with bold and adventurous ingredients such as tamarind, coconut milk and mango. The handsome six-table interior features a glass waterfall and a bar that dispatches spot-on mojitos.

INTERNO

CARIBBEAN COAST | $$$ | COLOMBIAN
Cárcel San Diego, Calle Camposanto, Cartagena; 310-260-0134; www.restauranteinterno.com; 3-course set meal COP$90,000

Interno is a restaurant inside Cartagena's women's prison that raises money for the rehabilitation of its inmates, who run the show. Trained by a top Bogotá chef, the cooks prepare set meals that are delectable takes on modern Colombian cuisine. Reservations 24 hours in advance with passport number required (and you'll need to bring your passport along as well).

COURTESY RESTAURANTE ITACA

'Mini-Mal is an amazing gastronomic tour through the flavours and cultures of the jungle, the Andes mountains and Colombia's two seas.'
Eduardo Martinez, Mini-Mal

JOSEFINA'S

CARIBBEAN COAST | $$ | SEAFOOD
Capurganá; 322-592-4182; mains COP$22,000-40,000

Scour the coast and you won't find better seafood – or a warmer welcome – than at Josefina's, a simple beach shack on Capurganá's Playa Caleta. Her medium-sized *pargo* (red snapper) practically fills the plate and is a succulent joy, supported by coconut rice, tangy salad and crispy *patacones* (plantain chips); the *crema de camerón* (cream-of-shrimp soup) isn't far behind.

HELENA ADENTRO

ZONA CAFETERA | $$ | COLOMBIAN
Carrera 7 No 8-01, Filandia; 315 699 3130; www.helenaadentro.com; mains COP$23,000-34,000

Run by a talented young local chef and his Kiwi partner, this hip restaurant serves up some of the best food in the

Zona Cafetera, with innovative takes on traditional Colombian cuisine made with fresh ingredients from local farms.

CAFÉ BERNABÉ GOURMET

ZONA CAFETERA | $ | FUSION

Cnr Carrera 6 & Calle 3, Salento; 315-596-1447; www.facebook.com/pg/CafeBernabe; mains COP$17,000-36,000

There's a lot to love about a place that pushes the culinary boundaries of a small-town dining scene, with its ambitious pairings of flavours (salmon with coffee and passion-fruit reduction), beautifully seared steaks and excellent cocktails and coffee.

RESTAURANTE ITACA

MEDELLÍN | $ | COLOMBIAN

Carrera 42 No 54-60; 4-581-8538; www.facebook.com/RestauranteItaca; set lunch COP$14,000, mains COP$16,000-33,000

This tiny hole-in-the-wall on Medellín's outskirts prepares fantastic gourmet plates bursting with flavour. Vegetarians are well catered for while meat-lovers should not leave without trying a portion of homemade sausages, proclaimed Antioquia's best.

Previous spread: Asado at Restaurante Itaca; Dish from Restaurante Itaca.

MORA CASTILLA

CAUCA | $ | CAFE

Calle 2 No 4-44, Popayán; 2-838-1979; www.moracastilla.com; snacks COP$2400-4000

This upstairs cafe is always busy with chatting locals and prepares excellent fresh juices and traditional snacks, including *salpicon payanese* (fruit salad), *champus* (maize-based beverage), tamales and *carantantas* (toasted corn chips).

ZEA MAIZ

CALI | $ | COLOMBIAN

Carrera 12 No 1-21 Oeste; 311-846-2774; www.facebook.com/arepaszeamaiz; arepas COP$2000-9000

This colourful basement restaurant in Cali's San Antonio district stuffs their square-shaped arepas (corn cakes) with all kinds of goodness and serves them with four homemade sauces, the mango picante being particularly satisfying. Ardent anti-arepa crusaders have been known to change their tune after eating here.

WAUNANA

CALI | $$ | COLOMBIAN

Calle 4 No 9-23; 2-345-0794; www.facebook.com/waunanarestaurante; mains COP$25,000-37,000

The brave and often spectacular pairings of local ingredients (the seabass ceviche with tropical fruit stands out), flawless presentation, excellent cocktails and the original spin on Colombian cuisine make this one of Cali's top choices.

ANDRÉS CARNE DE RES

BOGOTÁ | $$$ | COLOMBIAN
Calle 3 No 11A-56, Chia; 1-861-2233; www.andrescarnederes.com; steaks COP$49,600-59,000

This legendary steakhouse blows everyone away with its surreal décor, design gimmicks and all-out fun atmosphere, which will leave you wondering what the hell happened last night. The 75-page menu of classics like *arepas* (corn cakes), ceviches and succulent steaks is totally overwhelming.

MINI-MAL

BOGOTÁ | $$ | COLOMBIAN
Carrera 4A No 57-52; 1-347-5464; www.mini-mal.org; mains COP$27,900-38,000

Sustainably sourced and fiercely artisan, this creative contemporary Colombian is an intriguing triumvirate of Caribbean, Altiplano and jungle-sourced food. Dishes such as beef braised with *tucupí* (a spicy, adobo-like sauce derived from poisonous yuca root, enhanced with chilies and ants) or wild mushrooms with coastal cheese and nasturtium pesto are all outstanding and totally without precedent.

ABASTO

BOGOTÁ | $$ | BREAKFAST
Carrera 6 No 119B-52; 1-215-1286; www.abasto.com.co; mains COP$20,000-37,000

This rustic-trendy choice wins top accolades in Bogotá for creative breakfasts. Inventive *arepas* (corn cakes) and seriously good egg dishes such as *migas* (scrambled eggs with bits of *arepas* and *hogao*, a concoction of onion, tomato, cumin and garlic) are washed down with organic coffee.

MERCAGÁN

SANTANDER | $$ | STEAK
Carrera 33 No 42-12, Bucaramanga; 7-632-4949; www.mercaganparrilla.com; steak COP$21,500-47,500

Often touted as serving the best steak in the whole of Colombia, this traditional *parrilla* (grilled-meat restaurant) drops perfect slabs of meat from their own farm in 200g, 300g or 400g (good luck!) sizes, on sizzling iron plates. It's all about the *lomo finito* (tenderloin). Don't let them butterfly it – you want it *en bloque*!

MERCADO MUNICIPAL

BOYACÁ | $$$ | COLOMBIAN
Carrera 8 No 12-25, Villa de Leyva; 318 3637049; www.facebook.com/mmvilladeleyva; mains COP$24,000-65,000

This chef-driven restaurant in the gardens of a colonial house (1740) has resurrected ancient techniques of cooking meat in a 1m-deep underground wood-burning *barbacoa* (barbecue). Among the specialities are rich, fall-off-the-bone pork ribs doused in apricot barbecue sauce.

WHERE TO DRINK...

COFFEE

Azahar Café, Bogotá
Possibly the finest shrine to coffee in Colombia, Azahar exudes taste, expertise and an undying passion for the country's extremely famous jitter juice.

Cafe Quindio, Armenia
No caffeine connoisseur should miss this temple to the coffee bean, dotted with baby coffee plants and serving highland coffee from the surrounding Zona Cafetera.

Hacienda Venecia, San Peregrino
Award-winning coffee plantation centered on a well-preserved paisa farmhouse turned boutique hotel with majestic views.

Pergamino, Medellín
Medellín's best coffee is brewed with top-quality beans sourced from small farms around the country.

WHAT TO EAT

Encebollado
Fish stew; usually cooked with tuna or albacore, fresh tomatoes, coriander, peppers and cassava leaves. Pickled red onion rings, avocado or plantain are common garnishes.

Llapingacho
Fried, mashed potato with a cheesy centre, served with pork, avocado, fried egg and salad.

Humitas
Ground corn smashed with onions, eggs, spices and sometimes cheese, wrapped in cornhusks and steamed. So in-demand they are cooked in their own specially-adapted pots!

Ceviche
Lime juice-marinated whitefish, shrimps and black clams are served in the juices they are cooked in, making the ceviche soupier than in neighbouring Peru.

PRICE RANGES
For a main course:
$ less than $8
$$ $8–$15
$$$ $15 or more

Tipping: 10%

ECUADOR

Ecuadorian food is a distillation of its three topographical regions. From the Andes comes corn, at its best steamed into humitas and tamales. The coastline contributes myriad seafoods, while coastal and rainforest areas produce bananas and some of the planet's finest chocolate.

URKO COCINA LOCAL

QUITO | $$$ | ECUADORIAN
Isabel La Católica N24-862, La Floresta; 02-256-3180; www.urko.rest; mains $10-25, tasting menu $78

Traditional Ecuadorian cuisine gets a contemporary twist at this sophisticated restaurant. Dishes usher you on a gastronomic tour of Ecuador, all prepared with fresh, ethically sourced local ingredients including herbs and veg from the restaurant's rooftop garden. Eat off the regular menu in the casual downstairs 'barra', or book a spot upstairs to sample the tasting menu, themed around the four *raymis* or ancient Andean astral cycles.

PARQUE DE LAS TRIPAS

QUITO | $ | ECUADORIAN
Parque Navarro, cnr Ladrón de Guevara & Iberia, La Floresta; mains $2-4

To enjoy some of Quito's most authentic traditional cooking, head to this La Floresta park for a real palate adventure. Every evening food stalls are set up selling freshly prepared *tripa mishqui* (grilled cow intestines), *seco de pollo* (chicken stew), empanadas and *morocho* (a kind of spiced corn porridge).

CAFÉ MOSAICO

QUITO | $$ | ECUADORIAN/GREEK/MEXICAN
Samaniego N8-95, Parque Itchimbia, Old Town; 02-254-2871; www.cafemosaicoecuador.com; mains $5-14

Grabbing a viewpoint pew for at least one meal in mountain-rimmed Quito is obligatory, and vine-trailed Mosaico

has magnificent views. Serving a mix of Ecuadorian, Greek and Mexican fare, it also has one of the city's best selections of picking platters and an open-sided terrace from which the Old Town vistas are pretty much perfect. There's live music on Friday and Saturday evenings.

ZAZU

QUITO | $$$ | FUSION

Aguilera 331, New Town; 02-254-3559; www.zazuquito.com; mains $14-43

Among Quito's best restaurants, Zazu serves beautifully prepared seafood dishes, grilled meats and ceviches in a stylish setting of light brick, ambient electronica and an inviting, backlit bar. The menu showcases reimagined versions of the best of Ecuadorian cuisine with dishes such as ceviche with naranjilla emulsion or guinea pig with peanut ravioli.

MASAYA BISTRO

QUITO | $ | BISTRO

cnr Venezuela & Rocafuerte, Old Town; 02-257-0189; www.masaya-experience.com/en/hostel-quito; light meals $3-9

Masaya has enlivened Quito Old Town no end with its beautiful bistro and upmarket budget accommodation alike. The eating area is a large, inviting space with bare brick pillars and long wooden tables spilling onto a serene enclosed garden. Ecuadorian-international food is served in this

'URKO combines local produce and the talent of a young team to create a unique experience based on an indigenous worldview.'
Daniel Maldonado, URKO Cocina Local

COURTESY URKO COCINA LOCAL

relaxed setting, where beef in *chimichurri* (South American garlicky parsley sauce), quinoa croquettes, Ecuadorian-style ceviche, burgers, wraps and pastas are all possibilities.

COSA NOSTRA

QUITO | $$ | ITALIAN

cnr Baquerizo Moreno & Almagro, Mariscal Sucre; 02-252-7145; https://pizzeriacosanostra.ec; pizzas $9.50-17.80

Italian-owned Cosa Nostra has a pleasant front patio, cosy dining room and nearly three-dozen varieties of pizza piled with generous toppings and fired up in a brick oven – just about the best in town. It has white pizzas for those who don't dig tomatoes, good gnocchi and other pastas, and tantalising tiramisu for dessert.

COURTESY URKO COCINA LOCAL

ISVEGLIO

QUITO | $ | CAFE
Isabel La Católica N24-682, La Floresta; 02-603-9590; www.isveglio.com; coffees/snacks $2-6

The standard of artisan coffee has been on an upward trajectory in Quito and slick Isveglio is at the forefront of the movement. Cafe, coffee education centre and barista training school, it serves organic brews from Ecuador's various coffee-growing regions, plus some beans from further afield.

EL QUETZAL

MINDO | $ | CAFÉ
Av 9 de Octubre; 02-217-0034; www.elquetzaldemindo.com; snacks from $2, mains $7-12

This laid-back cafe-cum-restaurant is the largest and most atmospheric in Mindo town, surrounded by swooping verdant cloud forests. The coffee is excellent, but the locally grown chocolate steals the show. Try it in dishes (macadamia chicken with ginger squash and chocolate bonbons for a main; the delicious brownies for desert); or buy it (a handy tasting table helps you decide what's best!). There are other Ecuadorian main courses too.

FUSSION LOUNGE & RESTAURANT

OTAVALO | $$ | INTERNATIONAL
Sucre near Quiroga; 09-8743-0082; www.facebook.com/fussionlounge; mains $8-15

Chef Javier, who studied culinary arts in Peru, painted this place in the famous market town of Otavalo in Caribbean pastels, and the same artful imagination goes into his recipes: smoked ribs with ginger, beef à la pimienta cooked in reduction of white wine and balsamic vinaigrette, and an array of pasta and vegetarian platters. Hungry for post-market breakfast? How about rainforest crepes in passion-fruit sauce?

MOLIENDO CAFÉ

CUENCA | $ | COLUMBIAN
Vásquez 6-24; 07-282-8710; mains $4-8.50

Fancier places come and go in Cuenca, but this is one of the best, brightest little eateries you'll find in Ecuador – and thus Moliendo Café is always rammed. The hearty arepas (maize pancakes, from $4.50) come from Ecuador's northern neighbours Columbia but are a speciality here, topped with anything from beans and cheese to slow-cooked pork. The moreish, filling set lunches ($2-3) are also a smashing deal.

SHAMUICQ ESPAI GASTRONOMIC

SARAGURO | FUSION
cnr Loja & 10 de Marzo; 07-220-0590; small plates $3-8

A surprising find in ultra-traditional Saraguro, this unpretentious but sophisticated spot is masterminded by a local chef trained in some of Europe's

Previous spread: URKO Cocina Local; Dish from URKO Cocina Local.

best restaurants. Bold cuisine falls somewhere along the lines of highland Ecuadorian–European tapas, inspired by the grains grown around Saraguro and straight-from-the-market produce that melds into tasty but uncomplicated plates. It's an essential stop-off between Cuenca and Loja in the Southern Highlands.

LO NUESTRO

GUAYAQUIL | $$$ | ECUADORIAN
Av Estrada 903-A; 04-462-7233; www.lonuestro.com.ec; mains $7.90-22.90

Ensconced in a century-old mansion complete with wooden shutters and period furniture, Lo Nuestro is Guayaquil's leading culinary light. Come to feast on ceviche, sea bass with crab and other seafood dishes plus a stunning array of original soups, like shrimp-stuffed green plantain ball soup. Musicians play on weekend evenings, when reservations are recommended. Leave room for a homemade cake and a glass (or bottle) from the good wine selection.

EL MORRO RESTAURANT

PLAYAS | $ | ECUADORIAN
Pier, Puerto El Morro; 09-8141-0236; mains $3-8

Look for this delicious nameless eatery on the 2nd floor (the 1st floor is another restaurant) of the orange-and-white house at Puerto El Morro's pier, 10km east of Playas. It serves the best crab soup you'll ever eat. Get there early – when it's gone it's gone. Fishermen land their daily catches at the pier, and this is the first place they sell to, meaning the seafood is as fresh as can be.

COCO SURF

GALÁPAGOS | $$$ | SEAFOOD
Cnr Avs Antonio Gil & 16 de Marzo, Puerto Vilamil; 05-252-9465; www.facebook.com/Coco-Surf-1475105102783725; mains $15-24

This sidewalk cafe dishes up some of the tastiest seafood dishes in the Galápagos, and you'll hardly notice the high prices once the live band starts jamming out jazzy island tunes. The tuna tartare and *patanachos mar y terra* (appetiser platter with an assortment of seafood and meat) are highly recommended.

THE OASIS

GALAPAGOS | $$$ | SEAFOOD
Cnr Cormoran & Pinzon Artesano, Puerto Vilamil; 09-8684-3554; mains $15-35

Esmeraldas native Geanny Bennett Valencia cooks up some of the best dishes in Puerto Vilamil – or the archipelago, for that matter. Mouth-watering *encocados* (coconut stews) are the favourite, served in versions like *camarones* (shrimp), *langosta* (lobster) or *pescado* (fish). The catch: the restaurant only opens by reservation; call ahead or stop by during the day.

WHERE TO EAT...

ECUADORIAN CHOCOLATE

Cacao & Cacao, Quito
Little café-shop selling chocolate made from organically grown local cacao.

Chocolate & Art Tour, Casa Museo Guayasamín, Quito
Legendary painter Oswaldo Guayasamín's former home is today a museum hosting this tour that marries artworks with tastings of To'ak Chocolate

El Quetzal de Mindo, Mindo
Small bar-restaurant filled nightly with a buoyant crowd all happy to be enjoying delectable food and the best fruity alcoholic beverages in Havana.

Yumbo's Chocolate, Mindo
Yumbo's work with an all-female cooperative of cacao growers to bring you Mindo's best-tasting chocolate caliente (hot chocolate). Also available are a succinct chocolate tour, a shop selling chocs and even chocolate stout.

PERU

Celebrity chefs have catapulted Peruvian cuisine to international stardom and, with Virgil Martinez' London-based Lima restaurant, Michelin recognition. Michelin doesn't cover Peru but would have its work cut out if it did. Where to begin? With the iconic citrus-marinated fish ceviche, 300-odd chilli varieties or bedazzling array of jungle fruits.

WHAT TO EAT

Ceviche
Peru's national food is raw fish or shellfish marinated in lime with onions and chilli slivers.

Cuy
Guinea pig is an Andean delicacy.

Pachamanca
Medley of pork, chicken, alpaca and guinea pig cooked with potato, cassava and corn in an oven of hot stones.

Papas a la huancaína
One of myriad ways to try Peru's astonishing diversity of potatoes (the potato originated here once upon a time), in this instance boiled and served with hard-boiled egg in cheese sauce.

Juanes
Spiced rice, meat and olives wrapped in a jungle leaf and steamed.

PRICE RANGES
For a main course:
$ less than S20
$$ S20–60
$$$ S60 or more

Tipping
10% in touristy places

CALETA LA PUNTA

LIMA | $$ | CEVICHE

Malecón Pardo 180, La Punta, Callao; 01-453-1380; mains S40-65

This is a must for original, well-prepared ceviche, not only because the vegetarian mango ceviche won best at Lima's prestigious Mistura food festival, but also because this *cevichería's* setting, at waterfront La Punta neighbourhood, just makes the experience brilliant. Delectable *tiraditos* (marinated fish slices) and whole fried fish with ample garlic are served, along with *maíz chullpi*, a typical table snack of crunchy corn.

ORIGEN TOSTADORES DE CAFÉ

LIMA | $ | CAFE

Av Bolívar 1199, Pueblo Libre; 01-261-8280; www.origentostadoresdecafe.com; coffees S6-10

Several Lima coffee shops are now stylishly showcasing Peru-cultivated coffee but this artisan place is ahead of the pack, breaking coffee-making down to a science and with all the chemistry-set-style machines to prove it. Just blocks from one of Lima's best museums, Museo Larco, Origen offers that trifecta of wi-fi, quiet spaces and hot/iced caffeinated beverages. But the real pride is in the beans: these guys work directly with local producers.

ASTRID Y GASTON CASA MOREYRA

LIMA | $$$ | FUSION

Av Paz Soldan 290, San Isidro; 01-442-2775; www.astridygaston.com; mains S50-100

The standard-bearer of *novoandina* cooking in Lima, Gastón Acurio's flagship French–influenced restaurant, now run by Lima native Diego Muñoz, remains a culinary tour de force. The seasonal menu features traditional Peruvian fare, but it's the exquisite fusion specialities that make this a sublime fine-dining experience. The 28-course tasting menu showcases the depth and breadth of possibility here – just do it.

ÁMAZ

LIMA | $$ | AMAZONIAN

Av La Paz 1079, Miraflores; 01-221-9393; www.amaz.com.pe; mains S30-70

Chef Pedro Miguel's wonder is wholly dedicated to the abundance of Peru's Amazon. Start with tart jungle-fruit cocktails and oversized *tostones* (plantain chips). Banana-leaf wraps, aka *juanes*, hold treasures such as fragrant Peking duck with rice. There's excellent *encurtido* (pickled vegetables) and the generous vegetarian set menu for two is a delicious way to sample the diversity.

LA MAR

LIMA | $$$ | SEAFOOD

Av La Mar 770, Miraflores; 01-421-3365; www.lamarcebicheria.com/en/Lima; mains S49-89

This Gastón Acurio outpost is a polished cement patio bursting with VIPs, and a good-time *cevichería* with outstanding service. There are wonderful

'We want to humbly take on the great challenge of getting to know this beautiful country, replete with unique ingredients, landscapes, culture, tradition, and history.' *Rodrigo Cabrera, Central*

COURTESY SALAMANTO

ceviche and *tiraditos* (Japanese version of ceviche) but also try the the seafood shells, the delicious riff of their bloody Mary and all. Desserts are swimmingly good too. It does not take reservations.

MAIDO

LIMA | $$$ | JAPANESE

San Martín 399 cnr Colón, Miraflores; 01-313-5100; www.maido.pe; mains S25-110

True artistry and exquisite flavours make Maido an excellent stop for top-notch *nikkei* (Japanese–Peruvian) fare that has put it on World's Best lists. The menu of chef Mitsuharu 'Micha' Tsumura ranges from sushi to tender 50-hour ribs, *okonomiyaki* (Japanese pancake) and ramen, with a Peruvian accent. Desserts – such as the yucca *mochi* or a white-chocolate egg with sorbet yolk – delight.

CENTRAL

LIMA | $$$ | PERUVIAN
Av Pedro de Osma 301, Barranco; 01-242-8515; www.centralrestaurante.com.pe; mains S50-100, 12-course tasting menu S568

Part restaurant, part laboratory, Central reinvents Andean cuisine and rescues age-old Peruvian ingredients not used elsewhere. Chef Virgilio Martinez wants you to taste Peru's Andes. He paid his dues in Europe and Asia's top kitchens, but his work here simply dazzles, with dishes such as the charred octopus starter or suckling pig served with pickled vegetables and spiced squash. Central's menu is supplied by sustainable fishing and organic gardens.

ISOLINA

LIMA | $$ | PERUVIAN
Av San Martín 101, Barranco; 01-247-5075; www.isolina.pe; mains S35-78

This is home-style *criollo* (spicy Peruvian fare with Spanish and African influences) food at its best. Isolina doesn't shy away from tripe and kidneys, but also offers loving preparations of succulent ribs, *causa escabechada* (whipped potato dishes with marinated onions) and vibrant green salads on the handwritten menu. Family-sized portions come in old-fashioned tins, but you could make a lighter meal of starters such as marinated clams or ceviche.

FIESTA CHICLAYO GOURMET

NORTH COAST | $$$ | PERUVIAN
Av Salaverry 1820, Chiclayo; 074-20-1970; www.restaurantfiestagourmet.com; mains S40-90

This famous, architecturally impressive spot has exacting culinary standards. Take their divine rice dish *arroz con pato a la chiclayana*, made with farm-raised duck that must be black-feathered and no more than three months old. Or take their *ceviche a la brasa* (citrus-marinated fish served warm and unforgettable in corn husks after an 11th-hour searing). The lowdown on Northern Peru's much-lauded cuisine is outrageously great, with pisco sours constructed tableside and exquisite service. Book ahead.

EL CELLER DE CLER

NORTH COAST | $$ | PERUVIAN
cnr Gamarra & Independencia, Trujillo; 044-31-7191; www.facebook.com/elcellerdeclerrestaurant; mains S18-48

This atmospheric spot is the only place in Trujillo to enjoy dinner (coupled perhaps with one of their amazing cocktails) on a 2nd-floor balcony – the wraparound number dates to the early 19th century. The food is upscale, featuring pasta and grills, and delicious. Antiques fuel the decor, from a 1950s-era American cash register to an extraordinary industrial-revolution pulley lamp from the UK.

Previous spread: MIL; Salamanto.

LA SIRENA D' JUAN

NORTH COAST | $$ | PERUVIAN
Piura 316, Máncora; 073-25-8173; www.facebook.com/laSirenaDeJuan; mains S30-50

Local boy done good Juan has turned his intimate little main-drag seafooder into northern Peru's best restaurant. Yellowfin tuna fresh from Máncora's waters is the showstopper, whether prepared as a *tiradito* (Peruvian sashimi) in yellow curry or grilled with mango-*rocoto*-red pepper chutney. There are also several Peruvian classics given foodie upgrades (baby goat in black beer, for example). Service in the small, French-farmhouse-style space is personalised and on point.

EL BATÁN DE TAYTA

NORTHERN HIGHLANDS | $$ | AMAZONIAN
La Merced 604, Chachapoyas; www.facebook.com/ElBatanDelTayta; mains S20-50

Exotic is the word here, from the decor (Amazonian creepers, bamboo table umbrellas and furry seat covers), to the food ('drunk' guinea pig, duck and edible ants in a vanilla and cognac cocktail, for example!) and the implements it's served on (model boats, mini-drums, or if you're lucky, a terracotta roof tile). Despite the theatrics, the food is plentiful and well executed.

DOÑA ZULLY

NORTHERN HIGHLANDS | $$ | AMAZONIAN
San Pablo de la Cruz 244, Tarapoto; 042-50-7632; www.facebook.com/DonaZully; mains S20-45

The *parrilla* (charcoal grill) masters here rustle up some of the best barbecues in the Peruvian Amazon using the staple ingredients of *cecina* (smoked pork) and *doncella* (an Amazonian river fish), among others. The tilapia, steam-cooked in a banana leaf with sides of fried plantain and avocado salad, is also sensational. Service is attentive and the atmosphere refined.

INTI-MAR

SOUTH COAST | $$ | SEAFOOD
Contiguo Puerto General San Martín, Punto Punto Pejerrey, Paracas (El Chaco); 981-318-866; www.inti-mar.com; mains S40-55

One of the Peruvian coastline's best eateries, this working scallop farm across the bay from El Chaco offers tables right alongside the sea. Its seafood dishes astound and delight, but the fresh scallops served *natural* with lemon and olive oil are phenomenal. Or plump for the *conchas a la parmesana*, oven-baked in their shells with a Parmesan covering. By the water, some loungers entice you to linger for post-meal drinks.

WHERE TO EAT...

CEVICHE

Caleta La Punta, Lima
The waterside La Punta neighbourhood is a Mecca for lunchtime ceviche aficionados and seafood at Caleta La Punta is so good it has won awards.

El Pescador, Chiclayo
This little locals' secret packs in the droves for outstanding seafood dishes at outstandingly good prices.

ChillOut Carnes y Pescados, Iquitos
First prize in the keenly-fought battle for number one in Iquitos' *cevichería* (ceviche restaurant) contest: massive ceviche platters are often made with river fish, like *doncella*.

Inti-Mar, Paracas
This working scallop farm serves them at their freshest, with lemon and olive oil, plus several other ceviches, in a stellar seafront setting.

RESTAURANTE CAMPESTRE LA CHOZA DE OMAR

CENTRAL HIGHLANDS | $$ | PERUVIAN
Obrajillo; 996-963-062; www.facebook.com/Obrajillo; mains S25-35

This rustic outdoor restaurant where road meets river in idyllic Obrajillo entices droves of weekending Lima residents, who go crazy over the huge plates of carnivorous fare while their kids run amok in an expansive emerald-green garden. Try the *pachamanca* (meat and tubers baked on hot stones in the ground) and don't miss playing *sapo*, Peru's equivalent of a pub sport. Verdant mountains rise all around in this balmy introduction to Andean life.

MIL

SACRED VALLEY | $$$ | PERUVIAN
Moray ruins, near Maras; 946-948-088; www.milcentro.pe; 8-course tasting menu S340

Opened in 2018, this lauded Virgilio Martinez restaurant is more an experience than a meal. A set menu showcases the incredibly diverse local Andean ingredients using cutting-edge cooking techniques. Lunch is eight 'moments,' small plates, paired with beverages. Built on the flanks of the Moray ruins, its location is superb.

CICCIOLINA

CUZCO | $$ | INTERNATIONAL
2nd fl, Triunfo 393; 084-23-9510; www.cicciolinacuzco.com; tapas S10-35, mains S30-55

Within a lofty colonial courtyard mansion, Cicciolina may be Cuzco's best restaurant. The eclectic food is divine, starting with house-marinated olives, and continuing with the likes of crisp

COURTESY MIL

This page: Corn, MIL. Opposite page: Preparing drinks in MIL.

polenta squares with cured rabbit, charred octopus, red trout in coconut milk, beetroot ravioli and tender lamb. Dine in the more casual tapas bar (no reservation necessary) or restaurant (reserve beforehand). In either, the impeccable service and cosy ambience are deal-clinchers.

CHICHA

CUSCO | $$ | PERUVIAN
2nd fl, Regocijo 261; 084-24-0520; www.chicha.com.pe/en/cusco; mains S30-70

A Gastón Acurio venture serving up haute versions of Cuzco classics in an open kitchen. Its riff on *anticuchos* (beef skewers) is a delectable barbecued octopus with crisp herbed potato wedges. Other contenders include papas *rellenas* (stuffed potatoes), curried alpaca with quinoa and *chairo* (lamb and barley soup) served in a clay pot.

SALAMANTO

AREQUIPA | $$ | PERUVIAN
San Francisco 211; 054-57-7061; www.salamanto.com; mains S40-60, 10-course tasting menu S107/137 without/with snacks

The innovative, beautifully plated contemporary Peruvian creations at Salamanto bolster Arequipa's reputation as a foodie destination. The 10-dish degustation is unmissable with highlights that could be trout carpaccio, alpaca steak with pisco mustard or *cuy* with goose puree, rocoto pepper jelly, mushrooms, oysters and spiky green Latin American peppers called *caiguas*. There are only three wines (Argentinian and Peruvian) to choose from but they have been carefully selected.

'Chicha is about regional food: the produce, traditions and culture from each location elevated with good culinary techniques, working with responsibility and the hand of local producers.'
Chicha

BELÉN MERCADO

AMAZON BASIN | $ | AMAZONIAN
cnr Prospero & 9 de Diciembre, Iquitos; meals S1-10

Iquitos' floating shantytown, Belén, is flanked by this chaotic labyrinth of stalls sprawling over a huge area, including parts often submerged by the Itaya river. Here, a menú, including juice made with wondrous jungle fruits, costs S5. Look out for specialities including meaty Amazon worms, *ishpa* (simmered sabalo fish intestines and fat) and *sikisapa* (fried leafcutter ants), watch your wallet and prepare for a voyage into the unknown.

COURTESY MIL

BRAZIL

Brazil's incredible domestic bounty, coupled with waves of immigration from Europe, Africa, the Middle East and Asia, make it South America's most diverse and delicious culinary destination. Regional specialities abound: Delectable freshwater fish from the Amazon and the Pantanal, unique African-influenced dishes in Bahia, European influences in the south (German, Italian) and down-home comfort classics (beans, pork) from Minas Gerais.

WHAT TO EAT

Feijoada
The national dish, this hearty stew marries black beans with various salted beef and pork cuts seasoned with garlic, onions, bay leaves and even *cachaça* (local firewater).

Moqueca
An African-influenced seafood stew slow-cooked in a traditional clay pot with coconut milk, palm or olive oil, onions, tomatoes, garlic and cilantro.

Picanha
Brazil's most succulent cut of beef, traditionally served in all-you-can-eat barbecue restaurants known as *churrascarias*.

Coxinha
A boteco (neighbourhood bar) classic: shredded chicken meat fried in batter, often doused with hot sauce.

Pão de queijo
Traditional cheese bread made with sweet and/or sour tapioca starch.

PRICE RANGES

$ less than R$30
$$ R$30–75
$$$ R$75 or more

Tipping: 10%

FLOR DO LUAR

AMAZONAS | $$ | BRAZILIAN

Av Presidente Getulio Vargas 129, Novo Airão; 93 99418-0865; www.facebook.com/flor.luar.75; mains R$26-45

Flor do Luar sits on a floating pontoon on Amazonas state's Rio Negro and serves fabulous food and cold beers. The speciality is the phenomenal *banda de tambaqui assada*, a local fish cooked on the grill with plantains.

BANZEIRO

AMAZONAS | $$$ | BRAZILIAN

Libertador 102, Manaus; 92 3234-1621; www.restaurantebanzeiro.com.br; mains R$75-140

This one-of-a-kind experience is a destination-worthy Amazonian highlight. Freshwater fish varieties such as *pirarucú*, *tambaqui* and other Amazonian specialities are served in various preparations, from cheese and banana to parsley and *formigas* (ants).

AMAZÔNICO PEIXARIA REGIONAL

AMAZONAS | $$ | SEAFOOD

Av Darcy Vargas 222, Manaus; 92 3236-0546; www.amazonico.com.br; mains R$36-98

However you get your tambaqui (perhaps the tastiest of all Amazonian fish) prepared here – stewed, grilled, ribs – the execution is perfect. It's one of the best meals you'll have in the Amazon.

QUIOSQUE DA PRAÇA

PARÁ | $ | STREET FOOD

Praça Barão de Santarém, Santarém; 93 99418-0865; from R$8

This small kiosk serves one of the Amazon's best *tacacá*, a soup made from *jambu* (a mouth-numbing indigenous herb), *tucupi* (a manioc broth) and dried shrimp.

REMANSO DO BOSQUE

PARÁ | $$$ | AMAZONIAN

Travessa Perebebuí 2350, Belém; 91 3347-2829; www.restauranteremanso.com.br; mains R$38-140

Chefs Thiago and Felipe Castanho are single-handedly responsible for putting Amazonian cuisine – and Belém – on the worldwide foodie map, turning their culinary wizardry inwards to the incredibly diverse jungle bounty to create some of Brazil's most exciting and innovative haute cuisine. Stunning regional Amazonian delicacies include filhote fish roasted over hot coals and Paraense-style duck rice.

CANTA MARIA GASTRONOMIA

RIO GRANDE DO SUL | $$ | ITALIAN

Parnaíba 777, Bento Gonçalves; 54 99159-9996; www.facebook.com/pg/cantamariagastronomia; buffet R$53.80-87

This is the best of Rio Grande do Sul's famed restaurants specialising in the *comida típica italiana* buffet: *capeletti* (meat-filled pasta) soup, salad, pasta, *galeto* (rotisserie spring chicken), *linguiça* (garlicky pork sausage), pork ribs, polenta and fried cheese. Clear your schedule!

'Maní's cuisine has direct links to personal memories, real and imagined; to sensitive perspectives on simple everyday things; to Brazil, its stories and ingredients.'
Helena Rizzo, Maní

COURTESY CASA DO BARREADO

OSTRADAMUS

SANTA CATARINA | $$$ | SEAFOOD

Rod Baldicero Filomeno 7640, Ribeirão da Ilha; 48 9990-5711; www.ostradamus.com.br; oysters R$35-45, mains for 2 R$135-195

Slurp local oysters over a dozen ways at Santa Catarina's best and most famous seafood restaurant, but don't fill up on those – the outstanding and incredibly presented seafood dishes here are a vacation highlight. From the skewered grilled shrimp tower to the perfectly grilled fillet of *pescada-amarela* with artichokes, asparagus, potatoes and shrimp – everything is beautiful and devastatingly tasty.

ABENDBROTHAUS

SANTA CATARINA | $$$ | GERMAN

Henrique Conrad 1194, Blumenau; 47 3378-1157; www.abendbrothaus.blogspot.com; meals R$76

This Sunday-only feast is the most coveted table in Santa Catarina's German and Italian–heavy Vale Europeu for *marreco* (stuffed Garganey); in fact, the menu's only item begins its journey to your stomach at 6am, when Josefa Jensen begins a sunrise recipe ritual handed down from her grandmother.

CASA DO BARREADO

PARANÁ | $$ | BRAZILIAN
José Antônio da Cruz 78, Paranaguá; 41 3423-1830; per person incl dessert R$40

In her own home a few blocks behind Paranaguá's centro histórico, Norma cooks up real-deal *barreado* (rib-sticking meat stew) true to its original recipe (simmered for 24 hours in an earthen clay pot). Do not miss finishing with the *chico balanceado*, a sweet concoction of bananas, meringue and *manjar branco* (coconut pudding).

MAR E SOL

PARANÁ | $$ | SEAFOOD
Praça Felipe Valentim, Ilha do Mel; 41 3426-8021; meals R$29-38

This dead-simple, family-run seafooder on Paraná's atmospheric sand-street island getaway, Ilha do Mel, serves spectacular fish, shrimp and crab *moquecas* (seafood stews) and seafood risottos. Junior, the resident pet parrot, gives flyby recommendations.

MANÍ

SÃO PAULO | $$$ | BRAZILIAN
Joaquim Atunes 210; 11 3085-4148; www.manimanioca.com.br; mains R$51-110

Rustic-chic Maní and the 2014 Veuve Cliquot World's Best Female Chef, Helena Rizzo, will astound you. The inventive slow-cooked egg (1½ hours at 63°C) is more famous, but the house-cooked potato chips topped with *filet mignon*, or hearts of palm taglierini with creamed Tulha cheese are true culinary coups.

MOCOTÓ

SÃO PAULO | $ | BRAZILIAN
Av Nossa Senhora do Loreto 1100; 11 2951-3056; www.mocoto.com.br; mains R$39-60

Chef Rodrigo Oliveira took over his father's simple emporium and started churning out seriously incredible Northeastern comfort food at friendly prices – *dadinhos de tapioca* (fried tapioca squares), braised pork leg and the vegan *Sertaneja moqueca* (with boiled cashews, ground banana, gherkin, pumpkin and greens) – are favourites, chased with hundreds of *artisan cachaças* (sugar cane alcohol beverages).

PATUÁ DA BAIANA

SÃO PAULO | $$$ | BAHIAN
Luis Barreto 74A; 11 3115-0513; www.facebook.com/patuadabaiana; mains R$46-167

Previous spread: Dish from Casa do Barreado.

Bá's 'secret' underground restaurant in her home is a priceless experience: you must call ahead and know someone who knows someone. If Bá digs your vibe, she greets you with open arms, cooking up scrumptious Bahian specialities (seafood stews, shrimp in manioc sauce, shrimp fritters – she chooses the dishes, not you!). File under unforgettable.

A CASA DO PORCO

SÃO PAULO | $$ | BRAZILIAN
Araújo 124; 11 3258-2578; www.acasadoporco.com.br; mains R$48-72

Chef Jefferson Rueda's casual temple of swine is a wonderful descent into all things pork. Delicious and decadent specialities such as *porco San Zé* offer the full treatment, carved from an eight-hour whole slow-roasted hog and served in perfectly crispy/decadently succulent squares with side dishes such as *tutu de feljão* (beans thickened with cassava flour). Heart-stoppingly satisfying.

ESTADÃO

SÃO PAULO | $ | FAST FOOD
Viaduto 9 de Julho 193; 11 3257-7121; www.estadaolanches.com.br; sandwiches R$7-33

This classic downtown *lanchonete* (snack bar) serves one of Sampa's gastronomic musts: a signature *pernil* (pork loin) sandwich, smothered in the cheese (go for provolone!) and sautéed onions.

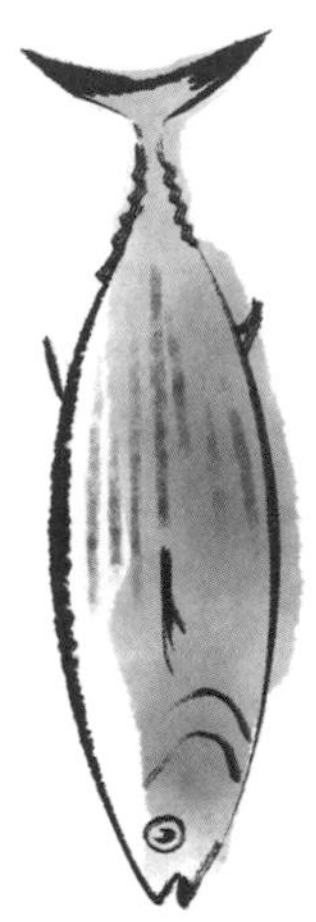

'Chef Jefferson Rueda's casual temple of swine is a wonderful descent into all things pork.'
A Casa do Porco

TORDESILHAS

SÃO PAULO | $$ | BRAZILIAN
Alameda Tietê 489; 11 3107-7444; www.tordesilhas.com; mains R$63-87

Chef Mara Salles creates some of the very best contemporary Brazilian cuisine in the country at dependable Tordesilhas. There is a palpable lean on specialities from the Amazon such as *pato no tucupí* (roasted duck flavored with juice of the manioc plant and *jambu*, a mouth-numbing indigenous herb) and grilled Amazonian fish, as well as Brazil-wide regional dishes.

LAMEN KAZU

SÃO PAULO | $$ | JAPANESE
Tomás Gonzaga 51; 11 3277-4286; www.lamenkazu.com.br; mains $29-47

It's not as famous (or cheap) as some of its neighbours, but take the hint: the 99% Japanese clientele should tell you something. The fiery *kara misso lamen* (spicy pork noodles), doused with the homemade chilli sauce, is a revelation; as is everything on the menu. This is the culinary epicentre of Liberdade, São Paulo's Japantown.

LEGGERA PIZZA NAPOLETANA

SÃO PAULO | $$ | PIZZERIA
Diana 80; 11 3862-2581; www.pizzerialeggera.com.br; pizza R$34-42

Brazilian-Italian-American *pizzaiolo* Andre Guidon imports everything humanly possible from Italy – and

this small, family-run affair epitomises the Brazilian–Italian diaspora. The 20 individual-sized, uncut pies here (plus a few calzones) are easily the best among a sea of options in one of the world's most serious and fantastical pizza cities.

VELOSO BAR

SÃO PAULO | $ | BOTECO

Conceição Veloso 56; 11 5572-0254; www.velosobar.com.br

Arrive early to this outstanding *boteco* (neighbourhood bar), where crowds fight over tables for some of the city's best bar snacks: Shockingly good *coxinhas* (battered and fried shredded chicken, catupiry cheese and spices), doused in Brazil's best homemade hot sauce, chased with memorable São Paulo's best caipirinhas.

CASA DO OUVIDOR

MINAS GERAIS | $$ | MINEIRA

Direita 42, Ouro Preto; 31 3551-2141; www.casadoouvidor.com.br; mains R$29-69

Ouvidor has garnered numerous awards for its authentic comida mineira over the past four decades, with specialities like tutu à mineira (mashed beans with roast pork loin, crackling, collard greens and boiled egg). Bring an empty stomach – portions are immense!

EMPÓRIO SANTO ANTÔNIO

Minas Gerais | $$ | Mineira

Bélica 133, Tiradentes; 32 3355-2433; mains R$50-64, all-you-can-eat weekend buffet R$60

Run by the same family for nearly two decades, everything at this Tiradentes staple is lovingly homemade – roast chicken, pork cheeks, artisanal *linguiça* (garlicky pork sausage), home-smoked trout and classic Mineira specialities.

This page: Dish from Camarões Potiguar.

The real tour de force is the sumptuous all-you-can-eat weekend buffet, which includes everything from *leitão a pururuca* (crispy roast marinated pork) to homemade cookies.

XAPURI

MINAS GERAIS | $$ | MINEIRA
Mandacarú 260, Belo Horizonte; 31 3496-6198; www.restaurantexapuri.com.br; mains R$48-75

Run by the affable Dona Nelsa, this long-standing local institution 15km northwest of Belo Horizonte is renowned for its fabulous comida mineira (typical Mineira cuisine). Everything is served at picnic tables under a thatched roof, with many dishes emerging from the traditional wood stove blazing up front.

ROCKA BEACH LOUNGE

BÚZIOS | $$$ | SEAFOOD
Praia Brava; www.rockafish.com.br; 22 2623-6159; mains R$79-86

Argentine chef Gustavo Rinkevich calls on sustainable fish and organic vegetables from the garden for standout dishes like miso-marinated fresh catch with jam foam and Amazonian bean vinaigrette at this casual-chic seafood eatery perched directly above Praia Brava. Beachcombers linger all day.

ACONCHEGO CARIOCA

RIO DE JANEIRO | $$ | BRAZILIAN
Barão de Iguatemi 245; 21 2273-1035; mains for two R$80-120

Aconchego Carioca consistently ranks as one of the best places in town to eat traditional Brazilian cuisine. The cosy setting has a casual neighbourhood vibe, but attracts diners from across the city who come for *bobó de camarão* (shrimp in manioc sauce), pork ribs with guava sauce, and a cachaça-tinged flan for dessert.

APRAZÍVEL

RIO DE JANEIRO | $$$ | BRAZILIAN
Aprazível 62; 21 2508-9174; www.aprazivel.com.br; mains R$90-130

Aprazível offers beautiful views across Rio's charming Santa Teresa neighbourhood and a lush garden setting. Grilled fish and roasted dishes showcase the country's culinary highlights from land and sea. Standout choices include the grilled heart of palms starter and standout main courses like delectable *moquequinha* (seafood stew) or roast pork with pineapple chutney and polenta.

PARAÍSO TROPICAL

BAHIA | $$$ | BAHIAN
Edgar Loureiro 98B, Salvador; 71 3384-7464; www.restauranteparaisotropical.com.br; mains R$53-98

This Salvador destination restaurant has long been considered one of the Bahia's top picks for beautifully prepared regional cuisine with a gourmet twist. If you want to experience a

moqueca Bahiana (Bahian–style seafood stew), this is a detour-worthy choice.

50 SABORES

CEARÁ | $ | ICE CREAM

Av Beira Mar 2982, Fortaleza; 85 3023-0050; www.50sabores.com.br; 1/2 flavours R$14/20

One of Brazil's most famous ice cream shops, though with a terribly misleading name: there are actually 150 flavours here! Don't let anyone tell you one scoop of tapioca, one scoop of açaí isn't the perfect combination.

CAMARÕES POTIGUAR

RIO GRANDE DO NORTE | $$ | SEAFOOD

Pedro da Fonseca Filho 8887, Natal; 84 3209-2425; www.camaroes.com.br; mains for two from R$81-131

This creative homage to shrimp is arguably Natal's best dining experience. Start with a traditional shrimp-and-Catupiry cheese *pastel* (fried, stuffed dough pastry), then follow up with anything from shrimp in pumpkin to the coveted Bonfim (sauteed with cashews, *coalho* cheese and fragrant *biquinho* peppers with *vatapá* risotto).

CHICA PITANGA

PERNAMBUCO | $$ | SEAFOOD

Petrolina 19, Recife; 81 3465-2224; www.chicapitanga.com.br; per kg lunch weekday/weekend R$77.40/82.10, dinner R$65.50

'Leggera transports patrons to modern Naples on the back of the best of Paulistano hospitality.'
Andre Nevoso Guidon, Leggera Pizza Napoletana

Pitanga offers a changing array of diverse, near gourmet-level *por kilo* (pay-by-weight) dishes every day. The dozen or so salad options might, for example, include tabbouleh or mango salad, while duck rice or shrimp in spinach sauce might appear among the hot dishes. Most dangerous pay-by-weight restaurant in Brazil!

CRUZEIRO DO PESCADOR

RIO GRANDE DO NORTE | $$ | SEAFOOD

Cnr Av Baía dos Golfinhos & Concris, Praia da Pipa; 84 3246-2026; www.cruzeirodopescador.com.br; mains R$65-85, for two people R$125-230

What looks like a typical mess of a house hides a don't-miss culinary experience. Chef Daniel does everything with homemade and homegrown finesse, from the poetically handwritten menus and the romantic candlelit setting to the products from his own garden. The flavours of his cooking – some pinched from India and Bahia – are delicious.

MESA DA ANA

FERNANDO DE NORONHA | $$$ | BRAZILIAN

Estrada do Atalaia 230, Vila do Trinta; 81 3619-0178; dinner per person R$250

Husband-and-wife team Ana (Cordon Bleu grad) and Rock (pronounced 'hockey;' Noronha's resident artist eccentric) serve 12 or less people a four-course, fish-heavy feast dictated by the local catch (no advance menu) at this rustic island gem.

GUYANA

Rainforest swathed, largely road-free Guyana is for the most part a wilderness still some way from attracting foodies, but its charmingly dilapidated Caribbean capital Georgetown nevertheless boasts some enjoyable dining experiences, many of which come from the country's large Indian minority.

WHAT TO EAT

Pepperpot
Guyana's beloved national dish is stewed meat flavored with cinnamon and cassareep, a thick black liquid made from cassava root.

Metemgee
This popular Guyanese–Creole stew is made from vegetables and starches such as yams, cassava and plantains.

Cook up rice
A mixture of rice, meat, coconut milk and lots of herbs.

Roti
Soft Indian flatbread served with delicious fillings.

Cow heel soup
Soup made with split peas, vegetables, dumplings and cow heels.

Fried Bora
These very long and thin green beans are a delicious accompaniment to any meal, normally fried in a little salt.

PRICE RANGES

For a main course:
$ less than G$1000;
$$ G$1000–2000;
$$$ G$2000 or more

Tipping: 10–15%

BACKYARD CAFÉ

GEORGETOWN | $$$ | GUYANESE

Rose St, West Ruimveldt; 663-5104; www.facebook.com/backyardcafeonline; meals G$4000-6000

Anyone interested in Guyanese cooking simply must head to Delven Adam's makeshift backyard restaurant, where tailored menus are prepared for his guests each night. It's even possible to accompany Delven when he goes shopping at the market beforehand. The extraordinarily varied and creative feasts include dishes such as lightly friend breadfruit, pumpkin soup, sea bass served with mangoes and his famous passion fruit cheesecake. Call several weeks ahead to arrange a table.

AAGMAN INDIAN RESTAURANT

GEORGETOWN | $$$ | INDIAN

28 Sherif St, Campbellville; 654-7693; www.aagmanrestaurant.com; mains G$2000-3500

This is the best Indian fine dining restaurant in Georgetown and well worth the detour to get here from the city centre. The menu is huge and focuses on Mughlai cuisine, with outstanding dishes including Duck Rogan Josh and the Paneer Sholay Kebab, paneer flavoured with saffron and other Mughlai herbs and spices then roasted in a clay oven. The restaurant is white tablecloth smart and as formal as Georgetown gets.

SHANTA'S

GEORGETOWN | $ | INDIAN

225 Camp St; mains from G$500-1000

For more than a half century, simple street food vendor Shanta's has been filling Georgetown's bellies with the best roti, curries and *chokas* (roasted vegetables) this side of India. Don't miss the boneless chicken curry in roti, the dhaal or the cassava bread. It's unbelievably inexpensive and at lunchtime you'll be squeezing into any available space at the plastic tables.

SURINAME

Suriname is a cultural unicorn, its ethnic melting pot a rich palimpsest of indigenous, European, African and Asian influences. While the food scene here is still in its infancy, the capital Paramaribo nevertheless offers some interestingly diverse dining experiences.

SOUPOSO

PARAMARIBO | $$ | FUSION

Costerstraat 20A; 420-351; www.facebook.com/souposo; mains SR$25-100

From delicious daily soups (do not miss the peanut one if they're serving it during your visit) to mains like duck leg confit in masala and an amazing pesto pasta topped with home-smoked *bang bang* (freshwater fish) and sundried tomatoes, the food here would stand out anywhere, but in Parbo it's exceptional. Brunch includes omelettes, fresh juices and salads. The heritage-home garden setting makes the experience even lovelier.

DE GADRI

PARAMARIBO | $ | CREOLE

Zeelandiaweg 1; 420-688; mains SR$27-45

This quiet restaurant overlooking the river and nestled in the shadow of Paramaribo's historic Fort Zeelandia offers the best creole food in town along with exceptionally friendly service. It's not a particularly atmospheric spot, but try the delicious soup of the day – peanut, cassava or banana accompanied by roast chicken and pom, a kind of casserole, and you'll see why locals line up for takeaway at lunchtime.

BODEGA & GRILL DE WAAG

PARAMARIBO | $$$ | INTERNATIONAL

Waterkant 5; 474-514; www.dewaag.sr; mains SR$75-200

This gorgeously realised addition to Parbo's eating choices has seen the transformation of an old waterfront building into a smart and stylish indoor-outdoor eating space and bar, with a great menu focused on (but not limited to) steaks, all of which come US Department of Agriculture (USDA) certified and are the best in the city. Also available are good salads, tapas, soups and breakfasts.

WHAT TO EAT

Bakabana
This popular dish, which originates from Indonesia, is battered and fried plantain that is then dipped in spicy peanut sauce.

Bojo cake
A thick, damp dessert made from grated cassava and coconut and flavoured with rum and cinnamon.

Moksi-alesi
Literally 'mixed rice', *moksi-alesi* is traditionally made from leftover rice and cooked with salted meat, fish or shrimp, sometimes with coconut milk.

Pinda bravoe
Don't leave Suriname without trying this deliciously spicy peanut soup, hailing from West Africa.

Roti
These grilled Indian flatbreads stuffed with spicy meats, potato or vegetables are a popular lunchtime snack.

PRICE RANGES

For a main course:
$ less than SR$50
$$ SR$50–100
$$$ SR$100 or more

Tipping: 10%

FRENCH GUIANA

This slice of Gallic *je ne sais quoi* in the heart of the Amazon allows you to enjoy perfect croissants in the tropics and enlivens French food with a surprising array of local influences running from Amerindian to Lao.

WHAT TO EAT

Cod fritters
Normally served as snacks before dinner, alongside the ubiquitous ti' punch, a sweet rum-based cocktail apéritif.

Blaff
This spicy fish chowder is a breakfast staple.

Awara broth
This light brown soup is made by mixing smoked chicken and smoked fish with the pulp of the awara fruit and reduced in a big pot over a period as long as 36 hours.

Callaloo
Popular across the Caribbean and of West African origin, callaloo is a soup like stew made from the taro root (*dasheen*) or *amaranth* in French Guiana, and normally served with meat as a main course.

PRICE RANGES
For a main course:
$ less than €12
$$ €12–20
$$$ €20 or more

Tipping: Not generally expected.

RESTAURANT PARIS CAYENNE

CAYENNE | $$$ | FRENCH
59 rue Lallouette; 0594-317617; www.pariscayenne.fr; mains €23-36

Cayenne's chicest dining spot and almost certainly French Guiana's best restaurant hums with ambience and white-table clothed elegance, and the dining room is hung with abstract art and has the feel of a private members' club. The menu is sublime and includes Gallic mainstays such as foie gras, as well as more Caribbean dishes like octopus and conch fricassee, and the superb wild Guianese shrimp, served flambé or grilled.

LA PETITE MAISON

CAYENNE | $$$ | CREOLE
23 rue Félix Eboué; 0594-385839; www.restaurantlapetitiemaison.com; mains €17-36

One of Cayenne's most charming haunts for lunch or dinner, La Petite Maison really lives up to its name and is found in a traditional stone and wood Cayenne house, decorated with an elegant feel and serving an innovative Creole menu. Dishes include eggplant crumble, shrimp *moqueca* (seafood stew), pork in honey sauce, and sublime homemade ice cream.

LA GOÉLETTE

ST LAURENT DU MARONI | $$ | CREOLE
Riverfront; 0594-342897; mains €16-23

Easily the best restaurant in French Guiana's second city of St Laurent du Maroni, 'the Schooner' is indeed built boat-like over the Maroni River with great views towards Suriname. The food is excellent, focusing on locally caught fish and seafood, with choices including fried mussels in white wine and Roquefort sauce, seafood risotto and *moqueca royale* cooked in coconut milk with seafood and coriander.

BOLIVIA

Bolivia is an emerging foodie destination, now with a celebrity ambassador in Claus Meyer, the man behind multi-Michelin–starred Noma, who founded a restaurant here in 2012. Potato- and corn-driven in the highlands and more yucca and fruit-driven in the jungle, Bolivian food remains satisfyingly simple at heart.

WHAT TO EAT

Salteñas
These piping hot pastry shells are Bolivia's best, most ubiquitous snack. Beef, pork or chicken are mixed in a sweet, juicy, slightly piquant sauce containing olives, raisins and potatoes.

Sonso
Yucca pureed with salty cheese and cooked, typically grilled on a skewer.

Pique a lo macho
One of several Bolivian hangover-fix dishes, this is beef, sausage, eggs, peppers and onions piled over potato fries.

Llajua
Tomatoey salsa created with locotos, rare chilli peppers endemic to Bolivia and Peru. It spices up plain potato- and bread-based meals country-wide.

Mamá qonqachi
Frisbee-like cheese bread.

PRICE RANGES
For a main course:
$ under B$30
$$ B$30–60
$$$ B$60 or more

Tipping: 5–10%

ALI PACHA

LA PAZ | $$$ | VEGETARIAN
Colón 1306, Casco Viejo; 02-220-2366; www.alipacha.com; tasting menus B$200-300

Locals thought it absurd to open a high-end vegetarian restaurant with degustation menus in La Paz's down-trodden Casco Viejo neighbourhood. And it is absurd. Fantastically so! Even carnivores will swoon over the creative plant-based creations and herbaceous cocktails. You're guaranteed to taste Bolivia's flavours like never before.

GUSTU

LA PAZ | $$$ | BOLIVIAN
Calle 10 No 300, Calacoto; 02-211-7491; www.gustu.bo; mains B$95-130, dinner tasting menu B$480-580

Credited with sparking the city's culinary renaissance, and launched by Danish culinary entrepreneur Claus Meyer (of four-time best-restaurant-in-the-world Noma fame), this ground-breaking establishment works to both rescue and showcase underutilised Bolivian ingredients. In a gorgeous building rich with Andean textiles, it offers everything from Ande-an grains to caiman from the Amazon. Even wine pairings are from Bolivia.

LOS QÑAPÉS

LA PAZ | $ | BOLIVIAN
René Moreno 1283, San Miguel; 7201-1122; www.facebook.com/losqnapes; snacks B$6-15

Snack on Bolivian favourites like *cuñapé* (a cheesy yuca bread), *humitas* and *masacos* (plantains or yucca mashed with meat or cheese) at this always-busy cafe. All ingredients are organic and Bolivian.

NAMAS TÉ

LA PAZ | $ | VEGETARIAN
Zoilo Flores 1334, San Pedro; 02-248-1401; www.namastebolivia.com; mains B$5-25

Tea-lovers take note: the tea menu at this lovable lime-green veggie restaurant is a staggering four pages long! There's also plenty of quinoa (in falafel, soup, tabbouleh salad) and even a raved-about tofu pad thai. Smoothies, juices and sandwiches round things out. It's all cleverly done, not least the restaurant name (*Namaste* = respectful greeting in Hindu, *Té* = tea in Spanish).

PACEÑA LA SALTEÑA

LA PAZ | $ | BOLIVIAN
Loayza 233, Casco Viejo; 02-220-2347 www.pacenalasaltena.com; B$5-10

Eating a *salteña* (a baked pastry stuffed with out-of-this-world meat and vegetable goodness) is a not-to-be-missed local experience. Whilst this is possible at many impromptu stalls around the city, award-winning Paceña La Salteña, with its peach walls, chintz curtains and gold trimmings, gives the fare a gilded edge. Vegetarian versions are available too. *Salteña* juice does tend to dribble down one's face, but thankfully lots of triangular napkins are on hand.

POPULAR COCINA BOLIVIANA

LA PAZ | $$ | BOLIVIAN
Murillo 826, Rosario; 6561-3649; www.facebook.com/popularlapazbolivia; 3-course lunch B$65

You'll often need to queue to get in the door at aptly named Popular, where good-value seasonal three-course menus put a gourmet spin on the city's humble lunch spots. Ingredients are market-fresh and the plates are true works of art.

'Ali Pacha is born from the concern to develop a different gastronomic concept: one that highlights haute cuisine and Bolivian ingredients under a vegan proposal.'
Luis Fernandez Salazar, Ali Pacha

ISLA PEÑON

LAKE TITICACA | $$ | SEAFOOD
Chañi; mains around B$30

Do as the locals hereabouts do and make a weekend trip to this faux floating island, also known as a part of the Islas Flotantes de Chañi. It's attached to a rocky outcrop with sweeping views, and the famously moreish Lake Titicaca trout comes from right beneath your feet. Chañi village is 5km north of central Copacabana, Lake Titicaca's main town.

LAS VELAS

LAKE TITICACA | $ | INTERNATIONAL
By Yumani, Isla del Sol; mains B$50-70

Want a candlelit dinner of organic vegetarian pizza at 4000m? Head to this beloved hilltop restaurant with wonderful westerly views. There are also pastas and exquisite trout and kingfish. Board games, cards and musical instruments keep you amused whilst you wait for the slow-cooked, well-cooked food. Take the path to Yumani and turn left into the forest at the sign for Las Velas (bring a flashlight).

EL SECRETO DE MAMA

AMAZON BASIN | $ | BAKERY
Cosme Gutiérrez between Beni Mamoré & Santa Cruz, Riberalta; 7399-3010; www.facebook.com/elsecretodemama.bo; snacks from B$3

This pretty-in-pink bakery offers table upon table of delectable local treats

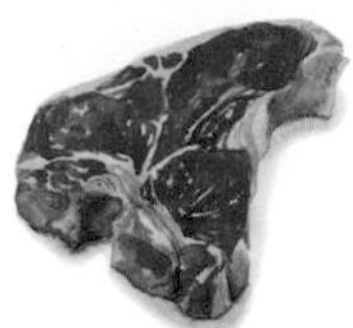

like empanadas, *cuñapes* (cheese and yuca balls), *bombitas* (cream-filled pastries) and *sonso* (a cheesy yuca bread). Wash them down with hot chocolate made from pure Beni-grown cacao. You'll never look at teatime the same way again!

CHURRASQUERIA LA ESTANCIA

AMAZON BASIN | $$ | STEAK
Ibare between Av. Pedro Ignacio Muiba & Hermán Velarde Rojas, Trinidad; www.facebook.com/ChurrasqueriaLaEstancia; mains B$45-75

Ask anybody in Trinidad where to get a good bit of beef and you'll be sent here. With its palm roof and coal-fire barbecue hamming up the ranch-house setting, the succulent and juicy cuts will make you wonder how other restaurants even dare to call themselves *churrasquerías* (grilled-meat restaurants).

CLEMENTINA

CENTRAL HIGHLANDS | $$ | INTERNATIONAL
Juan Caprile between Santa Cruz & Pantaleón Dalence, Cochabamba; 04- 425-2151; www.clementina.com.bo; mains B$39-98

A corrugated shipping container facade conceals this intimate, sophisticated scene. Dishes include creative salads, like quinoa with tandoori chicken, burgers and a dozen pasta dishes (gluten-free upon request). Lamps hanging in mason jars and a dimly-lit back patio give it a romantic vibe.

CAFÉ GOURMET MIRADOR

CENTRAL HIGHLANDS | $$ | CAFE
Pasaje Iturricha 297, Mirador de la Recoleta, Sucre; 04- 643-3038; meals B$25-50

Best cafe in Bolivia? Settled in a lounge chair looking out over Sucre's rooftops and surrounding mountains, you'll certainly be inspired to scour the classifieds for local real estate. No matter the time it feels quite Edenic – catching up on your reading, sipping an espresso or smoothie and snacking on a sandwich or tortilla.

EL HUERTO

CENTRAL HIGHLANDS | $$$ | INTERNATIONAL
Av Cabrera 86, Sucre; 04-645-3587; www.elhuertorestaurante.net; mains B$65-85

Set in a lovely secluded garden, El Huerto has the atmosphere of a classy lawn party, with sunshades and grass underfoot. There is great service, and stylishly presented traditional plates (especially the chorizo) that don't come much better anywhere in the country. Other specialities are the prawns, Peruvian- and Bolivian-caught fish, chateaubriand and an excellent wine selection.

Opposite page: Dish from Ali Pacha.

COURTESY ALI PACHA

CAFÉ JARDÍN

SANTA CRUZ REGION | $$ | HEALTH FOOD

Samaipata; 03-944-6362; www.lavispera.org/wp/en/cafejardin; mains B$40-60

Gaze at this organic garden at laid-back farmstay Finca La Víspera from the sun-filled café, a wood-panelled conservatory with patio seating, and see staff hurrying to pick your salad fresh from the ground. Famed for its slow food, this vegetarian cafe serves all-day breakfasts and lunches. Finish off with a tea infusion made with homegrown herbs. It's an easy 15-minute walk southwest of Samaipata's plaza.

BODEGA CASA VIEJA

SOUTH-CENTRAL BOLIVIA | $$ | BOLIVIAN

La Concepción, Tarija; 04-666-2605; www.lacasavieja.info; mains B$20-60

Home to some of the best *patero* (foot-trodden) wine in Bolivia, this atmospheric winery has a lovely restaurant with a trellis-covered courtyard and covered outdoor patio with captivating mountain views. Classic Chaco dishes like *saice* (spicy ground beef over potatoes and rice) and *chancho de la cruz* (whole hog) are served. La Concepción is in Bolivia's winemaking heartland, Valle de la Concepción, about 30km from Tarija.

WHERE TO EAT...

ULTIMATE BOLIVIAN MARKET FOOD

Mercado Central, Potosí
Great window into life in high-altitude Potosí: grab sublime empanadas here until mid-afternoon and, come evening, *humitas* (steamed corn filled with cheese, onion, egg and spices). Excellent juices too.

Mercado Central, Sucre
Don't miss the fresh juices: vendors make delicious concoctions, like *jugo de tumbo* (unripe passion-fruit juice). Cheap, tasty meals are fried up and served day and night.

El Puente Night Market, Tarija
By the river, from late afternoon apron-clad women serve local specialities like *falso conejo* (ground meat with vegetables, onions and rice), *saice* (spicy diced beef and vegetables) and *sonso*.

CHILE

Hearty and traditional sums up Chile's gastronomic landscape. Expectedly, excellent seafood features throughout; along the way, various culinary microclimates shake up the country's flavour profile. Ancestral Mapuche cuisine, German-influenced Southern Chile and the distinctive gastronomic traditions of the island of Chiloé keep things interesting – often unique – guiding your palate on its epicurean crusade exploring the world's longest and narrowest country.

WHAT TO EAT

Pastel de choclo
Layered beef, chicken and maize casserole baked in an earthenware *paila*.

Chupe de Jaiba
A crab soufflé originating in Santiago jazzed up with smoked merquén chile and parmesan cheese.

Curanto al hoyo
A hearty stew of mussels, clams, chicken, pork and three types of potatoes, traditionally simmered for hours in an underground heath covered by *nalca* (a rhubarb-like plant) or *pangue* (a native plant of Chile).

Asado
Traditional barbeque, often with Ribeye steaks and Patagonian lamb.

Cazuela marina
A heartwarming seafood and vegetable stew served along the coast.

PRICE RANGES

For a main course:
$ less than CH$7000
$$ CH$7000–12,000
$$$ CH$12,000 or more

Tipping: 10%

LA KALETA

EASTER ISLAND (RAPA NUI) | $$ | SEAFOOD

Caleta Hanga Roa, Hanga Roa; 32-255-2244; mains CH$9000-16,000

Santiago's El Mercurio newspaper crowned La Kaleta the best regional restaurant in Chile in 2016 and the seafront tables have been packed with vacationing Chileans ever since. The menu changes with the season to reflect the freshest ingredients from the sea, but typically includes ceviche, grilled fish and seafood pastas.

BALTINACHE

ANTOFAGASTA | $$$ | CHILEAN

Atienza 2, San Pedro de Atacama; 9-3191-4225; 3-course menu CH$15,000

Thick adobe walls hung with geoglyph-inspired artwork and flickering candles set the scene at this elegantly understated gem. The nightly changing menu features high-quality local products like river trout, vegetable soup with grated goat's cheese, rabbit and desserts made from desert fruits.

EL WAGÓN

TARAPACÁ | $$$ | CHILEAN

Thompson 85, Iquique; 57-234-1428; mains CH$9000-17,000

Almost single-handedly taking on the task of preserving the region's culinary traditions, this rustically decked-out dining hall serves up a fantastic collection of seafood plates, with inspiration for recipes coming from grandma's classics to port-workers' and miners' staples.

DELICIAS DEL SOL

COQUIMBO | $$ | CHILEAN

Villaseca Village, Vicuña; 9-3230-3382; mains incl wine CH$7000-8000

Don't miss lunch at this restaurant 5km southeast of Vicuña, where a group of women discovered a groundbreaking way to cook with sunrays instead of hard-to-find firewood. Locally raised *cabrito* (goat) is the speciality, paired with lovely vineyard views.

EL PERAL

VALPARAÍSO | $$ | CHILEAN
El Peral 182, Valparaíso city; 32-336-1353; mains CH$8000-10,000

The menu at this beloved cafe above Ascensor El Peral is written on chalkboards each morning and typically includes the freshest ingredients from the sea. Pair your food with invigorating fruit juices, local craft beers or pisco sours in intriguing flavors.

BORAGÓ

SANTIAGO | $$$ | CHILEAN
Av Nueva Costanera 3467; 2-2953-8893; www.borago.cl; tasting menu from CH$50,000

Chef Rodolfo Guzman earned a coveted spot among the World's 50 Best Restaurants by elevating Chilean cuisine to new heights at this Vitacura restaurant. The multicourse tasting menus, which include little-known endemic ingredients, sweep you away on an unforgettable culinary adventure from the Atacama to Patagonia.

PEUMAYEN

SANTIAGO | $$$ | CHILEAN
Constitución 134; 9-6683-5598; www.peumayenchile.cl; tasting menu CH$12,500

One of the most unusual culinary experiences in Chile, this upstart is innovating Chilean cuisine by looking back to the culinary roots of the Mapuche, Rapa Nui and Atacameños people. The tasting menu is served on a stone slab and features modern takes on traditional indigenous fare, such as llama, lamb tongue, sweet breads, horse and salmon.

'My kitchen was born from the need to reclaim the cuisine of grandmothers, families and the territory; it's not simply food, it's history and knowledge.'
Anita Epulef, Anita Epulef Cocina Mapuche

SALVADOR COCINA Y CAFÉ

SANTIAGO | $$ | CHILEAN
Bombero Ossa 1059; 2-2673-0619; www.facebook.com/SalvadorCocinaYCafe; mains CH$7700

This no-frills two-storey lunch spot packs a surprising punch with market-focused menus that change daily and highlight unsung dishes (and exotic meats) from the Chilean countryside.

MERCADO CENTRAL

SANTIAGO | $ | SEAFOOD
Cnr 21 de Mayo & San Pablo; 2-2697-3779; www.mercadocentral.cl

Santiago's wrought-iron fish market is a classic for seafood lunches (and hangover-curing fish stews like the tomato- and potato-based *caldillo de congrio*, Pablo Neruda's favourite). Skip the touristy restaurants in the middle and head for one of the tiny low-key stalls around the market's periphery.

EL HOYO

SANTIAGO | $ | CHILEAN

San Vicente 375; 2 2689 0339; www.elhoyo.cl; mains CH$2900-14,700

Since 1912, 'the Hole' has captivated Santiaguinos with its long-simmered whole *pernil* (pork leg), *arrollado* (pork-stuffed pork roll) and, for the more adventurous, its famous cow's tongue. It's all washed down in city's most traditional working men's cantina with a jar of *terremoto* (sweet, fermented white wine called *pipeño* with pine-apple ice cream).

EL CHIRINGUITO DE PULLAY

ÑUBLE | $$ | SEAFOOD

Playa Pullay, Pullay; 9-6159-6922; www.facebook.com/ElChiringuitoDePullay; mains CH$6000-8000

Fresh seasonal ingredients sourced from local farmers and fishers – that's the philosophy behind this low-key beachfront restaurant with colourful wooden furniture.

ANITA EPULEF COCINA MAPUCHE

LA ARAUCANÍA | $ | CHILEAN

Camino al Curarrehue, Curarrehue; 9-8788-7188; menú CH$10,000

Mapuche chef Anita Epulef turns seasonal ingredients into adventurous vegetarian Mapuche tasting menus. You can sample such indigenous delicacies as *mullokiñ* (bean puree rolled in quinoa), sautéed *piñones* (the nut of the araucaria tree – in season only!) and roasted corn bread with an array of salsas – all excellent and unique.

TRAWEN

LA ARAUCANÍA | $$ | FUSION

Av O'Higgins 311, Pucón; 45-244-2024; www.trawen.cl; mains CH$6200-16,800

This time-honoured favourite does some of Pucón's best gastronomic work for the price, boasting innovative flavor combinations and fresh-baked everything. Highlights include excellent smoked-trout ravioli in spinach-cream sauce, bacon-wrapped venison, *merkén* (Mapuche spice) octopus risotto and salads from the restaurant's own certified-organic gardens, the first in southern Chile.

¡ÉCOLE!

LA ARAUCANÍA | $ | VEGETARIAN

Urrutia 592, Pucón; 45-244-1675; www.ecole.cl; mains CH$4800 to CH$5400

The eco-conscious ¡école! is a meeting point for conscientious travelers and a tranquil and artsy hangout that has long been Pucón's most interesting place to stay, but its excellent vegetarian restaurant (open to non-guests) is one of Chile's best.

Opposite page: Dish from Peumayen.

TRADICIONES ZUNY

LA ARAUCANÍA | $ | CHILEAN
Tucapel 1374, Temuco; 9-9795-5280; meals CH$5000

Temuco's best-kept secret is an underground locals' haunt specialising in the fresh, simple food of the countryside served out of an indigenous-themed home. It's hard to find – look for the colourful duck/basketball mural – but the cheap, Chilean-Mapuche organic fusion cuisine is a showstopper.

LA ÚLTIMA FRONTERA

LOS RÍOS | $ | SANDWICHES
Pérez Rosales 787, Valdivia; 63-223-5363; sandwiches CH$3000-5300

This restobar hidden quietly away in a restored mansion is a long-standing Valdivian favourite. It boasts a distinctly bohemian vibe while producing loads of outside-the-box sandwiches, fresh juices and local craft beer – 15 or so on draft (Cuello Negro, Totem, Valtare, Duende).

CHILE PICANTE

PUERTO MONTT | $$ | CHILEAN
Vicente Pérez Rosales 567; 9-8454-8923; www.chilepicanterestoran.cl; menu CH$10,500

With expansive city and sea views as the backdrop, chef-owner Francisco Sánchez Luengo offers just a few choices in his always-changing, three-course menu, all bursting with the day's market flavours. There's a fascinating emphasis on out-of-the-box preparations of native ingredients: *nalca* (Chilean rhubarb), *cochayuyo* and *ulte* (sea plants), *michuña* (native Chiloé potato) etc.

LA MARCA

LOS LAGOS | $$$ | STEAK
Ruta 225, KM 1.5, Puerto Varas; 65-223-2026; www.lamarca.cl; steaks CH$7200-13,300

This is the spot in Southern Chile for devout carnivores to delight in seriously outstanding slabs of perfectly grilled beef. Order a bottle of reasonably priced Carménère and save room for some of the best churros you'll ever have.

EL HUMEDAL

LOS LAGOS | $$ | FUSION

Turismo 145, Puerto Varas; 65-223-6382; www.humedal.cl; mains CH$7600-12,300

In an adorable and cosy German-style home perched on a hilltop over town, El Humedal (oddly, it means 'Wetland') serves up some of Puerto Varas' sexiest fusion comfort food (Thai conger eel, green quinoa bowls, pumpkin gnocchi and other Asian curries and stir-fries).

LA COCINERÍA DALCAHUE

CHILOÉ | $ | SEAFOOD

Pedro Montt 105-138, Dalcahue; 65-264-1594; www.cocineriasdalcahue.blogspot.cl; mains CH$3000-8000

Tucked behind the Dalcahue's crafts market, this collection of stalls – run by grandmotherly types who dish hearty stews, soups and seafood, pound out *milcao* (potato bread) and dole out Chilote sweets – is Dalcalhue's don't-miss. Seek out Camila – Donde Lula, whose *cazuela* (hearty meat and vegetable soup) with beef and *luche* (algae) is outstanding.

CAZADOR

CHILOÉ | $$ | CHILEAN

Ernesto Riquelme 1212, Castro; 9-4408-6823; www.facebook.com/marycanelachiloe; mains CH$7000-14,000

This groundbreaking bistro specialises in heartier dishes and game, many of which arrive sizzling in cast-iron skillets. Start with a beautiful *queso de campo* (country cheese) or smoked ham seared in apple vinegar with chorizo and potatoes, then move on to heartier dishes like duck or goose with red wine, smoked pork ribs or the seafood of the day.

'There are three basic things to learn to cook well: know who you are, where you come from and what you have around you.'
Rodolfo Guzmán, Boragó

RUCALAF PUTEMÚN

CHILOÉ | $$ | FUSION

Km 3.6 de la Ruta a Rilán, Castro; 9-9579-7571; www.rucalafputemun.cl; mains CH$7900-12,500

In a colourful and cosy cabin-like room, enjoy scrumptious contemporary Chilean fare – excellent ceviche, merluza (hake) with pesto and dehydrated tomato, free-range escabèche-style chicken.

RESTAURANT TRAVESÍA

CHILOÉ | $$ | CHILEAN

Lillo 188, Castro; 65-263-0137; www.facebook.com/restaurantravesia; mains CH$6000-13,000

Two locals (a historian and a chef) are behind Castro's most authentic restaurant. Its menu features resurrected island recipes transformed into gourmet Chilote cuisine using staunchly local ingredients (algae like *luche* and *lamilla*, for example). Favourites include *chanchita tentación* (braised smoked pork), *congrio* soup (smoked pork, *luche*, razor clams) and *murta* (strawberry myrtle) sours.

EL CHEJO

CHILOÉ | $ | CHILEAN
Diego Bahamonde 251, Quemchi; 65-269-1490; meals CH$4000-9800

A family-run treasure, El Chejo offers honest food prepared with love by a family that fawns over its patrons. There's no menu – you get what's good that day. That could mean starting with the excellent *empanada de centolla* (a fried pastry filled with king crab) followed by a choice of several locally caught fish, washed down with a sampling of Chilote fruit liqueurs (try the murtado, a medicinal berry).

COCINERIA TRADICIONES MORELIA

CHILOÉ | $$ | CHILEAN
Sector Quilque, Parque Nacional Chiloé; 9 9997 6311; mains CH$6500-9500

This cosy, fireplace-heated restaurant on Lago Cucao beckons hungry adventurers with a daily-changing menu focused on local produce: think strawberry juice with *nalca* (giant Chilean rhubarb), *cazuela* (clam stew) with *macha* and smoked pork stew with *luche* (red algae).

COCINERÍAS COSTUMBRISTAS

LOS LAGOS | $ | SEAFOOD
Portales 258, Chaitén; 9-8170-8983; meals CH$3000-8000

Apron-clad community *señoras* in tiny kitchens serve up piping-hot seafood empanadas, fish platters and fresh *paila marina* (shellfish soup). Fills up fast.

MARTÍN PESCADOR

LOS LAGOS | $$$ | SEAFOOD
Balmaceda 603, Futaleufú; 65-721-279; mains CH$10,000-13,000

This locavore eatery is taking some exciting risks with a rotating menu featuring local products you will see nowhere else served in low-lit ambience with a roaring log fire. Think honey from local michay flowers, forest mushrooms, nalca fruit, rabbit and traditional Huilliche seafood.

EL RINCÓN GAUCHO

AISÉN | $$ | INTERNATIONAL
Parque Nacional Patagonia; 65-297-0833; mains CH$7000-17,000

With fine wood details and big picture windows, this is a handsome setting for meals or drinks, with an on-site greenhouse supplying most of the fresh produce and local lamb served. In addition to the gourmet set menu, there are sandwiches, takeout lunches and tea.

AFRIGONIA

PUERTO NATALES | $$ | CHILEAN
Magallanes 247; 61-241-2877; mains CH$12,000-14,000

Outstanding and wholly original – you won't find Afro-Chilean cuisine on any NYC menu. This romantic gem serves up fragrant rice, fresh ceviche, mint roasted lamb and special desserts.

WHERE TO DRINK...

PISCO SOURS

Chipe Libre, Santiago
Learn about the big sour over pisco – and who made it first – at the only bar in Santiago dedicated to the South American brandy.

Moscatel, La Serena
This stylish, upscale pisco bar serves more than 40 varieties, including rare types you won't find elsewhere.

La Taberna, Punta Arenas
The opportunity to sip pisco sours in this classy mansion shouldn't be missed.

Distileria Pisco Mistral, Pisco Elqui
Where better to try Chile's national cocktail than inside one of its most famous pisco distilleries?

PARAGUAY

Paraguay rivals Argentina over the sky-high quality, insane popularity and ubiquity of its beef, which generally reaches the table as *asado*, barbecued meat that is the acme of almost all socialising. Otherwise, corn and manioc flour-themed snacks keep consumers energised in-between meaty binges.

PAULISTA GRILL

ASUNCIÓN | $$$ | BARBECUE
Av San Martín near Spano; 21-60-8624; www.paulistagrill.com.py; weekday/weekend buffet 85,000/100,000G

One of the city's most famous all-you-can-eat restaurants, specialising as a churrasquería (roughly translating as barbecue, Paraguay's favourite food by a country mile). There are more than 15 different cuts of mouth-watering meats at this attentively run joint plus salad, pasta and sushi bars to peruse and some creative desserts. Barbecue is so advanced in Paraguay that the term often needs further elaboration. Paulista Grill does Brazilian-style barbecue.

LA CABRERA

ASUNCIÓN | $$$ | BAR
Av Sta Teresa 2495; 0984-50-5178; www.facebook.com/LaCabrera Paraguay; meats from 50,000G

This time, it's the Argentines that get in on the grill action, at this restaurant with delicious meat dishes accompanied by an astonishing array of mini-salads, sauces and garnishes. Book ahead for Sundays, especially at lunchtime. It gets busy fast!

MILORD

ENCARNACIÓN | $$$ | EUROPEAN
cnr Av Francia & 25 de Mayo; 71-20-6235; www.facebook.com/milordrestaurant; mains from 40,000G

With a chef who studied in Paris, formal waiters and a more refined atmosphere than other Encarnación restaurants, Milord, forming part of a boutique hotel of the same name, is widely regarded as the place to be seen by fine diners. The menu is varied and inventive with a French–Italian bent and, despite the slightly elevated price tag, you won't feel that you've overspent.

WHAT TO EAT

Asado
Grilled meats, invariably in the form of beef that rivals that of Paraguay's southern neighbour Argentina, are the focal point of every social event.

Chipa
Bread made with manioc flour, eggs and cheese. The best bet for Chipa is the southern town of Coronel Bogado, where chipa-sellers board buses with their breads in a bid to give you your fix.

Chipa guasú
Hot corn pudding with cheese and onion.

Vori-vori
Beef is boss in Paraguay, but corn could be number two foodstuff, as indicated by this chicken soup festooned with cornmeal balls.

PRICE RANGES

For a main course:
$ less than 15,000G
$$ 15,000–55,000G
$$$ 55,000G or more

Tipping: 10–15%

URUGUAY

Uruguayan cuisine revolves around grilled meat. *Parrillas* (restaurants with racks of meat roasting over a wood fire) are everywhere, and weekends mean *asados* (barbecues). Seafood is excellent on the coast and sweet treats come laden with *dulce de leche*.

WHAT TO EAT

Chivito
Steak sandwich piled high with toppings, typically cheese, tomatoes, olives and mayo.

Chivito Canadiense
The 'Canadian' version of the chivito sandwich crams bacon, egg and onion on top of the usual ingredients.

Pasta con salsa Caruso
Caruso sauce – made from cream, ham, cheese and mushrooms – was created in Montevideo in the 1950s. It's named after Neapolitan tenor Enrico Caruso.

Torta frita
A round, flat fried snack, usually sprinkled with sugar and accompanied by *dulce de leche* and *mate* (a bitter, tea-like beverage).

PRICE RANGES

For a main course:
$ less than UR$300
$$ UR$300–500
$$$ UR$500 or more

Tipping: 10%

NARBONA WINE LODGE

WESTERN URUGUAY | $$$ | ITALIAN

Hwy 21, Km 268, Carmelo; 4540-4778; www.narbona.com.uy; dishes US$25-34

Set amid vineyards and orchards 13km from Carmelo, this restaurant in a restored 1908 farmstead serves gourmet pasta, Uruguayan beef, organic vegetables and fabulous *tannat* and *grappamiel* (honey-infused grape brandy) from Narbona's award-winning cellars. Inside, browse shelves stacked with local olive oil, peach preserves and *dulce de leche* (milk caramel).

CHARCO BISTRÓ

WESTERN URUGUAY | $$$ | INTERNATIONAL

San Pedro 116, Colonia del Sacramento; 4523-5000; www.charcohotel.com; mains UR$420-680

Outstanding both for its location and its food, this bright and airy eatery with a contemporary aesthetic is tucked down a cobbled side street and has a spacious deck overlooking the Río de la Plata's grassy shoreline. Tantalising treats such as steak with chimichurri, grilled salmon, and homemade ravioli come complemented by superb mixed drinks and ample glasses of local wine.

ESCARAMUZA

MONTEVIDEO | $$ | CAFÉ

Pablo de María 1185; 2401-3475; www.escaramuza.com.uy; mains UR$270-450

Tucked into a beautifully restored Cordón home, Escaramuza impresses on many levels. Cross the threshold to discover one of Montevideo's most beautiful bookshops. A few paces further and you've entered the seductive high-ceilinged cafe and back-patio restaurant, where patrons linger over superbly prepared, reasonably priced Uruguayan specials with health-food overtones; *milanesas* (breaded cutlets) and buttery mashed potatoes, meet kale salad!

LA FONDA

MONTEVIDEO | $$ | HEALTH FOOD
Pérez Castellano 1422; 2917-1559; www.facebook.com/lafondauy; mains UR$375-500

Grab a table on the pedestrianised street, or enter the high-ceilinged, brick-walled interior to watch the wild-haired chefs bantering to cool jazz as they roll out homemade pasta, carefully lay asparagus spears atop risotto or grab ingredients from the boxes of organic produce adorning their open kitchen. The ever-changing chalkboard menu always includes one vegan option.

CANDY BAR

MONTEVIDEO | $ | TAPAS, BURGERS
Durazno 1402; 2904-3179; www.facebook.com/candybarpalermo; tapas UR$150, mains UR$270-300

At this cool corner eatery, colourful folding chairs fill the sidewalk beneath a spreading sycamore tree, while the chefs inside mix drinks, whip up meals and juggle fresh-baked bread behind a countertop overhung with artsy lampshades. Reasonably priced tapas and burgers (carnivorous and vegetarian) rule the menu, complemented by artisan beers and mixed drinks.

ESTRECHO

MONTEVIDEO | $$ | INTERNATIONAL
Sarandí 460; 2915-6107; mains UR$350-490

Grab a seat at the long stoveside counter and watch the chefs whip up delicious daily specials at this cosy Ciudad Vieja lunch spot. The international menu includes baguette sandwiches with steak or smoked salmon, a variety of salads, fresh fish of the day and divine desserts.

MERCADO DEL PUERTO

MONTEVIDEO | $$$ | PARRILLA
Pérez Castellano; 291-68410; www.mercadodelpuerto.com; mains UR$300-700

This converted market on Ciudad Vieja's waterfront remains a Montevideo classic. Take your pick of the densely packed *parrillas* and pull up a stool. Weekends are ideal for savouring the market's vibrant energy.

LA PULPERÍA

MONTEVIDEO | $$ | PARRILLA
cnr Lagunillas & Nuñez, Punta Carretas; 2710-8657; www.facebook.com/lapulperiamvdeo; mains UR$300-475

The epitome of an intimate neighbourhood *parrilla*, this corner place doesn't advertise its presence (drop by before 7pm and you won't even find a sign outside); instead, it focuses on grilling prime cuts of meat to perfection, and relies on word of mouth to do the rest. Grab a barstool by the blazing fire or a table on the sidewalk.

EL CHANCHO Y LA CONEJA

EASTERN URUGUAY | $$$ | URUGUAYAN

Calle 12/Nina Miranda, Punta del Este; 4277-2497; www.facebook.com/Elchanchoylaconeja; mains UR$460-600

Owners Horacio (the pig) and Karina (the rabbit) named this rustic backstreet hideaway for their Chinese zodiac animals. Well-chosen blues and jazz numbers, yellow brick walls, artsy light fixtures and distressed-wood benches set an atmospheric backdrop for delicious grilled meat and fish, homemade pasta (try the ricotta, basil, walnut and bacon pierogi, inspired by Karina's Polish grandmother) and more.

PARADOR LA HUELLA

EASTERN URUGUAY | $$$ | SEAFOOD

Playa Brava, José Ignacio; 4486-2279; www.paradorlahuella.com; mains UR$520-760

For a classic taste of José Ignacio's rarefied atmosphere, drop in at this chic beachside eatery, where you can mingle with the town's beautiful people over sushi, grilled fish and clay-oven-fired pizza, all served up with dreamy ocean views.

LA OLADA

EASTERN URUGUAY | $$$ | URUGUAYAN

Calle José Ignacio btwn Soria & Focas, José Ignacio; 4486-2745; mains UR$550-690

Hidden away on a residential back street (look for the life preserver out front), La Olada embodies José Ignacio's casual-chic vibe. People play ping-pong on the front patio, while inside, candlelight and wood-burning clay ovens cast a cosy glow on diners enjoying grilled meats and fish, fresh-baked bread, *chipirones* (squid), homemade ravioli, pizza and local wines.

LO DE DANY

EASTERN URUGUAY | $$ | URUGUAYAN

Playa Norte, Cabo Polonio; 099-875584; www.facebook.com/lodedani.cabopolonio; mains UR$180-450

This straightforward orange snack shack is run by one of Polonio's few year-round resident families. It's a welcoming, affordable spot for everything from homemade *buñuelos de algas* (seaweed fritters) to *rabas* (fried squid) and *chivitos* (steak sandwiches piled high with toppings).

RESTO–PUB 70

EASTERN URUGUAY | $ | ITALIAN

Playa de los Pescadores, Punta del Diablo; 099-103367; www.facebook.com/restopub70/; Mains UR$275-350

Run by an Italian family, this portside eatery serves divine, reasonably priced homemade pasta such as *lasagne alle cipolle* (veggie lasagna with walnuts and caramelised onions), accompanied by house wine. Afterward, don't miss the *cantucci con vino dolce* (almond biscotti dipped in sweet wine) and *limoncino* (an artisanal liqueur).

WHERE TO EAT...

CHIVITOS

Rustic Resto Bar, Punta del Este
The *chivito* originated in Punta del Este, where, legend has it, in 1946 a hungry woman requested a goat sandwich (*sándwich de carne de chivito*) and was instead served a beef steak sandwich piled high with toppings, presented as a '*chivito*'. Sink your teeth into one at this friendly lunch spot.

Los Farolitos, Colonia del Sacramento
This simple street-side stand is renowned for its *chivitos*, but also sells other low-cost, fast-food including hot dogs and *milanesas* (breaded cutlets).

La Bodeguita, Colonia del Sacramento
Nab a table out back on the sunny two-level deck and soak up the sweeping river views.

ARGENTINA

Argentines are artists at the grill. From beef produced at the famous cattle ranges of the Pampas grasslands to Patagonian lamb, meat takes centre stage in most Argentinian cooking. But vegetarians need not despair: owing to the Italian roots of much of the population, the pasta and gnocchi is invariably fresh, and the gelato sublime. Empanadas are a delicious, every-day treat.

WHAT TO EAT

Bife de chorizo
A classic sirloin steak, cooked on the *parrilla* (grill).

Choripán
Barbecued sausage served in a fluffy white baguette, usually with *chimichurri* (an oil, garlic and parsley sauce).

Empanadas
Savoury pastry turnovers stuffed with a range of fillings.

Locro
A hearty corn or mixed-grain stew with meat. Popular in the Andean northwest.

Facturas
Sweet pastries, some filled with jam or custard, including *medialunas* (croissants).

Alfajor
Round, crumbly cookie sandwich filled with *dulce de leche* (milk caramel) and often covered with chocolate or meringue.

Tipping: 10%

EN MIS FUEGOS

PATAGONIA | $$$ | PATAGONIAN

Av Gales 32, Puerto Madryn; 0280-460-3342; www.gustavorapretti.com.ar

It's rare to get a taste of Patagonia beyond roast lamb, but at En Mis Fuegos chef Gustavo Rapretti delivers a broader vision of the region with an enticing menu that emphasises local ingredients: look out for white salmon with *wakame* seaweed, trout with homemade pickles, melt-in-your-mouth pork and outstanding rabbit confit.

BUENOS CRUCES

PATAGONIA | $$ | ARGENTINE

Espora 237, El Calafate; 02902-492698; www.facebook.com/BuenosCrucesRestaurante

This dynamic family-run enterprise brings a modern twist to Argentine classics. Start with a warm beet salad with balsamic reduction, then try the nut-crusted trout, the guanaco meatloaf or the baked ravioli crisped at the edge and bubbling with Roquefort cheese.

PURA VIDA

PATAGONIA | $$ | ARGENTINE

Libertador 1876, El Calafate; 02902-493356

Featuring the rare treat of Argentine home cooking, this offbeat, low-lit eatery is a delight. Its longtime owners can be found cooking up buttery spiced chicken pot pies or filling wine glasses. Don't skip the decadent chocolate brownie with ice cream and warm berry sauce.

MAFFIA

PATAGONIA | $$ | ITALIAN

Av San Martín 107, El Chaltén; 02966 74-7011

In a gingerbread house, this pasta specialist makes delicious stuffed *panzottis* and *sorrentinos*, with creative fillings like trout, aubergine and basil or fondue. There are also homemade soups and garden salads, and flan for dessert. Service is professional and friendly.

LEGUA 50

PATAGONIA | $$$ | INTERNATIONAL
cnr Belgrano & San Martín, Esquel; 02945-452875; www.facebook.com/legua50

Considered Esquel's best restaurant, Legua 50 is certainly the city's most elegant address, with ivory leather booths, cascading lights and stained glass in the bar. Extraordinary rib-eye steak, green salads and moist trout in black butter are artfully presented. There's an excellent wine list, too.

ALTO EL FUEGO

BARILOCHE & THE LAKE DISTRICT | $$ | PARRILLA
20 de Febrero 451, Bariloche; 0294-443-7015; www.altoelfuego.com.ar

The most frequently recommended *parrilla* in town offers the killer combination of great cuts of expertly seared meat and a well-chosen wine list. Inside a wooden house built in 1941, the elevated grill takes centre stage in an informal dining room. If weather permits, take advantage of the breezy outdoor deck area.

BUTTERFLY

BARILOCHE & THE LAKE DISTRICT | $$$ | FUSION
Hua Huan 7831, Bariloche; 0294-446-1441; www.butterflypatagonia.com.ar

'I find comfort in the flame and what it means to put all of my energy into the act of cooking.'
Gustavo Rapretti, chef at En Mis Fuegos

A chandelier gently spins, casting soft shadows on the rough stone walls. A fire crackles in the fireplace and an almost reverential hush reigns as diners tuck into the seven-course tasting menu that changes frequently but may comprise the likes of red cabbage, goat's cheese and almond salad, panko-coated shrimp and a beautifully seared sirloin with mango emulsion.

IL GABBIANO

BARILOCHE & THE LAKE DISTRICT | $$ | ITALIAN
Av Bustillo, Km24, Parque Nacional Nahuel Huapi; 0294 444-8346; www.facebook.com/ilgabbiano.bariloche

At the best Italian restaurant in the region, chef Mimi Barchetta imbues each plate with plenty of amore, and it shows. Standout dishes include gnocchi with octopus ragout, *tagliatelle alla boscaiola* (with mushrooms and tomatoes), rigatoni with lamb ragout and beautifully seared meats. A convivial, easy vibe reigns and it's a great place for a romantic tête-à-tête.

MORPHEN

BARILOCHE & THE LAKE DISTRICT | $$ | FUSION
Av San Martín 151, San Martín de los Andes; 02972-422545; www.morphen.com.ar

Enter Morphen, and you enter a wonderland of Banksy graffiti, surreal sculpture, swirling murals and unusual mobiles suspended from the ceiling. The food is a pleasant deviation from the meaty standards touted by most restaurants in San Martín de los Andes. Feast on vegan 'hamburgers,' pizza-caccia with pesto, and pumpkin ravioli with shrimp in curry sauce, and wash it all down with craft beer.

OSADÍA DE CREAR

THE CENTRAL ANDES | $$$ | ARGENTINE

Cochabamba 7801, Agrelo, Luján de Cuyo; 0261-498-9231; www.susanabalbowines.com.ar

At the renowned Susana Balbo winery, Osadia's five-course 'Argentina from the mountains to the sea' wine-paired lunch is one of the area's best. Susana Balbo is the first female Argentine winemaker and the winery is known for its torrontés whites. The restaurant itself is elegantly designed with rustic features and mountain views.

CASA EL ENEMIGO

THE CENTRAL ANDES | $$$ | ARGENTINE

Aranda 7008, Maipú; 0261-341-1729; www.elenemigowines.com

The passionate and philosophically inclined husband-and-wife team who created El Enemigo wines have now mastermnided this similarly unique and inspired dining experience. It combines a stunning setting, architecturally interesting bodega, warm and professional service and expertly conceived dishes elevated above the norm; the pea soup and lamb goulash are favourites.

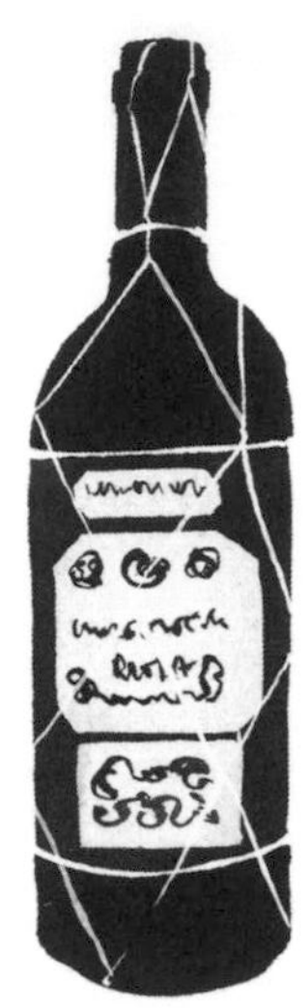

'Siete Fuegos, or "seven fires", describes Francis Mallmann's collection of open-flame cooking techniques, inspired by Argentine gauchos.'

Siete Fuegos

FUENTE Y FONDA

THE CENTRAL ANDES | $$ | ARGENTINE

Montevideo 675, Mendoza; 0261-429-8833; www.fuenteyfonda.com.ar

This restaurant's tagline – eat like you're at your grandma's house – says it all: this is Argentine comfort food at its best. Portions of dishes like lasagne, ravioli and casseroles are huge, and come with bread, salad, a side and dessert, all served in farmhouse dishware.

AZAFRÁN

THE CENTRAL ANDES | $$$ | FUSION

Av Sarmiento 765, Mendoza; 0261-429-4200; https://azafranresto.com

Classic gourmet Mendoza-style, Azafrán has a rustic-chic decor true to its roots as an ordinary deli. It serves innovative versions of classic Argentine meat dishes, enormous steaks (of course) and good fish dishes. Head to the restaurant's 500-label wine cellar with the sommelier to choose just the right bottle for your meal.

SIETE FUEGOS

THE CENTRAL ANDES | $$$ | ARGENTINE

RP 94, Km 11, Valle de Uco; 0261-461-3910; www.vinesresortandspa.com

Siete Fuegos the flagship restaurant of celebrity chef Francis Mallman. Its location at the luxurious Vines of Mendoza Resort & Spa makes it something of a destination restaurant, and there's no arguing with the juiciness of the steaks or the long-roasted lamb. Best go easy on the bread and starters, including pumpkin soup and empanadas, lest you bust a gut after the meal.

EL PAPAGAYO

THE CENTRAL SIERRAS | $$$ | ARGENTINE

Arturo M Bas 69, Córdoba; 0351-425-8689; www.elpapagayo.com.ar

For a special dining experience, book a table inside this sleek two-floor restaurant, set in a narrow but light-flooded passageway. Chef Javier Rodriguez conjures up a gastronomic feast showcasing small plates that combine typical Argentine flavours with a Mediterranean touch, all prepared in wood-fired ovens or on a charcoal grill.

SABÍA QUE VENÍAS Y PREPARÉ UN PASTEL

THE CENTRAL SIERRAS | $$ | INTERNATIONAL

Pueyrredón 681, Capilla del Monte; 0354-848-2699; www.sabiaquevenias.com.ar

The couple behind this amazing restaurant met while working as chefs in top Buenos Aires restaurants; now, at their own culinary playground, they experiment with creative recipes prepared with high-quality ingredients. The huge menu features regional specialities such as trout and goat, as well as great soups, sandwiches and baked goods.

MARTHA DE BIANCHETTI

THE NORTHEAST | $ | CAFÉ

9 de Julio 1198, Corrientes; 0379-442-3008; www.marthadebianchetti.com

This old-fashioned Italian-style bakery and cafe serves home-baked pastries and excellent coffee as well as *chipacitos* (little cheese scones). When the doors open a lovely smell wafts down the block, and inside the glass-fronted counter displays tray upon tray of tempting cookies and cakes.

ZAZPIRAK BAT

THE NORTHEAST | $$ | BASQUE

Entre Ríos 261, Rosario; 0341-440-3780; www.zazpirakbat.com

From outside, this Basque cultural centre gives few clues that there's a restaurant inside, and the menu seems a little humdrum at first glance. But what a place this is. Fish and seafood are prepared to give maximum expression to the natural flavours; it's all delicious, quantities are enormous and the salads are particularly praiseworthy.

ESCAURIZA

THE NORTHEAST | $$ | SEAFOOD

cnr Bajada Escauriza & Paseo Ribereño, Rosario; 0341-454-1777; www.escaurizaparrilla.com.ar

Backing Florida beach, this legendary place is one of Rosario's best spots for fish. The enormous indoor-outdoor dining area is redolent with the aromas of chargrilling river catch like surubí;

WHERE TO TASTE...

WINE

Carinae, Maipú
A small winery producing a lovely rosé and some good reds. Tour fees are deducted from any wine purchases you make.

Reancer, Luján de Cuyo
Virtual-reality glasses – used to show various stages of the wine production process – enhance visits to this Chilean-owned winery.

Andeluna Estate, Valle de Uco
Tastings of the wonderful wines produced here take place in a charming old-world, style tasting room.

Alta Vista, Chaceras de Coria
A medium-sized operation owned by a French family with over 350 years of winegrowing tradition and 350 hectares of vines spread over five farms.

start with some delicious seafood empanadas. Service, quality and quantity are all highly impressive.

DE LA FONTE

THE NORTHEAST | $$$ | ITALIAN
cnr Corrientes & 1 de Mayo, Puerto Iguazú; 03757-420625

This exquisite hotel restaurant, domain of a maverick creative talent, is strong on presentation, whether its homemade pasta or inventive creations with a touch of molecular gastronomy. Tropical flavours are seamlessly intertwined with prime cuts of carefully sourced meat or fish. The tasting menu showcases great culinary ability, and the menu always includes an innovative vegan option.

SOPRA TUTTO

THE NORTHWEST | $ | ITALIAN
Rivadavia 404, Catamarca; 0383-445-2114; www.facebook.com/SopraTutto2.0trattoria

Homemade pasta plates, beautifully presented and flavoursome, are produced in this warm, cosy corner trattoria that doubles as a pasta shop. Family owned and operated, it stuffs delicate cannelloni with *choclo* (creamed corn) or spinach and fresh cheese, its bolognese is rich with red wine and gravy, and the house-made empanadas are special too.

PACHA

THE NORTHWEST | $$$ | FUSION
Guemes Sur 143, Cafayate; 03868-426033; www.pachacocinadeautor.com

Contemporary street-art style murals of Andean women greet diners at Pacha, symbolising the melding of the traditional with the new. Chef Tomás Casado sources seasonal ingredients and local wines carefully and crafts a menu with inventive departures from traditional Argentine fare; the excellent pastry section is the domain of his wife Soledad. Casado also bakes his own sourdough bread with yeast he's been fermenting for years.

This page: Vegan pasta from Chirimoya. Opposite page: Dish from Butterfly.

COURTESY BUTTERFLY

CHIRIMOYA

THE NORTHWEST | $$ | VEGAN

España 211, Salta; 0387-431-2857; www.facebook.com/chirimoya.vegetariano

Colourful and upbeat, this artsy, world-class vegan restaurant is the most inventive and consistently excellent kitchen in the entire region. Here pasta is fashioned from zucchini, cannelloni are made from corn flour and stuffed with cauliflower florets, and mushrooms are transformed into high culinary art. Even the beer and wine are all natural and well curated. Portions are generous, and it's all delicious.

ÉPOCA DE QUESOS

THE PAMPAS | $$ | ARGENTINE

cnr San Martín & 14 de Julio, Tandil; 0249-444-8750; www.epocadequesos.com

The romantic restaurant at Época de Quesos has rustic style to spare, but the food is the main draw: generous *picadas* (sharing plates of local cheeses and cured meats), craft beer and wine. It's worth perusing the shop and sampling the goods, before grabbing a table in the cosy, tumble-down dining room (candlelit at night) or leafy patio.

TISIANO

ATLANTIC COAST | $$$ | ITALIAN

San Lorenzo 1332, Mar del Plata; 0223 486-3473; www.facebook.com/tisianoristorante

WHERE TO EAT...

ICE CREAM

Helados Juaja, Bariloche
The best ice cream in Bariloche. Of the 60 or so flavours, there are usually a couple of dozen in rotation at any given time.

Domo Blanco, El Chaltén
Flavours include lemon ginger and berry marscarpone made with fruit harvested from a local estancia and calafate bushes in town.

De Buen Humor, Rosario
Rosario's residents claim their ice cream to be Argentina's finest. Head to this cheery ice cream parlour to put it to the test.

Cadore, Buenos Aires
This classic *heladería* (ice-cream parlour) is famous for its *dulce de leche* (milk caramel) ice cream.

There's a reason Tisiano is known across Argentina. Up front is a cocktail bar serving daily specials at affordable prices. Step into the stone dining room if it's the sensational house-made pasta that you crave: fresh raviolis and a range of rich sauces. The pizzas are wood-fired and have thin crusts: watch the chef spinning his dough in front of the oven.

I LATINA

BUENOS AIRES | $$$ | LATIN AMERICAN
Murillo 725; 011-4857-9095; www.ilatinabuenosaires.com

Located in a lovely antique house on a residential block in the Villa Crespo neighbourhood of Buenos Aires, i Latina takes diners on a culinary journey from Mexico to Patagonia. The set menu consists of seven courses, all exquisitely prepared and presented, inspired by Latin American cuisines: think fresh fish with coconut, Oaxacan mole, and beef cheek marinated in Colombian coffee. Wine pairings are optional.

CAFÉ SAN JUAN

BUENOS AIRES | $$$ | INTERNATIONAL
Av San Juan 450; 011-4300-1112; www.facebook.com/pg/CafeSanJuanOficial

After studying in Milan, Paris and Barcelona, chef Leandro (Lele) Cristóbal took the helm at Café San Juan in the San Telmo neighbourhood of Buenos Aires. The bustling bistro is known for its bold flavours. Start with tapas, then delve into the grilled Spanish octopus and pork *bondiola* (deliciously tender after nine hours' roasting).

PROPER

BUENOS AIRES | $$$ | ARGENTINE
Aráoz 1676 | 011-4831-0027 | www.properbsas.com.ar

Industrial might be a buzzword in interior styling, but converting a former car-repair workshop into a restaurant takes the paired-back theme to a new level. Behind the garage door, chefs Augosto Mayer and Leo Lanussol prepare small plates in an open kitchen; most items are cooked in a wood-fired oven. The menu varies according to what's in season and available locally. Just a few expertly combined ingredients form each plate.

DON JULIO

BUENOS AIRES | $$$ | PARRILLA
Guatemala 4691; 011-4832-6058; www.parrilladonjulio.com

Classy service and a great wine list add an upscale bent to this traditional – and very popular – corner steakhouse. The *bife de chorizo* (sirloin steak) is the main attraction here, but the baked goat cheese *provolone, bondiola de cerdo* (pork shoulder) and gourmet salads are a treat as well.

ARAMBURU

BUENOS AIRES | $$$| MODERN ARGENTINE

Vicente López 1661; 011-4811-1414; www.aramburu已resto.com.ar

Chef Gonzalo Aramburu's seasonal 17-course dinner is astounding; each artistically created plate is just a few bites of gastronomic delight. The kitchen is open to allow diners to watch the chefs at work, using a combination of experimental chemistry-lab-like techniques and traditional cooking methods. Expect enlightening tastes, textures and smells, plus unique presentations – all will translate into a highly memorable dining experience.

EL CUARTITO

BUENOS AIRES | $ | PIZZA
Talcahuano 937; 011-4816-1758

At one of Buenos Aires' oldest pizzerias, order your slice of doughy pizza and cold glass of beer to have standing at the counter. You'll feast alongside local office workers and longtime neighbourhood residents, with a good view of the old sports posters and soccer shirts hanging on the walls. The empanadas are great, too.

KALMA RESTO

TIERRA DEL FUEGO | $$$ | INTERNATIONAL
Valdéz 293, Ushuaia; 02901-425786; www.kalmaresto.com.ar

This Ushaia restaurant presents Fuegian staples like crab and octopus in a creative new context. Black sea bass is paired with a tart tomato sauce; there's stuffed lamb seasoned with pepper and rosemary; and the summer greens and edible flowers come fresh from the garden. It's gourmet at its least pretentious. Service is stellar, with charismatic chef Jorge Monopoli making the rounds and sharing his enthusiasm for harvesting local ingredients.

'This warm and cosy former general store is a peek inside the real Ushuaia.' *Almacen Ramos Generales*

ALMACEN RAMOS GENERALES

TIERRA DEL FUEGO | $ | CAFÉ
Av Maipú 749, Ushuaia; 02901-424-7317; www.ramosgeneralesush.com.ar

With its quirky memorabilia, this warm and cosy former general store is a peek inside the real Ushuaia. Locals hold their powwows here. There's local beer on tap, a wine list and light fare such as sandwiches, soups, stews and quiche. Croissants and crusty baguettes are baked daily.

KAUPÉ

TIERRA DEL FUEGO | $$$ | INTERNATIONAL
Roca 470, Ushuaia; 02901-422704; www.kaupe.com.ar

For an out-of-body seafood experience, head to this candlelit house overlooking the bay. Chef Ernesto Vivian uses the freshest of everything and service is impeccable. The tasting menu features two starters, a main dish and dessert, with standouts such as king crab and spinach chowder or sea bass in blackened butter.

EURO

PE

WHAT TO EAT

Humar
What Icelanders call 'lobster' the rest of the world calls langoustine. Often grilled or used in soup, they're a treat.

Lamb
Thanks to summers spent munching grasses and herbs, Icelandic lamb is tender and slightly gamey. You'll commonly find it smoked, pan-fried or in fillets.

Þorskur
'Half of our country is the sea', runs an Icelandic saying, and cod is something of a delicacy. Fillets are popular, though the cheeks and tongues are a favourite.

Skyr
This delicious yoghurt-like concoction is technically a cheese. Despite its rich flavour, it's low in fat and high in protein.

PRICE RANGES
For a main course:
$ less than 2000kr
$$ 2000–5000kr
$$$ 5000kr or more

Tipping: Round up the bill or leave a small tip for good service.

ICELAND

Think Icelandic food, and the boundary-pushing likes of fermented shark or sheep's head might spring to mind. But Iceland has another, far more rewarding culinary side. Here you can find delicious, fresh-from-the-farm ingredients, seafood hauled from icy waters, innovative dairy products (hello, *skyr*!) and historic food-preserving techniques that are finding new favour with today's much-feted New Nordic chefs.

DILL

REYKJAVÍK | $$$ | ICELANDIC
Laugavegur 59; 552 1522; www.dillrestaurant.is; 7 courses 13,900kr

Exquisite New Nordic cuisine is the major drawcard at Reykjavík's elegant Michelin-starred bistro. The skilled chefs use a small number of ingredients to create highly complex dishes in a parade of courses – Arctic char with kale might be followed by murre (guillemot) with soft potatoes and onions, before skyr with celery and fried oats. The owners are friends with Copenhagen's famous Noma clan and take Icelandic cuisine to similarly heady heights. It's hugely popular; book well in advance.

GRANDI MATHÖLL

REYKJAVÍK | $ | STREET FOOD
Grandagarður 16; 787 6200; www.grandimatholl.is; mains from 1200kr

Once functional port districts, Reykjavík's Grandi and Old Harbour have transformed into cultural hotspots in recent years. Nowhere encapsulates the changes better than this old fish factory turned pioneering street-food hall. Long trestle tables sit beside stalls selling everything from lamb and cod to kimchi, Cuban sandwiches and sourdough pizza, plus sparkling wine and craft beer. Look out for the Gastro Truck: its succulent signature chicken burger has an addictive jalapeño kick.

SÆGREIFINN

REYKJAVÍK | $ | SEAFOOD
Geirsgata 8; 553 1500; www.saegreifinn.is; mains from 1500kr

Sidle into this green harbourside shack ('the Sea Baron') for the most famous lobster soup in the capital. You can also choose from a fridge full of fresh fish skewers to be grilled on the spot – trout, salmon, cod, scallops, redfish and plaice are on offer, alongside veggie options. The original sea baron sold the restaurant some years ago, but the place retains its unfussy, down-to-earth charm, with benches inside and out.

DUNHAGI

WESTFJORDS | $$ | ICELANDIC
Sveinseyri, Tálknafjörður, 662 0463; www.cafedunhagi.is; mains 1800-4000kr

Set on a wild peninsula with rolling hills and a wide fjord, Dunhagi delivers a true taste of the Westfjords. A beautifully restored historic house, with rough-hewn wood floors, comfy booths and vintage photographs, sets the scene for Icelandic lamb, trout fresh from the fjord, and seaweeds and salads picked from the neighbouring beach by affable owner Dagný herself. It's open late May to August.

TJÖRUHÚSIÐ

WESTFJORDS | $$ | SEAFOOD
Neðstakaupstaður 1, Ísafjörður; 456 4419; www.tjoruhusid.is; mains 2500-6000kr

Set in one of Ísafjörður's many 18th-century timber buildings, warm, rustic Tjöruhúsið offers some of the best seafood around. The menu changes daily, but typically includes soup, fish such as cod, halibut, wolffish and spotted catfish (fresh off the boat from the nearby harbour), and desserts such as chocolate mousse. There's outdoor seating on benches when it's sunny, which are great for breathing in the Westfjords bracing beauty. Dinner is deservedly popular, so book in advance.

'Our cuisine is very seasonal with regional ingredients. We use old methods combined with new techniques and love working with the nostalgic palate of Icelanders.'
Slippurinn

BJARGARSTEINN MATHÚS

WEST ICELAND | $$ | SEAFOOD
Sólvellir 15, Grundarfjörður; 438 6770; www.bjargarsteinn.is; mains 2800-5200kr

This superb restaurant has a lovely location on the waterfront in Grundarfjörður, a small town that's backed by waterfalls and surrounded by ice-capped peaks. Its seasoned owners have created a lively menu of Icelandic dishes, with an emphasis on fresh seafood such as cod, mussels, salmon, and hearty fish soup. Desserts are delicious, and pretty too. The seasonal menu is always changing, the decor is quaint, and views to Kirkjufell are stupendous.

VIÐ FJÖRUBORÐIÐ

SOUTHWEST ICELAND | $$$ | SEAFOOD
Eyrarbraut 3a, Stokkseyri; 483 1550; www.fjorubordid.is; mains 2960-8150kr

This large seafood restaurant is a place of pilgrimage for lovers of langoustines. It sits just back from the sea in Stokkseyri, a quirky village that's home to an elf museum. The lobster bisque (langoustine tails sautéd in garlic and butter) is among the best in Iceland. Slurp your soup alongside

Opening spread, clockwise from top left: Le Cochon Aveugle (x2), Riverstation, Portuguese pastries, Le Cochon Aveugle. This page: Siglunes Guesthouse Restaurant. Opposite page: Slippurinn.

COURTESY BACON ON THE BEECH, LE COCHON AVEUGLE, RIVERSTATION, MATT MUNRO/ LONELYPLANET ©

chatting locals, glass fishing buoys and marine memorabilia. There are good homemade cakes and desserts too. Reserve for dinner.

SLIPPURINN

HEIMAEY | $$ | ICELANDIC

Strandvegur 76; 481 1515; www.slippurinn.com; lunch 2800-3500kr, dinner mains 3000-5000kr, set menu 4000-6500kr

Off Iceland's south coast stand the Vestmannaeyjar, 15 jagged islands created by underwater volcanoes. Only one of them, Heimaey, is inhabited, and it's home to one of the most creative restaurants in the country. Lively Slippurinn, open May to September, fills the upper storey of a beautifully remodelled old machine workshop that once serviced the ships in the harbour and now has great views. Delicious Icelandic dishes such as seaweed salad, lamb with rhubarb and cured halibut combine local ingredients in exquisite fashion.

SIGLUNES GUESTHOUSE RESTAURANT

NORTH ICELAND | $$ | MOROCCAN

Lækjargata 10, Siglufjörður; 467 1222; www.hotelsiglunes.is; mains 3000-4000kr, 3-course menu 6700kr

Tröllaskagi (Troll Peninsula), a place of craggy mountains, deep valleys and gushing rivers, couldn't feel more classically Icelandic. But come to the remote fishing village of Siglufjörður, and you're in for a surprise. In the wood-lined restaurant at Siglunes Guesthouse, Moroccan chef Jaouad Hbib prepares delicious, from-scratch Moroccan cuisine. Tajines sizzle with heat, and starters are a well-conceived blend of delicate salads and exquisite homemade cheeses. Top it off with crème brûlée for dessert.

VOGAFJÓS

NORTH ICELAND | $$ | ICELANDIC

Rte 848, Reykjahlíð; 464 3800; www.vogafjos.net; dishes 2000-5900kr

Lake Mývatn is the stark, otherworldly jewel in North Iceland's crown, and east of its shores a working farm is home to one of the region's finest restaurants. Its menu is an ode to local produce: smoked lamb, home-made mozzarella, dill-cured Arctic char, geysir-baked bread, home-baked cakes and homemade ice cream. It's

COURTESY SIGLUNES GUESTHOUSE RESTAURANT

COURTESY SLIPPURINN

all delicious. While you eat, you can enjoy views of the lush surrounds or the dairy shed itself.

KAFFI KÚ

AKUREYRI | $ | CAFE

Rte 829; 867 3826; www.kaffiku.is; dishes 1000-2500kr

Set 11km southeast of Iceland's second city, Akureyri, this is a perfect pastoral pit stop. The cafe sits above a high-tech cowshed – you can watch through the internal windows as the cows queue to be milked by a 'robot', or book a tour. The homemade food majors on the farm's own produce, with excellent beef goulash and roast-beef bagels, plus waffles that pair perfectly with farm-fresh cream.

NORÐ AUSTUR SUSHI & BAR

EAST ICELAND | $$ | SUSHI

Norðurgata 2, Seyðisfjörður; 787 4000; www.nordaustur.is; small dishes 790-2590kr, set menu 4900-6300kr

Locals rave about this place, and with good reason: the salmon, trout and char come straight off the fishers' boats and into the hands of accomplished sushi chefs with international pedigree. The set tasting menus offer excellent value; the decor is cool, as are the cocktails and sake. Bookings recommended. It's located in Seyðisfjörður, an arty, picturesque town in the Eastfjords, famous for its blue church and ferry link to the Faroes.

WHERE TO DRINK...

CRAFT BEER

Beljandi Brugghús, Breiðdalsvík
This genial microbrewery in tiny Breiðdalsvík offers pales, porters and IPAs. There's occasional live music and sports event.

Bryggjan Brugghús, Reykjavik
Roomy microbrewery in the Old Harbour with 12 taps, beer tours, happy hours and vintage pub paraphernalia.

Kaldi, Reykjavik
Effortlessly cool with mismatched seats and banquettes, Kaldi offers its own awesome microbrews – not available elsewhere.

Ölstofa Akureyrar, Akureyri
A great spot for draught and local offerings, this convivial bar offers a lounge where you can sample Einstök beers fresh from the brewery.

SCOTLAND

Traditionally, Scotland has been all about comfort food: solid, nourishing fare, often high in fat, that will keep you warm on a winter's day spent in the fields or at sea. But this nation of hills, glens, rolling farmland and urban enterprise has been a frontrunner in Britain's culinary revolution, and an inspiring array of local and sustainable produce is also on offer.

WHAT TO EAT

Haggis
Scotland's national dish – the finely chopped lungs, heart and liver of a sheep, mixed with oatmeal and onion and stuffed into a sheep's stomach – tastes surprisingly good.

Smoked fish
Salmon is the best known, but Arbroath smokies (haddock) and kippers (herring) are an excellent way to start the day.

Scottish breakfast
Bacon, sausage, black pudding, tomato, mushrooms, potato scones, eggs and plenty of tea.

Cullen skink
A thick and delicious soup of smoked haddock, potato, onion and milk.

Beef steaks
From local cattle breeds – including Aberdeen Angus – Scottish beed is justifiably renowned.

PRICE RANGES
For a main course:
$ less than £10
$$ £10–20
$$$ £20 or more

Tipping: 10–15%

BABA

EDINBURGH | $$ | MEZZE
130 George St; 0131-527 4999; www.baba.restaurant; mains £8-15

Located on Edinburgh's premier George Street and connected to the chic Principal hotel, Baba specialises in hip and sophisticated Levantine cuisine. The menu is short but exquisite, featuring stunning mezze (Beiruti burrata, anyone?), and flavour-packed plates delivered straight off the charcoal grill, from date- and barbecue-glazed chicken leg to charred broccoli, lentils and hazelnuts with pomegranate. Baba ghanoush doesn't get more smoky, addictive or beautifully presented than this.

KITCHIN

EDINBURGH | $$$ | SCOTTISH
78 Commercial Quay; 0131-555 1755; www.thekitchin.com; 3-course lunch/5-course dinner £36/90

Fresh, seasonal, locally sourced Scottish produce is the philosophy that has won a Michelin star for this elegant but unpretentious Leith restaurant. The menu moves with the seasons, so expect fresh salads in summer and game in winter, and shellfish dishes such as baked scallops with white wine, vermouth and herb sauce when there's an 'r' in the month.

OX & FINCH

GLASGOW | $$ | FUSION
920 Sauchiehall St; 0141-339 8627; www.oxandfinch.com; small plates £4-15

This fashionable place could almost sum up Glasgow's thriving modern eating scene, with a faux-pub name, sleek but comfortable decor, tapas-sized dishes and an open kitchen. Grab a cosy booth and be prepared to have your taste buds wowed by innovative, delicious creations such as chicory with apple and comté, or miso-cured monkfish with plum and ginger. They're best shared, and draw on French and Mediterreanean influences while focusing on quality Scottish produce.

UBIQUITOUS CHIP

GLASGOW | $$$ | SCOTTISH
12 Ashton Lane; 0141-334 5007; www.ubiquitouschip.co.uk; 2-/3-course lunch £20/24, mains £20-30, brasserie mains £13-30

A pioneering champion of Scottish produce, Glasgow's Ubiquitous Chip is legendary for its fine cuisine and lengthy wine list. Named to poke fun at Scotland's culinary reputation, it offers a French touch but resolutely Scottish ingredients, carefully selected and following sustainable principles. The elegant courtyard space offers some of Glasgow's best dining, while the cheaper brasserie above is exceptional value for money. Two bars, including the cute 'Wee Pub' down the side alley, offer plenty of drinking pleasure.

NINTH WAVE

MULL | $$$ | SCOTTISH
Bruach Mhor, Fionnphort; 01681-700757; www.ninthwaverestaurant.co.uk; 3-/4-/5-course dinner £48/56/68

This excellent restaurant in a stylishly converted bothy on the Isle of Mull is owned and operated by a lobster fisherman and his Canadian wife. The daily menu makes use of locally landed shellfish and crustaceans, vegetables and salad grown in the garden, and quality local meats with a nose-to-tail ethos. There's also a superb cheeseboard and handmade chocolates infused with locally foraged flavours. It's open between May and September, and advance bookings are essential; no under-12s.

'Since opening in 1971, provenance has been at the core of our philosophy, and we've become synonymous with sourcing local produce.'
Ubiquitous Chip

CÔTE DU NORD

NORTHERN HIGHLANDS | $$ | MODERN SCOTTISH
The School House, Kirtomy, near Bettyhill; 01641-521773; www.cotedunord.co.uk; degustation £31-50

Innovative cuisine, whimsical presentation and an emphasis on local ingredients distinguish the excellent gastronomic degustation menu here. Tucked down a country lane near Scotland's northern tip, this is not your normal gourmet restaurant – the chef is none other than the local GP. His forages for wild herbs and flavours in between surgery hours result in dishes such as sea bass with onion, lamb's belly with haggis ice cream and a modern twist on the cornetto. It's tiny and offers excellent value, so reserve well ahead.

CAPTAIN'S GALLEY

NORTHERN HIGHLANDS | $$$ | SEAFOOD
Scrabster, near Thurso; 01847-894999; www.captainsgalley.co.uk; 5/6-course dinner £57/£65, 3-course lunch or early dinner in the Seafood Bar £35

The classy but friendly Captain's Galley offers local and sustainably sourced produce prepared in delicious ways that let the natural flavours shine. And given the location – by the ferry to Orkney, a few miles from Thurso, the UK's northernmost town – the focus is unsurprisingly on seafood. The chef picks the best fish off the local boats, and the menu describes exactly which fishing grounds your morsel – which might be Scandinavian seafood tapas or razor clams with a creamy vegetable vermouth – came from. The Seafood Bar offers the same ingredients in a less formal setting.

LOCH LEVEN'S LARDER

CENTRAL SCOTLAND | $ | SCOTTISH

Channel Farm, off the A911 near Kinross; 01592-841000; www.lochlevenslarder.com; mains £8-12

Three miles east of Kinross, this family-run farm shop and (daytime-only) restaurant overlooking Loch Leven is the ideal place to enjoy fresh local food, much of it from the family's own farm. You can settle down to a breakfast of smoked salmon and scrambled eggs, a platter of Scottish cheeses, or a lunch of Cullen skink or afternoon tea for two. There's a terrace with a panorama over the loch, a children's playground, and a footpath that connects to the Loch Leven Heritage Trail, making it an ideal break on a walking or cycling circuit of the loch.

THE NEWPORT

NORTHEAST SCOTLAND | $$$ | SCOTTISH

1 High St, Newport-on-Tay; 01382-541449; www.thenewportrestaurant.co.uk; mains £20-30, 7-course tasting menu £55

Set just across the water from Dundee, the Newport is a gorgeous place, with vast windows overlooking the Firth of Tay. The quirky recycled decor includes the clever use of an old piano to store cutlery and wine glasses. You can graze on small plates showcasing the best of local produce, opt for a main, or try the tasting menu. Dishes might include Jerusalem artichoke crisps, Black Isle lamb or heritage carrots with whey, curd and yeast.

COURTESY CÔTE DU NORD

This page: Dish from Côte du Nord. Opposite page: Dishes from Ox & Finch.

COURTESY OX & FINCH

88 DEGREES

NORTHEAST SCOTLAND | $ | CAFE
17 High St, Kirriemuir; 01575-570888; www.facebook.com/88kirriemuir; mains £4-8

This tiny deli serves some of the best cafe food in Scotland – superb coffee (the cafe is named for the ideal temperature of an espresso), delicious cakes, french macarons and tray bakes, plus soups, quiche and salad. It's in Kirriemuir, an Angus village that was the birthplace of JM Barrie.

COBBLES

SOUTHERN SCOTLAND | $$ | BISTRO
7 Bowmont St, Kelso; 01573-223548; www.thecobbleskelso.co.uk; mains £10-30

This inn off the main square in the prosperous Borders town of Kelso is a cracking place, and so popular you will need to book a table at weekends. It's cheery, very welcoming and warm, and serves excellent upmarket pub food in generous portions, with dishes such as 'chip shop' fish and chips, Aberdeen Angus steaks and pea and mint ravioli. There's home-made ice cream and craft ales from Cobbles' own brewery.

WHERE TO DRINK...

WHISKY

Ballygrant Inn, Ballygrant
The knowledgeable owners at this attractive Islay bar can guide you through the 700-plus malts. There are also quality ales and good food.

Bow Bar, Edinburgh
This lovely Old Town pub has a vast selection of whiskies, plus excellent real ales and Scottish craft gin.

Òran Mór, Glasgow
Set in a former church in the West End, this likeable spot offers 300 single malts in its bar, plus a restaurant and theatre.

Quaich Bar, near Aberlour
This cosy nook offers around 900 different single malts. It's in the Craigellachie Hotel, a charmingly old-fashioned Speyside lodge.

NORTHERN IRELAND

Northern Ireland's food scene has flourished in recent years, with new restaurants opening to rave reviews and the region's fine local produce – from seafood and dairy to bread and lamb – shining through in street eats, pubs and inventive fine dining.

WHAT TO EAT

Seafood
Oysters, mussels, monkfish, lobster, hake, crab and squid are among the fishy highlights.

Champ
Mashed potatoes are mixed with green onions, butter and milk to produce a rich and filling staple.

Ulster fry
Fried bacon, sausages, black pudding, white pudding, eggs, tomatoes and fadge (potato bread) should give you fuel enough for the day ahead.

Beef and lamb
Whether served up in a classic Irish stew or served as steak or cutlets, Northern Ireland's livestock can be truly first class.

Barm brack
This sweet and fruity bread is as popular in the north as it is in the Republic.

PRICE RANGES
For a main course:
$ less than £10
$$ £10–20
$$$ more than £20

Tipping: 10–15%

SAPHYRE

BELFAST | $$$ | MODERN IRISH
135 Lisburn Rd; 028-9068 8606; www.saphyrerestaurant.com; mains lunch £12-20, dinner £20-32, 5-course tasting menu £50

Spectacularly set inside the 1924 Ulsterville Presbyterian Church (behind an interior-design showroom), Saphyre serves some of the most sophisticated cooking in Belfast. Menus change seasonally, and masterpiece mains might include stone bass with leek, mustard and mussels, or beef with oxtail, leek, cauliflower.

MUDDLERS CLUB

BELFAST | $$$ | MODERN IRISH
Warehouse Lane; 028-9031 3199; www.themuddlersclubbelfast.com; 6-course tasting menu £55

Industrial-style decor, friendly service and rustic dishes that allow fresh local ingredients to shine are a winning combination at one of Belfast's best restaurants. Dishes might include halibut with courgette and romesco sauce and cauliflower with miso and onion. The venue is named after a society of Irish revolutionaries co-founded by Wolfe Tone who held meetings at the same spot in the 1790s.

PYKE 'N' POMMES POD

DERRY| $ | STREET FOOD
Behind Foyle Marina, off Baronet St; 028-7167 2691; www.pykenpommes.ie; mains £4-16

Stop by this quayside shipping container to sample Kevin Pyke's delectable street food: his signature Notorious PIG (pulled pork, crispy slaw, beetroot and crème fraiche), the Vegenderry burger (chickpeas, lemon and coriander), the Legenderry Burger (wagyu beef, pickled onions and honey-mustard mayo), and tacos. In addition to the quayside POD, Pyke 'n' Pommes now has a licensed restaurant, @57.

HARRY'S SHACK

COUNTY LONDONDERRY | $$$ | BISTRO

Portstewart Strand, Portstewart; 028-7083 1783; www.facebook.com/HarrysShack; mains £12-19

Bang on Portstewart Strand beach, this wooden shack is one of the north coast's best restaurants. Harry's uses fruit, vegetables and herbs from its organic farm plus local meat and seafood in simple but sensational dishes like megrim sole with cockles and seaweed butter, and Mulroy Bay mussels in Irish cider. The drinks list includes craft beers from seven local breweries including Lacada Brewery in Portrush and Northbound from Derry.

URSA MINOR

COUNTY ANTRIM | $ | BAKERY

45 Ann St, Ballycastle; www.ursaminorbakehouse.com; dishes £2.50-7, loaves £3.30-4.20

Artisan bakers Dara and Ciara Ó Hartghaile use only three ingredients in their excellent sourdough loaves: flour, water and salt. You can see the bread being made in the downstairs bakehouse. Upstairs, a bright cafe serves veggie breakfasts and lunches such as beetroot fritters with labneh and smoky coconut bacon salad, as well as pastries and excellent coffee.

'Muddlers Club is named after a society of Irish revolutionaries co-founded by Wolfe Tone who held meetings at the same spot in the 1790s.'
Muddlers Club

HARA

COUNTY DOWN | $$ | MODERN IRISH

16 Lisburn St, Hillsborough; 028-7116 1467; www.harahillsborough.co.uk; mains £15-20

Located in elegant Hillsborough, south of Belfast, Hara gets even the little details right: the wheaten bread is served warm from the oven and the side orders are divine. The menu changes regularly, but usually features unusual and creative dishes - try loin of velvet pork with sweetcorn and smoked black pudding or grilled pear with sheep's cheese and oats - alongside classic Irish cooking, all of it highlighting local ingredients. Service is chatty and the dining room is bright and modern. Book ahead.

BALLOO HOUSE

COUNTY DOWN | $$ | MODERN IRISH

1 Comber Rd, Killinchy; 028-9754 1210; www.ballooinns.com; mains £14-28, Sun lunch 2-/3-course £22/26

Just west of Strangford Lough, Balloo House has long been one of County Down's best restaurants. Casual, modern Irish fare – try burgers with beer-battered pickles or monkfish wellington – is available in the nook-and-cranny-filled, stone-floored downstairs pub, which centres on a warming range stove. Upstairs, partner restaurant Overwood offers fine dining Thursday to Saturday. There's bluegrass in the bar on Wednesdays.

IRELAND

Ireland's rich waters, green fields and regular rainfall provide a fine natural larder. There's a real focus on local food here, a revival that began in the 1970s and has gone from strength to strength. Now, farmers markets showcase the best of regional produce, and restaurants all over the country highlight locally sourced ingredients.

WHAT TO EAT

Potatoes
The mashed-potato dishes of colcannon and champ (with cabbage and spring onion, respectively) are two of the tastiest recipes in the country.

Meat and seafood
Beef, lamb and pork are common options. Seafood is often excellent, especially in the west, as are oysters, trout and salmon, particularly if they're direct from the sea or river.

Soda bread
This tasty Irish classic is made with buttermilk and bicarbonate of soda (to make up for soft Irish flour that traditionally didn't take well to yeast).

Black pudding
Made from cooked pork blood, suet and other fillings, this thick, rich blood sausage is a ubiquitous part of an Irish cooked breakfast.

PRICE RANGES
For a main course:
$ less than €12
$$ €12-25
$$$ €25 or more

Tipping: 10–15%

ASSASSINATION CUSTARD

DUBLIN | $ | CAFE
19 Kevin St; 087-997 1513; www.facebook.com/assassinationcustard; mains €6.50-12

This compact cafe may not look like much, but it's one of the tastiest treats in Dublin. The small menu is influenced by Italy and the Middle East and changes daily – think pumpkin with tahini and fermented black beans, or sardines with aioli and pickled radish. The name comes from the custard – made by James Joyce's wife Nora – served to Samuel Beckett after his 1938 stabbing by a Paris pimp. It's open Tuesday to Friday lunchtimes, and is cash only.

CHAPTER ONE

DUBLIN | $$$ | IRISH
18-19 N Parnell Sq; 01-873 2266; www.chapteronerestaurant.com; 2-course lunch €36.50, 4-course dinner €80

Flawless haute cuisine and a relaxed, welcoming atmosphere make this Michelin-starred restaurant in the basement of the Dublin Writers Museum the best dinner experience in town. The regularly changing menu is French-inspired contemporary Irish, with dishes like guinea hen terrine with pickled green strawberries, and turbot with fennel, baby squid and purple potato.

CLANBRASSIL HOUSE

DUBLIN | $$ | IRISH
6 Upper Clanbrassil St; 01-453 9786; www.clanbrassilhouse.com; mains €19-29

With an emphasis on family-style sharing plates, this intimate restaurant consistently turns out exquisite dishes, cooked on a charcoal grill. Think miso-glazed monkfish with chorizo and chickpeas, or cauliflower, vadouvan butter, white beans and hazelnuts. The hash-brown chips are a thing of glory, too, and there are some great brunch options to settle into.

FUMBALLY

DUBLIN | $ | CAFE
Fumbally Lane; 01-529 8732; www.thefumbally.ie; mains €7-12

This bright, airy warehouse cafe that serves delicious, healthy breakfasts, salads and sandwiches – while the occasional guitarist strums away in the corner. Specials might include Brooklyn Lager tempura cod in a corn tortilla or a seaweed spaghetti, carrot, plum and ginger salad with kale crisps. Its Wednesday dinner (tapas from €6) is an organic, locally sourced exploration of the cuisines of the world that is insanely popular with locals; advance bookings suggested.

REEL DINGLE FISH CO

COUNTY KERRY | $ | FISH & CHIPS
Bridge St, Dingle; 066-915 1713; www.reeldinglefish.com; mains €5-15

'Our philosophy is to create a menu that is not only exciting and innovative, but also sources the finest sustainable seafood.'
Henry Hunt, Smugglers Inn

COURTESY FUMBALLY

Locals queue along the street to get hold of the freshly cooked local haddock (or cod, monkfish, hake, mackerel, calamari, ray...) and chips at this tiny outlet. You can also choose from burgers made from local herds and sausages, and it's all fresh and very substantial. It's right by Dingle's popular harbour, and is one of the best chippies in the county and the country.

SMUGGLER'S INN

COUNTY KERRY | $$ | IRISH
Cliff Rd, Waterville; 087-392 9011; www.smugglersinn.ie; 3-course lunch & early dinner €29.50, mains €20-27

At this diamond find near the famous Waterville Golf Links, owner and chef Henry Hunt's gourmet creations incorporate fresh seafood and locally farmed poultry and meat, followed by artistic desserts (including homemade ice cream), served in a conservatory dining room with sea views. Half-board deals are available at the inn's 13 upstairs rooms, and cooked-to-order breakfasts (for guests and walk-ins) include a catch of the day.

PANTRY & CORKSCREW

COUNTY MAYO | $$ | IRISH

The Octagon, Westport; 098-26977; www.thepantryandcorkscrew.com; mains €17-24, early-evening menu €22/25

The heart of Mayo's slow-food movement is found at this narrow storefront with a turquoise exterior and interior walls crammed with pictures. The kitchen works culinary magic with seasonal, local and organic produce to rustle up stout-braised beef, maple-glazed pork, plus arancini with jalapeño and Aran Islands feta. The early-evening menu is superb value; book ahead.

LOAM

GALWAY | $$$ | MODERN IRISH

Fairgreen Rd; www.loamgalway.com; 091-569 727; 2/3/7/9 courses €45/55/119/159

Enda McEvoy is one of the most groundbreaking chefs in Ireland today (with a Michelin star to prove it), producing inspired flavour combinations from home-grown, locally sourced or foraged ingredients: dried hay, fresh moss, bone marrow, squid, edible flowers, wild oats, forest gooseberries, duck and hand-cut peat (which McEvoy uses in his extraordinary peat-smoked ice cream).

MORAN'S OYSTER COTTAGE

COUNTY GALWAY | $$ | SEAFOOD

The Weir, Kilcolgan; 091-796 113; www.moransoystercottage.com; mains €14-29, half-dozen oysters €12.50-16

Some of County Galway's finest seafood, including lobster in season, plus non-fish dishes such as wild mushroom risotto and honey-roast duck, is served in this atmospheric thatched pub and restaurant, set in a quiet cove. A terrace overlooks Dunbulcaun Bay, where the oysters are reared before they arrive on your plate.

RESTAURANT 1826 ADARE

COUNTY LIMERICK | $$ | MODERN IRISH

Main St, Adare; 061-396 004; www.1826adare.ie; mains €20-28, 3-course early-bird menu (€36

One of Ireland's most highly regarded chefs, Wade Murphy continues to wow diners at this art-lined 1826-built thatched cottage in famously picturesque Adare. His passion for local seasonal produce is an essential ingredient

Previous spread: Dessert from Lemon Tree; Fumbally.

in dishes such as pan-seared halibut with Connemara clams and pickled samphire or pasture-reared chicken with Ballyhoura Mushrooms and chive gnocchi.

DOOKS FINE FOODS

COUNTY TIPPERARY | $ | IRISH
Kerry St, Fethard; 052-613 0828; www.dooksfinefoods.ie; mains €5-14

A slice of culinary sophistication poised at the west end of sleepy little Fethard, a medieval village near Clonmel, bright and relaxing Dooks is a cornucopia of all that is good to eat. You can choose from breakfast sausages flavoured with rosemary, fennel and orange, lunchtime focaccia topped with garlic- and buttermilk-marinated chicken or salads scattered with nasturtium petals - or just drop in for sublime coffee and blissful cake.

GALLAGHER'S OF BUNRATTY

COUNTY CLARE | $$$ | SEAFOOD
Old Bunratty Rd, Bunratty; 061-363 363; www.gallaghersofbunratty.com; mains €15-30

Stone walls, exposed beams, timber panelling and a wood stove make this thatched cottage as enchanting inside as it is out. But the real reason to book is for some of Ireland's most magnificent seafood, such as fish and sorrel pie, lemon- and dill-crusted hake, or garlicky hot buttered crab claws. The set meals are excellent value. Lunch is only offered on Sundays, but the linked JP

'If you limit the palate of your ingredients, you force yourself to be more creative, you force yourself to find different flavours and different textures.'
Enda McEvoy, Head Chef, Loam

Clarke's Country Pub next door serves lunch and dinner daily, and has an extensive gin, whiskey and beer selection.

WOODEN SPOON

COUNTY TIPPERARY | $ | CAFE
Main St, Ballina; 061-622 415; www.facebook.com/WoodenSpoonKillaloe/; dishes €4-10

Formerly at home in Killaloe, this popular cafe has moved across the Shannon to a larger space with a sustainable lifestyle area. Savoury dishes include beef stews and towering jacket potatoes stuffed with Mediterranean vegetables and goat's cheese. Sweet treats take in brownies, scones and inspired carrot and coffee cakes. Gluten-free and vegan options are plentiful; it also brews excellent Cork-roasted Badger & Dodo coffee.

OARSMAN

COUNTY LEITRIM | $$ | GASTROPUB
Bridge St, Carrick-on-Shannon; 071-962 1733; www.theoarsman.com; mains lunch €10-15, dinner €15-27

Established in 1781, this upmarket, family run-pub is decorated with fishing paraphernalia and pottery and offers excellent seasonal and locally sourced dishes. Lunch features burgers, soup and gourmet sandwiches (chicken and pesto on garlic and rosemary bread or maple- and soy-marinated pork on brioche), while evening mains are more complex, like slow-cooked beef with beef-tail ragout, artichoke and

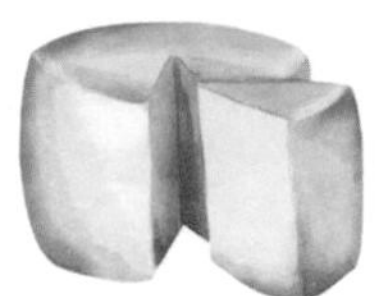

celeriac. Irish craft brews include local Carrig Brewing beers.

SPINNERS ON CASTLE ST

COUNTY OFFALY | $$ | IRISH
Castle St, Birr; 057-912 3779; www.spinnersbirr.com; bar mains €12-18, restaurant mains €14-27

By the castle wall in historic Birr, Spinners is part of a complex spanning five restored Georgian houses. The whitewashed bar is the perfect place for a cheeseboard or burger with black pudding and homemade relish, while the elegant restaurant's seasonal menu might feature Burren Smokehouse smoked salmon blinis followed by baked brill with creamed leeks. Service is excellent. Tables are set up in the tree-shaded enclosed courtyard in fine weather and there's occasional live music in the bar. It's closed on Mondays and Tuesdays.

NASH 19

CORK | $$ | INTERNATIONAL
Princes St; www.nash19.com; 021-427 0880; mains €12-21

A superb bistro and deli where locally sourced food is honoured at breakfast and lunch, either sit-in or take away. Fresh scones and full Irish breakfasts draw crowds early, while options like oysters, Italian meatballs and lamb's liver keep them coming for lunch – the Producers Plate (€21), a sampler of local produce, is sensational.

BASTION

COUNTY CORK | $$$ | MODERN IRISH
cnr Main & Market Sts, Kinsale; 021-470 9696; www.bastionkinsale.com; 8-course tasting menu €77.50, vegetarian tasting menu €67.50

Holder of a Michelin Bib Gourmand since 2016, this intimate bistro in foodie Kinsale offers diners a relaxed and informal entry into the world of

COURTESY LEMON TREE

This page: Dish from Lemon Tree.

haute cuisine. The tasting menu offers courses such as beef fillet with pickled mushroom and candied hazelnut or cauliflower with madras curry oil.

MANNING'S EMPORIUM

COUNTY CORK | $ | CAFE

N71, Ballylickey; 027-50456; www.manningsemporium.ie; mains €8-15.50

This gourmet deli and cafe is an Aladdin's cave of West Cork's finest food. Order at the counter – tasting plates are the best way to sample the local artisan produce and farmhouse cheeses, and there are toasted sandwiches, pizzas and a good wine selection too.

LEMON TREE

COUNTY DONEGAL | $$ | MODERN IRISH

32-34 The Courtyard Shopping Centre, Lower Main St, Letterkenny; 074-912 5788; www.thelemontreerestaurant.com; mains €18-24

This family-run restaurant in the market town of Letterkenny is one of the best places in the county to sample contemporary Donegal cooking. The innovative menu offers splendid fresh seafood, poultry and meat dishes sourced locally and prepared with French flair such as black pudding terrine, hake, with celeriac and mushroom arancini with parmesan and toasted onions.

'Our goal is to showcase Donegal for not only its breathtaking scenery but also its beautiful produce.' *The Lemon Tree*

CAMPAGNE

COUNTY KILKENNY | $$$ | MODERN IRISH

5 The Arches, Gashouse Lane, Kilkenny City; 056-777 2858; www.campagne.ie; 3-course lunch & early bird menu €38, 3-course dinner menu €60

Chef Garrett Byrne was awarded a Michelin star for this bold, stylish restaurant in his native Kilkenny. He's passionate about supporting local and artisan producers, and adds a French accent to memorable culinary creations such as roast partridge with pumpkin gnocchi or pear poached in butterscotch with a pecan and olive oil sponge. The early bird menu (to 9pm Wednesday to Friday, to 6pm Saturday) is a serious bargain.

TANNERY

COUNTY WATERFORD | $$$ | MODERN IRISH

10 Quay St, Dungarvan; 058-45420; www.tannery.ie; 2-/3-course menu lunch €26/33, dinner €45.50/58.50

At this old tannery building in pretty Dungarvan, lauded chef Paul Flynn creates seasonally changing dishes that focus on just a few flavours, such as charred trout with lemon-and-fennel arancini or crab crème brûlée. There's intimate seating downstairs and in the buzzing, loft-like room upstairs, and the service is excellent.

WALES

Historically, Welsh cuisine was hearty and wholesome, based on what could be grown locally and cheaply. In recent years, a quiet revolution has taken place: boosted by the abundance of fresh produce and a generation of young chefs with an innovative take on traditional Welsh recipes, the food scene is buzzing.

WHAT TO EAT

Cawl
This soupy stew of bacon, lamb, cabbage, swede and potato is one of those cosy dishes you long for when you're walking in the hills.

Meat and seafood
Welsh lamb (particularly from the Gower salt marshes) and black beef are rightly revered. On the coast, look for *sewin* (wild sea trout), Penclawdd cockles and Conwy mussels.

Cheese
Famous varieties include hard, crumbly Caerphilly, brie-like Perl Wen and the creamy blue Perl Las. Welsh rarebit is a classic take on cheese on toast.

Bread and cakes
Welsh cakes are laced with sugar and raisins and griddled, while *bara brith* is a heavy fruit loaf served with tea.

PRICE RANGES
For a main course:
$ less than £10
$$ £10 to £20
$$$ £20 or more

Tipping: 10–15%

PURPLE POPPADOM

CARDIFF | $$ | INDIAN
185a Cowbridge Rd East; 029-2022 0026; www.purplepoppadom.com; mains £11-20

Trailblazing a path for 'nouvelle Indian' cuisine, chef and author Anand George adds his own twist to dishes from Kashmir to Kerala. The setting is friendly and attentive and the emphasis is on the perfection of tried-and-tested regional delights, with offerings ranging from tiffin sea bass and North Indian murgh lababdar (tandoori chicken tikka with tomato and onion) to Keralan thoran (mixed vegetables with mustard and fresh coconut).

COURTESY THE WHITEBROOK

RIVERSIDE MARKET

CARDIFF | $ | MARKET
Fitzhamon Embankment; 029-2019 0036; www.riversidemarket.org.uk; mains £5-12

Every Sunday, the embankment across the Taff from Principality Stadium is lined with stalls for the Riverside Market. Independent producers show off their wares, from burgers, Indian street food and hefty cronuts to speciality cheeses, homemade sourdough, pizzas, jars of jam and cured meats. The seating lets you watch the river go by while sipping great coffee and eating your goodies.

COAST

PEMBROKESHIRE | $$$ | MODERN BRITISH

Coppet Hall Beach, Saundersfoot; 01834-810800; www.coastsaundersfoot.co.uk; mains £26-29, lunch menu £29, 5-course menu £59

The spectacular beachfront setting is more than matched by the wizardry emanating from chef Tom Hines' kitchen at this award-winning restaurant in quietly charming Saundersfoot. Whether you choose from the adventurous a la carte 'Tom's menu' (which features such rich delights as truffle polenta with chorizo and parmesan, and John Dory with saffron onions and fennel), the simpler lunch menu or the whole five-course shebang, prepare to be wowed. Local seafood shines, and the service is great, too.

PRYD O FWYD

CARMARTHENSHIRE | $$ | WELSH

Calon Y Fferri, Ferryside; 01267-240411; www.pryd.co.uk/; 1/2/3 courses: dinner £16/21/26, Sunday lunch £14/19/24

Don't be put off by the uninspiring exterior: Pryd o Fwyd ('bite to eat' in Welsh) is a welcoming place and the food, prepared by chef Guy, who's also the postmaster (the post office is in the same building), is excellent. The menu offers classics and innovative touches – pork loin comes with a chorizo and broad bean jus, and the vegetarian jalfrezi is a real highlight. It's just a five-minute walk from Ferryside train station but is slightly hidden away off Carmarthen Road, so ask a local for the post office if you get lost.

'There is everything to be learned from the people who grow, raise and catch the food we prepare – the whole animal is used, the whole plant.'
Ynshyr

COURTESY THE WHITEBROOK

WRIGHT'S FOOD EMPORIUM

CARMARTHENSHIRE | $ | CAFE

Golden Grove Arms, Llanarthne; 01558-668929; www.wrightsfood.co.uk; mains £8-11

Sprawling through the rooms of an old village pub, this hugely popular deli-cafe serves sandwiches, salads and massive antipasto platters packed full of top-notch local and imported ingredients. Wash it all down with a craft beer or something from its range of small-estate, organic wine, then browse shelves full of the area's best produce.

YNYSHIR

POWYS | $$$ | MODERN BRITISH

Eglwysfach, Machynlleth; 01654-781209; www.ynyshir.co.uk; 20-course lunch/dinner £180

Foraged wild foods, the best local meat and seafood and his own

kitchen-garden produce give Gareth Ward of Ynyshir the foundations to concoct some of Wales' most wonderful food. A Michelin-starred restaurant within a luxurious country retreat, Ynyshir offers set menus, with a focus on quality local ingredients, that reach new heights for brevity ('mackerel', 'strawberry') but herald total gastronomic joy.

OSTERIA

GWYNEDD | $$| ITALIAN
26 Hole in the Wall St, Caernarfon; 01286-678460; mains £10-14

Two Florentine partners are behind this excellent Tuscan restaurant, housed in a compact whitewashed-stone building hard up against the city walls. Specialising in interesting carpaccios and *bruschette* (try the gorgonzola with walnuts and honey), they import many of their ingredients and wines from Tuscany and prepare daily specials such as stuffed vegetables and pasta with cod and cherry-tomato ragu.

GALLT-Y-GLYN

GWYNEDD | $ | PUB
A4086, Llanberis; 01286-870370; www.galltyglyn.com; pizzas from £7.50

Sure, it serves pasta, pies, burgers and salads, too, but almost everyone comes for the delicious choose-your-own-topping pizza and the fact that you get a free drink with every main course. Simply tick what you want on the paper menu and hand it over at the bar. This old pub near the foot of Snowdon is a bit shabby, slightly eccentric, very family friendly and utterly brilliant.

BISTRO BERMO

GWYNEDD | $$ | BISTRO
6 Church St, Barmouth; 01341-281284; www.bistrobermo.com; mains £19-22

Discreetly hidden behind an aqua-green shopfront, this intimate restaurant delivers a sophisticated menu chock-full of Welsh farm produce and fresh fish. Featuring dishes such as chargrilled lamb cutlets with minted gravy and halibut on sautéed oyster mushrooms, the cooking is classical rather than experimental, and generally excellent. There are only half a dozen tables, so book ahead.

PARISELLA'S OF CONWY ICE CREAM

CONWY | $ | ICE CREAM
Conwy Quay; www.parisellasicecream.co.uk; cone £2.50

This kiosk on Conwy's quay sells a selection of what may well be the best ice cream in Wales, using locally sourced milk and double cream. Among Parisella's 60-plus flavours are such delights as *stracciatella*, lemon curd, and amaretto and black cherry. It's a great spot for slurping a cone while gazing at the estuary and castle – just watch out for the seagulls. There's also a parlour at 12 High St.

Previous spread: Dishes from The Whitebrook.

GIGI GAO'S FAVOURITE

SWANSEA | $$ | CHINESE

18-23 Anchor Ct; 01792-653300; www.favouritechinese.co.uk; mains £13-15

In a centre-stage waterfront location, this passionately loved Chinese kitchen eschews the batters, all-purpose sauces and replica menus of many Westernised Chinese eateries to produce food that does justice to China's deep culinary treasures. Homemade organic noodles are served with unapologetically funky Beijing-style sauce, the pork is sweet braised Hunan style, and vegetarian dishes aren't just padding out the menu.

RESTAURANT JAMES SOMMERIN

VALE OF GLAMORGAN | $$$ | MODERN BRITISH

The Esplanade, Penarth; 029-2070 6559; www.jamessommerinrestaurant.co.uk; mains £21-32, 6/9 courses £75/95

James Sommerin's top-notch restaurant has views over the Severn Estuary and a Michelin star. Much that issues from the kitchen looks as exquisite as it tastes, marrying multiple textures, well-balanced flavours and tricksy molecular-gastronomy techniques. Welsh lamb comes with coconut, butternut squash, cumin and mint, while other offerings, such as langoustine with samphire and spices, make simpler magic.

CANTEEN

NEWPORT | $ | PIZZA

Cnr Market & East Sts; 01239-820131; www.thecanteennewport.com; mains £8-13

With names like Strumble Head, *Mae Hen Wlad Fy Nhadau* (Land of My Fathers) and Costa del Newport, the Canteen's lip-smacking range of thin, crispy, stone-baked pizza has been suitably Welshified with the addition of locally sourced quality toppings. This welcoming, informal spot also serves salads, good coffee, craft beer from Bluestone Brewing and cider brewed by Welsh Cider brewed by Gethin's in HaverfordWest.

THE WHITEBROOK

MONMOUTHSHIRE | $$$ | MODERN BRITISH

Whitebrook, near Monmouth; 01600-860254; www.thewhitebrook.co.uk; menu 3-/5 course lunch/6-course dinner £42/55/85

Hidden down green-canopied country lanes in a remote part of the Wye Valley, this wonderful Michelin-starred restaurant-with-rooms is well worth seeking out. Every plate is a little work of art, made largely with what can be sourced from within 12 miles and adorned with foraged herbs such as monkwort and nettles. Evening dishes might include squab pigeon with cauliflower and forced rhubarb or crown-prince pumpkin with purple sprouting broccoli, buttermilk and three-cornered garlic.

WHERE TO DRINK...

LOCAL BEER

Albion Ale House, Conwy
A collaboration between four Welsh craft breweries (Purple Moose, Conwy, Nant and Great Orme), this heritage-listed 1920s boozer is a beer-drinker's heaven.

Neuadd Arms Hotel, Llanwrtyd Wells
A great village pub, with tourist information, rooms, an interesting menu and excellent beers brewed in the stables out back.

Tiny Rebel Newport Centre
One of several bars run by this award-winning Welsh brewery – its Cwtch red ale is a cracker, and there's a good mix of styles on offer.

Brecon Tap, Brecon
A treasure trove of craft beer, traditional cider, estate wines and locally baked meat pies, with occasional live music.

ENGLAND

Wherever you travel in England, for every greasy spoon or fast-food joint, there's a local pub or speciality restaurant. You can still find postwar stodge, but it's no longer the default: instead, international options abound and reinvented classics are everywhere. London is now a global gastronomic capital, and it's increasingly easy to find excellent food options right across the country.

WHAT TO EAT

Cornish pasty
A mix of beef, potato, onion and swede baked in a pastry casing that's been crimped on the side. Invented as an all-in-one-lunch pack for tin miners.

Seafood
Fish and chips is the classic, but there's far more on offer, including prawns, oysters, mackerel, bass, crabs and scallops.

Roast dinner
Meat (or nut roast) usually served with roast potatoes, vegetables, gravy and Yorkshire pudding (a savoury batter rather than a sweet treat).

Chicken tikka masala
Just one famous example of Britain's embrace of foreign food, this creamy, spicy Anglo-Indian dish is perennially popular.

PRICE RANGES

For a main course:
$ less than £10 (London £12)
$$ £10 to £20 (London £12–25)
$$$ £20 (London £25) or more

Tipping: 10–15%

DINNER BY HESTON BLUMENTHAL

LONDON | $$$ | MODERN BRITISH
Mandarin Oriental Hyde Park, 66 Knightsbridge; 020-7201 3833; www.dinnerbyheston.com; 3-course set lunch £45, dinner mains £40-50

Sumptuously presented Dinner is a gastronomic tour de force, taking diners on a journey through British culinary history via the likes of spiced squab pigeon and roast cod. Dishes carry historical dates for context and are served with inventive modern inflections. The restaurant interior is a design triumph, from the glass-walled kitchen and its overhead clock mechanism to the large windows looking onto the park.

COURTESY MACKIE MAYOR

OTTOLENGHI

LONDON | $$ | MEDITERRANEAN
287 Upper St; 020-7288 1454; www.ottolenghi.co.uk; mains £17-22

Mountains of meringues tempt you through the door of this Islington deli-restaurant, where a sumptuous array of baked goods and fresh salads greets you. Meals are as light and bright as the brilliantly white interior design, with a strong influence from the eastern Mediterranean – roasted beetroot and coriander labneh salad, or slow-roasted goat, beluga lentils and green olive salsa. It's one of six London restaurants run by English-Palestinian chef Yotam Ottoleghi.

PADELLA

LONDON | $ | ITALIAN
6 Southwark St; www.padella.co; dishes £4-12.50

A fantastic part of the foodie enclave of Borough Market, Padella is a small, energetic bistro specialising in handmade pasta dishes, inspired by the owners' culinary adventures in Italy. The portions are small, which means that, joy of joys, you can (and should!) have more than one dish. Outstanding, but be prepared to wait (no reservations taken). There's also a virtual queue system accessed via the website which will notify you when a table is ready – not a bad option given the many fine pubs in the neighbourhood.

POTLI

LONDON | $ | INDIAN
319-321 King St; 020-8741 4328; www.potli.co.uk; mains £8-15

With its scattered pieces from Mumbai's Thieves Market, Indian-market-kitchen cuisine, homemade pickles and spice mixes, tantalising Potli deftly captures the aromas of its culinary home. Downstairs there's an open kitchen and service is friendly, but the alluring menu – where flavours are teased into a rich and authentic Indian culinary experience – is the real crowd pleaser. The paneer shashlik (cottage cheese, caramelised onions and peppers) and Kerala fish curry, with its mild yet full-flavoured accents, are both delectable, but this Hammersmith neighbourhood restaurant is assured throughout.

'Eating with us is special and memorable. Our food is simple, allowing the ingredients to be the hero.'
Nathan Outlaw, Restaurant Nathan Outlaw

COURTESY PADELLA

TOWPATH

LONDON | $ | CAFE
Rear 42-44 De Beauvoir Cres; 020-7254 7606; mains £7-9.50

Occupying four small units facing the Regent's Canal towpath in Hackney, this simple cafe is a super place to sit in the sun and watch the ducks and narrowboats glide by. The coffee and food are excellent, with delicious cookies and brownies on the counter and cooked dishes such as pork tenderloin and roast cauliflower with courgettes and monk's beard chalked up on the blackboard daily. It's closed in winter.

RESTAURANT NATHAN OUTLAW

CORNWALL | $$$ | FISH
6 New Rd, Port Isaac; 01208-880 896; www.nathan-outlaw.com; tasting menu £145

Port Isaac's prestige has skyrocketed since Cornwall's top chef, Nathan Outlaw, moved his main operation here from Rock. This is the place to experience Outlaw's passion for Cornish fish and seafood, and you'll see the likes of John Dory with soused beetroot and smoked paprika or turbot with sweetcorn and pickled red onions. His style is surprisingly classic, relying on top-notch ingredients rather than cheffy tricks. As you'd expect of a twice-Michelin-starred restaurant, you'll pay top dollar, but it's a tell-your-friends experience.

HIDDEN HUT

CORNWALL | $ | CAFE

Porthcurnick Beach, Portscatho, Truro; www.hiddenhut.co.uk; meals £4-12

Hidden indeed: this beach cafe is so tucked away, you might miss it even if you've been here before. The wooden cabin was built as a wartime lookout, but now serves delicious beach food from April to October: grilled mackerel, hot soups, proper cakes and 'beach salads'. During summer, there are pop-up communal 'feast nights' and beach breakfasts. The only seating is on benches, but with views like this, who wants to sit indoors? It's a 500m walk north to the hut from Portscatho.

RIVERSTATION

BRISTOL | $$ | BRITISH

The Grove; 0117-914 4434; www.riverstation.co.uk; mains £11-16

Riverstation's waterside location is hard to beat, with lovely views over Bristol's Floating Harbour from its balcony, terrace and bright interior. But it's the classical food that truly shines, from pan-fried trout fillet, baby beetroot, new potatoes and chard to cumberland sausages with savoy cabbage and mash.

THE CIRCUS

BATH | $$ | MODERN BRITISH

34 Brock St; 01225-466020; www.thecircusrestaurant.co.uk; mains lunch £14-17, dinner £17-24

Chef Ali Golden has turned this bistro into one of Bath's destination addresses. Her taste is for British dishes with a Continental twist, reminiscent of British food writer Elizabeth David: Hampshire boar, Wiltshire lamb and West Country fish are all infused with herby flavours and rich sauces. It occupies an elegant townhouse near the Circus. There's also a strong menu with vegetarian, vegan and dairy- and gluten-free dishes.

ELEPHANT

DEVON | $$$ | MODERN BRITISH

3 Beacon Tce; 01803-200044; www.elephantrestaurant.co.uk; lunch 2-/3-course menu £21.50/24.95, dinner mains £15-27

The jumbo on Torquay's fine-dining scene: Michelin-starred and critically lauded, Elephant belongs to chef Simon Hulstone, whose taste for seasonal food (much of it grown on his own farm) and delicate presentation takes centre stage. The food is modern

Previous spread: Dish from Mackie Mayor; Padella.

with classical underpinnings – though expect surprising flavour combos – and every plate looks as pretty as a painting. Lunch is a steal.

L'ENCLUME

CUMBRIAH | $$$ | MODERN BRITISH
Cavendish St, Cartmel; 015395-36362; www.lenclume.co.uk; set lunch £65, lunch & dinner menu £155

Set in a former wheel-makers and smithy, the 'Anvil' is run by the wildly imaginative Simon Rogan, and is frequently rated England's best restaurant. Known for his boundary-pushing cuisine and off-the-wall presentation, Rogan's dishes often have a focus on foraged ingredients such as sea buckthorn, juniper, dandelion seed and Douglas fir. The tasting menu is a great parade of plates, and might offer tomatoes preserved in rosehip with nasturtium and lobster tail or raw cornish mackerel and vegetables in coal oil.

FELLPACK

CUMBRIA | $$ | CAFE
19 Lake Rd, Keswick; 017687-71177; www.fellpack.co.uk; mains £10-20

This on-trend cafe in stunningly situated Keswick specialises in 'fell pots' – a Lakeland-style Buddha bowl, incorporating an all-in-one meal such as katsu curry, jambalaya or hake and butterbean stew, all freshly made and flavour-packed. Flatbreads and chunky soups are offered during the daytime. The owners are full of enthusiasm and the food is zingy and imaginative.

WRECKFISH

LIVERPOOL | $$ | MODERN BRITISH
60 Seel St; 0151 707 1960; www.wreckfish.co; mains £14-25

Restaurateur Gary Usher's crowd-funded restaurant is a marvellous example of Modern British cuisine at its best: nothing overly fussy, but everything done just right. From the open kitchen come fine dishes such as salt-baked swede with smoked garlic honey and a braised featherblade of beef with mushroom purée and tenderstem broccoli.

MACKIE MAYOR

MANCHESTER | $$ | FOOD HALL
1 Eagle St; www.mackiemayor.co.uk; mains £9-15

This restored former meat market in the Northern Quarter is now home to a superb food hall with a fine selection of 10 individual traders. There are divine pizzas at Honest Crust; drunken noodles, pad krapow and vegan green curry at Chilli B; fresh tacos and frozen margaritas at Pico's; and tasty steaks at Tender Cow. You eat at long shared tables, across two floors, and there's coffee, tea and craft beer too.

OX CLUB

LEEDS | $$ | GRILL
Bramleys Yard, The Headrow; 07470 359961; www.oxclub.co.uk; lunch mains £9-14, 2/3-course menu £19.50/£22.50

WHERE TO TAKE...

AFTERNOON TEA

Orchard Tea Garden, Grantchester
After an idyllic punt, walk or cycle along the Cam, flop into a deckchair under a leafy apple tree and wolf down cakes and sandwiches – set teas are named after Rupert Brooke and Maynard Keynes.

Ampersand Hotel, London
The capital has lots of high-end tearooms (Claridge's and Brown's are classics), but this luxury hotel instead goes high science, with petri-dish jam and chocolate spacemen among the award-winning offerings.

Rosylee, Manchester
A touch of Edwardian and Georgian elegance in the heart of the Northern Quarter, this gorgeous tearoom offers a superb afternoon tea as well as other British classics.

Arguably the best restaurant in Leeds, Ox Club occupies an intimate, minimalist space and champions local produce with a deceptively simple menu. Though it bills itself as a grill restaurant, the Modern British dishes are far more inventive than what you'll find in your average BBQ joint – sea trout with caviar cream and crispy seaweed or smoked celeriac with braised celery and lovage, for example.

HOUSE OF TIDES

NEWCASTLE | $$$ | MODERN BRITISH

28-30 The Close; www.houseoftides.co.uk; 0191-230 3720; tasting menus lunch £75, dinner £95

A 16th-century merchant's house on the river bank is now the home of Newcastle's most celebrated restaurant, the Michelin-starred House of Tides. Acclaimed Newcastle-born chef Kenny Atkinson incorporates premium ingredients – monkfish, salt-aged beef, wild blackberries, black truffles and nasturtiums – in regularly changing multi-course tasting menus. The food is deliciously intricate here, and the welcome warm.

RILEY'S FISH SHACK

NORTHUMBERLAND | $$ | SEAFOOD

King Edward's Bay, Tynemouth; 0191-257 1371; www.rileysfishshack.com; small dishes £5-12, mains £14-35

This rustic, tucked-away shack lies down steep timber stairs on the beach at Tynemouth, 9 miles from Newcastle. Phenomenal local seafood underpins wood-fired dishes from wraps to empanadas and mains like turbot with wild mushroom and bang-bang monkfish kebabs, served in environmentally friendly cardboard boxes. Indoor seating is limited; there's also a handful of stools outside and deckchairs spread on the sand.

LE COCHON AVEUGLE

YORK | $$$ | FRENCH

37 Walmgate; 01904-640222; www.lecochonaveugle.uk; tasting menu £60-85

Strawberry and elderflower sandwich? Scallop in sea urchin butter? Blowtorched mackerel with melon gazpacho? Fussy eaters beware – this small

This page: Opening a scallop in Le Cochon Aveugle. Opposite page: Smoking a rack of lamb in Le Cochon Aveugle.

BACON ON THE BEECH. COURTESY LE COCHON AVEUGLE

restaurant with huge ambition serves an ever-changing menu (no à la carte) of imagination and invention. You never know what will come next, except that it will be delicious. Bookings are essential.

CHATSWORTH ESTATE FARM SHOP CAFE

PEAK DISTRICT | $ | CAFE

Pilsley, Bakewell; www.chatsworth.org; dishes £7-13

One of the finest places to eat in the Peak District, this bucolic cafe serves hearty breakfasts (eggs Benedict with Chatsworth-cured bacon or salmon; strawberry-and-honey Chatsworth yoghurt with muesli) until 11.30am, segueing to lunches (steak-and-kidney suet pudding; traditional roasts) and afternoon teas. Over half the products at its adjacent farm shop are produced on the estate, and the stately home of Chatsworth House is about 2 miles away.

VAULTS & GARDEN

OXFORD | $ | CAFE

University Church of St Mary the Virgin, Radcliffe Sq; 01865-279112; www.thevaultsandgarden.com; mains £7-10.50

This beautiful lunch venue spreads from the vaulted 14th-century Old Congregation House of the University Church into a garden facing the Radcliffe Camera. Come early, and queue at the counter to choose from wholesome organic specials such as leek and potato soup, slow-roasted lamb shoulder, or spiced chickpea tajine. Breakfast and afternoon tea are equally good – the scones are delectable.

WHERE TO EAT...

SUNDAY ROAST

The Cross, Kenilworth
Prime cuts such as roast beef chateaubriand in a romantic 19th-century inn. The food at this garlanded Warwickshire gastropub is exquisite.

Star Inn, Helmsley
Cracking country dining with premium Yorkshire produce – Marwood's beef and Yorkshire pork star on the Sunday menu at this thatched country pub.

Pipe and Glass Inn, Beverley
Beef, partridge and inventive veggie options are among the Michelin-winning dishes in Yorkshire's East Riding. You can tour the herb gardens afterwards.

Hind's Head, Bray
Famously inventive super-chef Heston Blumenthal tackles an English classic on the Sunday set menus at his 15th-century Oxfordshire pub.

LE MANOIR AUX QUAT'SAISONS

OXFORDSHIRE | $$$ | MODERN FRENCH

Church Rd, Great Milton; 01844-278881; www.belmond.com/le-manoir-aux-quat-saisons-oxfordshire; 5-course lunch/7-course dinner £110/194

In a honey-coloured manor house 9 miles from Oxford, some of England's most wonderful – and most expensive – dishes are lovingly prepared. Chef Raymond Blanc has been working his magic here for over 30 years, presenting imaginative dishes that use ingredients from the amazing on-site kitchen garden. The various menus follow the seasons and span multiple courses: truffled egg with wild mushroom tea might be followed by spiced monkfish, alliums and aromatic cornish mussels. It's the holder of two Michelin stars.

SPICED ROOTS

OXFORD | $$ | CARIBBEAN

64 Cowley Rd; 01865-249888; www.spicedroots.com; mains £16-24

From black rice with pomegranates to oxtail with macaroni cheese and plantains – and, of course, spicy jerk chicken – everything is just perfection at this friendly Caribbean restaurant. There are plenty of vegetarian options too, as well as curried fish or goat, while adding a cocktail or two from the thatched rum bar is pretty much irresistible.

MIDSUMMER HOUSE

CAMBRIDGE | $$$ | MODERN BRITISH

Midsummer Common; 01223-369299; www.midsummerhouse.co.uk; 3-course lunch £50, 8-course dinner £135

At the region's top table, chef Daniel Clifford's double-Michelin-starred creations are distinguished by depth of flavour and immense technical skill. Savour transformations of sea bass, scallops and goat's cheese, before a sesame and white chocolate pyramid with guava sorbet, coconut, chilli and garlic. Vegetarian, vegan and pescatarian versions of the eight-course menu are available on request.

BRIDGE COTTAGE BISTRO

NORTH YORKSHIRE | $$ | MODERN BRITISH

East Row, Sandsend; 01947-893438; www.bridgecottagebistro.com; mains £12-30

This outstanding restaurant in the pretty coastal village of Sandsend, 3 miles north of Whitby, may well be the east coast's best eating experience. Its no-nonsense setting in a bare old cottage lets the food sing, and the spotlight is always on Yorkshire, with delights like hay-baked lamb, roast hake with tomato and pancetta, and Eccles cakes with Wensleydale ice cream. There are regular special nights, including a fish tasting menu on Fridays.

IYDEA

BRIGHTON | $ | VEGETARIAN
17 Kensington Gardens; www.iydea.co.uk; 01273-667992; mains £5-10

Even by Brighton's high standards, the food at this multi-award-winning vegetarian cafe is a treat. The daily-changing choices of curries, lasagnes, falafel, enchiladas and quiches are full of flavour and can be washed down with selected vegan wines, organic ales and homemade lemonades. If you're on the hop, you can get any dish to take away in plastic-free packaging.

SPORTSMAN PUB

KENT | $$$ | BRITISH
Faversham Rd, Seasalter; 01227-273370; www.thesportsmanseasalter.co.uk; mains £16-29

The village of Seasalter, 4 miles east of Whitstable, would hardly receive a trickle of visitors were it not for the deceivingly ramshackle, Michelin-garlanded Sportsman Pub. Local ingredients from sea, marsh and woods are crafted by Whitstable-born chef Stephen Harris into taste-packed creations. Oysters feature heavily in the starting line-up, and fish such as turbot, ray and mackerel dominate the mains, though good meat and veggie options are available too.

'We let the estuary, woods, marshland and fertile soils around the pub dictate what we cook – oysters, fish, meat, vegetables and game.'
The Sportsman

GROSVENOR FISH BAR

NORWICH | $ | FISH & CHIPS
28 Lower Goat Lane; www.fshshop.com; mains £5-9

At this groovy Norfolk chippy-with-a-difference, chips come with fresh cod goujons, a 'Big Mack' is a crispy mackerel fillet in a bread roll, and the 'Six Quid Squid' (squid rings with garlic aioli) really is £5. Either eat in the basement or they'll deliver to the likeable Birdcage pub opposite, so you can have a pint with your meal.

ALLOTMENT

DOVER | $$ | BRITISH
9 High St; 01304-214467; www.theallotmentrestaurant.com; mains £12-18

Dover's best dining spot plates up local fish, meat and vegan dishes from around Canterbury, seasoned with herbs from the tranquil garden out back, for breakfast, lunch and dinner. Cleanse your palette with a Kentish wine in a relaxed, understated setting as you admire the view of the Maison Dieu (13th-century pilgrims' hospital) directly opposite through the exquisite stained-glass frontage.

PORTUGAL

Settling down to a meal with friends is one of life's great pleasures for the Portuguese, who take pride in simple but flavourful dishes honed to perfection over the centuries. Seafood, roast meats, freshly baked bread and velvety wines are key staples in the everyday feast that is eating in Portugal.

WHAT TO EAT

Pastel de nata
These famous custard tarts are best served warm and dusted with cinnamon.

Seafood
Bacalhau (dried salt-cod), *caldeirada* (fish and shellfish in a rich broth) and escabeche (marinated vinegar fish stew) are highlights.

Pork
The Alentejo and northern Portugal are particularly partial to the pig – *porco preto* is a gourmet 'black pork' made from pigs that graze on acorns.

Bread
Integral to every meal. It also turns up in main courses such as *açorda* (bread stew, often served with shellfish) and *migas* (crumbled bread cooked with pork and other meats).

PRICE RANGES

For a main course:
$ less than €10
$$ €10–20
$$$ €20 or more

Tipping: 10% or just round up.

ALMA

LISBON | $$$ | MODERN PORTUGUESE

Rua Anchieta 15; 213 470 650; www.almalisboa.pt; mains €32-36, tasting menus €110-120

Two-Michelin–starred Henrique Sá Pessoa's flagship Alma is one of Portugal's destination restaurants and offers Lisbon's best gourmet dining experience. Original stone flooring and hardwood tables exude understated style, but it's Pessoa's outrageously good nouveau Portuguese cuisine that draws in the foodie flock. Seasonal menus focus on the freshest Iberian flavours possible. Standout dishes include charred red peppers in an exquisite red-pepper coulis and salted cod in coriander broth. Portions are bigger than average at this level and the sommelier isn't afraid to pick bold, unorthodox wines to round out your evening.

PASTÉIS DE BELÉM

LISBON | $ | PASTRIES

Rua de Belém 84-92; www.pasteisdebelem.pt; pastries from €1.10

Since 1837 this patisserie has been transporting locals to sugar-coated nirvana with heavenly *pastéis de Belém*. The crisp pastry nests are filled with custard cream, baked at 200°C for that perfect golden crust, then lightly dusted with cinnamon. Admire azulejos in the vaulted rooms or devour a still-warm tart at the counter and try to guess the secret ingredient.

MERCADO DA RIBEIRA

LISBON | $ | MARKET

Av 24 de Julho; www.timeoutmarket.com; dishes €5-24

Doing trade in fresh fruit and veg, fish and flowers since 1892, this domed market hall has been the word on everyone's lips since *Time Out* transformed half of it into a gourmet food court in 2014. Now it's Lisbon in chaotic culinary microcosm: Garrafeira Nacional wines, Café de São Bento steaks, Manteigaria Silva cold cuts and Michelin-star chef creations from Henrique Sá Pessoa.

SOL E PESCA

LISBON | $ | BAR

Rua Nova do Carvalho 44; www.facebook.com/solepesca; tinned fish €2-17

Rods, nets, hooks and fish charts give away this tiny bar's former life as a fishing-tackle shop. Cabinets are stacked with vintage-looking tins of sardines, tuna, mackerel and other preserved delicacies – a traditional snack now enjoying a new lease of life. Grab a chair, order a tin or two, add bread, olives and wine, and you have the makings of a fine and affordable meal.

RESTAURANT DA ADRAGA

GREATER LISBON | $$ | SEAFOOD

Praia da Adraga, Sintra; 219 280 028; www.restaurantedaadraga.com; seafood per kg €37-100

'The forest that surrounds us, along with the decoration and the crackling and comforting sounds of the fireplace in the winter, make this a magical space.' *Restaurante de Casa das Penhas Douradas*

MATT MUNRO/LONELYPLANET ©

This legendary seafood restaurant sits on the edge of a small beach below Almoçageme. No fancy techniques or overdressed dining room here – just incredibly fresh fish and seafood cooked to perfection, served in a casual, yellow-tableclothed setting with framed sea views. Call ahead to reserve a table by the window.

GAVIÃO NOVO

MADEIRA | $$ | SEAFOOD

Rua Santa Maria 131, Funchal; 291 229 238; www.gaviaonovo.pt; mains €8-17

Madeira's top seafood restaurant is an intimate affair at the heart of the Zona Velha, attracting tourists, locals and the Portuguese rich and famous, who come for one of the most authentic

dining experiences on the island. Fish from the waters around Madeira are complemented by Portuguese seafood air-freighted in every Saturday. Desserts are made fresh twice a day and only the best Portuguese olive oils are used.

A EIRA DO MEL

THE ALGARVE | $$ | PORTUGUESE
Estrada do Castelejo, Vila do Bispo; 282 639 016; mains €11-22, seafood plates €27-35

A rustic former farmhouse 9km north of Sagres is the atmospheric setting for José Pinheiro's lauded slow-food cooking. Seafood is landed in Sagres, with meats, vegetables and fruit sourced from local farms. Dishes such as octopus cataplana (cooked in a shell-like pan) with sweet potatoes, spicy piri-piri Atlantic wild shrimp, rabbit in red wine, and *javali* are accompanied by regional wines.

MONTE DA EIRA

THE ALGARVE | $$ | PORTUGUESE
N396, Clareanes; 289 438 129; www.restaurantemontedaeira.com; mains €8-16, 2-/3-course lunch menu €14.50/17.50

A former threshing mill's stables have been converted to house this charming restaurant with white-clothed tables spread over several rooms and two outdoor terraces. Refined rustic specialities, such as *estfado de javali* (wild boar stew with local herbs) and *caçarola de coelho e ameixas* (rabbit and prune casserole), are complemented by hundreds of Portuguese wines. It's 4km south of the pretty whitewashed village of Querença. The lunch menus offer superb value.

VILA JOYA RESTAURANT

THE ALGARVE | $$$ | GASTRONOMY
Estrada da Galé, Albufeira; 289 591 795; www.vilajoya.com; degustation menu €210

Helmed by Austrian chef Dieter Koschina, this fine-dining restaurant in the Vila Joya resort was Portugal's first to gain two Michelin stars. Koschina draws on a variety of culinary influences and premium Portuguese produce to create exquisite dishes such as Atlantic lobster with Thai curry and mango or Wagyu beef with pearl onions and green peppers.

TABERNA TÍPICA QUARTA FEIRA

THE ALENTEJO | $$ | PORTUGUESE
Rua do Inverno 16, Évora; 266 707 530; 3-course dinner €22.50-25

Don't bother asking for the menu since there's just one option on offer at this jovial eatery tucked away in the Moorish quarter. Luckily it's a stunner: slow-cooked black pork so tender it falls off the bone, plus freshly baked bread, grilled mushrooms (and other starters), dessert and ever-flowing glasses of wine – all served for one set price. Reserve ahead. Arched ceilings, checked tablecloths and the warmth of young owner João make this family-run place a favourite with out-of-towners.

***Previous spread:* Portuguese pastries; Tavern near Rossio. *Opposite page:* Street decorated for festival.**

GADANHA MERCEARIA E RESTAURANTE

THE ALENTEJO | $$ | PORTUGUESE

Largo Dragões de Olivença 84A; Estremoz; 268 333 262; www.merceariagadanha.pt; sharing plates €8-15, mains €18-24

The walled market town of Estremoz is popular for its marble and its food, and here traditional local produce is brilliantly merged with contemporary touches. Extraordinary *petiscos* (snacks) include *linguiça de porco preto* and *farinheira* with quail eggs (*farinheira* is a local speciality made of pork fat, herbs and flour). The daily lunch menu is highly recommended.

CASINHA VELHA

ESTREMADURA | $$$ | PORTUGUESE

Rua Professores Portelas 23, Leiria; 244 855 355; www.casinhavelha.com; mains €17.50-21.50

The best culinary experience in central Portugal begins insanely: an epic cow's, sheep's and goat's cheese cart, arranged regionally, along with black pork sausages and pumpkin jam, awaits at your table – you cut your own portions and pay what you cut. Mains include duck from the restaurant's own farm, served in *arroz de pato* (duck rice), with bacon, pineapple and dried fruits. The *creme de leite*, the Portuguese version of crème brûlée, is a beautiful mess on a plate. You

WHERE TO DRINK...

PORT & WINE

Prova, Porto
This chic, stone-walled bar offers tastings, wine and port by the glass and sharing plates of local hams and cheeses. Its port tonics are legendary.

Portologia, Porto
Over 200 different ports are on offer at this cosy bar. If you fall in love, you can usually buy a whole bottle (or even send a case home).

BA Wine Bar do Bairro Alto, Lisbon
The welcoming staff at Bairro Alto's best wine bar offer fantastic choices based on your tastes. There's artisan cheeses and charcuterie too. Reservations essential.

Epicur, Faro Over
250 Portuguese wines can be paired with charcuterie, cheese and oysters at this stylish bar in the Algarve.

won't forget this meal in a hurry – this is what people are talking about when they rave about Portuguese cuisine.

ALCOA

ESTREMADURA | $ | BAKERY

Praça 25 de Abril 44, Alcobaça; 262 597 474; www.pastelaria-alcoa.com; pastries €1.30-3

There's a branch in Lisbon too, but this heralded *pastelaria* (pastry shop) hails from Alcobaça. It's been hawking some of Portugal's most decadent *doces conventuais* (conventual sweets) from opposite the town's famous monastery since 1957. Loosen your belt: these award-winning cash-only pastries pack a sugary punch.

CAFE SANTIAGO

PORTO | $ | PORTUGUESE

Rua Passos Manuel 226; 222 055 797; www.caferestaurantesantiago.com.pt; mains €8-12

This is probably the best place in town to try Porto's classic gut-busting treat, the *francesinha* – a thick, open-faced sandwich piled with cheese, sausage, egg and/or assorted meats, plus a tasty, rich beer sauce. This classic is a meal in itself, and unless you've a big appetite you might want to share it with a friend.

EUSKALDUNA STUDIO

PORTO | $$$ | GASTRONOMY

Rua de Santo Ildefonso 404, Aliados & Bolhão; 935 335 301; www.euskaldunastudio.pt; 10-course tasting menu €95

Everyone loves surprises, especially edible ones prepared with flawless execution, experimental finesse and a nod to the seasons. Just 16 lucky diners (eight at the green marble counter peeking into the kitchen and eight at oak tables) get to sample Vasco Coelho Santos' stunning 10-course menus. It's more like a private gastronomic event than just another good meal. Santos' credentials, including a stint behind the stove at the legendary El Bulli, speak of a chef aspiring to culinary greatness – and he achieves it.

FLOR DOS CONGREGADOS

PORTO | $$ | PORTUGUESE

Travessa dos Congregados 11; 222 002 822; mains €9.50-17

Tucked away down a narrow alley, this softly lit, family-run restaurant brims with stone-walled, wood-beamed, art-slung nooks. The frequently changing blackboard menu goes with the seasons. Everything from lamb to bonito is cooked and seasoned to a T. Special deals offers bargains on the likes of a 'Terylene' slow-cooked marinated pork sandwich and a glass of sparkling Tinto Bruto red.

DOC

THE DOURO | $$$ | PORTUGUESE
Estrada Nacional 222, Folgosa, near Pinhão; 254 858 123; www.docrestaurante.pt; mains €15-34, menus €90-100

Architect Miguel Saraiva's ode to clean-lined, glass-walled minimalism, DOC is headed up by Portuguese star chef Rui Paula. Its terrace peering out across the river is a stunning backdrop. Dishes give a pinch of imagination to seasonal, regional flavours, from lobsters and sea bass to slow cooked pork and a good vegetarian selection – all are paired with carefully selected wines from the cellar.

CASA DE PASTO DAS CARVALHEIRAS

THE MINHO | $$ | FUSION
Rua Dom Afonso Henriques 10, Braga; 253 046 244; www.casadepastodascarvalheiras.com; small plates €5-15

This colourful restaurant with a long bar serves up delectable, weekly changing *pratinhos* (small plates) such as cod confit with bok choy and noodles, mushrooms with creamy polenta and tasty concoctions of *alheira* (a light garlicky sausage of poultry or game). Weekday lunch menus go for €9 or €12, depending on the number of dishes you order.

'Here, Rui Paula, with a modern and inventive look, makes the kitchen a historic laboratory based on several generations of culinary recipes.'
DOC

O MARQUÊS

THE MINHO | $ | PORTUGUESE
Rua do Marquês 72, Viana do Castelo; 258 828 069; meals from €6

A tremendous backstreet find in the Costa Verde's most appealing town, this place is generally absolutely jammed with locals for the *platos do dia*. There are only a couple of options a day, such as baked cod with white beans or roasted turkey leg with potatoes and salad. It's a friendly, satisfying, family-run affair.

RESTAURANTE DE CASA DAS PENHAS DOURADAS

THE BEIRAS | $$$ | GASTRONOMY
Penhas Douradas, Manteigas; 275 981 045; www.casadaspenhasdouradas.pt; fixed-price lunch/dinner menu €28/38

This smart restaurant, part of the fabulous Casa das Penhas Douradas hotel, is a world away from traditional village life. Its streamlined Scandinavian-style decor sets the scene for sophisticated modern cuisine based on seasonal local ingredients such as kid goat, trout, juniper berries and wild mushrooms. The fixed-price lunch menu comprises a starter, main and dessert, while dinner is a five-course feast. Gourmet picnics are also available to order. Penhas Douradas is a winding 12km northwest of Manteigas.

SPAIN

Spain is one of Europe's culinary powerhouses, a foodie destination of the highest order. Spanish cuisine has colonised the world, from tapas, paella, *jamón* and churros to Spanish wines and olive oils. But by visiting Spain you can go to the source – and enjoy Spanish cooking at its best and in all its infinite variety.

WHAT TO EAT

Tapas
Spain's classic small plates, usually ordered at the bar, can be based around fish, meat or vegetables, and be hot or cold, straightforward or sophisticated.

Paella
Named for the wide pan it's cooked in, this iconic rice dish comes in many forms – if you want to go authentic, try it at Valencia's waterfront Las Arenas district.

Seafood
Whether it's Galician *pulpo* (octopus), Cantabrian *anchoas* (anchovies) or Andalucian *pescaito frito* (fried fish), Spain serves up the sea's bounty in irresistible – and often surprisingly simple – ways.

PRICE RANGES
For a main course:
$ less than €12
$$ €12–20
$$$ €20 or more

Tipping: Many Spaniards leave small change in restaurants – 5% is considered generous;

DIVERXO

MADRID | $$$ | MODERN SPANISH
Calle de Padre Damián 23; 915 70 07 66; www.diverxo.com; set menu €250

The city's only three-Michelin-starred restaurant, DiverXo in northern Madrid is one of Spain's most unusual culinary experiences. Chef David Muñoz favours what he has described as a 'brutal' approach to cooking – his team of chefs appear as you're mid-bite to add surprising new ingredients. The carefully choreographed experience centres on plate-packed menus such as the 'Flying Pigs' and is utterly unlike the more formal upmarket dining options. The nondescript suburban setting and small premises (chefs sometimes end up adding finishing touches in the hallway) only add to the street-smart atmosphere. Bookings up to six months in advance are required.

ADRIENNE PITTS/LONELY PLANET ©

MERCADO DE SAN MIGUEL

MADRID | $ | TAPAS
Plaza de San Miguel; 915 42 49 36; www.mercadodesanmiguel.es; tapas from €1.50

This is one of Madrid's oldest and most beautiful markets, an inviting space that's strewn with tables and set within early-20th-century glass walls. All the stalls are outstanding, but you could begin with the fine fishy pintxos atop mini toasts at La Casa del Bacalao, follow it up with some *jamón* or other cured meats at Carrasco Guijuelo, cheeses, pickled goodies or the gourmet tapas of Lhardy. There are also plenty of places to buy wine, Asturian cider and the like; the Sherry Corner has sherry tastings with tapas.

TABERNA MATRITUM

MADRID | $$ | MODERN SPANISH
Calle de la Cava Alta 17; 913 65 82 37; www.tabernamatritum.es; mains €14-20

The next door Calle de la Cava Baja may be the buzzing heart of La Latina's tapas scene, but this little gem rewards those who explore further. The seasonal menu encompasses terrific tapas, salads and generally creative cooking – try the Catalan sausage and prawn pie or the winter calçots (large spring onions), also from Catalonia. The wine list runs into the hundreds and is sophisticated without being pretentious.

CAFÉ PALMELITA

TENERIFE | $ | CAFE
Calle Castillo 9, Santa Cruz de Tenerife; 922 88 89 04; www.palmelita.es; cakes €2.50-4

This delightful Tenerife cafe has vintage fittings inside and out, and was founded in the late 1960s with German origins. The coffee is excellent and elsewhere the focus is on serious indulgence, with hot chocolate with double cream, buttery pastries and traditional German cakes. It's all

'The finest Iberian ham, the freshest fish from Galicia, Mediterranean rice dishes, exquisite cheeses: you'll find all the highlights of Spanish cuisine here.'
Mercado de San Miguel

ADRIENNE PITTS/LONELY PLANET ©

designed to put a contented waddle in your step, and the cafe is also a superb breakfast spot.

QUINTA DE SAN AMARO

GALICIA | $$ | GALICIAN
Calle San Amaro 6, Meaño, near Cambados; 630 87 75 90; www.quintadesanamaro.com; mains €14-20

The bright, big-windowed restaurant at this country boutique hotel is worth a trip from anywhere in the region for its delicious updates on traditional Galician cuisine – preparations like Iberian pork sirloin with chestnut purée and caramelised apple, prawn and vegetable tempura, monkfish-and-prawn brochette, and some delectable desserts. There's a fine wine list with, naturally, an emphasis on the excellent local white, albariño. First-class

service, tastefully cheery decor and expansive countryside views further enhance a memorable experience.

O CURRO DA PARRA

GALICIA | $$ | GALICIAN
Rúa do Curro da Parra 7, Santiago de Compostela; 981 55 60 59; www.ocurrodaparra.com; mains €17-23, starters & medias raciones €5-15

With a neat little stone-walled dining room upstairs and a narrow food-and-wine bar below, always-busy Curro da Parra serves thoughtfully created, market-fresh fare, changing weekly. Everything is delicious; typical offerings might include line-caught hake with green peppers or roast lamb with rosemary potatoes and pistachios. The cheesecake with wild berry foam and lime has been a favourite ever since it opened. On weekday lunchtimes there's an excellent *menú mercado* (market menu).

ATRIO

EXTREMADURA | $$$ | CONTEMPORARY SPANISH
Plaza de San Mateo 1, Cáceres; 927 24 29 28; www.restauranteatrio.com; menús from €145

With a stunning location in the heart of old-town Cáceres, this is Extremadura's top restaurant. Chic contemporary design and service that's both formal and friendly back up the wonderful, inventive culinary creations. The focus is on local produce of the highest quality, via a 12- to 13-course degustation menu. Vegetarian and gluten-free menus are available with advance notice.

RESTAURANTE COCINANDOS

CASTILLA Y LEÓN | $$$ | MODERN SPANISH
Plaza de San Marcos, León; 987 07 13 78; www.cocinandos.com; set menus €50-90

The proud owner of León's only Michelin star, Cocinandos brings creative flair to the table with a menu that changes weekly with the seasons and market availability. Featuring up to 12 courses, the set menu might include smoked trout with leek and dill, chanterelle mushrooms with potatoes and beef, and chestnuts with foie gras and coffee. The atmosphere is slightly formal, but the young team puts diners at ease and the food is exceptional.

ARBIDEL

ASTURIAS | $$$ | ASTURIAN
Calle Oscura 1, Ribadesella; 985 86 14 40; www.arbidel.com; mains €28-32, set menus €55-88

Much-loved, Michelin-starred Arbidel is famous for chef Jaime Uz's reinvention of classic Asturian flavours and ingredients with a distinctly modern flair. Exquisitely prepped, locally inspired delights might feature green-apple gazpacho, black-pudding ravioli, or Asturian beef tenderloin with local Casín cheese and cassava. The tasting menus are the best way to sample the kitchen's wide-ranging creativity.

Previous spread: Madrid streets.

BAR-RESTAURANTE ESLAVA

SEVILLE | $$ | TAPAS

Calle Eslava 3; 954 90 65 68; www.espacioeslava.com; tapas €2.90-4.50, raciones €10.50-22.50

You'll almost certainly have to wait for a table at this fine tapas restaurant's bar, but it's so worth it, especially if you use the time to start on the excellent wine list. The tapas are superb: contemporary, creative, brilliantly executed and incredible value for money. Standouts include slow-cooked egg with a caramelized wine reduction, and a filo pastry cigar stuffed with cuttlefish and algae.

CRÉEME

SEVILLE | $ | ICE CREAM

Plaza del Museo 2; 954 91 08 32; www.facebook.com/creemehelado; cones & tubs €3-5

Owner Antonio makes ice cream using his pick of the season's produce (avocado, or rosemary and peach) and creates his own flavour combinations: murillo (almond, caramel and chocolate) and mi papi ('my dad' – almond and honey). It's some of the best ice cream in Spain. Sit inside or grab a bench in shady Plaza del Museo by the Bellas Artes museum.

MANU JARA DULCERÍA

SEVILLE | $ | PASTRIES

Calle Pureza 5; 675 87 36 74; www.manujara.com; pastries €1.60-4

'We like simple things. Traditional cuisine, with local and seasonal products. We want to keep and update our grandmothers' recipes, made with love.'
Restaurante Amelibia

This exquisite patisserie has heavenly cakes laid out in a traditional wood and tiled interior. Try the creamy *milohajas* (mille feuille, aka vanilla slice) with chantilly cream. There's another branch in Nervión by the Sevilla FC stadium, as well as Bocasú stall in nearby Triana Market.

EL MESÓN DE CERVANTES

MÁLAGA | $$ | TAPAS

Calle Álamos 11; 952 21 62 74; www.elmesondecervantes.com; medias raciones €4.50-8.50, raciones €7.50-14

Cervantes started as a humble tapas bar run by expat Argentine Gabriel Spatz, but has expanded into four bar-restaurants, all within a block of each other. This is the headquarters, where pretty much everything is a show-stopper – the lamb stew with couscous, pumpkin and mushroom risotto and the grilled octopus are all outstanding. Most things can be ordered as tapas or half or full portions, so you can try lots of dishes. Cervantes is still humble but now vastly popular; the newest bar of the quartet, La Taberna de Cervantes, sits opposite and is often less busy.

LA FÁBULA RESTAURANTE

ANDALUCÍA | $$$ | GASTRONOMY

Calle de San Antón 28, Granada; 958 25 01 50; www.restaurantelafabula.com; mains €24-34, tasting menus €80-95

It's hard to avoid the pun: Fábula is pretty fabulous. A formal restaurant set in the refined confines of the boutique Hotel Villa Oniria, it's the domain of chef Ismael Delgado López, whose artfully composed plates of contemporary Spanish cuisine will impress. Rock comes with artichokes and almonds, and lamb with avocado and baby onions.

PALACIO DE GALLEGO

ANDALUCÍA | $$ | SPANISH
Calle de Santa Catalina 5, Baeza; 667 76 01 84; www.palaciodegallego.com; mains €15-32

In the atmospheric setting of a 16th-century house, with tables on the delightful patio as well as in an old wood-beamed dining room, the Gallego serves up superb meat and fish dishes, barbecued and otherwise – lamb, beef, pork, octopus and morcilla are among the substantial options. There's a list of well over 100 Spanish wines, and you won't come across many starters better than the goat's cheese, orange and walnut salad. It's in the handsome country town of Baeza, which is home to some lovely renaissance buildings.

4 NUDOS

ANDALUCÍA | $$ | SEAFOOD
Puerto Deportivo, San José; 620 93 81 60; www.4nudosrestaurante.com; mains €15-20

San José has some great seafood restaurants, and the 'Four Knots' is the star. Aptly housed in the Club Náutico at the marina, it serves classic Spanish dishes – paella included – alongside more innovative creations such as baby-prawn ceviche and tuna marinated in soy sauce, ginger and rosemary.

CENADOR DE LAS MONJAS

CASTILLA-LA MANCHA | $$ | SPANISH
Calle de las Monjas, Pastrana; 949 37 01 01; www.cenadordelasmonjas.es; mains €12-20, set menus €35-40

The dining room in the 16th-century San José monastery offers beautifully prepared Spanish food that is anything but austere. Sit under a wood-beamed ceiling, overlooked by oil paintings of

BRUNO ABARCA/GETTY IMAGES ©

This page: Alley in Las Alpujarras. Opposite page: Bar-Restaurante Eslava.

COURTESY BAR-RESTAURANTE ESLAVA

severe-looking nobility and indulge in venison meatballs or tuna with a honey glaze. Abiding by monastic tradition, most of the vegetables are grown here.

BAR TORRECILLA

LA RIOJA | $ | PINTXOS

Calle Laurel 15, Logroño; 608 34 46 94; pintxos from €2

La Rioja is almost as well known for its food as its wine, and this bar in the atmospheric capital of Logroño might just have the best pintxos in town. Go for the melt-in-your-mouth foie gras or the mini-burgers, or anything else that strikes your fancy, at this modern bar on buzzing Calle del Laurel.

BAR JAVI

CANTABRIA | $ | TAPAS

Ardigales 42, Castro Urdiales; 942 78 35 30; www.barjavi.com; pintxos €2.50-3

¡Advertencia! The warning on the napkins at this sweet tapas bar in the seaside town of Castro Urdiales says it all: 'We take no responsibility for addiction to our pintxos'. Indeed, with daily specials ranging from delicately fried baby-squid croquettes to smoked turbot and codfish with braised mushrooms – all accompanied by reasonably priced glasses of top-quality wine – it's hard not to get hooked.

WHERE TO DRINK...

SHERRY

Tabanco El Pasaje, Jeréz
This 1945 institution has an excellent sherry selection, simple tapas and suitably raw flamenco sessions.

Taberna Manolo Cateca, Seville
Tiny, authentic spot with over 200 sherries by the glass, plus a meat- and cheese-heavy tapas spread.

Bodegas Osborne, El Puerto de Santa María
This gorgeous whitewashed *bodega*, home to the historic Osborne sherry winery, offers daily tours with tastings.

La Venencia, Madrid
Manzanilla (chamomile-coloured sherry) from Sanlúcar and sherry from Jeréz are poured straight from dusty wooden barrels at this atmospheric but low-key gem.

RESTAURANTE AMELIBIA

BASQUE COUNTRY | $$ | SPANISH
Barbacana 14, Laguardia; 945 62 12 07; www.restauranteamelibia.com; mains €15-22

This classy restaurant is one of the highlights of the medieval fortress town of Laguardia. Here, you can gaze out the windows at a view over scorched plains and distant mountain ridges while dining on sublime traditional cuisine. Think oxtail and wild mushrooms in red wine sauce, or boneless pork on a bed of apples.

LA VIÑA DEL ENSANCHE

BILBAO | $ | PINTXOS
Calle de la Diputación 10; 944 15 56 15; www.lavinadelensanche.com; small plates €5-15, set menu €35

Set with old-fashioned wood-panelled walls and framed postcards written by adoring fans over the years, La Viña del Ensanche remains one of Bilbao's best eating spots – no small achievement for a place that has been in business since 1927. Mouth-watering morsels of ham, tender octopus and crispy asparagus tempura are just a few of the many temptations.

BAR BORDA BERRI

BASQUE COUNTRY | $ | PINTXOS
Calle de Fermín Calbetón 12, San Sebastián; 943 43 03 42; pintxos from €2.50

The uber-popular Bar Borda Berri is a pintxos bar that really lives up to the hype. Amid mustard-coloured walls hung with old photos and strands of garlic, hungry diners crowd in for house specials like braised veal cheeks in wine, mushroom and idiazabal (a sheep cheese) risotto, and the decadent octopus.

MARTÍN BERASATEGUI RESTAURANT

BASQUE COUNTRY | $$$ | BASQUE
Calle Loidi 4, Lasarte-Oria; 943 36 64 71; www.martinberasategui.com; tasting menu €285, mains €75-88

This superlative restaurant, about 9km southwest of San Sebastián, holds three Michelin stars and is considered one of the best in the world. Chef Martín Berasategui approaches cuisine as a science – which means vibrant reductions, slashes of jus and bubbling froth, plus top-notch ingredients and exquisite presentation. The results are tastes you never knew existed. Hake loin and jaw comes with a cayenne and coffee; red mullet with saffron, fennel and squid ink.

CASA PARDINA

ARAGÓN | $$ | ARAGONESE
Calle Medio, Alquézar; 660 39 94 72; www.casapardina.com; set menus €31-40

Alquézar is a magnificent place, its tight labyrinth of streets coiled above the steep cliffs of the plunging Río Vero gorge. This very special restaurant offers lovely village views and traditional Aragonese home cooking, yet also exudes contemporary creativity. The setting is all soothing stonework and twinkling chandeliers, while the many dishes to choose from include slow-roast lamb, stewed venison with dates and honey, and a salad of mango, orange and smoked cod.

EL PASAJE DE ZABALBURU

MURCIA REGION | $ | TAPAS
Plaza San Pedro 3, Murcia; 622 62 21 67; www.facebook.com/elpasajedezabalburu; tapas €4-12

It's difficult to imagine tastier tapas than the inventive, exquisite creations at this bar on the west side of Murcia's strollable centre. Grab a pew at the long bar and enjoy fabulous fare presented with flair. Seafood is especially good here, with stellar grilled calamari, and you have to try the house speciality, pelochos – ham croquettes with a spiky noodle coating.

BAR GAUCHO

NAVARRA | $ | PINTXOS
Espoz y Mina 7, Pamplona; pintxos €2-5

This bustling bar serves multi-award-winning pintxos that, despite some serious competition, many a local will tell you are the finest in the city. Highlights include octopus with potato, egg with truffles and sea urchin served in its own shell.

EL PORTAL

ALICANTE | $$$ | SPANISH
Calle Bilbao 2; 965 14 44 44; www.elportaltaberna.com; mains €15-25, menus €39-70

Excellent in every way, this plush corner spot sports deliberately over-the-top decor that changes biannually but is always interesting. Grab a table or squeeze up at the bar to enjoy some of the Mediterranean coast's finest produce. Plump prawns, excellent tuna, fresh fish, mouthwatering ham; it's a feast for the palate. Excellent wines are available by the glass. The atmosphere is smart but relaxed with a DJ responding to the mood as seafood makes way for gin and tonics later in the day.

EL POBLET

VALENCIA | $$$ | GASTRONOMY
Calle de Correos 8; 961 11 11 06; www.elpobletrestaurante.com; weekday 3-course menu €62, degustation menu €125

This upstairs restaurant, overseen by famed Quique Dacosta and with Luis Valls as chef, offers elegance and fine gastronomic dining at prices that are very competitive for this quality. Modern French and Spanish influences combine to create sumptuous menus – the main degustation menu might see cured meats followed by blue-crab mochi, a classic cuttlefish stew and roasted peach. Some of the imaginative presentation has to be seen to be believed, and staff are genuinely welcoming and helpful.

WHERE TO EAT...

CHURROS

Chocolatería de San Ginés, Madrid
Popular with tourists during the day and clubbers in the early hours, this is one of the places to eat these sugary doughnuts with hot chocolate.

La Granja, Barcelona
Combines history (it dates back to 1872 and has a section of Roman wall at the back) with doughy churros and speciality coffees.

Casa Aranda, Málaga
Sat by the market, this cafe's sweet pastries and rich hot chocolate have proved so popular it's now taken over an entire alleyway.

Horchatería de Santa Catalina, Valencia
For churros with a twist: here buns known as fartóns can be dipped into a sweet, opaque drink made from tiger nuts called horchata.

NAVARRO

VALENCIA | $$ | VALENCIAN

Calle del Arzobispo Mayoral 5; 963 52 96 23; www.restaurantenavarro.com; rices €15-18

Valencia is the home of paella, and Navarro is the place to come for it. It's been a byword for the dish for decades, and is now run by the grandchildren of the original founders. It's open for lunch only, offering meat and fish dishes as well as its famous rice dishes (best ordered a day in advance). There's outdoor seating and helpful service.

DISFRUTAR

BARCELONA | $$$ | MODERN EUROPEAN

Carrer de Villarroel 163; 933 48 68 96; www.disfrutarbarcelona.com; tasting menus €155-195

Disfrutar ('Enjoy' in Catalan) is among the city's finest restaurants, with two Michelin stars. Run by alumni of Ferran Adrià's game-changing (now closed) El Bulli restaurant, nothing is as it seems, such as black and green olives that are actually chocolate ganache with orange-blossom water. The decor is fabulously on point, with latticed brickwork and trademark geometric ceramics from Catalan design team

COURTESY CASA DELFIN

This page: Casa Delfín. Opposite page: Seafood stew from Casa Delfín, Casa Delfín.

COURTESY CASA DELFIN

Equipo Creativo, and the service is faultless.

CASA DELFÍN

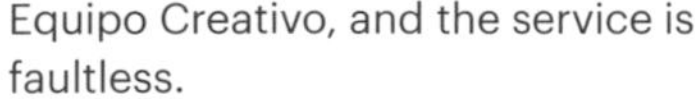

BARCELONA | $$ | CATALAN
Passeig del Born 36; 933 19 50 88; www.casadelfinrestaurant.com; tapas €5-12, mains €12-20

Casa Delfín is everything you dream about Mediterranean cooking in a traditional, wine-bottle-lined setting, with spot-on service and creative presentation lending a contemporary touch. Menus change depending on market produce, but might offer salt-strewn Padrón peppers, plump anchovies from L'Escala, suquet dels pescadors (Catalan fish stew) for two or hearty meat dishes such as roasted mountain lamb sprinkled with rosemary and thyme. For the finale, try the cheese-

'The dining room of a restaurant provides a cohesion few places can emulate. It is a universe of emotional connections, enriched with the feedback of proximity.'
El Celler de Can Roca

cake with a pistachio-biscuit base drizzled with a tangy mandarin sauce.

LA COVA FUMADA

BARCELONA | $ | TAPAS
Carrer del Baluard 56; 932 21 40 61; tapas €2-12

There's no sign and the setting is functional, but this tiny, buzzing family-run tapas spot always packs in a crowd. The secret? Mouth-watering pulpo (octopus), calamari, sardines, bombas (meat and potato croquettes served with aioli) and grilled carxofes (artichokes) cooked in the open kitchen. Everything is amazingly fresh.

COURTESY CASA DELFIN

LES COLS

CATALONIA | $$$ | CATALAN

Carretera de la Canya, Olot; 972 26 92 09; www.lescols.com; degustation menu €115

Set in a converted 19th-century masia (farmhouse) in lush, volcanic La Garrotxa, Les Cols is the queen of the region's fabulous restaurants. The interior has an avant-garde edge, with glass walls and glittery-gold decor. Two-Michelin-starred chef Fina Puigdevall's dishes are powered by local produce and prepared with a silken touch, from cooked and raw wild mushrooms to pork chop with quince and acorn.

EL CELLER DE CAN ROCA

COSTA BRAVA | $$$ | CATALAN

Carrer Can Sunyer 48, Girona; 972 22 21 57; www.cellercanroca.com; degustation menus €190-215

Ever-changing avant-garde takes on Catalan dishes have catapulted El Celler de Can Roca to global fame. Holding three Michelin stars, it was named the best restaurant in the world in 2013, 2015 and 2018. Each year brings new innovations, from molecular gastronomy to multi-sensory food-art interplay to sci-fi dessert trolleys, all with mama's home cooking as the core inspiration. Run by the three Girona-born Roca brothers, El Celler is set in a refurbished country house, 2km northwest of central Girona. Book online 11 months in advance or join the standby list.

GIRI CAFÉ

IBIZA | $$ | SPANISH

Plaça d'Espanya 5, San Juan; 971 33 34 74; www.cafe.thegiri.com; mains €12-28

This stunning cafe-restaurant, with an exquisitely stylish rustic-chic interior and a blissful garden, ticks all the right progressive foodie boxes: seasonal, locally sourced, sustainably produced and mainly organic ingredients. It walks the walk too: from Iberian ham platters and rosemary-sprinkled chips to falafel burgers and flamed sea bass drizzled with coconut sauce, these are imaginative and beautifully presented dishes. It's closed in the winter.

SA FÀBRICA DE GELATS

MALLORCA | $ | ICE CREAM

Avinguda de Cristòfol Colom 13, Sóller; www.gelatsoller.com; ice cream per scoop €1.30

This legendary ice cream shop offers around 40 trays of locally made flavours. Sóller has been known for its citrus groves for almost a thousand years, and fittingly enough the varieties using fresh orange or lemon juice are outstanding. There's a small patio with a handful of tables.

ANDORRA

Andorran cuisine is influenced by Catalonia first and France second. Hearty dishes revolve around earthy flavours and seasonal ingredients, like wild mushrooms, *cargols* (snails), mountain meats (including boar), and trout, served grilled with ham. *Pa amb tomàquet* (bread with tomato, garlic and oil) is another favourite.

BODEGA POBLET

ANDORRA LA VELLA | $$ | TAPAS

Carrer de l'Alzinaret 6; 862 722; tapas €6.50-17

Red walls, tall tables and scattered art create a casually fashionable vibe at this welcoming spot, specialising in creative, international bite-sized delights. Artistically presented dishes burst with flavour, including veggie-filled nems, zesty salads served in enormous golden bowls and deconstructed pa amb tomàquet (bread with tomato, garlic and oil). Staff are delightful, and there's a popular set lunch menu.

BORDA ESTEVET

ANDORRA LA VELLA | $$ | CATALAN

Carretera de la Comella 2; 864 026; www.bordaestevet.com; mains €15-25

This excellent place, at the southwest end of Andorra's busy capital, offers meaty, seasonal mountain fare with a strong Catalan twist. Highlights include steaks, cod and classic Catalan trinxat (potato and cabbage with a pork garnish). Conclude a great eating experience with a digestif from the liqueur-loaded table.

TABERNA ÁNGEL BELMONTE

ANDORRA LA VELLA | $$ | CATALAN

Carrer Ciutat de Consuegra 3; 822 460; www.tabernaangelbelmonte.com; mains €15-25

Feast on well-executed Catalan favourites showcasing seasonal ingredients at this friendly tavern-style restaurant, tucked back from busy Avinguda de Mertixell on the south side of the river. The cosily rustic wood-lined dining room sets the tone for the hearty likes of onion soup, mushroom ravioli, seafood paella and grilled mountain meats, and there are plenty of daily specials to choose from.

WHAT TO EAT

Escudella
This hearty stew of meat and vegetables is the Andorran national dish, and is particularly popular in winter. Typical ingredients include chicken, veal, meatballs, pork, potatoes, cabbage, chickpeas and pasta.

Embotits
These cured pork sausages and hams come in various forms, including *longaniza*, *donja*, *bisbe* and *morcilla*.

Crema Andorrana
This rich custard dish is closely related to the French crème brûlée and Catalan *crema Catalana* and is topped with whipped cream, in honour of Andorra's snowy terrain.

Chicory salad
A popular summer dish, in which chicory from the hillsides is combined with bacon and nuts.

PRICE RANGES

Main course:
$ less than €12
$$ €12–20
$$$ €20 or more

Tipping: 10%

FRANCE

Epicureans have a gourmet ball feasting on the natural flavours, regional variety and cooking styles of French cuisine. Seasonal ingredients – sourced from aromatic street markets, seaside oyster farms, sun-baked olive groves and ancient vineyards – are phenomenal. Then there are the chefs, in timeless village cafes, historic brasseries, modern neobistros and gastronomic temples, who combine the priceless know-how of earlier generations with the explosive creativity of the contemporary French kitchen to astonishing effect.

WHAT TO EAT

Andouillette
This fat, feisty sausage packs a punch with its rough-cut, pig-intestine packed body and cloying meaty aroma.

Escargots de Bourgogne
Snails in their shells, baked with garlic and parsley butter, are a Burgundy classic. Prize out the chewy gastropod and mop up the oil with bread.

Confit de canard
Seasoned duck joints are simmered for hours, then conserved in their own fat for months.

Macarons
Smartie-smooth and crafted in a rainbow of zany colours and flavours, ganache-filled *macarons* are made from whisked egg whites, sugar and almonds. Ladurée and Pierre Hermé are synonymous with France's finest.

PRICE RANGES
For a two-course meal:
$ less than €20
$$ €20–40
$$$ €40 or more

Tipping: 10%

LE VERRE VOLÉ

PARIS | $ | WINE BAR

67 rue de Lancry, 10e; 01 48 03 17 34; www.leverrevole.fr; mains €11-22

The tiny 'Stolen Glass' – a *cave* (wine cellar) with a few tables a hop and a skip from the fashionable Canal Saint-Martin – is one of Paris' most popular wine bar–restaurants, with outstanding natural and unfiltered wines and expert advice. Unpretentious, hearty *plats du jour* are excellent. Reserve in advance for meals, or stop by to pick up a gourmet sandwich (such as mustard-smoked burrata with garlic-pork sausage) and a bottle to enjoy canal-side.

BERTHILLON

PARIS | $ | ICE CREAM

29-31 & 46 rue St-Louis en l'Île, 4e; 01 43 54 31 61; www.berthillon.fr; cones from €3

Grab a cone to take away or linger in the timber-fronted *salon de thé* over a sumptuous sundae topped with whipped cream and fruit coulis at Paris' most esteemed glacier (ice-cream maker), on Île Saint Louis since 1954. Tempting seasonal flavours in

its 70-strong repertoire of all-natural, chemical-free embrace fruit sorbets (pink grapefruit, raspberry and rose) and velvety ice creams (salted caramel, candied Ardèche chestnuts, Armagnac and prunes, gingerbread).

LADURÉE PICNIC

PARIS | $ | DELI

15 rue Linois, 15e; 01 70 22 45 20; www.laduree.fr; breakfast/lunch menu €14.50/9.50, sandwiches/salads from €2.40/5.50

Ladurée Picnic specialises in exceedingly fine, gourmet picnics to take away in the celebrated Parisian pâtisserie's signature peppermint-green packaging. Luxury salads include lobster or aromatic salmon; mineral waters are flavoured ginger-coriander or mint-cucumber; and the rainbow of cakes and macarons included as dessert in good-value lunch deals are out of this world. Should you be in the market for breakfast, a croissant aux noix (walnut croissant) washed down with a goji berry and pomegranate juice is always a good idea.

THE FRENCH BASTARDS

PARIS | $ | BAKERY

61 rue Oberkampf, 11e; pastries from €1.50

Far from being irreverently named, this new generation Parisian bakery is evocative of the bâtard – a loaf with no definite shape. Casting an innovative spin on traditional French breads and pastries is what The French Bastards

PREMIER PHOTO/SHUTTERSTOCK ©

does. Watch savvy globetrotting bakers Emmanuel, Julian and David at work crafting cruffins (hybrid croissant-muffin), pains au chocolat-banane, snail-shaped cinnamon scrolls et al. Gourmet sandwiches too for bucolic picnics on the banks of nearby Canal St-Martin.

BALAGAN

PARIS | $$ | MIDDLE EAST

9 rue d'Alger, 1er; 01 40 20 72 14; www.balagan-paris.com; mains €24-34

Cool navy-blue-and-cream diamond tiling contrasts with the joyous party vibe bursting forth at this achingly trendy, Israeli–Middle Eastern club-style restaurant near the Jardin du Luxembourg. The Experimental group (of cocktail club fame) is the creative talent behind this sassy address and Balagan's adjoining cocktail bar provides

WHERE TO EAT...

CHEESE

Fromagerie Laurent Dubois, Paris
Buy unusual delicacies such as truffle-spiked St-Félicien, and rare, limited-production French cheeses like blue Termignon at this world-class *fromagerie* (cheese shop) in the capital.

Les Halles de Lyon Paul Bocuse, Lyon
Pick up a round of runny St Marcellin from legendary cheesemaker Mère Richard at Lyon's celebrated indoor food market.

Cooperative Fruitère Val d'Arly, Chamonix
A shopfront for 70 artisanal producers, this Savoy dairy stocks Reblochon, Raclette, Tomme de Savoie and other Savoyard cheeses.

La Ferme Bellonte, St-Nectaire
Buy cheese from the source and watch it being made at this multi-generational dairy farm in the Auvergne, central France.

the perfect dinner prelude. Tuck into deconstructed kebabs or onion confit Ashkenazi chicken liver, followed perhaps by octopus in red wine or smoked chicken with a mountain of herbs.

AU PASSAGE

PARIS | $$ | BISTRO
1bis passage St-Sébastien, 11e; 01 43 55 07 52; www.restaurant-aupassage.fr; small plates €8-24, meats to share €25-70

Rising-star chefs continue to make their name at this petit bar de quartier (little neighbourhood bar), with a timeless shabby-chic décor and 'punkitude' Spanish chef Luis Miguel Tavares Andrade currently in the kitchen. Choose from gourmet petites assiettes (tapas-style plates) of cold meats, raw or cooked fish, vegetables and so on, alongside feisty cuts of meat (slow-roasted lamb shoulder, rib-eye steak etc) to share. The choice of natural wines to accompany is exquisite.

SEPTIME

PARIS | $$$ | GASTRONOMY
80 rue de Charonne, 11e; 01 43 67 38 29; www.septime-charonne.fr; lunch/dinner menus from €60/95

This bijou neobistro in the edgy 11e arrondissement is a beacon of modern French cuisine. Alchemists in Bertrand Grébaut's Michelin-starred kitchen produce truly beautiful creations, served by blue-aproned waitstaff in a down-to-earth, veering-on-rustic interior. The menu reads like a curious shopping list: each dish is a provocative listing of three ingredients, while the mystery carte blanche dinner menu places diners in the hands of the innovative chef. Table reservations open three weeks in advance.

RESTAURANT GUY SAVOY

PARIS | $$$ | GASTRONOMY
11 quai de Conti, 6e; 01 43 80 40 61; www.guysavoy.com; lunch/dinner menus €130-250/478

The world-famous French chef at this triple-Michelin-star temple to gastronomy needs no introduction (he trained Gordon Ramsay, among others). Guy Savoy's flagship seduces with a sweeping red-carpeted staircase and a string of supremely elegant old-world dining rooms bejewelled with contemporary art works in Paris' historic mint, the 18th-century Monnaie de Paris. Monumental cuisine includes Savoy icons such as iced poached oysters and artichoke soup with black truffle and a layered truffle mushroom brioche.

LE VIVIER

BRITTANY | $ | SEAFOOD
rte du Prado, Côte Sauvage; 02 97 50 12 60; mains €9-30

The seafood is superb but almost secondary at this convivial but busy eatery, dramatically perched on a small cliff a short walk from Quiberon on Brittany's blustery Côte Sauvage. Bookings are essential for the top tables, squeezed onto a sunny terrace

Previous spread: Le Marais; cheese counter in the Bastille district.

hovering above the rocky coastline. The menu is plain and unpretentious – think fish soup, salads, mussels, smoked fish and tangy Breton oysters. End your meal with a dramatic meander down onto to the rocks to lap up the stunning surrounding scenery.

BREIZH CAFÉ

BRITTANY | $ | BRETON
6 rue de l'Orme, St-Malo; 02 99 56 96 08; www.breizhcafe.com; crêpes €10-15

Crêperie and cider bar Breizh Café might be fast becoming international, with outposts in Paris and Tokyo, but it is in St-Malo that the source of all that Breton crêpe-and-cider magic lies. Breton ingredients (local ham, organic eggs) fuse with Japanese flavours (seasoned pickles, seaweed, roast duck) to create a fabulous dining experience. Finish with a transcendent Amuse-Crêpe: a sushi-styled crêpe roll filled with melted Valrhona chocolate and ginger-spiced salted caramel.

L'ASSIETTE CHAMPENOISE

CHAMPAGNE | $$$ | GASTRONOMY
40 av Paul-Vaillant-Couturier, Tinqueux, Reims; 03 26 84 64 64; www.assiettechampenoise.com; lunch/dinner menus from €115/215

Heralded as one of Champagne's and France's finest tables, triple Michelin-starred L'Assiette Champenoise showcases the cuisine of chef Arnaud Lallement. His intricate creative dishes rely on exceptional seasonal French produce: scallops, sea urchins and turbot from Brittany, Marseillais green asparagus, milk-fed veal sweetbreads, truffles. Dining is formal, in a contemporary design interior with shimmering glass chandeliers and an al fresco terrace for aperitifs and after-dinner coffee.

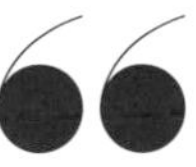

'Cuisine is the art of instantly transforming products rich with history into joy.'
Guy Savoy

CHEZ AUGUSTE

ALSACE | $ | BISTRO
11 rue Poincaré, Mulhouse; 03 89 46 62 71; menus €20-25

Overflowing with regulars, this casually sophisticated bistro in downtown Mulhouse always has a brilliant buzz. The concise menu excels in French classics, including scallops with orange-infused carrot purée and pistachio, confit pork cheeks slow-cooked for six hours, and an outrageously decadent, chocolate fondant to die for. Service is faultless.

AUBERGE DU PARC CAROLA

ALSACE | $$ | INTERNATIONAL
48 rte de Bergheim, Ribeauvillé; 03 89 86 05 75; www.auberge-parc-carola.com; menus €32-64

Quaint on the outside, slick on the inside, this picture-postcard auberge (country inn) is all about surprises. Much-lauded young German chef Michaela Peters is behind the stove, and flavours ring true in seasonal show-stoppers like roe deer with spiced red cabbage and Black Forest ham, and

RICHARD SEMIK/SHUTTERSTOCK ©

Alsatian wild boar tartine with Granny Smith apples. Tables spill outside beneath trees in warm weather – a bucolic setting for a long and lazy, quintessentially French summer lunch.

MA TABLE EN VILLE

BURGUNDY | $$ | BURGUNDIAN

50 rue de Strasbourg, Mâcon; 03 85 30 99 91; www.matableenville.fr; lunch/dinner menus from €19/41

Balancing gastronomy with a warm welcome, this husband-and-wife venture is a gem. Chef Gilles Bérard brings decades of experience in some of France's finest Michelin-starred restaurants to his market-fresh menus (Burgundy snails in red wine or duck filet in a blackcurrant vinegar sauce anyone?), while Laurence attends to diners in the contemporary dining room sporting bright artwork and fiery orange cushions. Wine lovers note: her knowledge of Mâconnais vintages by artisan producers is exhaustive.

LA MAISON DES CARIATIDES

BURGUNDY | $$$ | FRENCH

28 rue de la Chaudronnerie, Dijon; 03 80 45 59 25; www.thomascollomb.fr/la-maison-des-cariatides; lunch menus €19-25, mains €14-28

This 17th-century mansion with original beamed ceiling, soft-cream exposed

This page: Vergisson village and surrounding vineyards, Burgundy. Opposite page: Spicy French sausages, Lyon market.

stone walls and a refined modern decor (think on-trend scrubbed-wood tables, over-sized lampshades and open kitchen) is a much-loved spot in Burgundy's dashingly handsome capital for savouring top-of-the-line French and regional cuisine, complemented by an extensive selection of Burgundian wines. In warm weather the gourmet action spills onto a pretty terrace out back.

AU 14 FÉVRIER

BEAUJOLAIS | $$$ | FUSION
Le Plâtre Durant, St-Amour Bellevue; 03 85 37 11 45; www.sa-au14fevrier.com; menus €82-120

For a gastronomic experience in the Beaujolais area, reserve a table at this pearl of a fusion restaurant in the wine-producing village of St-Amour Bellevue, southwest of Mâcon. A true alchemist, Japanese chef Masafumi Hamano's magic formula lies in fusing French with Japanese to create a stunning colourful cuisine, perfectly matched with French wines. Dining is in a traditional maison de village, quaint outside, modern inside.

LE MUSÉE

LYON | $$ | BOUCHON
2 rue des Forces, 2e; 04 78 37 71 54; menus €19-32

Housed in the stables of the former Hôtel de Ville (city hall) in France's foodie capital Lyon, The Museum is the perfect example of a *bouchon* (Lyonnais bistro). Among the splendid array of meat-heavy Lyonnais classics on the daily-changing menu is a divine *poulet au vinaigre* (chicken cooked in vinegar) and several scrumptious desserts, all served on cute china plates at shared family-style tables. Don't miss the after-dinner tour of the *traboule* (passageway) out back conducted by the bistro's gregarious owner.

'We strive to honour French traditions in the experience ... pouring sauce on desserts at the table, suggesting Medoc Grands Crus wines by the glass to make them accessible ...'
Café Lavinia!

CINQ MAINS

LYON | $$ | NEOBISTRO
12 rue Monseigneur Lavarenne, 5e; 04 37 57 30 52; www.facebook.com/cinqmains; menus €20-35

When young Lyonnais Grégory Cuilleron and friends opened this neobistro in Vieux Lyon in 2016, it was an instant hit. And the new generation team continues to lure savvy foodies to their cool loft-like space with exposed stone

walls, taupe palette and enchanting mezzanine wholly evocative of Lyonnais architecture. Tantalizing, seasonal creations on the weekly-changing menu reflect what's at the market – contemporary Lyonnais bistronomie cuisine at its finest.

LE VIEUX LOGIS

DORDOGNE | $$$ | REGIONAL FRENCH

Trémolat; 05 53 22 80 06; www.vieux-logis.com; menus €55-130

Foodies travel from far and wide to experience Michelin-starred chef Vincent Arnould's refined, beautifully presented creative cuisine of the Périgord. The ceiling soars over the elegant dining room – a former tobacco drying barn – and summertime dining is alfresco beneath a canopy of sculpted trees. Every dish is a surprising treat, and the wine list matches. Winter ushers in elaborate dishes based around the region's black truffles.

GAROPAPILLES

BORDEAUX | $$ | NEOBISTRO

62 rue Abbé de l'Épée; 09 72 45 55 36; www.garopapilles.com; lunch/dinner menus from €35/ €90

Reservations are essential at this Michelin-starred neobistro with just 20 covers where vins d'auteur (carefully curated wines by small regional wine producers) accompany chef Tanguy Laviale's sensational market-driven cuisine à la hauteur (an elevated, tip-top cuisine). Dining is in an elegant, streamlined interior with dark wood flooring and little decorative distraction. In summer lunch is served in a bucolic, herb-fragranced courtyard garden.

LA TUPINA

BORDEAUX | $$$ | FRENCH

6 rue Porte de la Monnaie; 05 56 91 56 37; www.latupina.com; lunch/dinner menus from €18/64

Filled with the homely aroma of soup simmering inside a tupina ('kettle' in Basque) over an open fire, this vintage bistro opened by the gregarious Jean-Pierre Xiradakis in 1968 is feted for its southwestern French fare: calf kidneys with fries cooked in goose fat, milk-fed lamb, tripe, goose wings, Bordeaux's very own eel-like lamprey in red wine. Dining is old-world farmhouse-style, in several small elegant rooms decorated with B&W photographs, antique furniture and silverware.

CAFÉ LAVINAL

GIRONDE | $$ | FRENCH

place Desquet, Bages; 05 57 75 00 09; www.jmcazes.com/en/cafe-lavinal; menus €29-39

With Michelin-starred chef Julien Lefebvre from nearby Château Cordeillan-Bages in southwest France's prestigious Médoc wine region overseeing the menu and some 120 wines on the carte de vin, a brilliant bistro experience is guaranteed at this local winemakers' hangout in Bages, near Pauillac. Retro red banquet seating and a zinc bar evoke the 1930s and the menu mixes French classics (snails, veal kidneys, magret de canard, fish stew) with burgers, salads and charcuterie platters.

LA TERRASSE ROUGE

GIRONDE | $$ | FRENCH

1 Château La Dominique, St-Émilion; 05 57 24 47 05; www.laterrasserouge.com; menu €39

Dining on the chic terrace overlooking a field of Bordeaux-red glass pebbles and a sea of pea-green vines beyond at this vineyard restaurant is sublime. The Red Terrace was borne out of Jean Nouvel's designer revamp of Château La Dominique's wine cellars near St-Émilion wine region, and both menu and ambiance venerate local viticulture. Chefs source seasonal local produce to fuel inventive dishes (smoked Aquitaine sturgeon in lemon and chervil cream) and regional classics (lamproie à la Bordelaise or lamprey stew).

HÔTEL DE LA PLAGE

ATLANTIC COAST | $$ | FRENCH

1 av de l'Herbe, L'Herbe, Cap Ferret; 05 56 60 50 15; www.hoteldelaplage-cap-ferret.fr; mains €14-25

Built in the 1860s to feed and accommodate the first oyster farmers who came to settle on Cap Ferret, this attractive wooden mansion in the tiny oyster-farming village of L'Herbe on oozes historic charm and story. Bordelais restaurateur Nicolas Lascombes is the creative nous behind the hipster restaurant today, known far and wide for its seasonal oyster bar, seafood dishes, nod to tradition and buzzing beach vibe.

LA CO(O)RNICHE

ATLANTIC COAST | $$ | SEAFOOD

46 av Louis Gaume, Pyla-sur-Mer; 05 56 22 72 11; www.lacoorniche-pyla.com; lunch menus €63-68, seafood platters €40-85

There's no more glamorous address on the Atlantic Coast than this 1930s hunting lodge, reinvented by French designer Philippe Starck at the foot of the golden Dune du Pilat. Reserve a table by the infinity pool to feast on bold views of Europe's biggest sand dune and extravagant seafood platters piled high with lobster, crab, oysters, winkles, clams and other tasty crustaceans.

PICKLES

NANTES | $$ | MODERN FRENCH

2 rue du Marais; www.pickles-restaurant.com; lunch/dinner menus from €18/46

This inventive neobistro could be in Paris. Market-sourced, modern and wholly creative cuisine by English chef Dominic Quirke (a Newcastle lad wed to a French lass) is sensational. Dining is around tightly packed bistro tables or at a table d'hôte–style bar, and Dom invariably pops out the kitchen to chat food. Think beef pastrami with mackerel, walnuts and chicory perhaps

WHERE TO EAT...

FRENCH PÂTISSERIE

Jacques Genin, Paris
Velvety hot chocolate marries with an assembled-to-order *millefeuille* at the tearoom in the Le Marais showroom of wildly creative *chocolatier* and *pâtissier* Genin.

L'Éclair de Génie, Paris
Pastry chef Christophe Adam revisits the classic éclair. Like fashion, flavours change with the seasons.

L'Ourson qui Boit – Pâtisserie, Lyon
Japanese chef-in-Lyon Akira Nishigaki blends French savoir-faire with Japanese flavours to create yuzu tarts, green-tea cream filled *choux* (pastry puffs) and other sublime pastries.

Mireille Oster, Strasbourg
Handmade varieties of traditional Alsatian *pain d'épices* (gingerbread).

followed by quince spiked with chocolate, lime and black garlic.

LE SUQUET

LANGUEDOC-ROUSSILLON | $$$ | GASTRONOMY

rte de l'Aubrac, Laguiole; 05 65 51 18 20; www.brs.fr; menus €145-230, mains €49-90

Originally opened by superstar chef Michel Bras in the village of Laguiole, the cuisine here is steeped in the rustic, country flavours of his youth, reinvented in all kinds of outlandish ways. Unusual herbs and vegetables dominate and signature dish Le Gargouillou is an explosive fusion of plants like chickweed, pattypan squash and white borage. Now run by son Sébastien, it is worth a trip for the architecture alone: a modernist, plate-glass marvel with soul-soaring views over Aubrac's green hills in southwestern France.

BISTRO À CÔTÉ

CAMARGUE | $$ | BISTRO

21 rue des Carmes, Arles; 04 90 47 61 13; www.bistro-acote.com; menu €33

Gastronomic feasting at the double Michelin-starred flagship L'Atelier of Provençal chef Jean-Luc Rabanel is an undeniable treat. But for sensational bistro dining courtesy of the same chef, revel in this reassuringly casual space with wooden chairs, terrace-style tables and a blackboard menu of solid bistro classics. Dishes ooze that inimitable Rabanel style – go for something like veal with caramelised ginger and wild black Camargue rice, grilled duck breast or the signature salt-crusted *pintade* (guinea fowl).

LE SANGLIER PARESSEUX

PROVENCE | $$ | MODERN FRENCH

Caseneuve, Luberon; 04 90 75 17 70; www.sanglierparesseux.com; 2-/3-/4-course menus €32/39/59

In the heart of the Luberon, a detour to the hilltop village of Caseneuve, a 15-minute drive from Apt, rewards with one of the region's most talked-about tables. The Lazy Boar cooks up an inventive, unfussy, seasonal cuisine – sea bream tartare with kaffir mousse and truffle mayo, pork lacquered in lavender honey, goat cheese ice-cream with sweet onion chutney. The sweeping countryside view from the vine-shaded terrace is equally enthralling.

This page: Navette biscuits. Opposite page: Toulon vineyard.

LA BASTIDE DE MOUSTIERS

PROVENCE | $$$ | GASTRONOMY
chemin de Quinson, Moustiers-Ste-Marie; 04 92 70 47 47; www.bastide-moustiers.com; menus €65-90

As you'd expect from a Michelin-starred restaurant founded by chef supremo Alain Ducasse, this country-side inn with dreamy Provencal views is a temple to French cuisine. Much of the produce featured in his playful amuses bouches, rich sauce-heavy mains and indulgent desserts notably comes from the inn's lush kitchen garden and the velvety dark chocolate lacing many a dessert is crafted in Alain Ducasse's cocoa bean roastery and chocolate workshop in Paris.

PEIXES

NICE | $ | SEAFOOD
4 rue de l'Opéra; 04 93 85 96 15; mains €17-35

Chic modern Peixes ('Fish' in Portuguese) is the latest jewel in the crown of Niçois master restaurateur Armand Crespo. Decked out a white-and-turquoise nautical decor, the dangling fish eyeball light fixtures and murals of a tentacle-haired mermaid ensnaring a fishing boat are quite dazzling. In the open kitchen seafood chefs wave their creative wand to turn fresh local fish is

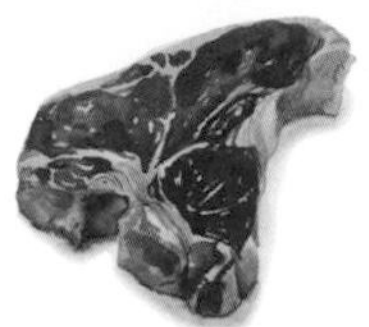

turned into delicious ceviches, tartares and Japanese-style tatakis bursting with world flavours.

RESTAURANT MIRAZUR

FRENCH RIVIERA | $$$ | GASTRONOMY

30 av Aristide Briand, Menton; 04 92 41 86 86; www.mirazur.fr; menus €160-260

Design, cuisine and sea views (the full sweep of the Med) are spectacular at this 1930s villa, northeast of Menton off the coastal road to Italy. This is the culinary kingdom of daring, triple-starred, Argentinian chef Mauro Colagreco who flavours his surprise culinary creations with a mesmerizing rainbow of herbs and flowers from the restaurant's garden, citrus orchard and veg patch. (Curious diners, when booking request a tour with the chief gardener – in itself a rare treat.)

U CASANU

MEDITERRANEAN | $ | CORSICAN

18 bd Wilson, Calvi; 04 95 65 00 10; mains €16-25

For an unforgettable lunch in the Corsican town of Calvi, grab a booth at this cosy hole-in-the-wall, cheerily decorated in yellow and green, and hung with watercolours by septuagenarian artist-owner Monique Luciani. Tuck into home-cooked fish couscous, roast lamb, codfish aioli or octopus salad, and don't miss the exquisite fiadone, a classic Corsican cheesecake made with lemon-scented Brocciu cheese soaked in eau de vie (brandy).

LA SASSA

CORSICA | $$ | GRILL

Tour de Nonza, Nonza; 04 95 38 55 26; www.lasassa.com; mains €20-40

In a magical setting, on a rocky spur immediately below Nonza's Genoese watchtower on Cap Corse, this entirely outdoor, summertime restaurant serves up succulent meat and seafood cooked on an open Argentinian-style grill. Colourfully spot-lit after dark, it puts on live music weekly, with DJs other nights. Both sea views and sunsets are unforgettable.

LE MATAHARI

CORSICA | $$ | SEAFOOD

Plage de l'Arinella, La Balagne; 04 95 60 78 47; www.lematahari.com; mains €18-37, dinner menu €45

White-clothed tables, strung along the sand and topped with straw parasols, evoke a tropical paradise at this romantic Corsican hideaway. It's location: on Plage de l'Arinella, in a serene cove tucked into the rocks, with dramatic views across the bay to the citadel of Calvi. Interior styling is shabby-chic, waiters wear white and boaters, and cuisine is Mediterranean fusion: spiny lobster with pasta, sesame-coated tuna steak, fish teriyaki.

WHAT TO EAT

Les Barbajuans
Deep-fried golden ravioli, stuffed with Swiss chard, ricotta, spinach, onions and rice, first created by a certain Barba Juan (Uncle John in local dialect).

Stockfish à la Monégasque
At the port, tuck into this fishy stew of pungent air-dried cod with tomatoes, red peppers and black olives.

Fougasse
Sweet olive oil- and orange blossom-laced flatbread, peppered with red-and-white sugared aniseed seeds evoking Monaco's country flag.

Petits farcis à la Monégasque
Stuffed vegetables – tomatoes, onions, red peppers and delicate courgette flowers – are served up in most traditional Old Town restaurants.

PRICE RANGES
For a two- or three-course set menu:
€ less than €20
€€ €20–40
€€€ more than €40

Tipping: 5–10%

MONACO

High-rolling, hedonistic Monaco might be the world's second-smallest country, but what it lacks in size it makes up for in attitude – including in its kitchen. Monagésque cuisine spoils with French and Italian nuances, and a dining scene embracing everything from pizza-joint casual to Michclin-starred gastronomy.

MARCHÉ DE LA CONTAMINE

MONACO | $ | MARKET
15 place d'Armes; www.facebook.com/marche-condamine; mains €8-12

Waltz tastebuds through the colourful Nicois, Provencal and Italian influences of Monégasque cuisine at this down-to-earth food court, tucked behind Monaco's outdoor food market. Highlights tucked into around a shared table include pasta from Maison des Pâtes, *socca* (chickpea pancake) and *pissaladière* (caramelized onion and anchovy tart) from Chez Roger; and pizza and seafood from Le Comptoir.

LA MARÉE

MONACO | $$$ | SEAFOOD
7 ave du Président JF Kennedy; 97 97 80 00; www.lamaree.mc; mains €21-135

La Marée's 'fish & chic' tagline says it all: if you're after seafood with a stunning sea view, then this swish rooftop restaurant at Monaco's Hôtel Port-Plage is the place. From turbot, red mullet, sea bass and monkfish to lavish seafood platters piled high with lobster, oysters, crab and other luxury crustaceans, pescatarians will be properly pampered here. Monaco's jet-set turn out in force for Sunday brunch.

LA MONTGOLFIÈRE

MONACO | $$$ | FUSION
16 rue Basse; 97 98 61 59; www.lamontgolfiere.mc; 3-/4-course dinner menu €49/56

Fresh seasonal produce and a fondness for Asian flavours form the backbone of this small, sought-after address, tucked down an alley in Old Monaco. Escoffier-trained, Monégasque chef Henri Geraci has worked in some of the Riviera's top restaurants, but home is now his own bistro with wife Fabienne front-of-house. Expect local dishes with exotic twists: stockfish, warm rock octopus salad, sensational miso-marinated black cod.

ITALY

Italy is the motherland of the modern culinary experience. No matter who you are or where you're from, Italian cuisine has permeated your palate and therefore your soul. Italy's gastronomic endeavours are copied, recreated and reinvented on every corner of the globe, day and night. But you haven't eaten any of it until you've eaten it in Italy. *Buon appetito!*

WHAT TO EAT

Pizza Napoletana
Rounded dough made from 0 or 00 wheat flour, topped with peeled San Marzano tomatoes and mozzarella cheese, baked for 60 to 90 seconds.

Pasta
Unleavened durum wheat flour (semolina) mixed with water (in the South) or eggs (in the north) and boiled, a staple since the 13th century.

Risotto
Arborio rice cooked with meat, fish, or vegetable broth slow-cooked to a creamy consistency, served with a variety of toppings.

Gelato
Impossibly creamy frozen dessert, similar to ice cream, made with milk and sugar in a palate-spinning variety of flavours.

PRICE RANGES
For two courses and a glass of house wine:
$ less than €25
$$ €25-45
$$$ €45 or more

Tipping: Not customary.

LA BRASSERIE DE BON BEC

VALLE D'AOSTA | $$ | ALPINE
Rue Bourgeois 72, Parco Nazionale del Gran Paradiso; 0165 74 92 88; www.hotelbellevue.it; meals €28-38

Bon Bec serves up outstanding mountain cuisine. Start off with house-smoked trout (sourced from nearby Lillaz) or classic Valdostan polenta, before moving on to grilled Angus beef or rich *tartiflette* (a dish from the Savoy made with potatoes, reblochon cheese, onions and lardons).

OSTERIA DEL BOCCONDIVINO

PIEDMONT | $$ | OSTERIA
Via Mendicità Istruita 14, Bra; 0172 42 56 74; www.boccondivinoslow.it; meals €28-38, set menus €20-24

On the 1st floor of the Slow Food movement's backstreet headquarters, this bottle-lined dining room was the first to be opened by the emerging organisation back in the 1980s. The daily-changing menu is expectedly a picture of precise providence and seasonality, with dishes that are beautifully prepared.

LA PIOLA

PIEDMONT | $$ | PIEDMONTESE
Piazza Risorgimento 4, Alba; 0173 44 28 00; www.lapiola-alba.it; meals €30-45

COURTESY CONSORZIO

The kitchen at La Piola is overseen by one of Italy's most respected chefs, Enrico Crippa. Expect wonderful produce – the vegetables and herbs all come from the family's own garden – and technique, along with a sense-grabbing flair. Don't miss their version of *vitello tonnato* (sliced cold veal and tuna sauce) and *bonet* (chocolate pudding): both the apotheosis of their respective genres.

MORE E MACINE

PIEDMONT | $ | PIEDMONTESE
Via XX Settembre 18, La Morra; 0173 50 03 95; meals €25-30

This is the Piedmontese kitchen at its most essential: come for a mountainous swirl of the signature fine *tajarin* pasta with *ragú*, risotto with whatever vegetable's in season, spicy sauced tongue or sliced octopus. Impressive Barolo by-the-glass list.

CONSORZIO

PIEDMONT | $$ | PIEDMONTESE
Via Monte di Pietà 23, Turin; 011 276 76 61; www.ristoranteconsorzio.it; meals €35-42, set menu €35

At this institution inside Turin's Quadrilatero Romano district, it can be almost impossible to secure a table. Reserve! Everyone is here for the pristinely sourced, spot-on Piedmontese cooking that's so traditional it's innovative.

TRATTORIA DAL BILLY

LIGURIA | $$ | LIGURIAN

'Tradition, local excellence and Slow Food philosophy characterize our osteria. Generational changes guarantee reinterpretation of dishes that keep the foundations of our cuisine intact.'
Andrea Bergesio, Osteria del Boccondivino

COURTESY CONSORZIO

Via Rollandi 122; 0187 92 06 28, Manarola; www.trattoriabilly.com; meals €30-40

Trattoria dal Billy fires up some of the best seafood dishes anywhere in Cinque Terre. Start off with a mixed appetiser platter – featuring 12 different hot and cold dishes (octopus salad, lemon-drizzled anchovies, tuna with sweet onion) – then tuck into lobster pasta or swordfish with black truffle. On clear days, book a table on the terrace for superb views. Reservations essential.

IL PESCATO CUCINATO

LIGURIA | $ | SEAFOOD
Via Colombo 199, Riomaggiore; 339 262 4815; snacks around €6

Riomaggiore's standout street food is a mound of fresh fried seafood – calamari, anchovies, shrimp, cod – stuffed

into a paper cone and served on the go. Take your seafood treat down to the waterfront for million-dollar views.

TRATTORIA DA MARIA

LIGURIA | $$ | TRATTORIA
Vico Testadoro 14r, Genova; 010 25 10 475; meals €10-20

This is a totally authentic, if well touristed, workers' trattoria and there's much squeezing into tiny tables, shouted orders and a fast and furious succession of plates plonked down. A daily hand-scrawled menu is a roll call of elemental favourites that keep all comers full and happy. Cross your fingers for *minestrone alla Genovese*, pesto lasagne or donkey *ragù* – pure Ligurian bliss.

REVELLO

LIGURIA | $ | BAKERY
Via Garibaldi 183, Camogli; 0185 77 07 77; www.revellocamogli.com; focaccia from €2

Revello is a suitably respectable choice if you had to choose just one *focacceria* to try in all of Liguria. Pick up slices of their famed *focaccia di Recco* – a slightly flaky variety stuffed with stracchino cheese – and sit in simple street food bliss by the seaside.

L'IMPERFETTO

SARDINIA | $$ | SARDINIAN
Via dei Genovesi 111, Cagliari; 070 461 99 09; www.facebook.com/imperfettoristorante; meals €30-40

If you have only one swank meal in Sardinia, make it at L'Imperfetto. Tucked into a quiet lane in the Cagliari's Castello district, this arched-stone dining room is both elegant and welcoming, with fantastic, fresh Sardinian fare. It's a chance to try the specialties of the island executed with flair and integrity.

IL TIRABUSCIÒ

SARDINIA | $ | SARDINIAN
Via Rosa Scoti 12, Calangianus; 057 559 54 74; www.tirabuscio.it; meals €30

Sardinian mountain fare at its finest, Il Tirabusciò ('the corkscrew)' is a cosy spot in the quaint village of Calangianus. Expect delicacies like wild-boar raviolini, duck with wild fennel or local artisanal cheeses with preserves.

LA TORRE DEGLI AQUILA

LOMBARDY | $$ | ITALIAN
Corso Strada Nuova 20, Pavia; 0382 2 63 35; www.latorredegliaquila.it; meals €30-40

It is almost worth a trip to Pavia just to eat in Dimo and Maria's medieval tower. Although rooted in tradition (farming sickles and antique pots adorn the walls), the sensational cooking is highly creative. Homemade pistachio bread is followed by tender black bean and potato gnocchi with prawns and sliced sirloin with prunes and *lardo di Colonnata* (lard from Colonnata).

Previous spread: preparing pasta in Consorzio; Consorzio.

LUINI

MILAN | $ | FAST FOOD

Via Santa Radegonda 16; 02 8646 1917; www.luini.it; panzerotti €2.80

This historic joint is the go-to place for *panzerotti*, delicious pizza-dough parcels stuffed with a combination of mozzarella, spinach, tomato, ham or spicy salami, and then fried up or oven baked (fried!).

RATANÀ

MILAN | $$ | MILANESE

Via Gaetano de Castillia 28; 02 8712 8855; www.ratana.it; meals €40-60

This neo-bistro run by chef Cesare Battisti and sommelier Federica Fabi turns out authentic Milanese flavours with a modern touch. Drawing on produce from Slow Food artisans, the menu offers up classics such as risotto *alla milanese* (saffron and bone marrow risotto) and a tender carpaccio of *Piedmontese* Fassona beef.

PASTICCERIA MARCHESI

MILAN | $ | BAKERY

Via Santa Maria alla Porta 11a; 02 86 27 70; www.pasticceriamarchesi.it; pastries from €1.50

Since 1824 the original Marchesi *pasticceria* (pastry shop) has been charming customers with its refined 20th-century features and picture-perfect petits fours. Indulge your sweet tooth with any number of *bignes* (cream puffs), pralines and sugared almonds, and sample some of the best panettone in Milan.

DURNWALD

SOUTH TYROL | $$ | ALPINE

Nikolaus-Amhof-Strasse 6, Val di Casies (Gsiesertal); 0474 74 68 86; meals €30-42

This family-run restaurant, specialising in ultra-fresh, locally sourced seasonal South Tyrolean cuisine, is hidden away in the pastoral South Tyrol's Val di Casies (Gsiesertal). Plates of venison goulash with polenta, pork medallions with chanterelles and porcini, spinach dumplings, house-cured meats and smoked trout mousse are all served with a smile and best finished off with scrumptious desserts such as home-made apple fritters.

CAFFETTERIA TORINESE

FRIULI VENEZIA GIULIA | $$ | ITALIAN

Piazza Grande 9, Palmanova; 0432 92 07 32; www.caffetteriatorinese.com; sandwiches €6-15, meals €40-45

Twice the winner of the best bar in Italy, Caffe Torinese is acclaimed for its coffee, baked goods and gourmet sandwiches, but it's also a rather refined restaurant. Be guided by charming owner Nereo, who will supply you with platters of charcuterie, foie gras burgers and monkfish with wild broccoli and lime.

WHERE TO EAT...

GELATO

Gelataria Bloom, Modena
Follows a fiercely farm-to-table philosophy, working directly with farmers who specialise in ancient fruits.

Gelateria Dondoli, San Gimignano
Think of it less as ice cream, more as art. Former gelato world champion Sergio Dondoli is known for creations including Crema di Santa Fina (saffron cream) gelato and Vernaccia sorbet.

Il Gelato Mennella, Naples
Smashing gelato from ingredients like prized Campanian nocciole (hazelnuts) from Giffoni and Sicilian pistachios from Bronte.

Caffè Adamo, Modica
There is great gelato and then there's gelato made by Antonio Adamo (even the Agrigento pistachios are ground on-site!).

ENOTECA DELLA VALPOLICELLA

VENETO | $$ | VENETIAN
Via Osan 47, Fumane, Valpolicella; 045 683 91 46; www.enotecadellavalpolicella.it; meals €25-35

Gastronomes flock to the town of Fumane, just a few kilometres north of San Pietro in Cariano, where an ancient farmhouse has found renewed vigour as a rustically elegant restaurant. The daily-changing menu is a showcase for fresh, local produce. Among the more unusual dishes is a risotto made using local Recioto wine and shredded chocolate.

CANTINE DEL VINO GIÀ SCHIAVI

VENICE | $ | VENETIAN
Fondamenta Priuli 992; 041 523 00 34; www.cantinaschiavi.com; cicheti €1.50

It may look like a wine shop and function as a bar, but this legendary canalside spot also serves the best *cicheti* (Venetian tapas) on this side of the Grand Canal. Chaos cheerfully prevails, with an eclectic cast of locals propping up the bar.

OSTERIA ALLA STAFFA

VENICE | $$ | VENETIAN
Calle dell'Ospedale 6397a; 041 523 91 60; www.facebook.com/alla.staffa.it; meals €30-40

LAURA EDWARDS/LONELY PLANET ©

This page: Brisighella.

With fish fresh from the Rialto fish market every morning and a preference for organic veg and cheese, chef Alberto does a take on Venetian classics that has flavourful foundations. This is traditional cooking taken to the next level, with artful presentation worthy of a modernist masterpiece.

RISTORANTE COCCHI

EMILIA-ROMAGNA | $$ | EMILIAN
Viale Antonio Gramsci 16a, Parma; 0521 98 19 90; www.ristorantecocchi.it; meals €27-45

This classy yet unpretentious restaurant's *Anolini in brodo* (round pasta pockets stuffed with beef and *parmigiano reggiano* in broth), trio *di tortelli* (a sampler of square pasta pockets stuffed with ricotta and spinach, pumpkin and potato with Fragno black truffles) and specials like pappardelle with rabbit *ragù* are reason to come to Parma.

TRATTORIA ERMES

EMILIA-ROMAGNA | $ | TRATTORIA

Via Ganaceto 89, Modena; 059 23 80 65; meals €20

This affordable little lunch spot is tucked into a single wood-panelled room at the northern edge of downtown Modena. This is authentic, daily-changing, unpretentious Emilian cuisine at its finest – proposals include lasagna on Monday, *gramigna alla salsiccia* (pasta with sausage) on Tuesday, *passatelli in brodo* (bread crumb and Parmesan cheese pasta in broth) on Thursday – actually, it doesn't make a difference, it's fabulous!

MERCATO ALBINELLI

EMILIA-ROMAGNA | $$ | MARKET

Via Luigi Albinelli 13, Modena; 059 21 12 18; www.mercatoalbinelli.it; meals €30-40

The best fresh market in Italy's most amazing food region – need we say more? You'll find a cornucopia of Emilian delights: Bible-sized hunks of *parmigiano reggiano*, bottles of Vecchia Modena Lambrusco or aged balsamic vinegar, just-stuffed *tortellini* and *tortelloni*, piles and piles of fresh produce, and a million other things you will be dying to try. You can assemble a picnic of Last Supper proportions here.

'Bertozzi teeter-totters between rowdy Bologna FC fan headquarters and devoted Emilian trattoria serving the city's best traditional recipes. We are ferociously dedicated to both!'
Alessandro Gozzi, Trattoria Bertozzi

TRATTORIA DA AMERIGO DAL 1934

EMILIA-ROMAGNA | $$$ | EMILIAN

Via Marconi 14-16, Savigno; 051 670 83 26; www.amerigo1934.com; meals €45-55, tasting menus €38-50

Emilia-Romagna's best dining experience awaits in truffle territory, the domain of legendary pastamaker Nonna Giuliana Vespucci, executive chef Alberto Bettini and his talented young apprentice, Giacomo Orlandi. *Tortelli* stuffed with *parmigiano reggiano* and wood-fired prosciutto, gnocchi with local truffles, a Parmesan basket-cradled poached egg with regional mushrooms and shaved truffles – showstoppers galore. One Michelin star, zero pretension.

TRATTORIA BERTOZZI

EMILIA-ROMAGNA | $$ | EMILIAN

Via Andrea Costa 84, Bologna; 051 614 14 25; meals €26-40

Often touted as Bologna's best restaurant by in-the-know culinarians – especially locals – this unassuming neighbourhood trattoria is both a rousing good-time and a deeply serious dive into Bologna's famed specialities. It's run by a jovial pair who excel as much with hospitality and wine-swilling as they do with *tagiliatelle al ragù*, meatballs with peas, and *gramigna* pasta with saffron, *guanciale* (cured pork cheeks) and zucchini.

OSTERIA ALL'BOTTEGA

EMILIA-ROMAGNA | $$ | OSTERIA

Via Santa Caterina 51, Bologna; 051 58 51 11; meals €36-41

At Bologna's temple of culinary contentment, owners Daniele and Valeria lavish attention on every table between trips to the kitchen for astonishing plates of *culatello di Zibello* ham, tortellini in capon broth, Petroniana-style veal cutlets (breaded and fried, then topped with *prosciutto di Parma* and *parmigiano reggiano*, and pan-sautéed in broth), off-menu speciality pigeon and other Slow Food delights.

IL LECCIO

TUSCANY | $$ | TUSCAN

Via Costa Castellare 1/3 , Sant'Angelo in Colle; 0577 84 41 75; www.illeccio.net; meals €30

Sometimes simple dishes are the hardest to perfect. And perfection is the only term to use when discussing this trattoria in Brunello heartland. Watching the chef make his way between his stove and kitchen garden to gather produce for each order puts a whole new spin on the word 'fresh,' and both the results and the house Brunello are spectacular.

***This page:* Artisan spaghetti, Tuscany. *Opposite page:* Vineyards, Chianti region.**

TRATTORIA MARIO

FLORENCE | $$ | TUSCAN

Via Rosina 2; 055 21 85 50; www.trattoria-mario.com; meals €25

Arrive by noon to ensure a spot at this noisy, busy, brilliant trattoria – a legend that retains its soul (and allure with locals) despite being overly publicised. Charming Fabio, whose grandfather opened the place in 1953, is front of house while big brother Romeo and nephew Francesco cook with speed in the kitchen. Local Florentines flock here for a brilliantly blue *bistecca alla fiorentina* (T-bone steak).

IL CEDRO

TUSCANY | $ | TUSCAN

Località Moggiona, Moggiona; 0575 55 60 80; www.ristoranteilcedro.com; meals €24

Utterly fantastic, 100% homemade *cucina tipica Casentinese* (typical Casentino cuisine) is the drawcard of this family-run village bistro. There is no menu – rather, seasonal, traditional dishes of the day are chalked on the board. Don't miss the signature *tortelli di patate* (potato-filled pasta cushions) or autumnal game with porcini mushrooms from the nearby forest.

NOVECENTO

UMBRIA | $$ | UMBRIAN

Corso Garibaldi 58, Spoleto; 0743 77 81 69; www.9centocasualrestaurant.com; meals €25-30

An oasis of modern design, this self-styled 'casual' restaurant marries kooky décor with inventive and astonishingly good-value Umbrian cuisine: Pecorino flan doused in lentil cream and crispy bacon, decadent plates of black Venere rice coated in cheese sauce and crowned by shavings of black truffles. *Spettacolare!*

ANTICA SALUMERIA GRANIERI AMATO

UMBRIA | $ | SANDWICHES

Piazza Matteotti, Perugia; sandwiches €3-4.50

Sitting inconspicuously in a no-fanfare grey kiosk on Piazza Matteotti is this Perugian street-food institution. Its speciality is succulent *porchetta* (herbed roast pork) piled high and served – crispy skin and all – in a crusty bread roll. Get in line!

DIVINPECCATO

UMBRIA | $$ | RISTORANTE

Strada Pievaiola 246, Capanne; 075 528 02 34; www.ristorantedivinpeccato.com; meals €35

Chef Nicola works culinary magic at this wonderful roadside restaurant some 27km southeast of Castiglione del Lago. The menu fizzes with seasonal oomph, featuring fresh springtime combos such as *gnocchi con fave e asparagi* (with broad beans and asparagus) and fantastic seafood creations.

WHERE TO DRINK...

APERITIVO

Bulgari Hotel, Milan
An intense slice of Milan life. Expertly mixed cocktails, vintage liquors and high-brow *aperitivo* in Italy's most famous city for it.

Bar Cavour, Turin
Historic room combining a magical, mirrored setting with a great collection of contemporary art and design savvy. Artfully prepared cocktails, quality snacks.

Caffè Poliziano, Montepulciano
Montepulciano's most atmospheric café is at its finest at *aperitivo* when the sunset view over Val di Chiana is simply magnificent.

Antica Cantina Sepe, Naples
Mamma Giovanna makes a small feast for DJ-fueled Thursday night *aperitivo* at this pocket-sized cantina and grocery store.

ANTICA OSTERIA DA LA STELLA

LE MARCHE | $$$ | OSTERIA
Via Santa Margherita 1, Urbino; 0722 32 02 28; www.anticaosteriadalastella.com; meals €45-50

Duck down a quiet Urbino side street to this elegant, wood-beamed restaurant, occupying what was once a 15th-century inn. Legendary in these parts, it serves a menu of updated regional dishes prepared with seasonal, locally sourced ingredients and dreamy, homemade pastas. Skipping dessert is unwise.

LA CIAMBELLA

ROME | $$ | ITALIAN
Via dell'Arco della Ciambella 20; 06 683 29 30; www.la-ciambella.it; meals €35-45

La Ciambella is set over the ruins of the Terme di Agrippa, visible through transparent floor panels, setting an attractive stage for interesting, imaginative food. Try a chickpea pancake, perhaps topped by *stracciatella* (creamy cheese) and anchovies, before a pasta dish of guinea fowl *ragù* and wild mushrooms, all accompanied by excellent Italian wine.

BONCI PIZZARIUM

ROME | $ | PIZZA
Via della Meloria 43; 06 3974 5416; www.bonci.it; pizza slices €5

Pizzarium, the takeaway of Rome's acclaimed pizza emperor Gabriele Bonci, serves Rome's best sliced pizza, bar none. Scissor-cut squares of soft, springy base are topped with original combinations of seasonal ingredients and served for immediate consumption. The freshly fried *supplì* (risotto balls) are also worth trying.

FLAVIO AL VELAVEVODETTO

ROME | $ | ROMAN
Via di Monte Testaccio 97-99; 06 574 4194; www.ristorantevelavevodetto.it; meals €30-35

This casual spot is celebrated locally for its earthy, no-nonsense *cucina romana* (Roman cuisine). Start with *carciofo alla giudia* (deep-fried artichoke) before moving onto *rigatoni alla carbonara* (pasta tubes wrapped in a silky egg sauce spiked with morsels of cured pig's cheek): And, of course: tiramisu.

50 KALÒ

NAPLES | $ | PIZZA
Piazza Sannazzaro 201b; 081 1920 4667; www.50kalò.it; pizzas from €5

That this trendy pizzeria's name roughly translates as 'good dough' in Neapolitan is no coincidence. Third-generation *pizzaiolo* (pizzamaker) Ciro Salvo, whose obsessive research into Naples' most famous edible translates into wonderfully light, perfectly charred wood-fired pizzas. Quality and location are key: ingredients are sourced directly from local and artisanal producers; and it's away from the tourist hordes.

PIZZERIA DA ATTILIO

NAPLES | $ | PIZZA

Via Pignasecca 17; 081 552 0479; www.pizzeriadaattilio.com; pizzas from €4.50

Its more-famous rivals might get much of the international press, but this come-as-you-are veteran dating to 1938 fires some of Napoli's best pies and is the go-to for many pizza connoisseurs the world over. Lording over the front-room pizza oven is *pizzaiolo* (pizzamaker) Attilio Bachetti.

ANTICA OSTERIA DA TONINO

NAPLES | $ | ITALIAN

Via Santa Teresa a Chiaia 47; 081 42 15 33; meals around €16

Wood-panelled, family-run Da Tonino has been feeding locals since 1880. Now run by the fifth and sixth generations, its gingham-print tables lure everyone from Rubinacci suits to old-timers and the odd Nobel Prize winner (Dario Fo ate here). The day's menu – hand-written and photocopied – offers simple, beautiful home cooking. If it's on offer, order the heavenly *polpette al ragù* (meatballs in tomato sauce).

PASTICCERIA MENNELLA

NAPLES | $ | PASTRIES

Via Carducci 50-52; 081 42 60 26; www.pasticceriamennella.it; pastries from €1.50

'My pizza is true Neapolitan, following a strict production discipline since 1938. The star-shaped Carnevale, with eight ricotta-filled tips, is my archetypal superstar.' *Attilio Bachetti, Pizzeria da Attilio*

If you eat only one sweet treat in Naples (good luck with that!), make it Mennella's spectacular *frolla al limone*, a shortbread pastry filled with heavenly lemon cream. Just leave room for the *mignon* (bite-size) version of its *sciù* (choux pastry) with *crema di nocciola* (hazelnut cream).

LA PALETTE

CAMPANIA | $$ | ITALIAN

Via Matermània 36, Capri; 081 837 9235; www.lapalette.it; meals from €35

Local *Caprese* ingredients are combined into the most flavour-filled, creative dishes possible here. Expect the delights of zucchini flowers stuffed with ricotta, fresh and tangy octopus salad, and an aubergine parmigiana that seems to taste so much better than everyone else's. An easy 10-minute walk from Capri Town, it has swooningly romantic bay views.

CORTEINFIORE

PUGLIA | $$ | SEAFOOD

Via Ognissanti 18, Trani; 0883 50 84 02; www.corteinfiore.it; meals €40-45

The decking, stiff tablecloths and marquee setting of this famed Trani seafood restaurant set hopes racing, and the food, wine and service deliver in full. Expect lots of seafood, and expect it to be excellent: try the *frutti di mari* (seafood) antipasti, or the Gallipoli prawns with candied lemon.

AL TRABUCCO DA MIMÌ

PUGLIA | $ | SEAFOOD

Localita Punta San Nicola, Peschici; 0884 96 25 56; www.altrabucco.it; meals €40-45

Sitting on wooden trestles beneath the *trabucco* (a traditional Pugliese wooden fishing platform) you'll eat the freshest seafood, prepared with expertise but no fuss, as you watch the sun sink behind Peschici. Local Gargano craft beers complete a relaxed experience.

OSTERIA NERO D'AVOLA

SICILY | $$ | SICILIAN

Piazza San Domenico 2b, Taormina; 0942 62 88 74; www.facebook.com/osterianerodavola; meals €40-50

Owner Turi Siligato fishes, hunts and forages for his smart *osteria*, one of Taormina's top eateries. Here seasonality, local producers and passion underpin outstanding dishes, such as grilled meatballs in lemon leaves, and fresh fish with Sicilian pesto.

LA BETTOLACCIA

SICILY | $$ | SICILIAN

Via Enrico Fardella 25, Trapani; 0923 2 59 32; www.labettolaccia.it; meals €35-45

Unwaveringly authentic, this on-trend Slow Food favourite, squirrelled away down a sleepy side street, is the hotspot to feast on spicy couscous with fried fish or mixed seafood, *caponata* (eggplant and sun-dried tomatoes with capers in a sweet-and-sour sauce), the catch of the day, and other traditional *Trapanese* dishes.

NANGALARRUNI

SICILY | $$ | SICILIAN

Via delle Confraternite 7, Castelbuono; 0921 67 12 28; www.hostarianangalarruni.it; meals €29-45

Famous throughout Sicily for its delicious dishes featuring forest mushrooms and wild boar, Giuseppe Carollo's eatery deserves equal renown for its splendid Sicilian wine selection. Spike your appetite with an array of local cheeses, then move on to mains featuring fresh ricotta, locally sourced vegetables and roast meats.

This page: Dining outdoors in Palermo.

SAN MARINO

Tiny and fiercely independent San Marino – the world's fifth smallest country – might be minuscule but this landlocked city-state is sandwiched between Emilia-Romagna, Italy's most important food region, and Le Marche (not too shabby, either).

WHAT TO EAT

Passatelli
An Italian pasta made with breadcrumbs, eggs and grated Parmesan cheese often served with local tweaks such as *stridoli*, a leafy herb.

Lasagna
Ristorante Righi's sublime signature lasagna, spread thin and topped with knife-cut *ragù* and pecorino fondue, is San Marino's most magical culinary moment.

Torta Tre Monti and Torta Titano
Two traditional Sammarinese cakes. Tre Monti tempts with five layers of round wafers filled with cocoa cream and hazelnuts, finished with dark chocolate; Titano with two layers of pastry made from almonds, peanuts and honey filled with chocolate and meringue.

PRICE RANGES
For two courses and a glass of wine:
$ less than €25
$$ €25–45
$$$ €45 or more

Tipping: Not expected.

OSTERIA LA TAVERNA

CITTÀ DI SAN MARINO | $ | SAMMARINESE

Piazza della Libertà 10; 0549 99 11 96; www.ristoranterighi.com; meals €25-30

San Marino's only Michelin-starred chef, Luigi Sartini, runs also this informal *osteria* where local dishes like *passatelli* (pasta made with breadcrumbs, eggs and grated Parmesan cheese) with broad beans and artichokes make for a casual – yet wonderful – lunch.

LA TERRAZA

CITTÀ DI SAN MARINO | $$ | SAMMARINESE

Contrada del Collegio 31; 0549 99 10 07; www.hoteltitano.com; meals €30-40

This gourmet choice serves up heart-stopping vistas from its perched position inside Hotel Titano. Starters like flan of radicchio, local ricotta, crispy pancetta and fossa cheese dazzle, as does the signature Fracosta beef *tagliata* (sliced steak) with coarse salt and rosemary – if you can turn away from the view, that is.

RISTORANTE RIGHI

CITTÀ DI SAN MARINO | $$$ | SAMMARINESE

Piazza della Libertà 10; 0549 99 11 96; www.ristoranterighi.com; meals €35-52, tasting menus €40-90

Don't miss Chef Luigi's Sartini's sublime signature lasagna at this Michelin one-star affair. Spread thin and topped with knife-cut *ragù* and pecorino fondue – it's the city-state's one must-eat. There are also plenty of themed tasting menus, too, including seafood and vegetarian options.

SWITZERLAND

WHAT TO EAT

Birchermüsli
This healthy, wholesome kickstart to the day, with rolled oats, yoghurt, seeds, nuts and apple or berries, is as Swiss as can be.

Schoggi
The Swiss are obsessed with their creamy milk chocolate.

Cheese
Seek out the holey stuff in Emmental, hard, nutty varieties in Gruyères, and mature, brine-cured kinds in Appenzell.

Bündnerfleisch
Air-dried beef is a sweet, exquisitely tender delicacy from Graubünden that is smoked and thinly sliced.

Rösti
Grated potatoes and onions pan-fried in butter sounds simple on paper, but for the Swiss getting Rösti right is a huge deal. Eat it in the German-speaking parts.

PRICE RANGES
For a main course:
$ less than Sfr25
$$ Sfr25–50
$$$ Sfr50 or more

Tipping: Round up for good service.

So it's all slopeside fondue and *Schoggi* (chocolate), right? Well, yes, Switzerland can deliver such cheesy, sugary goodness, but that's just tip-of-the-iceberg stuff. Gourmet picnics with air-dried beef and farm-fresh *käse*, wineries for quaffing zesty Chasselas white wines, refined restaurants with nods to over-the-border France, and slow-food, Italian-style feasts at rustic grotti taverns in Ticino – this gorgeous Alpine land has unexpected culinary edge.

LIVING ROOM

GENEVA | $$ | INTERNATIONAL
11 Quai du Mont-Blanc, Ritz Carlton, Geneva; 022 909 60 65; www.livingroombarandkitchen.com; mains Sfr31-65

With its gold-kissed, dove-grey dining room, glorious views of Lake Geneva, and menu bigging up seasonal, regional ingredients, Living Room is a class act. Chef Lénaïc Jourdren gets experimental with market-fresh Swiss and Mediterranean produce in palate-awakening dishes, from ceviche with raspberries and coriander to cider vinegar-glazed veal with Geneva lentils.

DENIS MARTIN

LAKE GENEVA & VAUD | $$$ | SWISS
Rue du Château 2, Vevey; 021 921 12 10; www.denismartin.ch; tasting menus Sfr190-360

If you're going to blow the budget, do it in serious style at this 17th-century mansion in lakeside Vevey. Chef Denis Martin is one of the country's hottest names in Swiss contemporary and molecular cuisine. His tasting menu walks the culinary high-wire, revolving around prime ingredients and starring the likes of prawns with coffee and hazelnut, cognac of beef, and chocolate with olives.

CHEZ BOUDJI

PAYS DE FRIBOURG | $$ | SWISS
Gite d'Avau 1, Broc, Gruyères; 026 921 90 50; www.boudji.ch; mains Sfr16-27

You're going to fall head over heels in love with this dreamy Swiss mountain chalet, with a panoramic terrace peeking across the Alps. Linger there in anticipation of the cheesy goodness you're about to consume. This is stodgy, hearty food: macaroni cheese, fondue, chalet soup and meringue with double cream for dessert! The rich flavour of the local cheese enlivening each simple dish is total indulgence.

GEORGES WENGER

THE JURA MOUNTAINS | $$$ | GASTRONOMY

Rue de la Gare 2, Le Noirmont, La Chaux-de-Fonds; 032 957 66 33; www.georges-wenger.ch; tasting menus Sfr165-265, mains Sfr62-85

Deep in the heart of the forested Jura Mountains rearing up above Lake Geneva, master-chef Georges Wenger works culinary magic, expertly transforming seasonal ingredients from trusted regional suppliers into delicate, beautifully presented dishes. Expect such gastro showstoppers as Breton scallops with endives and pink grapefruit, and roast venison with wild blueberries – presented with panache, served with finesse.

KORNHAUSKELLER

MITTELLAND | $$ | SWISS

Kornhausplatz 18, Bern; 031 327 72 72; www.bindella.ch; mains Sfr24-56

Soaring vaults and delicately frescoed arches make dining in this ornate former granary that bit special. The baroque backdrop, soft lighting and lively chatter make the cellar restaurant an incredibly atmospheric pick for a feast of region-driven dishes

'The baroque backdrop, soft lighting and lively chatter make the cellar restaurant an incredibly atmospheric pick for a feast of region-driven dishes'
Kornhauskeller

that swing from home-pickled Swiss Alpine salmon with herb salad to beef slowly braised in red wine served with tarragon polenta, and good-old fashioned potato Rösti crusted with Bernese cheese and bacon.

VOLKSHAUS BASEL

NORTHWESTERN SWITZERLAND | $$ | BRASSERIE

Rebgasse 12-14, Basel; 061 690 93 10; www.volkshaus-basel.ch; mains Sfr33-46

This stylish Herzog & de Meuron–designed venue is part resto-bar, part gallery, part performance space. For relaxed dining, head for the atmospheric beer garden in a cobblestoned courtyard decorated with columns, vine-clad walls and light-draped rows of trees. The menu ranges from brasserie classics (steak frites) to more innovative offerings (salmon tartare with citrus fruits and gin cucumber).

CHEZ VRONY

VALAIS | $$ | SWISS

Findeln, Zermatt; 027 967 25 52; www.chezvrony.ch; mains Sfr25-45

Ride the Sunnegga Express funicular to 2288m, then ski down or summer-hike to Zermatt's tastiest slope-side address in the Findeln hamlet, with pop-up views of mighty Matterhorn. Delicious dried meats, homemade cheese and sausage come from Vrony's own cows, grazing away the

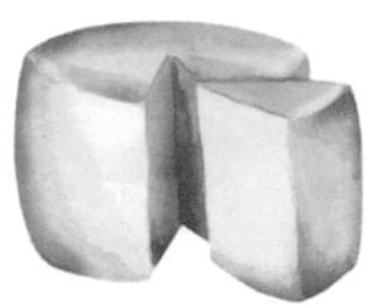

summer on the high Alpine pastures (2100m) surrounding it, and the Vrony burger is legendary. Advance reservations are essential in winter.

CHÂTEAU DE VILLA

VALAIS | $$ | SWISS

Rue Ste-Catherine 4, Sierre; 027 455 18 96; www.chateaudevilla.ch; fondue Sfr23-26, mains Sfr25-40

All turreted towers and centuries-old beams, Sierre's showpiece château rolls out a royal banquet of a raclette – taste five different types of raclette cheese from the Valais, washed down with perfectly matched local wines. September ushers in that fabulous old Valaisian favourite, La Brisolée, a tasting platter of roast chestnuts with regional cured hams, tangy cheeses and autumn fruits.

CAFE 3692

BERNESE OBERLAND | $$ | CAFÉ

Terrassenweg 61, Grindelwald; 033 853 16 54; www.cafe3692.ch; snacks & light meals Sfr7-25, mains Sfr35-38

Run by Myriam and Bruno, this rustic café is an Alpine delight, with entrancing views of the peaks of Eiger and 3692m Wetterhorn. Bruno (a carpenter) has let his imagination loose on the design: a mine-cart trolley has been transformed into a grill, and the ceiling is a wave of woodwork. Garden herbs and Grindelwald-sourced ingredients are knocked up into pastries, cakes, teas and season-focused specialities such as game in autumn.

MICHEL'S STALLBEIZLI

BERNESE OBERLAND | $ | SWISS

Gsteigstrasse 41, Gstaad; 033 744 16 83; www.stallbeizli.ch; mains Sfr21-26

Dining doesn't get more back-to-nature than at this converted barn in the swanky ski resort of Gstaad. In winter you can dig into the gooiest of fondues with Alpine herbs, prosecco or porcini mushrooms, or munch home-cured meat and cheese, with views of the cud-chewing cows and goats in the adjacent stable. Kids love it.

GASTHAUS RATHAUSKELLER

CENTRAL SWITZERLAND | $$$ | EUROPEAN

This page: Lugano. Opposite page: Kippel village, Valais.

Ober-Altstadt 1, Zug; 041 711 00 58; www.rathauskeller.ch; mains bistro/Zunftstube from Sfr20/45

You can't miss the late-Gothic Rathauskeller's frescoed façade in Zug's historic centre. The downstairs bistro serves high-end takes on classics like slow-cooked veal shanks and Rösti with shrimp, while the swanky upstairs restaurant, Zunftstube, has creaky floors, gilt Rosenthal crockery and season-driven delicacies like lobster ragout with summer truffles, and venison with porcini mushrooms.

OSTERIA CHIARA

TICINO | $$ | ITALIAN
Vicolo dei Chiara 1, Locarno; 091 743 32 96; www.osteriachiara.ch; mains Sfr34-45

Climb up a flight of steps from Locarno's lakefront to this family-run osteria and you won't regret it. It has a warm rustic feel, with granite tables tucked beneath a pergola, rough stonewalls and wooden tables gathered around a fireplace. And the food is love at first bite, be it cinnamon-infused crostini topped with chestnut cream, stuffed calamari with pecorino mousse, or meltingly tender veal osso buco with saffron-infused risotto.

GROTTO CA' ROSSA

TICINO | $$ | SWISS
Via Cantonale 34, Gordevio-Ronchini, Valle Maggia; 091 753 28 32; mains Sfr25-40

JONATHAN GREGSON/LONELY PLANET ©

With a flower-strewn garden in summer and a log fire blazing in winter, this highly memorable grotto is hidden deep in the mountainous Valle Maggia. Go for a home-cooked feast of Ticinese flavours: kicking off, say, with antipasti like wild boar salami, before moving onto the likes of gnocchi with local chestnuts, and butter-soft brasato (braised beef) in merlot.

BURESTÜBLI

GRAUBÜNDEN | $$ | SWISS
Hotel Arlenwald, Prätschli, Arosa; 081 377 18 38; www.arlenwaldhotel.ch; mains Sfr20-37

Warmed by a tiled oven, this dark wood-panelled chalet on the forest edge affords magical above-the-treetop views in the Alpine village of Arosa. Come winter, it's beloved by ruddy-faced sledders who huddle around pots of gooey fondue, butter-soft steaks and mugs of *Glühwein*

WHERE TO EAT...

FONDUE

La Tour de Gourze, Lavaux
For traditional fondue, cheesy *croûtes* (toasted bread smothered in melted cheese) and meringues with lashings of Gruyère double cream, this wooden chalet-restaurant is unbeatable. Dig in over views of vineyards, Lake Geneva and the Alps.

Café Tivoli, Châtel-St-Denis
Legendary fondue *moitié-moitié* (made with Gruyére and Vacherin Fribourgeois) is prepared up at this much-loved, family-run restaurant.

Café du Midi, Martigny
Guzzle Trappist brews and gorge on as much raclette as you can handle or dip into one of 10 different fondues – including with tomato, mushrooms or à la bière (beer fondue) – at this shabby-chic cafe with buzzing pavement terrace.

(mulled wine) before a floodlit dash through the snow.

CAFÉ SPRÜNGLI

ZÜRICH | $ | SWEETS

Bahnhofstrasse 21, Zürich; 044 224 46 46; www.spruengli.ch; sweets Sfr8-16

Feather-light *Luxemburgerli* macaroons in rainbow colours, fresh truffles, grand cru chocolate and fruit-topped tortes... Sprüngli has offered the Swiss sweet temptation since 1836. The refined café is a Zürich institution, lit by art deco globe pendants and overlooking Paradeplatz square. Go for a fabulous Sunday brunch or lunch mains like homemade gnocchi with walnuts, ricotta and sage.

ALPENROSE

ZÜRICH | $$ | SWISS

Fabrikstrasse 12, Zürich; 044 431 11 66; www.restaurantalpenrose.ch; mains Sfr25-37

Entering the Alpenrose is like rewinding the clocks a century. With its tall, stencilled windows, warm wood panelling and stucco ceiling, this is a proper blast of old-school charm in central Zürich. Swiss faves like herb-stuffed trout with homemade *Spätzli* (egg noodles), and venison ragout with seasonal veg, are exquisitely prepared and accompanied by carefully selected regional wines.

KRONENHALLE

ZÜRICH | $$$ | BRASSERIE

Rämistrasse 4, Zürich; 044 262 99 00; www.kronenhalle.ch; mains Sfr30-66

A haunt of city movers and shakers, the Crown Hall is a wonderfully old-world brasserie, with white tablecloths, dark wood and impeccably mannered waiters moving discreetly below Chagall, Miró, Matisse and Picasso originals. The cuisine straddles Swiss and international flavours, from one of the best *Zürcher Geschnetzeltes* (sliced veal) you're likely to taste to chateaubriand with *Rösti*.

WIRTSCHAFT ZUM FRIEDEN

NORTHEASTERN SWITZERLAND | $$ | SWISS

Herrenacker 11, Schaffhausen; 052 625 47 67; www.wirtschaft-frieden.ch; mains Sfr35-50

Locals have been eating, drinking and making merry at this wood-panelled inn since 1445. It's still an incredibly cosy choice today, with a tiled oven, tightly packed tables and old black-and-white photos. Chefs like to put an imaginative twist on regional ingredients, along the lines of tartare of butternut squash panna cotta, Aargau water buffalo with pecorino mash, and local wild boar steak in Sichuan pepper sauce.

LIECHTENSTEIN

Hemmed in by the Alps, little-but-lovely Liechtenstein looks towards neighbouring Switzerland and Austria, gastronomically speaking. In the mountains, food swings hearty, but in Vaduz you'll find everything from hip Scandi bistros to dark-timber taverns, and Michelin-starred menus paired with wines from the prince's own vineyards.

WHAT TO EAT

Hafalaab
Liechtenstein's hard-to-pronounce national speciality is a warming broth, flavoured with smoked ham and served with wheat and cornmeal dumplings.

Ribel
Similar to polenta, Ribel is made from cornmeal that's cooked in milk, roasted in butter and served with fruits, compotes or local sour cheese.

Zürcher Geschnetzeltes
Zürich is but a short hop away, hence Liechtenstein being a fan of its signature sliced veal in a creamy mushroom sauce laced with white wine.

Käsknöpfle
These tiny cheese dumplings – perfect on cold winter days – are served with a sprinkle of nutmeg and crispy fried onions.

PRICE RANGES
For a main course:
$ less than Sfr25
$$ Sfr25–50
$$$ Sfr50 or more

Tipping: Round up for good service.

TORKEL

VADUZ | $$ | SWISS

Hintergasse 9, Vaduz; 232 44 10; www.torkel.li; mains Sfr51-74, 5-course tasting menu Sfr128

Just above the Prince of Liechtenstein's vineyards in Vaduz sits His Majesty's ivy-clad, Michelin-starred restaurant. The garden terrace has wonderful views of the castle above, while the beamed, candlelit interior is fantastically cosy in winter. The menu makes the most of regional and seasonal flavours in ingredient-driven, exquisitely cooked dishes like summer venison with apple, hazelnut and lime, and white chocolate with peach and thyme.

NJORD

VADUZ | $$ | SCANDINAVIAN

Landstrasse 117, Mühleholz; 232 20 02; www.njord.li; mains Sfr23.50-36.50

A breath of fresh Scandi air, Njord has a coolly modern bistro look, with greys, cream panelling, wood floors and cheek-by-jowl tables. The menu wholly embraces the seasons in the likes of carpaccio of venison with cranberry jam, rocket, fig and chestnuts, Swiss veal ragout with calvados sauce and pumpkin gnocchi, and molten chocolate cake with blueberries and frozen yoghurt. Vegetarians and vegans are also well catered for.

ADLER VADUZ

VADUZ | $$ | SWISS

Herrengasse 2, Vaduz; 232 21 31; www.adler.li; mains Sfr22-40

Creaking wood floors, wainscoting and lilac walls festooned with quirky portrait plates create a nouveau-rustic backdrop for Swiss classics prepared with market-fresh ingredients at the Adler. Dishes like Zürcher Geschnetzeltes (sliced veal in a creamy mushroom sauce), Käsknöpfle (cheese dumplings) and seasonal game go nicely with a glass of Vaduz Pinot noir. Bag a seat on the terrace in summer for prime views of the high-on-a-hill castle.

AUSTRIA

Schnitzel with noodles might have been Maria's favourite, but there's way more to Austrian food nowadays thanks to a generation of new-wave chefs adding a pinch of imagination to seasonal, locally grown ingredients in farm-to-fork menus. Worldly markets, well-stocked wineries and a rising taste for organic, foraged flavours are all making Austria a culinary destination to watch.

WHAT TO EAT

Wiener schnitzel
Nothing says classic Austrian grub like Wiener schnitzel, a breaded veal cutlet that's often as big as a boot fried to golden perfection.

Tafelspitz
Tafelspitz (boiled beef) is a national fave. It's often served with root vegetables and *Apfelkren* (apple-horseradish sauce).

Salzburger Nockerln
Salzburg's beloved dessert is a massive soufflé-like baked concoction sprinkled with icing sugar.

Tiroler Gröstl
A hearty fry-up made from leftovers, usually potato, pork and onions, topped with a fried egg.

Steirischer Backhendl-Salat
Styria's delicious breaded chicken salad is drizzled with the local dark, nutty pumpkin oil.

PRICE RANGES
$ less than €15
$$ €15–30
$$$ €30 or more

Tipping: 10%

GASTHOF HIRSCHEN

VORARLBERG | $$ | AUSTRIAN
Hof 14; Schwarzenberg; 05512-29 44; www.hotel-hirschen-bregenzerwald.at; mains €15-31; 4-/6- course tasting menus €59/79

Romantically tucked away in the Bregenzerwald's forested hills, this woodcutter's dream of an inn has been going strong since 1755. Candlelight flickers in the dark timber-clad parlour, and the menu shouts of the seasons and local sourcing, with starters like cured trout, asparagus and nasturtium segueing into mains like braised hare with potato noodles, pumpkin and rosemary jus.

COURTESY SCHULHAUS

MUSEUM RESTAURANT

TYROL | $$ | AUSTRIAN
Rudi-Matt-Weg 10, St Anton am Arlberg; 05446-24 75; www.museum-restaurant.at; mains €18-37.50

You'll pray for the flakes to fall so you can retreat to this dream of a timber chalet, high above the ski resort of St Anton am Arlberg. The farm-to-fork menu swings seasonal: Vorarlberg goat's cheese with wild garlic in spring, say, or perfectly pink local venison with cranberry-juniper sauce in winter. The sorbets and ice creams from the village dairy are superb.

SCHULHAUS

TYROL | $$ | AUSTRIAN

Zellberg 162, Zell am Ziller; 05282-33 76; www.schulhaus.tirol; mains €15-34

On its panoramic perch above Zell am Ziller, this revamped schoolhouse is Tyrolean through and through. The larch-wood interior is drenched in honeyed light, the terrace commands views deep into the valley and to glacier-encrusted mountains beyond, while the menu plays up farm-fresh and foraged ingredients in dishes like Zillertal chanterelle ravioli and creamy organic goulash with potato dumplings.

AURACHER LÖCHL

TYROL | $$ | AUSTRIAN

Römerhofgasse 4, Kufstein; 05372-621 38; www.auracher-loechl.at; mains €13-28

Creaking with the weight of its 600-year history, this deliciously cosy, low-beamed restaurant is the one-time haunt of Tyrolean hero Andreas Hofer. The kitchen rolls out Austrian soul food: Kaspressknödel (cheesy dumplings), pork roast with lashings of onions, and, more novelly, Tyrolean tapas. A G&T in Stollen 1930, a medieval cave turned glam speakeasy, piques the appetite nicely.

DIE WILDERIN

LAKE DISTRICT | $$$ | MODERN BRITISH

Seilergasse 5, Innsbruck; 0512-56 27 28; www.diewilderin.at; mains €13.50-20

'Candlelight flickers in the dark timber-clad parlour, and the menu shouts of the seasons and local sourcing'
Gasthof Hirschen

SIMON RAINER, COURTESY DIE WILDERIN

Innsbruck takes a gastronomic walk on the wild side at this modern-day hunter-gatherer of a restaurant. Chefs take pride in using sustainably sourced regional, seasonal and foraged ingredients, be it pumpkin dumplings topped with mountain cheese or Tyrolean beef cooked until meltingly tender, served with kohlrabi and polenta. Lit by a huge chandelier, the gallery-style, post-industrial interior has a pleasingly relaxed boho vibe.

BÄRENWIRT

SALZBURGERLAND | $$ | AUSTRIAN

Müllner Hauptstrasse 8, Salzburg; 0662-42 24 04; www.baerenwirt-salzburg.at; mains €10 20

Sizzling and stirring since 1663, Bärenwirt is Austrian through and through. Go for hearty *Bierbraten* (beer roast), locally caught trout or organic wild-boar bratwurst. A tiled oven warms hunting-lodge-style interior in winter, while the river-facing terrace is a summer crowd-puller.

BLAUE GANS

SALZBURGERLAND | $$$ | AUSTRIAN

Getreidegasse 43, Salzburg; 0662-842 491 50; www.blaue-gans.com; mains €21-28, 4-course menus €58-65

In the 650-year-old vaults of one of Salzburg's chicest hotels, the Blaue Gans is a refined setting for creative takes on regional cuisine, such as Tauern lamb with braised romaine lettuce and beech fungus, or crispy organic pork belly with fennel and rhubarb, all married with full-bodied wines drawn from the cellar.

OBAUER

SALZBURGERLAND | $$$ | AUSTRIAN

Markt 46, Werfen; 06468-52 12; www.obauer.com; 3-course lunch €42, dinner menus €50-138

Besides the soul-stirring mountain views, the other reason to stop in the ludicrously pretty town of Werfen is to dine in Obauer's sophisticated restaurant or gardens. Regional ingredients are elevated to art forms in tasting menus taking you from the likes of chamois carpaccio with blueberry mustard, to curd cheese soufflé with anise foam and sorrel ice cream.

DER STEIRER

STYRIA | $$ | AUSTRIAN

Belgiergasse 1, Graz; 0316-70 36 54; www.der-steirer.at; mains €10-28.50

Exposed stone vaults, monochrome hues, cheek-by-jowl seating and the odd designer flourish give this neo-Beisl (bistro pub) a historic-meets-retro-cool feel. Wines of the month, highlighting flavour-of-the-moment Styrian vintners, are paired with spot-on trad dishes like crispy Backhendl (fried breaded chicken) and Tafelspitz (boiled beef with horseradish), as well as more creative mains like rack of wild boar with pumpkin-apple risotto.

LUKAS RESTAURANT

UPPER AUSTRIA | $$$ | AUSTRIAN

Unterer Stadtplatz 7, Schärding; 0664 341 3285; www.lukas-restaurant.at; 4-/6-course menu €75/99

White walls, bare floorboards, sheepskin-covered chairs and copper lighting set the stage for chef Lukas Kienbauer's ingenious riffs on Austrian cuisine. In the full-length open kitchen, he uses local meat, river fish and plants grown on his farm or foraged nearby in no-choice menus that might feature spruce macarons, nettle-wrapped zander parcels with wild thyme foam, and Alpine honey–marinated pork belly.

RESTAURANT LOIBNERHOF

THE DANUBE VALLEY | $$ | AUSTRIAN

Unterloiben 7, Dürnstein; 02732-828 90; www.loibnerhof.at; mains €15-26

On a scenic bend in the Danube and topped by a ruined castle where

Previous page: Schulhaus; Preparing dishes in Die Wilderin.

Richard the Lionheart was once imprisoned, Dürnstein has beauty, history and the Loibnerhof. Lodged inside a 400-year-old vaulted cellar revamped in minimalist style, the family-run restaurant keeps things regional, with the likes of herb-crusted lamb, Wachau apricot parfait and feisty nut schnapps. In summer, tables spill out into the orchard.

BITZINGER WÜRSTELSTAND AM ALBERTINAPLATZ

VIENNA | $ | STREET FOOD
Albertinaplatz; 0664 88 62 24 28; www.bitzinger-wien.at; sausages €3.50-4.80

Behind the Staatsoper is Vienna's cult sausage stand, often with snaking queues. Bitzinger offers the contrasting spectacle of ladies and gents dressed to the nines, sipping beer, wine or champagne while scoffing mustard-doused Bosna bratwurst and Käsekrainer cheese sausages at outdoor tables or the heated counter after performances. It's open until 4am, so perfect for late-night munchies.

VOLLPENSION

VIENNA | $ | CAFÉ
Schleifmühlgasse 16; 01-585 04 64; www.vollpension.wien; cake & light dishes €4-10

Vienna has many fancier coffeehouses, but cake is never made with more love than at this fabulous time warp of a cafe, where bare brick walls are festooned with old-school knick-knacks and faded photos. Wafts of butter and vanilla drift from the kitchen, where a cheerful team of *Omas* (grandmas) get baking to boost their meagre pensions. Come for a slice of strudel, a bowl of creamy goulash or a blowout breakfast.

MEIEREI

VIENNA | $$ | AUSTRIAN
Am Heumarkt 2a; 01-713 31 68; www.steirereck.at; set breakfasts €21-25, mains €19-28

In the green surrounds of Vienna's Stadtpark, this light-drenched, slickly minimalist former dairy is most famous for its goulash served with lemon, capers and dumplings, not to mention its selection of 120 cheeses. Served until noon, the bountiful breakfast features gastronomic show-stoppers like poached duck egg with forest mushrooms and pumpkin, and corn waffles with warm tomato salad and sheep's cheese.

LANDKIND

VIENNA | $ | MARKET
Schwendermarkt, Stand 16, Vienna; www.landkind.wien; dishes €5-14.50

Part organic market stall, part cafe, part community hangout, Landkind sources produce from small-scale sustainable farmers. Browse its shelves for regional fruits, vegetables, cheeses, wines, gins and cakes, or squeeze into the tiny space to dine on soups, strudels, salads or sharing platters, served on retro crockery.

WHERE TO EAT...

CAKE

Demel, Vienna
Once purveyor of confectionery to the royal court, this decorous café and cake shop is Vienna's sweet spot for the flakiest Apfelstrudel (apple strudel), with tangy apples, raisins and walnuts wrapped in a caramelised crust.

k.u.k. Hofbäckerei, Linz
Fritz Rath bakes mighty fine Linzer Torte at this frozen-in-time café. The crumbly tart with a lattice pastry top is filled with almonds, spices and redcurrant jam.

Café Sacher
With a battalion of waiters and regal air, this ruby-red, chandelier-lit café is the original home of Sacher Torte, an insanely rich iced-chocolate cake layered with apricot jam.

WHAT TO EAT

Black Forest gateau
You'll never forget your first forkful of *Schwarzwälder Kirschtorte*: a three-layered chocolate sponge cake filled with cream, morello cherries and *Kirsch* (cherry liqueur).

Matjes
Brine-pickled herrings whacked into a roll with raw sliced onions.

Bratwurst
Nothing says German food like the humble bratwurst, slathered in *Senf* (mustard) that's *süss* (sweet) or *scharf* (hot). Nuremberg's bite-sized ones (*Rostbratwurst*) are among the best.

Sauerkraut
Sausages and sauerkraut are a match made in heaven. Fermented cabbage seasoned with caraway seed is a big culinary deal here, accompanying most meat fests.

PRICE RANGES
$ less than €12
$$ €12–€22
$$$ €22 or more

Tipping: 5–10%

GERMANY

Germany's food scene has had a bumpy ride over the years, but boy have things changed. Beyond the whole sausage-cabbage-and-carbs shebang, even small towns are upping their culinary game, with farm-to-fork ingredients and menus singing of the seasons. Michelin stars shimmer in remote backwaters, cities dish up the world on a plate, and everywhere is going vegan and organic.

FISCHBRÖTCHENBUDE BRÜCKE 10

NORTHERN GERMANY | $ | SEAFOOD

Landungsbrücken, Pier 10, Hamburg; 040-3339 9339; www.bruecke10.com; sandwiches €4-10

There are a gazillion fish sandwich vendors in Hamburg, but this one is a true winner, with its nautical-themed whitewashed wood interior and tables out front overlooking the docks. Try a classic *Bismarck* (pickled herring) or *Matjes* (brined herring), or push the boat out with a bulging shrimp sandwich.

MATT MUNRO/LONELY PLANET ©

RESTAURANT KLEINEN BRUNNENSTRASSE 1

NORTHERN GERMANY | $$$ | EUROPEAN

Kleinen Brunnenstrasse 1, Hamburg; 040-3990 7772; www.kleine-brunnenstrasse.de; mains €20-26.50

Northern Germany's slow food heart beats in this crisply contemporary bistro. Menus change daily and always reflect what's in season, with clean, bright flavours in dishes like veal cheeks slow-braised in sage and lemon, perfectly pink duck breast with pear chutney and confit potatoes, and buckthorn, orange and basil sorbet. Snag a table on the tree-rimmed pavement terrace on warm days.

SÖL'RING HOF SYLT

NORTHERN GERMANY | $$$ | EUROPEAN

Am Sandwall 1, Rantum, Sylt; 04651-836 200; www.soelring-hof.de; 9-course tasting menu €184/224

From the terrace among the dunes you can hear the crash of the surf, muted by blowing grasses at Söl'ring Hof. Johannes King's two Michelin starred kitchen is equally alluring. Conjurer of textures and flavours, he keeps things as light and natural as the sea breeze, with the likes of Sylt royal oysters, and rack of venison with beetroot, blackberries and beech fungus, which you'll still be raving about years later.

FISCHER-HÜTTE

NORTHERN GERMANY | $$ | SEAFOOD

An der Mühle 12, Wieck; 03834-839 654; www.fischer-huette.de; mains €12-22

A real gulp of the briny blue, the 'fisherman's hut is endearingly rustic, with its red-brick, low-beamed interior crammed with lanterns, model boats, fishing nets and other nautical knickknacks. As you might expect, seafood is the big deal – and good it is, too, whether you opt for scallops with lentil curry, or chunky fillet of Baltic cod sliding into basil spaghetti. Boats pull up to the dock right outside.

BREMER RATSKELLER

LOWER SAXONY & BREMEN | $$ | GERMAN

Am Markt 11, Bremen; 0421-321 676; www.ratskeller-bremen.de; mains €14.50-29.50

Bremen's Ratskeller has been feeding hungry locals hearty, no-fuss German food and beer since 1405. High vaulted ceilings and candlelit cubbyholes ramp up the old-world atmosphere, just right for sampling local herrings and gut-busting classics like Bremen-style Seemannslabskaus (corned beef and mashed potatoes with pickled herring, two fried eggs, beetroot and gherkins).

'High vaulted ceilings and candlelit cubbyholes ramp up the old-world atmosphere, just right for sampling local herrings and gut-busting classics.'
Bremer Ratskeller

NATUSCH

LOWER SAXONY & BREMEN | $$$ | SEAFOOD

Am Fischbahnhof 1, Bremerhaven; 0471-710 21; www.natusch.de; mains €22.50-28.50

Decked out like a galleon, this dark-wood-panelled tavern is the real nautical deal, with model boats, figureheads and intimate booths for digging into fish hauled in fresh from the boat. Share an antipasti platter (a tasty mix of gravlax, oysters, prawns, scallops and locally caught shrimp) followed, say, by North Sea sole with melted butter and new potatoes.

SEESTEG

LOWER SAXONY & BREMEN | $$$ | SEAFOOD

Damenpfad 36a, Norderney; 4932-893 600; www.seesteg-norderney.de; 3-/4-/5-course dinner €65/80/95

Wow, what a view! Decked out in subtle monochromes and lit by candles, this Michelin-starred restaurant on the East Frisian island of Norderney gazes out across the stormy North Sea. Head chef Markus Kebschull takes pride in local sourcing, serving delicacies like skate with fennel, tomato, garlic and saffron, breast of pigeon with porcini and plums, and nutmeg ice cream with spiced pumpkin, with a dash of finesse.

MICHELBERGER

BERLIN & BRANDENBURG$ | INTERNATIONAL

Warschauer Strasse 39, Berlin; 030-2977 8590; www.michelbergerhotel.com; mains €8-18

Hailing from their own farm or regional forests and fields, organic ingredients shine at this lofty, white-tiled restaurant, ensconced in one of Berlin's coolest hotels. Pull up a chair at one of the communal tables for taste sensations like wild boar with miso, clams, cabbage and gooseberry, and wild venison pie with black pudding and spiced pear. It's also a sweet spot for breakfast or a light lunch.

KATZ ORANGE

BERLIN & BRANDENBURG | $$ | INTERNATIONAL

Bergstrasse 22, Berlin; 030-983 208 430; www.katzorange.com; mains €18-24

With its farm-to-table menu, country flair and creative cocktails, the 'Orange Cat' hits a gastro grand slam. It will have you purring for dishes like monkfish cheeks with sprouts and kumquat, and Duroc pork that's been slow-roasted for 12 hours (nicknamed 'candy on bone') served with garlic-and-lemon yoghurt. The castle-like former brewery setting is stunning, especially in summer when the patio opens.

GOLDIES

BERLIN & BRANDENBURG | $ | FAST FOOD

Oranienstrasse 6; 030-7478 0320; www.goldies-berlin.de; mains €5-11

Having trained in some of Germany's most celebrated Michelin-starred kitchens, Kajo Hiesl and Vladislav Gachyn started Goldies as a way of perfecting the humble French fry. Their trendy fast-food joint has since become an institution for hungry locals. Fries come with homemade sauces or loaded high with eclectic toppings such as slow-cooked pork knuckle with sauerkraut and crispy pig skin.

ORANIA

BERLIN & BRANDENBURG | $$$ | GERMAN

Oranienstrasse 40, Berlin; 030-6953 9680; https://orania.berlin/restaurant; mains €30-36

Punctilious artisanship meets boundless creativity at Orania, where a small army of chefs fusses around culinary wunderkind Philipp Vogel in the shiny open kitchen. The flair is cosmo-chic with food, cocktails and live music to match. Only three

Previous page: Wernigerode Castle.

ingredients find their destiny in each product-focused dish: codfish with green curry and burned leek, say, or liquorice, raspberry and dark chocolate. The signature Xberg Peking duck is represented in four courses.

SCHLOSSRESTAURANT LINARI

BERLIN & BRANDENBURG | $$$ | INTERNATIONAL

Schlossbezirk 6, Lübbenau; 03542-8730; www.schloss luebbenau.de; 3-course menu €30-45

In the Unesco-listed Spreewald forest, Schloss Lübbenau's restaurant has kept an air of palatial elegance, with antique wood furnishings, candlelight and oil paintings. The chef keeps the menu in flux with garden grown and regionally hunted-and-gathered ingredients in classics like port wine-braised beef cheeks and baked pike-perch served with parsley sauce. In summer, head out onto the terrace for pretty garden views.

MEET & EAT MARKT

COLOGNE & NORTHERN RHINELAND | $ | MARKET

Rudolfplatz, Cologne; www.meet-and-eat.koeln; light bites €5-12

A combination of farmers market and street-food fair, Meet & Eat draws locals of all ages to Rudolfplatz on Thursday evenings. Aside from fresh produce, you can pick up homemade pesto, chutney, organic cheeses and other artisanal products or sit down at a covered table for a vegan sausage or succulent burger.

BEI OMA KLEINMANN

COLOGNE & NORTHERN RHINELAND | $$ | GERMAN

Zülpicher Strasse 9, Cologne; 0221-232 346; www.beiomakleinmann.de; mains €13-24

Named for its long-time owner, who was still cooking almost to her last day at age 95 in 2009, this nicely chilled, picture-plastered haunt is often as busy as a beehive. It rolls out interesting riffs on enormous pork and veal schnitzels – from Bombay curry style to Olaf Maria (with sardines and capers). Grab one of the small wooden tables for a proper Cologne night out.

BRAUEREI IM FÜCHSCHEN

COLOGNE & NORTHERN RHINELAND | $$ | GERMAN

Ratinger Strasse 28, Düsseldorf; 0211-137 4716; www.fuechschen.de; mains €9-17

Boisterous, packed and big on local flavour, the 'Little Fox' in Düsseldorf's Altstadt is all you expect a Rhenish beer hall to be. The kitchen is especially famous for its mean Schweinshaxe (roast pork leg) served in a high-ceilinged interior that echoes with the mirthful roar of people enjoying their meals. This is one of the best Altbier breweries in town, in business since 1848.

WHERE TO EAT...

WURST

Historische Wurstkuchl, Regensburg
Right on the banks of the Danube, this cult hole-in-the-wall has been dishing out finger-size, wood-fired sausages with homemade sauerkraut for the past 500 years.

Curry 36, Berlin
Day after day, night after night, a motley crowd wait their turn at this popular temple to *Currywurst* (sausage topped with ketchup and curry powder) that's been frying 'em up since 1981.

Weisses Brauhaus, Munich
This rollicking beer hall is the go-to place for a Munich-style *Weisswurst* (white veal sausage) breakfast. Sluice down a skinned pair with a foamy *Weizen* (wheat beer), but only before noon.

ZUM WENIGEMARKT 13

ERFURT, WEIMAR & THURINGIA | $$ | GERMAN

Wenigemarkt 13, Erfurt; 0361-642 2379; www.wenigemarkt-13.de; mains €11-20

Lodged in 18th-century house on a small marketplace in Erfurt, this old-school, wood-panelled tavern dishes up traditional and updated takes on Thuringian cuisine, playing up regionally hunted and gathered ingredients where possible. Tender neck fillets of pork with sauerkraut and Thuringian dumplings and roasted char with potato-coconut purée are both menu stars.

RESTAURANT GENUSS-ATELIER

SAXONY | $$$ | GERMAN

Bautzner Strasse 149, Dresden; 0351-2502 8337; www.genuss-atelier.net; mains €25-30, 4-/5-/6-course surprise menu €49/59/69

Lighting up Dresden's culinary scene is this fantastic place that's well worth the short trundle on tram 11. The imaginative, ingredient-driven menu whacks out punchy flavours like pumpkin spelt and elderberry, and catfish with black pudding and apple. Arguably the best way to experience the 'Pleasure-Atelier', however, is to book the surprise menu and let the chefs show off their craft.

This page: Dresden.

RESTAURANT VINCENZ RICHTER

SAXONY | $$ | GERMAN

An der Frauenkirche 12, Meissen; 03521-453 285; www.vincenz-richter.de; mains €12-24

Despite the historic guns, hunting trophies and armour, the romance factor is high at this 16th-century inn thanks to attentive service, classy interpretations of Saxon cuisine, and crisp whites from the Richters' own wine estate. Loosen your belt buckle for deeply satisfying specialities like wild boar roast with apple, red cabbage and dumplings.

ZU DEN 12 APOSTELN

FRANKFURT & SOUTHERN RHINELAND | $$ | GERMAN

Rosenbergerstrasse 1, Frankfurt am Main; 069-288 668; www.12aposteln-frankfurt.de; mains €11-25

Glowing with sepia-toned lamplight, the 12 Apostles has ground-floor and cellar dining rooms bringing on regional faves like Matjes (herring) with sour cream, apple and fried onion; roast pork knuckle with pickled cabbage; Frankfurter schnitzel with Grüne Sosse (green sauce); and Käsespätzle (handmade cheese noodles with onions). It brews its own light and dark beers on the premises.

KLEINMARKTHALLE

FRANKFURT & SOUTHERN RHINELAND | $ | MARKET

Hasengasse 5-7, Frankfurt am Main; www.kleinmarkthalle.de

Aromatic stalls inside this bustling traditional market hall sell artisan smoked sausages, cheeses, breads, pretzels, loose-leaf teas, pastries, cakes and chocolates, along with fruit, vegetables, spices, fresh pasta, olives, meat, poultry and, downstairs, fish. It's unmissable for picnickers or self-caterers, or anyone wanting to experience Frankfurt life. The upper-level wine bar opens to a terrace.

URGESTEIN

FRANKFURT & SOUTHERN RHINELAND | $$$ | GERMAN

Rathausstrasse 6, Neustadt an der Weinstrasse; 06321-489 060; www.restaurant-urgestein.de; 5-/6-course menus €100/120, with paired wines €140/160

For a gastronomic extravaganza on the German Wine Road, book a table at Benjamin Peifer's Michelin-starred, vaulted brick cellar restaurant within a half-timbered house in Neustadt. Over 300 wines complement exquisite dishes like pickled trout with sauerkraut and horseradish, followed by steamed liver dumplings with Riesling foam, hay-roasted pigeon with foie gras mousse, and nougat ganache with hazelnut yoghurt.

ZUR HERRENMÜHLE HEIDELBERG

FRANKFURT & SOUTHERN RHINELAND | $$$ | GERMAN

Hauptstrasse 239, Heidelberg; 06221-602 909; www.herrenmuehle.net; mains €32.50-37.50, 3-/4-course menus €62/68

A flour mill from 1690 has been turned into an elegant and highly cultured place for refined spins on 'country-style' cuisine. Beneath weighty, 300-year-old wooden beams, at tables where candles flicker, try the likes of rack of venison with sherry jus and truffled Savoy cabbage, and saffron-crusted gilt-head bream with baby spinach and creamed potato.

ALTE ZUNFTSCHEUNE

FRANKFURT & SOUTHERN RHINELAND | $$ | GERMAN

Neue Rathausstrasse 15, Traben; 06541-9737; www.zunftscheune.de; mains €11-23

WHERE TO EAT...

SWEETS

Niederegger, Lübeck
It's the almond-to-sugar ratio that makes Lübeck Germany's marzipan mecca. Niederegger have been perfecting the stuff since 1806: coating it in dark chocolate and wrapping it in shiny red bars. Head to the café for marzipan-laced cakes, coffees and ice cream.

Alt-Aachener Café-Stuben, Aachen
For Aachen's riff on traditional Lebkuchen (gingerbread), try spicy, moreish Printen biscuits in a dozen varieties at this old-school café.

Striezelmarkt, Dresden
Christmas wouldn't be the same without Stollen – a spiced cake loaded with sultanas and candied peel, sprinkled with icing sugar and spruced up with a ball of marzipan – sold at this fairytale of a festive market.

Moselle-style dishes come into their own at this marvellous rambling attic of a restaurant, chock-full of rustic bric-a-brac and beautiful timber staircases. Its stone vaulted cellar still has its original 1890s lighting. Home cooking like black pudding and liver sausage, schnitzel with Riesling cream sauce, and juicy rump steak with asparagus and fried potatoes, keeps the place consistently rammed.

KALINSKI

FRANKFURT & SOUTHERN RHINELAND | $ | GERMAN

Kaltenbachstrasse 4, Saarbrücken; www.kalinskibrueder.de; dishes €2-8.50

Saarbrücken's hippest hang-out is this Wurstwirtschaft, which sizzles up street-food-style *Currywurst* (including a fabulous tofu and wheatgerm vegetarian sausage with spicy tomato sauce), pulled pork burgers, Spätzle, and meatballs, accompanied by potato or sweet-potato fries and craft beers and gins. Everything is preservative-free and made daily on the premises from local produce. Seats spill onto the front pavement.

CAFÉ SCHÄFER

STUTTGART & THE BLACK FOREST | $ | CAFÉ

Hauptstrasse 33, Triberg; 07722-4465; www.cafe-schaefer-triberg.de; cake €3-5

There are countless takes on Black Forest gateau, but there's only one original... Find it in the cuckoo-clock town where Germany's highest waterfall flows: Triberg. Here Claus Schäfer uses the original 1915 recipe to rustle up the most decadent torte layering kirsch-laced chocolate sponge with whipped cream and sour cherries, and wrapping it all in more cream and shaved chocolate.

DIE HALDE

STUTTGART & THE BLACK FOREST | $$ | GERMAN

Oberried-Hofsgrund; 07602-944 70; www.halde.com; mains €18-36, 4-/5-course menus €54/69

When it snows, the view from this rustic-chic retreat in the Black Forest is a Christmas card scene, with spruce-clad hills rippling into monochrome distance. Oil paintings, crisp white linen and fresh flowers dress the dark-timber parlours of the elegantly old-fashioned restaurant. Here chef Martin Hegar makes regional ingredients sing in showstoppers like trout with braised parsnips, apple and salsa verde, and venison with wild mushrooms, plums and *Spätzle* (egg pasta).

WEINSTUBE IM BALDREIT

STUTTGART & THE BLACK FOREST | $$ | GERMAN

Küferstrasse 3, Baden-Baden; 07221-231 36; mains €12.50-23

Squirreled away in the cobbled backstreets of the spa town of Baden-Baden, this old-world wine tavern opens onto an ivy-swathed courtyard in summer. Besides bang-on-the-money regional favourites like smoked pork cheeks with lentil ragout, expertly matched with local wines, you'll find nods to neighbouring Alsace in the likes of perfectly crisp Flammkuchen (tarte flambée) topped with Black Forest ham, Roquefort and pears.

RESTAURANT BAREISS

STUTTGART & THE BLACK FOREST | $$$ | MODERN EUROPEAN

Hermine-Bareiss-Weg 1, Baiersbronn-Mitteltal; 07442-470; www.bareiss.com; lunch menu €125, dinner menus €198-245

Claus-Peter Lumpp has consistently won plaudits for his flawlessly composed, French-inflected menus at three-Michelin-starred Restaurant Bareiss. On paper, dishes such as sautéed langoustine with almond cream, and fillet of suckling calf and sweetbreads with chanterelles seem deceptively simple; on the plate they become things of beauty, rich in textures and aromas and presented with an artist's eye for detail.

WEINHAUS NEUNER

BAVARIA | $$$ | BAVARIAN

Herzogspitalstrasse 8, Munich; 089-260 3954; www.weinhaus-neuner.de; mains €26-33

Bringing on the Bavarian charm with vaulted ceilings, dark wood and candlelight in a 15th-century listed building, this nostalgic dream of a wine tavern keeps its menu regional, with a few detours into neighbouring Austria. Simple yet lovingly prepared dishes like Munich market salad with walnuts, Allgäu goat's cheese and quince, and wild boar cooked two ways with forest mushrooms and herb gnocchi taste of the seasons and the terroir.

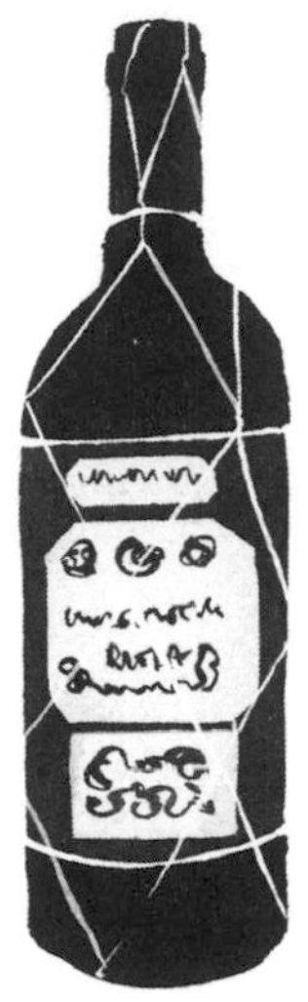

'Seared over a flaming beech-wood grill, the finger-sized Nürnberg Rostbratwurst sausages sold at this rustic inn arguably set the standard across the land'

Bratwursthäusle

BRATWURSTHÄUSLE

BAVARIA | $ | FRANCONIAN

Rathausplatz 1, Nuremberg; 0911-227 695; http://die-nuernberger-bratwurst.de; mains €8.50-15.50

Seared over a flaming beech-wood grill, the finger-sized Nürnberg Rostbratwurst sausages sold at this rustic inn arguably set the standard across the land. Eisbein (pickled ham hock) and Leberknödelsuppe (liver dumpling soup) also star on the meaty menu. Dine in the timber-beamed restaurant or on the terrace with views of the Hauptmarkt.

SCHLENKERLA

BAVARIA | $ | GERMAN

Dominikanerstrasse 6, Bamberg; 0951-560 60; www.schlenkerla.de; mains €7-13

Going strong since 1678, this fabulous half-timbered, flower-bedecked tavern has never lost its touch. Beneath frescoed vaults and wooden beams as dark as the superb *Rauchbier* (smoked beer) poured straight from oak barrels, locals gather to dig into Franconian specials like ham hock in smoked beer sauce, and crispy pork shoulder with sauerkraut and dumplings.

BELGIUM

Belgium is justifiably known for great mussels, double-fried chips and superb chocolate. The country's chefs were once famed for offering French cuisine in Germanic portions, but a new wave of gastronomy references flavours from world cuisines. Simultaneously, old Belgian home-cooking favourites, from meatballs to rabbit stews, have been iresurrected and given new zest, while seasonal game dishes remain popular in the Ardennes.

WHAT TO EAT

Mussels and chips
Eat a hearty portion of *moules-frites* local-style using an empty mussel shell as a pair of tweezers.

Chocolate
Belgian chocolate uses pure ingredients, and no cheap vegetable fats. The essential varieties are pralines and creamy *manons*, bite-sized filled chocolates.

Waffles
Belgium's signature semi-sweet snack, traditionally lightly dusted with icing sugar and eaten hot off the griddle. Brussels' waffles are light and crispy, while the *gaufre de Liège* has rounder edges and a breadier dough with a hint of cinnamon.

Stoemp
A home-cooking classic, *stoemp* is essentially boiled potatoes mashed together with vegetables.

PRICE RANGES
$ less than €15
$$ €15–25
$$$ €25 or more

Tipping: Not expected.

JULIA FISH & OYSTER BAR

DE PANNE | $$$ | SEAFOOD
Arthur Vanhouttelaan 2; 058 62 66 65; www.julia-baaldje.be; mains €19-40

This acclaimed restaurant – run by the fourth-generation, female-led fishmongers Mare Nostrum – secures its own supply of fresh seafood daily. If you love the humble bivalve, or are partial to ceviche or perch and chips, you simply must stop by. The walls are bare brick and the furnishings minimalist, putting all the focus on the food.

DE RUYFFELAER

YPRES | $$ | FLEMISH
Gustave de Stuersstraat 9; 057-36 60 06; www.deruyffelaer.be; mains €15-26

Traditional local dishes are served in an adorable wood-panelled interior with old chequerboard floors and *brocante* (vintage) decor including dried flowers, old radios and antique biscuit tins. Try the whimsical 'cod bathing in a vegetable pond', or classic boeuf Bourguignon.

WIJNBISTRO DI VINO

OSTEND | $$ | BISTRO
Wittenonnenstraat 2; 0473 87 12 97; www.wijnbistrodivino.be; mains €14-22

This intimate and candlelit wine-bistro reflects its owner's passion for food and wine. The menu is simple (fish or meat), seasonal, well priced and executed, and paired expertly with one of the best wine lists in Ostend. Wood panelling and weathered tables add to the relaxed charm of the place.

MOMENT!

DE HAAN | $$ | CAFÉ
Koninklijke Baan 29; 059 43 00 43; www.apartmoment.be; mains €9-20

Cheerful Moment! serves up some of the best breakfasts on the coast, served up on long shared tables. They do big English breakfasts as well as more traditional Continental fare, with waffles, eggs of every variety and excellent lunches too.

LIEVEN

BRUGES | $$ | BELGIAN
Philipstockstraat 45; 050-68 09 75; www.etenbijlieven.be; mains €23-36

You'll need to book ahead for a table at this extremely popular, excellent-value Belgian bistro. It works wonders with local ingredients, and is recognised by its peers from around the country. Simple dishes such as rib-eye steaks and sole with mussels are perfectly produced in a sleekly modern but relaxed environment.

HELEN CATH-CART/LONELY PLANET ©

'The recipes for our tarts have been passed from chef to chef at Arcadi for 30 years.'
Arcadi

HELEN CATHCART/LONELY PLANET ©

DE STOEPA

BRUGES | $$ | BISTRO
Oostmeers 124; 050-33 04 54; www.stoepa.be; mains €14-28

A gem of a place in a peaceful residential setting. It's got a slightly hippie/Buddhist ambience; oriental statues, terracotta-coloured walls, a metal stove and wooden floors and furniture give a homey but stylish feel. Best of all is the leafy terrace garden. Tuck into the upmarket bistro-style food including falafel burgers and Indonesian curries.

CARTE BLANCHE

GHENT | $$$ | FLEMISH
Martelaarslaan 321; 09-233 28 08; www.carteblanchepw.be; lunch menu €25, dinner menu €60

Lobster is a big feature at this intimate, elegant restaurant. It's the brainchild of partners Walter Goderis and chef Paul Rapati, who've been receiving

diners here for almost 25 years: Goderis serves and Rapati cooks. The dark-hued dining room feels very grown-up and the constantly evolving set menus, which focus on Rapati's take on traditional Flemish flavours, are beautifully presented.

HOLY FOOD MARKET

GHENT | $$ | FOOD HALL
Beverhoutplein 15; www.holyfoodmarket.be; snacks from €7

After transitioning from a church to a library, the 16th-century Baudelo Chapel has now morphed into Ghent's hottest dining destination – a glorified food court of the gourmet variety centred around a swanky bar. Dine on everything from fresh oysters to shrimp croquettes and Russian caviar.

ARCADI

BRUSSELS | $ | BRASSERIE
Rue d'Arenberg 1b; 02-511 33 43; www.arcadicafe.be; mains €12-16

The jars of preserves, beautiful cakes and fruit tarts at this classic and charming bistro entice plenty of Brussels residents, as do well-priced meals such as lasagne and steak, all served nonstop by courteous staff. With a nice location on the edge of the Galeries St-Hubert, this is a great spot for an indulgent, creamy hot chocolate.

COMME CHEZ SOI

BRUSSELS | $$$ | FRENCH
Place Rouppe 23; 02-512 29 21; www.commechezsoi.be; mains from €49

The name evokes cooking just like 'at home', but unless you have a personal chef crafting North Sea lobster salad with black truffles and potatoes, sole fillets with Riesling and shrimp mousseline or perhaps spicy lacquered pigeon breast with wild rice, it's nothing of the sort. This is extraordinary food from master chef Pierre Wynants' son-in-law, Lionel Rigolet, and the Art Nouveau surrounds are equally extraordinary.

MER DU NORD

BRUSSELS | $ | SEAFOOD
Rue Ste-Catherine 45; 02-513 11 92; www.vishandelnoordzee.be; items from €8

Well-reputed fishmonger's window catering to a wide cross-section of Brussels folk plus assorted visitors – place your order and when it's ready your name is called by staff with a brass megaphone. You eat standing up at tables on the cobbled square opposite. The scampi (not deep fried but soaked in herb dressing) is sublime.

LAURENT GERBAUD

BRUSSELS | $ | CAFE
Rue Ravenstein 2; 02-511 16 02; www.chocolatsgerbaud.be; snacks from €6

A bright and welcoming cafe with big picture windows that's perfect for lunch, coffee or hot chocolate

Previous spread: Beer at the waterfront in Bruges; Clams at Bruges Fish Market.

if you're between museums. Don't leave without trying the wonderful chocolates, which count as healthy eating in the world of Belgian chocs because they have no alcohol, additives or added sugar. Friendly owner Laurent also runs chocolate-tasting and -making sessions.

BOUCHERY

BRUSSELS | $$ | FRENCH
Chaussée d'Alsemberg 812a; 02-332 37 74; www.bouchery-restaurant.be; veg lunch buffets €18, 4-course menus €58

Using locally sourced and organic ingredients, award-winning chef Damien Bouchéry puts his own twist on French cooking: veal tartare with grilled nectarines and chickpea fries are among the delicate dishes to grace the four- to eight-course evening menus. Almost everything is homemade, from the bread and butter to the lacto-fermented goods. The décor is elegant, with wooden floors and bent-wood chairs and white lamps and bench seating. Weekday lunch is a vegetarian buffet.

KITCHEN 151

BRUSSELS | $$ | MIDDLE EASTERN
Chaussée de Wavre 145; 02-512 49 29; www.kitchen.onefiveone.be; mains €15-30

Standing at a culinary crossroads, Kitchen 151 offers a whole world of flavours from the Middle East. Drag thick, fluffy pitas through velvety hummus, or gorge on a veggie burger made with pumpkin, Portobello mushrooms, tahini and almonds. If you're sharing a mezze, be sure to try the smoky baba ganoush. Decor is funky bistro-style.

SAINT-BONIFACE

BRUSSELS | $ | FRENCH/BASQUE
Rue St-Boniface 9; 02-511 53 66; www.saintboniface.be; mains €12-18

An enchanting old-world restaurant near the eponymous church featuring gingham tablecloths, walls jammed with framed pictures, and authentic dishes from France's southwestern and Basque regions, notably *cassoulet*, Périgord duck, foie gras and *andouillette* (strongly flavoured tripe sausage – very much an acquired taste).

THE JANE

ANTWERP | $$$ | INTERNATIONAL
Paradeplein 1; 03-808 44 65; www.thejaneantwerp.com; tasting menu €170, Upper Room lunch plates €9-25

In a stunningly repurposed old military-hospital chapel, the Jane's sublime two-Michelin-star dining on dishes such as ceviche seabass with passion fruit is such an overwhelmingly fabulous experience that you'll need to book online exactly three months ahead...on the dot of 8am.

WHERE TO BUY...

BELGIAN BEER

De Biertempel, Brussels
As its name states, this shop is a temple to beer, stocking upwards of 700 brews along with matching glasses and other booze-related merchandise.

Beermania, Brussels
Shop complete with a tasting *café*, international delivery service and online sales.

2-Be, Bruges
A vast range of Belgian products sold in a snazzy, central location; check out their 'beer wall'. The canal-side bar terrace serves monster 3L draught beers.

Bacchus Cornelius, Bruges
Explore this cornucopia of 450 beers and rare *gueuzes* (lambic beer), as well as *jenevers* (gins) and liqueurs flavoured with elderflower, cranberries and cherries.

DE GRASPOORT

MECHELEN | $$ | FUSION

Begijnenstraat 28; 015-21 97 10; www.graspoort.be; pasta €16.50-23.50, mains €22.50-28

Despite her restaurant's improbable location down a dead-end residential alley, traveller-turned-chef Greet has a winning combination of Asian and Mediterranean flavours, market-fresh ingredients and lots of vegetables (some vegan options) that have made this place a locals' favourite for over a decade.

CACHET DE CIRE

TURNHOUT | $$$ | EUROPEAN

Guldensporenlei 23; 014-42 22 08; www.cachetdecire.be; mains €24-29, 3-/4-course menu €40/54

Superb attention to detail is evident in every little touch in this gently colourful restaurant, from the fresh market produce to the hand creams in the bathrooms. The cuisine and presentation are gourmet in quality, yet with generous portion sizes and at prices that are little more than those of a standard brasserie. Mains might include pheasant ravioli with truffle cream.

AMON NANESSE

LIÈGE | $$ | BELGIAN

Rue de l'Épée 4; 04-250 67 83; www.maisondupeket.be; mains $14-24

COURTESY LAURENT GERBAUD

This page: Chocolates at Laurent Gerbaud.

Just behind Place du Marché, this rambling antique house with bare-brick walls and heavy beams combines a lively bar specialising in *pékèt* (gin) shots ($3.50) with a restaurant serving satisfying local pub meals including *boulettes a la liégeoise* (meatballs in raisin-sweetened gravy).

LE PATCH

VERVIERS | $$ | BELGIAN

Chaussée de Heusy 173; 087 22 45 39; www.lepatch.be; mains €14-24

Appetising aromas of fried garlic intermingle with jazzy music, dangling creepers and a ceiling hung with cookery utensils to create a multisensory treat in this inviting delight. The menu concentrates on beautifully prepared salads, pastas and Walloon classics: the sauce of their home-style *rognons* (veal kidneys) is as good as any you're likely to taste anywhere in Belgium.

LUXEMBOURG

Luxembourgish cuisine takes cues from France, Germany and Belgium, but the seasons are ultimately top chef. River-caught trout, pike and crayfish cast fishy hues to springtime and summer menus, while restaurants warm winter cockles with earthy hare, boar, dandelion root and buxom *Quetschentaart* (plum tarts).

WHAT TO EAT

Träipen
Luxembourg's black pudding is prepared from hog's head and married with apple sauce.

Huesenziwwi
A feisty hunting-season dish, 'jugged hare' is cooked in lard, flambéed in brandy and served in a blood-thickened stew.

Kachkéis
A runny, sticky cheese made from cow's milk – so iconic it's the super-power source of Luxembourgish comic-strip hero Superjhemp.

Gromperekichelcher
Any market worth its salt has a stall selling these fritter-like, shredded potato pancakes.

Judd mat Gaardebounen
Smoked pork collar, soaked overnight then simmered with broad beans and served with boiled potatoes.

PRICE RANGES
$ less than €15
$$ €15–30
$$$ €30 or more

Tipping: 5–10%

BISTRO QUAI

MOSELLE VALLEY | $-$$ | LUXEMBOURGISH

3 Route du Vin, Grevenmacher; 24 55 87 75; www.quai.lu; mains €12.50-32

Chef Thomas Medves' glass-box dining room with al fresco deck gazing poetically across the Moselle to Germany is the perfect stage for feasting on premium local produce from the Moselle Valley: Riesling pâté, veal Cordon Bleu stuffed with tangy Luxemburgischer Münster, crayfish with *crémant* cream sauce. Perfectly paired wines cap off the staunchly local dining experience.

LA DISTILLERIE

MÜLLERTHAL REGION | $$ | VEGETARIAN

8 Rue du Château, Bourglinster; 78 78 78 1; www.bourglinster.lu; lunch/dinner menus from €60/120

Spectacularly set inside the turreted, storybook castle Château de Bourglinster, parts of which date from the 11th century, Michelin-starred La Distillerie is a full-blown gastronomic extravaganza. Notably vegetables are the star of executive chef René Mathieu's intricate tasting menus (there's no à la carte) and Mathieu forages for wild herbs in the castle's grounds.

RESTAURANT MATHES

MOSELLE VALLEY | $$$ | MODERN LUXEMBOURGISH

37 Route du Vin, Ahn; 76 01 06; www.restaurant-mathes.lu; menus €42-94

Possibly Luxembourg's finest dining experience, this stylized dining room sporting street-art-like murals opens onto a bucolic sun-drenched terrace overlooking the restaurant's very own vineyards. Intricately crafted menus courtesy of chef Arnaud Le Levier might see you sampling foie gras terrine with Gewürztraminer chutney, oven-baked *brochet* (pike) in a Riesling sauce, or John Dory with smoked fennel and *crémant* sorbet.

NETHERLANDS

With a recipe book brimming with traditional meat-potato-veg dishes and modern innovation, the Dutch foodie experience is far from dull. New wave chefs continually refine their humble culinary antecedents with contemporary twists, while urbanites like Amsterdam and Rotterdam cook up a cornucopia of world cuisines. Countrywide, every taste and budget is catered for with *eetcafés* (pub-like eateries), *friteries* (chip shops), on-trend bistros and gastronomic restaurants.

WHAT TO EAT

Herring
Sliding a raw, salted or pickled *Haring* head-first down the gullet at a street-side herring stall never fails to entertain.

Asparagus
A white and fleshy springtime joy cultivated in Limburg and Noord-Brabant.

Stamppot
'Mashed pot' mashes potatoes up with kale, endive or pickled cabbage and accompanies smoked sausage or pork strips.

Pea soup
A spoon stuck upright in the cooking pot indicates the perfect *Erwtensoep* – a feisty pea soup spiked with smoked sausage and bacon.

Kroketten
Deep-fried, crumb-coated dough sticks with different fillings are the ultimate Dutch drinking snack.

PRICE RANGES
For a main course:
$ less than €12
$$ €12–25
$$$ €25 or more

Tipping: 5–10%

VLEMINCKX SAUSMEESTERS

AMSTERDAM | $ | FAST FOOD
Voetboogstraat 33; www.vleminckxdesausmeester.nl; small/large €2.30/4.50

A queue stretching down the block flags Amsterdam's most famous friterie, a hole-in-the-wall takeaway shack where perfectly crisp and fluffy, Flemish *frites* (fries) have been fried since 1957. The standard order comes in a red-and-white checked paper cone smothered in a choice of 28 wildly different gloppy sauces, including apple, green pepper, curried ketchup, peanut, sambal, mustard and various mayonnaise types.

D'VIJFF VLIEGHEN

AMSTERDAM | $$ | DUTCH
Spuistraat 294-302; 020-530 40 60; www.vijffvlieghen.nl; mains €21-28

Time-travel to the Dutch Golden Age with 'Five Flies', a culinary jewel filling five 17th-century canal houses since 1939. Old-wood dining rooms feature Delft Blue tiles, gold-plated leather and original etchings by Rembrandt; chairs have copper plates inscribed with the names of famous guests (Walt Disney, Mick Jagger...). Exquisite dishes are made from wholly Dutch produce, predominantly organic: think Dutch herring with cucumber salad and borage-laced buttermilk, roast veal with mature Gouda cheese and hazelnuts.

RON GASTROBAR DOWNTOWN

AMSTERDAM | $$ | INDONESIAN
Rokin 49; 020-790 03 22; www.rongastrobarindonesia.nl; dishes €15-17.50

Beneath a striking curved glass-and-metal ceiling, superstar chef Ron Blaauw showcases cutting-edge Indonesian cuisine: *saté kambing* (goat skewers with peanut sauce), *udang peteh* (shrimp with bitter beans in coconut sauce) and *bebek mendoan* (slow-cooked duck with tempeh and green-sambal mayo). His signature *iga babi bakar* (BBQ spare ribs in a sambal sauce), served hot off the grill, are practically an Amsterdam legend. End with lush Indonesian-inspired cocktails in the jungle-themed bar and club.

DUDOK

ROTTERDAM | $ | CAFÉ

Meent 88; 010-433 31 02; www.dudok.nl; apple pie & cream €5

Ask any Rotterdammer to nominate their most treasured sweet treat, and there's a good chance they will opt for the cinnamon-spiced *Appeltaart met slagroom* (apple pie with cream) served here with lashings of whipped cream. Café-brasserie Dudok opened at this site in 1991 and was named after architect Willem Marinus Dudok, the creative mind behind the 1945 former bank building.

FOUQUET

SOUTH HOLLAND | $$$ | MEDITERRANEAN

Javastraat 31a, Den Haag; 070-360 62 73; www.fouquet.nl; menus €29.50-89

The three-course *Menu du Marché* offered at this elegant Den Haag restaurant is an excellent, bargain-priced introduction to chef and owner Sebastiaan de Bruijn's seasonally inspired French-Mediterranean fare.

'I do not accept compromises in the taste of my menus. That is why I use organic ingredients supplied by honest producers.' *Patrick Brugman, Restaurant In den Doofpot*

The menu changes daily, responding to what is fresh in the local markets – Zeeland oysters perhaps, veal with asparagus and forest-mushroom gravy, five-spice fried duck liver with sultanas and chocolate – and is prepared with love and great expertise. Presentation, service and the wine list are equally impressive.

RESTAURANT IN DEN DOOFPOT

SOUTH HOLLAND | $$$ | EUROPEAN

Turfmarkt 9, Leiden; 071-512 24 34; www.indendoofpot.nl; lunch/diner menus from €45/60

A white high-ceilinged interior with graceful vintage wall mirrors and expert wine pairings provide the stylish prelude to the outstanding Modern European cuisine of talented chef Patrick Brugman. Creative menus change

COURTESY DUDOK

monthly and feature seasonal dishes such as smoked tzatziki with green apple, pork belly with Dutch eel and miso, and sesame-crusted ox tail with ginger and shallot sauce. The ultimate treat: lunch aboard In den Doofpot's electric, peppermint-green canal boat.

SMIT BOKKUM

NORTH HOLLAND | $$ | SEAFOOD

Slobbeland 19, Volendam; 029-936 33 73; www.smitbokkum.nl; mains €18.50-28

Run by the sixth generation, Smit Bokkum has been smoking local eel, sea bass, oysters, mackerel and cockles at its smokehouse in the quaint fishing port of Volendam, 20km northeast of Amsterdam, since 1856. Aromatic treats served on the restaurant's sunny harbor-side terrace include eel fillets on toast, eel soup and the day's catch à la Smit-Bokkum (with red cabbage and eel butter). Dedicated foodies won't want to miss a 20-minute guided smokehouse tour with tastings.

MR & MRS

NORTH HOLLAND | $$ | BISTRO

Lange Veerstraat 4, Haarlem; 023-531 59 35; www.restaurantmrandmrs.nl; menus €40-60

Unexpectedly gastronomic cooking at this tiny Haarlem restaurant – with Mr in the kitchen and Mrs creating exciting wine pairings out front – is artfully conceived and presented. A succession of small hot and cold plates ensure a dining experience to remember: whiskey-poached oysters with candied sea vegetables, sea bass and olive mille-feuille, guinea fowl stuffed with walnut, pumpkin and Gorgonzola. End on a sweet note with raspberry and pineapple tarte tatin.

HÉRON

UTRECHT | $$ | EUROPEAN

Schalkwijkstraat 26-28; 030-230 22 29; www.heronrestaurant.nl; menus €36–46

This adorable 'petit restaurant', hidden on a quiet Utrecht back lane, presents expectant gourmets with a tantalizingly cryptic menu that reads something a shopping list of culinary curiosities: 'brains-chicory-brown butter' perhaps, or 'pigs trotters-rémoulade-kohlrabi'? Everything brims with imaginative flavours and 100% locally sourced – including foraged plants collected by the forester owner. Six lucky guests get to sit right at the central cooking counter and watch every move of the expert chefs.

DEN BOERENSTAMPPOT

NOORD BRABANT | $ | TRADITIONAL DUTCH

Schoolstraat 3-5, Breda; 076-514 01 62; www.facebook.com/denboerenstamppot; 1/3-course dinner €7/10

Joyously life-affirming proprietors Fred and Marloes van Weerd have been serving up good old homestyle Dutch

Previous spread: Appeltaart from Dudok.
Next spread: Seafood from Oost; Mr Mofongo.

dinners at this quaint, cottage-style eatery in Breda for 45-odd years. The die-hard traditional meal of choice is a huge plate of *stamppot* (potato mashed with veg of the day) topped with a choice of meatballs, *stofvlees* (beef stew), chicken, sausage, cutlet etc. For just a few euros more, add a soup or starter and dessert and congratulate yourself on the bargain fill-up.

DAMES PELLENS

NOORD BRABANT | $$ | FRENCH
Boschstraat 24, Breda; 076-887 69 29; www.damespellens.nl; lunch/dinner menus from €27.50/34.50

Creative, multicourse dining courtesy of chef Daan de Brouwer is the USP of this stylish wine bar in Breda, named after a wealthy pair of bon vivant sisters with a penchant for the good life – spot a B&W photo of the vintage pair on the window sill. Both wine selection and suggested pairings are superb, but the biggest draw is the food: up to four courses or a swift *plat du jour* at lunchtime, and a more gourmet, somewhat experimental 'chef-special' fine dining of up to seven courses come dusk.

FRITURE REITZ

MAASTRICHT | $ | FAST FOOD
Markt 75; 043-321 57 06; www.reitz.nl; takeaway small/large fries €3/3.50, mains €8.50–18.95

Join the takeaway queue at Maastricht's iconic snack bar, which has been turning Limburg potatoes cultivated in the surrounding countryside into crisp double-fried frites since 1909. Should the weather not oblige, duck inside beneath the cheery red-and-white canopy instead, snag a table with red banquet seating in the old-world interior, and tuck into a heart-warming local dish of *konijn in het zuur* (sour rabbit) or *Luikse gehaktballen* (meatballs) – accompanied, of course, by the world's perfect fries.

DE ZILTE ZEEMEERMIN

GELDERLAND | $ | SEAFOOD
Steenstraat 83a, Arnhem; 026-379 48 16; www.deziltezeemeermin.nl; small plates from €5

Hollandse Nieuwe or soused herrings (lightly brined, raw, young herrings), herring sandwiches, *gerookte meervalfilet* (smoked catfish fillet), oven-baked clams and freshly shucked oysters served with various sassy sauces sell like hot cakes at this wildly popular fish bar in Arnhem. *Visbroertjes* ('fish brothers') Luuk and Wiebe de Haan – famed for their oysters at local festivals – are the creative talent behind The Silent Mermaid.

CÈPES

GELDERLAND | $$ | EUROPEAN
Houtkampweg 1, Otterlo; 0318-591 228; www.cepes.nl; lunch/dinner menus from €30/39

With a parasol-shaded terrace overlooking flowery gardens and grassy fields beyond, this on-trend contemporary

WHERE TO TASTE AND BUY...

CHEESE

Proeflokaal Kef, Amsterdam
Tuck into a sandwich stuffed with Dutch aged sheep's cheese and fig compote at historic Fromagerie Kef's canal-side cafe in Amsterdam Noord.

Kaasmarkt, Almaar
Cheese trading began in Almaar in 1365 and Friday mornings (Apr–Sep) the Netherlands' most famous cheese market fills the town's canal-ringed centre.

Gestam, Edam
Sample 30 different cheeses at this warehouse established in 1916 for regional producers of the town's namesake cheese.

Kaasstad, Gouda
Join the crowd every Thursday in spring and summer to watch the pantomime-style cheese market in front of Gouda's historic *waag* (weighing house).

address right by the bucolic Hoge Veluwe National Park is a dreamy spot to linger in warm weather. Chef Robert Hartelman sources his fresh, organic produce from local farms, vegetable gardens and cheese dairies, to stunning effect. Begin with a tasty combo of potato, quail egg, wild garlic, asparagus and Olde Remeker cheese perhaps followed by lamb with creamy feta cheese.

OOST

FRIESLAND | $ | SEAFOOD
Fortweg 20, Strand Fortweg Vlieland; 06 1007 8585; www.oostvlie.nl; mains €10-15

On the Friesan island of Vlieland, there is no more fashionable *Strandpaviljoen* (beach pavilion) than fabulous Oost ('East'), a contemporary shoebox hidden between sand dunes and a swath of fine golden sand. Fish and shellfish from the North and Wadden Seas – with a creative fusion touch (lots of spices 'n seaweed) and baked in a charcoal oven – is what it does best. Think laidback beachy lunch by day, luxuriously romantic dinner at sunset.

RESTAURANT BY ÚS SENT

FRIESLAND | $$$ | DUTCH
Over de Kelders 24, Leeuwarden; 058-737 01 52; www.restaurantby-us.nl; 3-/4-/5-course menu €40/50/58

Organic Dutch cuisine celebrating Friesan produce lies at the heart of Michiel and Lilian's candlelit bistro in Leeuwarden, a funky address with

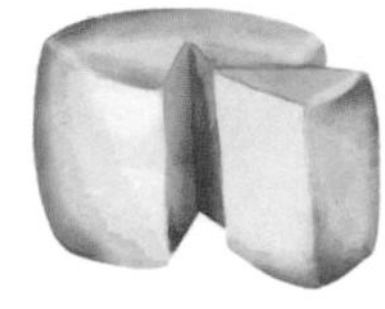

'Restaurant By Us is a restaurant that serves one menu – a surprise menu. We have chosen this to prevent as much waste as possible.'
Michiel en Lilian, Restaurant By Ús

wood-and-leather-meets-street-art interior and an equally fun dining experience. Pick how many courses you desire, state if you're vegetarian or have allergies, and leave the rest up to chef Michiel. The wine list is excellent, and faux furs and a wood-burning stove add a wonderful winter warmth.

SUNSET

AMELAND | $ | SEAFOOD
Oranjeweg 61, Hollum; 0519-554 280; www.thesunset.nl; mains €12–15

'If you're not barefoot, you're overdressed' is the strapline of this sizzling beach club, a summertime skip from Hollum's picture-book lighthouse on Ameland island. Lounge over cocktails, sunset views and freshly shucked oysters, and consider what else is required in life? All-day dining is equally tasty and packs a world-flavour punch: pulled-pork and felafel sandwiches, toasties and burgers alongside spicy tuna sushi, smoked mackerel with green-tea noodles or simply the catch of the day fresh from the North Sea.

JONATHAN ANDREW, COURTESY OOST

COURTESY MR MOFONGO

'T ZIELHOES

GRONINGEN PROVINCE | $ | DUTCH

Zijlweg 4, Usquert; Tel 0595-423 058; www.zielhoes.nl; mains €10.50-12.50

Traditional Dutch *stamppot* (stews), shrimp sandwiches, herrings on rye bread and eels on what feels like the edge of the world is the star turn of 't Zielhoes, a staunchly local address in the remote northernmost realm of the country. Unchanged for centuries, the former sluice-guard house sits at the foot of a sea dyke and is famed locally for its sweet *waddentaart* (a feisty fruit-and-rum pastry).

MR MOFONGO

GRONINGEN PROVINCE | $$ | WORLD CUISINE

Oude Boteringestraat 26, Groningen; Tel 050-314 42 66; www.mofongo.nl; mains €15-25

Hybrid dining–drinking spaces don't get cooler than Groningen's Mr Mofongo, named after an explorer the globetrotting owner (an underwater photographer) met at the Santa Lucia lagoon in Cuba after diving with bull sharks (it's true). The student-hip address combines buzzing street terrace with cocktail bar featuring a 'wall' of 56 homemade spirits (including traditional *jenever* or Dutch 'gin') tapped by a robotic arm, craft distillery and rooftop wine bar – all with a cosmopolitan menu to match. Think noodles, pasta, Javanese satay with peanut sauce, steaks and sticky ribs, ceviche et al.

WHAT TO EAT

New Nordic cuisine
Top-quality, seasonal Nordic produce prepared with groundbreaking creativity; find it on Michelin-starred menus and in more affordable haunts too.

Smørrebrød
As famous as the Little Mermaid, these Danish open-faced sandwiches come with a variety of toppings from shrimps to roast beef and remoulade.

Sild
Pickled, smoked or cured, herring is found all over the country, but it's a particular favourite on the island of Bornholm.

Pølse
Find the classic Danish hot dog at street stalls.

Kanelsnegle
These buttery 'cinnamon snails', drizzled with white glacé icing, are a perfect pick-me-up.

PRICE RANGES
For a main course:
$ less than 125kr
$$ 125kr–250kr
$$$ 250kr or more

Tipping: Round up for great service.

DENMARK

With its current cast of world-renowned chefs and clutch of Michelin stars, it's hard to believe the culinary scene in Denmark used to be as flat as its landscape. But a group of trailblazing chefs devised the New Nordic Manifesto in 2004, and the rest is history. Now top-notch food using the best local ingredients is everywhere, from the heady heights of Noma to the humblest street food stall.

HENNE KIRKEBY KRO

HENNE | $$$ | DANISH
Strandvejen 234; 75 25 54 00; www.hennekirkebykro.dk; lunch/dinner menu 625/1395kr

Michelin-starred Henne Kirkeby Kro is the kind of historic countryside inn that Copenhagen gourmands (and global food lovers) will happily travel hours to reach. The accomplished kitchen team is led by British-born Paul Cunningham, who has worked in many of Denmark's best kitchens, and the menu – which could feature dishes such as turbot, salted lemon & mushrooms – is a thing of beauty, drawing on the enormous kitchen garden and first-rate local produce.

KOLVIG

RIBE | $$ | DANISH
Mellemdammen 13; 41 82 37 27; www.kolvig.dk; lunch 119-179kr, dinner mains 229kr

Kolvig's alfresco terrace overlooks the river, offering prime Ribe-watching. The menu is the most ambitious in town, showcasing local produce; most interesting is the delicious tapas plate of Wadden Sea flavours, including shrimp, ham, smoked lamb and local cheese.

OLINICO

AARHUS | $ | INTERNATIONAL
Mejlgade 35; 86 25 05 70; www.olinico.dk; 3-courses 150kr

You may need to fight for one of the sought-after tables at OliNico (there's no reservations), a small, understatedly cool deli-restaurant with a menu of classic dishes at excellent prices. The daily-changing, three-course dinner menu may be Aarhus' best-kept food secret – braised pork with butternut squash gratin, anyone?

LANGHOFF & JUUL

AARHUS | $$ | DANISH

Guldsmedgade 30; 30 30 00 18; www.langhoffogjuul.dk; lunch 98-175kr, 3-course dinner menus from 368kr

Ticking all the right boxes, Langhoff & Juul is a rustic, informal space in the Latin Quarter, where the casual setting belies the accomplished food coming out of the kitchen, especially of an evening, with dishes such as chicken with salted, pickled rhubarb and cucumber salad. There's a super brunch spread every day, and smørrebrød and salads at lunch, plus polished service, great aesthetics, and a relaxed and enjoyable atmosphere.

FREDERIKSHØJ

AARHUS | $$$ | DANISH
Oddervej 19-21; 86 14 22 80; www.frederikshoj.com; 7-/10-course menu 1200/1800kr, with wine 1800/2500kr

Bookings are essential to experience this Michelin-starred restaurant's forested setting just south of Aarhus' centre, and to savour the gastronomic wizardry of Beirut-born owner-chef Wassim Hallal. His kitchen has a penchant for high-end headliners like lobster, caviar and oysters, with the majority of ingredients sourced from Jutland's bounty.

FALSLED KRO

FAABORG | $$$ | DANISH
Assensvej 513, Millinge; 62 68 11 11; www.falsledkro.dk; 4-/6-/8-course dinner menu 895/1095/1795kr, with wine 1790/2190/3290kr

'The kitchen's creations are nothing short of extraordinary, pushing superlative produce to enlightened heights'
Søllerød Kro

Book well ahead for a full-on gourmet experience, but with bigger portions and far warmer service than in so many upmarket places. Falsled Kro's cuisine focuses on prime, locally harvested ingredients cooked using French techniques with Nordic twists, such as scallops with cabbage and choucroute sauce, or Faaborg cod with sherry and autumn mushrooms. Dine on a lawn-front verandah or within the picture-perfect thatched inn (rebuilt 1851).

RESTAURANT GENERALEN

TRANEKÆR | $$ | DANISH
Slotsgade 82; 62 53 33 03; www.housepichardt.dk; lunch mains 95-249kr, dinner mains 225-275kr

At the western base of Tranekær Slot, Generalen has converted 19th-century stables into a stylish restaurant, maintaining the horse-box divisions between tables, though there's also cafe seating outside. Menus are typically Danish, concentrating on locally sourced produce and often reworking recipes from the castle's 1815 cookbook, such as lightly smoked Danish calf tenderloin with thyme, and butter-baked veal.

SØLLERØD KRO

HOLTE | $$$ | DANISH
Søllerødvej 35; 45 80 25 05; www.soelleroed-kro.dk; 2-/3-course lunch 395/495kr, 9-course dinner 1795kr

Michelin-starred Søllerød Kro is set in a beautiful 17th-century thatched-roof inn, located in an outer suburb of Copenhagen. The kitchen's creations are nothing short of extraordinary, pushing superlative produce to enlightened heights – dehydrated artichokes might be paired with hazelnut milk and smoke, for example. Yet, despite the adulation, Søllerød Kro keeps its feet firmly on the ground, ditching pomp and attitude for a genuine hospitality that's as much a highlight as its degustation menus.

TORVEHALLERNE KBH

COPENHAGEN | $ | FOOD HALL
Frederiksborggade 21, Israels Plads; www.torvehallernekbh.dk; dishes from around 55kr

This food market is an essential stop on the Copenhagen foodie trail. A delicious ode to the fresh, the tasty and the artisanal, the market's beautiful stalls peddle everything from seasonal herbs and berries to smoked meats, seafood and cheeses, smørrebrød, fresh pasta and hand-brewed coffee. You could easily spend an hour or more exploring its twin halls. You can eat here too; several of the vendors also prepare inexpensive meals.

DISTRICT TONKIN

COPENHAGEN | $ | VIETNAMESE
Dronningens Tværgade 12; 60 88 86 98; www.district-tonkin.com; baguettes 62kr, soups & salads 70-135kr

With a playful interior channelling the streets of Vietnam, casual, convivial District Tonkin serves up fresh, gut-filling bánh mì (Vietnamese baguettes), stuffed with coriander, fresh chilli and combos like Vietnamese sausage with marinated pork, homemade pâté and BBQ sauce. The menu also includes gorgeous, less-common Vietnamese soups, among them aromatic beef *pho*, and tomato-based *xíu mai* (with pork and mushroom meatballs).

REFFEN

COPENHAGEN | $ | STREET FOOD
Refshalevej 167a; www.reffen.dk; meals from 80kr

This harbourside street-food market is a veritable village of converted shipping containers, selling sustainable bites from across the globe. Options include organic polenta and pasta, dosas, burgers, sushi, satay skewers and Filipino BBQ. You'll also find a number of bars including an outpost of Copenhagen's cult-status

'Everything is cut to the bone, no frames but the few hanging on the walls. Simplicity with quality comes first, great details are just beneath.'
Relæ

COURTESY OLINICO

COURTESY PLUTO

microbrewery Mikkeller. Hands down one of the best spots to dine, drink and chill on a warm summer evening.

GASOLINE GRILL

COPENHAGEN | $ | BURGERS
Landgreven 10; www.gasolinegrill.com; burgers 75kr

Some of the city's most famous chefs join the queue at Gasoline, a petrol station-turned-burger takeaway. The menu is refreshingly straightforward: four burgers (one vegetarian), fries with a choice of toppings and home-made dips, and two desserts. The meat is organic and freshly ground daily, the buns brioche, and the flavour rich and decadent. The place closes when the burgers run out (usually around 6pm), so go at lunch to avoid disappointment.

SCHØNNEMANN

COPENHAGEN | $$ | DANISH
Hauser Plads 16; 33 12 07 85; www.restaurantschonnemann.dk; smørrebrød 75-185kr

A veritable institution, Schønnemann has been lining bellies with smørrebrød and snaps since 1877. Originally a hit with farmers in town selling their produce, the restaurant's current fan base includes revered chefs like René Redzepi; try the smørrebrød named after him: smoked halibut with creamed cucumber, radishes and chives on caraway bread. Other standouts include the King's Garden (potatoes with smoked mayonnaise, fried onions and chives).

WHERE TO EAT...

SMØRREBRØD

Schønnemann, Copenhagen
The undisputed master of the open-faced sandwich, enduringly popular Schønnemann has been serving up smørrebrød since 1877.

Aamanns Takeaway, Copenhagen
Pick up avant-garde flavour combinations (think blue cheese, cherry relish and fried buckwheat) at the takeaway arm of this revered restaurant.

F-Høj, Aarhus
If your budget doesn't stretch to Michelin stars, you can eat exquisite smørrebrød from the sister-restaurant of an anointed eatery instead.

Mortens Kro, Aalborg
High-end open sandwiches in elegant surrounds. Try the classic herring with apple puree or branch out with grilled ox fillet.

MANFREDS OG VIN

COPENHAGEN | $$ | DANISH
Jægersborggade 40; 36 96 65 93; www.manfreds.dk; small plates 90-120kr, 7-course tasting menu 295kr

Manfreds is the ideal local bistro, with passionate staffers, boutique natural wines and a regularly changing menu that favours organic produce (most from the restaurant's own farm) cooked simply and sensationally. Swoon over nuanced, gorgeously textured dishes like grilled spring onion served with pistachio purée, crunchy breadcrumbs and salted egg yolk. If you're hungry and curious, opt for the good-value seven-dish menu.

RELÆ

COPENHAGEN | $$$ | NEW NORDIC
Jægersborggade 41; 36 96 66 09; www.restaurant-relae.dk; 4-/7-course menu 475/895kr

Established by prolific chef Christian Puglisi, Relæ was one of the first restaurants in town to offer superlative New Nordic cooking without all the designer fanfare. One Michelin star later, it remains a low-fuss place, where diners set their own table, pour their own wine and swoon over soul-lifting dishes focused on seasonality, simplicity and (mostly) organic produce.

PLUTO

COPENHAGEN | $$ | DANISH
Borgergade 16; 33 16 00 16; www.restaurantpluto.dk/kbhk; mains 135-225kr

Loud, convivial Pluto is not short of friends, and for good reason: there's a superfun soundtrack, attentive staff and beautiful, simple dishes by respected local chef Rasmus Oubæk. Whether it's flawlessly seared cod with seasonal carrots or funky truffles and green beans in a mussel broth, the family-style menu lets the produce sing. There's a solid charcuterie selection, and some interesting natural wines, as well as bar seating (especially great for solo diners).

GERANIUM

COPENHAGEN | $$$ | NEW NORDIC
Per Henrik Lings Allé 4; 69 96 00 20; www.geranium.dk; tasting menu 2600kr, wine pairings 1600-15,000kr, juice pairings 1000kr

On the 8th floor of Parken Stadium, Geranium is the only restaurant in town sporting three Michelin stars. At the helm is Bocuse d'Or–winning chef Rasmus Kofoed, who transforms local, organic ingredients on the 17-course tasting menu into edible Nordic artworks like lobster paired with milk and the juice of fermented carrots and sea buckthorn, or cabbage sprouts and chicken served with quail egg, cep mushrooms and hay beer.

Previous spread: Dishes from Olinico; Pluto. Next spread: Preparing dishes in Egget.

HØST

COPENHAGEN | $$$ | NEW NORDIC
Nørre Farimagsgade 41; 89 93 84 09; https://cofoco.dk/en/restaurants/hoest; 3-/5-course menu 355/455kr

Høst's phenomenal popularity is easy to understand: award-winning interiors and New Nordic food that's equally fabulous and filling. The set menu is superb, with smaller 'surprise dishes' thrown in and evocative creations like birch-smoked scallops with horseradish and green beans, or a joyful blueberry sorbet paired with Norwegian brown cheese and crispy caramel.

NORDBORNHOLMS RØGERI

BORNHOLM | $ | SEAFOOD
Kæmpestranden 2, Allinge; 56 48 07 30; www.nbr.dk; dishes 60-115kr, buffet 194kr

Several of Bornholm's top chefs praise this smokehouse as the island's best. Not only does it serve a bumper buffet of locally smoked fish, salads and soup (ice-cream dessert included), but its waterside setting makes it the perfect spot to savour Bornholm's Baltic flavours.

FRU PETERSENS CAFÉ

BORNHOLM | $ | CAFE
Almindingensvej 31, Østermarie; 21 78 78 95; www.frupetersenscafe.dk; cake buffet incl drinks 150kr

Cake lovers, come hungry! This cute-as-a-button cafe draws sweet tooths from all over the island with its exceptional kagebord (cake buffet). Its Insta-worthy table groans under the weight of home-baked cakes, tarts, cookies, pastries and more. The rooms are a *hyggelig* (cosy) haven of antiques and trinkets, and there's pretty garden seating.

'From the beginning it was a traditional Bornholm smokehouse, which mostly made smoked herring for citizens in Copenhagen.'
Nordbornholms Røgeri

HALLEGAARD

BORNHOLM | $$ | TAPAS
Aspevej 3, Østermarie; 56 47 02 47; www.hallegaard.dk; hot dogs 65kr, tapas plate 200kr

The farmhouse deli-cafe at artisanal charcuterie Hallegaard offers a tapas plate with a selection of its products (six small samples plus bread, cheese and cake). Pair it with a drop from Hallegaard's small-batch brewery and you have one of Bornholm's best feeds. You can also get a fine hot dog.

KADEAU

BORNHOLM | $$$ | NEW NORDIC
Baunevej 18, Vester Sømarken; 56 97 82 50; www.kadeau.dk; lunch 550-700kr, 5-/8-course dinner 800/1100kr

Book ahead to experience one of Denmark's most exciting and innovative destination restaurants. The menu is a confident, creative celebration of Nordic produce and foraged ingredients. Lunch options are limited but inspired; the tour de force is dinner, where exquisite dishes celebrate Bornholm's nature and harvest and will leave you swooning. Kadeau now has a Michelin star to its name, and its star continues to rise.

NORWAY

Seafood fresh from the water, succulent game, forest-foraged berries and local producers crafting all manner of specialities from cheeses to the herb-infused spirit, *aquavit*, Norway's menu is full, flavoursome and will leave you wanting more. But forewarned is forearmed: food and drink is heart-stoppingly expensive for visitors, and you'll need a wallet as big as your appetite to enjoy the best the country has to offer.

WHAT TO EAT

Salmon
The omnipresent fish (*laks* in Norwegian) can be eaten myriad ways; try *gravlaks*, salmon marinated in sugar, salt and dill.

Reindeer
It's pricey, but the Sámi staple is at its most delicious when eaten roasted (*reinsdyrstek*).

Tørrfisk
You'll see racks of cod drying in the open air in the Lofoten Islands. Stockfish is used as an ingredient in dishes, or cut up to snack on.

Brunost
Norwegian 'brown cheese' is made using the whey of cow or goat's milk, and has a caramel-like flavour.

Waffles
Thin and fluffy, Norwegian waffles are a national obsession. Go sweet with sour cream and jam or savoury with cheese.

PRICE RANGES
For a main course:
$ less than 125kr
$$ 125kr–200kr
$$$ 200kr or more

Tipping: 5–10%

EGGET

STAVANGER | $$$ | BISTRO

Steinkargata 23; 984 07 700; www.facebook.com/eggetstavanger; menus from 795kr

In a clapboard building off Steinkargata, this ramshackle, rough-and-ready eatery is small in size but strong on ambition: the food is modern, creative and bang on trend, with an emphasis on freshness and seasonality. There's no set menu; dishes chalked above the bar might be anything from wild trout to kimchi, braised ribs or Asian slaws. Dishes are accompanied by the waiter's wine recommendations.

SYVERKIOSKEN

OSLO | $ | HOT DOGS

Maridalsveien 45; hot dogs from 20kr

It might look like a hipster replica, but this hole-in-the-wall *pølse* (hot dog) place is absolutely authentic and one of the last of its kind in Oslo. Dogs can be had in a potato bread wrap in lieu of the usual roll, or with both, and there's a large range of old-school accompaniments beyond sauce and mustard.

SENTRALEN RESTAURANT

OSLO | $$ | NEW NORDIC
Øvre Slottsgate 3; 22 33 33 22; www.sentralenrestaurant.no/restaurant; small plates 110-265kr

One of Oslo's best restaurants is also its most relaxed. A large dining room filled with old social-club chairs draws city workers, visitors and locals alike. The outstanding dishes are mostly riffs on Norwegian standards, and use Norwegian produce, but also incorporate international influences in subtle and surprising ways. Combinations may be bold but there's a lightness and prettiness to it all, and friendly, knowledgeable staff are happy to walk you through the menu.

BASS

OSLO | $$ | NEW NORDIC
Thorvald Meyers gate 26c; 482 41 489; www.bassoslo.no; dishes 80-190kr

In what might initially seem like just another corner cafe in the Grünerløkka neighbourhood, you'll find one of the city's best small-plate dining options, served beneath vintage seascapes on classic Norwegian ceramics. Most dishes are what might be called contemporary Norwegian-meets-international – from fried chicken and potato pancakes to deep-sea cod in sorrel butter and death-by-chocolate cake. There's also an impressive wine list, many of which can be had by the glass.

'To create the best atmosphere, we allow guests to participate by cutting, pouring and sharing.'
Sentralen

BRUTUS

OSLO | $$ | NEW NORDIC
Eiriks gate 2; 22 38 00 88; www.barbrutus.no; dishes 99-210kr, snacks 65-199kr

The cooking here is some of the most exciting and accessible in the city, and the dishes that emerge from the open kitchen are flavour bombs that highlight unusual local ingredients and incorporate pan-Nordic influences. The wine list features some of Europe's superstar natural producers and you can come here to just drink and snack. The space is pure Oslo: raw bricks, lushly painted wood cladding, simple vintage chairs and contemporary art.

KOLONIALEN

OSLO | $$$ | GASTRONOMIC
Sofiesgate 16; 901 15 098; www.kolonialenbislett.no; mains 180-289kr

When a venture is led by the ex-owner of three-Michelin-starred Maaemo, you expect the food to be extraordinary, and it is. The short menu is a mix of pan-European dishes – such as calves tongue with oyster mushrooms and red cabbage – done with a contemporary playfulness that stops short of quirky, care of the Australian chef. Kolonialen's almost-Mediterrean-feeling dining room and footpath tables bustle with contented neighbourhood locals day and night.

MARG & BEIN

BERGEN | $$$ | BISTRO

Fosswinckels gate 18; 55 32 34 32; www.marg-bein.no; mains 298-345kr

Bright and enormously inviting, 'Marrow & Bone' in the studenty area around Fosswinckels gate is a super place for supper. The tight, frequently changing menu is an exercise in taking well-loved traditional ingredients and giving them a modern spin; expect dishes such as braised ox cheek and bone marrow with beetroot. Rustic tables, big windows and Scandi furniture complete the swish package.

LYSVERKET

BERGEN | $$$ | NORWEGIAN

KODE 4, Rasmus Meyers allé 9; 55 60 31 00; www.lysverket.no; mains 349-399kr, 11-course menu 1095kr

Chef Christopher Haatuft is pioneering his own brand of Nordic cuisine at Lysverket, which he dubs 'neo-fjordic' – combining modern techniques with the best fjord-sourced produce. His food is highly seasonal (menus change daily), incredibly creative and full of surprising textures, combinations and flavours. The restaurant is housed in the offices of the city's power company (the name means 'light works'), and there are nods to industrial styling, from brass pendant lamps to huge, deco-esque windows.

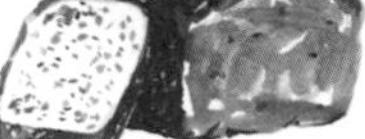

'The most exciting thing about baking, when it comes to cooking, is that there are no shortcuts.'
Morten Schakenda, Lom Bakery

TRE BRØR

VOSS | $ | CAFE

Vangsgata 28; 468 35 537; www.facebook.com/trebror; sandwiches & light meals 110-195kr

The Three Brothers is the heart of Voss's social scene, and rightly so – it's everything you want from a small-town cafe. There's super coffee from Oslo's Tim Wendleboe and Ålesund's Jacu Roastery, a great range of microbrewed beers from Voss Brewery down the road, and an on-trend menu of salads, soups, wraps and burgers. What's not to like?

LOM BAKERY

WESTERN CENTRAL NORWAY | $ | BAKERY

Sognefjellsvegen 7, Lom; 61 21 18 60; www.bakerietilom.no; loaves from 45kr, sandwiches/pizzas 66/170kr

Master baker Morten Schakenda, who makes all his breads using only natural ingredients and wood-fired ovens, is a culinary star in Lom. You can buy freshly baked baguettes, cinnamon twists and rustic loaves by the score, of course, but there are also delicious pastries and sandwiches, and the crispiest of pizzas too. Queues often stretch out the door. This might just be Norway's best bakery.

BRIMI BUE

WESTERN CENTRAL NORWAY | $$ | CAFE

Sognefjellsvegen 13, Lom; 468 54 262; www.brimiland.no/brimibue; mains around 180kr

This flashy establishment is the new home base for the town's top chef, Arne Brimi, and it's where everyone wants to eat when they pass through town. It's screamingly Scandi (all open plan with big glass windows and plain wood), the perfect setting for the cafe's speciality: gourmet platters of ham, cheese and fish, plus meats flame-grilled to perfection. The highlight is the nightly grill that's often hosted by Arne himself: bookings are essential.

SØDAHLHUSET

THE NORTHERN FJORDS | $$ | CAFE

Romsdalsvegen 8, Åndalsnes; 400 66 401; mains 125-285kr

Mix-and-match furniture, regular beer tastings and gigs, and a blackboard menu chock-a-block with delicious, homemade food made from locally-sourced ingredients. It's all par for the course at this cosy cafe where options range from sinful chocolate cake and *kraftkar* (blue cheese) burgers to more healthy options like quinoa, mango and avocado salad. As the sign says, it's run by three lovely ladies, and the welcome is warm.

VERTSHUSET TAVERN

TRONDHEIM | $$$ | NORWEGIAN

Sverresborg Allé 11; 47 51 59 00; www.vertshusettavern.no; mains 185-375kr

Once in the heart of Trondheim, this historic (1739) tavern was lifted and transported, every last plank, to the Sverresborg Trøndelag Folkemuseum on the outskirts of town. Tuck into rotating specials of traditional Norwegian fare or just graze on waffles with coffee in one of its 16 tiny rooms, each low-beamed, with sloping floors, candlesticks, cast-iron stoves and lacy tablecloths.

ANITAS SJØMAT

LOFOTEN | $ | CAFE

Sakrisøy, Moskenesøy; 958 56 525; www.sakrisoy.no/seafood; fish burgers 120-170kr

Part delicatessen and part waterside cafe, this fab place sells all sorts of stockfish snacks, Kong Oskar sardines and dishes such as uncommonly good fish soup, fish cakes, fresh shrimp, and fish burgers – our favourite is the pulled-salmon burger. Go on, be adventurous, try the seagulls' eggs...and don't be put off by the fearsome dried cod heads outside. If you like stockfish as much as they do, pick up its free Norwegian stockfish recipe pamphlet with five recipes.

KRAMBUA

LOFOTEN | $$$ | NORWEGIAN

Off E10, Hamnøy; 486 36 772; www.krambuarestaurant.no; mains 265-315kr

This fabulous restaurant inhabits an 1882 building and Noemi and Mikael Björkman serve up a seasonal menu

WHERE TO DRINK...

AQUAVIT

Grand Café, Oslo
Make like Norwegian playwright Henrik Ibsen, who headed to the Grand at 11am every day for a shot of *aquavit* to accompany a herring lunch.

Inderøy Brenneri, Trøndelag
Get rosy-cheeked with an exceptionally enjoyable and informative *aquavit* tasting tour at this working farm with its own distillery.

Skjenestova, Skorovatn, Trøndelag
There are 160 kinds of *aquavit* behind the bar at this surprisingly busy pub sited in a remote hamlet.

Baklandet Skydsstasjon, Trondheim
This cosy restaurant serving hearty Norwegian fare is just like eating at your granny's – if your granny offers dozens of varieties of *aquavit* to put hairs on your chest.

COURTESY GRUVELAGERET

This page: Dishes from Gruvelageret. Next spread: Dish from Rutabaga.

with the freshest fish imaginable. Try the smoked shrimp or cod tongues for starters. The menu usually includes expertly prepared tomato-based fish stew, lightly smoked Lofoten lamb and smoked Lofoten cod.

KAFÉ LYSSTOPERIET

LOFOTEN | $ | CAFE

Gammelveien 2, Henningsvær; 76 07 70 40; www.henningsvarlys.no; mains 98-149kr

This casual place in the heart of town is wildly (and deservedly) popular. The organic food ranges from Lofoten's best cakes and sweet treats to light meals such as soup, open sandwiches, pies, pasta salad and homemade pizzas. There are a couple of small outside tables, but the interior is warmly eclectic and filled with personality. There's great coffee, too.

FISKEKROGEN

LOFOTEN | $$$ | SEAFOOD

Dreyersgate 29, Henningsvær; 76 07 46 52; www.fiskekrogen.no; mains lunch 175-275kr, dinner 220-330kr

This smart dockside restaurant – a favourite of the Norwegian royal family – is Henningsvær's culinary claim to fame. Try, in particular, the outstanding fish soup, but there's everything else on the menu from fish and chips to fried cod tongues. Between 4pm and 5pm in summer it serves fish soup and seafood stew only. Quite right, too.

BØRSEN

LOFOTEN | $$$ | NORWEGIAN
Gunnar Bergs vei 2, Svolvær; 76 06 99 30; www.svinoya.no/restaurant; mains 295-375kr

Located in the Svinøya complex of *rorbuer* (traditional fisherman's huts), this is one of the town's top tables. A former fish house, it still retains atmospheric beams and wooden floors in its dining room, and it used to be called the 'stock exchange' after the bench outside, where the town's old geezers would gather to debate. Stockfish and Lofoten lamb are the specialities.

COAL MINERS' BAR & GRILL

SVALBARD | $$ | NORWEGIAN, INTERNATIONAL
Longyearbyen; 79 02 63 00; www.facebook.com/coalminerscabins; mains 135-345kr

A renovation of this former mining mess hall has transformed it into one of Longyearbyen's coolest venues. There's warming decor, fabulous charcoal-grilled meals (the spare ribs and burgers are excellent) and the humming backdrop of a happy crowd that often hangs around to drink long after the kitchen closes.

'Everything is cut to the bone, no frames but the few hanging on the walls. Simplicity with quality comes first, great details are just beneath.'
Relæ

HUSET

SVALBARD | $$ | NORWEGIAN
Longyearbyen; 79 02 50 02; www.huset.com; bistro mains 260-280kr, restaurant 5-/7-course Nordic tasting menu 1000-1200kr

It's something of a walk up here but it's worth it. Dining in the bistro is casual, with well-priced dishes such as meatballs with lingonberries on the menu. The Charcoal Burger of Svalbard is a meaty burger with all the trimmings; so juicy, we're told, that lonely scientists in their tents dream of it. Meanwhile the highly regarded sister restaurant serves up a Nordic tasting menu featuring locally sourced fare such as tartar of reindeer or Isfjord cod.

GRUVELAGERET

SVALBARD | $$$ | NEW NORDIC, INTERNATIONAL
Longyearbyen; 79 02 20 00; www.gruvelageret.no; 4-course set menu 895kr

Opened in the winter of 2015, Gruvelageret occupies a stunningly converted wooden mining warehouse and serves up an exceptional, seasonally updated set menu that might begin with Atlantic salmon, move on to borscht soup and reindeer fillet before climaxing with a gorgeous 'crushed cheesecake'. The location, high on a hill deep in the valley, is as splendid as the food.

SWEDEN

WHAT TO EAT

Köttbullar
Ikea took them worldwide, but it's still worth tasting classic pork-and-beef Swedish meatballs on home soil, along with potatoes and lingonberry jam.

Sill
Herring, often pickled and flavoured with dill, onions, mustard or garlic and eaten alongside crispbread, is the mainstay of a Swedish smörgåsbord.

Kanelbullar
Cinnamon buns are serious business here, with their own day of celebration (4 October).

Surströmming
This love-it-or-loathe-it fermented Baltic herring is a northern Swedish delicacy. Enthusiasts eat it with *tunnbröd* (a thin bread), boiled potatoes and onions at late-summer parties.

PRICE RANGES
For a main course:
$ less than 100kr
$$ 100kr–200kr
$$$ 200kr or more

Tipping: 10–15%

Sweden's cuisine is much like its style: understated, yet exceptionally well executed. Classics include herring, salmon and meatballs, but look beyond the obvious and you'll discover a vibrant culinary movement shining a light on quality Swedish produce. Whatever Swedish flavours you favour, just don't miss the daily ritual of *fika* – a pause for a coffee and something sweet observed with near religious fervour.

NAMU

MALMÖ | $$ | FUSION
Landbygatan 5; 040-12 14 90; www.namu.nu; mains 115-315kr

Brainchild of Masterchef Sweden winner Jennie Walldén, Namu (meaning 'tree') serves up artfully prepared Korean dishes adapted according to the availability of seasonal local ingredients, and presented in surroundings that beautifully merge Scandinavian design elements and traditional Korean styling. The result: a cultural and culinary synergy that fans of either genre won't want to miss.

BASTARD

MALMÖ | $$ | EUROPEAN
Mäster Johansgatan 11; 040-12 13 18; www.bastardrestaurant.se; mains 85-210kr

This hipster restaurant with its correspondingly hipster name is about as close as you'll get to a gastropub in Sweden. It serves predominantly small and sharing plates, ranging from gourmet dishes such as rabbit with violet artichokes, to pizza with taleggio cheese.

BOLAGET

GOTLAND | $$$ | FRENCH
Stora Torget 16, Visby; 0498-21 50 80; www.bolaget.fr; mains 210-310kr

Take a defunct Systembolaget (state-owned alcohol shop), chip the 'System' off the signage, and reinvent the space as a buzzing, French bistro–inspired hotspot. Dishes are suitably Gallic, from duck-liver terrine with butter-fried sourdough bread and fig marmalade, to smoked pork belly with sauerkraut and Dijon mustard. The summertime square-side bar seating is perfect for people watching.

THÖRNSTRÖMS KÖK

GOTHENBURG | $$$ | SCANDINAVIAN
Teknologgatan 3; 031-16 20 66; www.thornstromskok.com; mains 335-395kr, 4-/6-/8-course menu 675/895/1175kr

Classic technique, flawless presentation and a creative approach to local, seasonal ingredients helped chef Hakan Thörnström earn his Michelin star. Hidden away in a quiet side street, his dining den is one of Gothenburg's culinary highlights, where impeccably cooked duck might conspire with Jerusalem artichokes and dried apricots, or where cherries reach new complexity in the company of pine nuts, sage and chocolate.

'Take a defunct Systembolaget (state-owned alcohol shop), chip the 'System' off the signage, and reinvent the space as a buzzing, French bistro–inspired hotspot.'
Bolaget

BRYGGHUSET

BOHUSLÄN COAST | $$$ | SEAFOOD
Fiskebäckskilsvägen 28, Lysekil; 0523-222 22; www.brygghusetkrog.se; mains 205-325kr

Across the estuary from the Fiskebäckskil ferry terminal, this celebrated waterfront restaurant is lauded for its superb fish dishes that taste so fresh that the fish may as well have just leapt out of the harbour onto your plate. At lunchtime, have your herring eight ways – count 'em! – at the self-service buffet or grab a seafood soup.

LA NETA

STOCKHOLM | $ | MEXICAN
Barnhusgatan 2; 08-411 58 80; www.laneta.se; tacos & quesadillas 24-55kr

Competition for the title of 'Stockholm's Best Taqueria' is not fierce, but La Neta wins hands down. Fast-food pseudo-Mexican eateries are all over town, but this is the real deal, with homemade corn tortillas, nuanced flavours and zero frills in the dining area (unless you count the bowls of delicious salsa). It's great value for money and there's a perpetual line halfway around the block from the minute the place opens.

RUTABAGA

STOCKHOLM | $$$ | VEGETARIAN
Södra Blasieholmshamnen 6; 08-679 35 84; www.mdghs.se; menu small/large 595/895kr

At Rutabaga, celebrity chef Mathias Dahlgren pushes vegetarian cuisine into the realm of art: the menu features vividly colourful salads and other unusual combinations (an egg-truffle-white-bean dish, a mango and mozzarella salad, for example) which, as always, Dahlgren presents impeccably on the plate. Most dishes are meant for sharing (if you can bear to give any up).

EKSTEDT

STOCKHOLM | $$$ | SWEDISH
Humlegårdsgatan 17; 08-611 12 10; www.ekstedt.nu; 4/6 courses 980/1260kr

This Michelin-starred restaurant is frequently named among the best in the world, and dining here is as much an experience as a meal. Chef Niklas Ekstedt's education in French and Italian cooking informs his approach to traditional Scandinavian cuisine – but only slightly. Menus are built around ingredients such as reindeer and pike-perch. Everything is cooked in a wood-fired oven, over a fire pit or smoked in a chimney.

WOODSTOCKHOLM

STOCKHOLM | $$$ | SWEDISH
Mosebacketorg 9; 08-36 93 99; www.woodstockholm.com; mains 275-295kr

The menu's theme at this hip yet welcoming hotspot changes every seven weeks or so, with a focus that ranges from specific geographic regions to more abstract concepts. What remains unchanging is a commitment to smaller, sustainable, local producers and honest, beautifully textured dishes cooked with flair. The bar seats, reserved for drop-ins, are perfect for solo diners seeking a little bonhomie.

'We continue to explore age-old techniques and to learn more about a lost art of cooking.'
Niklas Ekstedt, Ekstedt

LA MAISON

STOCKHOLM ARCHIPELAGO | $ | BAKERY
Rådhusgatan 19, Vaxholm; 08-59 25 57 50; www.facebook.com/lamaisonvaxholm; pastries 30kr, sandwiches 70kr, dishes 95-105kr

After running a Parisian bakery, Kerstin Lekander decided to bring a little Gallic flair to Vaxholm. Decorated with rustic floorboards and a communal timber table, her island bakery lures the peckish with its freshly baked artisan loaves, baguette sandwiches, quiches, canapés and Alsatian-style pizza. The pastries are unashamedly buttery, with bite-sized versions for those who sin in moderation. Proper espresso to boot.

KAFÉ STRANDSTUGAN

VÄSTMANLAND | $ | CAFE
Storgatan 1, Nora; 073-840 01 61; www.noraglass.se/strandstugan; sandwiches 42-118kr

Down by the lake in Nora, this delightful wooden cottage is set in a flower-filled garden, where you can get coffee, sandwiches, quiches, desserts and other home-baked goodies, as well as Nora Glass ice-cream creations. If it's available, try the local speciality, *Bergslags paj*, a quiche made with venison, chanterelles and juniper berries.

MATILDAS

GÄVLE | $$ | FUSION
Timmermansgatan 23; 026-62 53 49; www.matildas.nu; mains from 200kr

The menu at this small, stylish bistro is short, sweet and seasonal, with a real depth of flavour to the dishes, wonderful attention to presentation and a relaxed ambience. You might feast on lobster tacos, oysters paired with champagne, crispy pork belly or homemade black pudding with lingonberry. The home-brewed beer, served by the delightful owners, goes down very smoothly.

HAVVI I GLEN

JÄMTLAND | $$$ | SAMI
Glen 530, Åsarna, Åre; 070-600 64 76; www.havviiglen.se; mains 190-275kr, tasting menu 1395kr

A proud standard-bearer for the Slow Food Sápmi movement, Havvi i Glen initiates you into the richness of mountain Sami cuisine, with game, mushrooms and berries featuring prominently on its seasonal menu. Expect the likes of thinly sliced reindeer steak with blueberry chutney, smoked Arctic char with sea buckthorn, and cloudberry sorbet.

WEDEMARKS KONDITORI & BAGERI

ÖSTERSUND | $ | CAFE
Prästgatan 27; 063-51 03 83; www.wedemarks.se; sandwiches from 69kr

This glorious cafe has been delighting its customers since 1924. Sink your teeth into classic Swedish treats like Princess layer cake topped with bright green marzipan or, in the warmer months, house-made Italian-style gelato. Savoury offerings include baguettes, panini and wraps, among them organic, house-made thin bread filled with hot-roasted salmon, cream cheese, mustard, salad and paprika. Bliss.

HANS PÅ HÖRNET

LAPPLAND | $ | CAFE
Storgatan 21, Arvidsjaur; 0960-102 10; http://hanspahornet.blogspot.se; lunch menu 95kr

This very local spot has a popular buffet lunch that changes each day and might include hearty options such as chilli con carne or herb-baked pork tenderloin. It also serves up inexpensive salads and sandwiches. This is the place to try *palt*, a Swedish meat-filled dumpling.

SPIS

KIRUNA | $$ | SWEDISH
Bergmästaregatan 7; 0980-170 00; www.spiskiruna.se; mains 195-295kr

With a top deli and bakery, breakfast and lunch buffets, and a quality dinner menu, SPiS is considered the best place to eat in Kiruna. The restaurant has won numerous awards with dishes such as icefish with almond potato puree, beets, browned butter, capers and horseradish green peas. The Meat Locker has amazing options including the 500g entrecôte.

WHERE TO ENJOY...

FIKA

Utö Bakgård, Stockholm Archipelago
Grab one of the outdoor tables and order a coffee and a cinnamon bun at this cute-as-a-button bakery near Utö's harbour.

St Jakobs Stenugnsbageri, Lund
All manner of exceptional baked goods weigh down the counters here, from cookies to bread to sugar-dusted pastries.

Bröd & Sovel, Växjö, Gotland
Highly regarded by those with culinary chops, the house-made cakes, sweets and pastries here are second-to-none on Gotland.

FiKA by SPiS, Kiruna
Loved by locals, this *konditori* has a delightful courtyard, tucked away at the back – perfect for *fika* with friends.

FINLAND

Though Finland has many old standards and ingredients (salmon, reindeer, berries) in common with its Scandinavian neighbours, they're used in subtly different ways to make Finnish cuisine characteristically Finnish. And these days, perhaps powered by their world leading coffee consumption (12kg per person per year!), fine-food-focused Finns are upping the ante to put gastronomic excellence at the heart of modern dining.

VANHA KAUPPAHALLI

HELSINKI | $ | MARKET

Eteläranta 1; www.vanhakauppahalli.fi

Alongside the harbour, this is Helsinki's iconic market hall. Built in 1888, it's still a traditional Finnish market, with wooden stalls selling local flavours such as liquorice, Finnish cheeses, smoked salmon and herring, berries, forest mushrooms and herbs. Stock up for a picnic.

STORY

HELSINKI | $ | CAFE

Vanha Kauppahalli, Eteläranta 1; www.restaurantstory.fi; snacks from €4, mains €12.50-19

At the heart of Helsinki's historic harbourside market hall, this sparkling cafe sources its produce from the surrounding stalls. Breakfast (oven-baked barley porridge, eggs Benedict) gives way to snacks (cinnamon buns, cakes) and hearty mains such as creamy salmon and fennel soup, aubergine ragout with couscous, and shrimp-laden *skagen* (Swedish-style open-faced sandwiches). Its outdoor terrace overlooks the water.

RESTAURANT OLO

HELSINKI | $$$ | FINNISH

Pohjoisesplanadi 5; 010-320-6250; www.olo-ravintola.fi; tasting menus short/long from €93/133, with paired wines €187/279

At the forefront of New Suomi (Finnish) cuisine, Michelin-starred Olo occupies a handsome, 19th-century harbourside mansion. Book a few weeks ahead to experience its memorable seasonal degustation menus, incorporating both the foraging ethos and molecular gastronomy. They may feature culinary jewels such as Icelandic salmon with wasabi and apple, or Finnish quail with forest mushrooms.

WHAT TO EAT

Karjalanpiirakka
Originally from the Karelia region, these savoury pastries have a rye crust and are filled with a rice porridge. They're often topped with egg butter.

Leipäjuusto
A mild cheese made from cow's milk which is curdled, set, then baked and cut into wedges and sometimes served with cloudberry jam. It's known variously as 'cheese bread' and 'Finnish squeaky cheese'.

Korvapuusti
These cinnamon (or cardamom) whirls made using a sweet dough with fresh yeast translate as 'slapped ears'.

Poronkaristys
Sautéed reindeer is most often found in Lapland, home of the indigenous Sámi reindeer herders; traditionally eaten with lingonberries.

PRICE RANGES

For a main course:
$ less than €17
$$ €17–€27
$$$ €27 or more

Tipping:
Exceptional service only.

MIKA HAMALAINEN, COURTESY VANHA KAUPPAHALLI

GRÖN

HELSINKI | $$ | BISTRO
Albertinkatu 36; 094-289-3358; www.restaurantgron.com; 4-course menus €64

Seasonal, often foraged ingredients are used in this 20-seat bistro's dishes. Choose from either the regular or vegan menu; stunning plates might include scallops cooked with red currant juice, herbs and vegetables, or grilled potatoes with chanterelle mushrooms, creamed corn, summer flowers and corn-husk velouté. Finnish artists provide the dining room's ceramic plates and paintings on the whitewashed walls.

PUB NISKA

ÅLAND | $ | PIZZA
Sjökvarteret, Mariehamn; 018-19151; www.pubniska.com; pizza €12-14

Star chef Michael 'Micke' Björklund of Smakbyn is the brains behind this *plåtbröd* (Åland-style pizza) restaurant. Toppings are diverse and delicious, including favourites such as cold-smoked salmon and horseradish cream. In true locavore spirit, the cheese is from Åland's dairy. The atmospheric interior feels like the inside of a ship, but the place to be is the glorious sunny terrace.

CAFÉ KVARNEN

BRÄNDÖ | $$ | CAFE
Jurmo; 040-506-4777; www.jurmo.ax/cafe.html; mains €13-27

It's worth a special trip to tiny Jurmo Island to sample the organic steak at wonderful Café Kvarnen, near the pier. The steak is sourced from local long-haired highland cattle and seasoned with island herbs. Other delicacies include homemade sausages, burgers, locally caught fish and fantastic Åland pancakes.

SMOR

TURKU | $$$ | GASTRONOMY
Läntinen Rantakatu 3; 02-536-9444; www.smor.fi; 5-/7-course set menu €62/72

A vaulted cellar lit by flickering candles makes a romantic backdrop for appetising, organic, locally sourced food, such as roast lamb with organic currant sauce or the catch of the day with organic shiitake mushrooms. Desserts are truly inspired: quark mousse with wild blueberries and oat ice cream or caramelised yoghurt with thyme cookies and honey could be options on the menu.

'What grows now determines our menu. This is a tribute to creativity, the wild and us all.'
Grön

BISTRO POPOT

LAHTI | $$ | BISTRO
Rautatienkatu 26; 010-279-2935; www.bistropopot.fi; mains €16-27, lunch buffet €12

Chef Andrew Smith learned his craft in the UK, France and Switzerland before relocating to Finland and wowing Lahti with his modern, seasonally driven cuisine. His menu roams Europe and ventures occasionally into Asia – everything is exquisitely presented, the service is friendly and assured, and the wine list is excellent.

PÖLLÖWAARI

JYVÄSKYLÄ | $$$ | FINNISH
Yliopistonkatu 23, Hotel Yöpuu; 014-333-900; www.ravintolapollowaari.fi; mains €22-29, menus €50-79, with wine pairing €78-136

We're of the view that Hotel Yöpuu's fine-dining restaurant is the best in the region. Its menu places a laudable emphasis on seasonality, and the kitchen's execution is exemplary. Choose one of the set menus or order à la carte – the main courses are exceptionally well priced considering their quality.

LINDS KÖK

NÄRPES | $$ | FINNISH
Bäcklidvägen 476; 040-510-8124; www.lindskok.fi; lunch menus from €20

Dine amid mandarin and lime trees, strawberries, herbs and tomatoes growing inside this lush greenhouse. Fresh-as-it-gets Finnish specialities include creamy tomato soup, fried Arctic char with aioli and bananas, and beef with red wine dressing and homemade barbecue sauce. The only appropriate dessert choice is the tomato ice cream.

GUSTAV WASA

VAASA | $$$ | FINNISH
Raastuvankatu 24; 050-466-3208; www.gustavwasa.com; mains €19-33, 7-course tasting menu €69, wine pairing €50

A former coal cellar is home to one of Finland's finest restaurants, with sublime seven-course tasting menus served in the intimate candlelit dining room. There's also a casual gastropub with wines by the glass and Finnish beers on tap, and you can even order food for the attached sauna.

CAFÉ FÄBODA

FINLAND'S WEST COAST | $$ | FINNISH
Lillsandvägen 263, Jakobstad; 06-723-4533; www.faboda.fi; sandwiches €13.50, mains €22-32

On a picturesque rocky perch overlooking the beach, this breezy spot open in the summer season is the best place to dine for miles around. Specialities include gourmet cheeseburgers on brioche buns, freshly caught whitefish with white wine–butter sauce, and steaks such as Chateaubriand in thyme-Madeira sauce.

Previous spread: Dish from Vanha Kauppahalli.

Coffee and dessert are also divine, as is the glorious view of sea and forest.

PEKKA HEIKKINEN & KUMPP

KAJAANI | $ | BAKERY, CAFE
Välikatu 7; 086-17890; www.pekkaheikkinen.fi; items €3-6.50

Opened in 1913 and run by the fourth generation of the same family, Pekka Heikkinen's loaves are made from Finnish flour and baked in birch pans in its wood-fired oven. Savoury golden-brown pastries include *juustosarvi* (filled with cheese) and *pasteijat* (with veggie or meat fillings); *korvapuusti* (cinnamon scroll) and *kääremunkki* (rye pastry with fruit) are among the delectable sweet varieties.

ROOSTER

OULU | $ | CAFE
Torikatu 26; 020-711-8280; www.rooster.fi; mains €13-19, weekday lunch buffet €11

Inside a beautiful wooden building, Rooster has a minimalist Finnish-design interior. Burgers are a speciality, such as its *Lohiburgeri* (salmon, marinated fennel and horseradish mayo), *Vuohenjuustoburgeri* (beef, grilled goat's cheese, watermelon and fig balsamic) and *Vegaanburgeri* (gado gado, mango, rocket and red-onion compote). Light lunch dishes include spicy sweet potato lasagne or nettle and pepper soup.

RAVINTOLA HUGO

OULU | $$$ | FINNISH
Rantakatu 4; 020-143-2200; www.ravintolahugo.fi; mains €20-28, 5-course menu €62, with paired wines €111

Innovative cuisine using locally sourced products makes this elegant restaurant, all white tablecloths and richly coloured walls, a real Oulu highlight. Some outstanding flavour combinations feature on the regularly refreshed menus, such as pike-perch with liquorice leaves and parsnip; lichen-smoked reindeer with wild mushrooms and powdered roast beetroot; and spruce and strawberry sorbet with clotted reindeer cream.

AANAAR

INARI | $$ | FINNISH
Tradition Hotel Kultahovi, Saarikoskentie 2; 016-511-7100; www.hotelkultahovi.fi; mains €21-36, 3-/5-course menu €46/62, with paired wines €64/87

A panoramic, glassed-in dining room overlooks the Juutuanjoki river's Jäniskoski rapids at Inari's best restaurant. Seasonal local produce is used in dishes such as morel and angelica-root soup, smoked reindeer heart with pine-needle vinaigrette; grilled Inari lake trout with white wine and dill sauce; and Arctic king crab with nettle butter. Don't miss amazing desserts like birch-leaf sorbet with lingonberry sauce, or a Finnish cheese platter with Aura Gold blue, Kolattu goat's cheese and Waldemar cheddar.

WHERE TO DRINK...

COFFEE

Lehmus Roastery, Lappeenranta
Try a shot of one of four organic coffees roasted on the premises at this award-winning roastery with views over Lake Saimaa.

Mokka Mestarit, Tampere
This style-conscious roastery and cafe in cultured Tampere offers caffeine hits espresso-style, but you can also geek out with cold-drip or Aeropress versions.

Kaffa Roastery, Helsinki
Watch the beans taking the heat as you sip the finished product at this large-scale roastery which has a coffee shop on the premises.

La Torrefazione, Helsinki
A no wi-fi zone, this locals' favourite insists the goods get your full attention. It creates roasting profiles and serves your beverage filter or drip-brewed.

RUSSIA

WHAT TO EAT

Okroshka
A cold soup made with chopped cucumber, potatoes, eggs, meat and herbs in a base of either *kvas* (a mild beer made from fermented rye-bread) or kefir.

Beef Stroganov
(bef Stroganov)
Beef, mushrooms and sour cream dish said to have been invented by a French cook employed by the St Petersburg noble Alexander Stroganov.

Chicken Kiev
(*kotleta po kievsky*)
Breaded chicken filled with butter, a staple since the 19th century.

Pelmeni
Ravioli-like dumplings stuffed with meat, fish or vegetables, served with sour cream, vinegar and butter, or in a stock soup.

PRICE RANGES
For a main course:
$ less than R300 (R500 in Moscow and St Petersburg)
$$ R300–800 (R500–1000)
$$$ R800 (R1000) or more

Tipping: 10%

Russia's dining scene has gone from strength to strength in the last decade, particularly in large cities, where international culinary mainstream mixes with the unique cuisines of the Caucasus and Central Asia as well as a powerful movement to reinvent traditional Russian gastronomy. Foodies will be thrilled by the dining options, from old-fashioned *haute-russe* to contemporary creations from local celebrity chefs.

UGLI (РЕСТОРАН УГЛИ)

KALININGRAD | $$$ | INTERNATIONAL
pr Mira 19-21; 4012-605 499; www.ugli-rest.ru; mains R300-1200

The menu here is all about things cooked over the eponymous *ugli* (coal) with steaks being the speciality. The chef does other meaty things very well, too, from home-smoked duck breast and salmon to baked bone marrow on rye toast, paired with some well-chosen wines. Decor is industrial warehouse meets cosy woodland cabin; there's friendly service, too.

MAYAKOVSKI (МАЯКОVSKИЙ)

KURSHSKAYA KOSA | $$ | SEAFOOD
Seafront promenade, Lesnoy; 800 200 4939; www.mayakovski-hotel.ru; mains R400-600

Even if you're not staying at the Mayakovski Hotel, be sure to plan a meal here. The pretty outdoor terrace has a nice view over the pool and lies within earshot of the roaring sea. The freshly prepared seafood, such as baked halibut over lemon risotto, is the best on the Curonian Spit.

ZAVOD BAR (ZAVOD-БАР)

VELIKY NOVGOROD | $$ | RUSSIAN
ul Germana 2; 8162-603 106; www.alkon.su; mains R270-560

GARY LATHAM/LONELY PLANET ©

Attached to the Alkon Distillery, Zavod is a chic and cosy restaurant with exposed brick, an open fire and great food. Go for the homemade *pelmeni* filled with fish and meats, or a sweeter strawberry and cottage cheese option. Pair your meal with a tasting set of the distillery's vodka or cranberry *nastoyka* (liqueur), with a plate of vodka snacks.

BANSHIKI (БАНЩИКИ)

ST PETERSBURG | $$ | RUSSIAN
Degtyarnaya ul 1; 8-921-941 1744; www.banshiki.spb.ru; mains R500-1100

Attached to a renovated *banya* (public baths) complex, this place serves nostalgic Russian fare at affordable prices. Everything is made in-house, from its refreshing *kvas* (fermented rye bread water) to dried meats and eight types of smoked fish. Don't overlook cherry *vareniki* (dumplings) with sour cream, oxtail ragout or the rich borsch.

CHEKHOV (ЧЕХОВ)

ST PETERSBURG | $$ | RUSSIAN
Petropavlovskaya ul 4; 812-234 4511; www.restaurant-chekhov.ru; mains R550-890

Despite a totally nondescript appearance from the street, this restaurant's charming interior perfectly recalls that of a 19th-century dacha. The menu, hidden inside classic novels, features lovingly prepared dishes such as roasted venison with bilberry sauce or Murmansk sole with dill potatoes and stewed leeks.

'I always want to find another definition for what we create here. Maybe 'theatre'? Indeed, everything that happens here looks like a play.' *Olesia Drobot, EM Restaurant*

COCOCO

ST PETERSBURG | $$$ | RUSSIAN
Voznesensky pr 6; 812-418 2060; www.kokoko.spb.ru; mains R650-1300

Cococo has charmed locals with its inventive approach to contemporary Russian cuisine. Your food is likely to arrive disguised as, say, a small bird's egg, a can of peas or a broken flowerpot – all rather gimmicky, theatrical and fun. The best way to sample what it does is with its tasting menu.

DUO GASTROBAR

ST PETERSBURG | $$ | FUSION
Kirochnaya ul 8a; 812-994 5443; www.duobar.ru; mains R350-500

Boasting a minimalist Scandinavian design scheme, Duo Gastrobar wows diners with its outstanding cooking that showcases quality ingredients in delectable plates such as crab bruschetta, spicy beef soup with beans, and scallops with buckwheat and smoked duck breast. Run by two experienced chefs, it's a great place to experiment with new flavours and combinations in a pleasant and friendly atmosphere.

EM RESTAURANT

ST PETERSBURG | $$$ | EUROPEAN
nab reki Moyki 84; 8-921-960 2177; www.emrestaurant.ru; set menu of three/six courses R2500/4500

Bookings are essential for this superb, intimate restaurant where the chefs

calmly prepare beautifully presented dishes in an open kitchen. Expect exotic elements such as reindeer, smoked perch, red cabbage sorbet and foie gras coloured with squid ink. Individual food preferences can be catered to and they also work their culinary magic on a vegan menu.

SEVERYANIN (СЕВЕРЯНИН)

ST PETERSBURG | $$ | RUSSIAN
Stolyarny per 18; 8-921-951 6396; www.severyanin.me; mains R620-1300

An old-fashioned elegance prevails at Severyanin. Amid vintage wallpaper, mirrored armoires and tasselled lampshades, you might feel like you've stepped back a few decades. Start off with the excellent mushroom soup or borsch (beetroot soup), before moving on to rabbit ragout in puff pastry or Baltic flounder with wine sauce.

YAT (ЯТЬ)

ST PETERSBURG | $$ | RUSSIAN
nab reki Moyki 16; 812-957 0023; www.eatinyat.com; mains R370-750

Perfectly placed for eating near the Hermitage, this country-cottage-style restaurant has a very appealing menu of traditional dishes, presented with aplomb. The *shchi* (cabbage-based soup) is excellent, and there is a tempting range of flavoured vodkas as well as a fab kids' area with pet rabbits.

KARELSKAYA GORNITSA (КАРЕЛЬСКАЯ ГОРНИЦА)

PETROZAVODSK | $$ | KARELIAN
ul Engelsa 13a; 8142-785 300; www.gornica.ru; mains R320-850

Claiming to be the first Karelian restaurant in the world, this ye-olde hot spot boasts excellent, hearty fare, including rabbit borsch and rich, gamey and fishy mains, washed down with its own *medovukha* (honey mead). The wild *mushroom soup* (pokhlebka gribnaya) is superb.

BJÖRN

MOSCOW | $$$ | SCANDINAVIAN
Pyatnitskaya ul 3; 495-953 9059; www.bjorn.rest; mains R700-1200

A neat cluster of fir trees on a busy street hides a Nordic gem that deserves a saga to glorify its many virtues. This is not an 'ethnic' restaurant, but a presentation of futuristic Scandinavian cuisine straight out of a science fiction movie. From salads to desserts, every dish looks deceptively simple, visually perfect and 23rd century.

CAFE PUSHKIN

MOSCOW | $$$ | RUSSIAN
Tverskoy bul 26a; 495-739 0033; www.cafe-pushkin.ru; mains R1000-3400

The tsarina of *haute-russe* dining in Moscow, offering an exquisite blend of Russian and French cuisines. Service

Previous spread: St Petersburg.

and food are done to perfection. The lovely 19th-century building has a different atmosphere on each floor, including a richly decorated library and a pleasant rooftop cafe.

DANILOVSKY MARKET (ДАНИЛОВСКИЙ РЫНОК)

MOSCOW | $$ | MARKET
Mytnaya ul 74; 495-120 1801; www.danrinok.ru; mains R400-600

A showcase of Moscow's ongoing gentrification, this giant Soviet-era farmers market is now largely about deli food cooked and served in myriad little eateries, including such gems as a Dagestani dumpling shop and a Vietnamese pho kitchen. Even if you're not shopping, it's entertaining to peruse the tables piled high with produce including homemade cheese and jam, golden honey and vibrant spices.

DELICATESSEN (ДЕЛИКАТЕСЫ)

MOSCOW | $$ | INTERNATIONAL
Sadovaya-Karetnaya ul 20; 495-699 3952; www.delicatessen.bar; mains R500-800

The affable owners of this place travel the world and experiment with the menu a lot, turning burgers, pizzas and pasta into artfully constructed objects of modern culinary art. The other source of joy is a cabinet filled with bottles of ripening fruity liquors, an asset which saw Delicatessen make the list of the World's Top 50 Bars in 2016.

DARBAZI (ДАРБАЗИ)

MOSCOW | $$ | GEORGIAN
ul Nikoloyamskaya 16; 495-915 3632; www.darbazirest.ru; mains R590-1500

The vast majority of Russia's Georgian restaurants focus on tried-and-true fare, such as shashlyk (meat kebabs) and *khinkali* (dumplings). This classy place goes far beyond these, listing less well-known delicacies with almost encyclopaedic meticulousness. Try the *chakapuli* (lamb cooked in white wine with tarragon) and *megreli kharcho* (duck in walnut sauce).

LAVKALAVKA (ЛАВКАЛАВКА)

MOSCOW | $$ | INTERNATIONAL
ul Petrovka 21 str 2; 8-495-621 2036; www.restoran.lavkalavka.com; mains R500-1100

All the food here is organic and hails from small farms from across the country where you can rest assured all the lambs and chickens lived a very happy life before being served to you on a plate. It's a great place to sample local ingredients cooked in an improvisational style as well as craft beers and different kinds of *kvas* (fermented rye-bread drink) produced on farms near Moscow.

MIZANDARI (МИЗАНДАРИ)

MOSCOW | $ | GEORGIAN

WHERE TO BUY...

CHOCOLATE

Chocolate Salon, Moscow
The factory outlet for several local candy makers, including the most famous, Krasny Oktyabr (Red October). The display case is brimming with all forms of tempting sweets and chocolates.

Alyonka, Moscow
Sample the products of Russian chocolatiers that's based in the old Red October factory. Alyonka is an iconic Soviet brand of chocolate with a picture of a rosy-cheeked peasant girl wearing a kerchief on the wrapper.

Kupetz Eliseevs, St Petersburg
St Petersburg's most elegant grocery store sells plenty of branded goods from tea blends to caviar and handmade chocolates as well as delicious freshly baked breads, pastries and cakes.

Bolotnaya nab 5, str 1; 8-903-263 9990; www.mizandari.ru; mains R300-500

Georgian restaurants in Moscow tend to be either expensive or tacky. This small family-run place is neither. Come with friends and order a selection of appetisers, such as *pkhali* and *lobio* (both made of walnut paste), *khachapuri* (Georgian cheese bread) and *kharcho* (rice with beef or lamb soup). Bless you if you can still accommodate a main course after all that!

GARMOSHKA (ГАРМОШКА)

VORONEZH | $$$ | RUSSIAN
ul Karla Marxa 94; 4732-525 759; www.cafe-garmoshka.ru; mains R380-880

Housed in a historic building, and done up like a wealthy merchant's home, Garmoshka is the fanciest night out in town. The atmospheric tone is traditional Russia, replete with antiques, a library filled with books of famous authors from the region, staff clad in traditional Russian dress and piano music filling the rooms. The menu is Russian classics, featuring exotic meats (including bear).

5642 VSOTA (5642 ВЫСОТА)

KISLOVODSK | $$ | INTERNATIONAL
Kurortny bul 13; 8-928-900 5642; www.5642-vysota.ru; mains R250-1000

This three-part venture from Moscow's Novikov group brings to the Caucusus spa town an excellent restaurant, bakery-cafe and burger bar (the latter two decorated with murals by street artist Misha Most). The restaurant has an open kitchen, appealing decor and mammoth menu featuring Adygean and Georgian cuisine. The burger bar's veggie Greenpeace burger is an inspired touch and the luscious fruit tarts in the bakery are hard to resist.

MINDAL (МИНДАЛЬ)

ASTRAKHAN | $$ | CENTRAL ASIAN
ul Ulyanovykh 10; 9275 699 913; www.mindal-astra.restoru.ru; mains R500-600

This is the ideal spot to sample the diverse cuisines of the Caspian Sea region. Choose from traditional Azeri, Persian, Kazakh and Russian dishes, starting off with a 'Tsar's fish soup', then dabbling with baked lamb or sturgeon steak, served on a bed of pomegranate seeds, and finishing up with baklava. The cosy setting has a Central Asian vibe.

GOSTINY DVOR (ГОСТИНЫЙ ДВОРЪ)

SUZDAL | $$ | RUSSIAN
Trading Arcades, Torgovaya pl; 49231-021 190; mains R450-550

There are so many things to like about this place: eclectic decor of rustic antiques and warm wood; outside terrace tables offering river views; hearty

Opposite page: Dish from Em Restaurant.

COURTESY EM RESTAURANT

Russian dishes (chicken, pike, *pelmeni* dumplings) prepared with modern flair; and friendly, attentive service, to start. Finish up with a tasting set of house-made *medovukha* (honey ale) while the kids amuse themselves in the playroom.

RESTORATSIA PYATKIN (РЕСТОРАЦИЯ ПЯТКИН)

NIZHNY NOVGOROD | $$ | RUSSIAN
Rozhdestvenskaya ul 25; 831-430 9183; www.pir.nnov.ru/pyatkin; mains R500

Pyatkin makes you feel like a merchant back in his mansion after a great trading day at the fair. The menu is full of Volga fish specialities; it brews the unusual apple *kvas* (fermented rye bread water) and has a children's menu.

TATARSKAYA USADBA (ТАТАРСКАЯ УСАДЬБА)

KAZAN | $$ | TATAR
ul Mardzhani 8; 843-561 0362; www.tatusadba.ru; mains R500

The 'Tatar Farmstead' is located adjacent to Kazan's Old Tatar Settlement and plays on traditional themes, both in the restaurant's decor and menu. There's a full range of Tatar classics, including several dishes with horsemeat and lamb, as well as hearty soups and stews, other mains and desserts. There's a good selection of Tatar pastries as well, including crunchy *chak chak*.

PASHTET (ПАШТЕТ)

YEKATERINBURG | $$ | RUSSIAN

WHERE TO EAT...
DUMPLINGS

Dukhan Chito-Ra, Moscow
The object of worship at this revered Georgian restaurant is *khinkali* – large, meat-filled dumplings – but the traditional veggie starters are also great.

Poznaya na Lenina, Irkutsk
With a stylishly dark interior and Buryat-themed modern paintings on the walls, this otherwise unpretentious cheapie is possibly the best place to sample *pozy* – Buryat-Mongolian dumplings.

Uralskiye Pelmeni, Chelyabinsk
This two-storey restaurant-cum-disco is all about *pelmeni*, small dumplings with plenty of fillings – such as rabbit, goose and eel – to choose from.

ul Tolmacheva 23; 343-228 0059; www.rest-pashtet.ru; mains R390-1550

Reinvented Russian classics are served in rooms designed to depict a traditional Russian summer dacha. Both the food and wine menus are extensive and the restaurant's house-made pâtés (*pashtet* in Russian) are definitely worth trying.

CHUM RESTAURANT-MUSEUM (РЕСТОРАН-МУЗЕЙ ЧУМ)

TYUMEN | $$$ | RUSSIAN
str Maligina 59/12; 3452-621 660; www.maxim-rest.ru; mains R600-900

Inside a faux Siberian hunters cabin lined with furs and skis, this unusual restaurant specialises in the cuisine of northern Siberia. Dishes include salted fish, elk, reindeer tongues and wild boar. However, whereas the average Siberian hunter probably just munches on a great hunk of meat, here the dishes are given a totally modern touch and presented with arty flamboyance.

FOOD & BAR 114

ABAKAN | $$ | ASIAN
ul Kirova 114/1; 3902-215 777; www.asia-hotel.ru/food-bar-114; mains R340-510

With its imaginative Asian-themed menu, this ain't your usual hotel restaurant. Turkish pea and quinoa salads provide relief to those suffering under Siberia's carnivore dictatorship. You can also go full Khakassian by ordering *potkhi* (warm sour cream dip) for starters, followed by *myun* lamb soup, *khan* blood sausage and *irben* tea with thyme, cream and honey.

PUPPEN HAUS

NOVOSIBIRSK | $$$ | RUSSIAN
ul Chaplygin 65/1; 383-251 0303; www.puppenhaus-nsk.ru; meals around R2000

The 'Puppet House', which specialises in refined traditional Siberian dishes, is both eccentric and divine. It consists of numerous little dining rooms and alcoves crammed with stony-eyed wooden puppets. The food is as memorable as the setting and if you've never tried elk steaks, Kamchatka lobster or – get this – boiled bear (!) then now is the chance.

REKA 827 (PEKA 827)

TOMSK | $$ | SEAFOOD
ul Kooperativnyy 2; 3822-902 020; www.reka827.ru; mains R700-900

If it's summer, sit out on one of the sun loungers on the deck of this sophisticated restaurant and eat great seafood while watching the locals swim in the river below. The fish dishes here are prepared with verve, which means you can look forward to tastes such as whole fried octopus and little fishy tapas-style dishes.

0.75 PLEASE

KRASNOYARSK | $$ | RUSSIAN

Next spread: Old Town Riga.

pr Mira 86; 391-215 2913; www.075please.ru; mains R480-640

This gem is two in one – a wine bar and an Arctic-themed restaurant that upgrades traditional Siberian staples to near-Michelin levels. *Nelma stroganina* (a kind of frozen ceviche) quite literally melts in your mouth. Reindeer steak with cheese and pear makes a star duo with homemade chokeberry liquor. Crème brûlée with sea buckthorn sorbet is nothing short of Elysian.

KOCHEVNIK (КОЧЕВНИК)

IRKUTSK | $$ | MONGOLIAN
ul Gorkogo 19; 3952-200 459; www.kochevnik-irk.com; mains R300-1200

Take your taste buds to the Mongolian steppe for some yurt-size portions of mutton, lamb and steak as well as filling soups and *buuzy* dumplings, sluiced down with a bottle from the decent foreign wine list. Smiley service, a picture menu, low prices and an exotically curtained summer terrace make this one of the most agreeable places to dine in Irkutsk.

RASSOLNIK (РАССОЛЬНИК)

IRKUTSK | $$ | RUSSIAN
130 Kvartal, ul 3 Iyulya 3; 3952-506 180; www.rassolnik.su; mains R300-700

This retro restaurant serves up a 100% Soviet-era menu (think upmarket *pelmeni*, *okroshka*, *shchi*, *kvas* and grandmother's pickles) in a plush Stalinist banqueting hall bedecked in nostalgia-inducing knick-knackery. Classic Soviet-era films are projected onto one wall, the menu is designed like a 1960s scrapbook and waiting staff are dressed for the occasion.

'Northern cuisine for me is cleanliness, simplicity, freshness. To create new dishes, I try to get the most out of every product ...'
Alexey Kuschenko, 0.75 Please

MUSCAT WHALE (МУСКАТНЫЙ КИТ)

KHABAROVSK | $$ | ITALIAN
ul Kalinina 82; 421-220 9770; mains R400-800

This gorgeous, chic, yet pleasantly unfussy place is a top choice for a meal in Khabarovsk. The large and luminous space has white-tiled walls, painted brick and lots of wooden fittings, while its menu boasts wonderful fresh salads, scrumptious pizzas, innovative meat dishes and a huge dessert list.

KVARTIRA 30 (КВАРТИРА 30)

VLADIVOSTOK | $$ | EUROPEAN
ul Pologaya 65b; 8904 627 4483; www.facebook.com/kvartira30vvo; mains R400-600

In an extremely unlikely location amid a hilltop housing estate, this hidden gem is run by the charming Olga Gurskaya, who also holds cookery classes here. With just five tables, it offers some of the most interesting and innovative Russian food in Vladivostok: try the aubergines marinated in lemon juice and chilli with toasted rye bread and *zefir*, a marshmallow-like dessert made from blueberries.

WHAT TO EAT

Rupjmaize
No mealtime is complete without a slice of buttered rye bread, and it's also used as the base for desserts such as *rupjmaizes kārtojums*, a bread trifle with jam and cream.

Pelēkie zirņi ar speķi
The national dish of stewed grey peas and speck (smoked pork belly) is the perfect winter warmer.

Smoked fish
You'll find an array for sale in markets across Latvia, but it's especially delicious and picnic-perfect from the smoke shacks of the Kurzeme coast.

Mushrooms
With over 300 edible species growing in Latvian forests, be sure to sample some mushroom-based dishes, but leave the foraging to the pros.

PRICE RANGES

For a main course:
$ less than €7
$$ €7–15
$$$ €15 or more

Tipping: 10%

LATVIA

With culinary traditions leaning towards the functional, rather than the artistic, stereotypical Latvian fare could be considered...stodgy. However, nature is bountiful in this diminutive country, and inventive foodsmiths are putting a modern slant on familiar flavours, creating menus featuring the freshest of produce alongside foraged mushrooms and berries.

KONDITOREJA DAIGAS

KULDĪGA | $ | BAKERY
Liepājas iela 23; 2646 3533; snacks from €1

Set back off a pedestrianised street, this small, one-woman bakery has fabulous baked goods at amazing prices. In between customers, the baker can be seen working her magic in the tiny kitchen. Tarts, pastries, rolls and more are fresh from the oven, and the choices vary throughout the day. The coffee is good and there are a couple of tables.

36.LINE

JŪRMALA | $$$ | LATVIAN
Līnija 36; 2201 0696; www.36line.com; mains €18-55

Popular local chef Lauris Alekseyevs delivers modern twists on traditional Latvian dishes and fresh seafood at this innovative restaurant occupying a perch above the sand at the eastern end of Jūrmala. Enjoy the beach, then switch to casual attire for lunch, or glam up for a dinner of, say, sake- and miso-marinated sablefish.

MIIT

RĪGA | $ | CAFE
Lāčplēša iela 10; 2729 2424; www.miit.lv; mains €4-7

Rīga's hipster students head here to sip espresso and blog about Nietzsche amid comfy couches and blonde-wood minimalism. Weekday breakfasts and the weekend pancake brunch are pure morning joy. The lunch menu changes daily (salads and hearty soups are a mainstay) and everything is vegetarian.

VALTERA

RĪGA | $$$ | LATVIAN
Miesnieku iela 8; 2952 9200; www.valterarestorans.lv; mains €18-28

The country comes to the city: that's the motto at this modern restaurant that works with a bevy of small-scale producers in Latvia's lush hinterlands. Meats, cheeses, vegetables, fruits, breads – they all have peerless provenance. The menu changes constantly, reflecting what's fresh, but could feature venison, stuffed quail or pike-perch, for example.

3 PAVARU

RIGA | $$$ | MODERN EUROPEAN
Torņa iela 4; 2037 0537; www.3pavari.lv; 2037 0537; mains €18-27

The stellar trio of chefs who run this show have a jazzy approach to cooking, with improvisation at the heart of the streamlined, ever-changing menu. Flavour combinations could include black quinoa with hazelnuts, cauliflower and aubergine, or tuna steak with hummus, sardines and fennel; the emphasis is on experimentation, seasonal freshness and an artful visual presentation that would have made Mark Rothko proud.

'I try to put the whole of the world on a plate, at the same time maintaining the dominance of a product's natural taste.'
Ēriks Dreibants, 3 Pavaru

APARJODS

SIGULDA | $$ | INTERNATIONAL
Ventas iela 1; 6797 4414; www.aparjods.lv/en/restaurant; mains €12-28

The namesake hotel's popular restaurant serves an excellent range of Latvian and European specials made with locally sourced ingredients, such as spicy tiger shrimps or venison medallions with wine and lingonberry sauce. Service is excellent and there's a good beer and drinks list. In summer the front opens up to the outside, while at other times a roaring fire warms the dark-wood dining room.

CAFE IMBIR

DAUGAVPILS | $ | CAFE
Saules iela 39; 2450 9965; www.facebook.com/pg/kafcimbir; mains €3-7

Resplendent in white, this city-centre cafe has a couple of tables out front on the street. Inside you'll find excellent coffee, daily specials, light meals and luscious baked goods, plus surprises like board games.

ESTONIA

While it's still quite possible to dine on old-school Estonian dishes featuring pork, pork and more pork, today's chefs look to their Nordic neighbours for inspiration, and modern restaurants in Tallinn and beyond are crafting exquisite dishes made from seasonally sourced ingredients to mouth-watering, wallet-friendly effect.

RETRO

KURESSAARE | $ | CAFE
Lossi 5; 5683 8400; www.kohvikretro.ee; mains €7-13.50

The menu at this stylish little cafe-bar is deceptively simple (mainly burgers, with a few wraps, soups and seafood dishes thrown in), but Retro's kitchen works hard: making its own ciabatta and burger buns, and using sterling produce. Desserts, such as warm chocolate cake with berry compote, are delectable, and there's a great selection of Estonian craft beer, perfect for supping on the large terrace out back.

KUUR

KÄRDLA | $$ | EUROPEAN
Sadama 28; 5689 6333; www.restokuur.ee; mains €13-16

The name means 'shed', but this delightful harbourside restaurant easily confounds any low expectations that name sets. Smoking its own fish, welcoming guests into a stylish 'beach shack' dining room–bar, and (most importantly) serving top-notch food alongside judiciously chosen wines, it's a real treat. The spicy seafood soup, a brick-red, piquant fishy broth poured over the local catch, is delicious.

ALEXANDER

MUHU | $$ | EUROPEAN
Pädaste; 454 8800; www.padaste.ee; 3/9 courses €74/131

Alexander is the culinary centrepiece of Muhu's ultra-luxe Pädaste Manor. Offering either a three- or nine-course prix fixe menu, it's a real culinary adventure, focusing on tastes peculiar to Estonia's western islands and the best of what's in season, with nods to New Nordic cuisine and molecular gastronomy.

MANTEL JA KORSTEN

TALLINN | $$ | MEDITERRANEAN
Poska 19a; 665 9555; www.mantel-korsten.ee; mains €13-19

WHAT TO EAT

Leib
Estonian black bread is rustic staple. The rich, dense, fermented rye loaf is a common accompaniment to meals, and tastes best with fresh salted butter.

Kiluvõileib
This sandwich of Baltic sprats marinated in herbs and spices is considered a delicacy; they're often served with a boiled egg.

Verivorst
Usually served up around Christmas, this sausage is made of pig's blood, barley and encased in in pig intestine.

Kama
A mix of barley, rye, oat and pea flours originally mixed with kefir or buttermilk to make a nutritious – if grainy – drink, but inventive chefs are now using it to make desserts.

PRICE RANGES

For a main course:
$ less than €10
$$ €10–20
$$$ €20 or more

Tipping: 10%

Tucked away in the leafy, weather-board-lined streets that merge into the greenery of Kadriorg Park, smartly painted 'Cloak and Chimney' offers up artfully prepared Mediterranean dishes such as lamb knuckle, white bean and chorizo stew. There are one or two inviting vegetarian dishes in each section of a menu heavy on seafood, poultry and seasonal produce.

MOON

TALLINN | $$ | RUSSIAN

Võrgu 3; 631 4575; www.restoranmoon.ee; mains €13-19

Quietly but consistently the best restaurant in Tallinn's Kalamaja neighbourhood, Moon (pronounced 'moan'; it means 'poppy') is a gem, expertly combining Russian and broader-European influences. The staff are friendly and switched-on, the decor is cheerily whimsical, and dishes such as *piroshki* (little stuffed pies) and reputation-transforming chicken Kiev showcase a kitchen as dedicated to pleasure as to experimentation.

MANNA LA ROOSA

TALLINN | $$ | GASTRONOMY

Vana-Viru 15; 620 0249; www.mannalaroosa.com; mains €12-23

Housed in a French-style villa built in 1872 and once used as a pharmacy, this restaurant-bar interior has a wacky interior, a kaleidoscope of sculptures, absurdist paintings and extravagant furnishings, sourced from around the world by revered Estonian

'We get our inspiration from the Nordic nature. Unpredictable seasons. The cold and grey Baltic Sea. Dark forests and their magical gifts.'
Restaurant Ö

designer Soho Fond. Thankfully the first-rate food (truffle risotto, and Moroccan-style mussels, for example), inventive cocktails and super-cool staff easily justify all the visual excess.

RESTAURANT Ö

TALLINN | $$$ | ESTONIAN

Mere pst 6e; 661 6150; www.restoran-o.ee; degustation menu €65

Award-winning Ö (pronounced 'er' and named for Estonia's biggest island, Saaremaa) has carved a unique space in Tallinn's culinary world, delivering inventive degustation menus showcasing seasonal Estonian produce. There's a distinct New Nordic influence at play, deploying unusual ingredients such as whey, rye and salted fat, and the understated dining room complements the theatrical but always-delicious cuisine.

LEIB

TALLINN | $$$ | ESTONIAN

Uus 31; 611 9026; www.leibresto.ee; mains €16-24

Pitch-perfect service and unimprovably simple dishes such as pike-perch from Pärnu Bay, paired with autumn vegetables and fennel-butter sauce, combine to produce the very best of Tallinn dining. A peerless rendition of *Leib* (Estonian black bread), thickly sliced and served with salt-flaked butter, is the ideal accompaniment to the delightful New Nordic ('New Estonian'?) food at this garden restaurant.

LITHUANIA

From fish straight out of the smoker to ultra-filling, meat-filled dumplings and hand-picked mushrooms, Lithuanian cuisine is as hearty as it is fresh. Traditional staples remain firmly on the menu, but new chefs on the block are freshening up the fare with a nod towards the Nordics.

WHAT TO EAT

Cepelinai
Infamously soporific Zeppelin-shaped potato dumplings filled with minced meat, mushrooms, or cheese, topped with a sauce made of butter, sour cream and onions.

Blyneliai
Sweet or savoury pancakes, either made with curd cheese and served with fruits, or from grated potatoes and served with savoury accompaniments.

Šaltibarsčiai
A refreshing, summery soup served cold and made with beetroot, buttermilk, cucumber and dill.

Kibinai
Pastries stuffed with ground meat – often lamb – and onions made by the Karaite community in Trakai.

Šakotis
A traditional 'tree cake', rotated on a spit to give it its characteristic spiky 'branches'.

PRICE RANGES
For a main course:
$ less than €7
$$ €7–14
$$$ €14 or more

Tipping: 10%

TIK PAS JONĄ

CURONIAN SPIT NATIONAL PARK | $ | SEAFOOD
Naglių gatvė 6-1, Nida; 8-620 82084; www.facebook.com/RukytosZuvysTikPasJona; mains €4-8

Picture the scene: you select mackerel or carp or eel from a traditional smoking rack, lay it on a paper plate with a slice of rye bread, and eat with your hands while watching the lagoon glow orange at sunset. This is the best spot on the Curonian Spit to feast on the region's famous smoked fish. Accompany it with cold beer or pint of *kvas* (a fermented drink made from rye bread).

MOMO GRILL

KLAIPĖDA | $$$ | STEAK
Liepų gatvė 20; 8-693 12355; www.momogrill.lt; mains €15-27

This tiny, modern, minimalist steakhouse has an equally minimalist menu. There are three appetisers, a handful of mains – including three cuts of prime beef, seared expertly on the Josper grill – a smattering of sides, two desserts (the pistachio panna cotta is marvellous) and a well-chosen wine list. Perfect.

UOKSAS

KAUNAS | $$$ | LITHUANIAN
Maironio gatvė 28; 8-686 38881; www.uoksas.eu; mains €18-23, 4-/6-course, tasting menu €30/40

COURTESY TIK PAS JONĄ

There's an organic quality to the decor (lots of plants, chairs covered in faux lichen), the menu changes according to the seasons, and chef Artūras Naidenko never repeats the same dish twice, but the menu might include choices such as lamb shank with chickpea puree, or grilled catfish with baby zucchini. There's a commitment to sustainable, seasonal ingredients from the Baltic Sea region and it's best to put yourself in Naidenko's hands by opting for the surprise tasting menus.

SENOJI KIBININĖ

TRAKAI | $ | KARAITE

Karaimų gatvė 65; 528-55 865; www.kibinas.lt; pasties from €1.50, mains €5-9

Draped with antiques, wall paintings and wood-carved finery, the interior of this traditional house is an understandably popular place for the full Karaite culinary experience. It's worth braving the crowds for the superlative *kibinai* (Karaite pasties) with multiple fillings, plus a supporting cast of soups, salads and dumplings.

SWEET ROOT

VILNIUS | $$$ | LITHUANIAN

Užupio gatvė 22; 8-685 60767; www.sweetroot.lt; 7-course degustation menu €75, with wine pairing €130

Led by the seasons, Sweet Root pairs locally sourced ingredients – pike and nettles, beetroot leaves and chanterelles – and presents them in a smart, modern dining room. It's an evening-long degustation experience, elevated to greater heights if you opt for wine pairing. A menu of ingredients for you to cross off as you go along adds a touch of whimsy.

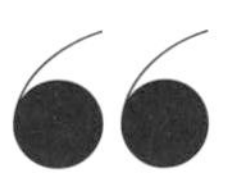

'It is our table, our traditions, our childhood on a plate, our seasons, and our feelings; in fact, it is who we truly are.'
Sweet Root

INNAFELKER/SHUTTERSTOCK ©

ROMNESA IGNALINA

AUKŠTAITIJA NATIONAL PARK | $ | LITHUANIAN

Strigailiškis, Ignalina; 8-600 26354; www.romnesa.lt/ignalina; mains €4-8

On the western outskirts of Ignalina, Romnesa really delivers when it comes to creative Lithuanian cuisine. The Old Testament–thick menu features such culinary delights as baked pike-perch with spinach, boletus stew, and pork chops with chanterelle sauce. Spuds in various forms are well represented and the homemade *gira* (kvas) is terrific.

WHAT TO EAT

Barszcz
The Polish versions of this soup can be either red (made from beetroot) or white (with wheat flour and sausage).

Bigos
This national dish is a hearty stew made with any kind of meat, but always with spicy Polish sausage, and sauerkraut.

Pierogi
Thinly rolled flour dough dumplings, stuffed with savoury or sweet ingredients, usually served with sour cream or melted butter.

Szarlotka
Classic Polish apple cake with a crumble topping.

Żurek
This hearty, sour rye soup, which can include sausage and a hard-boiled egg, is usually served in a hollowed-out, crusty bread bun.

PRICE RANGES
For a main course (add 10–20zł for Warsaw & Krakow):
$ less than 20zł
$$ 20–40zł
$$$ 40zł or more

Tipping: 10%

POLAND

Polish cuisine reflects the country's long agrarian tradition. Foraged wild ingredients, such as mushrooms and berries, add seasonal character to dishes in uniquely Polish ways. Warsaw and Kraków are among the most polished performers on the European culinary scene with creative chefs working with top-quality produce to create dishes that delight and earn Michelin stars.

RESTAURACJA JADKA

WROCŁAW | $$$ | POLISH
ul Rzeźnicza 24/25; 71 343 6461; www.jadka.pl; mains 67-87zł

Jadka takes creating fine Polish food very seriously – sourcing faultless local produce, working closely with the best suppliers, respecting the seasons and delving deeply into the history of Polish cooking yet accepting modern ways. Dishes such as smoked carp with cucumbers, nigella seeds and nasturtium, and venison with red cabbage and dumplings are an education and a delight.

KASZUBSKA MARINA

GDAŃSK | $$$ | POLISH
ul Długa 45; 73 412 6191; www.kaszubskamarina.pl; mains 36-59zł

This delightful place manages to evoke a rural theme without a single ancient agricultural knick-knack or trussed waitress in sight. Admire the crisp interior of heavy wooden furniture decorated with stylised Kashubian motifs and soothing scenes of the countryside, while sampling finely prepared regional dishes such as fish soup and duck stuffed with cranberries.

TATIANA

KATOWICE | $$$ | POLISH
ul Staromiejska 5; 32 203 7413; www.restauracjatatiana.pl; mains 55-79zł

Tatiana takes Polish food, particularly that of Silesia, and elevates it without uprooting it. Expect mains such as saddle of venison in burnt hay with barley-and-mushroom stuffed cabbage rolls and smoked plum mousse, and top-notch levels of food and wine service. Book ahead to be sure of a dinner-time table.

QUALE RESTAURANT

ŁÓDŹ | $$$ | INTERNATIONAL
Narutowicza 48; 72 312 3130; www.qualerestaurant.pl; set menu 180zł, mains 40-82zł

This elegant restaurant sets a gracious tone from the moment you set foot on the marble floor. The menu changes regularly, but always features classic Polish foods such as goose, duck, pork and trout, prepared in exquisite ways. The tasting menu is never the same twice and is great value for its quality and presentation.

SĄSIEDZI

KRAKÓW | $$ | POLISH
ul Miodowa 25; 12 654 8353; www.sasiedzi.oberza.pl; mains 40-80zł

A perfect combination of excellent Polish and international mains and unfussy, relaxed service. Dine downstairs in an evocative cellar, or in the secluded garden. The quality of the cooking rivals the best in this part of the city. If you've been hankering to try wild boar, goose leg confit or even horsemeat tenderloin, this is the place to give it a go.

ART RESTAURANT

KRAKÓW | $$$ | POLISH
ul Kanonicza 15; 537 872 193; www.artrestauracja.com; mains 60-90zł, seven-/nine-course tasting menu 239/289zł

'We rediscover forgotten polish cuisine and interpret it our way... We take the quality of fine dining and bring it to the bistro.'
Bez Gwiazdek

Easily the most ambitious restaurant in this part of Kraków, the Art is all white linens and swish service, but forget any notion of fusty food. The menu highlights farm-fresh ingredients and local sourcing, with plenty of unusual touches like red-pepper jam served with lamb saddle. Book on the terrace in nice weather. The lunch menu is great value.

ZAKŁADKA FOOD & WINE

KRAKÓW | $$ | BISTRO
ul Józefińska 2, Podgórze; 12 442 7442; www.zakladkabistro.pl; mains 35-45zł

Specialising in simple French-inspired cooking centred on veal, rabbit, fresh fish and mussels, as well as several vegetarian items, this is one of the best places in the neighbourhood. Expect courteous but formal service and an excellent wine list. The simplicity of the presentation extends to the decor: beige walls, black tables and wooden floors.

BEZ GWIAZDEK

WARSAW | $$$ | POLISH
ul Wiślana 8, Powiśle; 22 628 0445; www.bezgwiazdek.eu; set menus 100-180zł

'Without Stars' is a supremely successful expression of contemporary Polish cooking. Each month chef Robert Trzópek takes inspiration from a different province

MIKOLAIN/GETTY IMAGES ©

of Poland for his set menus, which include four to six courses and can be enjoyed with wine pairings. For creative, beautifully presented dishes in a relaxed environment this restaurant cannot be beat.

ZONI

WARSAW | $$$ | POLISH

pl Konesera 1, Szmulowizna; 22 355 3001; www.zoni.today; mains 68-160zł, tasting menu from 260zł

Chef Aleksander Baron pulls out all the stops with his contemporary take on old Polish dishes, such as Ruthenian *pierogi* (dried pike roe dumplings) and *zraz* (an aged beef roulade). Produce is seasonal and the presentation beautiful. The industrial chic setting, incorporating the five giant vodka stills of the old factory, is very impressive.

ALEWINO

WARSAW | $$$ | INTERNATIONAL

ul Mokotowska 48, Southern Śródmieście; 22 628 3830; www.alewino.pl; mains 56-65zł

A series of rustically chic rooms wrapped around a courtyard house one of Warsaw's best restaurants and wine bars. The wine selection is excellent and features some top Polish labels. The creative cooking uses seasonal produce and includes more than the usual throwaway vegetarian option. Service is relaxed and friendly.

SAM POWIŚLE

WARSAW | $$ | CAFÉ

ul Lipowa 7a, Powiśle; 600 806 084; www.sam.info.pl; mains 29-39zł

P262-3: Smoked seafood from Tik Pas Joną; Old town in Vilnius. This page: Jewish Quarter of Krakov. Opposite page: The bar at Quale Restaurant.

A large communal table dominates this slick bakery, deli and cafe that aims to use organic produce from local farmers and suppliers in its dishes. It's very popular for breakfast or lunch – make sure you book early in the week for a slot at the weekend or you may find yourself waiting in line for a while.

RESTAURACJA BUDA

KROSNO | $$ | POLISH
ul Jagiellońska 4; 13 432 0053; www.buda.krosno.pl; mains 28-40zł

This family-run restaurant is easily the best in Krosno. Expect excellent traditional Polish cooking such as duck fillet with potatoes and forest mushrooms alongside a smattering of international options such as spaghetti carbonara and 'Mexican' chicken. The atmosphere is refined but not stuffy, and service matches the standards set by the kitchen.

RESTAURACJA TEJSZA

TYKOCIN | $ | JEWISH
ul Kozia 2; 85 718 7750; www.tejsza.eu; mains 9-20zł

In the basement of the Talmudic House, this basic eatery serves excellent and inexpensive home-cooked kosher meals, including some fine pierogi and homemade *kuglem* and *kreplech*, a tasty beef and dumplings dish. There's an outdoor seating area. Save room for dessert.

W STARYM SIOLE

WETLINA | $$ | POLISH
Wetlina 71; 503 124 654; www.staresiolo.com; mains 25-40zł

This repurposed peasant's hut from 1905 is the setting for the best restaurant in this part of Poland. The attention to detail speaks volumes, from the custom woodworking in the dining room to the wine list and wonderful dishes, such as ribs in cabbage leaves and fire-grilled mountain fish and meats.

WHERE TO EAT...

VEGAN FOOD

Youmiko Vegan Sushi, Warsaw
Youmiko's freshly made vegan takes on sushi include toppings made from edamame beans, sweet potato and jackfruit. Put yourself in the chefs' hands and treat yourself to the degustation feast.

Eden Bistro, Warsaw
A temple of creative vegan food, third-wave coffee, organic wine and super-cool design. Sample its delicious take on laksa noodles made with sea buckthorn.

Veganic, Kraków
Cosy armchairs and an outdoor courtyard make for a welcoming setting for very good vegan food, like tofu burgers, pastas and stuffed cabbage leaves.

COURTESY QUALE RESTAURANT

BELARUS

Belarus' dining scene is firmly rooted in Central European flavours and culinary traditions. There's plenty of Georgian and Central Asian restaurants as well as a wide range of international options in the main cities including the capital Minsk.

WHAT TO EAT

Draniki
A staple of Belarus cooking, these grated potato and onion pancakes are traditionally served with fresh sour cream (*smetana*).

Khaladnik
A local variation on *borshch*, a soup made from beetroot and garnished with sour cream, served cold with chopped-up hard-boiled eggs and potatoes.

Dumplings
Belarusians love their dumplings which include *kletsky* (flour dumplings stuffed with mushrooms, cheese or potato) and *kolduni* (potato dumplings stuffed with meat).

Machanka
Also called *verashchanka,* this creamy stew of pork shoulder and sausage is served with *draniki*.

PRICE RANGES
For a main course:
$ less than €10
$$ €10–20
$$$ €20 or more

Tipping: 5–10%

JULES VERNE (ЖЮЛЬ ВЕРН)

BREST | $$ | INTERNATIONAL
Vul Hoholya 29; 44 5703 503; www.santarest.by/kafe-I-restorany/zhjul-vern; mains BYN10-25

Decked out like a traditional gentlemen's club and with a literary travel theme, this dark, atmospheric joint manages to be refined without being stuffy. It serves up cracking dishes, from mouthwatering Indian curries and French specialities to sumptuous desserts and the best coffee in Brest.

BISTRO DE LUXE

MINSK | $$$ | EUROPEAN
Vul Haradski Val 10; 44 7891 111; www.bistrodeluxe.by; mains BYN15-45

Housed in a gorgeous space with chandeliers, sleek brasserie-style furnishings, a chessboard floor and luxury toilets, Bistro de Luxe has charm and atmosphere in spades. The food is excellent – it leans towards French with dishes such as *escargot* (snails) and *steak haché* – and service is impeccable. Reservations are recommended, especially if you want to sit outside. Breakfast is served until noon.

KUKHMISTR (КУХМІСТР)

MINSK | $$ | BELARUSIAN
Vul Karla Marksa 40; 17 3274 848; www.kuhmistr.by

A stone's throw from the president's office, this charming place boasts wooden beams, a tiled fireplace, wrought-iron light fittings and antique knick-knacks. Staff are equally pleasant, and the menu is among the most authentically Belarusian in town. Order the house speciality, *zeppelins* (huge potato dumplings), or the *verashchanka* (pancakes with gravy and sausage).

ENZO

MINSK | $$ | INTERNATIONAL
Vul Kastrychnitskaya 23; 29 1770 088; www.enzo.by; mains BYN10-20

A hip and happening bistro worthy of the hip and happening Minsk street that it's on, Enzo is justifiably popular, mainly for its burgers and succulent steaks served on bread boards, but also for its towering salads and inventive desserts. Outside is prime people-watching, while inside classic-rock and alternative music videos are projected onto a brick wall behind the bar.

KAMYANITSA (КАМЯНІЦА)

MINSK | $$ | BELARUSIAN
Vul Pershamayskaya 18; 29 6945 124; www.kamyanitsa.by; mains BYN12-25

Come here for some of the best traditional Belarusian cuisine in Minsk. The *draniki* (potato pancakes) are top-notch, or go for the *kolduni* (potato dumplings stuffed with meat) or quirky house specials like Granny Dunya's Meat Pot. Terrific value, and the medieval Belarus theme is not overdone. Bonus: delicious *kvas* (a fermented drink made from old bread) is served by the litre.

PROVENCE (ПРОВАНС)

HOMEL | $$ | INTERNATIONAL
Vul Biletski Spusk 1; 44 7730 303; www.facebook.com/provanc; mains BYN10-20

With a prime location right on the Sozh River and an exciting contemporary menu, Homel's top restaurant is bringing dishes like salad Lyonnaise, gazpacho and honey-crusted Cornish game hen to this hidden corner of Belarus.

> 'A stone's throw from the president's office, this charming place boasts wooden beams, a tiled fireplace, wrought-iron light fittings and antique knick-knacks.'
> *Kukhmistr*

STAROE VREMYA (СТАРОЕ ВРЕМЯ)

HOMEL | $$ | BELARUSIAN
Vul Krestyanskaya 14; 44 7148 505; www.staroevremya.by; mains BYN5-20

'Old Times' flashes back to Soviet days, with waitstaff in pioneer and *provodnitsa* (female train attendant) get-ups and a tram car for a bar. Order a pure Russian dish like *selyodka pod shuboy* ('herring-under-a-fur-coat', fish and chopped veggies smothered in mayonnaise) salad for full effect – it's delicious. Added bonus: you can dress up like a Soviet functionary here and take goofy selfies.

KLYUKVA (КЛЮКВА)

VITSEBSK | $$ | FUSION
Vul Krylova 3; 33 3953 035; mains BYN5-20

With its sleek coffeeshop-like design and outdoor terrace on a quiet lane in Vitsebsk's Old Town, the 'Cranberry' is hard not to like. The breakfasts are the best in town, while the main menu works equally well for lunch – try the pizza-like *piccettas* – or dinner (tiger prawns, anyone?).

UKRAINE

Ukraine is the land of culinary abundance, with distinct regional variations. In recent years chefs have rediscovered the wholesome appeal of the national cuisine, and plenty of local restaurants now offer the chance to sample homestyle cooking that may surprise many with its finesse and flavours. Kyiv has arrived as a foodie destination, and dining out here is very reasonable compared to Western Europe.

KUKHNYA (КУХНЯ)

UZHHOROD | $$ | INTERNATIONAL

Vul Fedyntsya 19; 50 312 2232; www.facebook.com/kuhniabutik; mains 175-240uah

'The Kitchen' serves high-quality European food in a jazzy, contemporary dining room from where you can watch chefs prepping your meal. A few traditional Carpathian dishes make it onto the menu (eel, boar) but international favourites made using top-quality ingredients rule here. There are 45 types of wine to choose from and a huge selection of whisky for postprandial chill-out time.

BACZEWSKI (РЕСТОРАЦІЯ БАЧЕВСЬКИХ)

LVIV | $$ | EASTERN EUROPEAN

Vul Shevska 8; 032-224 4444; www.baczewski.virtual.ua; mains 100-330uah

Here's how you compress your Lviv cultural studies into one evening out. Start with Jewish forschmak (herring pâté), eased down by Ukrainian *nalyvky* (digestifs) and followed by Hungarian fish soup. Proceed to Polish *pierogi* (dumplings) and finish with Viennese *Sachertorte* with Turkish coffee. Be sure to reserve a table for dinner at this mega-popular place which includes a conservatory packed with greenery.

GREEN

LVIV | $ | VEGETARIAN

Vul Brativ Rohatyntsiv 5; 97 773 7700; www.green.lviv.ua

Billing itself as a 'vegetarian art café' Green has a relaxing, spacious dining room where you can tuck into meat-free, vegan and raw food. In the upstairs chill-out area, kick off your shoes and lounge around on cushions as you enjoy ice cream made on the

WHAT TO EAT

Borshch
A typical version of the national soup is made with beetroot, pork fat and herbs, but there's also an aromatic 'green' variety, with sorrel.

Bread
Dark and white varieties of *khlib* (хліб) are available every day, including the white *pampushky* (soft rolls rubbed with garlic and oil and then fried).

Holubtsy (голубці)
Cabbage rolls stuffed with seasoned rice and meat, stewed in a tomato and sour cream sauce.

Varenyky
These small, half-moon-shaped dumplings have more than 50 different traditional vegetarian and meat fillings. They're usually served with sour cream.

PRICE RANGES

For a main course:
$ less than 100uah
$$ 100–200uah
$$$ 200uah or more

Tipping: Round up to the nearest 10 or 50uah.

premises or a late breakfast. Also runs cookery courses and Friday is concert night.

TRAPEZNA IDEY (ТРАПЕЗНА ІДЕЙ)

LVIV | $ | UKRAINIAN

Vul Valova 18A; 032-254 6155; www.facebook.com/Trapeznaidey; mains 50-100uah

An unmarked door behind the paper-aeroplane monument leads into the bowels of a Bernardine monastery, where this lovely local-intelligentsia fave is hiding, together with a modern art gallery called the Museum of Ideas. People flock here for the hearty *bohrach* (a Ukrainian version of goulash) and *banosh* (Carpathian polenta with salty cottage cheese).

FAMILIA (ФАМІЛІЯ)

IVANO-FRANKIVSK | $$ | UKRAINIAN

Vul Nezalezhnosti 31; 0342-505 050; www.facebook.com/Familiya.if; mains 50-150uah

This fresh, casual bistro, with a leafy ambiance, is incredibly progressive for Ukraine. Enjoy meat, pasta, salads and eastern Slavic favourites such as *borshch* and Carpathian trout amid blonde wood and to a funky soundtrack. The 'gourmet' portion sizes are small, but the long drinks menu almost makes up for this.

FREESKYLINE/SHUTTERSTOCK ©

KANAPA (КАНАПА)

KYIV | $$$ | UKRAINIAN

Andriyivsky uzviz 19A; 068 044 3050; www.borysov.com.ua/uk/kanapa; mains 250-400uah

Sneak away from the busy road into this beautiful old wooden house with sliding-glass doors overlooking a lush ravine out back. Kanapa serves modern cuisine largely made from its own farm's produce. Traditional it is not: green *borshch* is made of nettles and chicken Kiev is not chicken but pheasant. Ukrainian mussels, caviar and pâté are other specialities.

KYIVSKA PEREPICHKA (КИЇВСЬКА ПЕРЕПІЧКА)

KYIV | $ | FAST FOOD

WHERE TO EAT...

DUMPLINGS

Komora, Poltava
Sample *halushky* – cubes of baked dough mixed with whatever is used as a filling in conventional dumplings – as well as many other types of dumpling here.

The Varenik, Kharkiv
Varenyky (triangular-shaped dumplings) are made by hand in an open kitchen here. Gorge on a variety of dumplings with different savoury and sweet fillings.

Puzata Khata, Kyiv
The upmarket *stolovaya* (self-serve cafeteria) chain is an excellent place for budget travellers to sample traditional Ukrainian cuisine, including dumplings.

Vul Bohdana Khmelnytskoho 3; perepichka 15uah

A perpetually long queue moves with lightning speed towards a window where two women hand out freshly fried *perepichka* – a mouth-watering sausage enclosed in crispy dough. An essential Kyiv experience, this place has been a local institution long before the first 'hot dog' hit town.

MUSAFIR (МУСАФІР)

KYIV | $$ | TATAR

Vul Saksahanskoho 57; www.musafir.com.ua; 099 409 4686; mains 85-125uah

The unmistakable scent of Crimean cooking wafts from the kitchen, where a *plov* (pilaf) master conjures a magic stew in the *kazan* (traditional wrought-iron bowl). Apart from the usual Tatar dishes, they make excellent *yantyk* (pie-like pastry) and Turkish coffee. The latter is served with lumps of sugar that you are expected to put straight in your mouth, rather than in your cup.

SHOTI (ШОТИ)

KYIV | $$$ | GEORGIAN

Vul Mechnykova 9; 044-339 9399; www.gusovsky.com.ua/restaurant/shoti; mains 160-480uah

This is modern Georgian cuisine at its finest. Try the fork-whipped egg-and-butter *khachapuri* (cheese bread) and a shoulder of lamb or charcoal-grilled catfish, all served with fresh, complimentary *shoti* flatbread. Huge racks of the finest Georgian wines, professionally decanted, tempt oenophiles. Sit outside on the broad veranda, or settle into the restaurant proper with its meticulously scuffed wood floor.

SPOTYKACH (СПОТИКАЧ)

KYIV | $$ | UKRAINIAN

Vul Volodymyrska 16; 044-586 4095; www.facebook.com/spotykach; mains 125-250uah

Sporting a Ukraininan revolutionary theme, with pictures of Taras Shevchenko and Bohdan Khelmytsky (and Che Guevara) Spotykach offers highly original takes on Ukrainian classics, including yellow-and-blue *varenyky* – the ultimate nationalist expression – and a *borshch* popsicle. *Spotykach* itself is vodka-based liquor made with different flavours, from blackcurrant to horseradish, and takes its name from the Russian for 'stumble'.

BUBA (БУБА)

ZHYTOMYR | $$ | GEORGIAN

vul Kyivska 10; 098 482 0089; www.facebook.com/buba.hinkalna; mains 60-120uah

As good as most Georgian restaurants in Kyiv and a third the price. The classic Caucasian stews and *khachapuri* (cheese bread) are well represented, only with modern twists. The English menu and an English-speaking waiter or two are rarities in these parts.

Previous page: Varenyky.

(БЕРНАРДАЦЦІ)

ODESA | $$$ | EUROPEAN

Odessa Philharmonic Hall, vul Bunina 15; 067 000 2511; www.bernardazzi.com; mains 200-420uah

This grand restaurant occupies the art nouveau dining room of an Italianesque palazzo (once a stock exchange, now the Philharmonic Hall) and is named after the building's architect. In addition to well-crafted Southern and Eastern European fare (including their so-called 'Beef Stroganoff 2.0' served with fried potato mousse with truffle), there's an award-winning wine list, occasional live music and a secluded courtyard for summertime chilling.

CITY FOOD MARKET (МІСЬКИЙ ПРОДОВОЛЬЧИЙ РИНОК)

ODESA | $$ | FOOD HALL

Rishelyevska 9A; www.facebook.com/odessa.cityfood.market; 048-702 1913; mains 100-200uah

Once an itinerant tribe, congregating here and there for irregular jamborees, Odesa foodies now have a rather palatial indoors base. The two-storey building is divided between shops, each with its own kitchen dedicated to a particular product – from the Vietnamese pho soup and Greek pita gyros, to grilled ribs and oysters. Vegetarians are not forgotten, with a dedicated shop called Vegan Hooligano and another one specialising in hummus.

'The highlight of the restaurant is the 'blind tasting', where guests put on blindfolds and are fully transferred to the world of aromas and subtle nuances of taste.' *Bernadazzi*

MYSHI BLYAKHERA (МЫШИ БЛЯХЕРА)

DNIPRO | $$ | UKRAINIAN

Pr Dmytra Yavornitskoho 46; 068-653 7907; www.mishiblyahera.com; mains 110-210uah

The name of this award-winning restaurant full of old books and local bohemians involves an overcomplicated pun about mice and a retired Jewish gangster's handwritten book of recipes. This hardened man apparently had a soft spot for fine pasta, Azov Sea fish and Danubian frogs, all of which may appear on their seasonal menus which include vegetables grown on an organic farm 40 km from Dnipro.

PLASTICINE CROW (ПЛАСТИЛИНОВАЯ ВОРОНА)

KHARKIV | $$ | UKRAINIAN

Vul Sumska 17; http://artvorona.com.ua; 066 557 5922; mains 80-170uah

Named after a beloved Soviet era animated cartoon, featuring a janitor and a crow, this restaurant involves some theatre. At the door a 'janitor' character will help you to guess the 'secret password'. Having succeeded, you'll be treated to excellent west Ukrainian food, including goulash and *banosh* (like polenta). The restaurant walls are covered with signs and pictures made with plasticine, and you'll be invited to leave your own creation.

CZECH REPUBLIC

Meat? Dumplings? Cuisine here is as carb-heavy as elsewhere in Central Europe, but subtle differences distinguish Czech food and three Michelin stars show it's no mere stodge. Meat, served marinated *and* roasted, is oh-so-soft and falls apart at a fork-twist. Dumplings can come bread-based, potato-based, savoury, sweet and in countless forms. And in the beer-mad nation that gave us Pilsner, many menus have 'with your beer' sections: yes, food specially tailored to accompany your beer!

WHAT TO EAT

Vepřové s knedlíky a kyselé zelí
Roast pork with dumplings and sauerkraut: the beating heart of Czech cuisine.

Houskové knedlíky
Bread dumplings made from flour, yeast, egg yolks and milk, with cubed baguette added to the mix. They're raised like bread dough, then boiled.

Svíčková na smetaně
Beef that has been marinated and roasted, making it succulently soft when served, often with sour cream sauce and cranberries.

Hermelín
Camembert-like cheese usually vended marinated in oil and pickles as an accompaniment to beer.

PRICE RANGES

For a main course:
$ less than 200Kč
$$ 200–500Kč
$$$ 500Kč or more

Tipping: 10% in touristy areas only.

LOKÁL

PRAGUE | $ | CZECH

Dlouhá 33, Staré Město; 734-283-874 www.lokal-dlouha.ambi.cz; 129-169Kč

It's hard to pick an 'if-you-only-have-time-for-one-meal-in-Prague-Old-Town' place, but this ever-busy classic Czech beer hall (albeit slickly refurbished) could be it. There is excellent *tankové pivo* (tanked Pilsner Urquell) and a daily-changing menu of traditional Bohemian dishes (from braised beef cooked in cream sauce with cranberries to carp fish patties, they execute everything very well). Efficient, friendly service helps.

CAFÉ LOUVRE

PRAGUE | $$ | CAFE

1st fl, Národní třída 22, Nové Město; 724-054-055; www.cafelouvre.cz; mains 139-349Kč

The French-style Cafe Louvre is arguably the most amenable of Prague's grand cafes, as popular today as it was in the early 1900s when it was frequented by Franz Kafka and Albert Einstein. It's as important to imbibe the atmosphere, which is wonderfully olde worlde, as it is sample the good breakfasts, cakes, coffee and wholesome Czech food for lunches (139-239Kč) and dinners (169-349Kč). Check out the billiard hall and ground-floor art gallery.

LEVITATE RESTAURANT

PRAGUE | $$$ | NORDIC/ASIAN
Štěpánská 611/14, Nové Město; 724-516-996; www.levitaterestaurant.cz; tasting menu 3000Kč

One of Prague's hidden treats, this gastronomy restaurant combines Asian traditions with Nordic flavours, using local ingredients. You simply can't come here 'just to eat'; it's a long, lovely experience spanning multiple courses and hours. A calm oasis near the bustling heart of Prague, this restaurant is aiming for the stars. Reserve in advance.

SANSHO

PRAGUE | $$ | ASIAN
Petrská 25, Nové Město; 739-592-336; www.sansho.cz; mains 190-250Kč, 6-course dinner 900-1200Kč

Friendly and informal' best describes the atmosphere at this groundbreaking restaurant where British chef Paul Day champions Czech farmers by sourcing all his meat and vegetables locally. There's no menu as such – waiters will explain what dishes are available, depending on market produce. Typical dishes include curried rabbit, pork belly with watermelon and hoisin, and 12-hour beef rendang. Reservations recommended.

'A calm oasis near the bustling heart of Prague, this restaurant is aiming for the stars.'
Levitate Restaurant

CAFÉ SAVOY

PRAGUE | $ | EUROPEAN
Vítězná 5, Malá Strana; 731-136-144; www.cafesavoy.ambi.cz; 119-179Kč

The Savoy is a beautifully restored belle-époque cafe, with smart, suited waiting staff and a surprisingly reasonable Viennese-style daily menu of hearty soups, salads, roast meats, schnitzels and traditional cakes. There's also a 'gourmet menu' (mains 300Kč to 800Kč) where the star is Parisian steak tartare mixed at your table, and a superb wine list (ask staff for recommendations).

MŮJ ŠÁLEK KÁVY

PRAGUE | $ | CAFÉ
Křižíkova 105, Karlín; 725-556-944; www.mujsalekkavy.cz; light meals 70-170Kč

A symbol of Karlín's up-and-coming, neighbourhood-to-watch status, 'My Cup of Coffee' uses Direct Trade beans prepared by expert baristas, and serves what is probably Prague's best caffeine hit. Add on an amiable, laid-back atmosphere, superb breakfasts and thought-through lunch dishes like pork stew with leek and wild rice, and you can see why it's often full. Reservations recommended at weekends.

BUFFALO BURGER BAR

PLZEŇ | $$ | AMERICAN
Dominikánská 3; 733-124-514; www.buffaloburger.cz; 200-350Kč

You might have come to Plzeň for the world's best lager, but this meat feast might become your best memory. Sample the country's tastiest burgers at this American-style diner where everything is freshly made, hand-cooked tortilla chips and guacamole through to the perfect French fries and juicy burgers themselves. The 'Hall of Flame' burgers are so hot you must sign a statement saying you eat them of your own free will!

MEDITÉ

MARIÁNSKÉ LÁZNĚ | $$ | SPANISH
Hlavní třída 7/229; 354-422-018; www.medite.cz; tapas 50-200Kč; sharing platters 400-500Kč

Czech owner David Böhm has transformed this unassuming spot into the Czech Republic's best tapas restaurant. Choose from a small menu of hot and cold tapas dishes, as well as authentic paella and pastas, and pair them with carefully-selected Spanish wines. The decor is colourful and minimalist – very different from this spa town's overwrought baroque.

NAŠE FARMA

ČESKÉ BUDĚJOVICE | $$ | CZECH
U Černé věže 15; 605-228-803; www.nasefarma.cz; mains 120-499Kč

The name of this restaurant (Our Farm) is a statement of its priorities – serving fresh local produce (mainly pork and beef) raised on organic farms in the surrounding region. Dishes are simple but delicious: maybe grilled pork chop with hollandaise sauce, pea purée and cauliflower florets, or meatloaf of confit beef with creamed potatoes and horseradish.

KRČMA V ŠATLAVSKÉ

ČESKÝ KRUMLOV| $ | CZECH
Horní 157; 380-713-344; www.satlava.cz; mains 95-295Kč

This medieval barbecue cellar is hugely popular with visitors. Your tablemates will more likely to be Austrian or Chinese than locals, but at one of the best, most atmospheric eateries in a candidate for the continent's prettiest town, you'll not mind. The grilled meats served up with gusto in a funky labyrinth illuminated by candles are excellent and perfectly in character with Český Krumlov. Advance booking is essential.

NONNA GINA

ČESKÝ KRUMLOV| $ | ITALIAN
Klášteriní 52; 380-717-187; www.facebook.com/pages/Pizzeria-Nonna-Gina/228366473858301; mains 130-200Kč

Authentic Italian flavours from the Massaro family feature at this long-established pizzeria, where food quality and service knocks the socks off Český Krumlov's many pricier restaurants.

Previous spread: Prague. Next spread: Bratislava old town.

Superb antipasti, great pizza and Italian wines at surprisingly low prices make for a memorable meal. Grab an outdoor table and pretend you're in Naples, or retreat to the snug, intimate upstairs dining room.

ŠUPINA & ŠUPINKA

TŘEBOŇ | $$ | SEAFOOD

Valy 155; 384-721-149; www.supina.cz; mains 264-399Kč

Many people come to Třeboň, a town known for the fish ponds producing much of the carp traditionally consumed country-wide on Christmas Eve, solely to eat here. It's possibly southern Bohemia's best fish restaurant in: even the menu is bound in fish skin! Šupina is fancier; Šupinka is cheaper and family-oriented. Both feature freshwater fish like pike, trout, eel and Třeboň carp. The kapří hranolky (pieces of battered carp and fries) are a national treasure.

PAVILLON

BRNO | $$ | INTERNATIONAL

Jezuitská 6; 541-213-497; www.restaurant-pavillon.cz; mains 280-550Kč

High-end (as in top-ten-in-the-country high) dining happens in this elegant, airy Brno space recalling the Moravian capital's heritage in functionalist architecture. Menus changes with the season, but usually features one vegetarian entrée as well as mains with locally sourced ingredients, such as wild boar or lamb raised in the Vysočina highlands. Daily lunch specials (200-300Kč) including soup, main and dessert, are good value.

ČERNÝ OREL

KROMĚŘÍŽ | $$ | CZECH

Velké náměstí 24; 573-332-769 www.cerny-orel.eu; Beers 34-49Kč, mains 169-489Kč

Some of the best food in this part of Moravia is served at this microbrewery on sleepy Kroměříž's main square. Choose from appetisers such as duck crackling and liver to a full gamut of game and fowl mains. Pair your meal with one of the house brews, such as the 17° dark with hints of caramel and coffee. Reservations essential.

SVATOVÁCLAVSKÝ PIVOVAR

OLOMOUC | $ | CZECH

Mariánská 4, 585-207-517; www.svatovaclavsky-pivovar.cz; beers 20-90Kč, mains 130-290Kč

This warm and inviting pub in the majestic Moravian university city of Olomouc makes its own beer and serves plate-loads of Czech specialities such as duck confit and beer-infused guláš (goulash). Stop by for lunch mid-week for an excellent-value soup and main course for around 150Kč. Speciality beers include unpasteurised wheat and cherry-flavoured varieties, and there is even a beer spa!

WHERE TO EAT...

TRADITIONAL CZECH FOOD

Restaurace U Veverky, Prague
Classic Czech pub with Prague's best-value homemade cooking. Roasted goose liver with red wine and caraway seeds, anyone?

Kolkovna, Prague
Stylish, modern take on traditional Prague pubs, with posh-but-hearty versions of classic Czech dishes like roast duck, Moravian sparrow and roast pork knuckle. Pilsner Urquell Brewery owns Kolkovna, so beers are first-rate.

U Zlaté Koule, Mariánské Lázně
Cosy-but-classy address with creaking beams, crisp table linen and a game-rich traditional menu. Order one day before for the showpiece: roast goose with apple stuffing and bread-and-bacon dumplings.

SLOVAKIA

Big cities lend cosmopolitan veneer to Slovak food but the real deal is a stodge-fest of potato-heavy, meat-heavy dishes swilled with beer, wine or fruit brandies: great to guzzle after time in Slovakia's many mountains. Find this nation's culinary soul in traditional countryside eateries or, better, by getting invited into a local's home.

WHAT TO EAT

Bryndzové halušky
Slovakia's national dish is potato dumplings cobbled together with sheep's cheese and diced bacon.

Kapustnica
Thick, complex sauerkraut-and-sausage soup, commonly flavoured with ham or mushrooms, then thickened with sour cream.

Pirohy
Pillowy dumplings with crimped edges, crammed with cheese, meat or mushrooms.

Placky and Lokše
Varying forms of hearty potato pancake, served with sauerkraut, sour cream or goose fat.

Šulance
Another of Slovakia's myriad dumpling dishes, yet this one is sweet: submarine-shaped dumplings doused in sugary, buttery sauce and poppy seeds.

PRICE RANGES
For a main course:
$ less than €7
$$ €7–12
$$$ €12 or more

Tipping: 10%

BRATISLAVSKÝ MEŠTIANSKY PIVOVAR

BRATISLAVA | $$ | SLOVAK
Drevená 8; 0944-512-265; www.mestianskypivovar.sk; mains €7-28

Continuing Bratislava's 600-year-old beer-making tradition, this brewery-cum-restaurant offers home-brewed and German beers to accompany its menu of Central European stomach-liners (sometimes infusing beer into dishes). Settle in at this vaulted, nook-and-cranny-filled hall and choose from beer-and-onion goulash, confit duck, beer-roasted chicken and moreish snacks from cheese platters to crackling pork.

JOYFULL/SHUTTERSTOCK ©

HRADNÁ HVIEZDA

BRATISLAVA | $$$ | SLOVAK
Bratislava Castle; 0944-142-718; www.hradnahviezda.sk; mains €10-30

Distinguished Slovak cuisine, like game goulash with dumplings, venison with rosehip sauce and risotto of barley and wild mushrooms, fills plates at this venerable venue. With a handsome setting in Bratislava Castle grounds, Hradná Hviezda is one of the city's top tables for romantic dinners.

BISTRO ST GERMAIN

BRATISLAVA | $ | INTERNATIONAL
Rajská 7; 911-331-999; www.facebook.com/BistroStGermain; sandwiches & light meals €4-10

Bratislava's fondness for French chic is fully satisfied by Bistro St Germain, a modish café emulating the City of Lights' 1920s heyday with its wonderfully tiled floors, bentwood chairs, chessboards and bookshelves. Food is more international than Parisian, with satisfyingly tall sandwiches, amazing burgers and cakes and delicious hot chocolate.

TRAJA MUŠKETIERI

BRATISLAVA | $$ | FRENCH/ SLOVAK

Sládkovičova 7; 0907-706-296; www.trajamusketieri.sk; mains €6-16

Medieval in decoration but French-leaning in food, the 'Three Musketeers' has a menu as poetic as its cellar setting, romping from Provençal fish soup to the rich and cream-garnished 'lady-in-waiting' pork. Artichoke tagliatelle and platters of French cheese make pleasant detours from meaty mainstays. There's a mostly Slovak wine list and courteous service, too.

KOLIBA PATRIA

HIGH TATRAS | $$ | SLOVAK

Eastern lakeshore, Štrbské Pleso; 052-784 8870; http://hotelpatria.sk; mains €8-18

On a lovely lakeshore perch with mountains swopping above, this terraced and turreted wood-built place is rustic but refined, introducing hungry travellers to true, traditional Slovakia. The menu offers familiar Slovak dishes done exceptionally well: perfectly spiced deer goulash, zesty sauerkraut and zander fillet on a buttery potato bed.

'Medieval in decoration but French-leaning in food, the 'Three Musketeers' has a menu as poetic as its cellar setting.'
Traja Muškatieri

ŽDIARSKY DOM

BELÁ TATRAS | $ | SLOVAK

Ždiar 55; 0907-468-034; www.facebook.com/restauracia.zdiarskydom; mains €3-11

Portions are big at this superb restaurant in fetching little Ždiar, a traditional, century-old settlement in the eastern Tatra Mountains. Pork ribs practically fall off the bone and the trout is mouthwatering. There's a cosy log-walled interior but the back terrace lures many, thanks to verdant mountain views that are quintessential Slovakia picturesque.

SLÁVIA

KOŠICE | $$ | SLOVAK/EUROPEAN

Hlavná 63; 0903-653-636; www.kaviarenslavia.sk; mains €8-17

Slávia is a show-stopping art-nouveau building on Košice's oval-shaped city square (Námestie) that is a great advert for Slovakian life, replete with buzzing restaurants, bars and grand edifices. This is the city's primo see-and-be-seen venue. Brunch options have gourmet twists (like scrambled quail's eggs and bacon from woolly mangalica pigs) while dinners are central European comfort food with five-star presentation, including schnitzels and beef stroganoff. Finish with a glass or three from the Slovak-dominated wine list.

HUNGARY

In culinary terms, Hungary is a Central-Eastern European trailblazer. Stodgy staples from surrounding Slavic nations play second fiddle here to feisty paprika-brightened stews and casseroles laced with smoked pork and beef. Hungarians historically lived nomadic lifestyles – goulash, the best-known dish, translates as 'herdsman's meal' – but these days, it's Michelin stars that fill the firmament.

WHAT TO EAT

Goulash
Hungary's most famous dish is a rich, belly-warming stew made with beef, vegetables, and paprika a-plenty.

Halászlé
This feisty fish soup splashed red with paprika is usually concocted with carp; southern cities Szeged and Baja are famous for it.

Csirke paprikás
With ingredients reading like a what's what of Hungarian cooking, this chicken dish is simmered in sour cream sauce containing paprika, peppers, garlic, onion and tomato.

Lángos
Snack on this deep-fried dough daubed with garlic and sour cream.

PRICE RANGES
For a main course (add 1500–3500Ft for Budapest):
$ less than 2000Ft
$$ 2000Ft–3500Ft
$$$ 3500Ft or more

Tipping: 10–15%

MANDRAGÓRA

BUDAPEST | $$ | HUNGARIAN
Kacsa utca 22, Castle District; 1-202-2165; www.mandragorakavehaz.hu; mains 3000-6500Ft

With a cosy basement location below a residential block, this wonderfully creative family-run restaurant has garnered loyal local fans with its excellent takes on Hungarian classics. Feast on menu eye-catchers like slow-cooked duck with beetroot, grey-cattle sausage or pearl-barley risotto.

KÉHLI VENDÉGLŐ

BUDAPEST | $ | HUNGARIAN
Mókus utca 22, Óbuda; 1-368-0613; www.kehli.hu; mains 1,000-4000Ft

Self-consciously rustic, Kéhli has some of the best and most authentic traditional Hungarian food in town. One of Hungary's best-loved writers, Gyula Krúdy (1878–1933), who lived in nearby Korona tér, moonlighted as a restaurant critic and enjoyed the Kéhli's *forró velőscsont fokhagymás pirítóssal* (bone marrow with garlic on toast) so much he included it in one of his novels.

BARAKA

BUDAPEST | $$$ | FUSION
V Dorottya utca 6, Belváros; 1-200-0817; www.barakarestaurant.hu; mains 7500-17,500Ft, 5-course tasting menus without/with wine pairing 23,500/38,000Ft

If you only eat in one fine-dining establishment in Budapest, make it Baraka. You're ushered into the monochrome dining room, where chef André Bicalho works his magic in the half-open kitchen. Seafood features heavily, with French, Asian and Hungarian hints to the beautifully presented dishes. The bar, with its array of Japanese whiskies and pan-Asian tapas, is a treat.

GERBEAUD

BUDAPEST | $ | CAFE

Vörösmarty tér 7-8, Belváros; 1-429-9000; www.gerbeaud.hu; cakes 750-1250Ft

On Pest's busiest square, chandelier-hung Gerbeaud has been the most fashionable meeting place for Budapest's elite since 1870. Along with exquisitely prepared cakes and pastries, it serves continental/full breakfast and a smattering of nicely presented Hungarian dishes with international touches. A visit is pretty much mandatory.

ONYX

BUDAPEST | $$$ | HUNGARIAN

Vörösmarty tér 7-8, Belváros; 0036-30-508-0622; www.onyxrestaurant.hu; 3/4/6-course lunches 19,900/21,900/27,900Ft, 6-course dinner tasting menus 33,900Ft

This Michelin-starred eatery adjacent to (and owned by) Gerbeaud has taken it upon its lofty shoulders to modernise Hungarian cuisine, and its six-course 'Within Our Borders' tasting menu suggests it's well on its way to achieving that goal. Expect seamless service and a piano to be quietly tinkling in the background. This one is for romance.

BORKONYHA WINEKITCHEN

BUDAPEST | $$$ | HUNGARIAN

'Chandelier-hung Gerbeaud has been the most fashionable meeting place for Budapest's elite since 1870.' Gerbeaud

Sas utca 3, Parliament & around; 1-266 0835; https://borkonyha.hu; mains 4250-7750Ft

Chef Ákos Sárközi's approach to Hungarian cuisine at this Michelin-starred restaurant is contemporary, and the menu here at one of the nation's top eateries changes regularly. If possible plump for the signature foie gras appetiser with apple and celeriac with a glass of sweet Tokaji Aszú wine and follow up with *mangalica* (Hungarian pork from woolly pigs!). There is also 200-odd types of fine Hungarian wine, most by the glass.

MÚZEUM

BUDAPEST | $$$ | HUNGARIAN

Múzeum körút 12, Southern Pest; 1-267-0375; www.muzeumkavehaz.hu; mains 3900-7900Ft

Going strong since 1885, this old-world restaurant melds exemplary service and top-notch cooking. One very suave spot, it is the place to come if you like dining in grand traditional style accompanied by live piano music. The goose-liver parfait is to die for; the goose leg and cabbage and roasted *fogas* (pike-perch) similarly stellar. A well-chosen selection of Hungarian wines stands by.

SZIMPLA KERT

BUDAPEST | $ | RUIN PUB

Kazinczy utca 14, Erzsébetváros; 0036-20-261-8669; www.en.szimpla.hu; mains 1400-2500Ft

Budapest's first *romkocsma* (ruin pub), Szimpla Kert remains a landmark place for sustenance, admittedly usually alcohol, but food too. It's a rambling complex filled with bric-a-brac, graffiti and art. Sit in an old Trabant car, watch a film in the open-air back courtyard, down shots or join in an acoustic jam session. Food is simple, but Szimpla Kert treats it seriously: ingredients for comfort food like burgers and wraps herald from Szimplakert Farmers' Market.

BISTRO SPARHELT

LAKE BALATON | $$$ | BISTRO
Szent István tér 7, Balatonfüred; 70-639-9944 www.sparheltbistro.hu; mains 3290-6990Ft

Balatonfüred is the oldest, trendiest resort town on lovely Lake Balaton and aptly the lake's best eating experience is here too. Chef Balázs Elek presides over a sleek, minimalist restaurant with a succinct menu that changes monthly, its dishes dictated by whatever is market-fresh. Expect the likes of duck liver with crab and wakame or leg of lamb with plum and sweet potatoes.

KISBUGACI CSÁRDA

KECSKEMÉT | $$ | HUNGARIAN
Munkácsy Mihály utca 10; 76-322-722; https://kisbugaci.hu; mains 2090-3100Ft

In the pretty city of Kecskemét halfway between Budapest and the southern border near Szeged is this classic country inn, or *csárda*. It trades on folksy charm, with its wooden benches and Gypsy music. But the food, which arrives in copious meaty portions, holds its own. Try the *Erdélyi flekken* (Transylvanian barbecue) or the *betyárpörkölt* (thief's stew).

TISZAVIRÁG RESTAURANT

SZEGED | $$$ | HUNGARIAN
Hajnóczy utca 1/b; 62-554-888; www.tiszaviragszeged.hu; mains 2950-6650Ft

The restaurant at this vibrant southern city's Tiszavirág Hotel serves exquisitely presented international and modernised Hungarian dishes, such as guinea fowl with Jerusalem artichokes, and pigeon with couscous and beetroot. There is a far-reaching selection of Hungarian wines by the glass and service is warm and efficient. It's all executed within a simple-but-elegant plant-filled space.

HORTOBÁGYI CSÁRDA

HORTOBÁGY NATIONAL PARK | $ | HUNGARIAN
Petőfi tér 1, Hortobágy; 52-589-010; www.hortobagyicsarda.eu; mains 1890-2690Ft

This is Hungary's most celebrated roadside inn, built at the end of the 18th century. Sit back and admire the Hortobágy kitsch taking up every place on the walls; Gypsy violinists often play as you tuck into your game dishes, goulash or *Hortobágyi bivaly csorba* (Hortobágy buffalo soup) with the inn's

Opposite page: Traditional Hungarian food at a food festival.

LARAMARCON/GETTY IMAGES ©

own sourdough. Don't miss the famous *Hortobágyi palacsinta* (pancakes) as an appetiser.

MACOCK BISTRO & WINE BAR

EGER | $$$ | HUNGARIAN

Tinódi Sebestyén tér 4; 36-516-180; www.imolaudvarhaz.hu/en/the-macok-bisztro-wine-bar.html; mains 3750-8400Ft

With its inventive menu and excellent wine cellar, this stylish eatery at the foot of Eger's castle is an ambience-rich contender for Hungary's best restaurant outside Budapest. The most scrumptious item on the menu could be the duck liver *brûlée*, or perhaps by a whisker the roasted rabbit with liver 'crisps'. Dine in a sleek inside space decorated in illustrations of the bistro's prized ingredients, or on an outside terrace.

IKON

DEBRECEN | $$$ | INTERNATIONAL

Piac utca 23; 30-555-7766; www.ikonrestaurant.hu; mains 3490-5990Ft

One of the finest restaurants in Hungary's handsome second city, Ikon commands a prominent position on the main square, but with its trimmed-down decor and classily clad staff, it remains discreet and upscale. Enjoy such inventive dishes as truffle risotto with sherry and sautéed mushrooms as well as rabbit cooked in *lecsó* (a sauce of tomatoes, vegetables and paprika) or venison with Jerusalem artichokes and hazelnuts. Tasting menus that can run to eight courses are 15,500Ft.

WHERE TO TAKE...

COFFEE AND CAKE IN STYLE

Hauer Cukrászda és Kávéház, Budapest
This enormous confectionery first opened in 1899 but only regained its fin-de-siècle splendour and scrumptious classic cake collection in 2016.

Gerbeaud, Budapest
Glamorous, not-to-be-missed cafe, hosting some of Budapest's most eminent souls – and tastiest cakes – since 1870.

Jókai Cukrászda, Pécs
Elaborate cheesecakes, pastries and eclairs at this bakery are a delight. Even macarons are Magyarised: try the poppy seed and blackcurrant ones.

Virág Cukrászda, Szeged
At the celebrated 'Flower Cakeshop', there's a museum-quality Herend coffee machine and meringues to die for.

SLOVENIA

A full-on foodie destination with culinary micro-regions like Istria and Prekmurje showing off their specialities through festivals and on menus, Slovenia is all about farm-fresh produce. Dining options span everything from classic restaurants and modern bistros to rustic inns and food trucks.

WHAT TO EAT

Kranjska klobasa
Large, round Carniolan sausage seasoned with garlic and pepper and usually served with a side of potato salad or pickled turnip.

Prekmurska gibanica
Pastry filled with poppy seeds, walnuts, apples and cottage cheese and topped with cream; hails from Prekmurje province.

Blejska kremna rezina
Also known as 'Bled cream cake' – a layer of vanilla custard topped with whipped cream and sandwiched between layers of flaky pastry.

Žganci
Slovenia's stodge of choice – groats usually made from *ajda* (buckwheat) but also barley or corn.

Štruklji
Sweet or savoury dumplings made with curd cheese.

PRICE RANGES
For a main course:
$ less than €15
$$ €15–30
$$$ €30 or more

Tipping: 10%

HIŠA FRANKO

KOBARID | $$$ | SLOVENIAN

Staro Selo 1; 05-389 4120, www.hisafranko.com; 6-/8-course set menu €125/150

Provenance is everything at this Soča Valley restaurant, one of the best in the country. Menus change with the seasons and showcase produce from chef Ana Roš's garden, plus berries, trout, mushrooms, cheese, meat and fish delivered by local farmers. The resulting dishes are innovative and delicious – how about a smoked-pork crème brûlée with sun-dried plums and horseradish? – and paired with top-notch wines.

PRI MARI

PIRAN | $$ | MEDITERRANEAN

Dantejeva ulica 17; 05-673 4735; www.primari-piran.com; mains €8-24

This stylishly rustic and welcoming restaurant run by an Italian-Slovenian couple serves the most inventive Mediterranean and Slovenian dishes in Piran. There's lots of fish to choose from – from shark fillet with polenta to pasta with spicy squid – and a good selection of local wines, from the Goriška Brda, Vipava Valley and Karst wine regions.

CANTINA KLET

PIRAN | $ | SEAFOOD

Trg 1 Maja 10; 05-673 3275; mains €5-10

This small wine bar sits pretty under a grapevine canopy on a central square in Piran. Order drinks from the bar (including cheap local wine from the barrel), then head to the self-service window to choose from a small blackboard menu of seafood dishes, such as fish fillet with polenta, fried calamari or fish tortilla.

ŠTRUD'L

LAKE BOHINJ | $ | SLOVENIAN

Triglavska cesta 23; 041 541 877; www.facebook.com/gostilnica.trgovinica.strudl; mains €6-12

For foodies keen to sample local specialities, this modern take on traditional farmhouse cooking is a must. Overlook its incongruous location in small Bohinjska Bistrica, and enjoy dishes like *ričet s klobaso* (barley porridge with sausage and beans) or go for the *hišni krožnik* (house plate) – a hearty sampling of native flavours, featuring ham, sausage, mashed beans and sauerkraut, potato mash and cooked buckwheat.

MONSTERA BISTRO

LJUBLJANA | $$$ | SLOVENIAN

Gosposka ulica 9; 040 431 123; www.monsterabistro.si; 3-course lunch €20, 7-course tasting menu €55

The concept bistro of star TV chef Bine Volčič delivers 'best-meal-of-the-trip' quality using locally sourced, seasonal ingredients and zero-waste food-prep concepts. Sample the roasted octopus, squid and mussels with organic polenta, cream buzzard and fennel salad, followed by the fig-leaf ice cream in blackcurrant sauce and egg foam with gin and juniper. The light-infused dining room, with white-brick walls and light woods, feels dressy but not overly formal.

'Monstera bistro follows the 'zero-waste' cuisine concept, which offers us a new dimension of thinking about food and cooking.'
Monstera Bistro

POP'S PLACE

LJUBLJANA | $ | BURGERS

Cankarjevo nabrežje 3; 059 042 856; www.facebook.com/popsplaceburgerbar; burgers €8-10

This centrally located craft-beer and burger bar has evolved into a must-visit in Slovenia's capital. The burgers, with locally sourced beef and brioche-style buns, are excellent, as are the beers. The dining area feels festive, with an open kitchen behind the bar and communal tables out front for diners to rub elbows. Avoid traditional meal times: it gets busy.

HIŠA DENK

POHORJE MASSIF | $$$ | EUROPEAN

Zgornja Kungota 11A; 02-656 3551; www.hisadenk.si; tasting menu €40-50

Gregor Vračko's restaurant, in the village of Zgornja Kungota north of Maribor, is all wood and floor-to-ceiling window minimalism. Its chic simplicity is a worthy contrast to the food. This is boldly creative fine dining with an added dash of eccentricity, elevating local Styrian produce to the highest level. There's no menu; just allow the chef to decide, settle back and expect a three-to-five hour dining extravaganza accompanied by an exceptional wine list.

WHAT TO EAT
Brodet
A Dalmatian favourite, this slightly spicy seafood stew served with polenta is also known as *brodetto, brudet* or *brujet*.
Gregada
Fish stew made with different types of white fish, potatoes, white wine, garlic and spices. Hvar island whips up the most famous version.
Fuži
Istrian hand-rolled pasta often served with *tartufi* (truffles) or *divljač* (game meat).
Zagrebački odrezak
Veal schnitzel stuffed with ham and cheese, then crumbed and fried – a calory-laden speciality of Zagreb.
Šaran u rašljama
Literally 'carp on a forked branch', roasted in its own oils over an open fire; a delicacy common in Slavonia region.

PRICE RANGES
For a main course:
$ less than 70KN
$$ 70–120KN
$$$ 120KN or more

Tipping: 10%

CROATIA

From grilled sea bass smothered in olive oil in Dalmatia to robust, paprika-heavy goulash in Slavonia, each corner of Croatia offers its own speciality. Foodie culture is on the rise here, with Istria region at the top of the gourmet ladder. Whether in a new breed of restaurants with up-and-coming chefs or traditional family-run taverns, savour the joy of slow-paced dining.

RESTAURANT ZIGANTE

LIVADE | $$$ | INTERNATIONAL
Livade 7; 052-664 302; www.zigantetartufi.com; 3-/6-course menu 435/900KN

Foodies from afar come to this place belonging to Istria's top truffle company and located just below Motovun in the village of Livade. Expect five-star fancy dining in an elegant setting, with truffles as the showcase in a seasonally evolving menu. Amidst all of the impressive nods to molecular gastronomy, the simple homemade fettuccine topped with shaved-at-the-table truffle is a showstopper.

KONOBA VELA VRATA

BERAM | $$ | ISTRIAN
Beram 41; 052-622 801; mains 45-100KN

Just outside Pazin, this rural tavern in a hilltop village serves some of the best handmade pasta, gnocchi and truffle dishes you'll taste in Istria. In winter the interior is a cosy affair; in summer head for the terrace with amazing views of the central Istrian countryside. Don't miss the incredible truffle chocolate cake.

PLAVI PODRUM

VOLOSKO | $$$ | CROATIAN

Obala Frana Supila 6; 051-701 223; www.plavipodrum.com; mains from 220KN

One of Kvarner region's best dining experiences, the 'Blue Cellar' – with an outdoor terrace right on the waterfront – does wonderful, innovative cooking perfectly paired with great wines and olive oils. Its standout dishes include sea bass and pumpkin-and-coriander purée, and scampi skewers with a dusting of coffee and black Istrian truffle accompanied by monkfish reduction and apple purée.

KONOBA BUKALETA

LOZNATI | $$ | CROATIAN

Loznati 9a; 051-571 606; mains 42-120KN

Cres island's *janjetina* (lamb) gets top billing at this down-to-earth village restaurant, just south of Cres Town, which has been run by the same family for well over three decades. Try the lamb breaded, grilled or roasted on the spit, or tuck into homemade gnocchi and pasta instead.

KONOBA NEBULOZA

RIJEKA | $$ | CROATIAN

Titov trg 2b; 051-374 501; www.konobanebuloza.com; mains 50-120KN

Straddling the line between modern and traditional Croatian fare, this slightly upmarket riverside restaurant – at the foot of the stairway leading to Our Lady of Trsat church – serves lots of seafood, along with selected beef and turkey dishes. Specialities include sous-vide swordfish and baby rump steak with prosciutto and cheese.

MODDYBLUES/SHUTTERSTOCK ©

'Nothing makes the senses feel more alive than the act of eating, and nothing makes more sense than to enjoy a good meal'
Zoi restaurant

KONOBA NONO

KRK TOWN | $$ | CROATIAN

Krčkih iseljenika 8; 051-222 221; www.nono-krk.com; mains 35-150KN

Just outside the old town on Krk island, this rustic place renowned for its local cooking style produces its own olive oil, as evidenced by the large traditional press around which tables are arranged. It also hangs its own prosciutto, which goes into some of the dishes. Generous portions and incredibly knowledgable staff make Nono worth seeking out.

KAŠTEL

ZADAR | $$ | MEDITERRANEAN
Bedemi zadarskih pobuna 13; 023-494 950; www.hotel-bastion.hr; mains 70-190KN

Hotel Bastion's fine-dining restaurant offers contemporary takes on classic Croatian cuisine, featuring octopus stew, stuffed squid, Pag cheese and more. France and Italy also make their presence felt, particularly in the delectable dessert list. Opt for the white-linen experience inside or dine on the battlements overlooking Zadar harbour for a memorable evening.

LIČKA KUĆA

PLITVICE LAKES NATIONAL PARK | $$ | CROATIAN
Rastovača; 053-751 014; mains 70-195KN

Built in traditional stone-walled style, Lička Kuća is touristy and extremely busy in high season, but the food is excellent. Specialities include slow-cooked lamb, dry-cured local prosciutto, and mountain trout, making it one of the best places for traditional dishes in the Northern Dalmatian interior.

PELEGRINI

ŠIBENIK | $$ | MEDITERRANEAN
Jurja Dalmatinca 1; 022-213 701; www.pelegrini.hr; mains 79-185KN, 3-/4-course set menu 570/690KN

Responsible for upping the culinary ante in Šibenik, this wonderful restaurant raids the globe for flavours, with influences from Japan and France, but its heart is in the Mediterranean. Among the menu highlights are codfish gnocchi and sea urchin pasta, while Dalmatian offerings are very well represented on the wine list. Call ahead to bag one of the tables on the patio with sea views.

MEDITERAN

PRIMOŠTEN | €€€ | MEDITERRANEAN
Put briga 13; 022-571 780; www.mediteran-primosten.hr; mains 98-270KN

Mediteran centres on a lovely old stone building, although in summer the action moves into the courtyard and up to the little first-floor terrace. Chef Pero Savanović's dishes offer a modern take on Dalmatian traditions and highlight delicious local produce. Visit when Istrian truffles are in season and you'll be in for a treat – try the monkfish with truffle sauce.

KLET KOZJAK

SVETI KRIŽ ZAČRETJE | $$ | CROATIAN
Kozjak 18a; 049-228 800; www.klet-kozjak.hr; mains 60-130KN

This adorable little cottage serves traditional food from Zagorje region – such as homemade nettle pasta with cheese and vegetable sauce – over sweeping

Previous spread: Vrbnik town; Grilled sardines, Split.

terrace views of the hills and valleys. Run by a local family that has been in the goat-breeding business for generations, it is known for its excellent goat's cheese and oven-baked kid goat.

BISTRO APETIT

ZAGREB | €€€ | EUROPEAN
Jurjevska 65a; 01-4677 335; www.bistroapetit.com; mains 132-202KN

High up on a villa-lined steet amid greenery, this restaurant run by chef Marin Rendić (who previously worked at Copenhagen's Noma) serves up Zagreb's suavest contemporary dishes. Start with tuna tartare with pear and sesame seeds, then move on to beef cheeks on bean spread, laced by carrot and pistachio. Opt for a degustation menu for flavour-packed feasting.

HERITAGE

ZAGREB | € | CROATIAN
Petrinjska 14; mains 18-39KN

Come here for tapas dishes, Croatian-style. This teensy place, with just one counter and a few bar stools, serves cheese and meat platters using all locally sourced ingredients. Try the flatbreads with prosciutto from Zagora, black-truffle spread and cheese from Ika, or the kulen (spicy paprika-flavoured sausage) with grilled peppers and cream cheese.

POJODA

VIS TOWN | €€ | DALMATIAN, SEAFOOD
Don Cvjetka Marasovića 10, Kut; 021-711 575; mains 50-115KN

Locals in the know rave about this seafood restaurant on Vis island, its leafy courtyard dotted with bamboo, orange and lemon trees. For a winter warm-up, try the pojorski bronzinić, a tasty peasant stew with squid, lentils and barley. In spring and summer the signature dish is orbiko, featuring orzo, peas and shrimp.

MALA HIŽA

MAČKOVEC | €€ | CROATIAN
Balogovec 1; 040-341 101; www.mala-hiza.hr; mains 65-135KN

Foodies from Zagreb travel to this village in Međimurje region, for its lauded and awarded seasonal cuisine done up with flair. Served in an old wooden cottage, the menu features snails, štrukli (baked cheese dumplings) and creative takes on local mainstays, plus over 150 wine labels including many from Međimurje.

ZOI

SPLIT | €€€ | MEDITERRANEAN
Obala hrvatskog narodnog preporoda 23; 021-637 491; www.zoi.hr; mains 120-180KN; 3-/5-course dinner menu 440/950KN

Accessed by a discreet door on the waterfront promenade, this is one of Split's most memorable dining spaces – simultaneously elegant and extremely hip, with a roof terrace, and the exposed walls of Diocletian's Palace offset with

WHERE TO DRINK...

WINE

Grgić Vina, Trstenik
The family vineyard of Californian wine-making legend Mike Grgich, this impressive winery on Pelješac Peninsula produces top-flight *plavac mali* and *pošip*.

Geržinić, Ohnići
This award-winning winery in Istria has been in the same family for a century. It cultivates 10 hectares of vineyards and produces a particularly good *malvazija*.

Lovrec Vineyard, Sveti Urban
Top winery in Međimurje region with 6-hectare vineyards and a 300-year-old cellar, producing *graševina* and other varietals.

Ilok Wine Cellar, Ilok
These old cellars in Slavonia region are a good place to taste *traminac*, a dry white wine served at the coronation of Queen Elizabeth II.

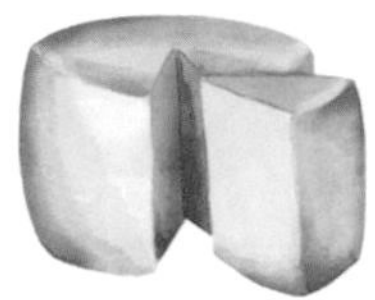

bright bursts of magenta. The sophisticated modern Mediterranean dishes, such as the crab, scampi and asparagus tagliatelle, look as divine as they taste.

KONOBA MATEJUŠKA

SPLIT | €€ | DALMATIAN, SEAFOOD

Tomića Stine 3; 021-814 099; www.konobamatejuska.hr; mains 75-140KN

This cosy, rustic tavern, in an alleyway minutes from the seafront, specialises in well-prepared seafood – as epitomised in its perfectly cooked fish platter for two. The grilled squid is also excellent, served with the archetypal Dalmatian side dish, blitva (Swiss chard with slightly mushy potato, drenched in olive oil).

VINOTOKA

SUPETAR | €€ | DALMATIAN

Ignjata Joba 6; 021-630 969; mains 70-150KN

Sit by the open fire in the stone-walled dining room of this Brač island konoba (traditional restaurant) or, when it warms up, grab a table on the street or in the glassed-in terrace across the lane. The seafood is excellent, particularly the green fettuccine with shellfish. With advance notice, they also serve succulent lamb or octopus *peka* (cooked beneath a domed lid).

KAPETANOVA KUĆA

MALI STON | €€ | DALMATIAN, SEAFOOD

Obala Ante Starčevića; 020-754 555; www.ostrea.hr; mains 95-140KN

The 'Captain's House' is one of the most venerable seafood restaurants on the Pelješac peninsula. Feast on Ston oysters and grilled squid on the shady terrace, but try to leave room for the Stonski makaruli, a macaroni cake that's a local speciality – it's unusual but surprisingly delicious.

RESTAURANT 360°

DUBROVNIK | €€€ | INTERNATIONAL

Sv Dominika bb; 020-322 222; www.360dubrovnik.com; 2/3 courses 540/640KN

Dubrovnik's glitziest restaurant offers fine dining at its best, with flavoursome, beautifully presented, creative cuisine, an impressive wine list and slick, professional service. Sample delicacies such as agnolotti with duck meat, pan-seared tuna, black pork neck, or mango chips and coconut sorbet. The setting is unrivalled – on top of the city walls with tables positioned so you can peer through the battlements.

This page: Zoi. Opposite page: Dish from Kaštel.

NAUTIKA

DUBROVNIK | €€€ | EUROPEAN
Brsalje 3; 020-442 526; www.nautikarestaurants.com; mains 290-360KN, 5-course tasting menu 820KN

Nautika comes pretty close to being Dubrovnik's finest restaurant. The setting is sublime, overlooking the sea and the city walls, while the faultless service is black-bow-tie formal but friendly. Classic techniques are applied to the finest local produce for sophisticated dishes such as the sea-bass fillet with cherry tomatoes and young spinach leaves. For maximum silver-service drama, order the salt-crusted fish.

BUGENVILA

CAVTAT | €€€ | EUROPEAN
Obala Ante Starčevića 9; 020-479 949; www.bugenvila.eu; mains 80-390KN

Bugenvila is not just the best place on Cavtat's seafront strip – with outdoor tables right on the promenade – but also one of the culinary trendsetters of the Dalmatian coast. Local ingredients are showcased in adventurous dishes served with artistic flourishes; try the scampi and strawberries risotto or pasta paccheri with porcini and truffles.

DIDIN KONAK

KOPAČEVO | €€ | SLAVONIAN
Petefi Šandora 93; 031-752 100; www.didinkonak.hr; mains 55-150KN

A quiet village on the edge of Kopački Rit Nature Park is home to this outstanding regional restaurant with a rustic, traditional vibe. The food is delicious – feast on the fish skewers of catfish and perch, or book in advance for the venison stew and meats baked under the *peka* (domed lid).

JOSIĆ

ZMAJEVAC | €€ | SLAVONIAN
Planina 194; tel 031-734 410; www.josic.hr; mains 29-90KN

On a historic *surduk* (wine road) that leads up a steep hill in Northern Baranja region, this village-based upmarket restaurant has tables set in vaulted cellars. Meat is the strong suit here – try the duck perkelt stew – and tastings of local graševina in the wine cellar shouldn't be missed.

WHERE TO BUY...

LOCAL PRODUCE

Fish Market, Split
A chaotic affair, Split's fish market is a spectacle to behold. Locals haggle for all their scaly and slimy requirements with their favourite vendors.

Sirana Gligora, Pag Island
Pag's award-winning cheese producer has a wonderful shop where you can taste dozens of cheeses before you buy. Other goodies include prosciutto and olive oil.

Miro Tartufi, Motovun
Truffles infuse olive oil, cheese and sausages in this cute Istrian shop. You can also arrange a truffle hunt, including lunch.

Uje, Dubrovnik
Uje specialises in olive oils, along with excellent jams, pickled capers, herbs and spices, figs in honey, and *rakija* (grappa).

WHAT TO EAT

Burek
Cylindrical or spiral lengths of filo pastry usually filled with minced meat. *Sirnica* is filled with cheese, *krompiruša* with potato and *zeljanica* with spinach.

Ćevapi
Minced meat (beef or pork) formed into cylindrical pellets and served in fresh bread with melting *kajmak* (thick semi-soured cream).

Sarma
Steamed parcels of rice and minced meat wrapped in cabbage or other green leaves.

Tufahije
Baked apples stuffed with walnut paste and topped with whipped cream.

Bosanska kava
Traditional Bosnian coffee, made and served in a *džezva* (small, long-handled brass pot) along with *lokum* (Turkish delight).

PRICE RANGES
For a main course:
$ less than 10KM
$$ 10–20KM
$$$ 20KM or more

Tipping: Up to 10%

BOSNIA & HERCEGOVINA

While you can stuff yourself with archetypal Balkan fast food all over Bosnia, Hercegovina strikes a balance between the grill joints of the interior and Dalmatian dining, focused on seafood, pasta and risotto. The capital Sarajevo buzzes with atmospheric eateries.

MALA STANICA

BANJA LUKA | $$$ | INTERNATIONAL
Kralja Petra I Karađorđevića bb; 051-326 730; www.malastanica.com; mains 15-35KM

Housed in a former train-station building, this upmarket restaurant with slick service is quite possibly the best in the Republika Srpska part of Bosnia. The menu features pasta, Istrian lamb, slow-cooked beef cheeks and Serbian specialities such as *Karađorđeva šnicla* (rolled, breaded and fried schnitzel stuffed with *kajmak*).

TIMA-IRMA

MOSTAR | $ | GRILL
Onešćukova bb; 066 905 070; www.cevabdzinica-tima.com; mains 5-11KM

Despite the constant queues at this insanely popular little grill joint, the staff maintain an impressive equanimity while delivering groaning platters of *ćevapi* (spicy beef or pork meatballs), *pljeskavica* (burger) and shish kebabs. Unusually, most dishes are served with salad.

ŠADRVAN

MOSTAR | $$ | BALKAN
Jusovina 11; 061 891 189; www.restoransadrvan.ba; mains 5-17KM

On a tree-shaded corner near Mostar's famous Stari Most (Old Bridge), this tourist favourite has tables set around a trickling fountain made of old Turkish-style metalwork. Obliging, costumed waiters can help explain the menu that covers many bases, from shish kebabs to baklava, and takes a stab at some vegetarian options.

SUPERFOOD

SARAJEVO | $$ | INTERNATIONAL
Husrefa Redžića 14; tel 033-977 797; www.facebook.com/SuperfoodStrEatArt; mains 5-27KM

Tucked away among much-graffitied apartment blocks, this hip cafe-restaurant wouldn't be out of place on the back streets of any Western metropolis. It's a great place for brunch or a lunchtime sandwich, and they're particularly proud of their gourmet hamburgers. Most of the ingredients are local, organic and free-range.

AVLIJA

SARAJEVO | $$ | EUROPEAN
Sumbula Avde 2; 033-444 483; www.avlija.ba; mains 7-15KM

Locals and in-the-know expats cosy up at painted wooden benches in this buzzing covered courtyard, dangling with trailing pot plants, strings of peppers and the odd birdcage. Local specialities are served, along with pasta, risotto and schnitzel; wash them down with inexpensive local draught beers and wines.

CAKUM PAKUM

SARAJEVO | $$ | EUROPEAN
Kaptol 10; 061 955 310; mains 7-26KM

A collection of antique suitcases, fringed lamps, gingham curtains and bright tartan tablecloths set the scene at this hip, wee restaurant with only half a dozen small tables. The food is simple but tasty – savoury pancakes, salads, a large range of pasta and a small selection of grills.

ŽELJO

SARAJEVO | $ | GRILL
Kundurdžiluk 19 & 20; 033-447 000; mains 3.5-7KM

Locals are willing to brave the tourist throngs at Željo as it's quite possibly the best place for *ćevapi* (spicy beef or pork meatballs) in Sarajevo. There are two branches diagonally across from each other – both have street seating, and neither serves alcohol.

> 'We prepare all our food with love using traditional recipes. The ambience of our old culture is an integral part of our restaurant.' *Tima-Irma*

SAČ

SARAJEVO | $ | BALKAN
Mali Bravadžiluk 2; 061 439 045; mains 3-4KM

Serving Sarajevo's best *burek* and *sirnica* (pastry with cheese), Sač bakes everything *ispod sača* – under a domed metal lid covered in charcoals. The result is delicious and not at all greasy. Grab a seat on the side alley, order a slice and wash it down with the traditional accompaniment, yoghurt.

PARK PRINČEVA

SARAJEVO | $$$ | BALKAN
Iza Hrida 7; 061 222 708; www.parkprinceva.ba; mains 14-30KM

Gaze out over a superb Sarajevo panorama from this hillside perch, like Bono and Bill Clinton before you. From the open-sided terrance, the City Hall is framed between rooftops, mosques and twinkling lights. Charming waiters in red waistcoats and bow ties bring out traditional dishes such as dumplings with cheese, veal *ispod sača* and skewers.

SERBIA

From Hungarian goulash to Turkish kebabs, Serbian gastronomy is a fusion of cultures. While grilled meats and fiery *rakija* (fruit brandy) are ubiquitous, an exciting New Balkan Cuisine is emerging along with a revival of ancient wine routes and Belgrade's hip craft-beer scene.

WHAT TO EAT

Roštilj
A catch-all term for grilled meats, usually pork or veal – from *ćevapi* (finger-sized skinless sausages) and *ražnjići* (shish kebabs) to *pljeskavica* (similar to a burger, usually eaten with onions).

Karađorđeva šnicla
Crumbed and fried, it's similar to chicken Kiev, but with veal or pork and lashings of *kajmak* (akin to salty clotted cream) and tartare sauce.

Svadbarski kupus
Literally 'wedding cabbage' – sauerkraut and hunks of smoked pork slow-cooked in giant clay pots; a must-try at Guča trumpet festival.

Komplet lepinja
Oven-baked flat bread filled with *kajmak* and scrambled egg and topped with gravy from the spit roast.

PRICE RANGES

For a main course:
$ less than 600RSD
$$ 600–1000RSD
$$$ 1000RSD or more

Tipping: 5–10%

FISH I ZELENIŠ

NOVI SAD | $$ | MEDITERRANEAN
Skerlićeva 2; 021 452 002; www.fishizelenis.com; mains 696-1979RSD

This snug little nook, decorated with checkered tablecloths and vintage knick-knacks, serves up the finest vegetarian and pescatarian meals in Vojvodina region, using only organic, in-season and locally sourced ingredients. Highlights include grilled trout served with potatoes and greens, and risotto with shrimp, squid and mussels.

SALAŠ 137

VOJVODINA PROVINCE | $$ | EASTERN EUROPEAN
Road 137, Čenej; 021 714 497; www.salas137.rs; mains 550-1650RSD

This rustic *salaš* (farmstead) 10km north of Novi Sad draws the crowds with traditional Vojvodinian feasting. Roll up your sleeves and help out in the organic garden, go for a carriage ride, feed the animals – you'll work up an appetite worthy of their famously huge meals. Sample delicacies such as *salašarski čekić* (dried plum, stuffed with cheese, wrapped in bacon and grilled) and *šnenokle* (meringue clouds bobbing atop milky custard).

BELA REKA

BELGRADE | $$$ | SERBIAN

Tošin bunar 179; 011 655 5097; www.restoranbelareka.rs; mains 650-1890RSD

In an ambience resembling a sophisticated home, Bela Reka is fiercely dedicated to the traditional craft of Serbian cuisine and is worth a trek to Novi Beograd, across the river from the old town. Meat-leaning dishes include perfectly spiced Pirot-style *uštipci* (meatballs), walnut-and-hazelnut-crusted monastery chicken and *homolje* (sausage stuffed with cheese). Traditional *somun* flatbread is fired up in a clay oven and the goat's cheese comes from the owners' farm.

ŠARAN

BELGRADE | $$$ | SEAFOOD

Kej Oslobođenja 53; 011 261 8235; www.saran.co.rs; mains 1050-2090RSD

Šaran (meaning 'carp') is rightfully renowned as the best quayside fish restaurant in Belgrade's Zemun neighbourhood. Freshwater river fish dishes like Smederevo-style pike (grilled, then baked under a flavourful smothering of tomatoes, garlic, onions and red peppers) are absolute standouts. Danube views and live tambourine music in the evenings add to the atmosphere.

IRIS NEW BALKAN CUISINE

BELGRADE | $$$ | NEW BALKAN

'Torn from the old cookbook pages and thus from oblivion, our recipes are the outcome of experience, craft and devotion of our grandmothers.'
Bela Reka

COURTESY BELA REKA

Sarajevska 54; 064 129 6377; www.newbalkancuisine.com/iris; tasting menu veg/nonveg 3500/3900RSD

Belgrade's best foodie bang for the buck clandestinely occupies a simple apartment south of the old central train station. Courses from the tasting menu are based around a single ingredient – whatever head chef Vanja Puškar has procured from organic farmers that week – and taken to new heights without leaving behind their Serbian origins. A memorable example: delightful fig-stuffed chicken roulade on triple-fried potato, with salty caramel and hop-orange foam.

AMBAR

BELGRADE | $$$ | BALKAN

Karađorđeva 2-4; 011 328 6637; www.ambarrestaurant.com; small plates 310-1150RSD

Innovative small-plate takes on Balkan cuisine are the go to at this chic spot in Belgrade's unglamorously named 'Concrete Hall' overlooking the Sava river. Everything from *ajvar* (spread made from roasted peppers, aubergines and garlic) to mixed grills has been given a contemporary spin; even the popular *pljeskavica* (burger) gets the five-star treatment.

MAYKA

BELGRADE | $$ | VEGETARIAN
Nikole Spasića 5; 011 3286 433; www.facebook.com/maykabeograd; mains 785-1050RSD

Among Belgrade's slim offerings for vegetarians, this gem in the city centre serves up worldly vegetarian specialities in a Serbian way. Dishes featuring the house-made seitan or stir-fried veggies with smoked sunflower cheese go down a treat, especially on the rustic front patio. The interior evokes a bar atmosphere and you can often come across live jazz and piano acts.

PEKARA TRPKOVIĆ

BELGRADE | $ | BAKERY
Nemanjina 32; 011 3611 268; www.pekaratrpkovic.co.rs; burek per 100g 32-55RSD

The fact that this family business has existed for over a century in Belgrade's competitive bakery market is quite an achievement. Trpković pastries and sandwiches are extremely popular, with grab-and-go queues especially for breakfast and lunch breaks. Sometimes there are two queues – one just for *burek* (flaky pie stuffed with meat, cheese or spinach and eaten with yoghurt).

ŠADRVAN

NOVI PAZAR | $ | GRILL
28. Novembra 12; 060 542 0400; meals 180-460RSD

Of all the fast-food spots in Novi Pazar, this 24-hour, no-frills joint (better known among locals as 'Kod Jonuza') right by the central fountain is the best for greasy-chinned grill gourmandising. Order *ćevapi* (minced veal or pork sausages) as a portion of five or 10 and wash them down with yoghurt.

STAMBOLIJSKI

NIŠ | $$$ | NEW BALKAN
Nikole Pašića 36; 018 300 440; www.restoranstambolijski.rs; mains 490-2050RSD

The upscale restaurant elegantly occupying a 19th-century Balkan-style house in Niš is easily southern Serbia's top dining destination. The accolades were showered on chef Saša Mišić for his modern takes on classics including *jagnjetina ispod sača* (lamb slow-cooked in a clay pot), coupled with creative dishes like pork neck with beer and honey.

Previous spread: Bela Reka; Dish from Bela Reka. Next spread: Pršut and cheese; Black risotto.

KOSOVO

A blend of Balkan culinary traditions, perfected through generations, Kosovo's dining revolves around delicious meat-heavy dishes. The international presence has brought world food to the macchiato-fuelled capital, though vegetarian requests are still met with puzzled looks outside Pristina.

WHAT TO EAT

Byrek
This filo pastry – usually filled with cheese or meat, and sometimes spinach – is an ever-popular snack.

Kos
Goat's-milk yoghurt eaten alone or with almost anything, particularly *byrek*.

Tavë
Meat baked with cheese or yoghurt and egg, oven-cooked in a clay pot; one locally flavoured version is *tavë Gjakova* (veal cooked with tomatoes and other vegetables).

Flija
A traditional Albanian dish, this flaky pie is slow cooked in a large covered pan over an open fire.

Baklava
Turkish in origin, this super-sweet pastry deep-fried and soaked in syrup is one of Kosovo's most common desserts.

PRICE RANGES

For a main course:
$ less than €5
$$ €5–10
$$$ €10 or more

Tipping: 10%

QARSHIA E JUPAVE

GJAKOVA | $$ | BALKAN
Rr Ismail Qemali 9; 039 0326 798; www.qarshiacjupave.com; mains €6

This cosy hotel-restaurant serves up big plates of cold cuts, including local cheeses and cured meats. For something more involved, try Albanian dishes such as the *tave Elbasan* (lamb cooked in yoghurt and garlic). Don't miss the underground wine bar across the alleyway.

TE SYLA

PRIZREN | $ | KEBAB
Shuaib Spahiu; 049 157 400; www.tesyla.com; kebabs €2-4

There's nothing pretentious about this riverside place, established in the 1960s by a street vendor who just sizzled up kebabs on the corner. From such humble beginnings grew a local classic. The kebabs are sensational, with the meat literally melting in your mouth.

RENAISSANCE

PRISTINA | $$$ | BALKAN
35 Rr Musine Kokollari; 044 239 377; www.facebook.com/Renaissancepristina; set meals €15

This might be Pristina's best-kept secret. Wooden doors open to a stone-walled dining room where tables brim with local wine, delicious mezze and meaty mains prepared by the family's matriarch. There's no menu – sit back and prepare for a leisurely meal.

SOMA BOOK STATION

PRISTINA | $$ | MEDITERRANEAN
4/a Fazli Grajqevci; 038 748 818; www.somabookstation.com; mains €5-11

Nearly all visitors to Pristina end up at this local institution at some point. The shady garden hums with activity at lunchtime, while the industrial-chic interior has a relaxed vibe. After tuna salad or grilled fish, settle at the bar area, among the best places to drink in town.

WHAT TO EAT

Pršut
Smoke-dried ham; the village of Njeguši on the edge of Mt Lovćen is famous for this delicacy. A true Montenegrin dish, such as *Njeguški ražanj* (spit-roasted meat), is stuffed with *pršut* and *sir* (cheese).

Lignje
Squid, either *na žaru* (grilled, with the crispy tentacles coated in garlic and olive oil) or *punjene* (stuffed with smoke-dried ham and cheese).

Crni rižoto
Black risotto, which gets its rich colour and subtle flavour from squid ink and includes pieces of squid meat.

Jagnjetina ispod sača
Lamb prepared by the traditional method of slow-roasting with vegetables under a metal lid covered with hot coals.

PRICE RANGES
For a main course:
$ less than €5
$$ €5–15
$$$ €15 or more

Tipping: Up to 10% at better restaurants.

MONTENEGRO

From the hearty comfort food of Montenegro's highlands to the fresh seafood offerings along the Adriatic coast, you're in for a treat. Local, seasonal and flavoured with wild herbs, the most memorable dishes are those enjoyed in a simple family-run *konoba*.

KONOBA FERAL

HERCEG NOVI | $$ | MEDITERRANEAN
Vase Ćukovića 4; 031-322 232; www.konobaferal.com; mains €8-20

A *feral* is a ship's lantern, so it's not surprising that seafood takes pride of place on the menu at this charming family-run restaurant with cozy wood-and-stone interior right by the Herceg Novi harbour. The grilled squid and homemade seafood tagliatelle are excellent; the wine list includes vintages from the nearby Savina Monastery.

KONOBA ĆATOVIĆA MLINI

MORINJ | $$$ | SEAFOOD
032-373 030; www.catovica-mlini.com; mains €12-25

This former mill masquerades as a humble *konoba*, but it's one of the Bay of Kotor's best restaurants. Watch the geese waddle while you sample the magical bread and olive oil, which appears unbidden at the table. Seafood is the focus, from cream soup with prawns to grilled octopus salad, but give the traditional Njeguši specialities (*pršut* and cheese) from the bay's hinterland a go too.

RESTAURANT CONTE

PERAST | $$$ | SEAFOOD

Obala Marka Martinovića bb; 067-257 387; www.hotelconte.me; mains €10-25

With its island views, table-top flowers and super-fresh oysters, this place in palazzo-filled Perast is ridiculously romantic. You'll be presented with platters of whole fish to select from; the chosen one will return, cooked and silver-served, to your table. Local delicacies include the black risotto with cuttlefish and the squid stuffed with *pršut* and cheese.

BELVEDER

CETINJE | $$ | MONTENEGRIN
Stari put bb; 067-569 217; mains €6-10

Occupying a scenic eyrie on the way from the old royal capital of Cetinje to Lipa Cave, this wonderful roadside restaurant serves traditional fare including freshwater fish, grilled squid, and lamb and veal slow-roasted *ispod sača* (under a domed metal lid topped with charcoal), accompanied by the smokiest paprika-laced potatoes you could hope for. The views from the wooden-roofed terrace gaze towards Lake Skadar.

STARI MOST

LAKE SKADAR NATIONAL PARK | $$ | MEDITERRANEAN
Rijeka Crnojevića bb; 067-339 429; mains €8-20

Perhaps surprisingly, given its sleepy village location, Stari Most is one of Montenegro's finest restaurants. It's

'Ćatovića Mlini provide a hideout from a busy life and time runs the way it suits you... harmonious like the order of perfect seafood specialities.'
Konoba Ćatovića Mlini

SVETLANASF/SHUTTERSTOCK ©

tucked away on the marble riverside promenade on the northwestern end of Lake Skadar, looking to the old bridge from which it derives its name. Fish (particularly eel, trout and carp) is the speciality here, and the *riblja čorba* (fish soup) alone is enough to justify the 26km drive from Podgorica.

KONOBA

KOLAŠIN | $$ | MONTENEGRIN
Trg Vukmana Kruščića 14; 069-609 144; mains €6-8

Sitting on the square that was the heart of the old Turkish town, this rustic eatery in Kolašin ski resort is a standard-bearer for Montenegrin mountain cuisine, designed to warm your belly on cold nights. Ease back and let your arteries clog over *kačamak* (polenta with mashed potato), *cicvara* (creamy buckwheat dish) or *popara* (bread-based porridge), and sample the roast lamb so tender it falls off the bone.

WHAT TO EAT

Fërgesë
Traditional dish made with green peppers, onions, egg and cheese, and occasionally meat or liver, baked in an earthenware pot; *fërgesë Tiranë* features offal, eggs and tomatoes.

Tavë
Meat baked in the oven with cheese and egg; *tavë Elbasani* is made with yoghurt and egg which are mixed with pieces of lamb or mutton.

Byrek
A ubiquitous Balkan snack, this filo pastry is usually filled with cheese, spinach or minced meat.

Midhje
Mussels, either wild or farmed in the Butrint lagoon, and often served fried.

Paçë koke
A thick soup made from the sheep's head, traditionally served for breakfast.

PRICE RANGES
For a main course:
$ less than 500 lekë
$$ 500–1200 lekë
$$$ 1200 lekë or more

Tipping: 10%

ALBANIA

From fancy Tirana gastronomy spots to beach shacks that grill the catch of the day, Albanian food is experiencing a renaissance. In coastal areas, the calamari and mussels will knock your socks off. Inland, the roast lamb is worth climbing a mountain for.

UKA FARM

TIRANA | $$$ | ALBANIAN
Rr Adem Jashari, Laknas; 067 203 9909; www.facebook.com/ukafarm; mains 900-2500 lekë

Along the road from Tirana to the airport, Uka Farm was founded by Albania's former Minister of Agriculture on a small plot of land. His son Flori, a trained winemaker and standout amateur chef, is now the driving force behind the restaurant. Guests can enjoy fresh, flavourful vegetables like zucchini and eggplant, locally sourced cheese and meat and quality home-made wine.

ERA

TIRANA | $$ | ALBANIAN, ITALIAN
Rr Ismail Qemali; 04 224 3845; www.era.al; mains 380-990 lekë

This Tirana institution in the heart of trendy Blloku neighbourhood serves Albanian and Italian fare. The inventive menu also features traditional dishes like *japrak* (spinach or grape leaf rolls stuffed with rice, minced meat and yoghurt). It's sometimes hard to get a seat, as it's fearsomely popular.

MULLIXHIU

TIRANA | $$ | ALBANIAN
Rr Lazgush Poradeci; 069 666 0444; www.mullixhiu.al; mains 800-1200 lekë

Around the corner from the chic cafes of Tirana's Blloku neighbourhood, chef Bledar Kola's Albanian food metamorphosis is hidden behind a row of grain mills and a wall of corn husks. The restaurant is part of Albania's 'slow food' scene; it's also a place of culinary theatre, with dishes such as risotto with Elbasan saffron and porcini served in treasure chests or atop teapots.

MET KODRA

TIRANA | $ | GRILL
Sheshi Avni Rustemi; qofta 100 lekë

One of the classics of Tirana dining, this tiny, smoky grill joint does one thing only – *qofta* (rissoles) – and the same family has been making them to exactly the same recipe since 1957. Grab a hunk of bread, a handful of olives and some goat's cheese from the market opposite for a perfect takeaway meal.

ONUFRI

BERAT | $ | ALBANIAN
Rr Shën Triadha; mains 200-300 lekë

In the village-like cobbled streets of Berat's *kalaja* (fortress), this is the closest you'll get to a home-style Albanian feast without gatecrashing a family lunch. Expect to be brought a heaving plate of stuffed peppers and aubergines, *byrek* (stuffed savoury pastries), *qofta* (rissoles) and grilled chicken. Finish up with a slice of homemade honey cake and you've got a meal to remember.

MUSSEL HOUSE

KSAMIL | $$ | SEAFOOD
Km 10, Rr Sarande-Butrint; 069 441 2617; www.the-mussel-house.business.site; mains 500-1000 lekë

With a winning view over the vast Butrint lagoon and fronting the famed mussel beds, this laid-back, beach-shack-like restaurant along the road to Saranda dishes up mussels in any style you might care to think of. It also serves excellent grilled fish and other seafood.

'The only way to pay tribute to our culinary roots is to build a sustainable future for Albanian food.' *Chef Bledar Kola, Mullixhiu*

MARE NOSTRUM

SARANDA | $$ | INTERNATIONAL
Rr Jonianët; 085 224 342; www.facebook.com/MareNostrumCuisine; mains 700-1200 lekë

This sleek restaurant immediately feels different from the others along Saranda's seafront: the elegant decor wouldn't be out of place in a major European capital, it buzzes with a smart, in-the-know crowd, and the imaginative menu combines the seafood and fish you'll find everywhere else with dishes such as Indonesian chicken curry and burgers.

ODAJA RESTAURANT

GJIROKASTRA | $ | ALBANIAN
Rr Gjin Bue Shpata; 069 880 7331; www.facebook.com/odajarestaurant; mains 250-600 lekë

Cooking up a storm since 1937, Odaja is a small, cute restaurant serving good, honest home-cooked Albanian mountain dishes. Tuck into the succulent meatballs with cheese, devour some stuffed peppers and relish the superb moussaka, and you'll understand just how good Albanian food can be.

NORTH MACEDONIA

Part Ottoman, part Mediterranean, North Macedonia's cuisine cherishes home growing and local foraging and perfectly embodies the 'slow food' credo. Traditional cooking in rural villages is a highlight, with endless bounty from the mountains and lakes ending up on local plates.

WHAT TO EAT

Šopska salata
Salad served with just about every meal – tomatoes, peppers, onions and cucumbers topped with grated *sirenje* (white cheese).

Tavče gravče
Baked beans cooked with spices, onions and herbs.

Ajvar
Spread made from roasted red peppers, aubergines and garlic; accompanies meats and cheeses.

Lukanci
Homemade chorizo-like pork sausages, laced with paprika.

Pita
Pie made of a coil of flaky pastry stuffed with various ingredients, usually local cheese and spinach or leek.

Uviač
Rolled chicken or pork wrapped in bacon and filled with melted yellow cheese.

PRICE RANGES
For a main course:
$ less than 200MKD
$$ 200–350MKD
$$$ 350MKD or more

Tipping: 10% in touristy areas.

LETNA BAVČA KANEO

OHRID | $$ | SEAFOOD
Kočo Racin 43; 070 776 837; www.kaneorestaurant.com; mains 220-650MKD

Virtually in the shadow of Lake Ohrid's sublime Church of Sveti Jovan at Kaneo, this is the best of the terrace restaurants by the water – the view is stunning, the food fantastic and the service professional. The traditional menu has had a facelift; truffle oil accompanies the potatoes, locally caught trout is both fresh and smoked, and courgettes are stuffed with aromatic herbs and rice.

HOTEL TUTTO RESTAURANT

JANČE | $$ | MACEDONIAN
042 470 999; www.tutto.com.mk; mains from 400MKD

Tutto's owner is the founder of North Macedonia's 'slow food' movement, and his enthusiasm for local produce is infused in the restaurant. Macedonian specialities such as slow-roasted lamb and pita (pastry stuffed with spinach and cheese) are a must; the fresh mushrooms on the menu are picked from the surrounding forest. The wonderful dining terrace looks onto the crumbling 19th-century stone village, high in the hills of Mavrovo National Park.

NADŽAK

SKOPJE | $ | MACEDONIAN
Orce Nikolov 105; 02 312 8113; mains from 100MKD

Nadžak may not look like much, but the food here is excellent, cheap and always fresh. All sorts of Macedonian specialities are on the menu, from *skara* (grilled meat) to *tavče gravče* (oven-baked beans in tomato sauce). Everything tastes great – order several dishes to share and grab a seat on the covered terrace in the heart of Skopje's hip Debar Maalo neighbourhood.

KEBAPČILNICA DESTAN

SKOPJE | $ | GRILL
Ulica 106 No 4; 02 322 4063; www.destan.mk; mains 180MKD

Skopje's best kebabs, accompanied by seasoned grilled bread, peppers and a little raw onion, are served at this classic Čaršija (Old Town) joint that's been attracting crowds of meat lovers for decades – no wonder the terrace is often full. Order 10 kebabs for a serious meat feast and pair them with *ajvar* (red-pepper spread) and a cabbage salad.

PIVNICA AN

SKOPJE | $$$ | MACEDONIAN
Kapan An; 02 321 2111; www.facebook.com/pivnicaan; mains 250-750MKD

Skopje's Čaršija (Old Town) is still home to a couple of *ans* – Ottoman-era inns, similar to caravanserai – and the Kapan An houses this restaurant. Try butter-soft *sarma* (stuffed cabbage leaves) or roasted pork ribs and feel the history echoing through the sumptuous central courtyard, where Pivnica's partially covered patio offers a tranquil bolthole.

'The taste of local dishes completes the contact with the region and makes stronger the overall impression left by the stay.'
Hotel Tutto Restaurant

AGROFRUTI/SHUTTERSTOCK ©

VILA RASKRSNICA

BRAJČINO | $ | MACEDONIAN
075 796 796; www.facebook.com/VilaRaskrsnicaBrajcinoPrespa; mains under 200MKD

It's worth detouring from the tourist trail just to stay at this utterly lovely village guesthouse in Pelister National Park – with a mountain-backed garden, rustic picnic tables and a peeping view of Lake Prespa – which offers lip-smacking country food. Your stay will probably start with homemade wine or sour cherry liquor, breakfast might include freshly baked *mekici* (fried dough), and dinner could be homemade paprika-laced pork-and-leek sausage.

BULGARIA

Bulgarians, along with their Turkish and Balkan neighbours, share a passion for grilled meats, fresh and unfussy salads, and slow-cooked oven concoctions baked and served in a clay pot. Lamb often shares menu space with pork and chicken. The local wines are invariably delicious, and meals traditionally start with a thimble-full of *rakia* — brandy made from grapes or plums.

WHAT TO EAT

Shopska salata
Signature salad composed of tomatoes, cucumbers, onions, red peppers and a black olive. It's often served with a shot of *rakia*.

Kebapche
Mildly spicy logs of grilled minced pork and beef, flavoured with cumin and pepper to lend a distinctive zing. Popular in summer.

Taratar
A chilled soup featuring the country's pride and joy, fresh yoghurt, and seasoned with cucumber, garlic and crushed walnut.

Kavarma
Traditional clay-pot dish, usually featuring chicken or pork. Recipes vary by region, but the pot is invariably filled with veggies and cheese, and brought out sizzling hot.

PRICE RANGES
$ less than 10 lv
$$ 10–20 lv
$$$ 20 lv or more

Tipping: 10%

MANASTIRSKA MAGERNITSA

SOFIA | $$ | BULGARIAN
ul Han Asparuh 67; 02-980 3883; www.magernitsa.com; mains 10-18 lv

Hard to believe this old-fashioned, inviting inn is located in the heart of busy Sofia. The enormous menu features recipes from monasteries across the country, with dishes like 'drunken rabbit' stewed in wine, as well as salads, fish, pork and game options.

MOMA BULGARIAN FOOD & WINE

SOFIA | $$$ | BULGARIAN
ul Solunska 28; 088562220; www.moma-restaurant.com; mains 10-24 lv

This on-trend re-imagining of the Bulgarian mehana (taverna) is one of Sofia's best, serving typical Bulgarian foods, such as grilled meats and meatballs, but within a more modern, understated interior. Start with a shot of brandy and a Shopska salata, and then move on to the ample main courses.

MADE IN HOME

SOFIA | $$ | BULGARIAN
ul Angel Kânchev 30a; www.facebook.com/madeinhomesofia; 0876884014; mains 14-23 lv

Worthy entry into the locally sourced, slow-food category (all items are made in-house). The cooking is eclectic, with dollops of Middle Eastern (like velvety hummus) and Turkish items, as well as plenty of vegetarian and vegan offerings. The playfully countrified interior feels straight out of Winnie-the-Pooh.

NIKO'LAS

SOFIA | $$$ | BULGARIAN
pl Rayko Daskalov 3; 0876888471; www.nikolas.bg; tasting menu 60/80 lv

The menu boasts a 'taste of the Balkans with an Asian twist', which undersells the amazing food on offer. Expect the likes of smoked trout topped with beetroot, goat cheese and poached pear, or grilled sea bass with Bulgarian caviar. The open kitchen allows for direct interaction with the chefs. The wood-clad walls are warm without being folksy.

MEHANA KASAPINOVA KÂSHTA

SOUTHERN MOUNTAINS | $$ | BULGARIAN

ul Yane Sandanski 4, Bansko; 0899948494; www.kasapinova-mehana.com; mains 8-15 lv

This 18th-century inn, just southeast of Bansko's main square, once entertained Bulgarian revolutionaries. These days, it's hungry hikers and skiers who file in for excellent barbecue. Atmospheric touches include colourful rugs and animal skins draped on the stone walls, best admired with a glass of locally made wine.

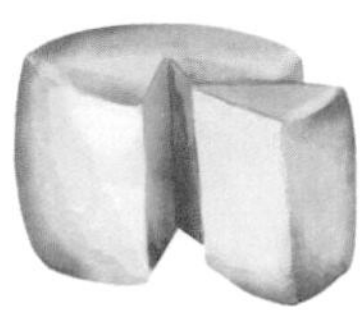

'I combine my roots in traditional Bulgarian food with a passion for foreign cuisines, especially Asian, using seasonal, mostly local ingredients.'
Tsvetomir Nikolov, owner and head chef

HADZHI HRISTO CORBADZHI/GETTY IMAGES ©

PAVAJ

BULGARIAN THRACE | $$ | BULGARIAN

ul Zlatarska 7, Plovdiv; 0878111876; www.facebook.com/pavaj.plovdiv; mains 10-15 lv

A tiny hole-in-the-wall that just happens to be one of the city's most happening restaurants. The formula for success follows international trends like using seasonal, farm-fresh ingredients and fusing them with local favourites like sausages, meatballs and baked lamb. The wine list is superb, but be forewarned: space is tight.

TAM'S HOUSE

BULGARIAN THRACE | $$ | INTERNATIONAL

ul Zagreb 4, Plovdiv; 0887242727; www.facebook.com/TamssHouse; mains 12-15 lv

A labour of love, fusing Bulgarian and South American cuisines by way of California. Expect a little of everything: steaks, burgers, tapas, and pilafs, prepared with care and given appealing, minimalist platings. Finish off with Tam's star attraction: a cheesecake 'egg' (mango cheesecake encased in white chocolate).

HAN HADJI NIKOLI

CENTRAL MOUNTAINS | $$$ | BULGARIAN

ul Rakovski 19, Veliko Târnovo; 062-651 291; www.hanhadjinikoli.com; mains 17-30 lv

Countless Veliko Târnovo inns were ransacked under Ottoman rule, as they were popular meeting places for revolution-minded locals. Fortunately, Han Hadji Nikoli survived, and the town's finest restaurant occupies this beautifully restored 1858 building. Well-executed dishes include 'Trakia' chicken (marinated in herbs and yoghurt), mussels sautéed in white wine, and exquisitely prepared pork neck.

SHTASTLIVECA

CENTRAL MOUNTAINS | $$ | BULGARIAN

ul Stefan Stambolov 79, Veliko Târnovo; 062-600 656; www.shtastliveca.com; mains 10-20 lv

Inventive dishes and amiable service have solidified the 'Lucky Man' as a favourite among locals and expats. Sauces pairing chocolate and cheese are drizzled over chicken, while strawberry and balsamic vinegar lend piquancy to meaty dishes. The nod to vintage style in its floral decor imparts a calming feel, and the downstairs tables enjoy the best views.

MAGNOLIA

CENTRAL MOUNTAINS | $$ | BULGARIAN

bul Nikola Petkov 1, Kazanlâk; 0431-89 546; www.magnolia-kazanlak.com; mains 7-14 lv

An old-fashioned inn, hidden within an unassuming peach-coloured building, features a menu of well-executed clay-pot medleys and mixed grills. Choose a table in the Bulgarian–Renaissance-style dining room or, better yet, the white-tiled courtyard, with walls draped in vines.

GARDEN RESTAURANT

THE DANUBE & NORTHERN PLAINS | $$ | BULGARIAN

bul Pridunavski 22, Ruse; 0886005658; www.hotel-riga.com; mains 6-12 lv

This outdoor restaurant is part of the Riga Hotel complex and features a beautiful view out over the Danube, water fountains and lots of calming greenery. Choose from a long list of grilled meats or fish. In the evening, the atmosphere borders on magical,

P302-3: Lake Ohrid; Spread of traditional Macedonian food. Previous page: Tsarevets Strongold; Banitsa with white cheese. Next page: Roast pork and potato dish.

as the brandy flows and the last rays of sun glint over the river.

BAY

BLACK SEA | $$ | MIDDLE EASTERN

Sveti Konstantin; 0887003003; www.thebay.bg; mains 15-25 lv

Discover the best food in Sveti Konstantin, and arguably in all of greater Varna, at this beachside Lebanese restaurant. Specialities include fish and barbecue, though the chef has added creative Middle Eastern touches, such as a mashed chick-pea salad, flavoured with yoghurt and eggplant. The grills are outstanding, as are the views out over a private beach.

MEHANA NEPTUN

BLACK SEA COAST | $$$ | BULGARIAN

ul Morski Skali 45, Sozopol; 0550-22 735; mains 15-30 lv

Occupying a promontory looking out onto the sea and Sveti Ivan Island in the distance, the romantic sea and sun-drenched views pair beautifully with delicious fish combinations, like mouth-watering stuffed squid. Book a sea-view table outdoors for around dusk for the full experience.

ETHNO

BLACK SEA COAST | $$ | SEAFOOD

ul Aleksandrovska 49, Burgas; 0887877966; www.facebook.com/EthnoRestaurant; mains 7-20 lv

This downtown Burgas restaurant does splendid things with seafood: the Black Sea mussels alone are worth a visit. Ethno effortlessly invokes a summery vibe with cheerful blue-and-white linens, tables and chairs that recall the city's Greek heritage.

ROSÉ

BLACK SEA COAST | $$ | INTERNATIONAL

bul Aleko Bogoridi 19, Burgas; www.facebook.com/roseburgas; 0885855099; mains 8-20 lv

Choose from a wide menu of grilled meats and fish, including a superlative lamb-shank offering, or fresh pasta at this upscale restaurant in the city of Burgas. Finish off with a cake or homemade ice cream. The smart interior is a pleasing mix of modern and antique and feels like a splurge.

STARIYA CHINAR

BLACK SEA COAST | $$ | BULGARIAN

ul Preslav 11, Varna; tel 052-949 400; www.stariachinar.com; mains 12-20 lv

This is upmarket Balkan soulfood at its best. Try the baked lamb, prepared according to an old Bulgarian recipe, or the divine barbecued pork ribs; it also boasts some ornate salads. Outdoor seating is lovely in summer; park yourself in the traditional interior when the cooler weather strikes.

WHERE TO DRINK...

BULGARIAN WINE

Vino Orenda, Sofia
This tiny, knowledgeable wine shop in the capital features the best of independent producers from around the country. Hosts regular tasting nights.

Damianitza, Melnik
Leading Melnik winemaker Damianitza offers free tastings of its signature dry-red 'Uniqato' or oaky 'No Man's Land' cabs.

Mehana Chavkova Kâshta, Melnik
A classic inn with all the trimmings affords the chance to sample some excellent local food and to wash it all down with some sublime Melnik reds.

Vino Culture, Plovdiv
Opening up from a 'blink-and-you'll-miss-it' exterior is an airy brick-walled space where the staff truly know their vintages.

ROMANIA

Romanian food draws liberally from Balkan, Turkish and Hungarian influences, elevated by fresh, organic ingredients and recipes honed over generations. Maize is abundant and polenta (called *mămăligă*) is a staple. Meals start with soup, usually soured with lemon or fermented wheat bran.

WHAT TO EAT

Ciorbă de burtă
Romanians have a special passion for tripe soup. The broth is flavoured with garlic and root vegetables – and vinegar to impart sourness.

Sarmale
These stuffed cabbage leaves hail originally from Turkey but conquered the national palate centuries ago. They're normally filled with minced pork and rice.

Mămăligă
Versatile cornmeal polenta can play the role of main course, side dish or even bread. It's an ideal accompaniment to stuffed cabbage leaves.

Papanași
Fried or boiled pieces of dough, dolled up with jam and sour cream. Beloved by kids, but a fitting, filling way to end a meal at any age.

PRICE RANGES
$ less than 20 lei
$$ 20–40 lei
$$$ 40 lei or more

Tipping: 10%

HOMEMADE

CRIŞANA & BANATS | $$ | ROMANIAN

Str Gheorghe Doja 40, Timişoara; 0730-832 299; www.facebook.com/pg; homemadetimisoara; mains 25-40 lei

Timişoara's most unusual restaurant is also its most memorable. The setting is a posh living room, with sofas, dark-green walls and antique rugs on parquet floors, like you've just crashed a 19th-century dinner party. The eclectic menu is more 21st century and runs from excellent burgers to intricate creations built around beef and pork.

ROATA

TRANSYLVANIAS | $$ | ROMANIAN

Str Alexandru Ciurea 6, Cluj-Napoca; 0264-592 022; www.facebook.com/restaurantroatacluj; mains 25-40 lei

Transylvanian cooking just like Granny made, in an under-touristed part of Cluj. Settle in beneath the vine-covered trellis outdoors and agonise between roast pork ribs and pike with capers. Or go all out with a 'Transylvanian platter', with homemade sausages, sheep's cheese and aubergine stew.

ROSECAS

CRIŞANA & BANAT | $$ | ROMANIAN

Str Traian Moşoiu 17, Oradea; 0756-260 185; www.rosecas.ro; mains 25-55 lei

Oradea is border country, and this upscale but welcoming place serves excellent home-cooked Romanian and Hungarian food. Choose from dishes like chicken paprika, goulash or duck, as well as delicious salads and a classic chicken soup.

CRAMA SIBIUL VECHI

TRANSYLVANIA | $$| ROMANIAN

Str Papiu-Ilarian 3, Sibiu; 0269-210 461; www.sibiulvechi.ro; mains 25-35 lei

The wine-cellar locale, white-linen tablecloths, candlelight and live mood-music lend an intimate feel. The traditional Romanian cooking, especially the minced meatballs and peasant's stew with polenta, is the best in Sibiu.

SZENTGYÖRGY PINCE

TRANSYLVANIA | $$| HUNGARIAN
Str Gábor Áron 14, Sfântu Gheorghe; 0267-352 666; www.szentgyorgypince.ro; mains 14-25 lei

Vaulted ceilings and brick walls bearing the crests of bygone nobles establish a regal tone within an old wine cellar. Plates are heavy with traditional Hungarian offerings, such as deer goulash and Transylvanian pork soup. Vegetarians are well served with rich dishes of paprika mushrooms and cheese-laden polenta.

'The unique "spoon tasting" menu gives you the chance to sample every dish in bite-sized portions.'
Artist

BISTRO DE L'ARTE

TRANSYLVANIA | $$| ROMANIAN
Piața Enescu 11, Braşov; 0720-535 566; www.bistrodelarte.ro; mains 32-40 lei

Tucked down a charming side street, this boho joint can be spotted by the bike racks outside shaped like penny-farthings. There's a Parisian feel in the arty decor and champagne breakfasts, though the menu selects the best from France, Italy and beyond: bruschetta, fondue, German-style cream cake and a hip cocktail list.

SERGIANA

TRANSYLVANIA | $$| ROMANIAN
Str Mureşenilor 28, Braşov; 0268-419 775; www.sergianagrup.ro; mains 30-45 lei

Steaming soups in hollowed-out loaves of bread, paprika-laced meat stews, and a polenta side dish with a more-than-generous ratio of cheese and sour cream. The subterranean dining hall, lined with brick and wood, is lively and casual – fuelled by ample German beer.

PILVAX

TRANSYLVANIA | $$| HUNGARIAN
Str Michael Weiss 16, Braşov; 0268-475 829; www.pilvax.ro; mains 25-60 lei

Braşov is home to a sizable Hungarian community, and centrally located Pilvax fuses the best of Transylvanian and Hungarian cooking. Go for baked stuffed peppers or braised spare ribs with polenta. The wine card, with Hungarian options from Tokaj and Villány, is among the best in the city.

ARTIST

BUCHAREST | $$$| ROMANIAN
Calea Victoriei 147; www.theartist.ro; 0728-318 871; Tasting menu from 78 lei

Located in a restored, eclectic 19th-century villa on posh Calea Victoriei, this is a top spot for fine dining in Bucharest. Chef Paul Oppenkamp marries modern food prep and plating standards with fresh Romanian ingredients. The unique 'spoon tasting' menu gives you the chance to sample every dish in bite-sized portions.

CARU' CU BERE

BUCHAREST | $$| ROMANIAN
Str Stavropoleos 3-5; 0726-282 373; www.carucubere.ro; mains 25-50 lei

Ignore the decidedly touristy atmosphere, with peasant-girl hostesses and sporadic traditional song-and-dance numbers. Bucharest's oldest beer house continues to draw a strong local crowd. The colourful belle-époque interior and stained-glass windows dazzle, as does the classic Romanian food.

LACRIMI ȘI SFINȚI

BUCHAREST | $$$| ROMANIAN
Str Șepcari 16; 0725-558 286; www.lacrimisisfinti.com; mains 30-60 lei

Lacrimi și Sfinți takes modern trends such as farm-to-table freshness and organic sourcing and fuses them to old-school Romanian recipes. The philosophy extends to the simple, peasant-inspired interior, where the woodworking and decorative elements come from old farmhouses.

'A former bread factory, up-cycled into a hip culinary destination. Our menu revolves around carefully selected steaks, wines and cocktails.'
Diana Podasca, co-owner, Q'usine

Q'USINE

BUCOVINA | $$| ROMANIAN
Str Dimitrie Cantemir 14, Câmpulung Moldovenesc; 0752-502 948; www.facebook.com/qusine2016; mains 25-40 lei

Youthful enthusiasm combined with a willingness to please energises this upmarket steakhouse and cocktail bar. The industrial setting, leavened by exposed wood, lots of greenery and cushioned Eames chairs, brings a welcome touch of urban sophistication to rustic Câmpulung.

IVAN PESCAR

DANUBE DELTA | $$| SEAFOOD
Str Gării 28, Tulcea; 0240-515 861; www.facebook.com/Ivan-Pescar-1456721501301741; mains 25-40 lei

An informal 'fish bar', perched on the side of the Danube River along Tulcea's bustling waterfront. Expect fresh, locally caught fish, including to-die-for fish soup, plus grills and stews.

MOLDOVA

Drawing on Romanian, Ukrainian and Turkish culinary influences, Moldovan food is simple, farm-fresh and filling. Mains are often built around pork and paired with a side of cornmeal polenta. Wines are invariably excellent; varietals feature native grapes like Fetească Albă and Rară Neagră.

WHAT TO EAT

Brânză
Moldova's most popular cheese is a slightly salty-sour sheep's milk product that's grated liberally on main courses, sides and savoury pastries.

Zeama
Hearty chicken soup, made of broth, egg noodles and veggies, and soured with lemon juice, is the go-to remedy for too much wine the night before.

Sarma
Cabbage leaves stuffed with ground pork or beef, vegetables and rice are the de facto national dish and eaten with a lashing of sour cream and side of polenta.

Plăcintă
Scrumptious pocket pastries served either sweet (stuffed with fruit) or savoury (filled with potatoes, cabbage or cheese).

PRICE RANGES
$ less than 90 lei
$$ 90–180 lei
$$$ 180 lei or more

Tipping: 10%

GOK-OGUZ

CHIŞINĂU | $$ | MOLDOVAN
Str Calea Orheiului 19a; 022 468 852; www.gok-oguz.md; mains 100-175 lei

Moldova packs a lot of diversity within a tiny landmass. This homespun Gagauzian restaurant features dishes from a Turkic-Christian minority located in the south of the country. Turkish influences are evident in dishes like baked mutton, lamb stew, and pastries with ewes'-milk cheese.

POPASUL DACILOR

CHIŞINĂU | $$ | MOLDOVAN
Str Valea Crucii St 13; 069 150 543; www.popasuldacilor.md/restaurant; mains 50-250 lei

Embrace the admittedly kitschy decor — with furs, totems and gnarled wood — and settle in for a traditional Moldovan feast with all the trimmings. Plates of smoked meats, cheeses, savoury pancakes and grills. A two-tonne door leads to a secret stash of rare local wine.

VATRA NEAMULUI

CHIŞINĂU | $$ | MOLDOVAN
Str Puşkin 20b; 022 226 839; www.vatraneamului.md; mains 75-300 lei

Old-world details like wood-beamed ceilings, white linens and traditional Moldovan music lend a romantic setting. The long menu of imaginatively dressed-up meats, like stewed pork with polenta or baked rabbit, and excellent wine list may prompt repeat visits.

KUMANYOK

TRANSDNIESTR | $ | UKRAINIAN
ul Sverdlova 37, Tiraspol; 0533 72 034; mains 50-125 Transdniestran roubles

One of the highlights of a visit to Moldova is to slip across the 'border' to the self-declared republic of Transdniestr. Ukrainian-style cooking dominates, and Kumanyok is the place to sample the spoils. The setting resembles a country house, where fleets of peasant-clad servers deliver armloads of dumplings and bowls of borsch.

WHAT TO EAT

Mayirefta
One-pot baked or casserole dishes, including *mousaka* (eggplant, minced meat, potatoes and cheese), *yemista* (vegetables stuffed with rice and herbs) and *stifadho* (sweet stewed meat).

Souvlaki
Arguably the national dish, from cubes of grilled meat on a skewer to pitta-wrapped snacks with pork or chicken *gyros* done kebab-style on a rotisserie.

Fish & seafood
Soupies (cuttlefish), calamari stuffed with cheese and herbs, and *psarosoupa* (fish soup) are highlights.

Mezedhes
Small dishes, often shared, including classics like tzatziki and taramasalata.

Loukoumadhes
Doughnuts drizzled with honey and cinnamon.

PRICE RANGES
For a main course:
$ less than €10
$$ €10–20
$$$ €20 or more

Tipping: 10% or round up.

GREECE

Greeks love eating out, sharing impossibly big meals in a drawn-out, convivial fashion. Whether you're eating seafood at a seaside table or sampling contemporary Greek cuisine under the floodlit Acropolis, dining out in Greece is never just about food, but the whole sensory experience. Bear in mind though that many village and island eating places are seasonal, and close for the winter.

KLIMATARIA

CORFU | $$ | TAVERNA
Benitses; 266 107 1201; www.klimataria-restaurant.gr; mains €8-16

This tiny, old-fashioned taverna, in a custard-coloured villa facing the main road, is worth a pilgrimage in its own right – every dish is delicious and superbly fresh, from the tender octopus and various mezedhes (appetisers) to the feta and olive oil. Call for reservations whatever the season.

ASTRA

EPIROS | $$ | GREEK
Megalo Papingo, Zahorhoria; 265 304 2108; www.astra-inn.gr; mains €11-16

This traditional restaurant and guesthouse represents everything delightful about Papingo in one place. The owners are passionate about local, organic ingredients and preserving food traditions. Nearly everything changes by the season, but year-round the *pita* pastry is hand-rolled, the trout is fresh and the *tsipouro* (brandy) is smooth. The stone house itself, wreathed in ivy, backed by mountains and surrounded by kitchen gardens, is wonderfully charismatic.

ELIES

THE MANI | $$ | GREEK
Kardamyli; 272 107 3140; www.elieshotel.gr; mains €9-14

Right by Ritsa Beach, 1km north of town, and nestled in an olive grove, this pretty and popular eating venue has the atmosphere of a provincial Mediterranean private garden. Thanks to owner-chef Fani, it presents a fine selection of top-notch Greek and Mani fare, including numerous scrumptious veggie dishes including pureed chickpeas with capers and stewed okra.

MOURGÁ

THESSALONIKI | $$ | GREEK

Christopoulou 12; 231 026 8826; mains €9-15

Elegant and relaxed, yet serious about everything that issues from its open kitchen, Mourgá is everything that's delightful about Greek food, Thessaloniki style. The grilled catch of the day is always excellent, while the raw anchovies with Cretan rusk and pickles is a stunning combination. While local producers are a focus, you can try cheeses and wines from across the country.

TRIGONA ELENIDIS

THESSALONIKI | $ | SWEETS

Cnr Dimitriou Gounari & Tsimiski; 231 025 7510; www.elenidis.gr; trigones €2.50

A veritable institution since 1960, Elenidis specialises in Thessaloniki's favourite pastry, the *trigona*. This sweet, flaky triangular cone, filled with tasty custard cream, is legendary in these parts, and was first created here. Locals emerge with 2kg boxes, but you might want to save room for the Greek halva (made with semolina) or homemade ice cream.

'At Astra we cook traditional dishes with meat and cheese from local farms, using herbs hand picked in the mountains. And we fish wild trout to serve to our guests.'
Astra

HOLGS/GETTY IMAGES ©

YPEROKEANIO

PIRAEUS | $ | MEZEDHES

Marias Hatzikiriakou 48; 210 418 0030; dishes €7-13

A fantastic and sweetly old-fashioned seafood mezedhopoleio, where you can sit at bistro tables out front and tuck into small plates of grilled sardines or steamed mussels. For dessert there's *kaimaki* ice cream – an old Asia Minor recipe made chewy with *sahlep* (orchid root) and flavoured with Chios mastic. Book ahead if possible; it's often packed.

KARAMANLIDIKA TOU FANI

ATHENS | $$ | GREEK

Sokratous 1, Psyrri; 210 325 4184; www.karamanlidika.gr; dishes €7-15

At this modern-day *pastomageireio* (tavern-deli) tables are set alongside the deli cases, and staff offer complimentary tasty morsels while you're looking at the menu. Beyond the Greek cheeses and cured meats, there's good seafood, such as marinated anchovies, as well as rarer wines and craft beers. Service is excellent, as is the warm welcome, often from Fani herself.

ELVIS

ATHENS | $ | GREEK

Plateon 29, Keramikos; 210 345 5836; skewers €2

This basic little souvlaki joint gets mobbed, and not just because the counter staff slide you a shot of booze while you're waiting. The meat quality is high, the prices are right and the music is great. Every skewer comes with good chewy bread and fried potatoes.

KOTTANI

THRACE | $ | TAVERNA

Km 9 Thermon-Kottani Rd, Xanthi; 694 500 9855; www.tavernakottani.blogspot.com; mains €7-10

High in the Rhodopi Mountains, this isolated taverna feels like a fairy tale, and the food is definitely magic: spicy *kebab romani* (beef patties), beans baked on the wood stove, excellent chilled red wine. Upstairs, where the kindly owner's grandfather was born, is a kind of museum of local cosiness, hung with traditional Pomak textiles.

ENALION

CYCLADES | $$ | GREEK

Pollonia, Milos; 228 704 1415; www.enalion-milos.gr; mains €10-18

The finest Greek produce is showcased at this wonderful little blue- and white-painted rustic restaurant. Grab a seat on the waterfront terrace and let the switched-on staff guide you through their top-notch selection of PDO (Protected Designation of Origin) olives, wine and cheese. Locally caught seafood features prominently on the menu, including a delicious *stifado* (stew) featuring octopus, tomatoes, onions, wine and Milos honey.

KATOGI

CYCLADES | $ | MEZEDHES

Hora, Ios; 698 344 0900; www.facebook.com/katogios; dishes €6-12

Entering Katogi feels like you've walked into a party in someone's quirky house, full of hidden nooks and plants and clamour. The original cocktails hit the spot, while the meze hit the spot: try their grilled *talagani* cheese with figs, or pasta purses filled with cheese and pear. Great atmosphere, though.

Previous page: Corfu's Old Town; Corfu's Old Town.

LAUDA

CYCLADES | $$$ | MODERN GREEK
Andronis Boutique Hotel, Oia, Santorini; 228 607 2182; www.laudarestaurant.com; mains €48-135

One of the top fine dining experiences in Santorini – natch, in Greece! – Lauda morphed from Oia's humble first restaurant into a destination in its own right. Chef Emmanuel Renaut combines local produce with international cooking techniques, with stellar results. Splurge on a tasting menu or go for fish marinated with caper leaves, or slow-cooked lamb with gnocchi. The sea-view terrace wreathed in bougainvillea is overwhelmingly romantic.

THALASSINO AGERI

CRETE | $$$ | SEAFOOD
Vivilaki 35, Hania; 282 105 1136; www.thalasino-ageri.gr; fish per kg €55-65

This solitary fish taverna among the vestiges of Hania's old tanneries in Halepa, 2km east of the centre, is one of Crete's top restaurants. Take in the sunset from a table right on the beach and peruse the changing menu, dictated by the day's catch, which is cooked over charcoal. The fried calamari melts in your mouth.

PESKESI

CRETE | $$ | CRETAN
Kapetan Haralampi 6-8, Iraklio; 281 028 8887; www.peskesicrete.gr; mains €9-15

It's almost impossible to overstate how good Peskesi's resurrected, slow-cooked Cretan dishes are, nor the beauty of the revamped Venetian villa in which you'll partake of them: this is Crete's finest culinary moment. Nearly everything is forged from heirloom produce and organic meats and olive oils from the restaurant's own farm: even the cocktails are made using must syrup, thyme-honey syrup or milk from the farm. Dishes such as goat with yoghurt dissolve in the mouth.

'Vacant 19th-century tanneries provide a wonderfully cinematic backdrop to a meal at Thalassino Ageri, and our dining tables sit right by the shore.' *Thalassino Ageri*

HOPE

CRETE | $$ | CRETAN
Mavrikiano, Elounda; 6972295150; mains €7-18

Clinging to a steep hillside in the ancient hamlet of Mavrikiano above Elounda, Hope has been a local fixture since 1938. The terrace where fishermen once gathered nightly to suss out the next day's weather is now packed with people getting giddy on wine, raki, homemade mezedhes, succulent lamb chops and the stupendous bay view.

KECHRIBARI OUZERIE

NORTHEASTERN AEGEAN | $$ | GREEK
Agion Anargyron 7, Chios Town; 694 242 5459; set meal €15

This cosy gem of an *ouzerie* (place that serves ouzo & light snacks) offers a variety of small plates in addition to excellent fish, mussels, baked potatoes and grilled meats. The choice is between two set menus featuring meat or fish; beyond that, you don't know exactly what you'll get. But that's all part of the appeal of this homey little place.

THEA'S RESTAURANT & ROOMS

NORTHEAST AEGEAN | $ | TAVERNA

Nas, Armenistis, Ikaria; 693 215 4296; www.theasinn.com; mains €7-11

There are a few fine tavernas in tiny waterfront Nas, but Thea's excels, serving up outstanding mezedhes, meat grills and a perfect veggie *mousakas* (baked layers of aubergine or courgette, minced meat and potatoes topped with cheese sauce). Good barrel wine and local *tsipouro* (distilled spirit of grape must) firewater complete the deal. An outdoor patio overlooks the sea.

TAVERNA MYLOS

DODECANESE | $$ | SEAFOOD

Agia Marina, Leros; 224 702 4894; www.mylosexperience.gr; mains €12-19

If there's one reason to visit Leros, it's to eat here, one of the best restaurants in the Dodecanese. Run by two passionate and knowledgeable brothers, this charming place is up there on the world's gastronomic scale. It features classic recipes with a modern twist: octopus carpaccio, peppery basil squid, and fabulous seafood pasta. And the seafront setting facing a traditional windmill is sublime.

This page: Mandraki. Opposite page: Rhodes Island.

KTIMA PETRA

DODECANESE | $$ | TAVERNA

Petra Beach, Patmos; 224 703 3207; mains €6.50-13

For one of Patmos' wholesome and genuine foodie experiences, don't miss this winner, located at Petra Beach. The setting – under a shaded terrace overlooking a vegetable garden – is idyllic. The restaurant, run by two hard-working brothers, sources its vegetables from their own adjoining plots. The result? Fabulous fresh and hearty traditional Greek cuisine.

TO PARADOSIAKON

DODECANESE | $ | BAKERY

Agia Marina, Platanos Leros; 224 702 5500; snacks €2.50-6

This patisserie and ice-cream bar, housed in an historic Italianate mansion on the waterfront, provides a sweet-toothed experience like no other. The knowledgeable owner Haris is an alchemist confectioner. He uses his grandmother's recipes to create traditional items, including *pastavouropita* (yogurt cake) and *pougakia* (almond and mandarin pastries). Don't miss the triple-layered chocolate gateau, spinach pie and homemade ice cream.

YEVSEA

DODECANESE | $$ | SEAFOOD

Paralia, Mandraki, Nisyros; 224 203 1066; www.facebook.com/geusea; €9.50-12

Meaning 'taste', this lovely, waterfront place is set to put Nisyros on the culinary map. Run by a passionate young duo, both *Masterchef* Greece contestants (one from Nisyros whose father is a fisherman), Yevsea serves up exceptional seafood and meat dishes featuring the masterful use of local ingredients (try the unique fish soup). Dragon fish, sea bream and other delights are served with painterly panache.

HOTZAS TAVERNA

CHIOS | $ | TAVERNA

Kondyli 3, Chios Town; 227 104 2787; mains €6-10

This comfortable, attractive taverna above Chios Town serves fine Greek standards with a twist, such as lamb kebab with yoghurt and rocket; white beans with tomato and mandarin; and dolmadhes with lemon. There's a variety of great veggie dishes, including risotto. Everything is *herisia* (handmade), from the pasta to the dessert.

MARCO POLO CAFÉ

RHODES | $$ | MEDITERRANEAN

Agiou Fanouriou 40-42, Rhodes Town; 224 102 5562; www.marcopolomansion.gr; mains €15-25

Despite being barely visible, or even signed, from the street, this irresistible dinner-only restaurant is filled nightly, with diners savouring exquisite culinary creations like sea-bream fillets on a 'risotto' of local wheat, pork loin with figs, or octopus sous vide with cream of beetroot. Linger over a romantic meal in the delightful lemon-fragrant garden courtyard.

WHERE TO...

MARKET SHOP

Kolonaki, Athens
Most Athens neighbourhoods have a weekly *laïki agora*, a street market. Local regulars come to buy fresh fruit, vegetables, fish, olives and honey.

Agora, Hania
Hania's cross-shaped market hall opened in 1913 and has stands selling traditional Cretan produce (herbs, honey, baked goods, raki, cheese).

Bazaar of Xanthi, Xanthi
A massive market held every Saturday at the base of Old Xanthi. Hear the hollers of vendors of giant cabbages, live snails and homemade booze.

Ergon Agora, Thessaloniki
Fresh fish and meat, cheeses, top-notch fruit and veg, bread, oils, honey and vinegars – it's all to be found in this high-end 'closed market'.

MALTA

Maltese cuisine is an exotic mix of flavours and ingredients brought to the islands by different occupiers through the centuries, with Italian, French, British and Arabic influences all playing important roles. There are plenty of excellent restaurants serving traditional Maltese dishes, as well as a growing crop of creative chefs inventing their own innovative twists on the cuisine.

WHAT TO EAT

Fenek (rabbit)
Malta's national dish, whether fried in olive oil, roasted, stewed, served with spaghetti or baked in a pie. A *fenkata* is a rabbit feast.

Pastizzi
A small parcel of flaky pastry, filled with either ricotta cheese and parsley, or mushy peas and onions. Arabic in origin, the tasty snack is served warm.

Ġbejniet
A small, hard, white sheep's or goat's milk cheese made on Malta's sister island of Gozo. Often steeped in olive oil and flavoured with salt and crushed black peppercorns.

Lampuka (dolphin fish)
Malta's favourite fish, typically baked with tomatoes, onions, black olives, spinach, sultanas and walnuts.

PRICE RANGES
$ less than €10
$$ €10–20
$$$ €20 or more

Tipping: 10%

OLEANDER

GOZO | $$ | GOZITAN
Pjazza Vittorja, Xagħra; 2155 7230; www.facebook.com/OleanderRestaurant; mains €11-25

Much-loved Oleander's alfresco tables make the most of its scenic location on a pretty square in Xagħra village. The menu specialises in the cuisine of Gozo, Malta's greener second island. Dishes including rabbit cooked in various ways, homemade ravioli with Gozitan cheese, and fresh fish of the day. Boneless quail stuffed with local figs and pistachios is a definite menu highlight.

OSTERIA SCOTTADITO

GOZO | $$ | ITALIAN
20 Triq Madre Ġ Camilleri, Nadur; 2733 3000; www.osteriascottadito.com; mains €10-24

Energetic owners from northern Italy run this excellent restaurant tucked behind Nadur's 18th-century church. Cuisine influenced by the Emilia-Romagna region of Italy is the focus, but many local and sustainable ingredients are used. Try the Scottadito lamb chops with a pecorino and wild fennel crust. It's an old shepherds' dish apparently, and it's best eaten with your hands.

CRYSTAL PALACE

CENTRAL MALTA | $ | PASTRIES
Triq San Pawl, Rabat; pastizzi €0.30

Spot it by the hordes outside, this hole-in-the-wall *pastizzerija* close to Mdina's city walls is a favourite with locals, renowned as one of Malta's finest purveyors of *pastizzi*. The little moreish stuffed pastry parcels are freshly baked throughout the night.

DIAR IL-BNIET

CENTRAL MALTA | $$ | MALTESE
121 Triq il-Kbira, Dingli; 2762 0727; www.diarilbniet.com; mains €13-25

Located in a historic farmhouse in the centre of Dingli village, this family-run restaurant is something special. All produce is seasonal and sourced from their 600-acre estate, or other local producers. Dishes include stuffed aubergines or courgettes, homemade pies and fried rabbit, followed by desserts such as date and anisette tart.

TARRAGON

NORTHERN MALTA | $$$ | MEDITERRANEAN
Triq il-Knisja, St Paul's Bay; 2157 3759; www.tarragonmalta.com; mains €25-32

Tucked above the harbour at St Paul's Bay, Tarragon combines sea views with a sophisticated Mediterranean-fusion menu. The white-tableclothed, wooden-floorboard style is both upmarket and informal, and seasonal standout menu items could include venison and pistachio ravioli or octopus with a cherry-tomato marmalade. The three-course degustation menu is a great way to experience the Tarragon magic.

BAHIA

CENTRAL MALTA | $$$ | MEDITERRANEAN
Triq Preziosi, Lija; 9999 1270; www.bahia.com.mt; mains €21-28

Named after a variety of oranges grown locally, Bahia is an innovative and stylish bistro near Lija's compact village square. Choose from just a dozen seasonal dishes. Seafood highlights could include red prawn and crab with confit potato and *dashi* (Japanese-style broth), while local fish with kimchi and burnt lemon introduces Asian flavours. Sunday lunch is very popular.

'Fond childhood memories flood our minds as we get a whiff of a fresh, homegrown dish leaving the kitchen.'
Diar il-Bniet

NONI

VALLETTA | $$$ | MEDITERRANEAN
211 Triq ir-Repubblika; 2122 1441; www.noni.com.mt; mains €21-33

Descend into Noni's stylish stone-lined basement space and be surprised by innovative modern spins on traditional Maltese and Mediterranean flavours. Dishes are prepared with a light touch and could include a silky smooth parfait of rabbit liver, or wonderfully tender slow-cooked octopus with Israeli couscous. An excellent wine list and craft beers from Malta and Belgium are other tasty diversions.

TERRONE

SOUTHERN MALTA | $$$ | MEDITERRANEAN
1 Triq il-Wilga, Marsaxlokk; 2704 2656; www.terrone.com.mt; mains €18-28

Seasonal, sustainable and local are all important at Terrone, where the menu is adjusted on a daily basis. Sit inside the chic interior enlivened with colourful tiles, or outside with views of fishing boats in Marsaxlokk's harbour, and enjoy dishes like tuna tartare, kingfish carpaccio and chargrilled octopus. A six-course seafood degustation menu is available.

CYPRUS

Take a handful of Greek recipes, throw in some Turkish cooking then add a pinch of Middle Eastern influences and you get Cypriot cuisine. This little island is the pot where the flavours of the eastern Mediterranean get stirred together.

WHAT TO EAT

Halloumi
This brined, white cheese is Cyprus' culinary gift to the world. The name stems from the word 'almi' – Greek for 'salty water'.

Sheftalia
(Called *şefteli kebapı* in northern Cyprus). These stubby caul-fat encased sausages are commonly made from lamb (in northern Cyprus) or pork (in the Republic of Cyprus) and served grilled.

Pirohu
Cypriot ravioli. Little dumplings stuffed with white cheese and mint, then topped with grated halloumi.

Snails
A late-autumn speciality, served either fried or stewed in a tomato and onion broth.

PRICE RANGES
$ less than €7
$$ €7–12
$$$ €12 or more

Tipping: 10% service charge is often added to restaurant bills.

MANDRA TAVERN

PAFOS | $$$ | TAVERNA
Dionysou 4, Kato Pafos; 2693 4129; www.mandratavern.com; mains €12.50-16.50

Many Pafos restaurants claim to serve authentic Cypriot cuisine but sneak in some international dishes. Not here. The speciality is their Greek *kleftiko* (lamb, slow-cooked with garlic and lemon) while the signature brandy pudding dessert, stuffed with dates and walnuts, is well worth leaving room for. The leafy courtyard setting, in the owner's family home, is a haven on a balmy summer's evening.

STOU KIR YIANNI

TROÖDOS MOUNTAINS | $$$ | MEDITERRANEAN
Linou 15, Omodos; 7000 0100; www.stoukiryianni.com; mains €12-28

Known for their pork-crackling cooked in Commandaria (Cypriot sweet wine), this restaurant, in a restored mansion with local art decorating whitewashed walls, serves up fresh Cypriot and Greek flavours. The vegan meze-platter highlights the island's fresh produce and the evening meze featuring dishes such as of halloumi in honey and sesame seeds, and *yaourtlou* (minced chicken meatballs served in herby yoghurt sauce) is a belt-loosening blow-out.

PIATSA GOUROUNAKI

NICOSIA | $ | GREEK
92 Aneromenis; 7778 7777; www.piatsagourounaki.com.cy; dishes €1.30-8.30

This contemporary-style *souvlakeri* dishes up some of the best Greek tastes in Nicosia, with charming service to boot. Pick the number of charcoal grilled meat-skewers you'd like, then choose from a long list of tasty meze and sides, featuring *bouyiourdi* (oven-baked feta and vegetables), pickled peppers and *tirokefteri* (spicy cheese dip). The street-side terrace gets crammed later in the evening.

ZANETTOS

NICOSIA | $$$ | TAVERNA
Trikoupi 65; 2276 5501; www.zanettos.com; meze spread per person €21

When you've been in business since 1938 you must be doing something right. This cavernous taverna, with black-and-white photographs covering its arched walls, offers the real-deal, meze experience. There's no menu, just a seemingly non-stop parade of dishes usually including pork belly, calf liver, *sheftalia* and snails. Come hungry and remember to pace yourself.

ART CAFE 1900

LARNAKA | $$ | CYPRIOT
Stasinou 6; 2465 3027; mains €9-14

With old photos covering the walls, shelves weighed down with bric-a-brac, and welcoming owners, Art Cafe 1900 is Larnaka's most atmospheric and friendly restaurant choice. Order the rustic stuffed cabbage leaves or the hearty *stifado* (beef and onion stew, simmered in vinegar and wine) then head downstairs to the cosy bar.

'A menu originated from Cyprus finest traditional tastes and products cultivated in our family's fruit orchards and market gardens.'
Stou Kir Yianni

NIAZI'S RESTAURANT

NORTHERN CYPRUS | $$ | KEBAB
Kordon Boyu Sokak 22, Kyrenia (Girne); 0392 815 2160; www.niazis.com; mains 32-80TL

Carnivore heaven. Niazi's is the inventor of the Cypriot 'full kebab' – a mixed grill and meze feast. Don't even think about ordering one unless your stomach is growling. For diners looking for something lighter, the rest of the menu romps through all the Turkish kebab classics plus more international choices such as king prawns in garlic butter.

ALEVKAYALI RESTAURANT

NORTHERN CYPRUS | $$ | SEAFOOD
Karpaz Yolu, Yenierenköy (Yiallousa), Karpas Peninsula; 0533 876 0911; mains 40-70TL

Calamari cooked to perfection, super-fresh fish and well-spiced *sheftali kebapı*, all served with oil-soaked meze dishes of pickled celery and fava beans. This shorefront terrace restaurant, with waves crashing into the rocks below, is a favourite lunch stop if you're driving up the Karpas Peninsula coastline.

WHAT TO EAT

Meze
Olive-oil-soaked appetisers accompany ouzo-like *rakı* (aniseed-infused grape spirit) or make up a whole meal.

İmam bayıldı
'The imam fainted': aubergine (eggplant), onion, tomato and peppers slow-cooked in olive oil.

Pide
Turkish pizza comes with a few classic toppings and is the ultimate snack.

Mantı
Meat-stuffed ravioli topped with yoghurt, tomato and butter.

Börek
These sweet or savoury filled pastries come in various forms, including *sigara böreği* (deep-fried cigar-shaped pastry filled with white cheese) and *su böreği* (lasagne-like layered pastry laced with white cheese and parsley).

PRICE RANGES
$ less than TRY25
$$ TRY25–40
$$$ TRY40 or more

Tipping: 10%

TURKEY

Turkish cuisine is about much more than döner and *şiş* kebaps, ranging from seafood restaurants and markets along the coast to Cappadocia village restaurants serving tapas-like meze with valley views. Meals are central to Turkey's family-focused culture and an art that has been perfected over centuries, with influences brought along the Silk Road during the Ottoman Empire. From *köfte* meatballs to *kokoreç* lamb intestines, every town has a speciality to try.

LĂL GIRIT MUTFAĞI

NORTH AEGEAN | $$ | GREEK

Altay Pansiyon Yanı 20, Cunda (Alibey Island); 0266-327 2834; mezes TRY20-30, mains TRY50

The road-connected island of Cunda, home to a Cretan community since the population exchanges between Turkey and Greece during the 1920s, is a magical setting for this Girit (Cretan) restaurant. Owner and chef Emine's grandmother taught her to cook the dishes, and the results are inspired. Expect her to emerge from the kitchen to explain the fresh, unusual and delectable dishes in the meze selection.

KAPLAN DAĞ RESTORAN

SOUTH AEGEAN | $$ | TURKISH

Kaplan; 0232-512 6652; www.facebook.com/kaplandagrestorantire; mezes from TRY10, mains TRY20-45

'Tiger Mountain' offers superbly prepared local dishes with lashings of olive oil and wild herbs. Enjoy seasonal mezes, such as fish in soya oil and stuffed zucchini flowers, and mains including *köfte* (meatballs) and *şiş* kebaps (roast skewered meat). It's tastefully decorated in a rustic style with gourds and dried herbs hanging from the roof beams and arty felt pieces on the walls. The views across the mountains are sublime.

ORFOZ

BODRUM | $$$ | SEAFOOD

Zeki Müren Caddesi 13; 0252-316 4285; www.orfoz.net; set menus from TRY150

Often cited as one of Turkey's best fish restaurants, this gem has views over Bodrum's eastern shore from its front terrace. It serves delectable seafood such as oysters with parmesan, smoked eel, sea snails with wine sauce, clams, scallops, sea urchins and blue crab, accompanied by an excellent selection of Turkish wines.

DERALIYE

ISTANBUL | $$$ | TURKISH
Ticarethane Sokak 10, Alemdar; 0532 655 4698; www.deraliyerestaurant.com; mezes TRY21-56, mains TRY48-135

Offering a taste of the sumptuous dishes once served in the great Ottoman palaces, Deraliye gives diners the chance to order delights such as the goose kebap served to Süleyman the Magnificent and Mehmet II's favourite lamb stew. Those with less adventurous palates can opt for modern standards such as kebaps. There's live music on Friday and Saturday evenings and Ottoman cooking classes too, close to Istanbul's major historical sights.

HAYVORE

ISTANBUL | $ | TURKISH
Turnacıbaşı Sokak 4, Galatasaray; 0212-245 7501; www.hayvore.com.tr; soups TRY10-15, pides TRY24-35, portions TRY14-30

Notable *lokantas* (traditional eateries serving readymade dishes) are rare in modern-day Beyoğlu, so this bustling place just off pedestrianised thoroughfare İstiklal Caddesi is to be wholeheartedly celebrated. Specialising in Black Sea cuisine, its delicious pilafs, pides, *hamsi* (fresh anchovy) dishes and vegetable and fish soups are best enjoyed at lunch.

'From the Danube and the Balkans to the Arabic Peninsula and the northern shores of Africa, different cultures blended into the Ottoman Empire and created Turkish cuisine.'
Neçati Yılmaz, Deraliye, Istanbul

PHIL WEYMOUTH/LONELYPLANET ©

BORSAM TAŞ FIRIN

ISTANBUL | $ | TURKISH
Güneşlibahçe Sokak 22, Kadıköy; 0216-337 0504; www.borsamtasfirin.com; lahmacun TRY7-10

The thin and crispy *lahmacun* (Arabic-style pizzas topped with minced meat, herbs and spices and served with a squeeze of lemon) that come out of the oven here are among Istanbul's best, and the pide are nearly as good. Eat one while walking through Kadıköy's produce market, or at the street-side tables with a view of this vibrant neighbourhood on the city's Asian side.

FATIH DAMAK PIDE

ISTANBUL | $ | PIDE
Büyük Karaman Caddesi 48, Fatih; 0212-521 5057; www.facebook.com/fatihdamakpide; pides TRY18-28

With a reputation for making the best Karadeniz (Black Sea)–style pide on Istanbul's historic peninsula, this *pideci*

offers standard toppings, including *sucuklu-peynirli* (sausage and cheese), and an unusual *bafra pidesi* (rolled-up pide). The pots of tea served with meals are a nice touch (the first pot is free, subsequent pots are charged) and, on weekends, the restaurant offers a Black Sea–style breakfast buffet.

KEBAPÇI İSKENDER

BURSA | $$ | KEBAB
Ünlü Caddesi 7; 0224-502 0056; www.iskenderiskenderoglu.com.tr; İskender portion TRY38

This *kebapçı* claims to have invented the nationally famous İskender (or Bursa) kebap, a döner kebap on fresh pide topped with tomato sauce and browned butter, back in 1867. The wood-panelled interior with tiled pillars and stained-glass windows creates a suitably heritage ambience in which to taste the renowned dish. There's no menu; diners simply order *bir* (one) or *bir buçuk* (1½) portions.

CIN BAL KEBAP SALONU

TURQUOISE COAST | $$ | BARBECUE
Kayaköy; 0252-618 0066; www.cinbal.com; mains TRY30-45

Cin Bal specialises in lamb *tandir* (clay oven) dishes and kebaps, with seating in its grapevine-covered garden courtyard. Most people choose from the choice cuts, then DIY barbecue on a little charcoal table grill, which waiters set up for you. Otherwise, leave it to the experts. The location is certainly atmospheric, next to the ghost town where Louis de Bernières set *Birds Without Wings*.

YÖRUK RESTAURANT

TURQUOISE COAST | $$ | TURKISH
Köprü Başı Mevkii, Çıralı; 0536 864 8648; gözlemes TRY10-12, pides TRY10-14, mains TRY16-30

On Turkey's sometimes touristy Mediterranean coast, this restaurant namechecking Yöruk nomads offers the opportunity to enjoy authentic Turkish food. Behind a counter heaving with mezes and seafood, the open kitchen turns out elongated pide, light and fluffy *gözleme* (stuffed flatbread), *mantı* (Turkish ravioli), kebaps and grills. Well priced and welcoming, with space for children to roam. Work it all off with a walk to Çıralı's eternal flame, the Chimaera.

CAPPADOCIA HOME COOKING

CAPPADOCIA | $$$ | ANATOLIAN
Ayvalı; 0384-354 5907; www.cappadociahomecooking.com; meal per person TRY25

Tolga and his family have swung open the doors to their home – surrounded by their organic garden and overlooking the village's deep gorge – to offer a taste of true home-style Cappadocian cooking. They provide meals and highly recommended cooking classes, guided by Tolga's tiny dynamo of a mother, Hava. It's a foodie haven amid Cappadocia's fairy chimneys.

P320: Mandra Tavern. Previous spread: Spice bazaar, Istanbul. Next spread: Dilijan; Spices at a market in Yerevan.

DIBEK

CAPPADOCIA | $$ | ANATOLIAN

Cami Sokak 1, Göreme; 0384-271 2209; www.dibektraditionalcook.com; mains TRY28-70, tasting menu TRY80

Diners sprawl on cushions and take a taste-bud tour of village food at this family restaurant in a 475-year-old building. Take our advice and order the *tadım* (tasting) menu plus a *testi kebapı* (meat and vegetable stew slow-cooked in a sealed terracotta pot). The latter is Göreme's best take on this local speciality, and there's tel *kadayıf* (dough soaked in syrup and topped with walnuts and tahini) for dessert.

OKYANUS BALIK EVI

BLACK SEA COAST | $$ | SEAFOOD

Kurtuluş Caddesi, Sinop; 0368-261 3950; www.okyanusbalikevi.com; mains TRY25-45

Above the co-owned family fish-monger, 'Ocean Fish House' is quite possibly the best fish restaurant on the Black Sea coast. As well as grilled or fried whole fish, a superb option is a panful of *iskorpit* (scorpion fish) fillets cooked as a *kavurma*, a delicious reduction of peppers, tomato, garlic and ginger. Owner Mert's mother leads the all-female chef team. Lovely rooftop terrace for a pre-prandial *rakı*, too.

AHMET BEY YÖRESEL EV YEMEKLERI

MALATYA | $$ | ANATOLIAN

Beşkonaklar Caddesi 41a; 0422-321 2000; www.ahmetbeyyoreselevyemekleri.business.site; Malatya tabağı TRY40

A charming older couple dishes up Malatya's foodie specialities, an authentic taste of eastern Anatolian flavours. You'll have to be rolled out the door after digging into *mumbar* (stuffed lamb intestines), *analı kızlı* (bulgur balls and chickpeas in a tomato stew) and *kiraz yaprağı köftesi* (bulgur-stuffed cherry leaves in a yoghurt sauce). Order the Malatya *tabağı* (plate) to try all five dishes on the menu.

AKÇAKALE ADA BALIK LOKANTASI

NORTHEASTERN ANATOLIA | $$ | SEAFOOD

Akçakale, Çıldır Lake; 0539-6759755; fish/salad TRY30/10

No need for a menu in this utterly unpretentious family restaurant, which sits right on a pretty bay: just order a portion of the superb fried lake fish, served in total simplicity with fresh bread and pomegranate sauce (*nar ekşisi sosu*) to dip it in. Dine in a rustic timber-ceilinged room or at one of a couple of basic tables under a tree right by the water's edge.

WHERE TO BUY...

FRESH MARKET PRODUCE

Kadıköy Produce Market, Istanbul
An aromatic and alluring showcase of Istanbul's best fresh produce – foodie central for locals on the Asian side of town.

Saturday Market, Selçuk
Suntanned farmers and their headscarf-wearing wives load the tables with oranges, tomatoes, big curly peppers, sheep's-milk cheese and wholesome picnic fodder.

Kemeraltı Market, İzmir
Labyrinthine 17th-century bazaar, home to caravanserais and tea gardens. Take a Culinary Backstreets walking tour to find the local secrets.

Tuesday Market, Fethiye
Mediterranean produce is on show at this large canal-side market, not far from the Lycian Way walking trail.

ARMENIA

Traditional dishes such as grilled meats, hearty soups and stews still created using delicious, locally grown produce can be enjoyed across the country. Enterprising Armenians are leaning on their locavore sensibilities to open eateries with a sustainable focus.

WHAT TO EAT

Khoravats
Skewered chunks of marinated meat flame-grilled over hot coals run the gamut from pork to lamb, beef or chicken.

Ishkhan
Fish isn't generally a speciality in landlocked Armenia, but trout from Lake Sevan, often grilled, is an exception.

Khash
Always eaten with others, this traditional winter soup is essentially slow-boiled cow or sheep parts (usually the feet), served with *lavash* bread and seasoned with salt and garlic at the table.

Spas
A yoghurt-based soup, most commonly made with wheat and coriander, that can be eaten hot or cold.

PRICE RANGES

For a main course:
$ less than AMD3000
$$ AMD3000–AMD5000
$$$ AMD5000 or more

Tipping: 10%

HERBS & HONEY

GYUMRI | $$ | CAFE
5 Rizhkov St; 093-644645; www.herbsandhoney.am; mains AMD1400-2800

Besides offering herbs and honey made by Armenian producers, the menu at this highly Instagrammable cafe includes wholesome salads, vegan dolma (stuffed grape leaves), 'detox' cocktails and tea concoctions for every ailment. Try the carrot cake for dessert – you won't regret it.

CHERKEZI DZOR

GYUMRI | $$ | ARMENIAN
1st Karmir Berd; 0312-65559; www.facebook.com/FishFarm.Restaurante; fish per kg AMD3500-5600

This fish restaurant is so popular some Russians have been known to fly here to try the fish and fly back the next day. Seating is in open pavilions surrounding the fish pools where your dinner will be caught fresh to order. Trout and sturgeon are available along with delicious salads and sides. Bread is freshly baked in on-site ovens.

CARAHUNGE

STEPANAVAN | $$ | CAFE
64 Sos Sargsyan St; 099-324300; www.facebook.com/CarahungeStepanavan; mains AMD1400-4000

Why the owners of this excellent cafe and bookshop chose to open in sleepy Stepanavan is a mystery, but it's a welcome sight for travellers passing through. The menu is a mix of Armenian and international fare, including pizzas, wings and *za'atar* (bread with green spices).

LAVASH

YEREVAN | $$ | ARMENIAN
21 Tumanyan St; 010-608800; www.lavash.restaurant/en; mains AMD1200-6000

It's tough to land a table without a reservation, but Lavash is worth the hype. The menu is fresh, from the *ghapama* (stuffed pumpkin) overflowing with dried fruit, nuts and lavash bread to the humongous 'Guinness World Record' *gata* cake you must see to believe (but never finish).

THE CLUB

YEREVAN | $$$ | INTERNATIONAL
40 Tumanyan St; 010-531361; www.theclub.am; mains AMD3300-9600

Fusing western Armenian and French cuisine, the seasonal menu at this fashionable basement restaurant includes salads, traditional village dishes such as dolma and *manti* (meat ravioli topped with yogurt), oven-baked fish and steaks sizzled on hot stones at the table. It's worth saving room for dessert, as these are particularly good.

ANKYUN

YEREVAN | $$$ | ITALIAN
4 Vardanants St; 010-544606; www.ankyun.am; mains AMD3600-8200

Ask local foodies to nominate the best Italian food in town, and they inevitably choose this place. The chef uses seasonal ingredients to create pizzas, antipasti, pasta, grills and excellent versions of classic desserts such as tiramisu and panna cotta. The decor

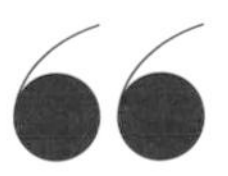

'Herbs & Honey is about creating the environment we want with each small step we take – from simple food consumption to the development of our country.' *Herbs & Honey*

SUN_SHINE/SHUTTERSTOCK ©

nods towards Tuscany, and the staff are both professional and friendly.

KCHUCH

DILIJAN | $$ | ARMENIAN
Myasnikyan St; 041-886010; www.facebook.com/KchuchDilijan; clay-pot dishes AMD1800-3500, pizzas AMD2500-3200

Kchuch is located in the middle of a lush park in the heart of Dilijan. Most of the food is baked inside brick ovens in *kchuch* (clay pots), and includes tasty meats like osso buco and chicken with dried apricots. Pizzas come in inventive flavours like the 'revolutionary pizza' loaded with grilled veggies.

AZERBAIJAN

Classic Azerbaijani fare might be heavy on the barbecued meat and hearty soups, but fresh fruits and vegetable dishes play a strong supporting role, and the country's restaurant scene is striding forward to offer a wider variety and refine traditional dishes for the modern palate.

WHAT TO EAT

Kəbab
The ubiquitous grilled meat can be found in many forms, from simple skewered cubes to spiced minced lamb.

Dolma
Minced meat (usually lamb), rice, coriander, mint and other seasonings, wrapped in vine or cabbage leaves or stuffed into aubergines, peppers or tomatoes.

Ləvəngi
Fish or chicken stuffed with walnuts and herbs and baked in the oven, most commonly found in southern Azerbaijan.

Plov
There are as many varieties of this rice and meat dish across the region as there are restaurants, but the Azerbaijani version often has chestnuts and dried fruit such as dates.

PRICE RANGES
$ less than AZN7
$$ AZN7–AZN15
$$$ AZN15 or more

Tipping: Up to 10% or round up.

CALĞALIQ RESTORANI

ZAQATALA | $$ | AZERBAIJANI
Aşağı Tala; 050-4147998; www.facebook.com/calgaliq; mains AZN4-15

The most characterful restaurant for miles around, Calğalıq is packed with more antique handicrafts than the average museum and the enchanted garden is all a-croak with frogs. There are some Georgian options and very local seasonal specialities like *maxara* (sac-cooked savoury pancakes).

CHALET

QƏBƏLƏ | $$$ | INTERNATIONAL
Yatmish Gozal, Tufandag Mountain Resort; 050-2902832; www.facebook.com/chaletsteakhouse; mains AZN10-22, steaks AZN25-90

At the top of a cable car station, Chalet is not just a great place to sit amid the mountain scenery, but also serves the best-quality Western food in Qəbələ, notably sizzlers, pasta and some exclusive imported steaks. Downstairs there's a rather hidden wine-bar.

TƏBƏSSÜM

LERIK | $ | KEBABS
Lənkəran–Lerik rd; 050-5082051; www.facebook.com/Tebessum27km; kebabs/tea from AZN4/3

Təbəssüm is a particularly appealing small-scale rural restaurant-resort that prides itself on not cutting down any trees. Indeed some foliage grows right 'through' the kitchen buildings. Long footbridges link dining pavilions that nestle into the mossy rocks, overlooking a small waterfall. The sensibly priced kebabs and tea hit the spot.

BORANI

LƏNKƏRAN | $$ | CAFE
Qala xiyabanı; 051-5850909; weekday lunch deals AZN5, mains AZN5-12

Borani brings Lənkəran an urban vibe with contemporary beats, handsome hipster waitstaff and an airy modern sense of 21st-century style. Its thin-crust pizzas are creditable (especially when served as *calzone*) but there are also various kebabs, Russian dishes, Georgian *khachapuri* (cheese bread) and salads.

FIRUZƏ

BAKU | $ | AZERBAIJANI
Əliyarbəyov küç 14; 012-4939634; www.firuzerestoran.az; mains AZN5-15, steak/fish AZN19/22, beer/fresh juice from AZN3/6

This long-lasting subterranean favourite is an attractive stone-walled basement draped in local carpets with tablecloths embroidered in a similar style. There's a phenomenally diverse Azerbaijani menu which includes some vegetarian options: try the garlic-rich *badımcan sırdağı* (an eggplant-potato-tomato dish).

PARIS BISTRO

BAKU | $$ | FRENCH
Zərifə Əliyeva pr 1/4; 012-4048215; www.facebook.com/ParisBistroAz; mains AZN10-19

It's hard to believe you're more than a few metres from the Champs-Élysées in this perfectly pitched French masterpiece. It hits all the right Parisian notes down to the plane trees curving out from an appealing park-facing street terrace. Waiters in claret aprons deliver garlic escargots, duck breast with tapenade or flaming crème brûlée.

ŞIRVANŞAH MUZEY-RESTORAN

BAKU | $$ | AZERBAIJANI
Salatın Əsgərova küç 86; 012-5950901; www.facebook.com/shirvanshahmuzeyrestoran; mains AZN5-15

'An unusual combination of flavors will give you the brightest gastronomic experience and will be remembered for a long time.'
SAHiL

On an unassuming backstreet, this enticing place started life as a 19th-century bathhouse but is now a veritable ethnographic museum of handicrafts and knick-knacks. Over a dozen rooms are themed to different historical eras from rustic craftsman's workshops to Soviet office. Reliable Azerbaijani food covers a similarly wide range, but you really come here for the atmosphere.

SAHIL

BAKU | $$$ | AZERBAIJANI
Neftçilər pr 34, Bulvar; 050-2850022; www.sahilbaku.az; mains AZN12-40

Faultless Azerbaijani and Persian cuisine in a suave-but-relaxed setting right on the Bulvar (seafront promenade). It's one of the few places to offer *shah plov* (a giant ball of mixed-ingredient rice pilaf) by portion, and *mirzaghassemi* (a delicious South Caspian eggplant and garlic mash).

PAUL'S

BAKU | $$$ | STEAK
Zərgəpalan küç; 055-5200092; www.pauls-baku.com; steak from AZN25.50-63, sides/dips AZN6/2

It's inconspicuous, comfortably unpretentious and the menu is short. But if you want perfectly cooked, top-quality steak, this German-Austrian yard-garden can't be bettered. Pork shashlik and Bratwurst are also specialities.

GEORGIA

Offering one of Europe's most enchanting and unexpectedly rich cuisines, Georgia has recently broken through as *the* Eastern European foodie destination of choice, with its fabulous viniculture and almost alchemical ability to enliven dishes with aubergine, walnuts and tomatoes.

WHAT TO EAT

Khachapuri
Sometimes described as a mere 'cheese pie', the *khachapuri* is the backbone of Georgian cuisine, and exists in dozens of forms.

Khinkali
A small bag of dough twisted into a hard nexus at the top, with a filling of spiced, ground-up meat, potatoes mushrooms or sometimes vegetables – and plenty of juice.

Pkhali
Popular Georgian pâtés made typically from either beetroot, spinach or aubergine paste with crushed walnuts, garlic and herbs.

Elarji
A unique dish made from cornmeal mixed with Sulguni cheese that has an almost unreal springy texture.

PRICE RANGES
For a main course:
$ less than 10 GEL
$$ 10–20 GEL
$$$ 20 GEL or more

Tipping: 10% in smarter places.

BABARESTAN

TBILISI | $$$ | GEORGIAN

Davit Aghmeshenebeli 132; 32-2943779; www.facebook.com/babarestan; mains 30-60 GEL

The extraordinary meals served in this rather formal dining room stuffed with antiques and art are based on an antique cookbook discovered at a market in 2015. Of the 900 'forgotten' Georgian dishes featuring rarely used ingredients such as rabbit, duck and crayfish, to date 230 have been recreated by chef Giorgi Sarajishvili and his team, who present a frequently changing menu of obscure delights. This is

Tbilisi's most innovative fine dining restaurant and an absolute must for any foodie visiting.

KETO AND KOTE

TBILISI | $$$ | GEORGIAN
Zandukheli 3; 555-530126; mains 16-27 GEL

Reservations are usually essential at this sumptuous restaurant overlooking the city. Choose between a table in the garden, on the terrace, or in the fabulous dining room, which is beautifully lit and glows in red accents from the painted beams on the ceiling. The menu is exceptional, with some favourites including the beef cooked in Roquefort and *adjika*, the mini meat *khinkali* in butter sauce and the wonderfully tender dolma.

CAFE LITTERA

TBILISI | $$$ | GEORGIAN
Machabeli 13; 599-988308; mains 28-38 GEL

In the lovely rear garden of the Georgian Writers' Union building, Café Littera serves simply superb 'nouveau Georgian' dishes in the most charming setting imaginable. Don't miss trying the assorted contemporary *pkhali* (their take on traditional Georgian pâtés combining vegetables with walnuts, garlic and herbs) as an appetiser, or main courses such as fried quail with wheat berry risotto, or pork belly with red adjika sauce. The wine list is also superb.

'Georgians say guests are a gift from god, and that inspired us to open a restaurant in the cellar of our family home.'
Toma Omiadze, Owner, Toma's Wine Cellar, Kutaisi

ALEXANDER SPATARY/GETTY IMAGES ©

CAFE STAMBA

TBILISI | $$ | INTERNATIONAL
Hotel Stamba, Kostova 14; 32-2021199; www.stambahotel.com; mains 11-36 GEL

This super-stylish all-day bar-cafe-restaurant, inside Tbilisi's best hotel, serves as the current meeting point for the capital's various cultural elites, and is equally suited to a relaxed breakfast, a blow-out *supra* (traditional feast) or top-notch cocktails prepared by the iconic Pink Bar. The menu skews Italian, with dishes such as black spaghetti with shrimp or mushroom risotto, as well as more Georgian *shkmeruli* (roast chicken in a creamy garlic sauce).

ALUBALI

TBILISI | $$ | GEORGIAN
Giorgi Akhvlediani 5; 555-459539; www.facebook.com/alubali-artisancafe; mains 10-45 GEL

Totally unmarked from the street and behind a slightly anonymous door cage, this delightful indoor-outdoor courtyard spot features its own jungle of plants and achingly hip lighting. Its deceptively simple and relatively short menu nevertheless boasts a number of delectable regional Georgian treats. Don't miss the Megrelian *elarji* (cornmeal mixed with *sulguni* cheese, creating a fabulously playful and addictive putty) or the mozzarella-like *gebzhalia* (cottage cheese in a minty yoghurt sauce).

PASANAURI

TBILISI | $ | GEORGIAN
Griboedov 37; 32-2988715; khinkali 0.75-0.95 GEL, mains 8-25 GEL

This modest place feels more like a pub than a restaurant, with its wood-boothed tables and frequent line out the door. Everyone comes for its superb *khinkali*, best of which is the meaty 'Pasanauri special', but there are vegetarian *khinkali* too, including cheese, mushroom and potatoes, which can be livened up by ordering the fabulous homemade *adjika* or sour cream. There's local beer on tap and a down-to-earth attitude guaranteed.

SALOBIE BIA

TBILISI | $$ | GEORGIAN
Machabeli 14; 32-2997977; mains 7-23 GEL

This unassuming lower-ground-floor restaurant decked out in Soviet Georgian posters is always full, so it's a good idea to reserve at any time of day. The handwritten menu revisits Georgian classics with a twist and takes you on a tour through the country's regional cooking, not least its *lobio* (bean stew), after which the place is named, and which comes in many guises. Other dishes not to miss are the chicken *shkmeruli* (with garlic cream sauce)

TOMA'S WINE CELLAR

KUTAISI | $$$ | GEORGIAN
Kldiashvili 34; 555-445140; www.facebook.com/tomaswinecellar; per person incl wine 40 GEL

One of the most accessible and enjoyable dining experiences available in a traditional Georgian home can be found at Toma's Wine Cellar in Kutaisi, where passionate young host Toma offers you the chance to sample his grandmother's home-cooked foods. Guests are all given the set meal, which is enormous, and includes Toma's homemade wine and dishes such as *jonjoli* (pickled wildflowers), *khachapuri*, and *gebzhalia* (cottage cheese in mint and sour cream).

Previous spread: Palaty; Khachapuri.

PALATY

KUTAISI | $$ | GEORGIAN
Pushkin 2; 431-243380; mains 10-25 GEL

This bohemian spot in Kutaisi's old town gets in all just right, with live but unintrusive piano music, pleasant low lighting and purposefully mismatched furniture all contributing to its intriguing atmosphere. The menu includes several departures from the norm, such as the huge sharing plate featuring a dozen different local specialities such as cheeses, sausage, and *pkhali*, the *lobio* (bean stew) with local ham, for the field mushrooms with walnut and Sulguni cheese.

PHEASANT'S TEARS

SIGHNAGHI | $$$ | GEORGIAN
Baratashvili 18; 355-231556; www.pheasantstears.com; mains 15-35 GEL

This Georgian-American joint venture makes top-class natural wines by the traditional *qvevri* method at its vineyards in rural Kakheti. At its eponymous restaurant in the town of Sighnaghi, it offers wine tastings paired with delicious meals prepared from fresh, organic produce, served in the cosy dining room or the pretty garden-courtyard. Sample dishes include raw beets with wild plum sauce, seasonal mushrooms with tarragon and grilled pork in white-wine sauce.

'Café Littera serves simply superb "nouveau Georgian" dishes in the most charming setting imaginable.'
Cafe Littera

UOLLI

BATUMI | $$ | GEORGIAN
Memed Abashidze 43; 593-059955; www.facebook.com/uollirestaurant; mains 12-30 GEL

With its stylish bar, lovely staff, plant-filled backyard hung with fairy lights and various attractive dining areas, Uolli is a notably attractive establishment on Batumi's eating scene. What's more, as well as a wide range of Georgian classics on the menu, you'll find plenty of vegetarian choice and a wide range of nontypical Georgian dishes, such as mussels cooked in white wine and beef-stuffed dolma.

DIARONI

ZUGDIDI | $$ | GEORGIAN
Gamsakhurdia 9; 415-221122; www.diaroni.ge; mains 12-15 GEL

Zugdidi's best-known restaurant is certainly one of its smartest, with a large dark-wood and brick interior and a shaded street-side terrace where you can watch the world go by. The food is excellent, with an extensive menu featuring many Megrelian specialities including *ghomi* (a cornmeal porridge), *elarji* (ghomi with Sulguni cheese) and *geblazhia* (cheese seasoned with mint).

AFRICA
MIDDLE

AND EAST

MOROCCO

Moroccan cuisine is a bubbling tajine of influences, a pot stirred by everyone from the Amazigh (Berbers) and Arabs to the colonial French and Spanish. In this country between the Mediterranean and the Sahara, where Africa and Europe converge amid mosques and medinas, you can breakfast on croissants, snack in the souk and sip mint tea or *café au lait*. The most important influence of all is the bounty of fresh produce.

WHAT TO EAT

Tajine
Stew cooked in a conical earthenware pot, with ingredients varying from fish to lamb.

Couscous
A fine, pale, grain-sized, hand-rolled pasta, lightly steamed with aromatic broth and served with vegetables, meat or fish in a reduction of stock and spices.

Pastilla
Savoury-sweet pie of wafer-thin *warqa* (filo-like pastry), traditionally containing pigeon.

Mechoui
A whole lamb, marinated and slow-roasted in an underground oven until the meat falls off the bone.

Amlou
The 'Moroccan Nutella' is an addictively sweet spread – a mix of argan oil, honey and almonds.

PRICE RANGES
For a main course:
$ less than Dh70
$$ Dh70–150
$$$ Dh150 or more

Tipping: Dh2 in cafes; 10% in restaurants

UMIA

ESSAOUIRA | $$$ | MEDITERRANEAN
22 Rue de la Skala, Medina; 0524783395; www.facebook.com/Umiarestaurantessaouira; mains from Dh180

This sleek, contemporary restaurant is one of seaside Essaouira's hottest, with both visitors and locals rushing to dine on the Mediterranean-influenced menu based around seasonal, Moroccan market finds. Perhaps a bowl of clams in a garlicky white wine sauce or *magret de canard* (seared duck breast) in a red wine jus, paired with a local wine and rounded off with an indulgent chocolate mousse.

LA TABLE BY MADADA

ESSAOUIRA | $$$ | MEDITERRANEAN
7 Rue Youssef El Fassi, Medina; 0524475512; www.latablemadada.com; mains Dh100-220

Style meets substance at one of Essaouira's best fine-dining restaurants, housed in an old almond warehouse. The interior is a blend of traditional Moroccan and modern European, and the menu focuses on seafood and fish dishes, alongside contemporary riffs on local favourites such as tajines and *pastilla*.

MANDALA SOCIETY

ESSAOUIRA | $ | VEGETARIAN
46 Ave d'Istiqlal, Medina; 0808506784; www.mandalamaroc.com; mains from Dh85

On the main drag of Essaouira's whitewashed medina, this Moroccan-Icelandic operation opened in 2019 and quickly developed a loyal following for its arty décor, organic meat-free menu and top-notch coffee. Expect smoothies, avocado on sourdough bread, sinfully good homemade chocolate cake, generous salad bowls and hot specials, such as tofu wok.

There's friendly staff and free wi-fi; it's plastic-free too.

À L'OMBRE DU FIGUIER

TIZNIT | $ | MOROCCAN
22 Passage Akchouch, Quartier Idzakri; 0528861204; www.facebook.com/ombredufiguier; mains Dh60-75

Follow the signs through alleyways and under low doorways to one of southern Morocco's best restaurants. Colourful tables are arrayed under the dappled shade of a sprawling fig tree. The menu is meat-heavy, with lamb, beef and turkey, but there's often a seafood plat du jour, while side dishes include a delicious cucumber and melon soup or Moroccan salad. For dessert, refresh the palate with chilled pineapple gazpacho.

DJEMAA EL FNA FOOD STALLS

MARRAKESH | $ | MOROCCAN
Djemaa El Fna, off Place de Foucald; mains Dh30-50

Grilled meat and tajines as far as the eye can see, plus Moroccan specialities of snail soup, sheep's brains and skewered hearts for the adventurous. Eating amid the mayhem of the food stalls and fresh orange juice stands on Marrakesh's carnivalesque main square is not to be missed. The whole shebang kicks off shortly before sunset, when around 100 small restaurants and their enthusiastic touts set up.

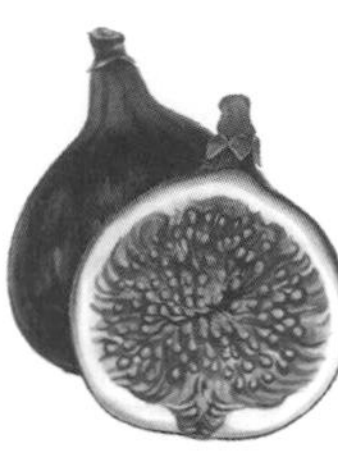

'Our chef finds daily inspiration in the catch of the day and fresh seasonal produce she sources from the nearby harbour and vegetable market.'
La Table by Madada

HENNA CAFE

MARRAKESH | $ | MOROCCAN
93 Arset Aouzal, Bab Doukkala; 0656566374; www.hennacafemarrakech.com; mains Dh40

Herbal teas, detox juices, henna tattoos, book exchange, Darija (Moroccan Arabic) classes...they're all on the menu at this intimate upstairs cafe, where a local *nquasha* (henna artist) draws intricate designs on hands and feet and you can munch on salads, falafel and *khleer* (cured lamb) sandwiches on the covered rooftop. All profits go to local residents in need.

AMAL CENTER

MARRAKESH | $ | MOROCCAN
cnr Rues Allal Ben Ahmad & Ibn Sina, Gueliz; 0524446896; http://amalnonprofit.org; mains Dh45-70

So many restaurants in Marrakesh reflect poorly on local cuisine, but here you get the real home-cooking deal. And, happily, it's all for a good cause: the Amal Center is a non-profit association that supports and trains disadvantaged Moroccan women in restaurant skills. The menu changes daily, but it generally includes a vegetarian option and the service is always warm. Meals are served in a leafy courtyard garden.

NOMAD

MARRAKESH | $$ | MEDITERRANEAN
1 Derb Arjan, Mouassine; 0524381609; www.nomadmarrakech.com; mains Dh100-130

Nomad's multitiered rooftop is one of the medina's buzziest venues, particularly at night when its lanterns twinkle over Rahba Kedima square. The small menu adds contemporary twists to North African ingredients and flavours, creating dishes such as Agadir calamari in a cumin-infused anchovy sauce or whole organic chicken in red chermoula. It's the brainchild of Marrakshi entrepreneur Kamal Laftimi, whose other restaurants include Le Jardin and Kilim.

RESTAURANT BRASSERIE LA BAVAROISE

CASABLANCA | $$$ | FRENCH
133 Rue Allah Ben Abdellah; 0522312203; www.restopro.ma/bavaroise; mains Dh160-230

Down a dishevelled street behind Casablanca's Marché Centrale, La Bavaroise has been serving an ultra-loyal local clientele since 1968 and shows no sign of losing its popularity. The speciality is grass-fed beef from the Atlas served in the form of steak with pommes frites, green salad and French-style sauces. Other highlights include oysters from Dakhla and decadent desserts. The stylish complex has several sections, including a bar and garden.

PÂTISSERIE BENNIS HABOUS

CASABLANCA | $ | BAKERY
2 Rue Fkih El Gabbas, Quartier Habous; 0522303025; pastries Dh5

Secreted in a lane in Casablanca's Souq Habous, this famous patisserie deserves a dedicated visit. Make your choice of traditional Maghrebi pastries such as *cornes de gazelle* (crescent-shaped cookies stuffed with almond paste and laced with orange-flower water) or *akda aux amandes* (almond macaroons) and then head to neighbouring Cafe Imperial to order a coffee and scoff your bounty.

RICK'S CAFÉ

CASABLANCA | $$ | MEDITERRANEAN
248 Blvd Sour Jdid, Old Medina; www.rickscafe.ma; mains Dh100-180

Opening spread, from left: Dishes from Dalida; Dish from Sufra; Chalkboard at Hickory Shack; Dish from Hickory Shack; Nomad. This page: Nomad. Opposite page: Café Clock.

OPENING SPREAD CREDITS: COURTESY OF DALIDA, SUFRA, HICKORY SHACK, NOMAD

COURTESY CAFE CLOCK

Immerse yourself in Bogart and Bergman's Casablanca at this reimagining of Rick's celluloid cafe. The art-deco interiors, the strains of 'As Time Goes By' and fez-clad bartenders will transport you to the famed gin joint, while you enjoy classic French and Moroccan dishes, accompanied by a live jazz soundtrack from 9.30pm. The film itself, of course, was shot almost entirely at Warner Brothers Studios in Burbank, California.

DOUYRIA

OUARZAZATE | $$ | MOROCCAN
72 Ave Mohammed V; 0524885288; www.restaurant-ouarzazate.net; mains Dh60-110

One of the best eateries in this provincial capital between the Atlas Mountains and the Sahara, Douyria wows diners with its rooftop terrace, candlelit tables and cushion-lined nooks perfect for sipping a cocktail. You can feast on richly flavoured local dishes, including unusual options such as tajine of roasted goat basted in argan oil and excellent pigeon or vegetarian *pastilla*. For dessert, there's house-made date or saffron ice cream.

NO 17 AT THE REPOSE

SALÉ | $ | MOROCCAN
17 Zankat Talaa, Ras Chejra, Medina; 0537882958; www.therepose.com; 3-course set dinner Dh200

Enjoy home-cooked vegetarian food and city views on the Repose medina guesthouse's plant-filled roof terrace, or in the cosy salon; non-guests just need to reserve ahead. The daily-changing menu makes the most of seasonal ingredients and flavours, but gives them a modern twist – perhaps date, carrot and orange salad or stuffed aubergine served with cous-cous, rounded off with a divine lemon parfait.

WHERE TO EAT...

FRESH SOUK PRODUCE

Souq Ableuh, Marrakesh
This tiny souk is dedicated to olives: green olives, black olives, purple olives, olives marinated in spicy harissa paste...

R'cif Market, Fez
A go-to for produce in the medina, R'cif's traders always have the freshest fruit, vegetables and meat.

Souqs Arabe and Berbère, Taroudant
At the main markets within the walled medina of 'Little Marrakesh', buy everything from tomatoes to textiles.

Tuesday Souk, Azrou
Mountain people from surrounding villages descend on one of the Middle Atlas' largest souks, bulging with local produce, livestock and clothes.

POPULAIRE SAVEUR DE POISSON

TANGIER | $$$ | SEAFOOD
2 Escalier Waller; 0539336326; fixed-price menu Dh200

This charming seafood restaurant is well worth the hype, offering an excellent, filling, four-course meal in rustic surroundings. First comes the fish soup, followed by inventive plates of fresh catch, olives and fresh breads. It's all washed down with a homemade juice cocktail made from a dozen fruits. Dessert is honey and almonds. Not just a meal, a whole experience.

MESÓN EL CORTIJO

CEUTA | $ | TAPAS
16 Calle Cervantes; 0956511983; tapas €2.80

In the Spanish enclave of Ceuta on the Mediterranean coast, this classic neighbourhood gathering place is heavy on tapas, *cerveza* (beer) and friendliness. Catch up on football, gossip and practise your español.

BLANCO RIAD

TETOUAN | $$ | MOROCCAN
25 Rue Zawiya Kadiria; 0539704202; www.blancoriad.com; mains Dh90, set menu from Dh155

The menu at this elegant riad at the foot of the Rif Mountains is a cut above the usual. A big change from the standard tajine menu, it features some innovative Moroccan dishes and is heavy on local seasonal produce. The garden is pleasant in summer, and the dining room has both Moroccan and Western seating.

EL JALEO

CHEFCHAOUEN | $ | MOROCCAN
Rue Ras El Maa; 0601403160; Dh40-80

El Jaleo, meaning 'the mess', serves the best cooking in mountainside Chefchaouen – by Nuura of Sofia restaurant – in a wonderfully atmospheric location above Oued Ras El Maa waterfall. The menu is unique, including steamed lamb, aubergine lasagna, *pinchos* (large tapas) and tajines. The lush garden is perfect for beholding sunset over the blue city after a long day exploring.

SOFIA

CHEFCHAOUEN | $ | MOROCCAN
Place Outa Hammam, Escalier Roumani; 0671286649; mains Dh30-80

The only female-owned restaurant in Chefchaouen, Sofia (named after the owner's daughter) is a revelation in a city where restaurants often neglect what's on the menu. Chef Nuura's cinnamon-hinted *pastilla* rolls are to die for and the vegetarian couscous has to be the best in town. Seating is outdoors on a few tables across from the small kitchen.

AUBERGE DARDARA RESTAURANT

CHEFCHAOUEN | $$ | MOROCCAN

Route Nationale 2; 0661150503; www.facebook.com/auberge.dardara; mains from Dh80, dinner set menu Dh120

This is the best restaurant in the area and worth the 10-minute taxi ride from town. The owner uses only the freshest ingredients from the garden, bakes his own bread and makes his own olive oil and goat's cheese. Try the superb salads, the venison cooked with dried figs or the succulent rabbit with quince.

RUINED GARDEN

FEZ | $$ | MOROCCAN
13 Derb Idrissi, Medina; 0649191410; www.ruinedgarden.com; tapas Dh35, mains Dh80-120

In this former merchant's house you can dine in the wild garden in summer or by a cosy fire in winter. Lunch has some bargain stews and 'tapas' (Moroccan salads), while dinner offers more elaborate dishes (prebook for the 1kg *mechoui* lamb). Veg options are especially good at lunch and, if you like what you eat, you can take part in a cooking class.

NUR

FEZ | $$$ | GASTRONOMY
7 Zqaq El Rouah, Medina; 0694277849; www.nur.ma; 10-course tasting menu Dh800

Born in Spain of Moroccan parents, chef Najat Kaanache has worked at restaurants such as Noma and travelled extensively. Her lovely fine-dining restaurant synthesises her experience into a dazzling, ever-changing tasting menu that highlights transatlantic culinary links and the medina's best produce. It's a bargain next to similarly ambitious global restaurants. Kaanache also offers cooking classes and culinary walking tours of the medina.

'The proud cultural and agricultural diversity of Morocco makes it the mouth of Europe, forged through its unique confluence of colonial cultures.' *Najat Kaanache, Nur*

CAFÉ CLOCK

FEZ | $ | CAFE
Derb El Magana, Talaa Kebira, Medina; 0535637855; www.cafeclock.com; mains Dh60-85

With a clientele of foreigners and creative young Fassis and a staff that's cheerful despite the maze of stairs in the multilevel space, this cafe and cultural centre is an ideal place to rest and nourish yourself. The menu is a Moroccan-Euro mix: a signature camel burger, lamb tajine and interesting vegetarian options, including aubergine and goat's-cheese quiche with spiced potato wedges. There are also branches in Marrakesh and Chefchaouen.

BULLS BURGER HOUSE

NADOR | $ | BURGERS
5 Blvd El Farabi; 0536603345; www.facebook.com/BullsBurgerHouse; burgers from Dh45

Somehow, one of the best burgers in Morocco has popped up in unremarkable Nador. Unbelievably soft buns hug perfectly spiced patties dripping with delicious sauces, and it all comes with garlic fries and homemade lemonade on the side. Shut your eyes and you might be in a trendy burger joint in any major city around the world.

ALGERIA

Although North African at its core – focused on stews and couscous, with dishes spiked with the Maghrebi spice-mix *ras al-hanout* – Algeria also mixes Middle Eastern, French, Spanish and Turkish influences into its cuisine. Outside Algiers, the dining-out scene is sparse.

WHAT TO EAT

Couscous
Steamed semolina balls, topped with various meat or vegetable stews. Couscous is considered Algeria's national dish.

Chorba Frik
A spicy *freekeh* (cracked green wheat), chickpea and tomato soup, traditionally eaten during Ramadan to break the fast.

Felfla
Also known as *Hmiss*, this simple vegetable dish of roasted red peppers, tomatoes and garlic is served with lashings of olive oil.

Maqroud
Diamond-shaped semolina pastries, stuffed with dates or figs, and then smothered in a honey and orange blossom water syrup.

PRICE RANGES
For a main course:
$ less than €5
$$ €5–€10
$$$ €10 or more

Tipping: 5–10% in better restaurants only.

RESTAURANT LA COMETE

NORTHERN ALGERIA | $$ | INTERNATIONAL
1 rue de la Paix, Oran; 041-294 584; mains DA1200

This faded favourite has waiters, wearing pristine suit jackets, that look like they've been doing the job for decades, and a clientele of old men who come back day after day to religiously sit at the same table. The menu is as charmingly old fashioned as the surroundings with steak, lots of seafood and a fantastic paella on Friday.

AUBERGE DU MOULIN

ALGIERS | $$$ | ALGERIAN
Rue Abane Ramdane, Chéraga; 023-358 326; www.aubergedumoulin.dz; mains DA1600-1900

This rambling, time-warp restaurant, with its dining room decorated with oil paintings, old farming implements and antique weaponry, is well worth the drive out of central Algiers. This is the place to try the North African speciality *mechoui*, (slow roasted lamb on the bone) and Algerian dishes such as *chorba frik* though there are plenty of classic French-style dishes on the menu as well.

BRASSERIE DES FACULTÉS

ALGIERS | $$$ | ALGERIAN
1 Rue Didouche Mourad; 021-492 458; mains DA1500-1800

On Algiers' main drag, this venerable spot offers Algerian and French classics from steaks to couscous. Algerians don't often go out to eat couscous – it's a dish usually cooked at home – so this is a fine alternative if you can't snag a dinner invite. The old fashioned and snug wood-panelled interior, with partial sea views, and selection of Algerian wine make this a favourite of well-to-do Algerians and foreign residents.

TUNISIA

Tunisian cuisine revolves around hearty, slow-cooked stew-style dishes, normally served loaded atop couscous and packed with a punchy amount of spice. Except in bigger cities, the dining scene is small; every Tunisian knows the best eating is found at home.

WHAT TO EAT

Harissa
This spice-mix is made into a paste, then added to everything from stews to briks. It's Tunisia's national condiment.

Tajine
No, not like Morocco's. In Tunisia, a tajine is a baked-egg dish, similar to a frittata, stuffed with vegetables and meats.

Brik
These triangular deep-fried pastries are commonly filled with egg, canned tuna, parsley and harissa.

Masfouf
Dessert couscous. Sugar and butter are mixed into the couscous and nuts and dates sprinkled on top for a sweet take on the ubiquitous grain.

PRICE RANGES
For a main course:
$ less than 10DT
$$ 10–25DT
$$$ 25DT or more

Tipping: 10%

LE SPORT NAUTIQUE

NORTHERN TUNISIA | $$ | SEAFOOD
Quai Tarak Ibn Ziad, Bizerte; 72 432 262; mains 14-30DT

This highly regarded restaurant with breezy terrace is quite simply one of the best dining spots in Tunisia's north. Fresh fish, cooked any number of ways – from simply grilled or baked to being smothered with cream and herbs or covered in a roasted almond crust – is the house speciality though meat eaters also have plenty to choose from.

FRANCESCO ROCCA/EYEEM/GETTY IMAGES ©

DOKEN

TUNIS | $ | MEDITERRANEAN
36 Rue des Libraires, Medina; 29 000 082; www.facebook.com/dokenmedina; mains 7-9DT, set menus 12-15DT

Slap amid Tunis' medina, this warm-coloured cafe, with tables spilling out into the alleyway outside, serves modern Mediterranean accented food including plenty of vegetarian options. For light lunches, after a morning of exploring the medina's squiggling lanes, their quiche is a treat while for dessert don't miss the tarte au citron – the chef has an expert hand with pastry. For a truly bargain meal, opt for a set three-course menu.

CAFÉ CULTUREL EL ALI

TUNIS | $$ | TUNISIAN
45 bis Rue Jemaa Zaytouna, Medina; 71 321 927; www.facebook.com/ElAliRestoEtCafeCulturel; mains 17-43DT

This cultured hideaway is all wood-beamed ceilings and stained-glass windows in the salons while the rooftop terrace is a serene spot to while away a few hours drinking tea or fruit smoothies. In the morning they do traditional Tunisian breakfast platters while at lunchtime diners dig into local dishes including vielle marmites (meats slow-cooked in terracotta pots).

DAR EL JELD

TUNIS | $$$ | TUNISIAN
10 Rue Dar El Jeld, Medina; 71 560 916; www.dareljeld.com; mains 25-40DT

Pass through the bee-yellow front door in this 18th-century mansion and an opulent courtyard dining space will be theatrically revealed. Start with the mixed appetiser plate which showcases Tunisia's fresh flavours and then order your main from a menu that stars local specialities such as *sebnekhia* (octopus with beans and spinach), *kabkabou* (fish and tomato stew) or *lahma m'jamra* (stuffed lamb shoulder). At dinner, there's live oud music. Bookings essential.

RESTO L'OMMIMA

CAP BON | $$ | TUNISIAN
Rue Moncef Bey, Hammamet Sud, Hammamet; 52 358 569; www.facebook.com/Resto.lomima; mains 21.5DT

This diner, where gingham red-and-white tablecloths clash with traditional North African tiles, is worth seeking out while holidaying in Hammamet. Even if you think you've sampled plenty of local grub, L'Ommima's homemade meals are miles above standard Tunisian restaurant offerings. The menu, written on a street-side chalkboard, changes daily, with options that've included everything from fish soup to stuffed sheep's stomach with couscous.

RISTARANTE BELLARIVA DALLA LINA

CAP BON | $$ | ITALIAN
265 Rue de la Plage, El Haouaria; 21 882 411; mains 5-35DT

El Haouaria sits snug on the tip of the Cap Bon Peninsula, the closest point in Tunisia to Italy, so this bona fide trattoria is an apt dining choice. The handmade pasta dishes, carefully crafted by owner Lina, steal the show but make sure to leave room for dessert which includes a decadent and gooey tiramisu.

RESTAURANT MERIEM

MAHDIA | $$ | ITALIAN
Ave Taher Sfar, Zone Touristique; 58 178 610; mains 8-30DT

Multilingual chef Sofian worked in Italy for a decade before returning home to open this clean and bright pizzeria and restaurant on Mahdia's Corniche. Most people eat here for the pizza and pasta but as Sofian's brother is a fisherman and supplies the restaurant with fresh fish daily, the Tunisian–style fish dishes on the menu are also an excellent choice.

Previous spread: Tajine dishes.

RESTAURANT LE CORAIL

SFAX | $$$ | TUNISIAN

39 Rue Habib Maazoun; 74 227 301; mains 20-48DT

Known for its ultra-fresh seafood, this upmarket restaurant offers private dining rooms downstairs and a vast restaurant space on the 1st floor. The food is a romp through traditional Tunisian cuisine and European classics. Start with the brik and then move on to grilled fish, risotto or spaghetti with fruit de mer (seafood). Their speciality (which needs to be ordered in advance) is a seafood couscous.

RESTAURANT DAR DEDA

TOZEUR | $ | TUNISIAN

Ave Abdulkacem Chebbi; 98 694 198; www.facebook.com/pg/restaurantdardeda; mains 5.5-9DT

Popular with tourists and locals alike for its friendly service and intimate candlelit atmosphere, Restaurant Dar Deda's menu is a run-through of reliably good Tunisian favourites. Think couscous, stick-to-your-ribs stews (including one using camel meat) and fresh salads. Don't forget the starters – the *doight de Fatima* (finger-shaped briks – fried pastries stuffed with potato) are the pick.

RESTAURANT FRUIT DE MER

GABÈS | $$ | SEAFOOD

Ave Hedi Chaker; 98 507 323; mains 7-17DT

Always packed, this open-sided restaurant, near the port in Gabès, serves up the best seafood in town and has plenty of staff on hand to efficiently keep the crowds happy. The grilled fish or braised mussels and octopus are both worth your time, as is the *calamari farçi*, a Tunisian favourite of squid stuffed with rice, greens and chilli.

RESTAURANT LA LUNA

GABÈS | $ | INTERNATIONAL

Ave Farhat Hached; 23 805 263; mains 7-22DT

This modest restaurant is where you come in Gabès to tuck into hearty classic European dishes of steak and beef stroganoff. Their seafood plates are fresh and tasty and the kitchen also whips up amply portioned pasta dishes and decent pizzas.

CAFÉ PATISSERIE BEN YEDDER

DJERBA | $ | CAFE

Pl Farhat Hached, Houmt Souk; 53 364 750; gâteaux 2-3DT, sandwiches 2DT

The outdoor terrace here is where you come in Djerba for fresh-from-the-oven sweet and savoury pastries, and a slice of cake. All washed down with coffee made from Cafés Ben Yedder beans or a freshly squeezed juice. It's a prime people-watching spot.

WHERE TO DRINK...

MINT TEA

Café Chaouachine, Tunis
Sip mint tea and smoke shisha under the vaulted arches of the atmospheric Souq des Chechias in Tunis medina.

Dar Hassine Allani, Kairouan
This late-18th-century dar, run by friendly women, offers tours of the house and tea on the rooftop with sweeping views over Kairouan's medina.

M'Rabet, Tunis
After tackling Tunis' medina maze, you can't beat mint tea overlooking the Zitouna Mosque's minaret on the two-tiered terrace or downstairs amid the painted columns.

Café Maure Diwan, Sfax
Inserted into Sfax's medina wall, this atmospheric cafe is perfect for relaxing with *thé au pignons* (mint tea with pinenuts).

SENEGAL

Senegal mixes French influence with home-grown recipes, using everything from baobab fruit to fish hooked by its Atlantic fishermen. The cosmopolitan capital, Dakar, and coastal tourist towns from Saint-Louis down to Cap Skirring have an array of restaurants serving pizzas and cold Flag beers to diners with sand between their toes. Elsewhere, it's a diet of African staples, including some excellent Senegalese specialties, and you may find yourself eating with your fingers.

WHAT TO EAT

Thiéboudienne
Rice cooked in a thick tomato sauce and served with fried fish and vegetables.

Poulet or poisson yassa
Grilled chicken or fish in lemon sauce with onions. A speciality of the Casamance region.

Mafé
Peanut-based stew, often beef or chicken.

Bissap
Tart purple soft drink made from water and hibiscus flowers.

Bouyi
Soft drink made from the fruits of the bulbuos baobab tree. The fruits have taken off as a superfood, thanks to high levels of nutrients and antioxidants.

PRICE RANGES

For a main course:
$ less than CFA3000
$$ CFA3000–6000
$$$ CFA6000 or more

Tipping: 10% at pricier restaurants.

LE LAGON I

DAKAR | $$$ | SEAFOOD
Rte de la Corniche-Est; 33 821 5322; www.lelagondakar.com; mains CFA9000-15,000

Perched on stilts over the bay, Le Lagon is one of Dakar's top seafood spots, with a spread of culinary treasures – oysters, sea urchins, chargrilled fish, pastas with mixed seafood. You can dine outside on the breezy waterside deck, or in the classy dining room, amid hanging swordfish, brass sailing instruments and a vintage diving suit. There's a small private beach right next to the restaurant.

RESTAURANT FARID

DAKAR | $$$ | LEBANESE
51 Rue Vincens; 33 823 8989; www.restaurantfarid.com; mains CFA6000-10,000, mezze for two CFA28,000

This little inner-city Dakar oasis serves the best Lebanese mezze this side of Beirut, including classics from babaganoush to tabouleh, as well as quality grilled meat and fish. You'll also find friendly service, courtyard dining and occasional live music and belly dancing.

ESTENDERA VIVIER BEACH

DAKAR | $$$ | INTERNATIONAL
Corniche des Almadies; 78 459 8181; www.facebook.com/estendera.vivierbeach; mains CFA7000-12,000

A charming little eatery with tables overlooking the crashing waves, Estendera has a small, well-executed menu of seafood, grilled meats and Italian plates. A typical meal here might start with barracuda carpaccio, then move on to seafood tagliatelle, chicken with porcini mushrooms or oven-baked lasagne – all with your feet in the sand.

LE BIDEEW

DAKAR | $$ | INTERNATIONAL
89 Rue Joseph Gomis; 33 823 1909; www.facebook.com/lebideew; meals CFA5500-7500

In the cool shade of the garden of the Institut Français, this colourful arts cafe is perfect for a break from central Dakar. The varied menu features dishes such as vegetable curry, octopus salad, chargrilled pork and grilled prawns with *bissap* (hibiscus-flower) chutney. The African buffet, offered most Fridays, and the variously themed Tuesday buffet are great deals.

LE DJEMBÉ

DAKAR | $$ | AFRICAN
56 Rue St Michel; 33 821 0666; dishes CFA3500-5500

'Located upstairs in the seaside village of Saly, Le Soleil offers the most "typically typical" view of the Petite Côte near Dakar.'
Mamadou Basse, Le Soleil de Saly

This inviting, colourful eatery is the whispered insider tip for anyone in search of a filling platter of *thiéboudienne*. There's also chicken in *yassa* and *mafé* form, as well as *bissap* juice, attracting a lively mix of Dakarois, expats and fans of authentic Senegalese cooking.

CABANE DU PÊCHEUR

DAKAR | $$$ | SEAFOOD
Plage de N'Gor; 33 820 7675; www.facebook.com/cabanedupecheurngor; dishes CFA7000-10,000

One of Dakar's best seafood restaurants, it serves freshly grilled fish dishes that you'll find hardly anywhere else in the city. The menu also features a few meat and vegetarian choices, including mozzarella and pesto ravioli, and the beach location is a relaxing winner.

LA POINTE DES ALMADIES

DAKAR | $$$ | INTERNATIONAL
Rte des Almadies; 33 820 0140; www.facebook.com/Www.lapointedesalmadies.sn; 2-/3-course menu CFA6500/8000

This popular, breezy spot draws a mix of expats and locals, who come for a meal and perhaps a swim in the pool. There's a wide range of appetisers and a surprising medley of international dishes, from mussels and frites to chicken couscous via saffron shrimp and spaghetti bolognaise.

LA GUINGETTE

PETITE CÔTE | $$$ | FRENCH

Saly; 77 158 0808; www.facebook.com/laguinguettedesaly; mains from CFA6000

Tucked down a small sandy lane, La Guingette earns good reviews for its colourful garden setting and its delectable, market-fresh cuisine, using ingredients gathered daily at nearby M'bour Market. A great day out down the wild Atlantic coast from big-city Dakar.

LE SOLEIL DE SALY

PETITE CÔTE | $$ | AFRICAN

Saly; 33 958 2865; www.lesoleildesaly.com; mains CFA4000-6000

'The Sun of Saly', a buzzing favourite on the main drag, serves up tasty pizzas and grilled meat and fish dishes. There's live African or French music three nights a week, normally Thursday through Saturday. Owner Mamadou Basse is easy to spot: look for the kind-hearted man in the fedora.

CASA RESTO

CASAMANCE | $$ | INTERNATIONAL

Cap Skirring; 77 796 2071; mains CFA3500-5000

Set on the main road through this sleepy southern seaside town, Casa Resto compensates for its lack of sea views with some of Cap Skirring's best meals, not to mention Senegal's best pizzas. The menu has a bit of everything, from steaks to seafood, and the thatched, open-fronted building is a pleasant hangout.

LA KORA

SAINT-LOUIS | $$ | AFRICAN

402 Rue Blaise Diagne; 77 637 1244; www.facebook.com/lakorachezpeggy; mains CFA4000-8500

La Kora has earned a stellar reputation for its fabulous cooking, the warm welcome chez Peggy and staff, and the lovely setting – complete with a baobab tree in the vine-trimmed courtyard and a stylish dining room slung with old photos of Saint-Louis. Steak tartare, fish fillet, crepes and pizza are all on the menu. La Kora also hosts occasional concerts.

LA LINGUÈRE

SAINT-LOUIS | $$ | AFRICAN

Rue Blaise Diagne; 33 961 3949; mains CFA1500-4000

A reliable local eatery that serves up tasty poulet yassa, thiéboudienne and other Senegalese classics. Friendly service and attention to details (including cleanliness) make all the difference. It's a basic-looking dining room, but dishes such as beef *mafé* impress diners, as does the *bissap*.

Previous spread: Poulet Yassa. Spread P356-7: Groundnut stew; Jollof rice.

THE GAMBIA

Gambians eat a lot of fish on the coast, which is also where the tourist resorts and the best restaurants are found. Elsewhere, even in capital Banjul, there are slim culinary pickings and visitors often dine at their accommodation. Rice is a staple, mixed with various sauces and vegetables.

WHAT TO EAT

Domoda
Groundnut sauce, made from peanuts with tomato paste, mustard, black pepper and onions. Mixed with rice, it's The Gambia's national dish. This 'peanut butter stew' is found under other names elsewhere in West Africa.

Benachin
Rice cooked in tomato, fish and vegetable sauce.

Fresh seafood
Available along the Atlantic coast, including outstanding grilled ladyfish, barracuda and butterfish.

Niebbe
Spicy red beans that are served with bread.

Akara
Black eyed peas ground to flour, deep fried and seasoned to make fritters, which are served for breakfast with baguette-like *tapalapa* bread.

PRICE RANGES
For a main course:
$ less than D250
$$ D250–500
$$$ D500 or more

Tipping: 10%

SEA SHELLS

ATLANTIC COAST RESORTS | $$$ | INTERNATIONAL

Bertil Harding Hwy, Kololi; 7760070; www.facebook.com/seashellsgambia; mains D400-650

This local legend is well worth a visit for its creative and beautifully presented dishes, despite its location on the coastal highway. Pop by at lunchtime for fresh vegetable tarts, curried chicken salad, salmon burgers with beetroot chutney and other light fare. At night, the menu shines with coconut-dusted prawns, roast ladyfish with a crab salad, and a famous beef Wellington. Like the best events, the décor is smart casual.

BUTCHER'S SHOP

ATLANTIC COAST RESORTS | $$$ | MOROCCAN

130 Kairaba Ave, Fajara; 4495069; www.facebook.com/TheButchersShopGambia; mains D435-675

Driss Bensouda, a Moroccan celebrity chef (star of TV's *Driss's Kitchen*), fires up some of the best cooking in The Gambia at this elegant eatery with terrace seating on busy Kairaba Ave. You'll find perfectly grilled fish and juicy steaks, along with global dishes such as rich Moroccan tagines, beef bourguignon and comfort classics such as steak and Guinness pie.

GIDA'S GARDEN

ATLANTIC COAST RESORTS | $$ | INTERNATIONAL

off Atlantic Blvd, Fajara; 3999756; www.facebook.com/gidasgarden; mains D375-695

This hidden oasis is best known for its delectably prepared grilled meats (beef fillet medallion with blue cheese, barbecue pork ribs), though you'll also find an array of seafood, a few vegetarian dishes and excellent desserts. It's a magical and tranquil setting by night, with low-lit tables overlooking the flower-filled gardens, where the Bang-Bang shrimp starter and ribeye steak inspire loyalty.

CAPE VERDE

Cabo Verdean cuisine includes Portuguese niceties such as imported olives and Alentejo wines, but it's built on a firm African base, with *milho* (corn) and *feijão* (beans) the ubiquitous staples. Thanks to the many Italian tourists and expats, good pizzas and pastas are available in even out-of-the-way places.

WHAT TO EAT

Cachupa
A filling blend of beans, boiled corn, *mandioca* (cassava), sweet potato and sometimes pork or chicken; the national dish.

Seafood
Atum (tuna), *garoupa* (grouper fish), *lagosta* (lobster), *polvo* (octopus) and *serra* (sawfish) are popular.

Caldeirada
Meat or fish stew.

Meat dishes
Carne de vaca (beef), *frango* (chicken), *porco* (grilled pork) or *cabrito* (goat), with sides such as *arroz* (rice) or *batatas fritas* (French fries).

Pudim
A flan-like dessert.

Island drinks
Grogue (sugarcane spirit), *ponch* (rum, lemonade and honey), Fogo wines, bottled Strela beer and coffee from the slopes of Mt Fogo on Santo Antão.

PRICE RANGES

$ less than CVE700
$$ CVE700–1200
$$$ CVE1200 or more

Tipping: 10–15%

CALETA

SANTO ANTÃO | $$ | SEAFOOD
Ponta do Sol; 2251561; mains CVE800-1300

At this bistro-like restaurant, with its boat-shaped bar, cool blue walls and sidewalk tables on the waterfront, the Cabo Verdean and European specialities incorporate prime local products. Start with the fried-goat-cheese cakes or sweet-potato soup and move on to risotto with seafood, sautéed king prawns or grilled pork chops. With regular live music, this is the place to toast the vertiginous cliffs up here at the end of the road.

CASA CAFÉ MINDELO

SÃO VICENTE | $$$ | BISTRO
Rua Governador Calheiros 6, Mindelo; 2313735; www.casacafemindelo.com; mains CVE1300-2500, lunch specials CVE400-500

Near the waterfront, this buzzing place serves up some of the best cooking in the islands' cultural capital, amid chunky wooden tables, industrial light fixtures and traditional artwork. The chalkboard menu lists changing specials, such as pasta with lobster, mussels in white wine and Portuguese-style seafood stew, and there's live music most nights. The tables on the square out front are Mindelo's favourite spot for an espresso or cocktail.

RESTAURANTE MARACUJÁ

SANTIAGO | $$ | FUSION
Tarrafal; 9138854; mains CVE550-950

One of the best eateries on the archipelago's largest island, Maracujá (Passion Fruit) serves up delicious seafood and grilled fish plates, with French accents. The *arroz de marisco* (seafood rice) is renowned. With its deceptively simple decor, the restaurant is a fast favourite for its caipirinhas, fish and veg soup and *polvo grelhado* (grilled octopus) alike. Leave room for melt-in-your-mouth crêpes for dessert.

GUINEA BISSAU

Seafood is the highlight of this former Portuguese colony spread between the tropical Bissagos Islands and a chink of the mainland. The restaurant scene is negligible outside capital Bissau, with regional specialities such as *jollof rice* (rice with tomatoes and spices) the mainstay, alongside local and European cuisine.

WHAT TO EAT

Seafood
Shrimp, oysters and meaty *bica* (sea bream), best served sautéed with onion and lime. Also *siga* (onion, okra and chilli with seafood or meat).

Chabeu
Deep-fried fish served in a thick palm-oil sauce; a national favourite.

Street food
Brochettes (small pieces of beef, sheep or goat meat skewered and grilled over a fire), lumps of roast meat and *bâton de manioc* (yucca fries).

Stews
Calderaida (thick stew, usually with meat base), *mancarra* (peanuts, often in a broth) and *cafriela* (grilled chicken or lamb with onion, lemon and chilli).

PRICE RANGES
$ less than CFA5000
$$ CFA5000–10,000
$$$ CFA10,000 or more

Tipping: 10–15% in upscale restaurants.

SALDOMAR

ARQUIPÉLAGO DOS BIJAGÓS | $$ | PIZZA
Bubaque town, Ilha de Bubaque; 245 5496826; pizza CFA5000

The Bissagos Islands' largest town is the setting for this alfresco eatery, which serves authentic wood-oven pizza, other Italian favourites, fish and veggie dishes in its rustic clifftop perch. With the feel of Robinson Crusoe's secret seaside garden, it's a short walk from the terminal for the archipelago's only ferry connection with the mainland.

PAPA LOCA

BISSAU | $$ | INTERNATIONAL
Av Francisco Mendes; 689 22 22; mains CFA3500-8000

Fittingly for a restaurant with hodgepodge decor, Papa Loca's menu ranges far and wide: from thin-crust pizzas and burgers to omelettes and crepes, with local specialities in the mix. Say *obrigado* and raise a Super Bock beer to the slow but well-intentioned service that holds it all together.

O BISTRO

BISSAU | $$ | ITALIAN
Rua Eduardo Mondlane; 245 3206000; mains from CFA5000

This well-established hangout serves up all the right ingredients, against a quirky decor that includes a bust of Vladimir Lenin: excellent, reasonably priced mains, including pizzas, ravioli, gnocchi and mixed grills; a well-stocked bar; and a warm ambience that transcends the air-con. The tables on the veranda are pleasant for a cold Cristal beer, if you don't forget your mosquito repellent.

GUINEA

Eating in impoverished Guinea is dominated by cassava, with perhaps some fish or chicken and a sauce to add some flavour. Good restaurants are hard to find, even in capital Conakry, and confined to the handful of hotels patronised by business travellers and the Guinean elite.

WHAT TO EAT

Riz gras
Rice fried in oil and tomato paste and served with fried fish or meat.

Fou for
Near-solid, sticky glob of cooked cassava (manioc) flour – like mashed potatoes mixed with gelatin. Grab a portion (with your right hand), form a ball, dip it in the sauce and enjoy.

Plantains
As in other coastal West African countries, cooking or green bananas are deep-fried and served as a sweet side dish.

Saka Saka
Guineans make a dark green sauce from chopped and stewed cassava leaves, add meat or fish and serve with rice.

PRICE RANGES

For a main course:
$ less than GFr45,000
$$ GFr45,000–90,000
$$$ GFr90,000 or more

Tipping: 10% in Conakry's best restaurants.

LE SOGUE HÔTEL

ÎLES DE LOS | $$ | SEAFOOD
Île Room; 664 276 411; www.lesoguehotel.com; meals GFr100,000

On a short stretch of private white-sand beach, this gorgeous hotel is one of the best in Guinea. The beachfront restaurant, which is filled with the artistic flotsam and jetsam of the ocean currents, serves African and French cuisine. There is also a strong focus on seafood, thanks to the local fishing community. A meal here adds to the experience of visiting the beaches and jungle-clad interior of tiny Île Room.

LE CÉDRE

CONAKRY | $$ | LEBANESE
7th Ave, Kaloum; 664 531 415; mains around GFr90,000

Near the tip of the peninsula containing the Guinean capital, this tucked-away spot offers a cool, quiet respite from the searing sun and noise outside. It serves a range of Lebanese starters and mains that fuse French and Middle Eastern tastes. The hummus, steak, fish and calamari receive favourable reviews from the travellers who occasionally pass through Conakry, and overlook Le Cédre's decorative shortcomings to focus on the food.

HOTEL SIB

DALABA | $$ | INTERNATIONAL
Quartier du Chargeur; 622 278 280; www.facebook.com/HotelSiB; dinner menu GFr90,000

If the SiB were anywhere else on Earth, it would have been converted into a luxury heritage hotel. As it is, this 1930s colonial building, originally constructed to house soldiers recuperating from WWII, is a creaky, character-laden place, dripping in yesteryear romance. The in-house restaurant, which puts on set three-course dinner menus, is easily the best place to eat in Dalaba, while the bar is an atmospheric 1930s mirror-lined masterpiece.

SIERRA LEONE

The coastal country nicknamed 'Sweet Salone' is known for its cuisine, and every town has a cookery (basic eating house) serving *chop* (meals). Fish is a dominant feature of capital Freetown's chop houses, beach barbecues and restaurants, while meals inland revolve around cassava and rice with sauces and stews.

WHAT TO EAT

Rice and sauce
The staple accompanied by *plasas* (pounded potato or cassava leaves, cooked with palm oil and often fish or beef), okra sauce or groundnut stew.

Street food
Fried chicken, roasted corn, chicken kebabs, plantain chips and *fry fry* (simple sandwiches).

Cassava bread
Made using flour from the starchy root crop; often fried and served with oily fish sauce.

Jollof rice
Fried rice with beans, a spicy onion-based sauce and meat or fish.

Potato leaf stew
Spinach-like leaves mixed with spices and fish stock and served with goat, chicken or smoked fish.

PRICE RANGES
For a main course:
$ less than US$5
$$ US$5–10
$$$ US$10 or more

Tipping: 10–15% service charge sometimes included

TESSA'S

FREETOWN | $$ | AFRICAN
13 Wilkinson Rd; 076 800085; www.facebook.com/TessasRestaurant; mains Le50,000-85,000

Authentic Sierra Leonean dishes such as black-eyed beans with plantain, palm-oil stew, *fufu* (fermented cassava, cooked and puréed) and jollof rice are on the lunch menu here, along with European dishes, served up in either the simple dining room or the garden.

OASIS

FREETOWN | $$ | RESTAURANT
33 Murray Town Rd, near Boyle Lane; 076 605222; www.freetownoasis.com; sandwiches Le30,000, small/large plates from Le35,000/60,000

This charming little guesthouse cafe is an oasis indeed, set in a garden that feels hundreds of miles from the chaos of Freetown. Famous for its smoothies, the food here is also excellent and wholesome – think black-bean soup, Thai chicken curry and indulgent brownies. There's a cosy dining room, a breezy porch, complete with whirring fans and brightly pattered rattan furniture, and sea views from the garden.

FRANCO'S

FREETOWN PENINSULA | $$ | ITALIAN
Florence's Resort, 20 Michael St, Sussex Village; 076 744406; www.florencesresort.com; mains Le50,000-100,000

Half an hour's drive across the peninsula from Freetown is this beloved resort restaurant and lagoon-side hangout. Run by an Italian–Sierra Leonean family, Franco's specialises in seafood and pasta, and its wine list makes it a local favourite for a long Sunday lunch.

LIBERIA

Coastal capital Monrovia has Liberia's only notable restaurant selection, although many serve Lebanese and other international cuisine within hotels. On the bright side, visitors can enjoy a burger without feeling like a philistine, as Liberia was founded by liberated American slaves. Rice and spicy meat sauces or fish stews are popular local dishes.

WHAT TO EAT

Rice and sauce
Local versions of this classic West African combo include palm butter with fish, *palava* sauce (plato leaf, dried fish or meat and palm oil) and *jollof* rice (rice and vegetables with meat or fish).

Fufu
A popular way to serve the staple cassava, which is pounded or grated and cooked to a sticky, near-solid glob. To eat, form it into a ball with your right hand and dip in sauce.

Beef Internal Soup
This strange-sounding appetiser is typically Liberian for combining meat, fish and veg in one pot: beef, dried codfish, other smoked fish, tripe and red pepper.

Liberian spinach
Boiled cassava or potato leaves.

PRICE RANGES

For a main course:
$ less than US$5
$$ US$5–15
$$$ US$15 or more

Tipping: 10%

THE GALLERY

MONROVIA | $$$ | INTERNATIONAL
Mamba Point Hotel, United Nations Dr, Mamba Point; 0775 554 444; www.mambapointhotel.com; mains from US$15

Conveniently located in the capital's best hotel, the Gallery's seafood, meat, pasta and vegetarian dishes come in global styles, including Italian, Lebanese and Indian. Contemporary art and candelabras set the fine-dining tone, but before you write it off as just another hotel restaurant, try the signature pizzas cooked in a clay oven with mango wood. Also here are a sushi bar, coffee lounge, pool bar, sports bar and seafront terrace.

DIANA RESTAURANT

MONROVIA | $$ | LEBANESE
Broad St; 0886 563 333; mains US$7-16

With simple decor and an extensive menu of shawarma, sandwiches, kebabs, falafel and more, Diana is a bustling lunchtime stalwart in downtown Monrovia, where relatively efficient service keeps 'em dining and dashing. One dish is big enough to share and the escalope wrap is recommended.

EVELYN'S RESTAURANT

MONROVIA | $$ | LIBERIAN
Gibson Ave, Sinkor; 0886 710 104; www.facebook.com/evelynslib; mains US$10-15

Monrovia has several excellent hotel restaurants serving international cuisine in plush surrounds, but head to the eastern Sinkor neighbourhood to meet the locals over some hearty Liberian dishes. A go-to for chicken and collard greens, Evelyn's Liberian selection includes palm butter and rice, split peas and pork with gravy, and cassava with fish sauce, eddoes and plantain. Going since 2008, it also serves a good shrimp alfredo and barbecue pork, but we recommend going Liberian.

CÔTE D'IVOIRE

Côte d'Ivoire is blessed with a cuisine that's lighter and more flavoursome than those found in some of its neighbours. Economic capital Abidjan has a lively dining scene, while the most popular eateries nationwide are *maquis* – budget open-air restaurants, usually under a thatched roof, that grill meats each evening.

WHAT TO EAT

Kedjenou
The national dish of slowly simmered chicken or fish with peppers and tomatoes.

Poisson braisé
Delicate dish of grilled fish with tomatoes and onions cooked in ginger.

Staples
Pretty much everything comes with rice, *fufu* (a dough of boiled yam, cassava or plantain, pounded into a sticky paste) or *attiéké* (grated cassava, with a couscous-like texture).

Aloco
Ripe bananas fried with chilli in palm oil; a popular street food.

PRICE RANGES

For a main course:
$ less than CFA3000
$$ CFA3000–6000
$$$ CFA6000 or more

Tipping: 10–15%, unless a service charge has been added

BUSHMAN CAFÉ

ABIDJAN | $$$ | AFRICAN

Riviera 4; 59-496651; www.facebook.com/BushmanCafe; mains from CFA10,000

This rooftop terrace restaurant is Abidjan's number one for gastronomic delights and a meal under the stars. The menu is simple and focused on local flavour, with dishes ranging from octopus salad and fish tartare to charcoal-grilled meat and *yassa poulet* (chicken in lemon sauce with onions).

LE MECHOUI

ABIDJAN | $$ | LEBANESE

Athletic Club, Blvd de Marseille, Zone 4; 21-246893; www.facebook.com/mehouiabidjan; meze from CFA4000

In an elegant setting that overlooks the lagoon, Le Mechoui serves fantastic Lebanese food. All the ingredients are fresh, the taste is top-notch, and the range of meze is simultaneously authentic and imaginative. Try the lamb tartare, tangy tabbouleh and the classic, creamy hummus – and a serving of hot Lebanese bread. 'The Grill' is run by a local Lebanese family, who will gladly recommend a selection of meze.

LE NANDJELET

ABIDJAN | $ | AFRICAN

Blokosso; 09-930400; mains from CFA2000

Make a beeline for the outdoor tables on the edge of the lagoon – they offer a breathtaking panorama of the Abidjan skyline by night. The thatched interior hosts live music and performances among its colourful murals, making this a go-to for a cold Flag beer as much as the *kedjenou*, *poisson braisé* and Ivoirian *escargot* (snails).

GHANA

Typified by servings of starchy staple with fiery sauces and oily soups, Ghanaian food is as enjoyable as meeting the West African nation's warm people. Stews and snacks such as yam chips and plantain fries elevate Ghanaian cuisine above those of other African countries. Accra also has a cosmopolitan restaurant scene.

WHAT TO EAT

Groundnut stew
A warming, spicy dish cooked with liquefied groundnut paste, ginger and either fish or meat.

Palm-nut soup
Tomatoes, ginger, garlic and chilli pepper, as well as palm nut, with a bright-red colour from palm oil.

Jollof rice
A spicy dish cooked with a blend of tomatoes and onion and usually served with meat.

Red-red
A bean stew normally served with fried plantain.

Fufu
Cooked and mashed cassava, plantain or yam, usually served with hot sauces and soups.

Banku
Fermented maize meal, another starchy staple.

PRICE RANGES

For a main course:
$ less than C20
$$ C20–50
$$$ C50 or more

Tipping: 10–15% in upscale venues

VIEW BAR & GRILL

KUMASI | $$$ | INTERNATIONAL

39 Melcom Rd, Ahodwo; 024 4668880; www.facebook.com/theviewbarandgrill; mains C20-125

The best restaurant in Ghana's second city serves delicious and beautifully presented food in stylish surroundings, with expansive windows taking in views over the city. The steaks are the stars of the menu, but there are also good chicken, fish and burger options. The cocktails are excellent and there are regular DJ parties on the roof terrace.

TIMAGES/SHUTTERSTOCK ©

BAOBAB VEGETARIAN MORINGA RESTAURANT

CAPE COAST | $ | VEGETARIAN

Baobab Guesthouse, Commercial St; 054 0436130; www.baobab-children-foundation.de; sandwiches C11-21, mains C12-24

A tiny organic food bar with a wholesome touch, Baobab serves up great veggie stews and curries, black-bread sandwiches and refreshing juices, smoothies and shakes. The patio, built in traditional Ghanaian style, has a great view over the sea and busy Commercial St. Profits from the restaurant, attached guesthouse and gift shop go to the Baobab Children Foundation, which runs a school for disadvantaged children.

CHUCK'S BAR & RESTAURANT

TAMALE | $$ | INTERNATIONAL

Mariam Rd; 055 3997379; www.facebook.com/ChucksTamale; mains C30-55

You won't see many locals in here, but as far as expat havens go, this restaurant and craft brewery in northern Tamale has it covered. A wood-burning pizza oven produces excellent pizzas and the menu also includes pastas, burgers and decadent desserts. There's regular live music and events, including karaoke and screenings of soccer matches. The large beer garden is perfect to sink a cold drink or two.

KHANA KHAZANA

ACCRA | $$ | SOUTH INDIAN

Kojo Thompson Rd; 027 5834282; www.khanakhazanagh.com; mains C20-30

One of the Ghanaian capital's first Indian restaurants, this outdoor eatery is cheap, delicious and has long opening hours to satisfy curry cravings at any time of day. One of the house specialities is the *dosa* (savoury parcel made of rice flour normally eaten for breakfast), while the menu also lists classic meat and veggie curries. Sunday is *thali* (set meal) day.

SANTOKU RESTAURANT & BAR

ACCRA | $$$ | JAPANESE

Villaggio Vista, North Airport Rd, East Dzorwulu; 054 4311511; www.yoloxperiences.com; mains C70-170

Stunning Japanese food, impeccable service and elegant decor make Santoku one of the best restaurants in Ghana. The team behind Nobu in London and Dubai worked with Santoku to create a range of dishes, from Otsumami snacks and Zensai sharing dishes to soups and noodles. The décor merges contemporary Western style and Eastern philosophy in its traditional Japanese woodwork and bamboo ceiling. A consistent achiever in the capital's dining scene.

'Our restaurant evokes the excitement, lifestyle and landscapes of Africa. The calm and scenic setting sets the tone for the West African culinary experience.'
Buka, Accra

AFFINI4/SHUTTERSTOCK ©

BUKA

ACCRA | $$ | AFRICAN

10th St, Osu; 024 4842464; www.thebukarestaurant.com; mains C30-50

Ever-popular Buka serves some of the best West African food in Accra, in stylish surroundings to boot. Hearty plates of *jollof* rice, grilled tilapia, goat stew and palm-nut soup are served on a pretty terrace, which fills up with the local office crowd every lunchtime. Ghanaian and Nigerian specialities dominate, but Togolese and Ivorian flavours also feature.

TOGO

Good restaurants are scarce in Ghana's smaller eastern neighbour, with most found in capital Lomé and serving the cuisine of their former colonisers, France and Germany, as well as West African specialities. As Lomé is right on the Gulf of Guinea, seafood features on the capital's menus, while brochettes and chicken are common.

LE FERMIER

KPALIMÉ | $$ | AFRICAN

Route de Kusuntu; 22 34 58 74; mains CFA4000-5000

This low-roofed, intimate spot on the northwestern outskirts of Kpalimé, capital of Togo's coffee-growing country, serves excellent African and French food – the *fufu* (pounded yam) served in a clay pot comes recommended. The lure of the best pizza in town also makes this a likely place to meet other travellers.

CÔTÉ JARDIN

LOMÉ | $$ | INTERNATIONAL

Rue d'Assoli; 22 42 19 82; mains CFA5500-7500

Hands-down the most atmospheric eatery in the Togolese capital, Côté Jardin has an exotic pleasure garden replete with tropical plants and woodcarvings and an eclectic menu featuring everything from fish curry to chicken supreme on the blackboard.

HÔTEL NAPOLÉON LAGUNE

LOMÉ | $$ | INTERNATIONAL

Route 20 Bé; 22 27 07 32; www.napotogo.com; mains CFA4500 to CFA7200

Perched on a lively stretch of the Bé lagoon, the Napoléon Lagune is one of Lomé's best hotels. Its excellent restaurant serves daily and a la carte menus of European cuisine and African specialities, amid thatched roofs and hanging gourds. Try the famous crocodile sauce if you dare.

HÔTEL COCO BEACH

LOMÉ | $$ | INTERNATIONAL

Coco Beach; 22 71 49 37; www.hotel-togo-cocobeach.com; meals CFA6700 to CFA8100

East of central Lomé, this beachfront hotel is in need of some TLC, but the restaurant specialising in seafood makes a good stop en route to Benin or as an excursion from town.

WHAT TO EAT

Pâte
A dough-like substance made of corn, cassava or yam. Togolese dishes are typically based on a starch staple such as this, accompanied by sauce.

Fufu
Yam served with vegetables and meat.

Djenkoumé
Pâte with cornflour and spices served with fried chicken.

Snacks
Outside Lomé, sit-down restaurants are uncommon, so travellers often fill up at snack bars, market stands and street stalls serving bites such as *aloko* (fried plantain), *koliko* (yam chips), *gaou* (bean-flour fritters), *wagasi* (a mild cheese fried in hot spice) and fresh fruit.

PRICE RANGES

For a main course:
$ less than CFA4000
$$ CFA4000–7000
$$$ CFA7000 or more

Tipping: 10% in upmarket restaurants

WHAT TO EAT
Igname pilé
A starchy staple from ground plantain or cassava.
Atlantic fish
Southern Benin is on the Gulf of Guinea and fish is a highlight of local cuisine. It's usually barracuda, dorado or grouper, and is usually served grilled or fried.
Wagashi
A soft cow's-milk cheese made by the semi-nomadic Fulani people of northern Benin. Available in places such as Parakou, it has a red rind and a mild flavour, and is widely used in Beninese kitchens.
Agouti
Also known as 'grass cutter', rabbit-like cane rats are a common local dish, found on the menus of even upmarket restaurants.

PRICE RANGES
For a main course:
$ less than CFA3000
$$ CFA3000–5000
$$$ CFA5000 or more

Tipping: 10% in upmarket restaurants

BENIN

Benin is more famous as the West African birthplace of voodoo than for its food, but Nigeria's western neighbour has one of the region's best cuisines. Its staple dishes are similar to those of neighbouring Togo, albeit with different names, while French colonial influence lives on in the restaurant menus of capital Cotonou.

CHEZ MAMAN BÉNIN

COTONOU | $ | AFRICAN
Rue 201A; 21 32 33 38; meals CFA2000-3500

Have your fish grilled, fried or stewed at this friendly, longstanding no-frills canteen off thoroughfare Blvd St Michel, where a large selection of West African dishes are scooped from steaming pots. There's no decor except for a couple of TVs showing the latest football action.

LE PRIVÉ

COTONOU | $$$ | FRENCH
Ave Clozel; 97 29 17 17; www.facebook.com/LePrive.Resto; mains CFA15,000

Centrally located between the bridge over the River Cotonou and the Catholic cathedral, this quiet achiever impresses even critical European palates with its well-presented international dishes and contemporary decor. While not the most authentically Beninese restaurant, visitors and locals enjoy coming here for a celebratory meal.

L'IMPRÉVU

COTONOU | $$ | INTERNATIONAL
Ganhi; 66 97 40 40; www.facebook.com/limprevuBJ; mains CFA4500

This light and airy guesthouse restaurant is a minimalist haven from the hectic Beninese capital, where brunches and coffees invite lingering. The menu runs the global gamut from Beninese to Italian, with a good line in seafood and chips. The wine selection and outdoor gazebo make it a popular expat haunt.

LE SECRET DE LA VIEILLE MARMITE

PARAKOU | $ | BENINESE
66 22 29 39; meals CFA2000-3500

In central Benin, this basic restaurant with a lively ambience does some of the best Beninese grub around. For travellers en route between Cotonou and northern Benin's wildlife parks, it's a welcome first taste of authentic local cuisine after the capital's hotel restaurants. Expect rice, chicken and sauces.

NIGERIA

Nigerians like their food *chop*, meaning hot and starchy. Herbs and spices are thrown around in abundance, as well as palm nut and groundnut oil. Cutlery isn't generally used – use your right hand to dine, with yam or cassava soaking up the juices of the stew.

WHAT TO EAT

Jollof
A one-pot peppery rice, cooked with palm oil and tomato, that's the proud centrepiece of many a Nigerian meal.

Banga soup
This rich stewy soup is made from palm fruits, and often contains beef. It's eaten alongside starchy *fufu*.

Pate
A northern Nigerian meal consisting of ground corn with vegetables, onions and assorted meats.

Miyan Kuka
Another northern Nigeria dish, this is a soup made from ground baobab leaves and spices.

Garri
Fermented cassava tubers, grated and formed into balls and served alongside soups and stews, or used as a thickener.

PRICE RANGES
$ less than N1500
$$ N1500–3000
$$$ N3000 or more

Tipping: 10%

ART CAFÉ

LAGOS | $$ | CAFE
282 Akin Olugbade Street, off Idowu Martins Street, Victoria Island; 811 888 8887; snacks N2000

Hung with vintage posters and mirrors, splashed with scarlet paint and with a reclaimed wood bar, the Art Café cuts a Continental dash on Victoria Island. It's a funky stop for a coffee, plus they serve pastries, chicken suya and pizza.

BOGOBIRI HOUSE

LAGOS | $$$ | NIGERIAN
9 Maitama Sule St, Ikoyi; 706 817 6454; mains N4400

This charming boutique hotel, beautifully decorated with paintings and sculptures by local artists, serves as the hub of the vibrant art and cultural scene in Lagos. The restaurant, where there is often excellent live music, serves some of the best Nigerian favourites in the city including Yoruba speciality *efo riro*, a soup with fresh tomatoes and cray fish, plus egusi melon seed soup, ofado rice and a range of meats and seafood. Bogobiri's side-street location provides a calm escape from the Lagos buzz.

CACTUS

LAGOS | $$ | BAKERY
Maroko Rd; https://cactus-lagos.business.site; mains from N1200

This place labels itself primarily as a patisserie, but it also serves up proper meals throughout the day. Breakfasts of pancakes or bacon are good, as are the pizzas, and the club sandwiches with salad and chips are simply huge – excellent value at N1800. Giant fresh juices cost N1200.

INDIGO

LAGOS | $$ | INDIAN
242b Muri Okunola St; 0805 235 9793; www.indigolagos.com; mains N1800

Subtly flavoured Indian food served in a refined atmosphere in lovely metal dishes. There's a picture window onto the traditional clay oven, where fresh bread is baked at high speed. Lots of choice for vegetarians.

TERRA KULTURE

LAGOS | $$$ | NIGERIAN
Plot 1376 Tiamiyu Savage St; 810 422 4137, https://terrafoodlounge.com; mains N4500

Close to Bar Beach, this welcoming arts centre with a high bamboo roof has a traditional restaurant which is one of the best and most attractive places to eat in town: try the catfish with pounded yam and spicy soup. There's an art gallery, a bookshop with funky crafts, literary readings and events, and a theatre.

SHIRO

LAGOS | $$$ | FUSION

'Our daily challenge is to find the highest quality ingredients, and to reinterpret traditional Nigerian recipes for guests at Terra Kulture.'
Terra Kulture

RED CONFIDENTIAL/SHUTTERSTOCK ©

3/4 Water Cooperation Road, Landmark Village, Victoria Island; 818 629 8888; mains N4000

This is an elegant spot, its dining room dominated by a stone mask sculpture: the restaurant brands itself as an 'experience', with DJ nights and cocktails as well as fine dining. Their food is an intriguing mix of Japanese, Indonesian and Thai: the sushi platters are a winner.

WAKKIS

ABUJA | $$ | INDIAN
171 Aminu Kano Cres; www.wakkis.com; mains N2800

A pointy-roofed brick building housing an excellent Indian restaurant: there's a charcoal pit in the open kitchen for cooking up tandoori classics such as spice-roasted chicken. They also create fragrant biryani specials, and there's plenty for vegetarians.

CAMEROON

Throughout Cameroon you'll find homely restaurants dishing up a starchy staple alongside grilled meat or fish and greens. Breakfast is generally a treat, with French-style pastries, fresh fruit and juices. Travellers can buy roadside snacks and sample local beer, drunk at shacks from dawn to dusk.

WHAT TO EAT

Ndole
A fragrant stew made with bitter leaves and spinach with ground nuts or peanuts, plus garlic and possibly beef, shrimp or crayfish.

Ekwang
Grated and spiced cocoyams, wrapped in leaves with dried fish or crayfish, and cooked in the pot.

Achu soup
This flavourful yellow soup contains pounded cocoyams and possibly meat, with the colour coming from palm oil.

Kati
Kati Hugely popular grilled and spiced chicken dish.

Puff puff
A street food favourite often sold alongside beans, puff puff are little flour and yeast balls, ideal for soaking up juices.

PRICE RANGES
For a main course:
$ less than CFA5,000
$$ CFA5,000–10,000
$$$ CFA10,000 or more

Tipping: 5–10%

IYA

BUEA | $$ | FUSION
Former Alliance Franco, Grand Stand; 6 65 00 10 00; www.iyabuea.com; mains CFA3000-6800

A rarity in Cameroon: a chic restaurant with warm attentive service. The minimal interior has white walls brightened with feathered hats and geometric basketwork from the northwest highlands. The menu is also traditional with a contemporary twist, featuring imaginative reinterpretations of Cameroonian standards. *Ndole* and *kati-kati* never looked – or tasted – this good.

LA FOURCHETTE

DOULA | $$$ | INTERNATIONAL
Rue Franqueville; 2 33 43 26 11; mains CFA7000-18,000

La Fourchette is a smart and tasteful option, and its menu is out of this world if you're used to the more normal Cameroonian choice of chicken or fish. Here you'll find steak tartare, grilled *zebu* fillet, goat's-cheese ravioli and stuffed crab, with prices to match. Service is charmingly formal: you should dress to impress and booking ahead is a good idea.

SAGA AFRICAN RESTAURANT

DOULA | $$ | AFRICAN
Blvd de la Liberté; 2 33 42 23 81; mains CFA4000-7500

Atmospheric and upmarket, Saga offers an interesting mix of African dishes with some local classics such as *ndole*, plus pizza, Chinese dishes and pasta. It's nicely decked out, with an open-air area at the front and a cool glass-fronted dining room behind.

AUBERGE DU PHARE

KRIBI | $$ | CAMEROONIAN
Off Rte de Campo; 6 75 64 04 64; mains CFA6000

Located immediately south of beachfront paradise Kribi, this great little hotel has rooms opening onto a palm-edged pool and beach. Its waterfront restaurant with sunset views is excellent, serving shrimp cooked in coconut milk and other fishy treats such as barracuda, sea bass and calamari. Wash it down with one of their delicious fresh juices.

AU PLAISIR DE GOUT

KRIBI | $$$ | FRENCH/ITALIAN
Rte de Campo; 6 75 08 08 45; www.auplaisirdugout.com; mains CFA8000–16,500

A gorgeous beachfront place with a wooden terrace perched over the sands. Au Plaisir de Gout dishes up fine French food, including crevettes, calamari and grilled fish: they also have a wood fired oven for pizzas. Sweets include cholate fondant and tarte aux pommes.

LA PAILLOTE

YAOUNDÉ | $$ | VIETNAMESE
Rue Joseph Essono Balla; mains CFA3500-6500

This stylish Vietnamese restaurant has a charming shaded terrace and a smart dining room inside, both of which attract a loyal crowd of Yaoundé expats. The dishes are delicious and service is excellent; try their spring rolls, tempura shrimp, caramelised pork or lemon grass beef and round things off with an iced coffee.

'Saga offers an interesting mix of African dishes with some local classics such as *ndole*.'
Saga African Restaurant

CALAFATAS

YAOUNDÉ | $ | BAKERY
Rue de Nachtigal; 2 22 23 17 29; www.calafatas.com; baked goods CFA200-2000

This historic place is part of the cultural fabric of Cameroon's capital. Concealed in a synthetic wooden cabin but founded way back in 1935, it is Yaoundé's best bakery, selling scrumptious madeleines, palmiers and croissants.

LE SAFOUTIER

YAOUNDÉ | $$$ | INTERNATIONAL
Boulevard du Mai; 2 22 23 36 46; buffet from CFA10,000

Named for Cameroon's safou fruit tree and located in the swish Hilton hotel overlooking their gardens, this swish modern place is a good bet for its generous international buffets at breakfast, lunch and dinner. It's not the place to catch any local flavours, but if you're missing pastries, pizza or creamy French desserts then it will hit the spot.

EQUATORIAL GUINEA

Eating in Equatorial Guinea, spread across mainland Rio Muni and five scattered Atlantic islands, is varied, but it's fair to say the restaurant scene is minimal outside the island-based capital, Malabo, and the mainland hub, Bata. Spanish, Portuguese and French are all official languages and restaurants serves these cuisines, while fish, tropical fruit and root crops are local staples.

WHAT TO EAT

Succotash
Lima beans and vegetables sautéed with butter and herbs. This American import (thanks to slavery) is the national dish.

Nutty flavours
Chicken in peanut sauce over rice, and the condiment andok (dika nut or wild mango).

Seafood
Fish in many forms, including grilled and served with pumpkin seeds in leaves and *pepesup* (spicy fish soup). Also lobster and *bilolá* (a huge snail).

Guinea fowl paella
Combining Spanish colonial influence and game meat, which both crop up on many menus.

Staples
Cassava, yams, sweet potatoes, bananas plantains, coconuts, mangoes and various leafy greens.

PRICE RANGES

For a main course:
$ less than CFA5000
$$ CFA5000–7500
$$$ CFA7500 or more

Tipping: 10%

L'ATELIER

BIOKO ISLAND | $$$ | AFRICAN
Calle Waiso, Malabo; 222 000 030; www.mvmlatelier.wixsite.com/mvmlatelier; mains from CFA7500

All wood, brick and leopard print, this modish restaurant, bar and cabaret lounge is the place to be seen. The menu features international dishes and tastes from mainland West Africa, including Cameroonian *ndolé* (peanut stew), Senegalese *poulet yassa* (grilled chicken in lemon sauce with onions) and Ivorian *kedjenou pintade* (guinea fowl with peppers and tomatoes).

LA LUNA COMPLEX

BIOKO ISLAND | $$$ | INTERNATIONAL
Calle de Argelia, Malabo; 333 096 096; www.lalunamalabo.com; mains from CFA7500

Superb sea views from the wide terrace complement good food, ranging from smoked salmon tagliatelle and king prawns to duck breast and vegetable couscous. The menu is mostly French with a few African options, including shrimp *ndolé*. There's a *menú del día*, Sunday buffet, live music on Friday and Saturday nights, daily happy hour and, the clincher, a swimming pool.

RESTAURANTE LE BOUKAROU

RIO MUNI | $$ | SEAFOOD
Hotel Carmen, Carretera del Aeropuerto, Bata; 222 254 473; www.facebook.com/batahotelcarmen; mains from CFA5000

Restaurants and beach clubs come and go in Bata, but Boukarou has become a favourite for its classic seafood, tiki bar, pool and beach combo.

GABON

Libreville and Port-Gentil, Gabon's coastal centres, have a selection of restaurants serving both local and European flavours, with croissants and café au lait widely available in this bastion of Françafrique. The Gabonese typically eat simple dishes of fish or meat (beware bushmeat upcountry), sauce and stewed veg or a staple such as cassava or yam.

WHAT TO EAT

Seafood
Poisson braisé (bass or redfish braised with chilli) with rice, *bouillon de poisson* (fish stew), *poisson salé* (salted cod stew) and *crabes farcis* (stuffed crab).

Sauces
Gabon's beloved *nyemboué* (crushed palm nuts) or *odika* (crushed acacia seeds, known as 'chocolate').

Fruit and veg
Okra, spinach and palm oil are widely eaten, and there are wonderful tropical fruits, especially bananas and mangoes.

Staples
Cassava (manioc) is usually pounded, mixed with water, formed into sticks and boiled. Also fried plantains, yams and rice.

PRICE RANGES
For a main course:
$ less than CFA5000
$$ CFA5000–9000
$$$ CFA9000 or more

Tipping: 10% in upmarket restaurants

LE BISTROT

PORT-GENTIL | $$ | FRENCH
Ave Savorgnan de Brazza; 062 67 61 39; www.facebook.com/lebistrotpog; mains from CFA9000

Funky decor, friendly staff, a lovely garden terrace and a cool interior make this the best find in Gabon's second city. Add to that the excellent food and it's hard to keep away. Try the succulent *coupé-coupé* (cubed fillet of beef) or good fresh salads and pastas. The ambience remains relaxed despite the occasional prospectors gassing away and sealing oil deals over Régab beers.

L'ODIKA

LIBREVILLE | $$$ | AFRICAN
Blvd Joseph Deemin, Quartier Louis; 01 73 69 20; mains from CFA8000

This lovely colonial-style veranda restaurant in the heart of the capital's nightlife hub is very attractive. You'll find tempting dishes such as beef *ndolé* (a Cameroonian dish with peanuts, spices and ndolé bitter leaves), *colombo du porc* (lightly spiced Mauritian pork dish) and seafood brochettes with odika sauce. Polished timber floors, fresh flowers and local art on the walls complete the picture.

LA DOLCE VITA

LIBREVILLE | $$ | ITALIAN
Port Môle; 01 72 42 38; www.facebook.com/ladolcevitalibreville; mains from CFA7000

Ocean views, a great bar, and fabulous seafood, pastas and pizzas make this local institution within the passenger port a Libreville favourite. Good specials (including the time-honoured three-course lunch menu), friendly staff and huge portions keep people coming back again and again. Try the skewered prawns grilled over a wood fire. Turning pizzas since 1996, it has overcome the drawback of its somewhat spooky alleyway location and opened two more branches.

SÃO TOMÉ & PRÍNCIPE

This tropical island nation's best restaurants offer a sophisticated fusion of local and European flavours, underpinned by super-fresh seafood and produce. Meat is limited to the chickens, goats and pigs you see wandering around villages, but few diners complain amid all the fresh barracuda, bananas and breadfruit.

WHAT TO EAT

Fish
Types include many pelagic species, such as sailfish, wahoo, rainbow runner and barracuda, often served as a thick grilled steak.

Seafood
Generally served with boiled vegetables and fried banana or breadfruit chips, forming the most common restaurant meal.

Calulú
The traditional São Toméan dish, a stew of smoked fish and vegetables, takes five hours to prepare.

Tropical fruit
Banana, papaya, pineapple, starfruit, guava, jackfruit, mango and more exotic specimens abound, particularly at breakfast.

PRICE RANGES

For main dishes:
$ less €5
$$ €5–10
$$$ €10 or more

Tipping: Not customary, but 5% goes a long way locally

ROÇA SÃO JOÃO

SÃO TOMÉ | $$$ | FUSION

EN-2, São João dos Angolares, Southern Coast; 992 9475; www.facebook.com/rocasaojoao; tasting menu €25

This well-known restaurant, an ever-popular weekend drive from São Tomé city, occupies a sprawling deck at a classic plantation house. The food is a mélange of European, African and São Toméan tastes, best when it sticks to creative takes on local fare. Run by TV chef João Carlos Silva, it's the perfect lunch stop if you're heading south.

PAPA FIGO

SÃO TOMÉ | $$ | SEAFOOD

Cnr Aves das Nações Unidas & Kwame Nkrumah, São Tomé city; 222 7261; www.facebook.com/papafigo.st; mains Db150,000-300,000

This charming and well-kept tin-roofed patio restaurant is laid-back in style, but no slouch in the kitchen. Everything on the menu has an interesting new twist. The thick fish steaks are world class: don't miss the barracuda. Tasty sides and special drinks round out a great seafood meal, while pizza and steaks also get a delicious makeover.

BOM BOM RESORT

PRÍNCIPE | $$$ | INTERNATIONAL

Bom Bom; 996 9990; www.bombomprincipe.com; menu €30

While the term 'tropical paradise' is highly overused, it certainly applies to Bom Bom's golden sand and swaying palms. The resort has an extraordinary location on a coastal peninsula, connected to tiny Bom Bom island, where the excellent farm-to-table bar-restaurant is, by a long wooden bridge flanked by two gorgeous beaches.

REPUBLIC OF CONGO

If you eat out in Brazzaville or Pointe-Noire you'll have an interesting choice of local and international cuisines. Northern Congolese are meat eaters (sadly, often bushmeat) while southern Congolese love their fish. Both get their protein almost exclusively from cassava.

WHAT TO EAT

Moambe chicken
Republic of Congo's national dish is chicken cooked in a sauce made from the pericarp of palm nuts to which peanut butter is normally added.

Fufu
A thick dough made from cassava or maize flour mixed with green plantain and then dipped in a spicy sauce or peanut soup.

Goat stew
A traditional main course in Congo, normally served with *fufu* or cassava.

Pili pili
Fiery chilli sauce, the accompaniment to most Congolese meals.

Cassava
Also known as manioc, cassava is a staple food in Congo and is normally cut into cubes and cooked in stews.

PRICE RANGES
For main dishes:
$ less than CFA6000
$$ CFA6000–12,000
$$$ CFA12,000 or more

Tipping: 5–10%

ILYS

BRAZZAVILLE | $$ | CONGOLESE

Rue Mouléṅda, Plateau des 15 Ans; 04 411 6863; www.facebook.com/ilysrestaurant; mains CFA7000-15,000

This little-known, low-key Brazzaville oasis offers Congolese, Senegalese and European dishes from its very unlikely location on a sandy backstreet. Dishes include a superb *bouillon sauvage*, a stew of several different fish, as well as *n'goki à la moambe*, pieces of crocodile in palm-and-mushroom sauce.

MAMI WATA

BRAZZAVILLE | $$$ | INTERNATIONAL

La Corniche; 05 534 2879; www.facebook.com/mamiwatarestaurant; mains CFA7,000-16,000

Hands down Brazza's finest restaurant, the 'Mermaid' has the best and breeziest river terrace in town, with truly epic views across the mighty Congo River from your table. Its Italian- and French-leaning menu attracts a wealthy crowd of locals and expats, but it also has an excellent value three-course lunch menu served daily. Try the *porc roti à la moutarde*, the fatoush or the wood-fired pizza.

IL PEPE NERO

POINTE-NOIRE | $$ | ITALIAN

Ave de l'Emeraude; 05 030 6467; mains 9000-15,000CFA

A sleek and stylish garden with tables scattered across a terrace await you at this Italian restaurant, which is certainly one of Pointe-Noire's best and a favourite for expats who crowd the place at lunch. Dinner is a rather quieter affair, but the traditional Italian home cooking is worth coming for at any time of day. Don't miss the crab and avocado salad or the shrimp tagliatelle.

DEMOCRATIC REPUBLIC OF CONGO

Despite its myriad problems, the DRC enjoys some of Central Africa's best cuisine, and those on a quest to discover some of the least known flavours and spiciest dishes on the continent will enjoy exploring the restaurants of Kinshasa and Goma.

WHAT TO EAT

Fufu
A thick dough made from cassava or maize flour mixed with green plantain and then dipped in a spicy sauce or peanut soup.

Poulet à la moambé
Chicken served in a sauce made from the outer layer of palm nuts.

Pili pili
This fiery chilli sauce is the accompaniment to most Congolese meals.

Goat stew
A traditional main course in the DRC, normally served with *fufu* or cassava.

Cassava
Also known as manioc, cassava is the staple food for most people in Congo and is normally cut into cubes and cooked in stews.

PRICE RANGES
For main dishes:
$ less than US$10
$$ US$10–20
$$$ US$20 or more

Tipping: 5–7% in smarter restaurants only

CHEZ FLORE

KINSHASA| $$ | CONGOLESE
Ave Tombalbaye; 970 404 777; mains US$12-20

You can expect to wait a while for your food at this Kinshasa institution, but if you're looking for a Congolese restaurant with a local crowd, this is it. The friendly staff will explain the large menu, in Lingala for the most part, and you can enjoy the enormous portions of dishes such as whole fish cooked in cassava and pumpkin leaves.

A CASA MIA

KINSHASA | $$$ | ITALIAN
70b Ave Uvira; 084 035 5657; mains US$20-35

A very refined option that is hugely popular with Kinshasa's foreign community, A Casa Mia has a gorgeous ornamental pool on its front terrace, and a dining room in the back that's half-open to the elements. The top-notch menu features superb wood-fired pizzas, wonderful pastas and fresh ingredients flown in from Italy – where else can you eat burrata in the Congo?

LE CHALET

GOMA | $$$ | INTERNATIONAL
Ave de la Paix; 011 261 8235; mains US$20-40

It's hard to imagine anything further from the chaos of downtown Goma than Le Chalet, a tranquil oasis of tropical gardens on a strip of super-exclusive lakeshore favoured by the DRC political classes. The interesting menu runs beyond the standard meat dishes, with excellent wood-fired pizza and good set-meal offers.

WHAT TO EAT

Seafood
Dishes making the most of fresh catches include *mufete* (freshwater tilapia stuffed with onions and lemon) and *calulu de peixe* (stew of fish, okra, palm oil and vegetables).

Funge
Cassava flour porridge, the traditional local staple.

Moamba de galinha
Spicy stew of chicken, chilli, okra, vegetables, garlic and red palm oil (or peanut sauce), normally served with *funge*.

Feijoada
This Portuguese bean stew with pork chunks was invented by slaves on the Brazilian plantations, who added their occasional meat rations to the staples of beans and rice.

PRICE RANGES
For a main course:
$ less than KW5000
$$ KW5000–10,000
$$$ KW10,000 or more

Tipping: 10% maximum in upmarket restaurants

ANGOLA

As well as typical African dishes of a starchy staple with sauce, Angolan cuisine has Portuguese influence dating back to the colonial era. The best restaurants are found in the coastal capital, Luanda, with a few more in the southern tourist town of Lubango.

CAFE DEL MAR

ILHA DE LUANDA | $$$ | INTERNATIONAL

Av Murtala Mohamed; 923 581 333; www.coconutsluanda.co.ao; meal with drinks US$100

On a typical summer weekend, Luanda locals head out of town to Ilha de Luanda, the spindly strip of land across Luanda Bay from the city. Casually chic Cafe del Mar is the most popular of the restaurants lining the beaches here, with a glamorous crowd of affluent Angolans dining on seafood, steak and chips and other international dishes. It's pricey but certainly worth the trip for a cocktail in the Atlantic breeze.

PIMMS

LUANDA | $$$ | PORTUGUESE

Rua Emílio M'Bidi 112; 926 648 028; www.pimmsangola.com; mains KW10,000-19,000

This upmarket Portuguese restaurant has been going since 2000, which means it has witnessed the end of the Angolan civil war followed by Luanda's oil boom and more recent decline. With a formal dining room patronised by businessmen at lunchtime, it's the place to try classic Portuguese dishes such as *bacalhau* (dried and salted cod) and *feijoada*. Both are popular throughout Portugal and its former colonies.

GALERIA DOS PÃES

TALATONA | $$ | PIZZA

Via A2; 949 838 641; www.facebook.com/gpcluanda; pizzas KW5000

Apart from the beach, the only place that can draw most Luandans out of town is the city's new extension, Talatona. Being a pizzeria, the smart 'Bread Gallery' is an expat hangout of note. The expat community may have shrunk since the end of the Angolan capital's boom, but this local institution isn't going anywhere. Humongous pizzas, seafood dishes and cold beers keep the regulars coming back.

NAMIBIA

Namibia may be mostly desert but it conjures up many ingredients and cuisines from its parched terrain. Hit the *konditoreien* (cake shops) in Windhoek and Swakopmund, the country's best culinary destinations, to taste sweet German and Afrikaner inventions. Fish, steaks and game abound on restaurant menus.

WHAT TO EAT

Meat and fish
Atlantic fish, including kingklip and kabeljou, and game meats, such as eland, oryx (gemsbok) and kudu.

Local produce
Gem squash, varieties of pumpkin such as butternut squash, oranges, and papayas served with a squeeze of lemon or lime.

Pastries
German *Apfelstrudel*, *Sachertorte* and *Schwartzwälder Kirschtorte* (Black Forest cake), and the Afrikaners' sweet *koeksesters* (small doughnuts dripping with honey) and *melktert* (milk tart).

Traditional staples
Oshifima, a dough-like paste made from millet, usually served with stew; *oshiwambo*, a combination of spinach and beef; and mealie pap, maize porridge.

PRICE RANGES
For a main course:
$ less than N$75
$$ N$75–150
$$$ N$150 or more

Tipping: 10–15%

THE RAFT RESTAURANT

WALVIS BAY | $$ | SEAFOOD
Esplanade; 064-204877; www.facebook.com/theraftrestaurant; mains N$77-227

This Walvis Bay landmark sits on stilts offshore, and has a great front-row view of the ducks, pelicans and flamingos. Here you can expect high-quality meats and seafood, as well as pizzas, burgers, spectacular sunsets and ocean views. The high-ceilinged, beamed interior would be appealing even if it wasn't suspended above the tide.

AS FOOD STUDIO/SHUTTERSTOCK ©

ANCHORS @ THE JETTY

WALVIS BAY | $$ | INTERNATIONAL
Esplanade, Waterfront; 064-205762; www.anchors-the-jetty-restaurant.business.site; mains from N$100-175

The food is good at the Anchor but the real attraction is the location overlooking the water. It makes a lovely spot for lunch or dinner, a Namib Dunes craft beer or a cocktail, with waterside tables watching boats bob in the bay. Seafood dominates the menu, but there are lots of other choices, from sticky spare ribs and flame-grilled rump steak to burgers and chicken livers.

ENOTECA RESTAURANT

SWAKOPMUND | $$ | INTERNATIONAL
Sam's Giardino Hotel, 89 Anton Lubowski Ave; 064-403210; www.giardinonamibia.com; dinner N$280

Sam's Giardino Hotel is a wonderfully personal place in the backstreets emphasising superb wines, fine cigars and relaxing in the rose garden. The daily five-course gourmet dinner, inspired by Swiss and other continental European cuisine, incorporates fresh and seasonal regional produce, including Atlantic fish, green asparagus from the Swakop River Valley, fruit from local and South African orchards, and herbs from Sam's gardens.

THE TUG

SWAKOPMUND | $$$ | SEAFOOD
Arnold Schad Promenade, off Strand St; 064-402356; www.the-tug.com; mains N$145-255

Housed in the beached tugboat Danie Hugo near the jetty, the Tug has been an obligatory destination for Swakopmund restaurant-goer for decades. Regarded by many as the best restaurant in town, it's an atmospheric, upmarket choice for meat and seafood, though a sundowner cocktail with oysters from nearby Walvis Bay will do just fine.

LEO'S AT THE CASTLE

WINDHOEK | $$$ | INTERNATIONAL
Hotel Heinitzburg, 22 Heinitzburg St; 061-249597; www.heinitzburg.com; mains N$250

Leo's has a regal setting in Heinitzburg Castle, built by Count von Schwerin for his fiancé in 1914, and welcomes guests to its stylish dining room with chandeliers and views across the Namibian capital. The formal settings of bone china and polished crystal glassware are almost as extravagant as the food itself, which spans cuisines and continents, land and sea.

'Nestled between the cold Atlantic Ocean and the harsh Namibian coastline, dining here takes you on a rustic culinary journey.'
The Tug, Swakopmund

COURTESY LEO'S AT THE CASTLE

PURPLE FIG BISTRO

GROOTFONTEIN | $$ | INTERNATIONAL
19 Hage Geingob St; 081 124 2802; www.facebook.com/purplefigbistro; mains N$50-120

In the remote eastern town of Grootfontein, this casual country bistro is a welcome sight for dust-caked travellers. Eat under the eponymous fig tree or in the purple interior. Light meals take the form of salads, wraps and toasted sandwiches, but there are also burgers, steaks and pancakes. Servings are large, staff are friendly and it's easily the best place to eat in town. Next stop Etosha National Park!

SOUTH AFRICA

South African food is as diverse as the rainbow nation's people, ranging from African staples such as mealie pap (maize porridge) to Cape Malay cuisine's mix of Asian spices and Dutch heartiness. One culinary ritual that's as pervasive as supporting the Springboks is firing up the braai (barbecue), known as *shisha nyama* in townships. Culinary tours of the townships or Cape Town's Bo-Kaap, traditionally the Cape Malay area, are a fun experience.

WHAT TO EAT

Braaivleis
Braaied meat: a steak, snoek or *sosaties* (spiced meat skewers) with grilled sides including mealies (corn cobs), sweet potatoes, *roosterkoek* bread and *braaibroodjies* (cheese, tomato and onion sandwiches).

Bobotie
A sweet and spicy Cape Malay dish of curried mince with raisins, topped with beaten egg baked to a crust.

Boerewors
Spicy 'farmer's sausage', another braai staple. Try the meat in dried form as *dröewors* or opt for leaner jerky-like biltong.

Melktert
Delicious dessert include milk tart, a light, cinnamon-dusted custard pie, and coconut-sprinkled dough *koeksisters*.

PRICE RANGES
For a main course:
$ less than R100
$$ R100–200
$$$ R200 or more

Tipping: 10–15%

CHEF'S WAREHOUSE & CANTEEN

CAPE TOWN | $$$ | TAPAS
Heritage Sq, 92 Bree St; 021-422 0128; www.chefswarehouse.co.za; tapas for 2 people R800

This restaurant and culinary shop serves a generous spread of small plates from chef Liam Tomlin and his talented crew. Flavours zip around the world, from a squid with a tangy Vietnamese salad to comforting *coq au vin*. Capetonian chefs come here to shop for ingredients and kitchen items, so diners can browse the shop afterwards for a great selection of cookbooks and other culinary treats.

KYOTO GARDEN

CAPE TOWN | $$$ | JAPANESE
11 Lower Kloof Nek Rd, Tamboerskloof; 021-422 2001; www.kyotogarden.co.za; mains R195-260

Beechwood furnishings and subtle lighting lend a calm, Zen-like air to this superior Japanese restaurant with an expert chef turning out sushi, sashimi and tempura, as well as mains from the land and sea. Splurge on the sea urchin and try their peppy Asian Mary cocktail.

KITCHEN DELI

CAPE TOWN | $ | DELI
111 Sir Lowry Rd, Woodstock; 021-462 2201; www.lovethekitchen.co.za; sandwiches & salads R60-75

Of all the swanky restaurants in Cape Town, it was in this little charmer that Michelle Obama lunched in 2011, proving the ex-First Lady has excellent taste. Tuck into plates of divine salads, rustic sandwiches made with love, and sweet treats with tea served from china teapots. The eclectically decorated deli is Woodstuck's best lunch choice, so come before 11.30am or after 2pm to avoid the midday rush.

LAPO'S KITCHEN

CAPE TOWN | $$$ | ITALIAN
13 Boundary Rd, Newlands; 071 804 7181; www.laposkitchen.com; 6-course dinner R690

Passionate Italian chef Lapo Magni hosts a Friday supper club, with seating at one long table in an atmospheric 19th-century watermill on the Liesbeek River. Recipes are mostly Italian, but the spotlight is firmly on sustainably sourced local produce, and his introductions to each course are a big part of the special and inspiring evening. Tapas plates also come out for Lazy Sundays in summer.

TAUREN STEAK RANCH

SPRINGBOK | $$ | STEAK
2 Hospital St; 027-712 2717; mains R70-180

Meat-lovers rejoice: Tauren serves steaks weighing up to a kilogram, with a host of delectable sauces. The menu also features burgers, a few vegetarian choices and pizzas with toppings including biltong and boerewors

'We are breaking down the barriers between chef, server and customer, creating a unique space where openness and interaction are not only encouraged, but celebrated.'
Lapo Magni, Lapo's Kitchen

(farmer's sausage). The ambience is country-relaxed, with *boeremusiek* on the stereo and the happy hum of contented diners in the air.

HICKORY SHACK

THE OVERBERG | $$ | BARBECUE
N2, Elgin Valley; 021-300 1396; www.hickoryshack.co.za; mains R95-185

This country ranch is more barbecue than braai, with its Texan technique of smoking dry-rub meat in a pit of local woods and organic chips. The magic happens slowly in the smokehouse, where the pit crew toils for hours to cook ribs, brisket, wings and pulled pork to perfection, with sauces added afterwards. Downhome sides include homemade baked beans, and for brunch there's Redneck Ranch Eggs and Texan-style link sausages.

LA PETITE COLOMBE

FRANSCHHOEK | $$$ | FUSION
Leeu Estates, Dassenberg; 021-202 3395; www.lapetitecolombe.com; dinner menu with/without wine R2650/1550

After a stint in the Cape Winelands' most elegant town, the Franschhoek branch of Cape Town's award-winning restaurant has moved out of town to a garden setting with river and mountain views. Diners can opt to pair each of the several courses on the French-inspired chef's menu with a different local wine. Vegetarian and reduced lunch menus are also offered.

COURTESY MUNDO VIDA

101 MEADE

GARDEN ROUTE | $$ | FUSION
101 Meade St, George; 044-874 0343; www.101meade.co.za; mains R125-250

Whether you're after freshly baked bread and good coffee to start the day, inventive tapas to share, a gourmet sandwich for lunch or heavier evening fare, such as Kashmir lamb curry or mushroom ravioli, the excellent cuisine and minimalist decor make this George's top eating option.

ILE DE PAIN

GARDEN ROUTE | $$ | CAFE
Thesen Island, Knysna; 044-302 5705; www.iledepain.co.za; mains R55-115

Ile de Pain is a wildly popular bakery and cafe that's as much a hit with locals as it is with tourists. There's an excellent breakfast menu, fresh salads, some inventive lunch specials and quite a bit for vegetarians. Expect to queue for a table at weekends or in peak season – reservations are not accepted.

REMO'S

PORT ELIZABETH | $ | ITALIAN
2 Alabaster St, Baakens Valley; 060 998 0789; www.remos.co.za; mains R50-115

What was once a warehouse in a derelict area is now a snazzy restaurant with an industrial-chic decor. One of South Africa's best Italian restaurants, it's quite a find. Start with fabulous *antipasti* (starters), then delve into the amazing pastas, salads or wood-fired pizzas. Don't miss the homemade pastries for dessert (the chocolate croissant is particularly good). There's also first-rate coffee, vitamin-packed fruit juices and splendid breakfasts.

SEVEN ON RESTAURANT

BLOEMFONTEIN | $$ | INTERNATIONAL
2 Waverley Rd; 051-447 7928; www.facebook.com/sevenOnKellner; mains R80-165

Previously located at 7 Kellner St and called Seven on Kellner, this broad-ranging restaurant has retained its relaxed, intimate atmosphere, making it a date-night favourite in Bloem. Poultry, meat and seafood dishes are expertly prepared, as are the pasta, pizza and vegetarian choices such as Indian chickpea curry.

O'S RESTAURANT

PARYS | $$ | INTERNATIONAL
1 de Villiers St; 056-811 3683; www.osrestaurant.co.za; mains R95-200

***P360-1:** Egusi soup and yam; Banga soup. **P370-1:** Koeksesters; Leo's at the Castle. **This page:** Dish from Mundo Vida. **Opposite page:** Clementines Restaurant.*

In this stylish, thoroughly satisfying restaurant down by the Vaal River, you might enjoy some deep-fried calamari strips followed by Portuguese-style peri-peri steak, or fillet flambé prepared at your table. The pizza menu is also worth a browse, and there are some kids' meals, too. Dine in the elegant interior, out on the river deck or amid the foliage in the gorgeous garden.

CAFÉ CHOCOLAT

FICKSBURG | $ | CAFE

9 Fontein St; 082 920 5551; mains R65-140

Part restaurant, part chocolate factory and part theatre, this is Ficksburg's top eatery and de facto cultural centre. Popular items include homemade pastas, pizzas and Maluti trout, and there's a good selection of deli items and fresh, homegrown salads. In the chocolate shop, the owners whip up Belgian truffles with all-organic ingredients, and have created the brand McKinley Chocolates. Upstairs, Gin-ger Bar offers more than 50 different gins.

COURTESY CLEMENTINES RESTAURANT

CALEXICO VINYL LOUNGE AND RESTAURANT

JOHANNESBURG | $$ | TEX-MEX

44 Stanley Ave; 011-482 5791; www.calexico.co.za; mains R88-295

A California-inspired Tex-Mex restaurant with a hint of craft beer and vinyl mixed in. The mix is delightful. The simple menu (nachos, ribs, quesadillas), the album covers, the neon signs, the Lucha Libre mural and the sprawling outdoor seating area combine to create the best vibe in the 44 Stanley complex.

URBANOLOGI

JOHANNESBURG | $ | FUSION

Mad Giant, 1 Fox St; 011-492 1399; www.urbanologi.co.za; mains R60-120

The fabulous Mad Giant brewery's restaurant serves an inventive range of delicious Asian-inspired tapas dishes. You can't go wrong with taste sensations such as the Yakitori chicken with spicy chimichurri sauce, which have suggested beer pairings. The setting in the 1 Fox Precinct, a regenerated gold-rush mining camp and tram depot, makes this a vibey spot for a bite and a pint of Killer Hop pale ale.

WHERE TO DRINK...

CRAFT BEER

Banana Jam, Cape Town
This Caribbean-themed temple to craft beer is worth the trip to Cape Town's Southern Suburbs for over 100 draught and bottled beers.

Mad Giant, Johannesburg
A sexy piece of urban regeneration in downtown Jo'burg, this brewery makes insanely drinkable beers with mad names such as Jozi Carjacker.

Tuk Tuk Microbrewery, Franschhoek
Cape Winelands microbrewery with permanent house beers on tap, ever-changing experimental brews and beers from Cape Brewing Company in Paarl.

Clarens Brewery, Clarens
In the Free State's prettiest town, sample permanent and seasonal beers in cosy surrounds.

GROUNDED AT ECHO

PRETORIA | $ | CAFE

Shop 1, 353 24th Ave, Villiera; 012-329 0159; www.groundedat.co.za; sandwiches & salads R60-100

It's easy to love this design-savvy cafe run by the nonprofit Echo Youth Development. It's a great spot for breakfast, with a variety of granolas alongside some tempting egg dishes. The coffee and tea are top class, as are the immunity-boosting winter smoothies and shots. A wall of the cafe acts as a gallery for local artists and next door it also runs a co-working space.

FERMIER

PRETORIA | $$$ | INTERNATIONAL

Karoo Yard, 141 Lynwood Rd, The Willows; 076 072 5261; www.fermierrestaurant.com; menu R650, wine pairing R350

Some of South Africa's best contemporary cooking is being served in a large mud-walled and tin-roofed shed in the east of Pretoria. Chef Adriaan Maree conjures up a fabulous multiple-course, three-hour-long culinary journey with an underpinning ethos of minimum food waste, sustainability and a celebration of fine local produce. The series of small, creative dishes is magnificent.

CLEMENTINES RESTAURANT

CLARENS | $$ | INTERNATIONAL

cnr Van Zyl & Church Sts; 058-256 1616; www.clementines.co.za; mains R85-195

The food at this souped-up country kitchen tastes just as good as it looks on the gourmet international menu, featuring everything from rainbow trout to Cape Malay lamb curry. Professional service, intimate ambience, local craft beer, veggie pasta dishes and daily specials on the blackboard are more perks.

WILD FIG TREE

SABIE | $$ | SOUTH AFRICAN

cnr Main & Louis Trichardt Sts; 013-764 2239; www.facebook.com/wildfigtreesabie; mains R70-170

There's a meat-driven menu and a warm atmosphere here, amid candles, wildlife photos and artworks. It's a great place to sample traditional South African dishes, especially game meat – from ostrich kebabs to *bobotie*. Ploughman's or trout platter, pizzas, tramezzinis and toasted sandwiches are also on offer. Spontaneous song and dance from the staff, and good selections of South African wines and craft beers, ensure a fun evening.

POTLUCK BOSKOMBUIS

BLYDE RIVER CANYON | $$ | SOUTH AFRICAN

off Rte 532; 071 539 6773; www.facebook.com/littleboskombuis; mains R95-185

This 'bush kitchen' is hidden down by the Treur River – diners must look out for a South African flag and follow a red-dirt track to find it. At the end of the road is a makeshift shelter beneath gnarly boulders and trees decorated with animal skulls, its terrace nudging the rocks in the river. Enjoy a cold craft beer and dishes from steaks to beef *potjie* stew, cooked without electricity.

MUNDO VIDA

KWAZULU-NATAL NORTH COAST | $$ | INTERNATIONAL

1 South Beach Rd, uMdloti Beach; 031-568 2286; www.mundovida.co.za; mains R100-250

Enjoy seafood and bistro dishes in unpretentious surroundings at this excellent coastal restaurant, where traditional recipes have a modern twist. For a taste of everything fishy try the seafood medley or, if your pockets are deep, tuck into the deluxe version.

'The idea is to close the gap between produce, farm, and the final product. Guests can see the produce growing, where it comes from and the versatility of each product.'

Adriaan Maree, Fermier

KUKA CAFÉ

HAZYVIEW | $$ | INTERNATIONAL

Perry's Bridge Centre, Rte 40; 013-737 6957; www.kukasoup.co.za; mains R85-200

Its blue-grey walls hung with artwork and cage lampshades, Kuka's glass doors open onto a terrace decorated with fairy lights. It's a contemporary setting for cocktails, tapas, pizzas, seafood, sushi and grills; house specials include slow-braised springbok shank and kudu fillet. The house Kuka lager is pleasant drop and there's a lunch menu featuring burgers, wraps and sandwiches. A pleasant surprise in the lowveld just outside Kruger National Park.

TSHOKWANE

KRUGER NATIONAL PARK | $ | INTERNATIONAL

Tshokwane Picnic Site, Satara-Skukuza Rd; 012-428 9111; www.sanparks.org/parks/kruger; mains R30-70

The addition of a restaurant has transformed this attractive picnic spot into a popular stopover on the drive between Kruger National Park's central and southern sections. Set in an open-sided, thatched lapa, the restaurant serves light meals, such as boerewors roll or kudu wors, jaffles and homemade pies, as well as other sausages off the braai and salads.

LESOTHO

The world's highest country, with the loftiest low point at 1380m, survives on trout from the mountain rivers, starchy staples, chicken and beef. Although Basotho shepherds are a common sight, sheep and goats are farmed more for their wool than meat. Good restaurants are exclusively found in Maseru and the better lodges.

WHAT TO EAT

Trout
Caught in the Highlands and, in good restaurants, served with accompaniments such as lemon and caper butter sauce.

Oxtail
Tastes much better than it sounds when slow-braised and served in red wine gravy.

Motoho
Fermented sorghum porridge. Also the maize equivalent, mealie pap.

Maluti
The national lager, brewed in capital Maseru, with a logo featuring the conical Basotho hat.

Home-brewed beer
If you have a strong constitution. Watch for coloured flags hung in villages – white is for sorghum beer, yellow for ginger sorghum beer.

PRICE RANGES
For a main course:
$ less than M75
$$ M75–150
$$$ M150 or more

Tipping: 10–15%

NO.7 RESTAURANT

MASERU | $$ | INTERNATIONAL
Lesotho Football for Hope Centre, Nightingale Rd; Tel 2832 0707; www.kick4life.org; dinner mains M90-130

Connected to football-focused NGO Kick4Life, No.7 pumps its profits back into Kick4Life's charitable work and the team includes young locals training for a career in hospitality. The stylish restaurant has city views and a menu fusing European sophistication with Basotho touches, offering dishes such as fillet steak and butternut risotto. There are separate pizza and burger menus, making this a vibey spot for a beer and a bite.

MALIBA LODGE

TS'EHLANYANE NATIONAL PARK | $$ | INTERNATIONAL
6361 6152; www.maliba-lodge.com; bistro mains M55-130

Amid the rugged wilderness of Ts'ehlanyane National Park, Maliba ('Madiba') is Lesotho's only five-star lodge. The excellent restaurant serves two- and three-course menus, including the likes of braised lamb shank, grilled ostrich fillet and pan-fried Lesotho Highlands trout. The walk-in bistro is a more casual affair with steaks, salads, burgers and chops on offer. Views of the snow-capped Maluti Mountains are on the menu at both.

SKY RESTAURANT

AFRISKI MOUNTAIN RESORT | $$ | INTERNATIONAL
5954 4734; www.afriski.net; mains M90-170

Overlooking the ski slopes, Africa's highest restaurant (3010m) reflects the Afriski resort's international sheen with its stylish wood finish and big red pizza oven. Choices include pizzas, burgers, steaks and a few vegetarian dishes. Admittedly the competition is not exactly stiff, but Sky is Africa's best ski resort restaurant, open year-round. During winter, there's also a lively cafe-bar at the foot of the gondola.

ESWATINI

Traditional Swazi cuisine revolves around thick porridges with meat stew or vegetables, while braais (barbecues) at minibus taxi stations churn out mealies (corn on the cob). There are several good restaurants in Mbabane and the neighbouring Ezulwini and Malkerns Valleys, serving South African and Portuguese dishes, the latter courtesy of neighbouring Mozambique.

WHAT TO EAT

Emasi
Sour milk: raw cow's milk, fermented and strained to remove the whey. In the popular dishes *emasi etinkhobe temmbila* and *emasi emabele,* it's mixed with ground mealies and ground sorghum respectively.

Umncweba
eSwatini's take on neighbouring South Africa's famous, jerky-like biltong. Also look out for *umkhunsu*, for which the meat is cooked before drying.

Mealies
Corn is king, whether as mealie pap (maize porridge), roasted cobs or *tinkhobe* (boiled cobs).

Vegetarian
You'll find plenty of bean, peanut and other legume dishes, usually offered with vegetables.

PRICE RANGES

For a main course:
$ less than E75
$$ E75–150
$$$ E150 or more

Tipping: 10–15%

EDLADLENI

MBABANE | $$ | SWAZI

Manzini/Mbabane Hwy; 2404 5743; www.edladleni.100webspace.net; mains E55-80

Delicious food, a serene setting and cracking views – if you're after an authentic Swazi experience, eDladleni is hard to beat. Charismatic owner Dolores Godeffroy is committed to reviving traditional recipes based on local produce.

RAMBLAS RESTAURANT

MBABANE | $$ | INTERNATIONAL

Mantsholo St; Tel 2404 4147; www.ramblasmbabane.com; mains E85-160

The Swazi capital's top choice for good cuisine and a buzzing ambience is just a ball's flight from the golf course. It's well worth the trip out of central Mbabane for an eclectic menu including great salads, meat dishes, pizzas, burgers and daily desserts.

LIHAWU RESTAURANT

EZULWINI VALLEY | $$$ | FUSION

Royal Villas; 2416 2042; www.lihawu.co.sz; mains E95-230

Within the swish Royal Villas resort nestles eSwatini's most elegant restaurant. The menu is Afro-fusion, with meaty signature dishes such as oxtail stew and pork belly, plus a couple of vegetarian options. The accompanying list of South African and French wines is top class and the adjoining cigar and whisky bar is another drawcard.

MALANDELA'S RESTAURANT

MALKERNS VALLEY | $$ | INTERNATIONAL

Malandela's complex, MR27; 2528 3115; www.malandelas.com; mains E80-150

The Malkerns Valley's most reliable option, the restaurant opened by farmer Peter 'Malandela' Thorne serves grilled meats, seafood dishes, frondy salads and scrumptious house desserts.

BOTSWANA

Being mostly covered by the Kalahari, Botswana's food scene is less of a highlight than its Big Five wildlife watching. Foreign visitors also generally find themselves eating international dishes in safari lodge restaurants, although there are one or two places to try Batswana dishes, including Gaborone's the Courtyard. One plate where local and international tastes converge is in the local obsession with steaks, best eaten from a braai (barbecue) under the stars.

WHAT TO EAT

Bogobe
This porridge made from *mabele* (sorghum) forms the centre of most Batswana meals. It's often replaced by imported maize meal, sometimes known by the Afrikaans name, mealie pap (or just plain pap).

Meat and vegetable sauces
Seswaa (shredded goat or lamb), *morogo* (wild spinach) and *leputshe* (wild pumpkin).

Breakfast dishes
Pathata (like an English muffin) and *megunya*, also known as fat cakes. The latter are little balls of fried dough that are like doughnuts minus the hole.

Steaks
Botswana's cattle industry is well regarded and its steaks are available in restaurants in most cities and larger towns.

PRICE RANGES
$ less than US$10
$$ US$10–20
$$$ US$20 or more

Tipping: 10%

HILARY'S

MAUN | $$ | INTERNATIONAL
off Mathiba I St; 686 1610; www.hilaryscoffeeshop.wordpress.com; breakfast P38-98, light meals P52-78

This homey place offers a choice of wonderfully earthy meals, including homemade bread, homemade lemonade, filter coffee, baked potatoes, soups and sandwiches. Ideal for vegetarians and anyone sick of greasy sausages and soggy chips, it's a welcome sight after leaving Maun Airport, gateway to the Okavango Delta.

THE PALMS

MAUN | $ | FRENCH
Sedia Riverside Hotel, Sir Seretse Khama Rd; 686 0177; http://sedia-hotel.com; mains P85-120

Head here for French and Middle Eastern cuisine in a lovely garden setting, including meze from falafel and hummus to beef kofta and pork confit. The exotic menu also features lamb or vegetable tajine, beef shawarma, pizzas and Moroccan- or Beirut-style pide. Run by a delightful French owner and driven by a far-ranging passion for new tastes, it has beautiful old fashioned décor with palm trees and a large, 18m-by-8m pool.

DUSTY DONKEY CAFE

MAUN | $ | CAFE
Airport Rd; 680 0736; breakfast P20-45, light meals P30-45

The former Wax Apple Cafe serves some of the best cappuccinos, homemade treats, and light meals from sandwiches to veggie burgers, on this side of the Okavango Delta. All are most welcome in dusty Maun, where good food is rarer than the Big Five. With a lovely casual atmosphere, the Donkey is handy for Maun Airport, 100m away.

THAMALAKANE RIVER LODGE

MAUN | $$ | INTERNATIONAL
Shorobe Rd; 680 0217; www.trlmaun.com/restaurant;

With a beautiful setting on a sun-drenched curve of the Thamalakane River, overlooking wading hippos and waving reeds (when there's enough water), Thamalakane wins in the location stakes. The boma bar-restaurant serves some of the best food in Maun, accompanied by South African wines and the sounds of the African bush. Okavango bream, seswaa and a mouth-watering fillet steak are among the chef's specials, while lighter lunches include pizzas and burgers.

OLD HOUSE

KASANE | $$ | INTERNATIONAL
President Ave; 625 2562; www.oldhousekasane.com; breakfast P50-80, light meals P40-80, mains P50-115

This open-air bar-restaurant close to the Chobe River is every bit as good as the guesthouse it inhabits. The menu contains all the usual suspects, including the best pizzas in town – perfect for a celebratory meal and cold St Louis beer after crossing the Zambezi from nearby Zambia. It's next to Kasane's quirky gold course, where warthogs are regularly spotted on the fairways.

PLANET BAOBAB

GWETA | $ | INTERNATIONAL
off A3; 021-855 0395 in South Africa; www.planetbaobab.co; meals P70-120

In the shimmering flatlands of the Makgadikgadi and Nxai Pans area, a huge concrete aardvark marks the turn-off for this inventive lodge. Planet Baobab forsakes masks and wildlife photos, replaced by a great open-air bar-restaurant filled with vintage travel posters, metal seats covered in cowhide, beer-bottle chandeliers and the like. In this former inland ocean, enjoy a sundowner at the water hole followed by a braai (barbecue) dinner beneath the giant marula tree.

'Our aim at Botswanacraft is to share culture and traditional Setswana food is a big part of that.'
Courtyard Restaurant, Gaborone

COURTYARD RESTAURANT

GABORONE | $$ | AFRICAN
Western Bypass, off Airport Rd; 392 2487; http://botswanacraft.com; mains P75-120

In the garden area at the rear of Botswanacraft, Botswana's best craft emporium, this tranquil spot serves up imaginative African cooking, including guinea-fowl pot, *seswaa sa pudi* (pounded goat) and Setswana chicken. It also offers the chance to try local staples such as oxtail stew and tripe. Salads, sandwiches, burgers and breakfasts and so on make an appearance and there's occasional live music.

CAFE DIJO

GABORONE | $$ | CAFÉ
Kgale Hill Shopping Mall, Lobatse Rd; 318 0575; www.facebook.com/CafeDijo; mains from P79

This classy but casual place is a favourite daytime haunt in Gabs. The lunch menu changes regularly, but toasted sandwiches, burgers, wraps and salads are usually on the blackboard. With Botswana's best carrot cake and great coffee, you could easily spend hours here.

CARAVELA PORTUGUESE RESTAURANT

GABORONE | $$ | PORTUGUESE
Mokgosi Close, off Independence Ave, Extension 4; 391 4284; www.thecaravela.com; mains from P79

One of Gabs' most popular expat haunts, Caravela serves up assured Mediterranean cooking in a pretty garden setting. It's close to the city centre, but tucked away in a residential corner, which adds to the happy feeling that this is a quiet legend among people in the know. Seafood, all manner of platters and dishes such as Portuguese steaks make this a terrific place to eat.

SANITAS TEA GARDEN

GABORONE | $$ | CAFE
off Samora Machel Drive, Gaborone Dam; Tel 393 1358; www.sanitas.co.bw; mains from P65

Inhabiting a corner of the capital's best plant nursery and close to the dam, this lovely and relaxed outdoor spot is popular with families. The food includes home-grown vegetables, wood-fired pizzas, light meals and made-on-site gelato. The location is certainly a lunchtime conversation starter, as Gabs locals discuss dam levels the way Brits talk about the weather.

BULL & BUSH

GABORONE | $$ | INTERNATIONAL
Off Sebone Rd; 397 5070; www.facebook.com/bullandbushbotswana; mains P55-126

This local institution, almost as old as Gabs itself, serves a smorgasbord of steaks and even manages the odd salad. Located near the famous Three Chiefs Monument, it does that trio of 19th-century heroes proud with its frontier-town atmosphere, which draws thirsty locals to the beer garden for a pizza and a pint. Entertainment and specials with names like Beer, Braai & Beats are offered most evenings.

This page: Basilico. Opposite page: Oxtail stew with sides from Courtyard Restaurant. Next spread: Dried kapenta.

BEEF BARON

GABORONE | $$ | BUFFET
Grand Palm Resort; 363 7777; www.grandpalm.bw; mains P75-215

With a name like this, there's no mystery about the menu, with the finest cuts from Botswana's healthy beef industry served in upmarket surrounds. Among these cane-backed chairs, sepia photos and wood-panelled walls, it's almost possible to forget the setting in a casino complex. The best steakhouse and fine-dining experience in Gabs.

BASILICO

GABORONE | $$ | ITALIAN
Kgalagadi Way, Extension 11; 311 1202; www.basilico.club; mains P130-180

A 500-sq-m farmhouse in Gaborone's diplomatic quarter is the setting for this restaurant and deli run by two Italian widows. Amid elegant Italian farmhouse décor, the menu features bruschettas, pizzas, pastas, meats and fish dishes, completed by Italian wines and homemade desserts and pastries. A candlelit dinner here might consist of beef carpaccio followed by seafood ravioli or Tuscan chicken and finally tiramisu.

COURTESY COURTYARD RESTAURANT

BARBARA'S BISTRO

FRANCISTOWN | $$ | INTERNATIONAL
Francistown Sports Club; 241 3737; www.facebook.com/BarbarasBistro; mains from P75

Located on Francistown's – as well as Botswana's – eastern edge, this leafy spot is a fabulous choice with 25 years of history. Barbara, the German owner, is a charismatic host and loves nothing better than to sit down and run through the specials. The food is easily Francistown's best – German specialties such as *eisbein* are recurring themes, while other European and Southern African dishes also feature. Jägermeister shots are not compulsory, but recommended.

WHERE TO EAT...

ON THE EDGE OF THE WILD

Mokolodi Nature Reserve, Gaborone
The thatched lapa among the trees is Gaborone's most atmospheric setting for a meal, with likely glimpses of zebras and giraffes.

Old Bridge Backpackers, Maun
When the Thamalakane River is flowing, this is the perfect spot to escape the heat, complete with a swimming pool.

Chobe Safari Lodge, Kasane
Between Kasane and Chobe National Park, this lodge restaurant overlooking the Chobe River has a high, breeze-friendly thatched roof.

Elephant Sands, Nata
Just off the solitary road through northwest Botswana, this poolside bar-restaurant serves a la carte daytime meals, set dinners and elephant sightings.

ZIMBABWE

With local specialities ranging from Zambezi bream to Zimbabwe's famous beef, it's possible to eat well in Zim's garden cafes and formal restaurants. International cuisine is generally on the menu, along with plentiful meat, fish and some vegetarian options. Harare, Bulawayo and Victoria Falls have the best choice of restaurants.

THE BOMA

VICTORIA FALLS | $$$ | AFRICAN

Victoria Falls Safari Lodge, Squire Cummings Rd; 083 284 3211; www.theboma.co.zw; buffet US$45

Enjoy a taste of Africa at this buffet restaurant set under a massive thatched roof. Here you can dine on smoked crocodile tail, peppered impala, Zambezi bream and wood-fired spit roasts; and the more adventurous can try a mopane worm (you'll get a certificate from the chef for your efforts). The accompanying carnival of entertainment includes traditional dancing, interactive drumming, fortune telling, face painting, hair braiding and acapella singing.

BULAWAYO CLUB

BULAWAYO | $$ | INTERNATIONAL

Cnr Eighth Ave & Fort St; 029-2881964; www.bulawayoclub.com; mains from US$8

Chandeliers, silverware, marble pillars, gleaming hardwood floors and the grand staircase might have diners thinking they need to dust off their blazer. Not to worry: this hotel restaurant's dining room may be decked out for Rhodesian high society, but the former gentlemen's club is welcoming to all. Its retro menu card offers British-style classics such as pie with gravy, chips and peas, or pavlova for dessert.

MOIRA JANE'S BLUE BIRD CAFE

MASVINGO | $ | CAFE

50 Robertson St; 0773-272473; meals from US$3

A good reason to stop by the country town of Masvingo, this attractive little garden cafe does excellent gourmet burgers, steak rolls, creamy garlic chicken and toasted sarnies. They serve good coffee from Zimbabwe's Eastern Highlands and home-baked cakes, too. There are picnic tables at the front

WHAT TO EAT

Charcoal-grilled meats
T-bone steaks, chicken or Zambezi bream served with greens and a starch, such as chips or sadza.

Sadza
A white maize meal made into either porridge or something resembling mashed potato, and served with tomato-based relishes, meat and/or gravy. Locals eat the staple with their fingers.

Exotic game meats
Try crocodile, kudu and warthog.

Fish
Trout from rivers or dams in the Eastern Highlands and bream or the whitebait-like dried kapenta, another staple, are plentiful in Lake Kariba.

Beef
Zimbabwe, once one of the world's great beef producers, still has good beef widely available.

PRICE RANGES

$ less than US$5
$$ US$5–10
$$$ US$10 or more

Tipping: 10%

or try the smart cafe decorated with old movie posters. Out the back is a second-hand clothing and goods shop to browse.

AMANZI

HARARE | $$$ | FUSION

158 Enterprise Rd, Highlands; 0242-497768; www.amanzi.co.zw/restaurant.php; mains $15-25

Amanzi is a class act and the special night out for the Zimbabwean capital. In a stunning colonial house with African decor, local art and an amazing garden, it serves delicious international fusion dishes. The outdoor patio is ridiculously atmospheric with a nearby garden waterfall and crackling fire brazier. Tapas is served all afternoon and the bar is also good. Regular events include Friday's farmers market and live music on Thursday evenings.

'The energy and vibe will captivate you the moment you arrive, when you are ceremoniously dressed in your *chitenge* (sarong) and welcomed by traditional dancers.'
The Boma

KWAMAMBO

HARARE | $$ | CAFE

40 Cork Rd, Belgravia; 078 587 5587; www.facebook.com/kwamambo; breakfast/lunch from US$6/10, coffee US$3

An attractive house-turned-restaurant with a relaxed garden setting, KwaMambo serves quality breakfasts and lunches, and brews one of the best coffees in Harare. Also here is its Tutti Gelati, serving excellent homemade gelato, and a quality craft shop. The international roster of lunch mains includes Portuguese chicken, Thai beef stir-fry, oxtail and mushroom fettuccine.

PORTUGUESE RECREATION CLUB

MUTARE | $$ | PORTUGUESE

9 Hosgood Ave; 020-61518; chicken & chips US$10

With an honours board dating to the 1950s, this old-school club was set up for the Portuguese/Mozambique community in this Eastern Highlands hub, a chorizo's throw from the Mozambican border. Unsurprisingly, the peri peri chicken here is as good as you'll get anywhere. It has an atmospheric front bar, and a busy dining area around the back with gingham tablecloths.

ZAMBIA

Food is not up there with Victoria Falls on Zambia's list of highlights, but nearby Livingstone and capital Lusaka have respectable dining scenes, while park lodge restaurants keep safarigoers happy. International staples bulk out most menus, with opportunities to try traditional Zambian dishes.

WHAT TO EAT

Nshima
This local staple is a thick maize porridge that's bland but filling. It's eaten with your hands and accompanied by beans or vegetables and a hot relish, and sometimes meat or fish.

Ifinkubala
Caterpillars, boiled, fried in oil and served tomatoes, onion and *nshima*. Also known as *ifishimu*, *vinkubala* or mopane worms. Also look out for *inswa*, flying ants, yum.

Michopo
Zambia's take on the great Southern African braai (barbecue), with grilled meat such as beef or goat served with tomatoes, onions and other sides.

Mosi
Zambian lager, named after Mosi-oa-Tunya aka Victoria Falls.

PRICE RANGES
$ less than ZMW75
$$ ZMW75–150
$$$ ZMW150 or more

Tipping: 10%

CAFE ZAMBEZI

LIVINGSTONE | $$ | AFRICAN
217 Mosi-oa-Tunya Rd; 0213-323189; www.facebook.com/cafezambezi; mains ZMW72-88

Head straight through to the courtyard, sunny by day and candlelit by night. Bursting with local flavour, the broad menu covers African favourites such as goat meat, peri-peri crocodile and caterpillars. Authentic wood-fired pizzas are a winner or sink your teeth into Zambian beef stew or aubergine-and-haloumi burgers. Its old school front coffee shop is a good breakfast spot too.

DA CANTON

LIVINGSTONE | $ | GELATO
Mosi-Oa-Tunya Rd; 0953 709666; pizza from ZMW35

While the Italian food here is tasty and authentic, it's the homemade gelato that has locals raving. The Italian owner makes all 18 flavours, including all the classics and some original concoctions. Pizzas, pastas and plenty of drinks, including cocktails, are also on the menu in the large, thatched-roof building.

GOLDEN LEAF

LIVINGSTONE | $$ | INDIAN
1174 Mosi-Oa-Tunya Rd; 0213-321266; mains ZMW55-100

As soon as those aromas hit you upon arrival, you'll realise this is the real deal for authentic Indian food. It's a good option for vegetarians, with choices including house-made paneer dishes, creamy North Indian curries and tandoori dishes. The setting in a colonial-style building, with a wraparound verandah surrounded by a garden, adds to an enjoyable meal here, as do the beers ranging from Namibian Windhoek to Stella Artois.

OLGA'S ITALIAN CORNER

LIVINGSTONE | $$ | ITALIAN
cnr Mosi-oa-Tunya & Nakatindi Rds; 0213-324160; www.olgasproject.com; pizza & pasta ZMW60-115

Olga's does authentic wood-fired thin-crust pizzas and focaccia, as well as delicious homemade pasta classics, all served under a large thatched roof. Numerous great options for vegetarians include the lasagne, and desserts range from tiramisu to gelato. Profits go to the YCTC community centre for disadvantaged youth.

MANGO TREE CAFÉ

LIVINGSTONE | $$ | CAFE
ZigZag, 693 Linda Rd, off Mosi-oa-Tunya Rd; 0213-322814; www.zigzagzambia.com/the-mango-tree-cafe; mains from ZMW75

Named after ZigZag lodge's many mango trees, the on-site cafe occupies a rustic red-brick open space with inviting couches and garden seating. It does drool-inducing homemade muffins, excellent Zambian coffee and smoothies using fresh fruit from the garden. Its changing menu of comfort food is all made from scratch, and you can expect anything from drop scones (pikelets) with bacon and maple syrup to thin-crust pizzas and burgers.

LATITUDE 15°

LUSAKA | $$$ | INTERNATIONAL
Leopards Lane, Kabulonga; 0211-268802; www.15.latitudehotels.com; dinner mains ZMW200

The capital's trendiest restaurant is part of a designer-boutique hotel-cum-art-gallery in leafy southeast Lusaka.

'We source all our fresh food from local farmers and our coffee is from one of the best coffee farms in Zambia.' *Mango Tree Café*

Grab a seat on its outdoor terrace overlooking the lawn or industrial chic interior to enjoy globally inspired, locally sourced dishes, including grilled kingklip or oxtail hot pot. There's also a luxurious pool diners can use.

RHAPSODY'S

LUSAKA | $$ | INTERNATIONAL
Circolo Italiano Di Lusaka, Showgrounds, Nangwenya Rd; 0211-256705; www.rhapsodys.co.za; mains ZWM75-235

Part of a small Southern African chain, Rhapsody's is a Lusaka go-to for breakfast, cocktails and everything in between. The menu runs the global gamut from oxtail to chicken curry, with pasta and vegetarian dishes, seafood and stir-fries thrown in. The spacious dining room with warm colours wins local fans.

THE DELI

LUSAKA | $ | CAFE
Lunzua Rd, Rhodes Park; 0211-253539; www.facebook.com/DeliZambia; mains from ZMW45

A good place to plant yourself for a few hours, with good coffee and a garden setting, supplemented by local art displays. The kitchen turns out lovely breakfasts, light meals, burgers and cakes, ensuring there's a bite here for every time of day.

MOZAMBIQUE

Mozambique's cuisine is a head-on collision of African, Indian and Portuguese influences best exemplified in the spicy piri-piri sauce: a Swahili word for a Portuguese recipe made with Mozambique grown chilli peppers. The country is especially noted for its seafood.

WHAT TO EAT

Matapa
Ground cassava leaves slow-cooked with garlic, onion, coconut milk and cashews.

Matapa de siri siri
Mozambique Island's take on the standard *matapa* recipe that substitutes the cassava leaves with a local seaweed. Prawns are sometimes added to the mix.

Galinha á Zambeziana
Chicken with a sauce of lime juice, garlic, pepper and piri-piri.

Chamusas
Samosas; triangular wedges of fried pastry, filled with meat or vegetables.

Seafood
Popular dishes include piri-piri prawns, lobster curry, crayfish and *lulas* (calamari).

PRICE RANGES
$ less than Mtc325
$$ Mtc325–650
$$$ Mtc650 or more

Tipping: 10–20% at upmarket and tourist establishments

IBO ISLAND LODGE

IBO ISLAND | $$$ | SEAFOOD
Rua Bela Vista; 21 785 2657; www.iboisland.com; mains Mtc500-1000

Part of a luxury boutique hotel – the most upmarket accommodation on Ibo Island – this place is housed in three restored 19th-century mansions in a prime setting overlooking the water near the dhow port. The food on the top-floor terrace reflects the nuances of Ibo's past (Swahili, Indian, Portuguese and African) with the primary focus being locally caught fish. Feast your eyes over honey steamed lobster and ginger crab curry.

COURTESY IBO ISLAND LODGE

RICKSHAWS CAFÉ

MOZAMBIQUE ISLAND | $$ | INTERNATIONAL
Rua dos Trabalhadores; 82 678 0098; mains Mtc495-610

This terracotta-tinted *pousada* (inn) with its open-to-all restaurant has nabbed a beautiful sunset location on Mozambique Island's western flank where you can sit alfresco and relish a menu that mixes Mozambican favourites like lobster curry with fish tacos, brownies and burgers. It's American-run but staffed by young locals. The name harks back to the bicycle taxis that were once ubiquitous here.

KARIBU

MOZAMBIQUE ISLAND | $$ | SEAFOOD
Barrio do Museu; 84 380 2518; mains Mtc400-800

This handsome history-evoking restaurant in atmospheric Stone Town specialises in the island's seafood bounty. Tuna, prawns, marlin and lobster are all done to perfection overseen by the hands-on Portuguese owner. Choose from the chalkboard menu and sit alfresco in front of artfully arranged antiques in the window.

CAFÉ DEL RIO

TETE | $$$ | INTERNATIONAL
84 746 3740; www.cafedelrio.co.za; mains Mtc500-1000

When Tete's heat has melted you to a runny pulp, revive your spirits at Cafe del Rio, a beautiful thatched restaurant furnished like an upmarket African safari lodge that catches gorgeous sunsets over the Zambezi River. You can easily while away a whole evening here playing chess, smoking cigars, knocking back cocktails and enjoying steak or the local speciality, *pende* fish.

'Join us on our grand patio for sunset views and ice-cold beverages after a day of trekking or cozy up to the fire with a warm cup of Café Makua', *Rickshaws Café*

RESTAURANTE MAÚA

CHIMOIO | $$$ | AFRICAN
Feria Popular, EN6; 258 25 125 045; mains Mtc500-800

Tap any local with taste buds and they'll probably tell you that this place – located in a rustic retail complex off the main Beira Corridor highway – serves the best food in Chimoio, possibly even central Mozambique. The menu leans heavily towards Mozambican flavours, with excellent tiger prawns, piri-piri chicken, steak and *matapa* (cassava leaves sauteed with cashews and coconut milk). The atmosphere and temperature are both pleasantly chilled.

MARISQUEIRA SAGRES

MAPUTO | $$$ | SEAFOOD
4272 Avenida Marginal; 21-495201; seafood mains Mtc500-950

An oceanside seafood joint northeast of Maputo's downtown that's popular for dinner and Sunday lunch, with a large menu of well-prepared seafood platters, plus meat grills and continental fare. Décor is a mix of seafaring motifs and international football scarves, but the real eye-catcher is the adjacent beach lapped by the warm waves of the Indian Ocean.

MADAGASCAR

WHAT TO EAT

Romazava
A beef stew in a ginger-flavoured broth. It contains *brêdes mafana*, a green leaf reminiscent of Indian *saag* in taste that will make your tongue and lips tingle.

Ravitoto
A well-loved Malagasy dish, it is a mix of fried beef or pork with shredded cassava leaves and coconut milk.

Zebu meat
Prepared in much the same way as European cattle beef – in stews, kebabs (known locally as masikita, often tiny in size) and as succulent steak.

Seafood
Seafood is found in abundance. Gorge yourself at whim on fish, freshwater crayfish, prawns, lobster and even tiny oysters (from Morondava).

PRICE RANGES

For a main course:
$ less than Ar12,000
$$ Ar12,000–15,000
$$$ Ar25,000 or more

Tipping: 10–15%

Food is taken seriously in Madagascar, where French, Chinese and Indian influences have blended with local eating traditions into an exciting and often mouth-watering cuisine. Regional variations are many, with an array of fruit, vegetables and seafood dictating local tastes and recipes.

LA VARANGUE

ANTANANARIVO | $$$ | INTERNATIONAL
17 Rue Prince Ratsimamanga; 020 22 273 97; www.hotel restaurant lavarangue-tananarive.com; mains Ar23,000-40,000

Justly revered for its real gourmet cuisine, La Varangue serves an elaborate melange of French gastronomy and Malagasy flavours. Meals are served either in the beautiful dining room, with its low lighting and fabulous antique collection, or on the terrace overlooking a charming garden. Highlights from the menu include zebu fillet in rosemary sauce or chicken flavoured with truffle.

LA SAKA

ANTANANARIVO | $$ | FUSION
Hôtel Sakamanga, Rue Andrianary Ratianarivo; 020 22 358 09; www.sakamanga.com; mains Ar15,000-32,000

Striking the perfect balance between gastro French and straightforward local cooking, Le Saka is a Tana institution. The restaurant is housed in a gorgeous wooden house full of old black-and-white photos and local artwork. The chef whips up some mighty desserts using Malagasy chocolate. Make sure you finish your meal with a house rum or coconut punch.

LOKANGA

ANTANANARIVO | $$$ | INTERNATIONAL
Lokanga Hotel, Haute Ville; 020 22 235 49; www.lokanga-hotel.mg; mains Ar25,000-26,000

In a stunning setting whichever way you look – the 19th-century building or the city views from the terrace – Lokanga serves a mix of Malagasy and international dishes. Try the duck breast with pineapple reduction, seafood *romazava* or zebu *chimichurri*. Professional service rounds out a fine culinary experience.

LA TABLE D'ALEXANDRE

NOSY BE | $$$ | CAFETERIA

Ambaro; 033 14 247 22; www.facebook.com/latabledalexandrenosybe; mains Ar28,000-46,000

For a decadent lunch on a day trip around Nosy Be, Alexandre's fits the bill. The debonair French chef here serves exquisite cuisine in a dining room that wouldn't have looked out of place on the set of *Out of Africa*: a gazebo perched on a low hill overlooking mangroves and Nosy Sakatia, decorated with traditional china and 19th-century paintings.

CHEZ SAMSON

ÎLE SAINTE-MARIE | $$$ | SEAFOOD
Baie d'Ampanihy; 020 57 914 01; mains Ar28,000-46,000

Samson trained as a chef in the best kitchens of Madagascar and he decided early on that the remote and stunning location of his restaurant would be no obstacle to fine dining. You're therefore guaranteed to be treated to the most delicious (and fresh) seafood, salads and indulgent desserts, all beautifully presented and with views of the Baie d'Ampanihy.

OCEAN 501

TAMATAVE (TOAMASINA) | $$ | SEAFOOD
Blvd Ratsimilaho Salazamay; 032 64 147 43; www.ocean501.biz; mains Ar15,000-25,000

Laid-back beach-shack restaurant with beautifully prepared and well-presented seafood dishes. However, you'll be so focused on the waves lapping the sands of the beach right in front of you that you probably won't even notice the splashes of thought that have gone into each dish.

'You'll be so focused on the waves lapping the sands of the beach right in front of you that you probably won't even notice the splashes of thought that have gone into each dish.'
Ocean 501

TSARE BE RESTAURANT

DIEGO SUAREZ (ANTSIRANANA) | $$$ | MALAGASY
36 Rue Colbert; 032 04 940 97; mains from Ar26,000

French cuisine with a touch of Madagascar, set off with a twist of Thai flavours, make this restaurant a crowd-pleaser. It's the sort of place where locals dress up and go to celebrate. There are dark-red walls, white tablecloths, good service and a wide range of cocktails and wines, with tables spilling out onto the street.

BLEU SOLEIL

MORONDAVA | $$ | INTERNATIONAL
Rue de l'Indépendance; 033 06 010 07; mains Ar7000-18,000

Winning the prize for the best beach views of any restaurant in Morondava, this breezy place serves everything from tagliatelle to zebu brochettes, grilled fish and a mean smoked-fish salad.

CHEZ MADAME CHABAUD

MAJUNGA (MAHAJANGA) | $$ | FUSION
Off Ave du Général de Gaulle; 032 40 530 05; mains from Ar15,000

Small, intimate and oh-so-delicious, Chez Madame Chabaud is a Majunga institution. Christiane (the original Madame Chabaud's daughter) prepares a divine fusion cuisine mixing Malagasy, Creole and European influences that befit the city's heritage. Try the *camaron* (large freshwater prawn) or the *ouassous* (a huge crayfish) and the mean cocktails.

CHEZ JENNY

ANTSIRABE | $$ | INTERNATIONAL
Rue Labourdonnais; 034 44 990 22; mains Ar14,000-18,000

Chez Jenny is a winning combination of colourful decor (including some captivating Zafimaniry wood carvings), delicious food, warm service and atmosphere, complete with a well-stocked bar and a cosy fireplace for cold winter nights. The duck in three pepper sauce is divine and the thick-crust pizzas are super tasty.

SHARON

TANAMBAO | $ | MALAGASY
Rue Labourdonnais; mains Ar2,500-4000

This cheap and cheerful eatery heaves with young locals every night of the week. It serves melt-in-the-mouth *brochettes* (kebabs), cooked on a street-side BBQ (don't miss the peanut dipping sauce). The huge *mi sao* (a traditional dish that combines noodles or pasta with meat, prawns and soya sauce) is the house's other signature dish.

P388-9: Ibo Island Lodge; Pizza from Rickshaw's Cafe. This page: La Varangue.

COMOROS

The trade winds have brought a range of culinary influences to this Islamic former French colony, where diners can find an Indian-style curry as easily as a bifteck (steak) on Grande Comore, the archipelago's largest island. East African and Arabic influences abound in the abundant use of cloves, cinnamon and nutmeg, as well as plantains, bananas, cassava and coconut milk.

WHAT TO EAT

Seafood stews
Langouste à la vanille (grilled lobster in a rich vanilla sauce), *m'ts-olola* (fish and green plantains stewed in coconut milk), roti *ya ya houma pampa* (cod slow-cooked in tomato and onion) and *ntrovi ya nazi* (steamed or fried fish with bananas and coconut stew).

Ambrevades au curry
It's a straight shot to India from here, and the subcontinent's influence can be tasted in dishes such as this pigeon pea (legume) curry flavoured with cardamom.

Side dishes
Mkatra foutra (fried yeast-leavened bread made with coconut milk), spinach-like *mataba* (cassava leaves), *achard aux legumes* (pickled vegetable salad) and poutou hot sauce all accompany main dishes.

PRICE RANGES
$ less than FC3000
$$ FC3000–6000
$$$ FC6000 or more

Tipping: 10%

L'ESCALE

GRANDE COMORE | $$ | FRENCH

Rue de la Corniche, Moroni; 333 57 96; www.facebook.com/lescale.moronicomores; mains FC4000-7000

Moroni's favourite French restaurant serves creatively presented cuisine in an attractive environment of wooden screens, shutters, pillars and beams. The scattered arts and crafts beneath ceilings of thatch and corrugated iron add extra earthiness, but the food bursts with contemporary ambition. Starters might include smoked swordfish with mango tartare, or vegetable tempura, followed by fillet steak and pommes frites or skewered fish medallions with seasoned rice.

LE NEW SELECT

GRANDE COMORE | $$ | AFRICAN

Place de France, Moroni; 773 00 31; www.facebook.com/newselect2016; mains FC3000-6000

This local hangout lies well inland, a location that suggests an authentic experience is on offer, and the kitchen indeed specialises in Comorian cuisine. A daily selection of island favourites is available, including pilaou (a spicy meat and rice dish), langouste à la vanille, chicken curry and m'tsolola. The front terrace and live music ensure popularity among young locals.

LE CORAYA

GRANDE COMORE | $$$ | INTERNATIONAL

Bandamadji Itsandra; 358 88 88; www.facebook.com/lccoraya; mains FC4000-8500

Take a drive up the coast from national capital Moroni to reach this wonderfully located restaurant, which juts out onto the azure Indian Ocean like a yacht setting sail for Tanzania. Le Coraya serves an ever-popular menu of seafood fresh from the Mozambique Channel, vividly coloured salads and heartier brochettes and curries.

MAURITIUS

A rich and delicious mix Chinese, French and African influences peppered with Indian spices, Mauritian food can be sampled across the island – except in Rodrigues. Less spicy but with more fresh fruit and beans, Rodrigues cuisine makes for an intriguing culinary detour.

WHAT TO EAT

Dhal Puri
Ground yellow split peas seasoned with curry, *rougaille* (tomato-based hot-pot), chutney and chillies, wrapped in *farata* (flat bread).

Seafood
Octopus appears in salads, cooked in saffron or in a curry with green papaya while smoked marlin is a national favourite of this fish-eating island.

Game
Venison and wild boar are mainstays of Chinese and French cuisine (especially around Mahébourg), with the distinctive creole sausage served up at the island's many *table d'hôte* (privately hosted meals).

Boulettes
Top billing for street food, *boulettes* are tiny steamed Chinese dumplings.

PRICE RANGES
$ less than Rs400
$$ Rs400–800
$$$ Rs800 or more

Tipping: 10–15% sometimes added at top-end restaurants

RESTAURANT LE BARBIZON

THE WEST | $$ | MAURITIAN

Ste Anne Rd, Chamarel; 483 4178; lebarbizon@yahoo.fr; mains from Rs450

Barbizon may not look like much, but it's a gem. Marie-Ange helms the kitchen, whipping up traditional Mauritian flavours from her family's cookbook, while Rico L'Intelligent (what a name!) entertains at the tables. He doesn't give you a menu. Instead, he offers a feast of rum punch, rice, five vegetables, and fish or chicken. This is the best Rs450 you'll spend on the island.

FRENCHIE CAFE

THE WEST | $$ | CAFE

483 6125; www.frenchiecafe.mu; mains from Rs400

One of the coolest places on the island, French-run Frenchie does quick bites and more substantial (but reasonably priced) mains, as well as breakfasts and an outstanding Sunday brunch (11am to 4pm). It's also a stylish cocktail bar with Saturday-night DJs. On the road to the Black River Gorges Visitor Centre; the turn-off is almost opposite La Balise Marina.

BOULETTE TI KOULOIR

THE NORTH | $ | MAURITIAN

School Rd, Off Royal Rd, Grand Baie; 263 5645; mains from Rs90

As the name suggests, this tiny outlet really is just a ti couloir (little hallway), where Yvonne and friends cook up *boulettes* (small steamed dumplings) and piled-high bowls of fried noodles to lines of locals. For the *boulettes*, diners choose among chicken, pork, fish, calamari and lamb.

LA CLEF DES CHAMPS

CENTRAL PLATEAU | $$$ | MAURITIAN

Queen Mary Ave, Floréal; 686 3458; www.laclefdeschamps.mu; set menu Rs1250

In the Floréal area, it's worth seeking out the *table d'hôte* (privately hosted meal) of Jacqueline Dalais. Known for her impressive library of self-created recipes, Jacqueline has earned quite the reputation locally for her unparalleled cuisine. Dishes served in her quaint dining room lean towards Provençal flavours and the presentation is exquisite. Jacqueline is regularly called upon to cater for government functions, especially when foreign dignitaries are in town.

ESCALE CRÉOLE

CENTRAL PLATEAU | $ | MAURITIAN
off Bois Cheri Rd, Moka; 5422 2332; www.escalecreole.net; mains from Rs250

This charming garden *table d'hôte* serves Mauritian specialities such as homemade creole sausages and octopus bouillon with coconut chutney. The hosts are the friendly mother and daughter team of Majo and Marie-Christine. Book at least a day in advance.

CHEZ ROBERT ET SOLANGE

RODRIGUES | $ | SEAFOOD
St François; 5733 1978; mains from Rs50

With expertly cooked food that offers the essence of Rodrigues, this casual venue specialises in fresh fish and vegetables prepared simply – the Rodrigues way. By the sea (it's 100m through the trees from the beach), this casual eatery doesn't bother with a menu: you'll be offered whatever is going (usually grilled chicken, fish or octopus served with papaya salads). Reasonably priced lobster is also often on offer.

ST AUBIN TABLE D'HÔTE

SOUTH COAST | $ | MAURITIAN
Off A9, Rivière des Anguilles; 626 1513; mains from Rs300

The height of the St Aubin experience is a meal at this heritage *table d'hôte*. The dining room is one of the island's best colonial keepsakes: dainty chandeliers cast ambient light over the white tablecloths and antique wooden furniture. The set menu showcases the fruits of the plantation: hearts of palm, pineapple, mango and chilli. Reservations are essential.

LE CAFÉ DES ARTS

THE EAST | $$$ | MAURITIAN
Victoria Rd, Trou d'Eau Douce; 480 0220; www.maniglier.com; set menu from Rs2900

This intriguing dining option is located within an old mill that has been transformed into Victoria 1840, an eccentric gallery space with canvases of wicked brushstrokes adorning the cracked brick walls. The food, an exquisite modern nod to traditional island flavours, mirrors the contemporary retro surrounds. Tapas-like snacks are offered with the pre- and after-meal aperitifs and a CD of music is thrown in for free.

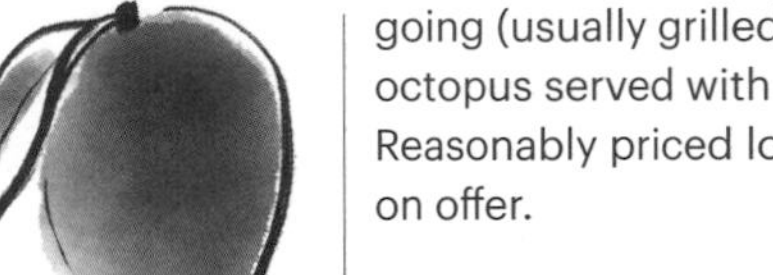

'A landmark in the island's gastronomic landscape, guests come to the restaurant… for the sense of family.'
La Clef des Champs

SEYCHELLES

The real beauty of Seychellois cuisine is its freshness and simplicity. As befitting a nation comprising many islands, fish appear as a principal ingredient. Cultural influences are stirred into the pot, with a blend of European (French and Italian) and African flavours.

WHAT TO EAT

Fish

Fish and rice. This is Seychelles' most common culinary combination (*pwason ek diri* in Creole patois). Bourgeois, capitaine, parrotfish and caranx are served smoked, salted, baked and stewed. Local shellfish (especially *trouloulou* and *teck teck*) are also widely available.

Tropical fruit and spices

Mango, breadfruit and carambola often make their way into flavourful *chatini* (chutney) while vanilla, cinnamon and nutmeg are used to flavour stews.

Bat curry

The local delicacy, *civet de chauve souris* (curried bat), can be sampled at La Grande Maison.

PRICE RANGES

$ less than Rs150
$$ Rs150–300
$$$ Rs300 or more

Tipping: 10–15% sometimes added at top-end restaurants

COURTESY THE STATION

LA GRANDE MAISON

MAHÉ (EAST COAST) | $$$ | CREOLE

East Coast Rd, Takamaka Distillery, La Plaine St Andre; 2522112; www.facebook.com/LGMsey; mains from Rs350

The home kitchen of Christelle Verheyden, arguably the country's most talented chef, La Grande Maison offers a top culinary experience in a country that boasts more than its share of fine restaurants. Housed in a restored colonial house opening onto a tropical garden, the best local (often organic) ingredients are carefully selected for house favourites such as creole *bouillabaisse*, and pork rum and raisin.

OSCARS – THE BAR & GRILL

MAHÉ (WEST COAST) | $$ | SEAFOOD

West Coast Rd; 2773919; mains from Rs200

For fresh grilled fish, Oscars is hard to beat. The menu includes grouper, sailfish, marlin and red snapper but a local favourite is the yellow-fin tuna seared, served rare and marinated in the house concoction of herbs and spices. The garden tables have beautiful coastal views.

THE STATION

MAHÉ | $$ | CAFÉ

Sans Souci, Morne Seychellois National Park; 4225709; thestationseychelles.com; mains Rs155-265, 3-course Sat lunch Rs450

The Station offers an attractive pit-stop on an inland island tour. With a health-promoting ethic underpinning the menu, dishes range from salads, soups and bruschetta to mezze and savoury pancakes. The three-course, adults-only 'Letting Go Saturdays' lunch is fast becoming an island institution.

POMME CANELLE RESTAURANT

MAHÉ (EAST COAST) | $$ | CREOLE
East Coast Rd, Domaine de Val des Prés; 4376100; mains from Rs 200

Occupying one of a number of heritage creole buildings in this complex of artisan stalls, the Pomme Canelle serves up a well-priced creole buffet that is particularly popular for a weekend lunch. There's no additional charge for the cooling breeze – these old creole buildings were built to maximise natural 'air-con'.

'Perfect retreat for the soul where wholesome food and a quiet, laid-back ambience will suit even the most stressed-out traveller.'
The Station

CAFÉ DES ARTS

PRASLIN | $$$ | INTERNATIONAL
Anse Volbert; 4232170; mains from Rs440

Praslin's most stylish restaurant is in the Le Duc de Praslin hotel. Flickering candles, colourful paintings, swaying palms, a breezy terrace and the sound of waves brushing the shore provide a romantic setting for the refined cuisine. Flavoursome Seychellois favourites, such as red-snapper fillet in passionfruit sauce or marinated chicken with tropical fruits, are beautifully presented. A reputable art gallery is housed in the same complex.

CHEZ JULES RESTAURANT

LA DIGUE | $$ | CREOLE
Anse Banane, 2584432, 2510384; mains from Rs230

This beachfront, roadside shack may be on the casual side, but it serves up some of the finest meals on the island of La Digue. The octopus curry and tuna steak with coconut sauce are two particularly successful dishes. Seats are readily available for breakfast (omelettes and fresh juices and smoothies) or lunch, but dinner should be booked by 3pm. Cash only.

MALAWI

Despite being separated from the nearest ocean by Mozambique and Tanzania, Malawians eat a lot of fish. It all comes from Lake Malawi, and restaurant kitchens have found inventive uses for fish such as chambo. *Nsima* (maize porridge) and chicken are also ubiquitous.

WHAT TO EAT

Nsima
Malawi's staple food. Made from ground corn, it is ubiquitous and served with a sauce or alongside meat and vegetables.

Lake fish
Enjoy a wealth of fish from Lake Malawi, with favourites including chambo (similar to bream), *mpasa* (like salmon) and *usipa* (like sardines). Seafood is often presented in curry or with a plate of fries.

Mbatata
Cinnamon and sweet-potato cookies.

Steaks
South African influence is felt in the braai (barbecue), and you can eat some great steaks at reasonable prices in the cities and better lodges.

PRICE RANGES
$ less than MK3650
$$ MK3650–7300
$$$ MK7300 or more

Tipping: 10% in the best restaurants, unless a service charge has been added to the bill

AMA KHOFI

LILONGWE | $$ | CAFE
Four Seasons Centre, Presidential Way; 0211 222222; mains MK7000

This delightful Parisian-style garden-centre cafe has wrought-iron chairs, a bubbling fountain and leafy surrounds. The menu offers salads, main courses such as burgers and beef panini, and homemade sweet treats including cakes and ice cream. The great caffeinated pick-me-ups include iced coffee, perfect for hot days.

THE MUSHROOM FARM

LIVINGSTONIA | $$ | VEGETARIAN
Chitimba Rd; 0884 273435; www.themushroomfarmmalawi.com; lunch MK2000-4000, dinner MK5000

Perched on the edge of the Livingstonia escarpment, this permaculture ecolodge is worth the arduous ascent from the lakeshore for the warm welcome and views that will have you manually closing your jaw. The bar-restaurant serves organic veggie fusion dishes such as tortilla wraps and Asian noodle salad. As well as roasting their own coffee, growing their own greens and baking their own bread, they support local farmers.

MACONDO CAMP

MZUZU | $$ | ITALIAN
Chimaliro 4; 0991 792311; www.macondocamp.com; mains MK4000-8000

Serial African overlanders Luca and Cecilia, two members of Malawi's sizeable Italian expat community, run this excellent restaurant in their guesthouse. They offer treats such as homemade pasta made daily, Parmesan flown from Italy and live music on the stoep. Dishes include pizza, focaccia, steaks and the ever-popular ravioli with blue cheese, which can be accompanied by a good selection of Italian and South African wines.

HOSTARIA RESTAURANT

BLANTYRE | $$$ | ITALIAN

Sharpe Rd; 0888 282828; www.hostariamalawi.com; pizza/mains MK7000/9000

In an atmospheric old house with black-and-white floors and a large veranda overlooking a lawn, Hostaria offers Italian recipes and fresh produce that attract local expats in the know. Come for a relaxing evening and wood-fired pizzas, homemade pastas and steaks.

CASA MIA

BLANTYRE | $$$ | INTERNATIONAL
Kabula Hill Rd; 0996 963110; www.blantyreaccommodation.com; mains MK6000-11,500

Don your smarts for dinner at this classy guesthouse restaurant. The wine-stacked interior, with its antique Cinzano prints, white tablecloths and expat clientele, is a pleasant environment for dishes ranging from steaks and bulled beef lasagna to peri-peri prawns and pork spareribs. Lunch on the breezy terrace is more casual. The Sunday braai (barbecue) and buffet is a popular local fixture.

CAFE MANDALA

BLANTYRE | $ | CAFE
Mandala House, Kaoshiung Rd; 01-810932; mains MK5000-7000

Encased in wraparound verandas and set in lovely gardens, this quietly grand colonial house is Malawi's oldest building, built in 1882 as a home for the managers of the African Lakes Corporation. Sit on a breezy stone terrace or inside at this chilled cafe adorned with artworks and guidebooks. Regulars love the Italian cuisine, fillet steak, Thai chicken, freshly brewed coffee, iced tea and gelato. A real oasis.

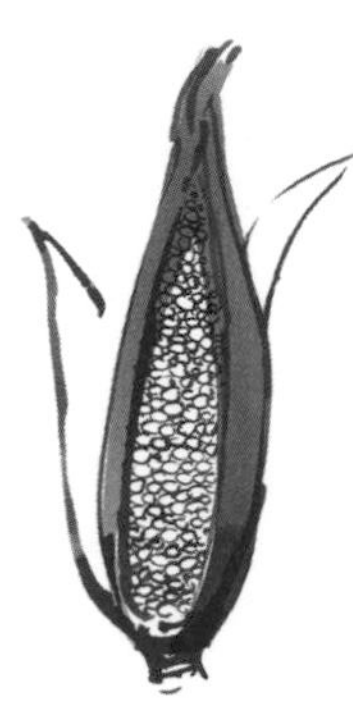

'Simplicity is key. We cook over firewood-burning stoves and bake our own bread in a cob oven (made of clay, mud and straw).'
The Mushroom Farm

HUNTINGDON HOUSE

SHIRE HIGHLANDS | $$ | FUSION
Satemwa Tea and Coffee Estate, Thyolo; 0993 121854; www.huntingdon-malawi.com; lunch/dinner MK7000/12,000

Lunch or afternoon tea at this historic guesthouse on a beautiful tea estate makes an unbeatable pit stop on the drive between Blantyre and Mt Mulanje. Dishes such as Asian beef noodles and beetroot burgers are served on the veranda, as are teas including white nectar and green velvet from the surrounding fields. Tastings in the tea factory and tours of the coffee fields are also offered.

CASA ROSSA

ZOMBA | $$$ | ITALIAN
Mountain Rd 5; 0991 184211; www.casarossamw.com; mains MK5000-10,500

In an atmospheric old colonial house, this Italian-owned guesthouse restaurant serves the best pasta dishes this side of Naples, including unique local variations such as chambo and ginger ravioli. The ingredients come from the local market, and rich dishes such as ravioli filled with beef cooked in red wine, served with butter and rosemary, exude a passion for Italian cuisine.

TANZANIA

Tanzania offers a variety of eating options, from sidewalk stalls to European-style restaurants, and dining here can be wonderful. This is especially so along the coast, where the seaside ambience, spices and mix of flavours enhance each meal, and in upmarket safari lodges, where meals seem even tastier against the wild bush backdrop. Tasty Indian cuisine is widely available.

WHAT TO EAT

Ugali
The Tanzanian national dish. It's a thick staple, made of cassava or maize flour, or both. Rice and *ndizi* (cooked plantains) are other staples.

Mishikaki
These marinated, grilled meat kebabs and *nyama choma* (seasoned roasted meat) are widely available. There's plenty of seafood, often grilled or (along the coast) cooked in coconut milk or curry-style.

Uji
A thin, sweet porridge made from bean, millet or other flour. Watch for ladies stirring bubbling pots of it on street corners in the early morning.

Vitambua
Small rice cakes resembling tiny, thick pancakes.

PRICE RANGES

For a main course:
$ less than Tsh10,000
$$ Tsh10,000–20,000
$$$ Tsh20,000 or more

Tipping: 10–15%

ORION TABORA HOTEL

TABORA | $$ | TANZANIAN, EUROPEAN
Station Rd; 026-260 4369; meals Tsh6000-15,500

Tabora's top dining spot, located in a colonial villa, has a mix of local and Continental food, with pizza and Indian available during dinner. There's dining indoors and in the outside bar area, which has a pool table, and live bands play on Friday, Saturday and Sunday. Even more vital, the bar has the skills, technology and ingredients to make a margarita.

MAUA CAFÉ & TOURS

MBEYA | $ | CAFE
13 Mwabenja St; 0786 248199; mains Tsh7000

A brick homestead turned cafe serving big breakfasts, including granola and fresh coffee (Tsh10,000); wraps, burgers and toasties for lunch (from Tsh5000); and pizza, fish and salads for dinner. Sit outside by the hibiscus

COURTESY UTENGULE COFFEE LODGE

bush on benches with bright fabric cushions. It has an excellent ethical craft shop and a small backyard campground and owner Amelia organises a range of tours.

UTENGULE COFFEE LODGE

MBEYA | $$$ | EUROPEAN

Utengule; 025-256 0100; www.riftvalley-zanzibar.com; mains Tsh16,000-25,000

If you have your own transport, this wonderfully green spot 20km west of Mbeya is the place to go for fine dining, with both a daily set menu and à la carte, and a bar. Speciality coffees (including to take home) are a feature. It also has a swimming pool and a pool table, meaning you can spend a good chunk of your day here.

'Neema is the place to be. You can even learn some Swahili sign language – our kitchen is staffed by deaf trainees.'

Neema Crafts Centre Cafe

MAMA IRINGA PIZZERIA & ITALIAN RESTAURANT

IRINGA | $$ | ITALIAN

Don Bosco area; 0753 757007; mains Tsh9000-16,000

Delicious Italian food – pizzas cooked in a wood-fired oven, gnocchi, lasagne and more, plus salads – are served in

P396-7: Dish from The Station; View from The Station. Previous spread: Ugali, fish and greens; Utengule Coffee Lodge. Next spread: Dish from Calafia; Dishes from The Terrasse.

the quiet courtyard of a former convent decked out with beautiful African fabrics. Mama Iringa sits about 3km from the town centre.

HASTY TASTY TOO

IRINGA | $ | TANZANIAN, INTERNATIONAL
Uhuru Ave; 026-270 2061; mains Tsh6000-13,000

This long-standing and cheerful Iringa classic has good breakfasts, yoghurt, samosas, shakes and reasonably priced main dishes, including a divine chickpea curry. The little foliage-fringed cafe is popular with local and expat clientele. You can get toasted sandwiches packed to go and arrange food for camping safaris.

NEEMA CRAFTS CENTRE CAFÉ

IRINGA | $ | CAFE
Hakimu St; 0783 760945; www.neemacrafts.com; mains Tsh3000-14,000

Located upstairs at the Neema Crafts disability project, this cafe is justifiably popular, with local coffees and teas, homemade cookies, excellent cinnamon buns, cakes, soups, and a selection of sandwiches and light meals. The noticeboard is great for finding out about safaris and Swahili classes, and the breezy terrace hung with bunting is one of the town's best hang-outs.

KHAN'S BARBECUE

ARUSHA | $ | BARBECUE
Mosque St; 0754 652 747; meals Tsh9000-10,000, mixed grill Tsh14,000

This Arusha institution is an auto-spares shop by day (look for the Zubeda Auto Spares sign) and the best known of many earthy roadside barbecues around the market area by night. It lays out a heaped spread of grilled, skewered meat and salad. If you want to experience Arusha like a local, this is a fine place to begin.

KILIMANJARO COFFEE LOUNGE

MOSHI | $$ | CAFE
Opposite the Nakumatt Shopping Centre, Kaunda Street; 0754 610892; www.kilicoffeelounge.webs.com; meals Tsh8000-17,000

This cafe's semi-garden setting is back a bit from the road, bringing a semblance of peace, and the food ranges from pizza and Mexican dishes to salads, sandwiches, burgers and steaks, alongside excellent milkshakes and juices. There are the makings of a travellers' classic here.

BLUE HERON

ARUSHA | $$ | INTERNATIONAL
Haile Selassie Rd; 0785 555127; www.facebook.com/pizzaheron; mains Tsh12,500-25,000

The pick of the garden restaurants that are a recurring theme in Arusha's east, the Blue Heron gets the tricky combination of lounge bar and family restaurant just right. Sit on the leafy verandah or out on the lawn tables to enjoy a menu ranging from panini and soups to beef tenderloin and various creative specials. The smoothies are divine.

CHAPAN BHOG

DAR ES SALAAM | $ | INDIAN
Kisutu St; 0685 401417; www.facebook.com/56Bhog; meals Tsh6000-15,000

Chapan Bhog's Gujurati dhoklas (savoury steamed chickpea cakes), South Indian dosas (fermented crêpes) and thalis are a vegetarian nirvana in a sea of *nyama choma* (roasted meat). The all-vegetarian menu is extensive, and the restaurant has a prime position on temple-lined Kisutu St.

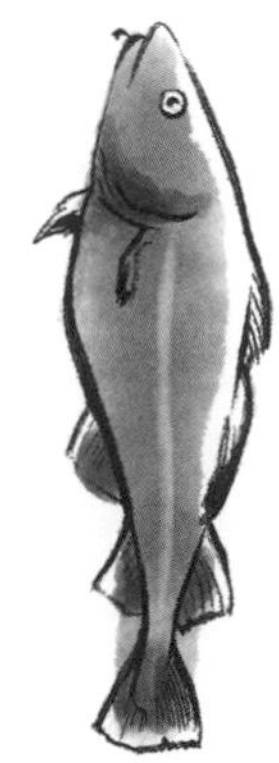

'If you want to experience Arusha like a local, this is a fine place to begin.'
Khan's Barbecue

MAMBOZ CORNER BBQ

DAR ES SALAAM | $ | BARBECUE
Cnr Morogoro Rd & Libya St; 0784 243734; mains Tsh5000-12,000

This streetside place is home to what many claim is Dar's best grilled chicken, including spicy gujarr chicken, lemon chicken and chicken *sekela* (with tamarind sauce), as well as dry fried fish and bowls of *urojo* (Zanzibar mix).

LUKMAAN RESTAURANT

ZANZIBAR | $ | ZANZIBARI
New Mkunazini Rd; meals Tsh5000-7000

Probably the best local restaurant for quality Zanzibari food. There's no menu: just make your way inside to the 1950s counter and see what's on offer. Servings are enormous and include various biryanis, fried fish, coconut curries and freshly made naan.

RWANDA

Sharing the East African penchant for *ugali* (maize meal) and *matoke* (cooked plantains), rural Rwanda offers a chance to try *tilapia* (Nile perch) and goat brochettes. In the cities, Rwanda's French roots are evident in the daily plat du jour.

WHAT TO EAT

Tilapia (Nile perch)
Not in itself the most flavoursome fish, it is blended into delicious creations. It is the national staple and the base of almost every meal.

Brochettes
In a country where meat is still something of a treat on high days and holidays, the ubiquitous brochette (kebab, or meat on a stick) is a very good way of making a little go far.

Matoke (cooked plantains)
For those who thought bananas were strictly a fruit to be packed in a lunchbox, think again! As a staple of the Rwandan diet, plantains redefine the banana as a flexible savoury food source.

PRICE RANGES
$ less than RFr4000
$$ RFr4000–RFr8000
$$$ RFr8000 or more

Tipping: 5–10%

CALAFIA

NORTHWESTERN RWANDA | $ | CAFE
off Ave de la Révolution, Gisenyi (Rubavu); 0787938145; www.calafiacafe.com; mains from RFr3000

On the lakefront road near the DRC border, this converted mansion now hosts a superb cafe – a labour of love for the expat friends who run it. Fish tacos, frittatas, delicious sandwiches and green salads are followed by freshly baked pastries and accompanied by ethically produced local coffee.

VOLCANA LOUNGE

NORTHWESTERN RWANDA | $$ | ITALIAN
NR 4 Rd, Musanze (Ruhengeri); 0728300753; mains from RFr4500

With a roaring wood fire and a relaxed, bush lodge ambience (despite being on Musanze's main street), this is one of the most atmospheric places to dine outside Kigali. The menu consists primarily of Rwandan versions of pizza and pasta; not for the epicurean perhaps, but many travellers will relish the local influence. Leave space for the chocolate mousse!

VOLCANOES RESTO-BAR

NORTHWESTERN RWANDA | $ | CAFETERIA
Volcanoes National Park; 0788495604; mains from RFr1300

This small cafeteria, arranged around attractive gardens, dishes up simple

meals and sells soft drinks and fruits. Frankly, it wouldn't matter what it served: after the euphoria of spotting gorillas in this magical national park, any food tastes divine. Boots and other equipment are rented out from here for hikes on Bisoke.

THE TERRASSE, HOTEL DES MILLE COLLINES

KIGALI | $$$ | AFRICAN, INTERNATIONAL

KN 6 Ave; 0788192530; www.millecollines.rw; Mains from RFr10,000

Welcome to Hotel Rwanda! While a colonial South African hotel was used in the film, the real deal is more of a utilitarian construction. It nonetheless shelters a beautifully landscaped garden and this excellent poolside restaurant that serves local treats while the band plays African beats.

'A light of hope in the darkness for a terrified crowd...saved by the hotel opening its doors in 1994.'
The Terrasse, Hotel des Mille Collines

AFRIKA BITE

KIGALI | $ | RWANDAN

KG 674 St; 0788503888; mains from RFr3500

This homely restaurant in a villa surrounded by an enchanting garden offers the capital's best opportunity to sample authentic Rwandan food in a congenial atmosphere. The popular lunch and dinner buffets feature tilapia and brochettes: arrive early.

HEAVEN RESTAURANT

KIGALI | $$$ | INTERNATIONAL

COURTESY THE TERRASSE

KN 29 St; 0788486581; www.heavenrwanda.com; mains from RFr10,000

This capital highlight has a relaxed, open-air bistro with a broad deck. It's hugely popular with expats and travellers looking to enjoy the innovative cuisine. Combining local flavours with international panache, the weekend brunch is a particular winner.

NEHEMIAH'S BEST COFFEE

SOUTHWESTERN RWANDA | $ | CAFETERIA

NR 1 Rd, Huye (Butare); 0783880153; no website; mains from RFr1300

On the main drag between 'town and gown', this sociable cafe is a hit with university students. Serving delicious omelettes, burgers, freshly made smoothies, pastries and great coffee it is one of the best spots in the region for a light lunch. There's bonus access to fast wi-fi.

KENYA

Most Kenyan meals are centred on ugali, a thick, dough-like mass made from maize and/or cassava flour. While traditional fare may be bland but filling, there are some treats to be found. Many memorable eating experiences in Kenya are likely to revolve around dining al fresco in a safari camp, surrounded by the sights and sounds of the African bush.

WHAT TO EAT

Ugali
The national staple food is a starchy corn porridge, often eaten (with the right hand) from a communal pot).

Nyama choma
This barbecued meat dish is a red-blooded, hands-on affair; most places have their own on-site butchery. It'll be brought to you in small bite-sized bits, often with greens.

Sukuma wiki
Braised or stewed spinach; the name in Kiswahili means 'stretch the week', the implication being that it's super-affordable.

Matoke
Mashed green plantains that, when well prepared, can taste like buttery, lightly whipped mashed potato.

PRICE RANGES

For a main course:
$ less than KSh500
$$ KSh500–1000
$$$ KSh1000 or more

Tipping: 10% service charge is often added.

GREEN GARDEN RESTAURANT

KISUMU | $ | INTERNATIONAL
0727738000; mains KSh380-550

Surrounded by colourful murals and potted palms, the Green Garden is an oasis of culinary delight set in an Italian-themed courtyard. As you would expect, it's an expat hotspot and the word is that the tilapia in spinach and coconut sauce is the way to go. Be prepared to wait a while for your meal.

SUNJEEL PALACE

ELDORET | $$ | INDIAN
0720554747; sunjeelpalace.atspace.cc; mains KSh400-650

This formal, dark and spicy Indian restaurant serves superb, real-deal curries. Portion sizes are decent and if you mop up all the gravy with a freshly baked butter naan, you'll be as satisfied as Ganesh himself.

HYGIENIC BUTCHERY

NAKURU | $ | KENYAN
Tom Mboya Rd; mains KSh180-300

Great name, great place. The Kenyan tradition of *nyama choma* (barbecued meats) is alive and well here at this joint (pun intended). Sidle up to the counter, try a piece of tender mutton or beef and order half a kilo (per person) of whichever takes your fancy, along with chapatis or ugali (no sauce!).

CLUB HOUSE

LAKE NAIVASHA | $$$ | INTERNATIONAL, KENYAN
Sanctuary Farm; 0722761940; www.sanctuaryfarmkenya.com/index.php/kitchen; lunch KSh3000, dinner KSh3500

Farm-to-table sustainable cuisine is more exciting when there are giraffes and hippos to spy on in the distance. The signature eatery at Sanctuary

Farm is relaxed but stylish, with tables strewn over a wooden verandah. Inside, there are framed black-and-white posters and Rift Valley wines. Expect dishes such as beetroot salad, red-pepper chicken, home-baked focaccia and baklava with pineapple sorbet. Reservations only.

KAREN BLIXEN COFFEE GARDEN

NAIROBI | $$$ | INTERNATIONAL, KENYAN
Karen Rd; 0733616206; www.karenblixencoffeegarden.com; mains KSh990-3000

The Coffee Garden offers diners five areas in which to enjoy its varied menu, including the plush L'Amour dining room, the historic 1901 Swedo House and the recommended main section, a casual restaurant set in a veritable English country garden. Dishes range from gourmet burgers to Swahili curries from the coast. The Sunday lunch buffet is popular and excellent value.

TALISMAN

NAIROBI | $$$ | INTERNATIONAL
320 Ngong Rd, Karen; 0705999997; www.thetalismanrestaurant.com; mains KSh1400-2400

This classy cafe-bar-restaurant remains fashionable with the in-crowd and it rivals any of Kenya's top eateries for imaginative international food. The comfortable lounge-like rooms mix modern African and European styles,

'Our approach at Sanctuary Farm is to keep it simple, fresh and local. We cook the produce of our garden, brimming with herbs, fruit and vegetables.'
Club House

while the courtyard provides some welcome air. Classics such as feta and coriander samosas and twice-cooked pork belly perk up the palate no end.

MAMA OLIECH

NAIROBI | $$ | KENYAN
Marcus Garvey Rd; 0723925604; mains KSh800-1350

Fish dominates the menu at this cheery neighbourhood joint: the whole fried tilapia from Lake Nakuru is the signature dish, especially when ordered with *ugali* (a maize or cassava-flour staple) and *kachumbari* (tomato-and-onion salsa). Wildly popular, the restaurant is considered one of Nairobi's best – the sort of place that locals take first-time visitors to the city.

CARNIVORE

NAIROBI | $$$ | BARBECUE
Langata Rd, Langata; 020-5141300; www.tamarind.co.ke/carnivore; buffet from KSh4000

Love it or hate it, Carnivore serves up Kenya's most famous *nyama choma* (barbecued meat) – it's been an icon for tourists, expats and wealthier locals for over 25 years. At the entrance is a huge barbecue pit laden with real swords of beef, pork, lamb, chicken and farmed game meats such as crocodile and ostrich. It's a memorable night out.

LE RUSTIQUE

NANYUKI | $$ | INTERNATIONAL

Mt Kenya Rd; 0721609601; www.lerustique.co.ke; mains KSh700-1500

This one-time Nairobi favourite has upped sticks and headed north to a leafy spot in Nanyuki. The fare, overseen to every last detail by owner Maike Potgieter, is superb, with pizzas, crêpes and an excellent wine list. But the atmosphere is as much of a draw-card, with an open fireplace for those cold Laikipia evenings or the quiet garden for warmer days.

SAILS

DIANI BEACH | $$$ | SEAFOOD

Diani Beach Rd, Almanara Luxury Villas Resort; 0716863884; www.almanararesort.com/sails; mains KSh1400-2700

By far the most stylish place to eat in Diani, Sails is gorgeous: a canopy of billowing white canvas separates the restaurant from the stars, while waiters serve up fine dishes, particularly seafood, including Zanzibar-style snapper, steamed ginger crab and smoked Malindi sailfish. Reservations highly recommended in the evening.

SHEHNAI RESTAURANT

MOMBASSA | $$ | INDIAN

Fatemi House, Mwindani Rd; 0722871111; mains KSh800-1500

This reputable *mughlai* (North Indian) curry house is popular with the local Indian community and does delicious dishes such as *gosht palakwalla* (lamb with masala and spinach) and a superb

DENNIS PRESCOTT/COURTESY TALISMAN

chicken biryani. The staff are friendly and the entire place has an air of gentility absent elsewhere in Mombasa, with filigree wooden screens and lamps hanging from the high ceiling. There's no alcohol.

MONSOONS

MTWAPA | $$$ | ITALIAN

Jumba la Mtwana; 041-2012666; mains KSh950-2800

As you stumble over the tangled tree roots of the Jumba la Mtwana ruins, delicious smells propel you towards the beach. A thatched hut perched above the blue of the Indian Ocean is not where you'd expect to find the region's best Italian restaurant, but there it is! Grilled seafood is the speciality here, paired with Italian wines.

CRAB SHACK

MIDA CREEK | $$ | SEAFOOD
3km inland from Turtle Bay Hotel; 0725315562; mains KSh800-1200

Crab samosas, grilled calamari and steamed fish await at the end of a mangrove boardwalk, overlooking Mida Creek. This lovely Giriama-run spot is a favourite for sunset-watching, too. It's a 3km walk or boda-boda (motorcycle taxi) ride along the road directly opposite Turtle Bay Hotel.

BAHATI GELATERIA ITALIANA

WATAMU | $ | GELATO
Watamu Beach Rd; 0724079856; gelato scoop KSh170

In a village where gelato joints sit cheek by jowl, the oldest one is still the best, with Anna and Andrea enticing customers with scoops of rich chocolate pistachio and other flavours into their colourful cafe. Great pastries and coffee, too.

PILIPAN RESTAURANT

WATAMU | $$$ | FUSION
Turtle Bay Rd; 0736724099; mains KSh800-2500

Set on a breezy Swahili-style outdoor terrace looking down on mangrove-strewn Prawn Lake, Pilipan turns up Watamu's chic factor, particularly after sunset, when the place is lit with twinkling fairy lights and candles. The mostly-Indian-but-not-quite menu includes sambal squid, Camembert samosas, tuna carpaccio and malabar prawn curry.

BABY MARROW

MALINDI | $$$ | ITALIAN
Mama Ngina Rd; 0700766704; mains KSh850-2700

This standout restaurant is not only one of the best on the coast, but in the entire country. Think leafy, intimate setting, makuti roof (thatched roof of palm leaves), and bold contemporary art, while the charming staff bring you house specialities such as smoked sailfish, pizza bianca, vodka sorbet or Sicilian ice cream. The jungle bar is a good spot for a digestif.

COURTESY CARNIVORE

WHERE TO DRINK...

KENYAN COFFEE

Connect Coffee, Nairobi
One of Nairobi's best and coolest cafes, Connect brings coffee sourced directly from farmers in Kenya, Ethiopia and Uganda to your table, and the barista-prepared offerings range from pour-over filter coffee to a popular cold brew or simply a long black.

Whispers Café, Lamu
For real cappuccino, light meals, mega juices and smoothies and the best desserts in town, this cafe with a garden, set in the same building as the Baraka Gallery, is just the ticket.

Cafesserie, Nyali Beach
Inside Nyali City mall, breezy, chilled-out Cafesserie has the best selection of cakes and some of the best coffee on the coast.

UGANDA

There's an enormous variety of food to be found in Uganda, with each tribe in this multiethnic country having its own traditional dishes and plenty of influence felt from the Arab world, the Indian Subcontinent and from former colonial power Britain.

WHAT TO EAT

Rolex

The rolex (the name comes from 'rolled eggs') is a chapati wrapped around an omelet with tomatoes, purple onion and cabbage added. It's a scrumptious breakfast dish sold at stalls everywhere.

Nsenene

These are grasshoppers, a very popular crunchy treat, which is either boiled or fried, sold by street vendors from big buckets in April and November.

Posho

Known as ugali elsewhere in East Africa, posho is a high-energy food staple usually made from maize flour or cassava.

Matoke

A calorific stew made with cooked plantains, garlic, chilli, coriander and beef.

PRICE RANGES

$ less than USh18,000

$$ USh18,000-36,000

$$$ Ush36,000 or more

Tipping: 5–10%

GARDENS RESTAURANT

FORT PORTAL | $ | AFRICAN

Lugard Road; 0772-694482; mains USh10,000-30,000

This busy restaurant has a quality menu of foreign and local dishes including burgers, curries, pizza and African fare such as *firinda* (mashed skinless beans) and lots of *mochomo* (barbecued meat). There's a good drinks list and excellent local coffee too, though its large African lunch buffet is the main reason for most to come, with dozens on local dishes you won't find elsewhere prepared daily.

ELEPHANTE

GULU | $ | CAFE

Plot 75 Jomo Kenyatta Rd; 0783-115811; mains USh8000-18,000

Gulu's hipsters flood this cute garden cafe serving wood-fired pizzas, tasty burgers and surprisingly authentic Mexican fare. It's owned by a Portland native, which ensures quality espresso drinks and a good tea selection (in addition to craft beer and a small but good wine selection). The pizza takes a while, but it's well worth the wait.

KHANA KHAZANA

KAMPALA | $$ | INDIAN

20 Acacia Ave; 0414-233049; mains USh20,000-48,000

Regarded by many as the best Indian in Kampala and thus likely in the whole of Uganda, classy Khazana has a country club vibe with a beautifully tended tropical garden and is *the* place to treat yourself to a north Indian feast. Its atmospheric Rajasthani-style decor, crisp white tablecloths and professional waiters serving a menu full of tandoori dishes and creamy curries combine to make this an unmissable highlight of Uganda's capital.

PRUNES

KAMPALA | $$ | INTERNATIONAL

8 Wampewo Ave; 772-712002; www.facebook.com/prunes.restaurant.cafe.ug; mains USh20,000-32,000

A great spot for brunch, lunch or a laid-back dinner, Prunes is a popular expat hangout. It does great Ugandan coffee and comfort food such as toasties, burgers and healthy salads of beetroot, goat's cheese, apple and nuts. Saturday mornings take on a different feel with its buzzy farmers market, which is one of the best places in Kampala to shop for fresh produce.

MEDITERRANEO

KAMPALA | $$$ | ITALIAN

31 Acacia Ave; 0414-500533; www.villakololo.com/menu; mains USh30,000-90,000

This upmarket open-air Italian restaurant occupies a sprawling wooden deck in a tropical garden, lit at night with kerosene lamps. The Italian chef creates fantastic thin-crust pizzas and handmade pastas, such as pappardelle funghi with porcini imported from Italy. You can also dine on steak, grilled rock lobster, or deep-fried calamari and prawns, or just order the chef's special of beef roll stuffed with truffle paste, porcini mushrooms & almonds.

NURALI'S CAFE

MBALE | $ | INDIAN

5 Cathedral Ave; 0772-445562; mains USh15,000-20,000

This popular Indian restaurant delivers delicious flavours from the tandoor. Both the chicken tikka masala and the chana masala are stand out dishes, plus there's excellent palak paneer and naan with big chunks of garlic. Add to that fast service and spice that hums on the tongue, and this is easily the best restaurant in Mbale. The restaurant space itself won't win any design prizes, but it's still an excellent spot given its location.

'Classy Khazana has a country club vibe with a beautifully tended tropical garden and is *the* place to treat yourself to a north Indian feast.', *Khana Khazana*

DELI

JINJA | $ | CAFE

2 Main St; 0794-589400; mains USh10,000-15,000

This industrial-chic deli and cafe is just the trick for homesick travellers. Tasty espresso drinks, brownies, gigantic fresh salads, delicious nachos and all kinds of sandwiches on crusty bread have patrons lining up at lunchtimes. Seating is mostly at picnic tables on the shady front lawn. Definitely the best dining spot in Jinja, and as full of locals as travellers.

ETHIOPIA

WHAT TO EAT

Injira and Wat
The slightly sour taste and rubbery consistency of injera resists love-at-first-sight. Once initiated, however, this ubiquitous 'pancake' becomes irresistible, contrasting perfectly with the fiery vegetarian *wat* (curry) or *siga tibs* (strips of fried, spicy meat) it generally accompanies.

Kitfo
Minced and warmed in a pan with butter, *berbere* (a mix of 16 spices) and sometimes tosin (thyme), this beef dish is an Ethiopian favourite.

Tere sega and Siga Tibs
Raw meat is not always the healthiest choice (it can carry tape worms) but is considered a prized delicacy. Contrary to rumour, it's never been cut from a living animal!

Tipping: 10% if service charge not included.

Eating Ethiopian-style means redefining common expectations of African cuisine. That's because the foundation of almost every meal in Ethiopia is *injera*, a one-of-a-kind pancake. Replacing plates, bowls and utensils, *injera* is the main accompaniment for delicious spicy stews and farm-fresh vegetables.

FOUR SISTERS

NORTHERN ETHIOPIA | $ | ETHIOPIAN

Gonder; 0918-736510; www.thefoursistersrestaurant.com; mains from Birr70

Owned and operated by four sisters, this is one of the best restaurants in northern Ethiopia. The delicious 'national food' is beautifully served in a villa set in a leafy dell, the stone walls of which are decorated with paintings inspired by Debre Berhan Selassie. There's also a cultural performance each evening.

BLACK ROSE

NORTHERN ETHIOPIA | $ | EUROPEAN, ETHIOPIAN

Mekele; 0911-513984; mains from Birr81

This stylish outpost of an Addis lounge bar is one of Mekele's more intriguing dining options. Downstairs it serves excellent pizza, pasta and Ethiopian dishes in a sophisticated setting with world music playing in the background. There's a cocktail bar upstairs.

BEN ABEBA

NORTHERN ETHIOPIA | $ | EUROPEAN, ETHIOPIAN

Lalilbela; 0333-360215, 0922-345122; www.benabeba.com; mains from Birr45

One of Ethiopia's most contemporary restaurants, this Ethio-Scottish-owned, Dalíesque jumble of walkways, platforms and fire pits is perched on the edge of a ridge with 360-degree views. The food is tasty and wholesome (traditional bread is prepared in house), the goat burgers are a house speciality and at 11am each day guests can watch injera being made.

YOD ABYSSINIA

ADDIS ABABA | $$ | ETHIOPIAN
off Cameroon St; 011 661 2985, 091 121 6127; www.yodethiopia.com; Mains from Birr160

This tourist-oriented restaurant serves some of the best traditional food in the capital, Addis, and it's a good place to try *tej* (honey wine). Photographs help identify the common Ethiopian favourites, but there are some rarely seen dishes as well, such as goat cooked with onions, garlic and seasoned butter. At 7.30pm there's an impressive cultural show.

KATEGNA

ADDIS ABABA | $ | ETHIOPIAN
Off Bole Rd/Africa Ave; 091 152 0183; mains from Birr60

A pleasingly modern take on the traditional Ethiopian restaurant, Kategna has an urban cafe atmosphere with a soothing colour scheme, low wooden stools and well-to-do young crowd. The menu covers all corners of the Ethiopian culinary scene with the house *kitfo* one highlight among many.

'I wanted to celebrate the essence of Ugandan culture, by curating distinctive dishes that nevertheless make you feel at home.'
Ghada Ghotmeh, founder of Prunes, Kampala

SANA'A RESTAURANT

ADDIS ABABA | $ | MIDDLE EASTERN
Gabon St; 091 151 4899; mains from Birr65

Worth crossing town for, this busy establishment is a lunchtime institution – queues for a table extend well beyond the door. The restaurant's popularity rests on the authentic Yemeni fare, including spicy hot *salta* (a highland stew/soup seasoned with fenugreek) and the house special, Yemeni-style chicken and rice.

ITEGUE TAITU RESTAURANT

ADDIS ABABA | $ | ETHIOPIAN
014 282 1147; www.itegue-taitu.business.site; mains from Birr44

This charming restaurant is part of one of Addis's oldest hotels; built in 1907 at the whim of Empress Taitu, it thankfully survived a fire in 2015. The high-ceilinged building is virtually a museum of antique furniture and the refined Ethiopian fare served here may just convince the sceptical that *injera* is more than merely palatable. There's a bargain-priced vegan lunchtime buffet that's immensely popular with both foreigners and well-to-do locals.

HIRUT RESTAURANT

EASTERN ETHIOPIA | $ | ETHIOPIAN
New Town, Harar; 096 217 4799; mains from Birr75

WHERE TO DRINK...

ETHIOPIAN COFFEE

Ethiopia is thought to be the original home of coffee an attending a coffee ceremony is a cultural highlight – thanks to the Italian influence, enjoying a macchiato in one of the following hip cafes is another.

Galani Cafe, Addis Ababa
This contemporary space serves Ethiopia's finest barista-poured coffees, and doubles as a dynamic cultural art space.

Tomoco, Addis Ababa
Coffee is taken seriously at this high-stooled Italian cafe (around since 1953) in Piazza. The beans are roasted on-site and there's a coffee map on the wall.

Senait Coffee Shop, Gonder
Opposite the exit to the Royal Enclosure, this characterful outdoor cafe offers the country's best beans.

Decorated with traditional woven baskets and specialising in authentic local cuisine, this is the most atmospheric restaurant in Harar. Tasty *kwanta firfir* (dried strips of beef rubbed in chilli, butter, salt and *berbere*) and pizzas, salads and sandwiches are on offer. Choose to sit in the cosy lounge or a well-shaded garden to sample the Ethiopian wines.

FRESH TOUCH RESTAURANT

EASTERN ETHIOPIA | $ | ETHIOPIAN

New Town, Harar; 091 574 0109; mains from Birr80

Classy Fresh Touch is a favourite among well-heeled locals and visitors. That's all thanks to four winning details: its convenient location near the old town, the uplifting ambience, the attractive open-air terrace and the excellent something-for-everyone menu. The burgers are a particular highlight.

PARADISE LODGE – ABAYA RESTAURANT

SOUTHERN ETHIOPIA | $$ | EUROPEAN

Arba Minch; 046 881 2914; www.paradiselodgeethiopia.com; mains from Birr90

Inside Paradise Lodge, this lovely atmospheric ridgetop dining room offers menu choices such as poached fish or beef stroganoff. It's the best sundowner spot in Arba Minch and there's outdoor seating from which to enjoy the view.

CASTEL KURIFTU WINE HOUSE & RESTAURANT

SOUTHERN ETHIOPIA | $$ | INTERNATIONAL

Ziway; 046 441 2705; mains Birr120

Easily one of the most characterful restaurants in Ethiopia, the Castel Kuriftu is something of a surprise, given the rustic location. This huge venture, built from stone, wood and thatch, not only boasts eye-catching architecture, it is also noteworthy for the delicious food, especially the grilled tilapia, and a wide selection of Rift Valley wines.

VENEZIA

SOUTHERN ETHIOPIA | $$ | ITALIAN

Awasa; 046 220 0955; www.venezia.hawassaonline.com; mains from Birr110

Run by an Italian–Ethiopian couple, this upmarket trattoria-like venue wins top marks for its flawlessly prepared Italian specialities. There's a wide range of salads, bruschetta, pasta, grills and woodfired pizzas and a good selection of Italian and South African wines.

DJIBOUTI

For sheer choice and quality of food, Djibouti has to be one of the best places in East Africa, with a plethora of tasty restaurants. You'll find excellent seafood, rice, pasta and local meat dishes. In the countryside, choice is obviously more limited.

WHAT TO EAT

Cabri farci
Stuffed kid, traditionally roasted whole on a spit, is a speciality well worth tasting, especially in the countryside.

Seafood
The local seafood is certainly Djibouti's pièce de résistance. You'll find barracuda, grouper, tuna, dorado, wahoo, trevally as well as lobster and crab. Fish is sometimes cooked Yemen-istyle (oven-baked and served with a chapatti flat bread.

Mokbasa
A belt-bustingly good purée of honey and either dates or banana.

Pastries
Along with delicious baguettes, you'll find excellent croissants and other treats in Djibouti City – a testimony to the French presence.

PRICE RANGES

For a main course:
$ less than DFr1000
$$ DFr1000–2500
$$$ DFr2500 or more

Tipping: 5–10%

CAFÉ DE LA GARE

DJIBOUTI CITY | $$$ | FRENCH
Rue de Nasro Houmed Abro; 21 35 15 30; DFr3200-6000

Dining at this upscale gourmet restaurant is a treat. The elegant dining room is decorated with earthy tones and classy furniture, and Café de la Gare is justly revered for its refined French-inspired cuisine with a bow to local ingredients. Highlights include *magret aux girolles* (duck with mushrooms), beefsteak and king prawns.

RESTAURANT L'HISTORIL

DJIBOUTI CITY | $$ | INTERNATIONAL
Pl du 27 Juin 1977; 21 34 13 64; mains DFr2200-3500

Subdued lighting, a soothing blue colour scheme and an ample selection of taste-bud-titillating specialities have made this restaurant one of the most popular in town for a fancy meal. Among the many winners are the rib of beef, steak tartare, fillet of grouper and grilled kingfish. Tempting desserts, too.

LA MER ROUGE

DJIBOUTI CITY | $$$ | SEAFOOD
Rte Nelson Mandela, Ambouli; 21 34 00 05; www.lamerrougedj.com; mains DFr2500-8500

La Mer Rouge is considered Djibouti City's premier address for crustaceans and fish. The menu revolves around whatever happens to flop onto the quayside. If they're on offer, plump for the *gambas* feta (king prawns with feta cheese) or splash out on a supersized seafood platter.

LE PIZZAIOLO

DJIBOUTI CITY | $$ | ITALIAN
Rue d'Ethiopie; 21 35 44 39; mains DFr1300-3000

Feast on palate-blowing Italian specialities in this zingy trattorialike venue. The menu roves from faultlessly cooked pizzas to pasta and from salads to meat dishes. A homemade pie or a chocolate mousse will finish you off sweetly.

WHAT TO EAT

Tibsi
Sliced lamb, pan fried in butter, garlic, onion and sometimes tomato.

Injera
This one of its kind pancake made with the indigenous Eritrean cereal *tef* is the national staple. On top of it sit anything from spicy meat stews to colourful dollops of boiled veg and cubes of raw beef.

Seafood
Along the Red Sea coast, the Arabic influence is evident. Fish kebabs and Yemeni-style charcoal-baked fish are both widely available (and succulent).

Spaghetti
A legacy left by the Italians, pasta dishes are available in all restaurants throughout Eritrea.

Capretto
Roast goat, sometimes served like a rack of lamb.

PRICE RANGES
For a main course:
$ less than Nfa50
$$ Nfa50–100
$$$ Nfa100 or more

Tipping: No tipping.

ERITREA

From spicy curries served over spongy *injera* bread to Italian classics straight from the old country, there's plenty of good food to be had in Eritrea. Eat well in Asmara, the capital, and don't miss the seafood in Massawa.

NAPOLI PIZZERIA

ASMARA | $$$ | PIZZA
36 Adi Hawesha St; 01 123784; mains Nfa70-150

If pasta offerings or pizzas make your stomach quiver with excitement, this trattoria-like venue with a cosy atmosphere is an optimal choice. If Italian fare isn't doing it for you, delve into fish dishes or Eritrean staples cooked to perfection.

AMERICAN BAR

ASMARA | $ | FAST FOOD
47 Harnet Ave; 01 205435; mains Nfa10-50

This snazzy fast-food joint serves up decent burgers and explosively fruity cocktails. The streetside terrace allows for a dash of people-watching panache with the historic Opera House in the background.

SWEET ASMARA CAFFE

ASMARA | $ | PASTRY SHOP
106 Harnet Ave; mains Nfa10-50

This sleek pastry shop is a treasure-trove for the sweet tooth, with a tempting array of diet-busting little treats in a central location on the main drag – great for soaking up some city vibes. Keep up your strength with a macchiato and a delectable cake.

SALLAM RESTAURANT

MASSAWA | $$$ | SEAFOOD
Old Town; 01 552187; mains Nfa100-180

It doesn't look like much from the outside (plastic chairs and dim lighting), but this is the culinary gem of Massawa. Here you can relish the Yemeni-style fresh fish sprinkled with hot pepper and baked in a tandoori oven. The fish, served with a chapatti flat bread, is absolutely superb. While eating you'll be surrounded by plenty of cats expecting a titbit.

SUDAN

Sudanese food is simple and not particularly varied but it's generally fresh, tasty and healthy. It's based around a few staples with spices used only sparingly. Along the Red Sea coast and the Nile, you can sample excellent fish dishes.

WHAT TO EAT

Fuul
Sudan's staple consists of broad beans stewed for hours in a large metal cauldron. The broth is ladled out into small plates and served with a dash of oil, a bit of spice, and a round of bread.

Fasuliya
This is the Sudanese version of baked beans.

Ta'amiya
This popular street snack is known elsewhere as felafel. The chickpea balls are served in a dry bread roll.

Fish
Fish dishes are widely available along the Nile. Nile perch and tilapia are usually filleted before being fried and are accompanied with bread and a chilli dipping sauce. Open-sea fish can be found along the Red Sea coast.

PRICE RANGES
For a main course:
$ less than S£50
$$ S£50–100
$$$ S£10 or more

Tipping: Not expected

AL-HOUSH

KHARTOUM | $$ | SUDANESE
El Seref Complex, Omdurman, Nile St; 156 76 76 76; www.al-housh.com; mains S£50-120

Everyone, from cabbies to well-heeled families, flocks to this legendary eatery in Omdurman. Loosen that belt for succulent *agashi* (fish or meat seared over charcoal), heaping helpings of salads and perky meatballs. The enormous dining room has bags of character. At dusk, you can sit on the terrace at the back to watch the sun go down over the Nile – a special experience.

ASSAHA VILLAGE

KHARTOUM | $$ | LEBANESE
Africa St; 183 48 19 19; www.assahavillage.com; mains S£50-130

With its vaulted dining room, brick walls and elegantly set tables, Assaha is poised to take patrons on a culinary magic-carpet ride. Nibble on a platter of olives while perusing the huge menu, perhaps settling on delicious *meze* (with great hummus) followed by a classic shwarma. The attractive terrace at the back is highly sought after at dinner.

AMWAJ

KHARTOUM | $$ | SUDANESE
Africa St; 91 828 88 90; www.facebook.com/amwajrests; mains S£40-140

A Khartoum institution. The waiters are snappy, ingredients are fresh, and prices are reasonable for scrumptious dishes such as grilled chicken, roast lamb and shwarma. Those who enjoy a sweet at the end of the meal will be impressed by the delicious baklava and other treats on offer. Some might find the decor a bit too hospital-like but that's the only gripe.

EGYPT

Egyptian cuisine is hearty peasant fare that elevates pulses to a central role and includes dishes with roots that stretch as far back as the Pharaonic era. Food is at the heart of family life but Egypt's wholesome home-cooking can be difficult to source as restaurants commonly concentrate on grilled meat. Conversely, the street food scene is a cheap-eat wonderland.

WHAT TO EAT

Kushari
Noodles, rice, black lentils and chick-peas are smothered in tomato sauce, sprinkled with fried onions and then doused with garlic-vinegar and chilli sauce.

Molokheya
An earthy stew of dried mallow-leaves, spiked with coriander, garlic and butter. Fatimid Caliph Al-Hakim was so obsessed with this soup that he banned everyone else from eating it.

Fuul mudammas
Egyptian breakfast staple. Slow-cooked, mashed fava beans in a garlicky tomato sauce.

Hamam mahshi
Roasted pigeon served stuffed with with *freekeh* (cracked green wheat) or bulgur. An Egyptian delicacy since the Pharaonic era.

PRICE RANGES

$ less than LE50
$$ LE50–150
$$$ LE150 or more

Tipping: 10%

ZEPHYRION

MEDITERRANEAN COAST | $$ | SEAFOOD

Sharia Al Geish, Aboukir; 03-562 1319; fish per kg LE75-210

This old school taverna (the name is Greek for 'sea breeze) has been serving fresh fish dishes on its sweeping blue-and-white terrace overlooking Aboukir Bay since 1929. Frills are few. Instead, this old timer has survived because of its succulent seafood and Mediterranean seafront setting. On summer weekends, when Zephyrion's regular clientele make the short jaunt north from Alexandria to Aboukir for long lazy lunching, the terrace buzzes with families.

COURTESY ZOOBA

FISH MARKET

ALEXANDRIA | $$$ | SEAFOOD
Al Corniche; 03-480 5119; mains LE60-300

An Alexandria institution for the hoity-toity set, Fish Market's dining room is in a prime position slap on the Mediterranean, with big picture windows overlooking the sea. Choose from the vast array of fishy mains displayed in the cabinets and then select a variety of mezze dishes (served with excellent Lebanese-style bread) to munch while you wait.

MOHAMMED AHMED

ALEXANDRIA | $ | EGYPTIAN
17 Sharia Shakor Pasha; 03-487 3576; mains LE2-12

The perfect lunch stop to scoff fuul and falafel. Mohammed Ahmed is Alexandria's undisputed king of spectacularly good and cheap Egyptian standards. Select your *fuul* (the iskandarani, mashed up with lots of lime juice and spices, is the local favourite), add some falafel, choose a few accompanying salads and let the feasting begin.

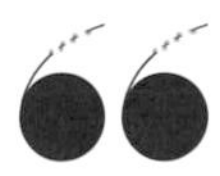

'Mohammed Ahmed is Alexandria's undisputed king of spectacularly good and cheap Egyptian standards.'
Mohammed Ahmed

ABU TAREK

CAIRO | $ | EGYPTIAN
40 Sharia Champollion, Downtown; 02-2577 5935; www.facebook.com/koshariabotarek; kushari LE10-25

King of kushari. If you want to try Egypt's carbohydrate-loaded national dish, beeline directly here. Abu Tarek has held Cairo's unofficial 'best kushari' title for decades. Head upstairs to eat in the always busy Egyptian-glitz dining room, and order your portion size; the 'special' is recommended for the all-important extra chickpeas and fried onions. When your kushari arrives douse it liberally with garlic-vinegar and chilli sauce and get stuck in.

FASAHET SOMAYA

CAIRO | $$ | EGYPTIAN
15 Sharia Youssef Al Guindi, Downtown; 020 9873 8637; www.facebook.com/FasahetSomaya; mains LE35-75

Egypt's best cooking happens at home. If you can't snag a dinner invite to a local's house, this six-table restaurant makes for a good substitute. Eschewing typical kebab-heavy menus, Fasahet Somaya instead serves up the rustic stews and stuffed vegetable staples of Egyptian family cooking, prepared like an Egyptian mother would. You'll have to dine early (it only opens 5pm to 7pm) and may have to queue.

O'S PASTA

CAIRO | $$ | ITALIAN
159 Sharia 26th of July, Zamalek; 010 0415 5756; www.ospasta.com; mains LE69-145

Squeeze – and we mean squeeze, there are only five tables – into this blue-and-green room to munch on Red Sea calamari pasta doused in a spinach and

cream sauce, or a distinctly North African–Italian fusion pasta dish of cumin spiked beef, dried figs and caramelised onions. The menu, with plentiful vegetarian options, is mainly pasta with some salads and antipasto thrown in for good measure plus a luscious sweet potato soup.

ZÖÖBA

CAIRO | $ | EGYPTIAN
Sharia 26th of July, Zamalek; 16082; www.facebook.com/ZoobaEats; dishes LE5-40

Egyptian street food gets a modern makeover. Whole-grain *kushari*, *ta'amiyya* (Egyptian falafel) sandwiches with beetroot-hibiscus tahini and pickled lemon *fuul* head up a menu of Egypt's classic cheap eats, given zesty contemporary tweaks. Eat in at the zinc-clad table amid eclectic decor, or take out. It's not just locals who love Zööba's take on Egyptian fast-food either. They won first place at London's 2016 Falafel Festival with their *ta'amiyya*.

RANGOLI

SOUTH SINAI | $$$ | INDIAN
Mövenpick Resort, Na'ama Bay, Sharm El Sheikh; 069-360 0081; www.movenpick.com/en/africa/egypt/sharm-el-sheikh; mains LE70-260

If you're a fan of the flavours of the subcontinent, don't miss Rangoli: perched within the cliff side tumble of the Mövenpick Resort with the sweep of Sharm El Sheikh's Na'ama Bay below. Thanks to the Mumbai-born chef, all the dishes here burst with authentically spicy flavour from the punchy black lentil dhal to the clay tandoori specialities. Book a balcony table for the best sunset view in town.

FARES SEAFOOD

SOUTH SINAI | $$$ | SEAFOOD
City Council St, Hadaba, Sharm El Sheikh; 069-366 3076; dishes LE40-300

There are loads of flashy seafood restaurants in Sharm El Sheikh. Long-timer Fares may be low on style-points but this is where Egyptian holidaymakers head for good-value seafood. Either order your fish priced by weight and choose how you want it cooked or pick one of the seafood *tagen* (stew cooked in a deep clay pot) menu options. The calamari and shrimp *tagen* is their speciality.

LAKHBATITA (RAMEZ & PAOLA)

SOUTH SINAI | $$ | ITALIAN
Waterfront Promenade, Mashraba, Dahab; 012 2557 9641; mains LE65-180

A slice of Italy on the Red Sea shore. Lakhbatita has been serving homemade pasta and wood-fired oven pizzas in Dahab, Egypt's dive-centric backpacker resort, since 1992. The food here is a cut above elsewhere on the waterfront. For the most relaxed dinner in town, sit back on the terrace, watching the sunset over the Red Sea, and dig into *spaghetti allo scoglio* (mixed seafood pasta) or vast bubbly crusted pizza.

P408-9: Dishes from Talisman; Carnivore. P412: Ben Abeba. Previous spread: Zööba. Next spread: Dish from Dalida.

SOFRA RESTAURANT & CAFÉ

LUXOR | $$ | EGYPTIAN
90 Sharia Mohammed Farid; 095-235 9752; www.sofra.com.eg; mains LE45-115

One of Egypt's top tables for classic Egyptian cuisine. Come here to first feast on mezze dishes of *ta'amiyya*, marinated grilled liver and pickled aubergines, then move onto mains of *hamam mahshi*, Egypt's famed dried mallow leaf stew *molokheya*, or Sofra's signature stuffed duck. Dine either in the intimate salons of this old villa sprinkled with original tilework and antique furniture or on the spacious rooftop terrace.

MARSAM RESTAURANT

LUXOR | $$ | EGYPTIAN
Marsam Hotel, Luxor west bank; 010 0342 6471; www.marsamluxor.com; mains LE50-100

Luxor's most serene restaurant, the Marsam sits amid the west bank's patchwork of farming plots and archaeological sites. Dine in the courtyard, under the shady trees, and look out at the backs of the mammoth Colossi of Memnon statues in the distance. The food is mostly hearty, fresh Egyptian fare with simple grilled fish and chicken dishes and plenty of mezze choice for those who want a light lunch.

ABEER

ASWAN | $$ | EGYPTIAN
Sharia Abtal At Tahrir; 011 0086 4739; mains LE40-80

Follow the smokey smell of grilled meat all the way down the road to find Aswan's most popular kebab restaurant. The canteen-style dining rooms, spread over a side alley, may be a tad scruffy but here it's all about the meat, expertly grilled over hot coals. Their speciality is *hamam mahshi* but if you're not up for trying pigeon, opt for the succulent grilled chicken, kofta (meatballs) or mixed grill.

1902 RESTAURANT

ASWAN | $$$ | EUROPEAN
Sofitel Old Cataract Hotel, Sharia Abtal At Tahrir; 097-231 6000; www.sofitel.com; mains LE200-410

The Old Cataract Hotel has several top-end restaurants but none grander than the 1902. Under its Moorish-inspired dome, the chefs – trained both in Egypt and France – serve sophisticated, French-style nouvelle cuisine. There is usually duck and cheese from France, fish from the Red Sea and a serious wine list from around the world. Guests are invited to play their part by dressing for the occasion.

WHERE TO DRINK...

AHWA (ARABIC COFFEE)

Fishawi's, Cairo
In business since 1773, Fishawi's is Cairo's most celebrated coffee-shop. Drink *ahwa* or tea amid the clouded mirrors and copper table-tops for old-world ambience aplenty.

Trianon, Alexandria
Sip *ahwa* within the 1930s grandeur of faded wall-panels and ornate ceiling. This cafe was once the haunt of Greek poet Cavefy.

Delices, Alexandria
Ahwa and cake in the high-ceilinged patisserie that was a favourite hangout of Allied soldiers during WWII.

Farsha Cafe, Sharm El Sheikh
All floor-cushions and lamps, Farsha is a place that travellers come for one ahwa and find themselves lingering four drinks and a *shisha* (water-pipe) later.

WHAT TO EAT

Sabich
This sandwich crams deep-fried aubergine, egg, boiled potato, cucumber, tomato, parsley and tahini into a pita. It hails from a Shabbat dish traditionally eaten by Iraqi Jews.

Kunafeh
Thought to have been first created in Nablus, then spread throughout the region, this Palestinian dessert consists of shredded *kadaif* pastry layered on top of sweet cheese and doused in syrup.

Challah
Traditional Jewish plaited-bread made from enriched dough; traditionally eaten at the Friday night dinner.

Shakshuka
Breakfast dish of spicy eggs and tomatoes with its roots in North Africa.

PRICE RANGES
$ less than 35NIS
$$ 35–70NIS
$$$ 70NIS or more

Tipping: 10%

ISRAEL & THE PALESTINIAN TERRITORIES

From innovative modern Mediterranean and creative fusion menus to simple canteens which solely concentrate on dishing up simple plates of hummus, Israel and the Palestinian Territories offers up the Middle East's most cosmopolitan dining scene. Eating out is a favourite social pastime and for both Israelis and Palestinians, food is the essential component around which all family life revolves.

MIZNON

TEL AVIV | $ | ISRAELI
30 King George St, City Centre; 03-631 7688; www.miznon.com; pitas 25-49NIS

A distinctly Mediterranean spin on fast food. This buzzy Tel Aviv street-food restaurant serves up massive pita breads stuffed with oil-soaked roasted vegetables, chicken, offal and meat as well as roasted-whole and spiced yam and cauliflower. Grab a beer and watch the frenetic action in the open kitchen while waiting for your order.

PORT SA'ID

TEL AVIV | $$ | MIDDLE EASTERN
5 Har Sinai St, South City Centre; 03-620 7436; www.facebook.com/pg/theportsaid; mains from 44NIS

The mothership for inner-city hipsters, this restaurant-bar next to the Great Synagogue is decorated with a library of vinyl records on wooden shelves and serves a menu of Middle Eastern–accented food with creative twists. Try the hummus made from lima beans, the oil-soaked roasted aubergines and the chicken livers.

ALI CARAVAN (ABU HASSAN)

TEL AVIV | $ | MIDDLE EASTERN
1 HaDolphin St, Jaffa; 03-682 0387; hummus 20NIS

If hummus is a religion, then Ali Caravan is its temple. Join the queue waiting patiently to squeeze into this simple canteen, near Jaffa Port in Tel Aviv, to dig into what many believe to be the best hummus in the country. The menu is simplicity at its best. There are just three hummus choices: plain, *fuul* (with mashed and spiced fava beans) or *masabacha* (with chick-peas and warm tahini).

DALIDA

TEL AVIV | $$ | FUSION
7 Zvulun St, South City Centre; 03-536 9627; www.en.dalidatlv.co.il; dishes 47-143NIS

Dalida is named after and inspired by the former Miss Egypt and iconic '60s singer who, like the food here, blended Arab, Italian and French styles. Chef Dan Zuaretz has added innovative tweaks to homely ingredients on a menu which stars dishes such as Arabic cabbage with champagne foam, and lamb heart with chilli jam and pickles. Eat inside the casual, bistro-style dining room or out on the courtyard.

LASHA BAKERY

THE NEGEV | $ | BAKERY

'All Kattan's dishes are rooted in traditional Middle Eastern cooking then tweaked with French gourmet techniques and style.'
Fadwa Cafe & Restaurant

COURTESY DALIDA

off Har Boker St, Spice Route Quarter, Mitzpe Ramon; 08-865 0111; www.lashabakery.com; pastries & sandwiches 15-25NIS

This small bakery-cafe is famed throughout the Negev Highlands for churning out scrumptious artisanal breads, sandwiches and stuffed pastries, and challah bread for Shabbat. Perch on one of the four counter chairs and munch your way through a *sabich* or focaccia bread topped with *shakshuka*.

URI BURI

AKKO | $$$ | SEAFOOD
HaHaganah St; 04-955 2212; mains 96-142NIS, half portions 54-85NIS

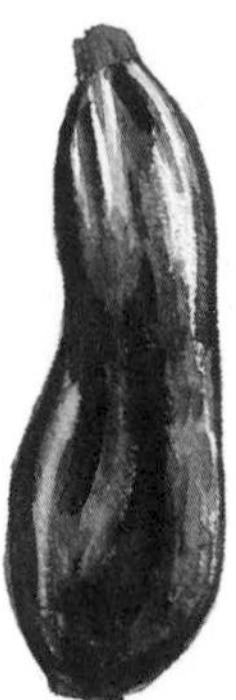

Eating at Uri Buri is enough of a reason to place Akko on your travel itinerary. The dining room may be cramped but seafood lovers will quickly understand why chef Uri is so legendary. Start with salmon sashimi freshened by wasabi sorbet, then move onto mains of prawns and artichoke swirled into buttery, black-rice noodles, or sea bass and apple simmered in coconut milk.

EIN EL WADI

HAIFA | $$ | LEBANESE

140 Derekh ha-Atsma'ut; 04-855 3353; www.facebook.com/Ein.alwadi; mains 55-80NIS

Dishes at this restaurant are as authentic as its ancient stone-cut arched cavern interior. Settle in for a feast of Lebanese and Palestinian dishes with a menu that stars Arab specialities such as *maglouba* (layered casserole of spiced rice, chicken and vegetables) and *shishbarak* (meat dumplings in a mint-spiked yoghurt stew). Attempt to leave room for the swimming-in-syrup *kunafeh* for dessert.

MAGDALENA

SEA OF GALILEE | $$$ | ARABIC

shopping mall, Migdal Jct, Rte 90, Migdal; 04-673 0064; www.magdalena.co.il; mains 75-195NIS

Innovative Galilean–Arab cuisine in sleek surroundings with views that stretch over the Sea of Galilee. Chef Zozo Hanna takes local ingredients and the recipes learned from his mother – in the Upper Galilee village of Rameh – and gives them a modern makeover on a menu that changes with the seasons but always highlights the best of the region's produce.

ALREDA

LOWER GALILEE | $$ | MIDDLE EASTERN

21 Al Bishara St, Nazareth; 04-608-4404; mains 50-100NIS

For an evening meal in Nazareth, imbued with the heady scent of yesteryear, head to this restaurant set within a Ottoman-era mansion. The menu focuses on traditional Nazarene recipes – some with Mediterranean twists – with specialities including seasonal dishes of okra (*bamya*) and wild thistle (*akub*), and fresh artichoke hearts filled with chopped beef, almonds and pine nuts.

ABU SHUKRI

JERUSALEM | $ | MIDDLE EASTERN

63 Al Wad (Hagai) St, Old City; 02-627 1538; hummus 25-30NIS

The hummus is so good at this little canteen, that it has spawned imitators all around Jerusalem. Order your hummus topped with either chickpeas, tahini, *fuul* or pine nuts and don't forget to add in a side order of falafel.

AZURA

JERUSALEM | $$ | MIDDLE EASTERN

4 Ha Eshkol, Iraqi Market, Downtown; 02-623 5204; mains 45-100NIS

In business since the 1950's, Azura is one of Jerusalem's best loved spots for slow-cooked comfort food. This kosher restaurant is where you head for hearty fare which you can see being cooked in huge pots over kerosene burners. Get stuck into a meat or vegetable goulash and don't leave without trying their signature Turkish-influenced dish of aubergine stuffed with minced beef in a cinnamon-spiced sauce.

MACHNEYUDA

JERUSALEM | $$$ | INTERNATIONAL
10 Beit Ya'akov St, Downtown; 02-533 3442; www.machneyuda.co.il; mains 76-161NIS

Owned by three of Israel's most acclaimed chefs, Machneyuda has won local plaudits for its playful menu which mixes modern-Mediterranean, New York bistro and Middle Eastern soul food. There's something for everyone from a classic mushroom risotto slicked with truffle oil, to an ode to offal called 'no brains, no worries'. The interior is as eclectic as the menu.

JALA JUNGLE

WEST BANK | $$ | MIDDLE EASTERN
El Makhrour St, Beit Jala; 05 8458 0207; www.jalajungle.business.site; mains 40-80NIS

On a hillside in Beit Jala, Jala Jungle serves home-style Palestinian food amid an organic farm, with clucking hens and views over the southern West Bank. Grab a table amid the trees and order wholesome vegetable dishes of spinach and aubergine or traditional favourites, *maglouba* (layered casserole of spiced rice, chicken and vegetables) and *mansaf* (lamb and rice doused in a sauce made from fermented dried-yoghurt).

FADWA CAFE & RESTAURANT

WEST BANK | $$ | MIDDLE EASTERN
Hosh Al Syrian Guesthouse, Old City, Bethlehem; 02-274 7529; www.hoshalsyrian.com/fawda-cafe-restaurant; mains 30-70NIS

Book ahead to sample chef Fadi Kattan's fusion of Franco–Palestinian food within the stone-cut dining room of Bethlehem's Hosh Al Syrian Guesthouse. All Kattan's dishes are rooted in traditional Middle Eastern cooking then tweaked with French gourmet techniques and style. The menu changes daily based on what produce is fresh and in season from local farmers and Bethlehem's market that day.

LA VIE CAFÉ

WEST BANK | $$ | INTERNATIONAL
Castel St, Ramallah; 02-296 4115; www.facebook.com/LaVieRamallah; mains 35-70NIS

Take a timeout at this casual cafe run by Saleh and Morgan. Inside, local art graces colourful walls while the shady garden is a relaxing respite from Ramallah's bustle. The menu skips from camel burgers and Middle Eastern mezze to pasta dishes and salads made from produce grown on the cafe's organic roof garden.

WHERE TO DRINK...

KUNAFEH

Jaafar Sweets, Jerusalem
Syrup-doused, sweet cheese *kunafeh* is the signature dish of this well-established Palestinian dessert vendor in Jerusalem Old City's Muslim Quarter.

Al Aqsa, Nablus
Head to this hole-in-the-wall bakery, next to the Al Kebir Mosque in Nablus, to taste what is considered to be the finest *kunafeh* in the Palestinian Territories.

Abd Al Hadi, Haifa
Middle Eastern pastries are piled high in this bakery, including excellent *kunafeh*. Add a strong Turkish coffee to your order, to offset the post-sugar slump.

Elmokhtar Sweets, Nazareth
This brightly lit sweets emporium offers up mouth-watering *kunafeh* along with baklava and homemade halva.

JORDAN

Crossroads of the Middle East, Jordan has absorbed both the classic recipes of pan-Arab cuisine and the family-feast dishes of its Bedouin roots. Whatever's on the menu, Jordanians are finicky about local produce, from ruby-red tomatoes grown in the Jordan Valley and olive oil direct from the producer, to the bread, enwrapping your falafel or *shawarma*, freshly baked that day.

WHAT TO EAT

Mansaf
This lamb and nut-spiked rice Bedouin dish is smothered in a sauce made from *jameed* (fermented dried yoghurt). Traditionally cooked for family celebrations.

Maglouba
A layered casserole of rice, chicken and vegetables. The pot is flipped upside down (*maglouba* is 'upside down' in Arabic) onto a platter to serve.

Zarb
A Bedouin barbecue. Meat and vegetables slow-cooked over coals in a metal drum buried under the sand.

Shrak
This Bedouin bread is rolled paper-thin, then cooked on a dome-shaped griddle called a *saj*.

PRICE RANGES
$ less than JD5
$$ JD5–10
$$$ JD10 or more

Tipping: 10%

UMM QAIS RESTHOUSE

JORDAN VALLEY | $$ | JORDANIAN

Umm Qais (ancient Gadara) archaeological site, Umm Qais; 02-750 0555; www.romero-jordan.com/um-qais.html; mains around JD7

Perched atop a hill in the Umm Qais ruins, the Umm Qais Resthouse has views that swoop over the Sea of Galilee, the Golan Heights and the peaks of Lebanon. After hiking around the ruins, come here for lunch on the outdoor terrace, surrounded by wildflowers, to dine on a seasonal menu of Jordanian dishes that highlights fresh produce, locally raised meats and regional wines.

LEBANESE HOUSE

NORTHWESTERN JORDAN | $$$ | MEZZE

Bab Amman, Jerash; 02 635 3330; www.lebanesehouse-restaurant.com; meals JD10-18

When Jerash families fancy a slap-up mezze spread, they head here. Known locally as 'Umm Khalil', this large

restaurant has been a national treasure since it opened in 1977. Do as the locals do and come here to feast on the best of Middle Eastern mezze from old favourites hummus and *wara ainab* (stuffed vine leaves), to *kibbeh* (ground lamb and bulgur wheat croquettes) and *makdous* (pickled aubergines).

REEM CAFETERIA

AMMAN | $ | MIDDLE EASTERN
2nd Circle, Jebel Amman; 06 464 5725; Shawarma JD1

There are hundreds of shoebox-sized *shawarma* (meat sliced off a vertical spit and stuffed in a pocket of pita-type bread with chopped tomatoes and garnish) sandwich kiosks in Amman but few that still have customers queuing down the street at 3am. To find out what all the fuss is about, look for the red-and-white awning (with milling crowd) at Amman's 2nd Circle roundabout, and join the queue.

SUFRA

AMMAN | $$$ | JORDANIAN
28 Rainbow St, Jebel Amman; 06 461 1468; www.romero-jordan.com/sufra.html; start from JD3.350, mains from JD10

Amman's top-spot for traditional Jordanian cuisine. *Mansaf* and *maglouba* are the Bedouin-rooted classics of Jordanian cooking but are generally reserved for family celebrations so can be difficult to find in restaurants but here, refined versions of both dishes are the stars of the menu. Dine either in the stone-cut rooms of this Ottoman-era villa or outside on the terrace garden with its sweeping views over the capital.

'They say nothing beats a home-cooked meal, and that's the spirit we offer you at Najla's, the true flavours of Jordan, preserved in this homey setting.'
Najla's Kitchen

WALEED_HAMMOUDEH/GETTY IMAGES ©

NAJLA'S KITCHEN

AMMAN | $$$ | JORDANIAN
16 Mohammed Ali Al Saedi St, Lweibdeh; 07 9515 5566; www.facebook.com/Najlashomemade; set meals JD15

The Haddad family offer a taste of Jordanian home cooking with their daily changing menu at this lunch-only restaurant named after their grandmother and inspired by her handed-down family recipes. Expect one rustic main and a series of fresh, seasonal sides. Even the bright, high-ceilinged interior radiates homey

ambience with its scatter of vintage furniture and decorative family knick-knacks.

HASHEM

AMMAN | $ | FALAFEL
Al Malek Faisal St, Downtown; 06 463 6440; www.facebook.com/Hashem.Restaurant.Amman; falafel JD3

Fellow falafel fans, beeline here. More than 50 years old, Hashem is an Amman institution. The menu choice is as simple as you can get – falafel, hummus and *fuul* (fava bean paste), all washed down with a glass of tea. It throngs with customers digging into these street food staples until the wee hours with tables spilling out of the plain dining room into the skinny alley outside.

JASMINE HOUSE

AMMAN | $$ | ITALIAN
Al Baouniyah St, Lweibdeh; 06 461 1879; www.facebook.com/JHA23; mains around JD7

The full-bodied flavours of the Mediterranean are served within the cactus-studded garden terrace and modernist-style rooms of this 1950s villa in Amman. The menu, which changes with the seasons, is small and focussed mainly on Italian cooking; expect home-made pasta dishes and classics such as parmigiana and lasagne. The villa is also a casual art gallery and the walls are often hung with works from their temporary exhibitions.

AL MANDI

MADABA | $ | MIDDLE EASTERN
Al Quds St; 05 325 3256; meals JD3

Al Mandi knows the adage: do one thing and do it well. Come to this simple canteen in Madaba to get stuck into an enormous plate of *mandi* (a Yemeni chicken and rice dish, topped with nuts and dried fruit and served with broth and a salad). Solo light-eaters might want to find a friend instead of attempting to polish off the entire portion by themselves.

HARET JDOUDNA

MADABA | $$$ | JORDANIAN
Talal St; 05 324 8650; www.haretjdoudna.com; mains JD8-15

Madaba's long-time favourite restaurant for fine quality Jordanian feasting is set in a restored Ottoman–era house, with a leafy courtyard for summer dining and roaring fire during winter. It's known for its *sawani* (meat and vegetables cooked on trays in a wood-burning oven) dishes but the menu offers the full caboodle of classic Middle Eastern mezze and kebab from smoothly whipped hummus to *shish tawouk* (grilled chicken kebab).

AL SARAYA RESTAURANT

PETRA (WADI MUSA) | $$$ | INTERNATIONAL
Mövenpick Hotel, Tourism St, Lower Wadi Musa; 03 215 7111; buffet JD20

Previous spread: Dishes from Sufra; Mansaf. Next spread: Dishes from Tawlet Ammiq.

Serving a top-notch international buffet in an elegant banquet hall inside Petra's Mövenpick Hotel, this is as opulent it gets for dining in Wadi Musa. It's worth leaving time for a nightcap in the grand, wood-panelled bar afterwards, which sports a roaring fire in the hearth in winter or a rooftop cocktail in summer.

ORIENTAL RESTAURANT

PETRA (WADI MUSA) | $$ | JORDANIAN

Tourism St, Lower Wadi Musa; 03 215 7087; mains JD6

After a day of hiking the trails of Petra, head to this super-friendly, simple spot, on the road leading to the site entrance, to refuel. Grab a spot on the narrow outdoor terrace, for prime people-watching, and order a mezze spread of hummus, *fatoush* (tomato, onion, mint and toasted bread salad) and *baba ghanoush* (aubergine and tahini puree) for a light dinner or dig into Jordan's national dish of *mansaf*.

AL MOHANDES

AQABA | $ | FALAFEL

At Tabari St; 07 9551 9904; mains JD1-2.50

Fast-food Middle Eastern style. This canteen is as unpretentious as they come and churns out crisp, but fluffy inside, falafel, olive oil-slicked hummus, fresh salads and hearty bowls of *fuul* (fava bean paste) to the masses all day long. If you're feeling fancy, add on one of their simple dishes of eggs, *shawarma* (meat sliced from a vertical spit) plates or grilled liver to your order.

CAPTAIN'S RESTAURANT

AQABA | $$$ | SEAFOOD

An Nahda St; 03 201 6905; www.captains.jo; mains JD8-18

Decorated in cheerful nautical style – think giant ship wheels as ceiling lighting and anchors hanging on the walls – Captains is where Aqaba locals come for a seafood blowout. The menu covers all the usual fishy bases from succulently grilled seabream to calamari and prawns. For a distinctly Middle Eastern take on fish cookery, order their speciality *sayadieh* (fish, delicately spiced, served with rice in an onion and tahini sauce).

BABA ZA'ATAR

AQABA | $ | BAKERY

As Sadah St; 07 9920 4006; mains JD1.25-4.50

Bakeries churning out *manakeesh* (baked flatbreads with various toppings) make for the best breakfast in Jordan. Baba Za'atar is a contemporary take on the traditional hole-in-the-wall, with a shaded picnic-table area outside for you to sit down and eat onsite. They do pizza as well but you're here for the fresh-from-the-oven, bubbly edged *manakeesh* topped with cheese, minced meat or tangy *za'atar* (spice mix of hyssop, sumac and sesame seeds).

WHERE TO EAT...

JORDANIAN HOME-COOKING

Al Ayoun Homestays, Orjan Village
The Al Ayoun Society's village homestays in Ajloun Forest Reserve are one of the best places in the country to dig into flavourful rustic home-cooking.

Beit Sitti, Amman
Learn the hearty recipes of Jordan's home cooks at these friendly cooking classes run by the Haddad family in Jordan's capital.

Galsoum's Kitchen, Umm Qais
Book in advance for a traditional north Jordanian feast, all created from seasonal, local produce and served in chef Galsoum's local home.

Petra Kitchen, Wadi Musa
Cook up a spread of Jordanian family favourites at this fun cooking class in Petra.

WHAT TO EAT

Hummus Beiruti
A creamier, more garlicky variation of hummus, spiked with herbs, green chilli and cumin.

Kibbeh nayyeh
Levantine cuisine's version of steak tartare. Minced raw lamb, mixed with mint, marjoram, onion, cayenne pepper, cinnamon and fine cracked wheat.

Shanklish
Ball-shaped aged, dried cheese (made from sheep or cow's milk) often rolled in *za'atar* (spice mix of hyssop, sumac and sesame) or Aleppo pepper.

Tabbouleh
Lebanon's classic salad and its national dish. Finely chopped parsley, mint, tomatoes and onions mixed with bulgur.

PRICE RANGES

$ less than LL15,000
$$ LL15,000 to LL30,000
$$$ LL30,000 or more

Tipping: 10–15%

LEBANON

Middle Eastern flavours at their most refined; food is central to Lebanese culture. A medley of cooking influences, from Armenian to Syrian, converged here to create the region's finest classical cuisine. Whatever your budget, it's impossible not to eat well.

ONNO

BEIRUT | $$ | ARMENIAN
Rue Badaro, Badaro; 70 383 203; www.facebook.com/OnnoBistro; mains LL12,000-26,000

The welcoming service at this wood-panel-framed bistro make Onno a local hit. The menu marries Armenian specialities such as *fishna kebab* (grilled lamb in sour cherry sauce) and *manti* (Armenian ravioli stuffed with spinach and topped with garlicky yoghurt) with Lebanese mezze classics. Adventurous eaters get a good look-in with lamb's brains, fried sparrows and beef tongue making menu appearances.

COURTESY TAWLET AMMIQ

CAFE EM NAZIH

BEIRUT | $ | CAFE
Rue Pasteur, Gemmayzeh; 76 711 466; www.saifigardens.com/en/cafe; dishes LL6000-18,000

This urban hideaway is a haunt of students, artists and foreign residents. In the day, people come for light lunches of mezze such as *hindbeh* (sautéed dandelion greens), *musakhan* (sumac-spiced chicken on flatbread) and *hummus beiruti*. After dark, it's a popular venue for cheap beer and *shisha* (water-pipe) with regular weekend gigs.

FALAFEL SAHYOUN

BEIRUT | $ | FALAFEL
Bechara El Khoury, Basta Tahta; 01 633 188; falafel LL3000

Beirutis have strong, often divisive opinions about where to find the best in class of any food, so it means all the more that this basic canteen is widely considered to make the best falafel in the city. Nothing fancy, simply crisp on the outside and fluffy inside falafel balls, served inside pita with fresh salad and hummus.

LIZA

BEIRUT | $$$ | LEBANESE
1st fl, Metropolitan Club, Rue Doumani, Achrafiych; 01 208 108, www.lizabeirut.com; mezze LL10,000-34,000, mains LL26,000-49,000

Expertly prepared nouvelle Lebanese food in chic surroundings – all tile-work, hanging-lamps and wall-frescoes – that have featured in international design magazines. Begin with mezzes of *hummus bi lahme* (hummus topped by pan-fried lamb), *kibbeh nayyeh* or *batrakh* (fish roe), then move on to signature dishes such as citrus-marinated chicken on *treekeh* (cracked green wheat). Prices are remarkably reasonable considering the quality – especially their daily lunchtime *plat du jour*.

FENIQIA

BYBLOS | $$ | LEBANESE
Rue Pepe Abed, Old Souk; 09 540 444; www.facebook.com/Feniqia; mains LL25,000-33,000

Set in a semi-open pavilion, neighbouring Byblos' ancient ruins, Feniqia serves classic Lebanese mezze and grills presented with fun, contemporary tweaks while the charismatic owner revs up a fun atmosphere. The dark tahini with toast-your-own-pita is a sensational free appetiser, while meat platters come arrayed on serious hardware.

COURTESY TAWLET AMMIQ

TAWLET AMMIQ

BEKAA VALLEY | $$ | LEBANESE
Ammiq Old Village, West Bakaa; 03 004 481; www.soukeltayeb.com; set weekend lunch US$44

Every weekend Lebanese foodies drive into the Bekaa Valley for a culinary adventure at Tawlet Ammiq where the test-kitchen gives local cooks the opportunity to refine and showcase traditional recipes. Diners choose from a buffet piled high with regional delicacies while admiring sweeping views of the western Bekaa from the terrace (in summer) or seated around the pot-belly stove when the weather is cool.

WHERE TO DRINK...

LEBANESE WINE

IXSIR, Basbina
This environmentally sustainable winery, in the hills above Batroun, is one of Lebanon's most impressive wine-operations and is the best-organised for tours and tastings.

Chateau Kefraya, Kafraiya
Bekaa Valley producer of quality reds and whites. Best for lunch in the restaurant and a tasting session in the shop though also runs tours.

Chateau Ksara, Ksara
This famous Bekaa Valley winery runs tours and tastings that include a visit to an atmospheric Roman-era cave complex where some of the wines are cellared.

Chateau Sanctus, Marmama
Book ahead for the weekend-only tastings and tours at this organic boutique winery.

SAUDI ARABIA

As the guardian of holy cities Mecca and Medina, Saudi Arabia attracts millions of visitors during *hajj* and *umra*. Catering for the faithful, restaurants across the country specialise in various expatriate cuisines, making for an eclectic dining experience for all.

WHAT TO EAT

Ramadan treats
You don't have to be a pilgrim to sample some of the treats associated with Saudi Arabia's Islamic traditions: Ramadan tents attached to hotels across the country offer many delicacies that are only available during the Holy Month.

Dates
With health-giving properties, dates are a traditional staple of the Bedouin who continue to roam Saudi Arabia's interior. To sample the myriad varieties, head to date markets in Buraydah and Al Hofuf.

Camel meat and milk
A favourite of high days and holidays, *hashi* (young camel) can be sampled in Riyadh restaurants while camel's milk is beginning to appear in supermarkets.

PRICE RANGES

$ less than SR30
$$ SR30–120
$$$ SR120 or more

Tipping: 10% in larger towns only

MAKKAH RESTAURANT

JEDDAH | $$ | MIDDLE EASTERN

Off King Fahad Rd, Sharafaya; 012 604 0016; mains from SR12

Styled as a traditional tent, with open sides to let the sea breezes in, this huge courtyard restaurant is decked with traditional couches – the perfect way to share a meal from a traditional serving platter. After-dinner diners puff on fruity shisha which adds to the scented Jeddah evenings.

AL ULA HERITAGE RESTAURANT

NORTHERN SAUDI ARABIA | $ | ARABIAN

Al Hameediya, off Route 375; 055 837 0888; mains from SR12

This busy little restaurant is set in a mock-traditional house, in keeping with the modern trend for retro. The chef's fresh *kunafeh* (a sweet vermicelli and soft cheese dish) is a local legend: in the evenings he shuttles the little metal *kunafeh* dishes non-stop onto the open burners. It doesn't get fresher than that!

AL TURATHI

CENTRAL NAJD | $ | MIDDLE EASTERN

King Abdul Aziz Rd, Hail; 016 531 0000; mains from SR16

Located in a beautiful mock traditional house, this part-museum, part-restaurant is stocked with vintage and antique items across its two storeys. There's no English menu, but the friendly staff help with the aid of pictures. The cuisine is local in emphasis with the chicken *mandi* (roast chicken and rice) particularly worth sampling.

GLOBE LOUNGE

RIYADH | $$$ | INTERNATIONAL
Al Faisaliah Tower, Rd 38, Al Olaya; 011 273 2222; www.alfaisaliahhotels.com; mains from SR210

One of five restaurants in Al Faisaliah Tower, the Globe Lounge has spectacular views over the city. Cosy and dimly lit, it's not only the most romantic spot in town, it also offers some of the best cuisine, including delicious Wagyu steaks and Canadian lobster.

NAJD VILLAGE

RIYADH | $ | MIDDLE EASTERN
Abi Bakr As Siddiq Rd, Al Mursalat; 9200 33511; www.najdvillage.com; mains from SR21

For Saudi food in a Saudi setting (some rooms even have a traditional fireplace), this is the perfect place to sample popular regional dishes such as *kabsa* (meat with rice) or *hashi* (baby camel). The set menu includes 14 mains, coffee, dates and *bakhoor* (incense).

AL SABAT BBQ

EASTERN PROVINCE | $ | MIDDLE EASTERN
Al Anwar, Al Qatif; 053 585 6668; mains from SR10

South of Al Qatif's centre, this beautiful, traditional restaurant is set around an open courtyard filled with greenery and a water feature. A family-run enterprise, it's hugely popular with locals. Grilled meat, served with clay-oven-baked flatbread and salad, is the order of the day and uniformly delicious.

'Our philosophy at Najd Village is based on providing you with a convenient place that is rich with history and heritage.'
Najd Village

PARKERS

EASTERN PROVINCE | $ | VEGAN
Prince Faisal Bin Fahd Rd, Dammam; 013 882 0260; mains from SR24

After an elaborate social media campaign launched this trendy restaurant, it has become the place to be seen for young, hip Saudis. With a garden, benches and a food truck, it's more East London than Eastern Province but the main restaurant serves up innovative comfort food like mac and Cheetos and corn on the cob with orange basil.

SEREI UNCLE IDRIS

JAZAN | $ | SUDANESE
King Fahd Rd; 055 765 9268; mains from SR12

Soldiers, Yemenis, elderly uncles and local *shebab* (teenage boys) all share the queue for the best Sudanese food in town: most ask for *lahm madfun* (buried meat) – grilled meat strips cooked in a spicy vegetable sauce and served with bread rolls. Given the delicious food, no one cares about the rough-and-ready plastic chairs and tables.

KUWAIT

In the heart of Kuwait City, Souq Mubarakiya unfolds into alleyways and courtyards in a maze of stalls selling spices, vegetables and fruits. The emphasis on 'bought fresh daily' is reflected in the country's now globalised but still wholesome cuisine.

WHAT TO EAT

Fish
There are plenty of reminders of Kuwait's seafaring history in the museums of the capital. What better place to sample Gulf seafood than in one of the boats traditionally used to catch it! Head to the hull of Al Boom to sample a typical catch.

Lebanese food
Of all the many expatriate nationalities who call Kuwait home, the Lebanese have left the biggest imprint on the country's taste buds. While almost all the best eateries are focused on the capital, Kuwait City, cafes in the interior can usually be relied upon to serve delicious mezze and grilled meats too.

PRICE RANGES

For main dishes:
$ less than KD5
$$ KD5–10
$$$ KD10 or more

Tipping: 10% in top restaurants only

GREENLAND VEGETARIAN RESTAURANT

KUWAIT CITY | $ | INDIAN

Souq Mubarakiya; 22422246; mains from KD2

A welcome relief from the Gulf emphasis on meat, this vegetarian restaurant in Souq Mubarakiya is decorated with Gandhi portraits and Indian street art. Highlights include South Indian *thali* with eight bowls of curry, dips, rice, paratha and poppadum.

MAIS ALGHANIM

KUWAIT CITY | $ | MIDDLE EASTERN

Arabian Gulf St; 22251155; www.maisalghanim.com; mains from KD3

With Arabian décor, heritage artefacts and a homely atmosphere, this family-run, seafront restaurant has heaps of character. They've been serving excellent Middle Eastern cooking here since 1953 and charcoal-grilled meats, seafood and rice dishes are menu highlights – if space allows after the delectable mezze.

BURJ AL HAMAM

KUWAIT CITY | $ | LEBANESE

Arabian Gulf St, Dasman; 22529095; www.burjalhamam.com.kw; mains from KD3.5

An unmissable waterfront venue with a sea-view terrace, this restaurant offers top mezze such as *dolma* (stuffed grape vine leaves), baked aubergine and aged *shankleesh* (mould-ripened cheese). The focus is Levant-inspired but other dishes (including testicles and brain) originate in Egypt and Armenia.

AL BOOM

KUWAIT CITY | $$$ | SEAFOOD

Radisson Blu, Taawen St, Rumaithiya; 25673430; www.radissonblu.com/en/hotel-kuwait/restaurants; mains from KD20

This atmospheric restaurant is housed in the hull of *Mohammedi II*, which took three years to build. Dishes include Omani lobster, Gulf shrimps and Kuwaiti zubeidi fish. There's no fear of seasickness – the boat is in dry dock.

BAHRAIN

If, as Rudyard Kipling contended, the best way to get acquainted with a country is to smell it, then a walk beyond Manama's Bab Bahrain – where coriander, cumin and hints of sesame pickle the air – quickly establishes Bahrain's culinary credentials.

WHAT TO EAT

Biryani
The large Pakistani community in Bahrain has contributed to the internationalisation of the country's cuisine with excellent meat, chicken or fish biryanis served in even the smallest cafes.

Coffee and cake
The Manama suburb of Adliya has a reputation for smart cafes. Here the Western tradition of coffee and cake has taken on a local flavour with Middle Eastern spices pepping up dessert menus.

Mixed grill
A staple of a Bahraini night out is the mixed grill. Marinated meats are arranged on unleavened flat bread and served with salad, hummus, limes and sliced onions.

PRICE RANGES
For main dishes:
$ less than BD3
$$ BD3–9
$$$ BD9 or more

Tipping: 10%

HOUSE OF COFFEE

MUHARRAQ ISLAND | $$ | INTERNATIONAL
Rd 918, Block 208; 17 322 549; www.shaikhebrahimcenter.org/en/houses/house-of-coffee-2; mains from BD3.5

Housed across three traditional Bahraini buildings, this coffee museum, cafe and restaurant serves international staples with a local flare, such as baklava cheesecake. They also offer an excellent traditional breakfast. Naturally, you'll want to end the meal with a coffee!

CAFÉ LILOU

MANAMA | $$ | CAFÉ
Rd 3803, Block 338, Adliya; 17 714 440; mains from BD3

This elegant balconied venue, with its velvet upholstery, wrought-iron banisters and polished-wood floors, is reminiscent of a 19th-century Parisian brasserie, and it's the perfect place for brunch. With mains like tamarind hammour, served with saffron-almond rice and rose petals in dried lime butter and chives, it deserves its fine reputation.

HAJI'S CAFÉ 1950

MANAMA | $ | MIDDLE EASTERN
Government Ave; 17 210 647; mains from BD2

Put your feet up (literally), order the house special and tuck into delicately spiced chunks of grilled meat served with a fresh salad and bread baked in a clay oven. The recipe of this 70-year old restaurant's success is that it has kept it simple.

MASSO

MANAMA | $$$ | INTERNATIONAL
cnr Mahooz Rd & Sheikh Isa Ave; 17 721 061; www.massorestaurant.com; mains from BD26

With creative use of fresh local ingredients, standout dishes at this sophisticated venue include chicken soaked in Earl Grey and harissa-marinated lamb chops. Western expats gravitate towards this sociable hotspot and the expert help with the wine menu.

WHAT TO EAT

International
From Turkish to Thai, there's every kind of cuisine available in Qatar's elegant modern capital. Current favourites are Doha's signature Japanese restaurants, Nobu and Morimoto.

Middle East sweets
For something distinctly regional, head to Souq Waqif. Many boutique-style restaurants focus on Middle Eastern fare, including Al Aker which specialises in trays of addictive *kunafeh* (crispy pastry filled with cheese).

Brunch
In common with Gulf neighbours, Qatar specialises in weekend brunch. This combination of Western breakfast, Lebanese lunch and Asian dinner, served buffet style from 11am to 3pm, is a hallmark of Doha's luxury hotels.

PRICE RANGES
For main dishes:
$ less than QR50
$$ QR50–150
$$$ QR150 or more

Tipping: 10%

QATAR

Once a dusty strip of pearling communities along the desert fringe, the capital, Doha, is now at the heart of luxurious living in the Gulf. Globalisation has brought international flavours to some of the region's top restaurants – an exclusively capital experience.

EVERGREEN ORGANICS

DOHA | $ | VEGAN
Palazzo 1, Mercato Qanat Quartier, The Pearl; 447 20437; www.evergreenorganics.qa; mains from QR35

Doha's first vegan cafe, Evergreen Organics is the brainchild of two young Qataris. With hardwood interiors and innovative, consciously sourced, artisanal wholefoods (date and pear granola, buckwheat pancakes and kale salads), this spot is right on message.

NOBU

DOHA | $$$ | JAPANESE
Four Seasons Hotel, Diplomatic St; 449 48500; www.noburestaurants.com; small plates & sushi QR90-295

This is the world's largest – and arguably most architecturally outstanding – branch of Nobu Matsuhisa's globally acclaimed dining experience. Shaped like a shell, there are stunning views from a rooftop bar. Prices are high, but this is once-in-a-lifetime fare.

BANDER ADEN

DOHA | $ | MIDDLE EASTERN
Souq Waqif; 443 75503; www.bandaraden.com; mezze QR10-50

A veritable institution in among Souq Waqif's trendier neighbours, this casual restaurant with traditional Yemeni cooking draws crowds of locals. Mounds of rice, all manner of meats, fish, stews, salads and fresh breads makes this the perfect venue for a mid-souq supper.

AL ODAID

MESAIEED | $ | MEDITERRANEAN
Sealine Beach Resort, Sealine Beach Rd; 447 65200; www.sealinebeachqatar.com/sealine-dining.html; mains from QR35

Wedged between sand dunes and the sea, diners here are reminded that there's more to Qatar than Doha. Order *shrimp jarish* cooked with ginger, garlic and Qatari herbs, or chicken *machboos* (aromatic rice with onions, tomatoes and spices), and savour Qatar's Bedouin heritage.

UNITED ARAB EMIRATES

Fuelled by cosmopolitan super cities Dubai, Abu Dhabi and Sharjah, along with a population counting itself 90% foreign, the wonderful foodscape of the United Arab Emirates is dominated by international cuisines. Far more challenging? Finding something Emirati to eat! But those willing to adventure beyond glitzy and glamorous hotels and high-rises will find much culinary treasure buried in the desert.

WHAT TO EAT

Harees
This porridge-like stew is made from cracked wheat and chicken or lamb slow-cooked in a covered clay pot with coal.

Kabsa
A fragrant, one-pot mixture of basmati rice, lamb or chicken, mixed vegetables and spices, often cooked mandi style (barbecued in a deep hole in the ground).

Camel
Burgers, chocolate (made from its milk) or stuffed whole at a special event, camel is bound to stumble across your palate.

Machboos
A meat or fish *casserole* with rice, onions and dried lemon (loomy) cooked in a spicy sauce.

Luqaimat
Deep-fried balls of dough doused in sugary-sweet date syrup.

PRICE RANGES
For a main course:
$ less than Dhs30
$$ Dhs30–90
$$$ Dhs90 or more

Tipping: 10%

LI BEIRUT

ABU DHABI | $$$ | LEBANESE
Corniche Rd (West), Jumeirah at Etihad Towers; 02 811 5666; www.jumeirah.com; mains Dhs80-210

Levantine mezze classics of *moutabel* (purée of aubergine mixed with tahini, yoghurt and olive oil) and *muhammara* (red chilli and walnut dip) soar; mains including rack of lamb encrusted with *zaatar* (a blend of spices that includes hyssop, sumac and sesame) or quail stuffed with *freekeh* (roasted green wheat) are superb. Lebanese wines – including famed Château Musar – and beers (Almaza, Beirut) complement what has to be one of the best meals in town.

CAFÉ ARABIA

ABU DHABI | $$ | MIDDLE EASTERN
Villa No 224/1, 15th St, Al Mushrif; 02 643 9699; www.facebook.com/cafearabia; mains Dhs25-90

Housed in a three-floor villa, this cafe is run by a Lebanese arts enthusiast, Aida Mansour. It tempts with vast breakfast choices from avocado toast to *shakshuka* (poached eggs in a spicy tomato sauce) and a mains menu that waltzes from sweet potato and feta salad to *harira* (Moroccan lentil soup), falafel platters and a locally loved camel burger.

CAFETERIA AL LIWAN

ABU DHABI | $ | SYRIAN
Lakeview tower, Next to ADNIF, Corniche Abu Dhabi; 2 622 9440; www.facebook.com/liwanabudhabi; mains Dhs20-40

This budget canteen will exceed your expectations. Discover Middle

COURTESY DAI PAI YONG

Eastern flavours Syria-nstyle, with some of Abu Dhabi's best hummus and *fuul* (mashed fava beans), falafel fried to crispy perfection and *kawaj* (tomato and mincemeat casserole) that would make a Damascene mamma proud.

AL MINA FISH MARKET

ABU DHABI | $ | SEAFOOD
Dhow Harbour; 02 670 3888; meals Dhs50

For a memorable lunch, suss out your fresh fish from the folk dressed in blue and take it to the folk dressed in red in the gutting and filleting station, then jostle with seafarers for your favourite spices and, finally, give everything to the cooks at one of the attached small canteens, who will make it into a fire-hot Kerala fish curry or simply grill it rubbed in salt and lemon. Phew!

BUTCHER & STILL

ABU DHABI | $$$ | STEAK
Four Seasons Abu Dhabi, Al Maryah Island; 02 333 2444; www.fourseasons.com/abudhabi; steak Dhs280-490

American chef Marshall Roth sources his meat for this outstanding 1920s Chicago-inspired steakhouse from the Temple Grandin-designed Creekstone Farms in Kansas (USA); when paired with his béchamel-creamed spinach, you have a perfectly executed classic combination. Don't even consider skipping the 99% lump crab cake as a starter, either!

BAIT EL KHETYAR

ABU DHABI | $ | JORDANIAN
Fatima Bint Mubarak St; 02 633 3200; mains Dhs6-37

This booming Jordanian restaurant boasts contemporary décor that could be considered rather chic compared to similar joints, but keep your eye on the prize: Two twin towers of shawarma (one chicken, one beef) that by all accounts is the city's best. Order it sandwiched, sliced or plated alongside the house hummus (with chickpeas, tomatoes, onions and parsley) and labneh (thick yoghurt) with garlic.

NOLU'S CAFE

ABU DHABI | $$ | CAFE
Al Bandar Marina, Al Raha Beach, Yes Island; 02 557 9500; www.nolusrestaurants.com; mains Dhs50-120

California meets Afghanistan at this cafe charmer where almond butter and chia pancakes are offered alongside *borani banjon* (oven-baked aubergines with mint-flecked garlic yoghurt) and hearty fodder like lamb shank with brown rice pilau. The Afghan menu-spin comes from the secret recipes of the owner's Afghan mother.

DAI PAI DONG

ABU DHABI | $$ | CHINESE

Rosewood Hotel, Al Maryah Island; 02 813 5552; www.rosewoodhotels.com; mains Dhs48-194, dim sum Dhs30-55

Dai Pai Dong's award-winning Chinese restaurant is where foodies chase Cantonese roasted duck, spicy braised chicken and wok-fried beef tenderloin with green tea and kumquat mojitos. When you've chowed down on its roasted pork buns or truffle and vegetable stuffed dumplings, you'll understand why Dai Pai Dong is known for its dim sum.

SUHAIL

ABU DHABI | $$$ | STEAK

Near Hameem, off E90 (Liwa Rd), Qasr Al Sarab Desert Resort, Liwa Oasis, Al Dhafra; 02 886 2088; www.anantara.com/en/qasr-al-sarab-abu-dhabi/restaurants/suhail; mains Dhs120-500

You really don't get more romantic than sitting on Suhail's terrace with the rolling dunes as your backdrop. The Qasr Al Sarab Desert Resort's fine-dining restaurant serves up an international menu of steaks and more modern-creative mains like duck with yuzu and passionfruit gel.

TANJORE

ABU DHABI | $$ | INDIAN

Al Salam St, Danat Al Ain Resort; 03 704 6000; mains Dhs35-115

Tandoori (clay oven) specialities like tandoori fish tikka and favourites like fiery chicken *chettinad* (yoghurt-and-chilli-marinated chicken) rival any curry in India, but the menu's standout stars are vegetarian dishes such as mirch *baigan kasalan* (chillies and aubergines in a peanut and coconut sauce).

AROOS DAMASCUS

DUBAI | $ | SYRIAN

Cnr Al Muraqqabat Rd & Al Jazeira St; 04 221 9825; www.facebook.com/Aroos.Damascus; sandwiches Dhs4-20, mezze Dhs14-35, mains Dhs15-50

A Dubai restaurant serving Syrian food to adoring crowds since 1980 must be doing something right. A perfect

COURTESY DAI PAI YONG

Opposite page: Dishes from Dai Pai Dong. This page: Dishes from Dai Pai Dong.

meal would start with hummus and a fattoush salad of toasted bread, tomatoes, onions and mint leaves before moving on to a plate of succulent grilled kebabs.

PAI THAI

DUBAI | $$$ | THAI
Madinat Jumeirah, King Salman Bin Abdul Aziz Al Saud St; 80 066 6353; www.jumeirah.com; mains Dhs55-175

An abra boat ride, a canalside table and candlelight are the hallmarks of a romantic night out, and this enchanting spot sparks on all cylinders. If your date doesn't make you swoon, then such expertly seasoned Thai dishes as wok-fried seafood and steamed sea bass should still ensure an unforgettable evening.

CLAYPOT

DUBAI | $$ | INDIAN
Citymax Hotel, cnr Mankhool & Kuwait Sts; 050 100 7065; www.citymaxhotels.com; mains Dhs45-75

The chef here has Dorchester and Ritz cred, and studied under nouvelle cuisine guru Michel Guerard. Kickstart your menu with the dahi puri (stuffed crispy puris), a fabulous Indian street food. The saffron-infused biryanis are also fabled, along with the paneer dishes and smoked kebabs.

'Food is the most expressive form of art and guests at Butcher & Still truly appreciate our carefully styled, 1920s cooking methods.'
Marshall Roth, Butcher & Still

RAVI

DUBAI | $ | PAKASTANI
Al Satwa Rd; 04 331 5353; mains Dhs8-25

Since 1978, everyone from cabbies to professional chefs has flocked to this Pakistani eatery, where you eat like a prince and pay like a pauper. Loosen your belt for heaped portions of grilled meats or succulent curries, including a few meatless options. Standouts include the daal fry and chicken tikka.

AL USTAD SPECIAL KABAB

DUBAI | $$ | IRANIAN
Al Musallah Rd; 04 397 1933; mains Dhs25-42

Sheikhs to shoe shiners clutter this funky, been-here-forever (since 1978, to be precise) kebab joint formerly known as Special Ostadi. Amid walls plastered with photographs of cheerful guests, a fleet of swift and quirky servers brings heaped plates of rice and yoghurt-marinated chicken into a dining room humming with chatter and laughter.

SAMAD AL IRAQI

DUBAI | $$ | IRAQI
Jumeirah Rd, Beach Park Plaza; 04 342 7887; www.samadaliraqirestaurant.com; mains Dhs50-95

This huge and fairly formal mall restaurant with decor inspired by ancient Iraq is locally adored for its excellent masgouf – wood-fired grilled fish, the country's national dish – but also serves Iraqi spins on traditional regional faves such as shawarma, biryani, kebab and grilled meats.

QWAIDER AL NABULSI

DUBAI | $$ | MIDDLE EASTERN

Al Muraqqabat St; 04 227 7760; mains Dhs28-50

Behind a garish neon facade, this place at first looks like a sweet shop (the kunafeh, a vermicelli-like pastry soaked in syrup, is one of Dubai's best), but don't discount its full menu of Middle Eastern delicacies like scrumptious *musakhan* (chicken pie) and sesame-seed-coated falafel *mahshi* (stuffed with chilli paste).

ZAROOB

DUBAI | $ | LEBANESE

Shop 1, Jumeirah Tower Bldg, Sheikh Zayed Rd; 04 327 6262; www.zaroob.com; dishes Dhs12-32

With its live cooking stations, open kitchens, fruit-filled baskets, colourful lanterns and graffiti-covered steel shutters, Zaroob radiates the urban integrity of a Beirut street-food alley. You'll find delicious no-fuss falafel, *shawarma* (spit-roasted meat in pita bread), flat or wrapped *manoushe* (Levant-style pizza) or *alayet* (tomato stew), all typical of the Levant.

SHABABEEK

SHARJAH | $$$ | MIDDLE EASTERN

Block B, Qanat Al Qasba; 06 554 0444; www.shababeek.ae; mains Dhs62-145

This chic space serves up contemporary Levantine dishes with creative flourishes. The mezze is what you want to focus on, with beetroot and walnut *moutabel* (purée mixed with tahini, yoghurt and olive oil), green lentil tabbouleh (salad of tomatoes, parsley and onions) and vine leaves soaked in *hosrom* (sour grape molasses).

SADAF

SHARJAH | $$ | IRANIAN

Al Mareija St; 06 569 3344; www.almadfoongroup.com; mains Dhs45-83

The Sharjah branch of this popular mini-chain enjoys cult status among locals for its authentic Iranian cuisine. The spicy, tender kebabs are particularly good, and the *zereshk* (rice with red barberries and chicken or lamb) is another solid choice.

REBOU LEBANON

FUJAIRAH | $$ | MIDDLE EASTERN

Corniche Rd, Khor Fakkan; 09 238 2522; mezze Dhs12-25, mains Dhs25-45

Right on the corniche, this little place is a winner for its mezze menu and hearty biryanis. Despite the name, Rebou also serves up pasta and a variety of steaks on a menu page titled 'West Food'. We'd suggest sticking to the Middle Eastern dishes.

WHERE TO EAT...

EMIRATI CUISINE

Logma, Dubai
Pair sandwiches made with traditional *khameer* bread at this funky Emirati cafe with a sweet *karak chai* (spiced tea).

Mezlai, Abu Dhabi
Locally sourced and organic traditional Emirati fine-dining in a Bedouin-tent-inspired atmosphere. Favourites include *medfoun* (shoulder of lamb cooked underground).

Aseelah, Dubai
Fantastic Aseelah often employs a local spice mix called *bezar* (cumin, fennel, cinnamon and dried chillies), including on its excellent date-stuffed chicken leg and camel stew.

Madfoon Al Sada, Ras Al Khaimah
The *mandi* (slow-roasted chicken or lamb served with rice and chilli sauce) at this humble haunt is among the best in the country.

OMAN

As a seafaring nation with a large Indian expatriate community, finding a chicken korma in the capital, Muscat, has traditionally been easier than tucking into the local lobster. But not anymore! Omanis have recently discovered that their taste for wafery flat breads, saucy spices and prize pomegranates is a welcome hit in the country's new indigenous eateries.

WHAT TO EAT

Lobster
Technically a crayfish, the delicious Omani lobster was until recently discarded as being a 'bottom-feeder'. This stigma now gone, it's offered grilled in seaside cafes from Mutrah to Masirah.

Harees
Mostly available in buffet tents during Ramadan, this glutinous savoury 'porridge' is usually laced with meat.

Shuwa
Traditionally baked in sand ovens, this melt-in-the-mouth mutton dish is best sampled in desert camps in Sharqiya Sands.

Umm Ali and Halwa
Bread-and-butter Umm Ali is offered on every hotel buffet; towns such as Barka and Sohar vie to produce the best *halwa* – a strictly national dates confection.

PRICE RANGES
$ less than OR5
$$ OR5–10
$$$ OR10 or more

Tipping: 10%, or leave loose change outside Muscat

AROOS MUSANDAM RESTAURANT

MUSANDAM | $ | SEAFOOD
Nr town centre, Khasab; 26831331; www.aroosmusandam.com; mains OR3

With an emphasis on the catch of the day (lobster, prawns, crab, fish of many varieties), delicious fresh juices (lemon-and-mint is a national favourite) and complimentary soup for larger orders, this unpretentious restaurant is a favourite among visitors to Oman's northern Peninsula.

CORNISH RESTAURANT

BATINAH COAST | $ | SEAFOOD
Corniche, Sohar; 93535077; Mains from OR2.5

In the heart of Sohar's busy fish market, this attractive, bright-windowed restaurant serves up the best of the catch, fresh from the incoming fishing boats. Preparations range from fish and chips to Indian and Chinese with plenty of non-fish and vegetarian options. Forget any thoughts of Cornish pasties – the name is a misspelling of Corniche.

AL MANDI AL DHAHABI

HAJAR MOUNTAINS | $ | MIDDLE EASTERN

Opp Nizwa Souq, Nizwa; 25414121; Mains OR2.5

A popular venue with Western expats and visitors, this friendly restaurant serves tasty Middle Eastern fare, with a vaguely Omani and Zanzibari flourish. The *mandi* (rice-and-meat) dishes are particularly authentic and tables on the roadside terrace sport magnificent views of Nizwa Fort and neighbouring souq.

AL BAHJAH RESTAURANT

NORTHERN COAST | $ | SOUTH INDIAN

off Wadi Bahayis St, Seeb; 24424400; www.rameehotels.com/our-hotels/oman; mains OR2

Seeb is a typical Omani town close to Muscat and has a large expat community from India, and this is reflected in the presence of this very good, ambiently-lit, Indian restaurant. It showcases dishes mostly from Kerala, in southern India, but there are also international options including chicken tikka masala all the way from Bradford, UK.

ROZNA

MUSCAT | $$ | OMANI

Al Maardih St, Airport Heights; 95522920; mains from OR4.5

'Omani food combines flavours picked from the path taken by Omani travellers during their long years of trading.'
Bait Al Luban

COURTESY BEACH RESTAURANT

As if Oman didn't have enough forts, they've just built a new one. Unlike its dusty old predecessors, however, with their all but empty interiors, this crenellated building has a covered courtyard with a flowing *falaj* and dining tables. This unique restaurant also offers traditional floor seating in the alcoves, a perfect setting for the tasty cuisine.

DUKANAH CAFÉ

MUSCAT | $$ | OMANI

Way 3709, behind GMC showroom, Al Ghubrah; 24502244; breakfast OR3

For a chance to sample not just Omani food but also a representation of an Old Muscat house, Dukanah Cafe is a fun destination, particularly for breakfast. Dishes of local cheese, beans, eggs and honey are served on large woven platters; with Muscat's Grand Mosque nearby, it's a perfect place to begin a Muscat tour.

KARGEEN CAFÉ

MUSCAT | $$ | MIDDLE EASTERN
Madinat Qaboos complex, Madinat Al Sultan Qaboos; 99253351, 24692269; www.kargeen.com; mains from OR4

With a choice of open-air and *majlis*-style dining (on sedans in small rooms), this Muscat favourite has spilt into a courtyard of illuminated trees to create a thoroughly Arabian experience. Make sure you try Kargeen's take on the traditional Omani *shuwa* – a succulent banana-leaf-wrapped lamb dish. Also worth a try are the hibiscus drinks and avocado milkshakes.

AL ANGHAM

MUSCAT | $$$ | OMANI
Opera Galleria, Sultan Qaboos St; 22077777; www.alanghamoman.com; Shatti Al Qurm; mains OR16

This exquisite restaurant next to the Royal Opera House in Muscat offers just the kind of refined fare demanded of a special occasion, such as a night at the opera. From the Omani silver napkin rings to the carved wooden ceiling, this stylish restaurant showcases national cuisine at its best.

BAIT AL LUBAN

MUSCAT | $$ | OMANI
Frankincense House, Hai Al Mina Rd, Mutrah; 24711842; www.baitalluban.com; mains OR6

You know you're somewhere unique when the complimentary water is infused with frankincense. This delightful restaurant is housed in a renovated *khan* (guesthouse), built 140 years ago, that used to charge by the bed not by the room. It serves genuine Omani cuisine (including vegetarian stews and mezze), but you could come just to savour the decor.

BEACH RESTAURANT

NORTHERN COAST | $$ | SEAFOOD
Muscat Hills Resort, off Al Jissah St; 24853000; www.muscathillsresort.com; mains from OR8

This elegant beachside restaurant, designed in shades of white with wood decking and sepia photographs, is a perfect venue for lunch. Oysters and lobster compete with other local seafood for pride of place on the menu. On the last Friday of each month the restaurant hosts 'Beats by the Beach', with a DJ (2pm to midnight).

BANK RESTAURANT

NORTHERN COAST | $$$ | ASIAN
Bank Beach Club, Jebel Seifah; 97368425; www.jebelsifah.com/dining/the-bank; mains OR10

Snacks and salads are served at this attractive beach club by day, but the restaurant really comes into its own at night when the pool pulses with colour and the rustling palms create a seductive ambience. The perfect spot, then, for their signature romantic dinner on the adjacent beach. Take a water taxi back to Muscat or sleep over at the neighbouring resort.

Previous spread: Seafood platter from Al Mina Restaurant & Bar; Beach Restaurant.

ANWAAR TIWI RESTAURANT

EASTERN COAST | $ | MIDDLE EASTERN

Main St, Tiwi; mains from 400 baisa

Located on a sharp bend in the middle of tiny Tiwi, this local-style restaurant serves Middle Eastern staples, including mezze and some Indian biryani and dal dishes. With goats jostling by, the terrace is a good place to drink a fresh mango juice before attempting the hike up neighbouring Wadi Shab – a national beauty spot.

SAHARI RESTAURANT

EASTERN COAST | $ | TURKISH

Main St, Ayjah (near Sur); 96281508, 25541423; mains from OR4

This popular Turkish restaurant, with its hand-painted murals and breezy terraces overlooking Sur's lagoon, is a delightful place to watch *dhows* (fishing boats) beaching at low tide. It also offers a convivial spot for some local music and freshly caught seafood, including prawns and squid and Turkish bread baked in-house.

DESERT NIGHTS CAMP

SHARQIYA SANDS | $$ | INTERNATIONAL

Access via Al Wasil; 92818388; www.desertnightscamp.com; mains from OR8

This luxury restaurant offers a 'shabby sheikh' ambiance for those who fancy seeing sand dunes...but preferably through a window with a glass of Chablis. The boutique furnishings, Omani antiques and fine dining comes as a welcome surprise at the end of a poorly graded road. There are luxury tents if driving back in the dark doesn't appeal.

AL MINA RESTAURANT & BAR

SALALAH | $$$ | MEDITERRANEAN

Al Baleed Resort, Al Mansurah Rd; 23228252; www.anantara.com/en/al-baleed-salalah/restaurants/al-mina; mains from OR12

One of the best restaurants in Salalah, this open-sided terrace-style restaurant has an exotic ambience, with the Arabian Sea thundering on the shore and moonlight captured in the adjoining infinity pool. Seafood and vegetarian dishes from Spain, Italy and Greece are given an Arabian flourish while jazz bands create an international vibe.

AL BALEED RESTAURANT

SALALAH | $ | MIDDLE EASTERN

As Sultan Qaboos St; 23227887, 91152518; mains from OR4

This local favourite (not related to the hotel of the same name) is a popular venue for an excellent Arabian brunch served between 9am and 1pm. The cavernous dining hall has some stylish Arabian features such as a lantern comprised of dozens of *kumar* (embroidered caps) and there's a huge deck overlooking Al Baleed *khor* (inlet) – a sanctuary for birds.

WHERE TO EAT...

AT HIGH ALTITUDE

Juniper Restaurant, Alila, Jebel Akhdar
Built of basalt and juniper, this superb canyon-rim restaurant offers locally grown fare while a roaring fire takes the nip out of the high-altitude air.

The View, Al Hamra
Serving international cuisine, this open-air restaurant lives up to its name with panoramic views of the desert floor, a dizzying 1400m below.

Restaurant, Wakan
Perching high above Wadi Mistal, this tiny mountain restaurant serves fish and chips – an Omani favourite – as an unlikely feature of a Hajar Mountain menu.

Misfah Old House, Misfah
Authentic dishes are cooked at this village home in an enchanted mountain plantation of dates, lemons and mangos.

ASIA

IRAN

Iranian food is a highlight of travelling in the country, with considerable variety on offer and places to eat varying from simple kebab stalls to luxurious restaurants. For many Iranians, eating is a social event. Don't miss relaxing in a *chaykhaneh* (teahouse), where Iranians go to socialise over tea and *qalyan* (water pipe) but also for meals.

WHAT TO EAT

Chelo kabab
Any kind of kabab served with *chelo* (boiled or steamed rice); the default option is *kubide*, a kebab of minced mutton, breadcrumbs and onion ground together.

Dizi
Also known as *abgusht*, this delicious and filling soup-stew of chickpeas, potatoes, tomatoes and soft-boiled mutton is named after the earthenware pot in which it is served.

Khoresht
A thick, usually meaty stew with chopped nuts.

Fesenjun
A classic of Persian cuisine: roast chicken and rice served with a sauce of pomegranate juice, walnuts, eggplant and cardamom.

PRICE RANGES

For a main course (for Tehran and central Iran add IR200,000):

$ less than IR200,000

$$ IR200,000–IR375,000

$$$ IR375,000 or more

Tipping: 10% in upmarket restaurants.

KOUROSH

RASHT | $$ | IRANIAN

Gilantur Lane; 013-3322 8299; www.kourosh-restaurant.ir; meals IR380,000

Sample the delights of Gilani cuisine right in the centre of Rasht. Start with the murky-looking but very tasty *zeitun parvardeh* (olives in walnut paste) and share some *mirza ghasemi* (dip-like pureed charcoal eggplant with garlic and tomato) before hoeing into a *torche kebab* (lamb and/or chicken in a sour marinade).

DIVAN

TEHRAN | $$$ | IRANIAN

7th fl, Sam Center, Fereshteh St; 021-2265 3853; www.facebook.com/divantehran; mains IR650,000

Chic furnishings, including striking portraits by Iranian artist Fataneh Dadkhah, set the luxe tone at this plush, popular northern Tehran restaurant. A tempting menu of traditional-with-a-twist Persian dishes, such as *fesenjun*, delivers both on flavour and presentation.

DIZI

TEHRAN | $$ | IRANIAN

52 Kalantari St; 021-8881 0008; set meal IR450,000

Serving Iran's favourite lamb, potato and chickpea stew for decades; it's the only thing on the menu but they do it damn well. The meal comes with fresh herb salad and a jug of the minty yoghurt drink dugh. No wonder this characterful restaurant, plastered with traditional paintings, is full practically from the moment it opens.

GILANEH

TEHRAN | $$ | IRANIAN

Saba Blvd, off Afriqa Blvd; 021-2205 5335; mains IR365,000-500,000

Rustic wooden beams, glazed tiles and a lively, friendly atmosphere all set the scene for the delicious Gilan-region food served at one of Tehran's most popular restaurants. Recommended are the mix of dips, the deep-fried zander (a type of fish), and either the duck or chicken *fesenjun*.

KOOHPAYEH

TEHRAN | $$ | IRANIAN
Khoopayeh Sq, Sarband, Darband Ave; 021-2271 2518; www.koohpaye.com; mains IR250,000-680,000

There's fierce competition for diners at the many restaurants and teahouses that line the babbling river flowing through Darband, but most in-the-know locals favour this elegant place near the start of the northern Tehran village. Sit on the outdoor terrace and enjoy the view as staff in red waistcoats deliver all kinds of kababs and other local dishes.

'The ingredients are bought fresh in the morning from local sources and are then prepared by our chef to have a home-made taste.'
Khoone

KHOONE

TEHRAN | $ | IRANIAN
Kaman Dead End, Shahidi St; 98 21 43937; www.facebook.com/restaurantkhoone; mains IR150,000-300,000

The next best thing to getting invited to a Tehrani's home for a meal is sampling the lovingly made dishes at this cute, cosy cafe. Khoone means ,home' in Farsi and the place is deliberately designed to put guests at ease. The short menu changes daily and features classic Iranian dishes such tahdig (crispy rice pies) and sweet drinks.

SHAHRZAD

ESFAHAN | $$ | IRANIAN
Abbas Abad St; 031-1220 4490; www.shahrzad-restaurant.com; mains IR500,000

Opulent Qajar-style wall paintings, stained-glass windows and battalions of black-suited waiters contribute to the Shahrzad's reputation as Esfahan's best restaurant. House specialities include lamb cutlets, and chelo fesenjan (pomegranate and walnut stew with rice). At the end of the meal complimentary pieces of gaz, a nougat flavoured with almond and rose water, complete the meal.

HAJ MAHMOOD BERYANI

ESFAHAN | $ | IRANIAN
Bazar Engelab Blind Alley; 031-3445 9006; www.beryaniazam.com; beryani IR140,000

Famous for its beryani (which is served with a glass of dugh; churned sour milk or yoghurt mixed with water), Azam has several branches. This one inside the bazaar is a recommended lunch option – the queuing, the shunting into seats, the quick turn-around and the chomping on whole onions is all part of the culinary experience.

ABBASI TEAHOUSE & TRADITIONAL RESTAURANT

ESFAHAN | $$ | IRANIAN
Abbasi Hotel, Shahid Medani St; 031-3222 6010; www.abbasihotel.ir; noodle soup IR200,000

Set into a flank of the Abbasi Hotel's elegant main courtyard, this delightful little restaurant (not to be confused with the hotel's main restaurant) attract legions of locals in the early evening. The signature dish is ash-e reshte (noodle soup with beans and vegetables; IR200,000) and big bowls of this wholesome meal fly out of the kitchen in record numbers when it's cold.

BASTANI TRADITIONAL RESTAURANT

ESFAHAN | $ | IRANIAN
Chaharsogh Maghsod Bazar, Naqsh-e Jahan (Imam) Sq; 031-3220 0374; mains from IR250,000

Esfahan's most atmospheric restaurant features an internal courtyard with fountain, tiled walls and painted vaulted ceilings with mirror inlay – truly gorgeous. Dishes such as *khoresh-e beh* (stewed lamb and quince) and *khoresh-e alu* (stewed chicken and plum) are consistently delicious. There's a cover charge for tea, worth paying just to enjoy the delightful interior.

MIRRORS RESTAURANT

KASHAN | $$$ | IRANIAN
Alavi St; 031-5524 0220; www.sarayeameriha.com; mains IR450,000

It is worth dining in this fabulous little restaurant for the sheer pleasure of sitting in pools of coloured light by day and under a canopy of mirrored stars at night. Ask for the daily stew and relax in the company of Kashanis enjoying a special occasion. The stone-floored antechamber lacks the dazzle of the main room's mirror work so book ahead.

GHAVAM

SHIRAZ | $ | IRANIAN
Rudaki Ave; 071-3235 9271; dizi IR210,000

This tiny restaurant, more shop than diner, is an absolute favourite with locals, foreign expats and the odd tour group whose guide is in the know. Would-be diners queue up on the street to find a place at the tightly packed tables, drawn to the delicious home-cooked fare. The *kashk-e bademjan* (aubergine dip) will delight vegetarians.

Opening spread, from left: Dish from Dyen Sabai; Rangoon Tea House; Nimtho Sikkim; Odette. Previous page: Dish from Shabhaye Talai.

SHATER ABBAS

SHIRAZ | $$ | IRANIAN
Sa'di St; 071-3227 1617; mains US$4-13

This restaurant is housed in a vast dining hall with giant murals on the wall and canteen-style salad bars. Hot bread is made near the entrance, luring potential diners in, and the lamb preparations – *shandiz lary kabab* (spiced lamb) or *kubideh* (minced lamb kabab) – are signature dishes. Fish dishes are available for non-meat eaters.

TALAR YAZD

YAZD | $$ | IRANIAN
Ghandehaeri Alley, off Jomhuri-e Eslami Blvd; 035-3522 6661; www.talareyazd.com; mains IR250,000

Elegant but uncomplicated, the Talar, with its prim white tablecloths and waiters wheeling trolleys, has a 1950s appeal. Its short menu of classic Iranian dishes, including slow-roast lamb, is delicious and the kababs are perfect. It's an 8km ride from central Yazd but worth it to spend time in the company of Yazdis out for lunch at the weekend.

KOLBEH DARVISH

KISH ISLAND | $$ | IRANIAN
Jahan Rd; mains IR150,000-320,000

This much-lauded eatery, specialising in traditional Iranian food and right on the seashore, is the perfect place to try out *kubide kabab* (minced mutton, breadcrumbs and onion, served with rice) or *ghorme sabzi* (diced meat with beans, vegetables and rice). Vegetarians will enjoy the delicious *mirza ghasemi* (mashed eggplant, squash, tomato and egg).

SHABHAYE TALAI

QESHM ISLAND | $$ | SEAFOOD
Zeytoun Park, Qeshm Town; 0936 397 4103; www.shabhayetalai.com; mains IR170,000-380,000

With top-notch views of the beach, Shabhaye Talai specialises in seafood, including lobster (from Larak Island) and shrimp, salads and burgers, all prepared to perfection. Vegetarian dishes are available, the menu is in English and there's a happening buzz in the evening.

HEZARDESTAN TRADITIONAL TEAHOUSE

MASHHAD | $$$ | IRANIAN
Jannat Lane; 051-3222 2943; mains IR287,500-540,500

One of Iran's most beautiful teahouse-restaurants, with a museum-like basement full of carpets, samovars, antique metalwork and countless knicknacks around a small fountain. The menu is limited to *ghorme sabzi*, chicken *kabab*, *dizi* or *halim bademjan* (lamb and mashed aubergine).

WHERE TO DRINK...

TEA

Shahriar Restaurant, Tabriz
There are several interesting rooms in this converted subterranean 19th-century bathhouse, though the qalyan-wafting *chaykhaneh* (teahouse) is the most exotic; it does very good dizi and kababs.

Azari Traditional Teahouse, Tehran
The dizi and *kashk-e bademjan* (eggplant fried and mashed and served with thick whey and mint) are excellent at this atmospheric tea house. In the evening there's live music.

Seray-e Mehr Teahouse, Shiraz
Decorated with painted panels and antiques on the wall, this split-level teahouse has a small menu of tasty favourites and a delightfully relaxed atmosphere in which to sit, eat and sip tea.

TURKMENISTAN

Though perhaps less well-explored than its Central Asian neighbours, Turkmenistan is equally rich in the foods of the steppe and Silk Road. Culinary output here is based on the once-nomadic subsistence diet of mainly meat, dairy and bread, consumed everywhere from streetside stalls and cafes, to *chaikhanas* (teahouses) and, in the capital, Ashgabat, high-end restaurants.

WHAT TO EAT

Dograma
Shredded meat, bread and onion stew.

Shashlyk
Skewered, grilled meats, best when cooked over the branches of a saxaul tree.

Samsa
Meat-filled pastries similar to a samosa.

Plov
Central Asian rice pilaf simmered with meat and carrots.

Fitchi
Large, round meat pastry.

Chorba
Soup of boiled mutton with potato, carrot and turnip.

Manty
Steamed dumplings served with sour cream.

PRICE RANGES

$ less than 20M
$$ 20–50M
$$$ 50M or more

Tipping: 10–20% may be included in upmarket restaurants, otherwise round up.

ÇEŞME

ASHGABAT | $$ | TURKISH

Lakhuti köçesi; per person for kebab & salads 60M

This charming red-painted cellar tucked down an Ashgabat backstreet is very welcoming. There's no menu: it's all about the sublime kebabs and choice of delicious accompanying sauces and salads – the staff brings a selection of these to choose from.

HOTEL ÝYLDYZ PANORAMIC RESTAURANT

ASHGABAT | $$$ | CENTRAL ASIAN

Bagtyyarlyk köçesi 17; +993 39 09 00; www.yyldyzhotel.com; mains 50-100M

On the 18th floor of Ashgabat's Hotel Ýyldyz, this lavish restaurant serves a mix of international cuisines – you'll find everything from French to Chinese on the menu. What really draws people in, though, are the views over the capital and the mountains.

COFFEE HOUSE

ASHGABAT | $$$ | INTERNATIONAL

Turkmenbashi şayoli 15A; +993 39 60 06; dishes 24-110M

Cool coffeehouse with solid breakfasts and decent coffee – salads, soups and burgers complete the menu. The interior is a masterwork of kitsch, with a bizarre patchwork of faux Corinthian columns, plastic bamboo reeds and gold wallpaper.

KÖPETDAG

ASHGABAT | $$ | INTERNATIONAL

Magtymguly şayoli 10; +993 27 67 20; mains 20-40M

Set in a charming garden, this is one of Ashgabat's most fashionable restaurants. The food takes second billing to the surrounds, but there's a huge menu of world foods (pizza, steaks) and local standards (grilled meats). Groups can book to dine in garish but imaginatively decorated yurts.

WHAT TO EAT

Plov
Uzbekistan's national dish: rice pilaf and vegetables simmered in broth.

Shahlyk
Skewered, grilled meats.

Non
Bread, comes in various types and shapes around Uzbekistan.

Somsa
Puff pastry stuffed with lamb meat and onion similar to a samosa.

Laghman
Long, flat noodles with tomato and meat sauce.

Salad
Most commonly tomato, cucumber and onion sprinkled with dill.

Beshbarmak
Flat noodles with horse meat and broth.

Naryn
Horse meat sausage with cold noodles.

PRICE RANGES
$ less than 10,00S
$$ 10,000S–20,000S
$$$ 20,000S or more

Tipping: 10–15% (often added automatically).

UZBEKISTAN

Uzbekistan is not known as a foodie destination, but that doesn't mean eating here can't be a pleasure – fresh produce, succulent grilled meats and bread warm from the oven are regular features of the Uzbek table. Uzbek cuisine is hearty and meat-heavy, utilising ingredients that can be cultivated on its dry, flat landscape. Dining options range from charming courtyard restaurants to vine-laden outdoor teahouses to smart, upmarket restaurants in the bigger cities.

AFSONA

TASHKENT | $$$ | UZBEK
Shevchenko 30; +998 71 252 56 81; www.facebook.com/afsonatashkent; mains 22,000-47,000S

This well-run restaurant aims to deliver Uzbek cuisine with a contemporary touch, breathing life into old favourites such as grilled meats, pumpkin *manty* (steamed dumplings), *cheburek* pastries and *hanum* (dough roll stuffed with vegetables). The decor is understated, with stylish geometric wood designs. The four-course set business lunch is a steal at 30,000S.

NATIONAL FOOD

TASHKENT | $$ | UZBEK
Gafur Gulom 1; +998 71 244 77 03; dishes 5000-15,000S

You'll be hard pressed to find a restaurant with more local colour – as you walk through the entrance you're greeted by giant kazans (cauldrons) filled with various national specialities. In addition to plov and laghman, you can sample *beshbarmak* (noodles with meat and broth), *dimlama* (braised meat, potatoes, onions and vegetables), *halim* (meat porridge) and *naryn* (horsemeat sausage served with cold noodles).

CENTRAL ASIAN PLOV CENTRE

TASHKENT | $ | UZBEK
cnr Abdurashidov & Ergashev; plov 7000S

EFESENKO/SHUTTERSTOCK ©

To sample Uzbekistan's national dish – *plov* (rice pilaf) –styles from various regions of the country, head to this celebration of all things plov. Walk past the mob of people crowding around steaming *kazans* (large plov cauldrons) and take a seat inside, where your order will arrive Uzbek-style on a single plate from which everybody eats. Get here before noon for the best selection.

PLATAN

SAMARKAND | $$$ | INTERNATIONAL

Pushkin 2; +998 66 233 80 49; www.platan.uz; mains 20,000-28,000S

Possibly the best restaurant in Samarkand, Platan has a classy interior and a summer terrace for shady al fresco dining. The menu includes some Middle Eastern and Thai influences alongside regional dishes like Russian-style red caviar and cooling *Uzbek chalop* (cucumber, dill, green onion and sour cream soup). The salad menu is particularly good: try the excellent *lobio* (a Georgian bean, walnut, garlic, lemon and parsley salad), the Thai beef salad or the zingy Bloody Mary salad.

OLD CITY

SAMARKAND | $$ | INTERNATIONAL

Abdurahmon Jomi 100/1; +998 93 346 8020; mains 14,000-16,000S

This charming place in Samarkand's Russian district offers interesting dishes, such as basturma cold smoked beef, *lavash* (flat bread) with feta-like brinza cheese, and over 40 salads, including a delicious beetroot and walnut option. Service is friendly and assured, the classy interior has a cosy fireplace, and while it caters largely to tourists, standards are high.

MINZIFA

BUKHARA | $$ | INTERNATIONAL

Hoja Rushnogi 6; +998 93 960 2326; mains 10,000-26,000S

Bukhara's most charming restaurant is this perennially popular place with a fantastic roof terrace overlooking the sunset-framed domes of the Sarrafon hammam. The menu stretches to dishes like chicken with cream sauce and walnuts, and has plenty of meat-free options such as vegetable shashlyk. Reserve at least a day or two ahead during high season. Be sure to save space for dessert (such as apples, pears and bananas with sour cream, honey and walnuts) or smoke a shisha while snacking on a selection of Uzbek traditional sweets like halva and sherbet.

TERRASSA CAFE

KHIVA | $$ | UZBEK

Ichankala, A Boltayev, 7; +998 91 993 9111; www.terrassa-cafe.com; mains 10,000-16,000S

Dining experiences in Khiva don't get better than a cool summer evening on this rooftop terrace, surrounded by the spotlit medressas and palace walls of the old town. The coffee is the best in Khiva and the food ranges from good local shashlyk to eggplant salad and grilled vegetables.

Previous page: Street in Khiva. Next spread: Plov; Laghman.

TAJIKISTAN

Tajik cuisine shares much with its neighbouring Central Asian countries. The restaurant scene is growing, especially in the capital Dushanbe, but in most parts of Tajikistan, small garden teahouses offer local dishes and ubiquitous, never-ending cups of tea. For travellers, eating is most often the joyous experience of sampling traditional fare prepared fresh at homestays.

WHAT TO EAT

Plov
Central Asian-style rice pilaf simmered with meat and vegetables.

Non
Crusty, round clay-oven-baked bread.

Kurutob
Bread morsels layered with onion, tomato, parsley and coriander and doused in a yoghurt-based sauce.

Laghman
Thick wheat noodles in tomato and meat sauce.

Shavlya
Vegetable and rice broth soup.

Chakka
Curd mixed with herbs, typically served with flatbread.

Nahud sambusa
Chickpea samosas.

Tuhum barak
Egg-filled ravioli coated with sesame-seed oil.

PRICE RANGES

For a main course:
$ less than US$5
$$ US$5–30
$$$ US$30 or more

Tipping: 10% in top-end restaurants (often included); round up elsewhere.

RUDAKI RESTAURANT

DUSHANBE | $$$ | INTERNATIONAL

Rudaki 14, Serena Hotel; +992 487 01 4000; www.serenahotels.com; breakfast/lunch/dinner buffet 140/185/220TJS

This upmarket restaurant in Dushanbe's Serena Hotel is a popular choice for a nice evening out (locals often host celebrations here). Most people aim for the huge buffet selection, which runs from local specialties to Russian and European dishes, though there's a full à la carte menu, also. Many evenings, dinner is accompanied by Persian dancing and folk music, and when it's not too windy, tables are set under the trees in the garden.

DELHI DARBAR

KHOROG | $$ | INDIAN

Azizbek 2; +992 3522 2 1299; ashok@delhidarbar.in; curries 25-30TJS, beer 15TJS

Legendary Delhi Darbar is the most popular meeting place in Khorog, and possibly the most well-trafficked restaurant in all of Tajikistan. In part, this is because it's exciting to find anyone even attempting to offer Indian cuisine in such a remote corner of Central Asia – but Delhi Darbar does a particularly good job, hiring chefs who hail from the Indian subcontinent. Go for the chicken tikka starter, deliciously crispy garlic naan bread and literally any of the curries. Cold beer is a further treat.

TRAKTIR KONSERVATOR

DUSHANBE | $$ | UKRAINIAN

1 projezd Tursunzade 4; +992 987 960505; mains 25-70TJS

In an unprepossessing alley near Dushanbe's Opera House, this surprisingly atmospheric restaurant is a treat both in terms of its rural Russian decor (think theatre posters, heavy beams and samovars) and extensive Ukrainian menu (pot-roasted pork, cutlets with

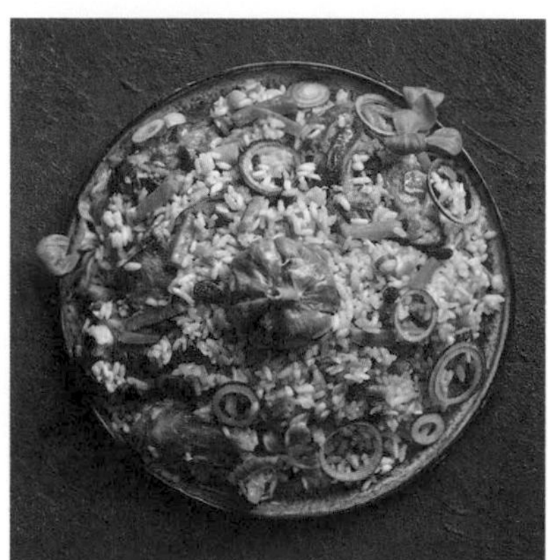
OLGA MAZYARKINA/GETTY IMAGES ©

buckwheat, sweet and sour pikeperch, and compote). A cosy outdoor terrace attracts a lively crowd in summer.

SAYOKHAT

PENJIKENT | $$ | CENTRAL ASIAN
Marvazi; +992 9277 4 0737; mains 15-25TJS

Penjikent's most imaginative eatery, this eccentric wooden structure boasts timber stairways and cosy booths and is festooned with traditional artefacts and beautiful Tajik textiles. The delightful owner, Sharif Badalov, goes out of his way to make guests feel welcome and is justly proud of the establishment's 'high-level plov'. The gharmij (wheat drink) is also worth trying.

SERENA INN RESTAURANT

KHOROG | $$ | TAJIK
Serena Hotel; www.serenahotels.com/serenakhorog; mains from US$7

'Our restaurant is a culinary journey showcasing the best in Tajik cuisine with views of the mountains, the Afghan border and the River Panj.'
Serena Hotels

This small restaurant on the outskirts of Khorog serves Tajik and international food in an upmarket environment with white linens. The showstopper is the terrace overlooking an attractive garden with views across the Panj River into Afghanistan. It makes a tranquil spot for a beer (21TJS) on the topchan (dining pavilion) in the summer and a cosy place to retreat from winter snow.

GHALABA

DUSHANBE | $ | CENTRAL ASIAN
Victory Park, Park Pobedy; mains 25-70TJS, beer 18TJS

For sweeping views over Dushanbe, it's hard to beat the rustic, vine-draped open-air booths and thatch-covered chorpoy (bed-like platform) at Ghalaba. Serving tea, beer and cocktails, it makes the perfect place to unwind at sunset.

KYRGYZSTAN

Kyrgyzstan's cuisine reflects the country's nomadic roots, with an emphasis on foods that could be cultivated on the move across the steppe. Kyrgyz dishes are primarily mutton-based and heavy on carbs – finding a meat-free meal is a tall order. In large cities though, a range of cultural restaurants, teahouses and Soviet-style cafeterias makes eating out a pleasure.

WHAT TO EAT

Shashlyk
Skewered, grilled meat.

Laghman
Mildly spicy, fat noodles served in soup.

Beshbarmak
Flat noodles in vegetable broth topped with meat.

Kesme
Thick noodle soup with potato, vegetables and meat.

Mampar
Tomato-based meat stew with gnocchi-like pasta pieces.

Plov
Pilaf of rice and fried vegetables.

Manty
Steamed dumplings filled with meat or vegetables.

Azu
Tatar dish of meat fried with pickles and vegetables, often served atop french fries.

Shorpa
Mutton soup.

PRICE RANGES

For a main course:
$ less than 250som
$$ 250–700som
$$$ 700som or more

Tipping: 10–20% only if included on the bill.

ASHLYAN-FUU

AK-SUU REGION | $ | CENTRAL ASIAN

Jusaev, Karakol; mains 50som

The regional specialty of Karakol is *ashlyanfu* – a Dungan-style spicy, cold soup with noodles and vinegar-chilli sauce, topped with chopped herbs. Locals head to this tin-roofed shack off Jusaev St for the best in the city, and perhaps the whole world. There's no menu, just bowls of *ashlyanfu* and *pirozhki* (fried bread). There's always a line, and they close up whenever the day's ingredients run out.

ZUBR CAFE

NORTHERN KYRGYZSTAN | $ | BARBECUE

Lenina, Naryn; mains 120-200som

This summertime tent-restaurant does excellent *shashlyk* and slightly chilled beer served in private, semi-open-air tarpaulin booths by the Naryn River. The aromas of grilling meats waft up from the barbecue as you approach.

CHAIKANA NAVAT

BISHKEK | $$ | TEAHOUSE

Kiev 141/1; (0)551-531111; www.navat.kg/en; mains 170-350som

Styled like an old teahouse, with atmospheric handicrafts lining the walls and *tapchan* (bedlike platforms) to dine on, this central Bishkek chain serves up Central Asian staples. Grilled meats are the highlight – the 'Barbecue Fantasy' is a giant, mixed platter of lamb ribs, chicken wings, veal and Caucasian-style 'lyulya' minced lamb kebabs.

SHASHLYK NO. 1

BISHKEK | $$ | GRILL

Karalaev 1a; (0)551-706080; www.shashlyk.kg; shashlyk 150-300som

It claims to be the best *shashlyk* in Bishkek...and might just be. Meaty treats-on-a-stick are the main event, but there's also a delightful mushroom kebab, all washed down with cold beer on the patio.

KAZAKHSTAN

Though Kazakhstan's food culture is firmly rooted in its nomadic past, particularly meat cultivated on the steppe, the post-Soviet era has seen a huge influx of upmarket, international restaurants. The neighbouring cuisines of Central Asia, Russia and even Korea have found their way onto Kazakh menus, resulting in a lively fusion cuisine.

WHAT TO EAT

Beshbarmak
Kazakhstan's national dish – chunks of long-boiled meat served in a huge bowl atop flat pasta with onions and potatoes.

Horsemeat
Long eaten by nomads on the flat northern plains. *Kazy, shuzhuk/shuzhak* and *karta* are all types of horsemeat sausage; horsemeat steak is also common.

Kuurdak
A fatty stew of potatoes, meat and offal from a horse, sheep or cow.

Shashlyk
Charcoal-grilled skewered meats usually eaten in an open-air restaurant.

Laghman
Long, stout noodles with tomato and meat sauce.

Manty
Steamed dumplings usually with lamb filling.

PRICE RANGES

For a main course:
$ less than 1500T
$$ 1500–3000T
$$$ 3000T or more

Tipping: Not customary.

LINE BREW

ALMATY | $$$ | INTERNATIONAL

Furmanov 187A; 701 742 06 86; www.line-brew.kz; mains 1650-6800T

This popular nationwide microbrewery attracts the carnivorously inclined with stone-cooked meats, an assortment of steaks, some of the juiciest shashlyk in the region and a supporting cast of salads and hot and cold appetisers. The beer on tap is the best in Kazakhstan. This is a good place to try horsemeat steak.

VOSTOK

EASTERN KAZAKHSTAN | $ | KAZAKH

Momyshuly 8, Semey; 7222 56 16 77; mains 700-1500T

Relaxed local joint in Kazakh heartland city Semey, Vostok serves shashlyk straight off the grill, heaping portions of *laghman* and other Kazakh staples are served in airy garden booths.

KOK-SARAY

SOUTHERN KAZAKHSTAN | $$ | UZBEK

Tauke-Khan 121, Shymkent; 7252 43 22 30; mains 900-1800T

Wood-carved pillars, murals and an airy front terrace create a warm atmosphere at this restaurant, which serves the best Uzbek food in lively southern city, Shymkent (and in all of Kazakhstan, claim locals). Don't miss the perfect *plov* (*tashkentsky* with white rice, *andizhansky* with black rice) or the superb *samsas* (samosas), which include a delicious pumpkin (*s tykvoe*) variety (in autumn only).

MYASO

NUR-SULTAN (ASTANA) | $$$ | STEAK

Bokeykhan 16; 701 522 2288; www.goodproject.kz; mains 3100-5800T

With a diagram on the exposed brick wall showing the different cuts of beef, fashion shows on the TV screen and a solid menu of (mostly) European wines, Myaso (whose name means, simply, "Meat") is the best steakhouse in the Kazakh capital. The menu runs from fillet mignon to charcoal-grilled horse steak. Chef Elena Kovaleva has worked across Kazakhstan and Russia, and brings her multinational background into the food concept.

OLIVIA

SOUTHERN KAZAKHSTAN | $$$ | ITALIAN

Rixos Khadisha Shymkent Hotel, Zheltoksan 17, Shymkent; 725 261 01 01; www.khadishashymkent.rixos.com; mains 2800-6500T

Visually a sultry cross between a stone-walled cellar and a library, with books on art and design on surrounding shelves, this gorgeous Shymkent restaurant serves beautifully executed pasta dishes, risottos and grilled meats from a short but sweet menu put together by the Michelin starred chef. An excellent Euro-centric wine list and professional service make this place hard to fault.

ASTANA NURY

NUR-SULTAN (ASTANA) | $$$ | GEORGIAN, AZERBAIJANI

Respublika dangyly 3/2; 7172-43 93 39; www.a-n.kz; mains 1800-9900T

This top-class Azerbaijani/Georgian restaurant has two lovely decks overlooking the Ishim River, as well as an inside dining room with beautiful Azeri decor. The many varieties of shashlyk, coal-grilled meats and Azeri *pilaw* (*plov*) dishes are among the best on the menu.

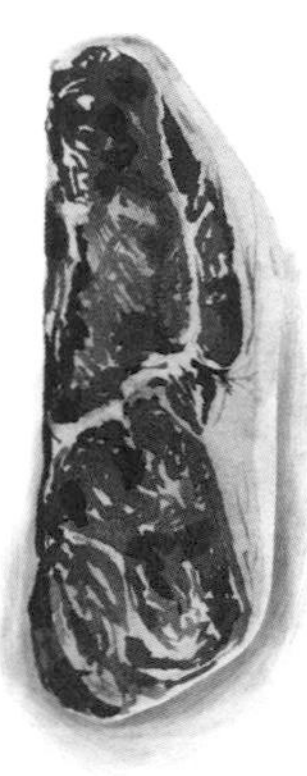

'Our cooking centres on our stone grill in the middle of the dining hall – the fire creates a feeling of comfort and the dishes cooked on this grill are perhaps the most delicious.'
Line Brew

BAKKARA

WESTERN KAZAKHSTAN | $$ | CENTRAL ASIAN

Mikrorayon 14, Aktau; 7292 31 46 44; mains 1500-3500T

Some of the best shashlyk in far western Kazakhstan – tender lamb, pork or sturgeon – are grilled up at this Aktau restaurant, which has no sign but is recognisable by the trees lining its perimeter. The shashlyk goes down a treat with chips, a salad and a mug of beer, especially in the shady garden in warm weather.

MONGOLIA

The nomadic Mongols have lived off their herds for centuries. Meat and milk are the staples, with seasoning used sparingly. Traditionally, Mongolian cooking is wok-frying or steaming, and roasting meats over a fire. Countryside meals are fuss-free and communal, though in the capital city, Ulaanbaatar, there's a growing cosmopolitan restaurant scene. *Saikhan khool loorai*! (That's 'Bon appétit' in Mongolian.)

WHAT TO EAT

Makh
"Meat"; boiled sheep bits with sliced potato and/or carrots.

Khorkhog
Chopped mutton cooked in a hot-stone urn.

Bortzig
Fried unleavened bread.

Hölte khool
Pasta slivers, boiled mutton and potato chunks in hot broth.

Buuz
Steamed dumplings filled with mutton, onion or garlic.

Khuushuur
Fried mutton pancakes.

Tsuivan
Steamed flour-noodle pasta with carrots, potato and mutton chunks.

Tsagaan idee
Dairy products, including yoghurt, milk, fresh cream, cheese and fermented milk drinks.

PRICE RANGES
For a main course:
$ less than T9000
$$ T9000–T16,000
$$$ T16,000 or more

Tipping: 10–20% in tourist-friendly restaurants.

FAIRFIELD CAFE & BAKERY

ARKHANGAI | $$ | CAFE
Tsetserleg; What3words: passes.turns.recounted; +976 9908 7745; www.fairfield.mn; mains T7000-9500

A godsend for those who've done the hard yards in the Mongolian countryside, this Australian-run cafe-restaurant bakes its own bread and cakes, to go with full English breakfasts (T15,500), egg-and-bacon rolls, roast beef with Yorkshire pudding, monstrous Aussie burgers, and vegetarian and Mongolian dishes to boot. There's proper fresh espresso-machine coffee, too.

URAN KHAIRKHAN

THE GOBI | $ | MONGOLIAN
Bayankhongor; What3words: reference.empire.shameful; mains T5000-8500

A ramshackle side entrance leads the way into jovial Uran Khairkhan, an atmospheric brick house with cosy booth dining. There's no English menu, but a heap of Mongolian favourites are on offer: tsuivan, goulash, bif-shtek (beef patty topped with a fried egg on rice), known collectively as tsagaan khool (white eats), along with a few Korean and Western dishes.

VERANDA

ULAANBAATAR | $$$ | MEDITERRANEAN
Jamyngun St 5/1; What3words: overdone.scared.finishers; +976 7710 2992; www.veranda.mn; mains T17,000-39,000

French and Italian cuisine served in a lovely location overlooking the Choijin Lama Temple Museum. While it's not particularly old, this fine-dining restaurant has an almost colonial air to it, with couch seating inside and a big porch with a view of the temple. The food is surprisingly good – the menu features an array of delectable main dishes that fuse Italian and French recipes served by uniformed waiters.

ETERNAL SPRINGS

BULGAN | $ | BAKERY

Sükhbaatar Gudamj, Erdenet; What3words: clasp.envies.headband; +976 7035 6004; meals T3200-5000, pizza T18,000

This cute-as-a-button Swedish-American bakery offers a daily selection of vegetable soups (pumpkin, broccoli), along with meatless pizzas, baked goodies and an extensive loose-leaf tea selection.

BULGOGI FAMILY

SELENGE | $$ | KOREAN

Darkhan; What3words: applause.banks.captions; +976 7037 7300; meals T8500-22,000

Bright, friendly Korean restaurant featuring *bulgogi* (grilled meat), spicy soups, tasty *bibimbap* (rice topped with meat, vegetables and an egg, choice of hot or cold) and noodle dishes. Mains are accompanied by an array of obligatory little side dishes. Alternatively, cook your own meal on the grill in the middle of your table.

BULL 3

ULAANBAATAR | $$ | HOTPOT

Baga Toiruu E, Blue Mon Bldg, 3rd fl; What3words: amps.heads.harmony; +976 7710 0060; meals T4500-9000

'We have a huge passion for food and wanted to open a new world, new tastes and new ingredients to Mongolians. We are always glad when our restaurant is full of happy people and our chefs are happy to see empty plates coming back.'
Tsolmon Sanj, owner of Veranda

DIBERTICUS/GETTY IMAGES ©

This elegant restaurant is always busy with well-dressed folk here for hotpot. Order an array of raw vegetables, sauces and thinly sliced meats brought to the table on platters, then cook them all in a personal cauldron of boiling broth. There's a heap of delectable meat and veg items, and a well-stocked bar to ensure a buzzy, social atmosphere.

MARVEL RESTAURANT & PUB

ÖMNÖGOVI | $ | KOREAN

What3words: Illusionist.toadstools.oboe; +976 7053 3035; mains T6000-7500

A tiny yet hip pub set down a pedestrian lane in Ömnögovi, with a nice menu of Mongolian favourites and Korean classics, including kimchi stew. They do some Western dishes, can arrange special-order vegetarian meals, and the Golden Gobi draughts are icy. It turns into a popular karaoke bar after dark.

CHINA

One of the world's most beloved and widely exported cuisines, Chinese cooking is so wide-reaching and so diverse that it defies definition. The Chinese themselves break their food into eight broad regional sub-cuisines, spanning from the numbing chillis of Sichuan to the northwest's hand-pulled noodles, and from hearty dumplings to delicate dim sum. Indeed, food is such a central part of the Chinese psyche that a common Mandarin greeting is *'Ni chifan le ma?'* ('Have you eaten?').

WHAT TO EAT

Hotpot
A savoury dip-ingredients-yourself soup.

Noodles
Fried (*chao mian*), cooked in soup, or hand-pulled (*lamian*).

Dumplings
Crescent shapes in the north (*jiaozi*), delicately steamed in the south (dim sum), or injected with soupy liquid in Shanghai (*xiaolongbao*).

Chuan
Charcoal-grilled skewers of cumin-covered meats and vegetables.

Stir-frying
Try *mapo dofu* (spicy tofu), *gongbao jiding* (Kungpao chicken) or *yuxiang rousi* (fish-flavoured shredded pork).

PRICE RANGES

For main dishes:
$ less than ¥50
$$ ¥50–150
$$$ ¥150 or more

Hong Kong & Macau
Two-course meal with drinks:
$ less than HK$200
$$ HK$200–500
$$$ HK$500 or more

Tipping: Not usual; high-end restaurants may add 15%.

YANG'S FRY DUMPLINGS

SHANGHAI | $ | DUMPLINGS
97 Huanghe Rd; dumplings from ¥12

Shanghai's most famous spot for sesame-seed-and-scallion-coated *shengjian* (fried dumplings). This is a no-nonsense affair: orders are taken at a counter, diners are brusquely shunted into any available plastic chair in the tiny dining room, and dumplings are consumed almost before they hit the table. Watch out for boiling meat juices that unexpectedly jet down your shirt.

KAM'S ROAST GOOSE

HONG KONG | $ | CANTONESE
226 Hennessy Rd, Wan Chai; 852 2520 1110; www.krg.com.hk; meals HK$80-200

Expect to queue for half an hour or more to worship at Kam's oily alter of perfectly roast goose. A spin-off from Hong Kong's famed Yung Kee Restaurant, Michelin-starred Kam's upholds the same strict standards in sourcing and roasting. The best cut is the upper thigh (succulent but less fatty), served with either rice or seasoned noodles.

BO INNOVATION

HONG KONG | $$$ | CHINESE
1st fl, 60 Johnston Rd, Wan Chai; 852 2850 8371; www.boinnovation.com; lunch set HK$750, tasting menu HK$900, dinner tasting menu HK$2280-2680

Presided over by the 'Demon Chef', Hong Kong's own Alvin Leung, who rips up the rule book and reimagines Chinese classics in bold and often outrageous ways. Set menus deliver deconstructed Hong Kong favourites, from molecular *xiaolongbao* dumplings to 'No shark fin', a similarly textured take on Hong Kong's unsustainable signature, crafted from yuzu, osmanthus, peach resin and dried persimmon.

TASTE OF DADONG

BEIJING | $$ | BEIJING
LG2-11, Parkview Green, 9 Dongdaqiao Lu,; 010 8563 0016; duck portion ¥118

Casual eatery by Peking duck maestro Dong Zhenxiang – of famed sister restaurant, Dadong – lets you enjoy a portion of the famously crispy roast fowl without having to order the whole bird. Dadong can't resist a bit of food theatre: a dusting of icing sugar on the sweet-and-sour ribs here, candyfloss 'flowers' there. And don't miss Dong's take on Beijing's beloved rustic noodle dish *zhajiang mian* – noodles with mincemeat sauce.

YUFUNAN

BEIJING | $$ | HUNAN
49 Gongmenkou Toutiao; 010 8306 3022; mains ¥58-117

One of the best modern Chinese dining experiences in Beijing, Yufunan is an insanely stylish spice fest, serving the sweat-inducing fare of Hunan province in an all-white, modernist dining space squeezed between hutong alleyway homes. *Duo lajiao* – spicy, pickled chillies – dominate almost every dish, with salt, sour and spice levels all cranked up to 11.

'Kam's Roast Goose commemorates our beloved late grandfather, Mr. Kam Shui Fai and father, Mr Kam Kinsen Kwan Sing. We are very proud of their accomplishments and they have given us great inspiration to carry on the Kam family's legacy.'
Kam's Roast Goose

LORD STOW'S BAKERY

MACAU | $ | BAKERY
1 Rua do Tassara, Coloane; 853 2888 2534; www.lordstow.com; egg tarts MOP$10;

Though the celebrated English baker Andrew Stow has passed away, his cafe and the original Lord Stow's Bakery here keep his memory alive by serving his renowned *pastéis de nata* (warm egg-custard tart with a flaky crust) and cheesecake in different flavours, including mango and green tea. The original bakery is an extremely simple take-away shop in Coloane with fluorescent lights and a worn tiled floor, but you can pop around the corner to Lord Stow's Cafe to sit in.

OLD CHANG'S SPRING ROLLS

HEILONGJIANG | $ | CHINESE
180 Zhongyang Dajie, Harbin; 0451 8468 5000; dishes ¥12-38

Hungry foodies line up for Old Chang's famous chunbing – DIY spring rolls, a northern Chinese speciality. The basement dining room is functional and clean – the star is the roll. You order wheat skins and a choice of fillings – crispy duck, eggs and veggies – then fold, tuck and gorge.

SAN QIAN LI COLD NOODLES

JILIN | $ | KOREAN
56 Xinhua Jie, Yanji; cold noodles ¥18-22

Yanji is home to a large ethnically Korean-Chinese population, and this bright local restaurant is one of the best places to slurp down the local dish: *leng mian* (cold noodles). Order and almost immediately a large bowl of chewy bean thread noodles appears, served in a cold beef broth that is addictively savoury and sweet with a fresh topping of shredded cucumber and cabbage.

LAOBIAN DUMPLINGS

LIAONING | $$ | DUMPLINGS
2nd fl, 208 Zhong Jie Lu, Shenyang; dumplings ¥16-60

Open since 1829, Shenyang's most famous restaurant is a 2nd-floor dumpling house with efficient staff who toss around picture menus featuring hundreds of flavours of boiled, steamed and fried treasures.

SHAGUO LI

TIANJIN | $$ | CHINESE
46 Jiujiang Lu; 022 2326 0075; most dishes ¥36-98, noodles from ¥20

Despite having walls adorned with photos of celebrities who've eaten here, this Tianjin icon remains refreshingly unpretentious. Locals still come for the speciality pork spare ribs in a sweet barbecue sauce – so tender they pull apart at the touch of a chopstick.

SHAWN TREN'S

SHANDONG | $$ | SHANDONG
216 Zhongshan Lu, Qingdao; 185 6276 1819; most dishes ¥20-40, seafood ¥35-90

Housed in a former Qingdao electrical office building dating from 1909, this super little restaurant, with big-window street views, knocks out delicious but affordable Shandong cuisine from its small open kitchen. There's a good selection of noodles, and an English-language menu makes ordering Qingdao's famous seafood a breeze.

'During a trip to Portugal in the late 1980s, Andrew had become familiar with their popular Pasteis de Nata – a kind of egg tart... [he] set forth, experimenting with his own version... and introduced the 'Portuguese' Egg Tart to Asia.'
Lord Stow's Bakery

LUCKY FULL CITY SEAFOOD

FUJIAN | $$ | DIM SUM
28 Hubin Beilu, Xiamen; dim sum from ¥16-34, meals from ¥70; 0592 505 8688

Waits to be seated can be extraordinarily long for this Xiamen institution.

A Cantonese culinary masterclass, dining here is about consuming stacks of exquisite dim sum, like egg buns, roasted pigeon and pork dumplings, seated at huge round tables in the even huger dining room.

ZHONGSHAN SOUTH ROAD FOOD STREET

ZHEJIANG | $ | MARKET
Zhongshan Nanlu, Hangzhou

Hangzhou is spoilt for choice when it comes to foodie streets, and this stretch of Zhongshan Nanlu overlooked by the Drum Tower is an absolute delight. Casual sit-down restaurants line the road, and stalls that run down its centre sell everything from fresh seafood and deep-fried insects to Beggar's Chicken and the absolute stinkiest of stinky tofu. Plastic tables and chairs cover the pavement area, often with giant beer dispensers in the middle.

GUSU CAI GUAN

JIANGSU | $$ | CHINESE
88 Caohu Xuxiang, Pingjiang Lu, Suzhou; dishes ¥30-130

This small restaurant has a classic Suzhou setting, overlooking a lovely canal and next to a picturesque stone bridge and a traditional teahouse. The menu is also traditionally Suzhounese, wish dishes designed for sharing, including the local specialty – sweet and sour squirrelfish (*songshu guiyu*) – and other fish caught in nearby Tai Lake.

PAUL YEUNG/SOUTH CHINA MORNING VIA GETTY IMAGES©

GAOTANG HUNDUN

ANHUI | $ | DUMPLINGS
1 Haidi Xiang, Tunxi; wontons ¥10

Down a little Tunxi alley is an ancient food cart inside an even more ancient Qing dynasty home – run by a 12th-generation *hundun* (wonton) seller and his family. The speciality is the wontons, made to order and with super-thin skin, though there are other dishes, like fried *jiaozi* (stuffed dumplings).

LAO SAN YANG

JIANGXI | $$ | JIANGXI
437 Chuanshan Lu, Nanchang; most dishes ¥16-45

WHERE TO DRINK...

TEA

Anxi Chaye Daguanyuan Quanzhou, Fujian
The famous Iron Buddha (Tieguanyin) oolong tea – known for its thick fragrance and floral sweetness – is grown on this 11-acre farm.

Longjing Tea Village Hangzhou, Zhejiang
Wander the lush hills near Zhejiang's capital city, where longjing (Dragon Well) tea is grown, then have a cuppa with a view of the plantations.

He Ming Teahouse Chengdu, Sichuan
Century-old, open-air teahouse in Chengdu's People's Park where locals fritter away afternoons with bottomless cups and mahjong.

Fuxi Teahouse Suzhou, Jiangsu
Chinese opera and local biluochun tea in a rickety old wooden house by a Suzhou canal.

Promising to 'keep the real taste of Old Nanchang', this wildly popular no-frills restaurant has a youthful vibe, a Communist Revolutionary theme and a menu full of spicy Jiangxi crayfish (xiao longxia), crab-claw noodles (xie-jiao laomian) and garlic chicken wings (suanxiang jichi). When spices get too much, there's palette-cleansing cold, slightly sweetened green-bean porridge (lü dou tang) and plenty of beer.

LUNA

GUANGXI | $$ | ITALIAN

26 Moon Hill Village (Li Village), Gaotian Town; 0773 877 8169; www.yangshuoguesthouse.com; mains ¥30-70

This fine rooftop restaurant is one of Yangshuo's best, thanks to its sublime view of Moon Hill. The food is well-rendered Italian: the rigatoni alla amatriciana (smoked bacon, onion and tomato), thin-crust pizza and home-made fennel sausage are fantastic.

BINGSHENG MANSION

GUANGDONG | $$ | CANTONESE

5th fl, 2 Xiancun Lu, Zhujiang New Town, Guangzhou; 020 3803 5888; dishes from ¥68

One of only eight restaurants awarded a star in the inaugural 2018 Guangzhou Michelin guide, this is the upscale flagship of the esteemed Bingsheng chain, serving creative riffs on Cantonese classics in an elegant dining space. A must-try for carnivores is the signature char siu pork, marinated for 24 hours, then roasted to charred, sticky loveliness. The small but exquisite selection of dim sum usually sells out by early afternoon.

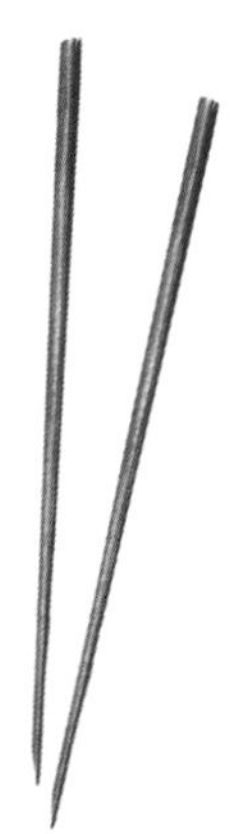

'Trained by Italian chefs, Luna's chefs Xiao Zhao and James create delicious pizzas, pastas, soups and salads to be enjoyed in the sun or under the stars on our open terrace opposite Moon Hill.'

Luna

HE JI

HENAN | $ | HENAN

3 Renmin Lu, Zhengzhou; noodle soup ¥17-29

For years, this Zhengzhou stalwart has been drawing raucous crowds for the nourishing local Henan noodles served in deliciously oily mutton broth (huimian). Orders are placed with green-shirted staff members: basic (youzhi) or deluxe (teyou), with a bit more meat, and there's a help-yourself tea station.

SHENJI SHAOKAO HAIXIAN

HUBEI | $$ | HUBEI

100-4 Jianghan Erlu, Wuhan; skewers ¥7-42, noodles ¥36-65

Bright, busy restaurant focusing on a special seafood version of a Wuhan specialty: huge bowls of reganmian (sesame noodles). This take on the classic noodles come with crab legs (xiejiaomian) or clams (shengzimian) – the literal translation of the latter is 'Jesus noodles'! There's also a menu of barbecue skewers (shaokao).

LAO CHANGSHA LONGXIAGUAN

HUNAN | $$ | HUNAN

72 Xiangjiang Zhonglu, Changsha; mains ¥10-30, crayfish ¥58-98

This cavernous and raucous warehouse-like dining hall (a bit more like a multi-storey car park) is the most enjoyable place to sample a signature Hunan dish: spicy crayfish (longxia). Crayfish are boiled and then covered in chilli, oil and garlic and served in large bowls to be cracked open and slurped out by hand.

A BO PO SALT ROASTED CHICKEN

HAINAN | $$ | HAINAN

Shop c1-10, Shuicheng Community B, Erdong Lu, Haikou; chicken from ¥88

A bo po means 'grandma' in Hainanese, and this amazing chicken is Indeed made by a 70-something grandma. She buries it in sea salt and bakes it for four hours, then seals it in plastic to pull in all the juices. plastic gloves are provided for encouraged eating with your hands – choose between spicy and non-spicy chicken, which comes with head and feet still attached.

OLD KAILI SOUR FISH RESTAURANT

GUIZHOU | $ | GUIZHOU

12 Shengfu Lu, Guiyang; 0851 8584 3665; dishes from ¥40

This Guiyang institution is the place to try a delicacy of the local Miao tribe: *suantangyu* (sour fish soup). Fish is picked from tanks at the back, cooked whole in a spicy and sour stew broth, then placed on a hot-plate at your table to continue bubbling. The atmosphere is raucous as big groups toast, gobble, spill and laugh.

'The goal was to eradicate the constraints that a traditional "A La Carte" restaurant's system imposes... I needed to shift control... Like at home, I'll pick the time, pick the menu... set the music, spark off the light.'

Paul Pairet, chef of Ultraviolet

ZENG LAO YAO YU ZHUANG

CHONGQING | $$ | SICHUAN

220 Changjiang Binjiang Lu; 023 6392 4315; mains ¥28-78

Outside, it's a seething mass of people crowded around tables. Inside, it's even more packed as you enter a former bomb shelter with white-tiled walls and a rock roof. This Chongqing institution is a unique, utilitarian dining experience, with all strata of society in search of the signature dish, carp (*jiyu*), and sublime spare ribs (*paigu*). It never closes.

CHEN MAPO DOUFU

SICHUAN | $$ | SICHUAN

197 Xi Yulong Jie, Chengdu; 028 8674 3889; mains ¥22-58

The plush flagship of a famous Sichuanese chain is famous for a reason – it's one of the best places in the world to sample one of China's most beloved dishes: *mapo doufu*. House tofu is cooked with a signature fiery sauce of garlic, minced beef, fermented soybean, chilli oil and numbing Sichuan peppercorns. The surroundings are suitably fancy, with red lanterns and dark-wood imperial-style decor.

ULTRAVIOLET

SHANGHAI | $$$ | GASTRONOMY BUND

www.uvbypp.cc; dinner from ¥5000

Paul Pairet's masterpiece and China's most conceptual dining experience revolves around Pairet's signature mischievous creations. Ten diners a night gather at a secret meeting point before being whisked away to a high-tech dining room for 22 courses accompanied by different sensory moods (sounds, scents and images). Think pairing up an illuminated apple-wasabi communion wafer with purple candles and a specially designed cathedral scent and visuals.

1 RESTAURANT

YUNNAN | $$$ | YUNNAN

14 Renli Lu, Shuhe Old Town, Lijiang; 888 513 6681; dishes ¥28-128

Built into a historic Lijiang courtyard house once owned by a Tea Horse Road trader, the menu here features Yunnanese and Naxi specialties like sweetcorn pancakes, pork with black fungus and dried yak with sliced potatoes, and even a few truffle dishes. In good weather, patio tables offer magical views of Shuhe old town.

GRANDMA

INNER MONGOLIA | $ | MONGOLIAN

Xilin Guole Beilu, Hohhot; 0471 333 0055; mains from ¥12

This Hohhot standout does a roaring trade in Mongolian specialities like sweet cheese, camel meat pie, cheese mooncakes, roast lamb ribs and handmade yoghurt. The bright, upstairs dining room is overlooked by a portrait of Genghis Khan and painted in colourful, Inner Mongolian motifs. Service is prompt and friendly.

JIA JIN YANG HELE NOODLES

SHANXI | $ | NOODLES

363 Shangnian St, Jincheng; 159 0356 6930; noodles ¥9-12

Hele noodles are a pressed noodle made from buckwheat, sorghum or oat flour that's commonly eaten in northern and northwestern China. This tiny, rustic shop run by a friendly couple does them well. The noodles –

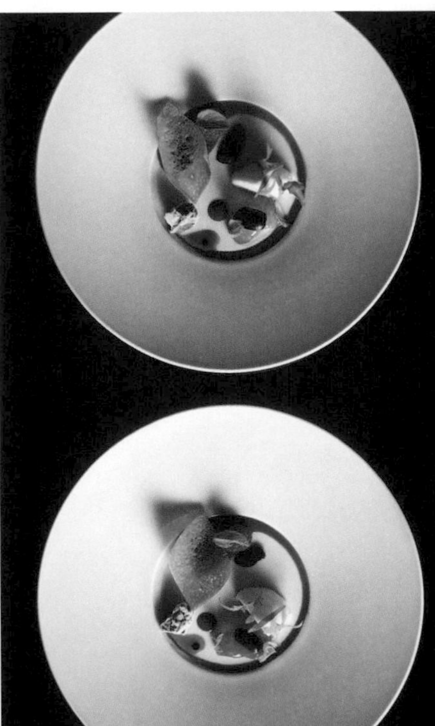

P461: Buuz. P464-5: Mapo tofu; Bo Innovation. This page: Dishes from Ultraviolet. Opposite page: Luna.

al dente and delicious – come in clear broth, or with pumpkin, preserved vegetables or braised pork. Illustrations on the walls show how the dough is pushed through a vessel with holes directly into boiling water.

MA HONG XIAOCHAO PAOMOGUAN

SHAANXI | $ | CHINESE ISLAMIC

46 Hongbu Jie, Xi'an; 133 5918 5583 dishes ¥17

One of Xi'an's most famous and beloved local joints for the city's favourite dish: lamb or beef *paomo* (flatbread stew). You have to get here before 11am, otherwise it's all elbows in ribs. Service is brusque and no-nonsense – pay, grab a well-worn plastic seat and break the round loaf of bread into tiny pieces (they must be small) to drop into the bowl of meat broth (spicy or mild), splashing over the crumbs.

TONG XIN CHUN

NINGXIA | $$ | CHINESE ISLAMIC

269 Funing Nanjie, Yinchuan; 0951 412 2991; main dishes ¥18-48

Situated on a Yinchuan street famous for lamb restaurants, locals regard this unassuming decades-old establishment as one of the best places to try Ningxia cuisine, in particular, mutton. The bonus is that it's one of the few Hui shops in Yinchuan that strictly enforces a no-smoking rule. The shou zhua roast lamb, eaten by hand, is sublime, succulent and melt-in-your-mouth, with the right lean-fat ratio.

MAZILU BEEF NOODLES

GANSU | $ | NOODLES

86 Dazhong Xiang, Lanzhou; 0931 845 0505; noodles ¥8

In business since 1954, this Lanzhou institution has locals flocking here for

WHERE TO EAT...

HOTPOT

Zhao'er Huoguo, Chongqing
Hotpot in its home city – nine-sectioned pots separate the flavours of raw ingredients; two-sectioned pots separate mild and spicy broths.

Yulin Chuanchuan, Xiang, Chengdu
Chengdu-style hotpot, where skewered meats and vegetables are dipped in fiery broth.

Fu De Yu Hotpot, Beijing
On Beijing's famous hotpot avenue, 'Ghost Street', the city's traditional non-spicy broth in battered, coal-fired cauldrons. Known for Inner Mongolian lamb and beef tripe.

Dandan Tongguoshuan, Hohhot, Inner Mongolia
Mongolian hotpot, with spicy or mild broths for scalding beef, lamb strips, piles of mushrooms and potatoes.

steaming bowls of the city's famous noodles: spicy, hand-pulled beef lamian. Orders are given at a counter, then diners take a ticket to the kitchen, where chefs prepare the noodles fresh. Lamian were taken home from China by Japanese students several centuries ago and eventually became ramen.

SNOW MOUNTAIN CREAMERY

QINGHAI | $$ | ICE CREAM

Bandao Buxingjie, Xining; 0971 827 8334; www.snowmountaincreamery.com; mains from ¥30

One of the most unusual foodie stories in China is this superb ice cream shop run by a charming American-expat family who have seven kids. They offer superb, hand-made ice cream and coffee in a cosy, two-tiered space. They also roast, grinds and brew their own coffee and the menu has a range of pizzas with local toppings like yak-meat pepperoni. The upstairs mezzanine is a recommended bolt-hole, surveying the vast coffee roaster and views out back while snuggling into a sofa that is hard to leave.

WORDO TIBETAN COURTYARD

TIBET | $$$ | TIBETAN

10 Zhade Xilu, Shigatse; 892 882 3994; dishes ¥50-70

Tibet is not known as a foodie destination, but the plateau's most charming dining experience can be had in this stylish Shigatse restaurant near the Summer Palace of the Panchen Lamas. In fine weather, you're seated in one of Tibet's loveliest courtyards, bedecked in swirling prayer flags, to sample super-fresh local specialities like curried potatoes and potato *momos* (dumplings), as well as more ambitious but equally well-rendered offerings like roast leg of lamb.

OU'ER DAXIKE NIGHT MARKET

XINJIANG | $ | UYGHUR

Ou'er Daxike Lu, Kashgar; meals from ¥10

Filled with the sounds of sizzling meats and the light of swaying bulbs, Kashgar's photogenic night market is a great place to sample a staple that's now favoured across China: chuan – charcoal-roasted meat skewers, typically coated in heaps of cumin and chili powder. Among other goodies are fried fish, chickpeas, kebabs, fried dumplings (*hoshan*) and bubbling vats of goat's-head soup, all topped off with fresh pomegranate juice.

NORTH KOREA

North Korean food draws on the Korean peninsula's long and rich culinary tradition. The country's modern history has taken its toll on the food scene today, but visitors eat sumptuously by North Korean standards, particularly in the traveller-ready restaurants of Pyongyang.

WHAT TO EAT

Kimchi
Spicy fermented cabbage served as a side or made into stew.

Rice
North Korea's staple food, usually served steamed.

Naengmyeon
Cold buckwheat noodles served with sliced meat, dried egg and hot sauce; a particular speciality of Pyongyang.

Bibimbap
Warm rice topped with vegetables, kimchi and sometimes meat.

Gangjeong
Sweet snack of rice puffs coated in honey, nuts, seeds or spices.

Tipping: Not expected anywhere in the country.

OKRYU

PYONGYANG | KOREAN

The most famous restaurant in North Korea, Okryu is a faux-traditional structure on the Taedong River that's famed for its naengmyeon (cold noodles) and is very popular with locals. Do as the locals do and slurp your noodles with gusto. The restaurant is mystifyingly divided into a cold-noodles section and a turtle-soup section. It's also known by the name 'Ongnyugwan'.

PYONGYANG NUMBER ONE DUCK BARBEQUE

PYONGYANG | KOREAN

Pyongyang Number One Duck Barbeque is one of the best places in Pyongyang and is often where group tours eat on their last evening in North Korea. The order of the day here is delicious strips of duck meat, which you cook on a grill at your table.

ITALIAN RESTAURANT

PYONGYANG | PIZZA

Kwangbok St

Pyongyang's imaginatively named first pizza joint caused a sensation when it opened in 2009 after Kim Jong-il reportedly sent a team of chefs to Italy to learn how to make the perfect pizza. The results are pretty decent, and there's a full range of pasta dishes, all to be followed by after-dinner karaoke.

LAMB BARBECUE RESTAURANT

PYONGYANG | KOREAN

The Lamb Barbecue Restaurant has some of the friendliest and most boisterous staff in the country. Once the delicious lamb barbecue has been served at your table, the servers burst into song and encourage diners to dance with them.

SOUTH KOREA

WHAT TO EAT
Kimchi
Pickled vegetables, usually spicy fermented cabbage.
Bibimbap
Rice with vegetables and/or meat.
Bulgogi
Pan-fried marinated beef or pork.
Chimaek
Double-fried chicken paired with beer.
Galbi
Beef ribs.
Jjigae
Stone-hotpot stew.
Gimbap
Rice, vegetables and/or meat rolled in dried seaweed.
Mandu
Meat/vegetable dumplings.
Hotteok
Fried dough filled with cinnamon and brown sugar.

PRICE RANGES
In Seoul:
$ less than ₩12,000 (less than ₩7000 elsewhere)
$$ ₩12,000–25,000 (₩7000–18,000 elsewhere)
$$$ ₩25,000 or more

Tipping: Not expected; high-end restaurants may add a service charge.

It stands to reason that any culture which bases its entire culinary output on fermented cabbage (kimchi) has something different going on. South Korea's food culture beats to its own drum, incorporating familiar Asian ingredients like soy sauce and rice, but doing everything in its own special way. Korean life revolves around food, whether fried snacks at a market stall, raucous chicken-and-beer with friends or an elaborate *jeongsik* banquet.

NORAN MAHURA

GYEONGSANGNAM-DO | $$ | SEAFOOD
60 Cheongsapo-ro 128beon-gil, Busan; 051 703 3586; set meals from ₩30,000

Not far from a lighthouse, locals flock to this seaside restaurant for sundowners and unexpectedly stay up all night enjoying the ambience. Meals include barbecued shellfish (조개구이; *jogae gui*) with an amazing salsa-like sauce. It tastes even better with *soju* (local vodka) at sunrise.

GEOIN TONGDAK

GYEONGSANGNAM-DO | $$ | CHICKEN
34 Junggu-ro 47beon-gil, Bupyeong-dong, Jung-gu, Busan; 051-246 6079; fried chicken ₩18,000

Three-hour lines aren't uncommon at Geoin Tongdak, one of the most acclaimed fried chicken eateries in South Korea. The crispy, double-fried chicken is battered and cooked in big fryers on the street, and consumed, along with pitchers of beer, at simple, crammed tables inside, where the decor stretches to fading wallpaper and decades-old posters of Korean TV shows.

GAEJEONG

GYEONGSANGBUK-DO | $$ | KOREAN
Daegu; dishes ₩6000-11,000

Divine and healthy traditional Korean food served over three floors since 1978. The (cold) spicy buckwheat noodles are supreme. Atmosphere is a bright, no-nonsense diner-style –

chopsticks and cutlery are stored in drawers under the table tops.

DDUNGBO HALMAE GIMBAP

GYEONGSANGNAM-DO | $ | KOREAN
325 Tonyeonghaen-ro, Tongyeong; 055 645 2619; per serving ₩5000

This simple restaurant, in business for 70 years, serves only one thing: *chungmu gimbap* (충무 김밥), a spicy squid-and-radish dish. Carrying Tongyeong's historical name, Chungmu, the dish is the town's signature. There's no menu, you just indicate how many portions you want and bowls are swiftly delivered without fanfare. Spice levels can test the red-pepper tolerance of even the hardiest Korean-food lover.

GOMANARU

CHUNGCHEONGNAM-DO | $$ | KOREAN
5-9 Baekmigoeul-gil, Gongju; 041 857 9999; meals ₩9000-25,000

This restaurant serves perhaps the prettiest *ssambap* (rice lettuce wraps with assorted ingredients) in Korea. Tables brim with piles of fragrant leaves, handfuls of colourful edible flowers, dried herbs and a rainbow of miniature sauce bowls and pickled vegetables ready to be wrapped. It's located across from Gongsan-seong, Gongju's hilltop fortress – window seats afford lovely views, especially when lit up at night.

COURTESY KOREA HOUSE

HANGUK-JIP

JEOLLABUK-DO | $$ | KOREAN
119 Eojin-gil, Jeonju; 063 284 2224; meals from ₩11,000

Jeonju's specialty dish is bibimbap, and some say this temple-like restaurant is the best best place to try it. The classic rice-bowl dish comes topped with bright yellow mung-bean jelly, a hearty dollop of chilli paste and wild greens. It's served either in a hot stone pot (*dolsot*; 돌솥) or topped with raw beef (*yukhoe*; 육회).

MINT

JEJU-DO | $$$ | INTERNATIONAL
93-66 Seopjikoji-ro, Seongsan-eup; 064-731 7773; set lunch/dinner from ₩45,000/60,000

WHERE TO DRINK...

MAKGEOLLI

Fermentation Kitchen, Busan
High-end bar serving special carbonated *makgeolli*.

Sorori Wolhyang, Seoul
Fruity, nutty artisanal *makgeolli* in a cosy basement bar.

Sansawon Brewery & Museum, Pocheon-si
Tasting sessions at a brewery producing high-quality, chemical-free *makgeolli* and other spirits, plus a museum of traditional equipment.

Muldwinda, Seoul
Seoul's most sophisticated *makgeolli* bar, set up by graduates from the nearby Susubori Academy.

Yetchon Makgeolli, Jeonju
Pair a kettle of wine with butter-soft pork belly or kimchi.

Dining inside celebrated Japanese architect Ando Tadao's Glass House is a delightful experience, one best enjoyed during the day when you can take in the coastal views through the floor-to-ceiling windows. The menu utilises high-grade local produce such as black pork and fish steak, as well as excellent pasta. Coffee and cake are also enjoyable reasons to linger.

YETNAL PATJUK

JEJU-DO | $$ | KOREAN

130 Seongeup Minseok-ro, Pyoseon-myeon, Seongeup Folk Village; 064-787 3357; mains from ₩6000

Everything about this restaurant, housed in a traditional building, is inviting. You're greeted by warm smiles and the sweet, earthy aroma of red beans. Soups and porridge are standout, including some made from lotus flowers, pumpkin and seaweed. Wooden tables, exposed beams and heavy earthenware add to the rustic charm.

WOLJEONG-RI GALBIBAP

JEJU-DO | $$ | KOREAN

46 Woljeong 7-gil, Gujwa-eup, Woljeong Beach; 064-782 0430; mains from ₩15,900

Is it the delicious *galbi* (barbecued beef ribs) and noodles or the large, chic neon space that guarantees a long queue here? Diners typically come early, jot their name on the waiting list and then explore the nearby beach to work up an appetite. The must-try dish is the *galbi* (beef ribs), a Woljeong speciality, served on heaping skillet plates.

Previous page: Dishes from Korea House.

KOREA HOUSE

SEOUL | $$$ | KOREAN

10 Toegye-ro 36-gil; 02-2266 9101; www.koreahouse.or.kr; set menu lunch ₩29,000-47,000, dinner ₩68,200-150,000, performances ₩50,000

A dozen dainty, artistic courses make up the traditional royal banquet served at elegant Korea House. The wooden *hanok* house, staff in formal Korean *hanbok* attire, *gayageum* (zither) music, and wooden platters and boxes the food is served in combine to make you feel like you're in a Korean period drama.

GWANGJANG MARKET

SEOUL | $ | KOREAN

88 Changgyeonggung-ro, Jongno-gu; www.kwangjangmarket.co.kr; dishes ₩4000-15,000

This sprawling fabric market is Seoul's busiest *meokjagolmok* (food alley), thanks to the 200 or so food stalls, kimchi and fresh-seafood vendors that have set up shop amid the silk, satin and linen wholesalers. Foodies flock here for the golden fried *nokdu bindaetteok* (mung-bean pancake) – paired beautifully with *makgeolli*. Most diners squeeze on to benches at tightly-packed vendors threading through the alleyways to munch on *mandu* (Korean dumplings), *jokbal* (braised pig's trotters), *bibimbap* and *boribap* (mixed rice and barley topped with veggies).

JUNGSIK

SEOUL | $$$ | KOREAN

11 Seolleung-ro, 158-gil; 02-517 4654; www.jungsik.kr; 5-course lunch/dinner from; ₩88,000/130,000

Neo-Korean cuisine hardly gets better than at Jungsik, voted number 25 in *Asia's 50 Best Restaurants* in 2018. At this Seoul outpost of the New York restaurant named after creative chef-owner Yim Jungsik, you can expect inspired and superbly presented contemporary mixes of traditional and seasonal ingredients over multiple courses, with an emphasis on seafood like abalone, octopus and black cod. Decor is pure minimalist fine dining.

I LOVE SINDANGDONG

SEOUL | $ | KOREAN

302-4 Sindang-dong, Dongdaemun; 02-2232 7872; www.ilovesindangdong.com; tteokbokki for 2 from ₩11,000

The *tteokbokki* (spicy rice cakes) at this raucous restaurant comes in bubbling saucepans as part of a witches brew of rice cakes, fish cakes, instant noodles, veggies, egg and tofu in a volcanic sauce. It's pure, junky comfort food and great fun; you can pay extra to go over the top adding seafood and cheese. Rounding it all out are *gimbap* (seaweed rice rolls), cheap draught beer and occasional live music.

'Owner Chef Jungsik Yim reinvents Korean cuisine using traditional and familiar ingredients, creating a brand-new genre of food: New Korean Fine Dining.'
Jungsik

BALWOO GONGYANG

SEOUL | $$$ | VEGETARIAN

5th fl, Templestay Information Center, 56; Ujeongguk-ro; 02-2031 2081; www.eng.balwoo.or.kr; set lunch ₩30,000, dinner ₩45,000-95,000

Balwoo Gongyang's fine temple-style cuisine has garnered a Michelin star. Dining here is not a rushed affair – subtle flavours and a mix of textures are meant to be savoured and meditated upon. Temple cuisine is necessarily vegetarian – standout dishes include rice porridge and delicate salads, dumplings, fried shiitake mushrooms and mugwort in a sweet-and-sour sauce.

JAHA SONMANDOO

SEOUL | $ | DUMPLINGS

12 Baekseokdong-gil; 02-379 2648; dumplings from ₩6500;

This posh mountainside *mandu* (dumpling) restaurant serves elegantly wrapped dough parcels stuffed with veggies, beef and pork. It's a little like eating in someone's home – the restaurant is in a hillside house with mountain views and you're asked to remove your shoes when you arrive. Dumpling recipes have been handed down from the proprietor's mother and grandmother. A cup of sweet cinnamon tea finishes the meal with a cleansing flourish.

JAPAN

Japanese food is highly seasonal and hyper local. Tokyo boasts more Michelin-starred establishments than any other city on earth. The good news is that wherever you go there are wonderful spots to dine – from humble street stalls and rustic *izakaya* (the Japanese equivalent of a pub) to the most cutting edge of restaurants all serving exquisite dishes.

WHAT TO EAT

Yakitori
Skewers of charcoal-grilled chicken and vegetables.

Sushi
Originated as a way to make fish last longer, the vinegar in the rice being a preserving agent.

Sukiyaki
Thin slices of beef briefly simmered in a broth of *shōyu* (soy sauce), sugar and sake, then dipped in raw egg.

Tempura
Lightly battered seafood and vegetables deep-fried in sesame oil.

Noodles
Ramen (curly egg noodles originally from China), soba (made from buckwheat flour) and udon (thick wheat noodles).

PRICE RANGES
For a main meal:
$ less than ¥1000 (less than ¥2000 in Tokyo and Kyoto)
$$ ¥1000 to ¥4000 (¥2000 to ¥5000 in Tokyo and Kyoto)
$$$ ¥4000 (¥5000 in Tokyo and Kyoto) or more

Tipping: Not usual; high-end restaurants tend to add 10%.

RYŪKYŪ RYŌRI NUCHIGAFŪ (琉球料理ぬちがふぅ)

NAHA | $$ | OKINAWAN

1-28-3 Tsuboya; 098-861-2952; set dinner from ¥3000

For a memorable, elegant meal, don't pass up dinner at the hilltop Nuchigafū. Formerly a lovely Okinawan teahouse, and before that a historic Ryūkyūan residence, Nuchigafū serves lunch and frothy *buku-buku* tea during the day and beautifully plated multi-course Okinawan dinners by night.

TŌSENKYŌ SŌMEN NAGASHI (唐船峡そうめん流し)

SATSUMA PENINSULA | $ | NOODLES

5967 Jūchō, Ibusuki; 0993-32-2143; sōmen ¥570

This sprawling restaurant in a riverside gorge near Ikeda-ko gets an estimated 200,000 annual visitors (!), paying tribute to the 1967 birthplace of *nagashi-sōmen* (flowing noodles). *Sōmen* (thin wheat-flour noodles) spin around tyre-shaped table-top tanks of swiftly flowing 13°C water; catch the noodles with your chopsticks and dip them in sauce to eat. Lots of fun and ultra-refreshing on hot days.

KAWASHIMA TŌFU (川島豆腐店)

KARATSU | $$$ | TOFU

Kyōmachi 1775; 0955-72-2423; www.zarudoufu.co.jp; lunch/dinner from ¥1500/5000

This renowned tofu shop has been in business since the Edo period and serves refined kaiseki (multi-course haute cuisine meals) starring tofu plus other seasonal specialities, around a 10-seat counter in its jewel box of a back room. Soft, warm, fresh – this is tofu as good as it gets.

TAKAMORI DENGAKU-NO-SATO (高森田楽の里)

ASO-SAN AREA | $$ | GRILL

2685-2 Ōaza-Takamori; 0967-62-1899; www.dengakunosato.com; set meals ¥1790-2850

At this fantastic thatch-roofed ex-farmhouse the staff use oven mitts to grill dengaku (skewers of vegetables, meat including Aso beef, fish and tofu covered in the namesake *dengaku*: sweet miso paste) at your own irori embedded in the floor. It's a few minutes drive from central Takamori and cash only.

HAKATAROU (博多廊)

FUKUOKA | $$ | JAPANESE

5th fl, SouthSide Terrace Bldg, 1-1-38 Daimyō; 092-687-5656; www.hakatarou.jp; most dishes ¥370-1800, 9-dish menus from ¥5000

Sample a wide range of regional foods at this elegant izakaya with friendly, kimono-clad staff Look for dishes like *karashi renkon* (spicy, deep-fried lotus root) and *basashi* (horsemeat sashimi) from Kumamoto, grilled Shimabara chicken, Kagoshima *kurobuta* (black pork), and Hakata ramen salad and *mizutaki* and *gameni* chicken stews, plus a huge selection of Kyūshū sake and *shōchū* (strong distilled liquor).

YABURE-KABURE (やぶれかぶれ)

SHIMONOSEKI | $$$ | SEAFOOD

2-2-5 Buzenda-chō; 083-234-3711; www.yaburekabure.jp;lunch/dinner sets from ¥3240/5400

The deadly, if not prepared properly, fugu (puffer fish) is the key item on the menu in this boisterous spot: pick from a range of fugu set menus, such as the dinner Ebisu course, which features the cute little puffer in raw, seared, fried and drowned-in-sake incarnations. Look for the blue-and-white pufferfish outside.

OKONOMI-MURA (お好み村)

HIROSHIMA | $ | OKONOMIYAKI

WHERE TO EAT...

RAMEN

Ichiran (一蘭), Fukuoka
This Fukuoka-born chain has a nationwide following. Fill out a form (available in English), requesting precisely how you want your noodles prepared, and eat at individual cubicles for zero distractions.

Mensho, Tokyo
Known for its innovative ramen recipes and the clean, contemporary design of its shops, at this branch of Mensho the concept is farm to bowl.

Menya Saimi (麺屋彩未), Sapporo
Often voted the best ramen shop in the city (and sometimes the country) – and it's not overrated. You will have to queue. Get the miso ramen.

2nd-4th fl, 5-13 Shintenchi; www.okonomimura.jp; dishes ¥800-1300

This Hiroshima institution is a touristy but fun place to get acquainted with *okonomiyaki* (savoury pancakes) and chat with the cooks over a hot griddle. There are 25 stalls spread over three floors, each serving up hearty variations of the local speciality. Pick a floor and find an empty stool at whichever counter takes your fancy.

KAPPŌ YANO (割烹矢野)

MATSUYAMA | $$ | SEAFOOD
2-5-8 Masaki-machi; 089-931-6346; www.aik4.shin-gen.jp; meals from ¥1500

Yano-san and his family have been serving traditional seafood-based meals at this popular joint for more than 30 years. Opt for the omakase courses where the chef will serve what's best that day, or go for a teishoku, a set meal that may feature sashimi (slices of raw fish and seafood) or *yakizakana* (grilled fish).

OFUKURO (おふくろ)

TAKAMATSU | $ | IZAKAYA
1-11-12 Kawara-machi; 087-862-0822; dishes ¥500-1500

This fabulous *washofu* (local eating house) in the heart of Takamatsu's entertainment district offers a well-priced and hearty dining experience. A number of delicious, pre-prepared vegetarian and fish dishes sit on the counter, served with salad and miso soup.

MUSEUM RESTAURANT ISSEN (ミュージアムレストラン日本料理一扇)

NAOSHIMA | $$$ | KAISEKI
Kagawa; 087-892-3223; www.benesse-artsite.jp; breakfast/lunch/dinner from ¥2662/2240/9680

The artfully displayed *kaiseki* (Japanese haute cuisine) dinners at this contrastingly austere restaurant in Benesse House Museum's basement (though with Andy Warhol works on the wall) are almost too pretty to eat. Courses feature local seafood, but there is a veg-dominated option (request a couple of days ahead) and the menu changes with the seasons.

MAMAKARI-TEI (ままかり亭)

KURASHIKI | $$ | SEAFOOD
3-12 Honmachi; 050-3373 6330; https://mamakaritei.gorp.jp; dishes ¥800-1200

Set in a 200-year-old warehouse, with chunky beams and long wooden tables, Mamakari-tei is famed for *mamakari*, the sardine-like local speciality. The tasty fish is supposed to induce bouts of uncontrollable feasting, so that people are obliged to *kari* (borrow) more *mama* (rice) from their neighbours to carry on their binge. Kaiseki-style course options are available at dinner, as well as an à la carte menu.

KŌBE PLAISIR (神戸プレジール)

KŌBE | $$$ | STEAK

Previous page: Miso Ramen from Menya Saimi.

2-11-5 Shimo-Yamate-dōri, Chūō-ku; 078-571-0141; www.kobeplaisir-honten.jp; lunch/dinner Kōbe-beef set menus from ¥7500/11,000

This is a great place to try Kōbe and Tajima beef prepared in a variety of styles, including *shabu-shabu* (thinly sliced beef cooked with vegetables in boiling water and then dipped in sauce). It's managed directly by the local agriculture cooperative, and courses include plenty of veggies, too.

CHIBŌ (千房)

OSAKA | $$ | OKONOMIYAKI

1-5-5 Dōtombori, Chuo-ku; 06-6212-2211; www.chibo.com; mains ¥885-1675

One of Osaka's most famous *okonomi-yaki* restaurants, Chibō almost always has a queue, but it moves fast because there's seating on multiple floors (though you might want to hold out for the coveted tables overlooking Dōtombori canal). The savoury pancakes made with cabbage and various toppings are all a treat here, but try the house special *Dōtombori yaki*, with pork, beef, squid, shrimp and cheese.

IMAI HONTEN (今井本店)

OSAKA | $$ | UDON

1-7-22 Dōtombori, Chūō-ku; 06-6211-0319; http://udon-imai.com; dishes from ¥800

Step into an oasis of calm amid Dōtombori's chaos to be welcomed by staff at one of the area's oldest and most-revered udon specialists. Try *kitsune udon* – noodles topped with soup-soaked slices of fried tofu. Look for the traditional exterior and the willow tree outside.

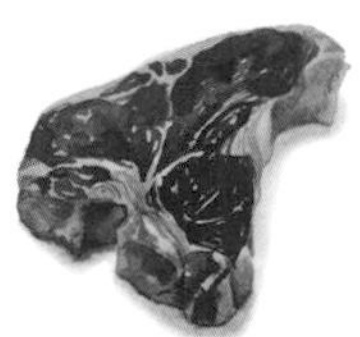

'Tajima beef is raised only in Hyogo Prefecture. The marbling is beautiful and the meat quality is good.'

Kōbe Plaisir

YOSHINO SUSHI (吉野鮓)

OSAKA | $$ | SUSHI

3-4-14 Awaji-machi, Chūō-ku; 06-6231-7181; www.yoshino-sushi.co.jp; meals from ¥2700

In business since 1841, Yoshino specialises in Osaka-style *hako-sushi* ('pressed sushi'). This older version of the dish (compared to the newer, hand-pressed Tokyo-style nigiri-sushi) is formed by a wooden mould, resulting in Mondrian-esque cubes of spongy omelette, soy-braised shiitake mushrooms, smokey eel and vinegar-marinated fish on rice. Reservations recommended.

YOTARO HONTEN (与太呂本店)

OSAKA | $$ | TEMPURA

3rd fl Nakanoshima Daibiru Building, 3-3-23 Nakanoshima, Kita-ku; 06-6147-2313; www.yotaro.co.jp; meals from ¥2500

This two-Michelin-starred restaurant specialises in exceptionally light and delectable tempura served at the counter, where you can watch the chefs, or in private rooms. The tasty sea bream dish serves two to three people and the filling tempura sets are fantastic value.

YURURI (ゆるり)

MIYAMA | $$$ | JAPANESE

15 Sano-mae, Morisato; 0771-76-0741; http://youluly.umesao.com; lunch/dinner menus from ¥3240/5400

Miyama's natural bounty is a big draw, and this restaurant in an elegantly updated thatched-roof farmhouse serves menus of seasonal local ingredients (such as mountain vegetables in spring and mushrooms in autumn). Reservations required (at least a day ahead), and only one party is served at dinner. You'll need a car to get here.

GIRO GIRO HITOSHINA (枝魯枝魯ひとしな)

KYOTO | $$$ | KAISEKI

420-7 Nanba-chō, Nishi-kiyamachi-dōri, Matsubara-sagaru, Shimogyō-ku; 075-343-7070; www.guiloguilo.com; kaiseki ¥4100

Giro Giro takes traditional *kaiseki* (Japanese haute cuisine) and strips any formality – you're left with great food in a boisterous atmosphere anh thousands more yen in your pocket. In a quiet lane near Kiyamachi-dōri, things liven up inside with patrons sitting at the counter chatting with chefs preparing inventive dishes. The seasonal menu consists of eight courses. Cash only.

KIKUNOI HONTEN (菊乃井)

KYOTO | $$$ | KAISEKI

459 Shimokawara-chō, Yasakatoriimae-sagaru, Shimokawara-dōri, Higashiyama-ku; 075-561-0015; www.kikunoi.jp; lunch/dinner from ¥10,000/16,000

Michelin-starred chef Mutara Yoshihiro serves some of the finest kaiseki (Japanese haute cuisine) in Kyoto. Located in a hidden nook near Maruyama-kōen, this restaurant has everything

This page: Yoshikawa. Opposite page: Sushi from Kizushi.

necessary for the most exquisite kaiseki experience, from setting to service to superbly executed cuisine, often with a creative twist. Reserve through your hotel at least a month in advance.

OMEN (おめん)

KYOTO | $ | NOODLES
74 Jōdo-ji Ishibashi-chō, Sakyō-ku; 075-771-8994; www.omen.co.jp; noodles from ¥1150

This elegant noodle shop, a five-minute walk from the temple Ginkaku-ji, is named after the signature dish – thick white noodles that are served in broth with a selection of seven fresh vegetables. Choose from hot or cold noodles, and you'll be given a bowl of soup to dip them in and a plate of vegetables (put these into the soup along with the sesame seeds).

YOSHIKAWA (吉川)

KYOTO | $$$ | TEMPURA
135 Matsushita-chō, Tominokōji, Oike-sagaru, Nakagyō-ku; 075-221-5544; www.kyoto-yoshikawa.co.jp; lunch/dinner from ¥3000/8000

This is the place to go for delectable tempura with a daily changing menu. Attached to the Yoshikawa ryokan, it offers table seating, but it's much more interesting to sit and eat around the small intimate counter (in what was once a traditional teahouse) and observe the chefs at work. Reservation is required for the private tatami room, and counter bar for dinner.

'Kikunoi's cuisine aspires for an aesthetic ideal found in tea ceremony called kireisabi, which can be translated as "rustic elegance".' *Kikunoi Honten*

©JUNICHI MIYAZAKI/LONELY PLANET

ATSUTA HŌRAIKEN HONTEN (あつた蓬莱軒本店)

NAGOYA | $$ | JAPANESE
503 Gōdo-chō, Atsuta-ku; 052-671-8686; www.houraiken.com; dishes ¥950, set menus from ¥2500

Atsuta Hōraiken has been in business since 1873 and is revered for good reason. Patrons queue during the summer peak season for *hitsumabushi* (eel basted in a secret *tare* (sauce) served atop rice in a covered lacquered bowl; add green onion, wasabi and *dashi* (fish broth) to your taste. Other *teishoku* (set meals) include tempura and steak.

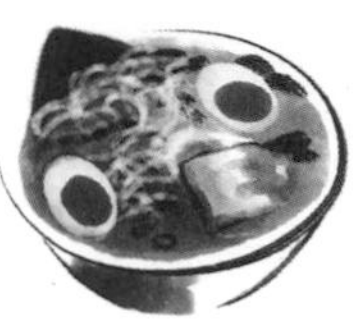

SENTŌ (仙桃)

KANAZAWA | $$ | CHINESE

2F Ōmichō Ichiba, 88 Aokusa-machi; 076-234-0669; http://kanazawa-sentou.com; dishes from ¥650, set menus from ¥980

Upstairs in Ōmi-chō Market, chefs from Hong Kong prepare authentic Szechuan- and Hong Kong–style dishes (including dim sum) from scratch. Delicious lunch and dinner set menus are excellent value. The spicy, salted squid is exquisite, and the *tantanmen* (sesame-and-chilli ramen) will have you coming back for a second bowl.

KYŌYA (京や)

TAKAYAMA | $$ | JAPANESE

1-77 Ōjin-machi; 0577-34-7660; www.kyoya-hida.jp; mains ¥800-5200

This Takayama institution specialises in regional dishes such as *hoba-miso* (sweet miso paste grilled on a magnolia leaf) and *Hida-gyū* (beef) *soba*. Sit on tatami mats around long charcoal grills, under a dark-timber cathedral ceiling. It's on a corner, by a bridge over the canal – look for sacks of rice over the door.

BANIKUMAN (バニクマン)

NAGANO | $$ | JAPANESE

1380 Kitaishido-chō; 026-228-0129; small plates from ¥500, horse meat from ¥1480

This is the place to come to try a Nagano speciality: horse meat. Try it as *basashi* (raw slices), in a *shabu-shabu* (hotpot) course or grilled. Don't be confused if you hear the words *sakura-niku* – sakura means cherry and is used euphemistically for horse meat. There's lots of tasty Nagano sake here, too!

FUJIYA GOHONJIN (藤屋御本陣)

NAGANO | $$$ | FUSION

80 Daimon-chō; 026-232-1241; www.thefujiyagohonjin.com; small plates from ¥750, courses from ¥4300

Gohonjin means 'a residence for the lords', and in the Edo period Fujiya Gohonjin played host to the feudal lords of the Maeda family. The present 1925 building was Nagano's Hotel Fujiya but has since been transformed into the city's most elegant function centre. The spectacular dining room, Wisteria, is Nagano's top Western-style restaurant serving dishes such as pasta and braised pork belly.

GOROSAYA (ごろさや)

SHIMODA | $$ | JAPANESE

1-5-25 Shimoda; 0558-23-5638; set menus ¥1700-3300

Gorosaya combines elegant, understated ambience and fantastic seafood. The isōjiru soup is made from more than a dozen varieties of shellfish and looks like a tide pool in a bowl. The *sashimi-don* (rice bowl), not on the English menu, is also excellent. Look for the wooden fish decorating the entrance.

MATSUBARA-AN (松原庵)

KAMAKURA | $$ | SOBA

4-10-3 Yuiga-hama; 0467-61-3838; www.matsubara-an.com/shops/kamakura.php; mains ¥960-1850, set meals from ¥3200

Dinner reservations are recommended for this upscale restaurant in a lovely old house near the beach. Try the *goma seiro soba* (al dente noodles served cold with sesame dipping sauce). Dine alfresco or indoors where you can watch noodles being handmade.

ARAIYA (荒井屋)

YOKOHAMA | $$$ | JAPANESE
4-23 Kaigan-dōri, Naka-ku; 045-226-5003; www.araiya.co.jp; set lunch/dinner from ¥1540/2970

Yokohama has its own version of the beef hotpot dish *sukiyaki*, called *gyū-nabe*. This elegant restaurant, established in 1895, is the place to sample it along with other premium grade beef dishes such as shabu-shabu.

ASAKUSA IMAHAN (浅草今半)

TOKYO | $$$ | JAPANESE
3-1-12 Nishi-Asakusa, Taitō-ku; 03-3841-1114; www.asakusaimahan.co.jp; lunch/dinner from ¥2000/8000

For a meal to remember, swing by this famous Tokyo beef restaurant, in business since 1895. Choose between courses of *sukiyaki* and *shabu-shabu*; prices rise according to the grade of meat. The building is modern but you'll dine in elegant traditional style rooms at low tables on tatami mat floors and be served by waitresses in kimono.

'The bounty of nature provides the inspiration for everything that we do here at Inua.'
Inua

INUA

TOKYO | $$$ | GASTRONOMY
2 -13-12 Fujimi, Chiyoda-ku; 03-6683-7570; https://inua.jp; set meals ¥19,800–29,800

Helmed by Noma alumnus Thomas Frebel and a crack team of young chefs and front-of-house staff, Inua focuses on sourcing amazing local produce – be it Japanese rose petals from Hokkaidō, long pepper from Okinawa or bee larva from Nagano. The 10- and 13-course set menus are a gourmet delight. Complementing the creative food is Inua's relaxed and spacious Scandi-meets-Nippon design, and superb service.

KIZUSHI (喜寿司)

TOKYO | $$$ | SUSHI
2-7-13 Nihombashi-Ningyōchō, Chūō-ku; 03-3666-1682; meals ¥3500-10,000

While sushi has moved in the direction of faster and fresher, Kizushi, in business since 1923, is keeping it old school. Third-generation chef Yui Ryuichi uses traditional techniques, such as marinating the fish in salt or vinegar, from back when sushi was more about preservation than instant gratification. The shop is in a lovely old timber-frame house in a characterful area of town.

SUSHI DAI (寿司大)

TOKYO | $$$ | SUSHI
3rd fl, Bldg 6, Toyosu Market, 6-5-1 Toyosu, Kōtō-ku; 03-6633-0042; course meal ¥4500

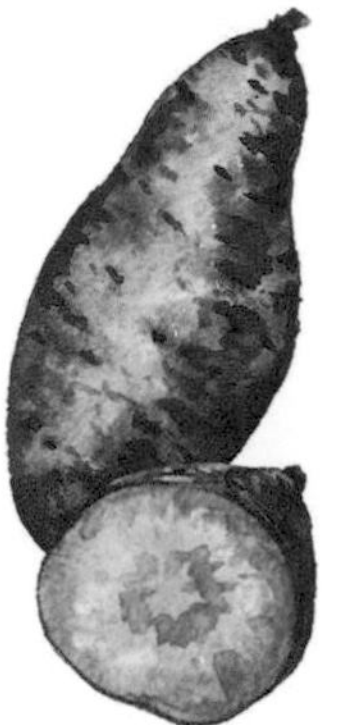

This page: Dish from Inua.

There is no better-value sushi in Tokyo than the *omakase* (chef's choice) course here. The menu changes daily (and sometimes hourly), but you're guaranteed to get 10 pieces of nigiri (hand-pressed) sushi made from seafood picked up from the fish market downstairs, prepared one at a time, pre-seasoned to perfection (and with zero boring fillers). Expect to queue.

TEMPURA KONDŌ (てんぷら近藤)

TOKYO | $$$ | TEMPURA

9th fl, Sakaguchi Bldg, 5-5-13 Ginza, Chūō-ku; 03-5568-0923; lunch/dinner course from ¥6500/11,000

Nobody in Tokyo does tempura vegetables like chef Kondō Fumio. The carrots are julienned to a fine floss; the corn is pert and juicy; and the sweet potato is comfort food at its finest. Courses include seafood, too. Reserve ahead.

TOFUYA-UKAI (とうふ屋うかい)

TOKYO | $$$ | KAISEKI

4-4-13 Shiba-kōen, Minato-ku; 03-3436-1028; www.ukai.co.jp/english/shiba; set meals lunch/dinner from ¥5940/10,800

One of Tokyo's most gracious restaurants is located in a former sake brewery, with an exquisite traditional garden in the shadow of Tokyo Tower. Seasonal preparations of tofu and accompanying dishes are served in the refined *kaiseki* style.

TONKI (とんき)

TOKYO | $ | TONKATSU

1-2-1 Shimo-Meguro, Meguro-ku; 03-3491-9928; meals ¥1800

Tonki is a Tokyo *tonkatsu* (breaded pork cutlet) legend, deep-frying with an unchanged recipe for nearly 80 years. The seats at the counter – where you can watch the perfectly choreographed chefs – are the most coveted, though there is usually a queue.

GYŌSHINTEI (尭心亭)

NIKKŌ | $$$ | KAISEKI

2339-1 Sannai; 0288-53-3751; www.meiji-yakata.com/en/gyoshin; meals ¥4180-6050

Splash out on deluxe spreads of vegetarian *shōjin-ryōri*, featuring local bean curd and vegetables served in delectable ways, or the *kaiseki* courses that include fish. The elegant tatami dining room overlooks a bonsai-filled garden, which is part of the Meiji-no-Yakata compound of chic restaurants close to the World Heritage Site.

KADARE YOKOCHŌ (かだれ横丁)

HIROSAKI | $ | FOOD HALL

2-1 Hyakkoku-machi; 0172-38-2256; www.kadare.info; dishes from ¥400

In the evening, university students flock to this nondescript office building housing eight tiny restaurants, most doubling as bars. It's a lively local hang-out. Hinata-bokko (日向ぼっこ), with the orange *noren* curtains, is particularly recommended, turning out excellent *hotate misoyaki* (grilled scallops in miso) and *ikamenchi* (fried minced squid). English-language menus are available for most of the stalls.

KIKUYO SHOKUDO (きくよ食堂)

HAKODATE | $ | SEAFOOD

Hakodate Morning Market; 0138-22 3732; www.hakodate-kikuyo.com/asaichi; mains from ¥1080

Inside Hakodate's seafood market, Kikuyo Shokudo got its start in the 1950s as a counter joint to feed market workers and is now one of the top reasons to come to Hakodate. The speciality is the *Hakodate tomoe-don*, rice topped with raw *uni* (sea urchin), *ikura* (salmon roe) and *hotate* (scallops), but you can also custom-make *kaisen-don* (raw seafood over rice) or sample another Hakodate speciality: *ika-sōmen* (raw squid sliced very thinly like noodles).

MUSU BAR + BISTRO (MŪSU バー+ビストロ)

NISEKO | $$ | BISTRO

190-13 Yamada; 0136-21-7002; www.musuniseko.com; mains ¥1000-1600

Musu offers great food, sweet service, and a lovely airy dining experience, plus easily the best cocktail menu in Niseko, with treats like the Yuzu Negroni or the Climber's Club, the latter using a shiitake-mushroom-infused brandy. The menu mixes European-inspired dishes such as beef cheek pasta and lemon tart, and local specialities such as Hokkaido potatoes and cod. Breakfasts, whether a flaky croissant with homemade jelly or a yoghurt and fruit plate, hit the spot.

WHERE TO EAT...

SOBA

Honke Owariya (本家尾張屋), Kyoto
In an old sweets shop in a traditional building, come here for *hourai* soba – a stack of five small plates of buckwheat noodles with a selection of toppings.

Uzuraya Soba (うずら家そば), Togakushi
Revered in Japan, this wonderful noodle shop claims that Togakushi is the home of soba.

Kosendō (古泉洞), Kakunodate
The house speciality at this noodle shop in the midst of the samurai district is *buke-soba* served with *takenoko* (bamboo shoots) and tempura-fried *ōba* (large Japanese basil leaf).

TAIWAN

There's a lot to love about Taiwanese cuisine, and a lot of it to love. It draws on the many cultures that have touched this island over the centuries: from Chinese styles like Hakka, Fujianese and Cantonese, through to Japanese, European and the gamey fare of the island's indigenous groups. Food experiences range from night market stick food to refined haute-cuisine and late-night stir-fries in a heaving *rechao* (izakaya).

WHAT TO EAT

Niurou mian
Beef noodle soup.

Cong zhuabing
griddle-cooked spring-onion pancakes.

Gua bao
Pork belly steamed bun.

Chou dofu
Stinky fermented tofu, usually deep-fried.

Fengli su
Pineapple shortcake.

Hezi jian
Oyster omelette.

Lu rou fan
Braised pork over rice.

Xiaolongbao
Soup dumplings.

Danzai mian
Noodles with pork mince in shrimp stock.

Boba naicha
Milk tea with tapioca pearls.

Xiansu ji
Salty fried chicken.

Fan tuan
Seaweed-wrapped rice ball.

PRICE RANGES

$ less than NT$200
$$ NT$200–600
$$$ NT$600 or more

Tipping: Not customary; 10–15% service charge sometimes added.

FLOWER SPACE

EASTERN TAIWAN | $$ | VEGETARIAN
140 Bo'ai St, Hualien; 03-831 4959; meal sets NT$250

Vegetarian meal sets with a multiplicity of ingredients and subtle flavours. The setting is relaxingly calm amid dangling pot plants, fresh flowers and owl statuettes, with semiprivate dining spaces arranged around a centrepiece of the owner's extraordinary collection of handmade dollhouse furniture.

DAXI FISHING HARBOUR

TAIWAN'S NORTHEAST COAST | $ | SEAFOOD
490 Binhai Rd, Sec 5, Toucheng; dozen oysters NT$200

Buy at the source in this two-storey food court beside Daxi's fishing harbour. Choices include all manner of fresh fish, grilled oysters (*shenghao*) and sea urchin (*haidan*) at bargain prices. Most vendors have the day's catch displayed in tanks to be grilled or fried, or you can buy direct off the boats and take it to a vendor for cooking.

MIAOKOU NIGHT MARKET

TAIWAN'S NORTHEAST COAST | $ | MARKET
Rensan Rd, Keelung; www.miaokow.org

The night market is one of Taiwan's culinary drawcards, and Keelung's Miaokou – sprawling outwards in yellow-lantern-lined streets around a temple – is one of its most famous. An absolute pilgrimage for any foodie, there are endless options from around 200 different stalls. Try thick crab soup (beloved from stall #5), sausage with garlic, sticky rice, fried dumplings, seafood and unique drinks like fresh-squeezed *ponkan* (Chinese honey orange) juice.

LAN JIA

TAIPEI | $ | TAIWANESE

3 Alley 8, Lane 316, Roosevelt Rd, Sec 3, Zhongzheng; 02-2368 1165; steamed buns NT$60

Lan Jia is widely regarded as having the best *yi bao* in Taiwan. The queue consistently snakes around the corner of this no-frills street shop for the savoury slow-braised pork hamburger with pickled mustard and ground peanuts stuffed inside a steamed bun. A cart out front sells them to go, or you can sit down inside the wonderfully faded, shabby dining room.

DIN TAI FUNG

TAIPEI | $$ | DUMPLINGS

194 Xinyi Rd, Sec 2, Da'an; 02-2321 8928; www.dintaifung.com.tw; dishes NT$90-260

Taipei's most celebrated Shanghai-style dumpling shop – repeatedly called one of the world's best restaurants, and beloved by the late Anthony Bourdain – is now a worldwide franchise. This is the place that started it all, and daily mealtime queues attest to its enduring popularity. Try the classic *xiaolongbao* (steamed pork dumplings) – perfect pasta pockets filled with a pork meatball and an injection of broth. Fuss-free and fast service; you can watch the master dumpling-makers at work through glass windows near the entrance.

SNOW KING

TAIPEI | $ | ICE CREAM

2nd fl, 65 Wuchang St, Sec 1, Zhongzheng; bowls from NT$95

Snow King is a legend, serving intensely flavoured homemade ice cream for more than 70 years. There are scores of wild tastes, from the expected (chocolate) to the downright bizarre (wasabi, pork knuckle or Taiwan Beer). Sit-in window pews mean you can have a bowl and admire the view of historical Zhongshan Hall across the way.

SMART FISH

WESTERN TAIWAN | $ | TAIWANESE

361 Zhongzheng Rd, East District, Chiayi; www.smartfish.com.tw; per person from NT$150

This hugely popular restaurant featured on Netflix's Street Food has been serving up fish head stew since 1953. Silver carp heads are deep-fried and simmered in a milky pork broth with vegetables, fungus and tofu – the most delicious of land and sea distilled into a bowl. Very unassuming spot with a street counter and busy tables inside – queues can be immense.

DUANCHUNZHEN BEEF NOODLES

NORTHERN TAIWAN | $ | NOODLES

135 Jiangong 1st Rd, Hsinchu; 03-574 8838; noodles from NT$80

WHERE TO EAT...

TAIWANESE INDIGENOUS FOOD

MiBaNai, Taitung
Taitung classic for indigenous cuisine, including stir-fried venison, roast salt fish, betel-flower salad and bacon-wrapped baby corn.

HuHu's Restaurant Taroko National Park
Meat or fish with local vegetables and sticky rice spiced with *maqaw* ('mountain pepper', *litsea cubeba*). To drink: a thimbleful of millet wine and blue-coloured pea water.

Ibu Kitchen, Meinong
Ingredients sourced from surrounding hills – mushrooms, plums for tofu sauce, zesty mountain pepper to add to steamed mullet.

Mu-Ming, Hualien
Multicourse Amis meals full of flavour-packed indigenous creativity.

Though it's located a few kilometres from downtown Hsinchu, committed foodies make the pilgrimage here for the Chungking-style beef noodles (*Chongqing niurou mian*). Just as hearty and full-flavoured are the stewed beef noodles (*hongshao niurou mian*), while beef noodles in tomato soup (*fanjia niurou mian*) are a tangy, non-spicy option. The atmosphere is smart but no-frills – dark wood tables and stools give some old-world Taiwanese flair.

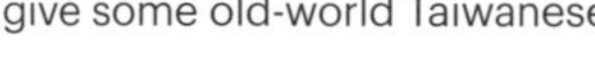

WANG'S FISH SHOP

TAIWAN'S SOUTHWEST COAST | $ | TAIWANESE

612 Anping Rd, Tainan; 06-228 8095; per person from NT$70

This white-tiled roadside shop, operated by a milkfish (*shimuyu*) farmer, slaughters the fish in the wee hours to prepare the popular breakfast of fish-meat broth (*yurou tang*). Fish belly (*yudu*) also comes braised or pan-fried. Fresh milkfish is rich and unctuous, utterly delicious but also filling – cold dishes laid out near the entrance help to cleanse the palate.

WU PAO CHUN BAKERY

TAIWAN'S SOUTHWEST COAST | $$ | BAKERY

19 Siwei 3rd Rd, Lingya District, Kaohsiung; 07-335 9593; www.wupaochun.com; loaf NT$350

The flagship store of the Taiwanese baker who won top prize (bread category) in the Bakery World Cup in Paris. And he did it with a wheat loaf that he embedded with Taiwanese millet wine, rose petals and dried lychees. Peruse piles of European-style breads, soft Asian pastries, tarts and cookies from shelves and baskets in the bakery's smart showroom of carbs.

'Bread is in my soul. Even after decades of baking, the smell of fresh bread makes me feel very kind and gives me endless inspiration and food for thought.'
Wu Pao-chun, master baker of Wu Pao Chun Bakery

ONE BAR

TAIWAN'S SOUTHWEST COAST | $$ | TAIWANESE

1 Lane 261, Qingnian 1st Rd, Kaohsiung; 07-331 3322; set meals NT$330

Inventive set meals of chicken or mushroom stew, braised pork and grilled fish set in an Eames-inspired dining area full of futuristic paraphernalia, plus

an oldies playlist, beaming you to the late-Japanese-colonial era.

SHUMIN KITCHEN

TAIWAN'S SOUTHWEST COAST | $$ | TAIWANESE

7 Yingxiong Rd, Kaohsiung; 07-215 5660; mains NT$200-700

This laid-back restaurant is known for well-executed Taiwanese dishes and above-average pricing. At lunch, it's full of middle-class families and couples. At night it morphs into a rechao (Japanese-style gastropub), attracting drinkers with a solid booze selection and dishes to pair, like blanched squid (*baiqie touchou*) and handmade fish cake (*shougong heilunpian*).

HOUSE OF CRAB

TAIWAN'S SOUTHWEST COAST | $$$ | SEAFOOD

93 Minsheng 1st Rd, Kaohsiung; 07-226 6127

This upmarket restaurant, owned by a native of Penghu Island, does some of the best seafood dishes anywhere in Taiwan. Predictably, the crab is the highlight, along with Penghu specialities, like stir-fried rice noodles with pumpkin (*chao nangua mixian*) and squid balls (*huazhiwan*). All served in a classy-but-simple dining room decorated in black, red and white.

LA TABLE DE MOZ

PENGHU ISLANDS | $$$ | FUSION

Bang Bang Banana, 6 Zhiping Rd, Magong; 0918-970 270; 4-course dinner NT$650-800

Superb, multi-course, candlelit dinners cooked by talented chef and owner, Moz. Sophisticated flavours and an emphasis on Penghu island ingredients come together in breathtaking fusion, served in a quirky, cosy dining room decorated in eclectic tables, couches and oddball wall hangings.

WHERE TO EAT...

MORE TAIWANESE INDIGENOUS FOOD

Qiuyue Restaurant, Sandimen
Cliffside cafe for Paiwan dishes like pork shank braised with red quinoa and mutton-and-mountain-pepper stew.

Epicurean Cafe, Lanyu
Open-air cafe serving Tao food – yams, wild vegetables, seafood and soup.

Nanfang Buluo, Shimen
Rustic Amis and Paiwan dishes like cinnamon chicken soup, mountain-pepper fish, and 'Lover's Tears' – an algae similar to Chinese black-ear fungus.

Taiya Popo, Wulai
Excellent if obscure indigenous dishes, such as bird's nest fern, betelnut salad and bamboo partridge.

PHILIPPINES

While other Southeast Asian cuisines are more ballyhooed, the Philippines is a sneaky-good food destination. As one might expect from an archipelago of 7000-plus islands, regional styles abound, so seek out the local speciality – *batchoy* (noodle soup with pork cracklings) in Iloilo, chicken *inasal* (a citrusy marinade) in Bacolod, *sisig* (sizzling pig jowl) in Pampanga and Spanish-influenced empanadas in Ilocos

WHAT TO EAT

Adobo
The signature Filipino sauce, comprising vinegar and soy sauce, slathered on anything under the sun (especially chicken).

Crispy pata
Deep-fried pork knuckle – shoot for the coveted *chicharon* (skin).

Halo-halo
The national dessert is a metaphor for the happy-go-lucky Philippines, an ebullient mash-up of fruit preserves served in shaved ice and milk.

Mangoes
Many think the Philippines has the best mangoes in the world. You be the judge.

PRICE RANGES

$ less than P200
$$ P200–400
$$$ P400 or more

Tipping: 5–10%

PENSION IVATAN

BATANES | $$ | FILIPINO

Basco, Batan Island; 0917 177 2022; www.batanespensionivatan.com; mains P150-450

This little oasis is a good bet to sample local Ivatan cuisine from the Batanes group of islands in the extreme north of the country. Regional delicacies like *payi* (lobster), *uved* (banana root balls with bits of garlic and fish) and *vunes* (minced taro stalks cooked with garlic) grace the menu, or opt for a full Ivatan sampler platter.

CALLE BREWERY

NORTH LUZON | $$ | FILIPINO

11 Encarnacion St, Vigan City, Ilocos; 0917 719 1694; www.facebook.com/callebrewery; mains P250-500

This home-grown craft brewery in a graceful 19th-century mansion doubles as the best restaurant in the historic city of Vigan. Head upstairs to the wine room and order the 12-course dégustation set (reserve ahead) of Ilocano classics like *pinakbét* (mixed vegetable stew), *bagnet* (deep-fried pork knuckle) and *poqui-poqui* (roasted aubergine). Downstairs is a smokehouse – pick your meat and a couple of sides and wash down with some excellent home brew.

CAFE BY THE RUINS

BAGUIO | $$ | ORGANIC

25 Chuntug St; 074-442 4010; www.facebook.com/cafebytheruinsph; mains P300-400

Rising from the ashes after a recent fire, Baguio's most beloved restaurant has reopened in a contemporary, glass-and-metal space. The menu is heavy on organic dairy and produce such as carabao (water buffalo) cheese, *etag* (smoked pork), mountain rice and jackfruit – all sourced from the surrounding Cordillera Mountains of North Luzon, one of the country's main indigenous areas.

LOCAVORE

MANILA | $$ | MODERN FILIPINO

5-7AB Forbeswood Rd, BGC; 02-8796 2017; www.locavore.ph; mains P300-700

Locavore uses locally sourced ingredients to stunning effect, creating French-inspired takes on Filipino classics like *Bicol exprés, kaldereta* (beef stew) and of course *halo-halo* (various fruit preserves served in shaved ice and milk). The signature *lechón* (roast suckling pig) and oyster *sisig* are to die for. It does not take reservations, so there's often a wait.

DAMPA SEASIDE

MANILA | $$ | SEAFOOD

Macapagal Blvd, Pasay; mains P250-500

A real local experience, here you trawl the attached palengke (wet market) for your desired ingredients (preferably crabs, shrimps, mussels and other seafood) and then choose one of several sleeves-up restaurants on the premises to cook your selection the way you like it. The prices are all very reasonable, and close seating quarters ensure that it's a social affair.

QUIK SNACK

MANILA | $ | CHINESE

Caravajal St, Binondo; 02-8242 9572; mains P150-250

A visit to Manila's Chinatown is a must for any true foodie. Also known as Amah (Grandma) Pilar's after its founding matriarch, Quik Snack has been serving its trademark *ku-tsai-ah* (Chinese empanadas), *lumpia* (spring rolls) and noodle soup for more than 50 years. It's hidden on atmospheric Caravajal St, a narrow alley in the heart of Chinatown that doubles as a wet market.

BISTRO REMEDIOS

MANILA | $$ | FILIPINO

1911 Adriatico St, Malate; 02-8523 9153; mains P300-600

This is one of the best places in Manila to sample dishes from the central Luzon province of Pampanga - widely considered the food capital of the Philippines. Adventurous eaters will revel in the chance to dig into exotic Kapampangan entries like *sisig pampabata*, fried *kamaru* (crickets), frog legs or *tidtad* (meat stewed in pig blood).

WAWAY'S

SOUTHEAST LUZON | $ | FILIPINO

Peñaranda St, Bicol; 052-480 8415; buffet P250

It's nothing fancy, but this buffet-style eatery in Legazpi offers a great primer on the delicious food of Southeast Luzon's Bicol region. Coconut milk and sili (hot chili peppers) spice up dishes like *Bicol exprés* (a fiery pork dish), *pinangat* (taro leaves wrapped around minced fish or pork) and *candingga* (diced pork liver and carrots sweetened and cooked in vinegar).

WHERE TO EAT...

BARBECUE

Malaspina Inasalan, Bacolod
Bacolod is the ancestral home of chicken inasal and a required stop on any Philippines food tour. Locals swarm this curbside eatery for their fix.

Mama's Grill, Siargao
Surfers converge on this shack along the highway to fuel up on chicken, beef and pork skewers.

Yakski, Cebu City
Casual place with a happy pig on its sign peddles meat on a stick (pork belly, chorizo, chicken) to the fawning masses.

Mercado, Malapascua
Open-air stalls grill fresh seafood and meat for hungry divers on this tiny Visayan island.

PRANA

BORACAY | $$ | ASIAN FUSION

Cnr Main Rd & Angol Rd, Angol; 036-288 5858; mains P300-450

Mandala Spa & Resort Villas' in-house restaurant is a model of sustainability on the environmentally challenged resort island of Boracay. An on-site organic herb garden is the source and inspiration for the tremendous salads and curries that emerge from the kitchen, and Prana further enhances its green cred by using kitchen scraps for fertiliser.

RICO'S LECHON

CEBU CITY | $$ | FILIPINO

N Escario St; 032-384 7151; www.ricoslechon.com; mains P300-400

Cebu is the place to eat that signature Filipino delicacy, *lechón* (spit-roasted suckling pig), and Rico's has the best in town. It's cooked every morning and shipped off to *lechón* addicts in Manila and abroad or served here at Rico's flagship eatery. A full complement of Filipino and Cebuano specialities like *ngohiong* (Cebuano spring rolls) is also offered.

BOHOL BEE FARM

BOHOL | $$ | ORGANIC

Southern Coastal Rd, Km 11, Panglao Island; 038-510 1822; www.boholbeefarm.com; mains P250-500

Started as a small-scale vegetable patch by a local environmentalist 20 years ago, Bohol Bee Farm has evolved into a full-scale resort with a sprawling oceanfront restaurant where you can nibble on organic squash muffins, home-baked bread and the likes of

Spread P488-9: Chou dofu; Gua bao. This page: Halo-halo. Opposite page: Adobo.

honey-glazed chicken on organic red rice. Tour the fecund garden overflowing with leafy munchables that go straight into the famous salads.

TAO FARM

PALAWAN | $$ | FILIPINO
Barangay San Fernando, El Nido; www.taophilippines.com; meals included in stay (2 nights US$250)

Legendary boat tour operator Tao Philippines has turned its organic farm in North Palawan into a resort. This is great news for foodies, as this is where Tao trains its chefs to prepare the most inventive food in the country. Drawing influences from the surrounding islands and using ingredients sourced from its farm and from local farmers and fishers, Tao brings Michelin-quality flavours to a remote corner of Palawan.

'We don't say "no" to anything the local farmers bring us. We buy it and make it work.'
Tao Philippines

KALUI

PALAWAN | $$ | FILIPINO
Address: 369 Rizal Ave, Puerto Princesa; 048-433 2580; mains P250-400

This shoes-off eatery is an institution in Palawan's bustling capital, Puerto Princesa. Choose from a few varieties of seafood, all served with veggies and a seaweed salad, or opt for the sumptuous set meal (P795), which includes coconut flan for dessert. Colourful paintings, sculptures and masks adorn the walls, and there's a general air of conviviality.

ALAVAR SEAFOOD HOUSE

MINDANAO | $$ | SEAFOOD
Don Alfaro St, Zamboanga City; 062-992 4533; mains P250-500

Head way down to the southern tip of Mindanao – practically the Philippines' last frontier before Borneo – to enjoy steamed *curachas*, the signature dish of Zamboanga. Alavar's, with its tangy trademark sauce, is the best place to sample these prehistoric-looking crabs, which prowl the depths of the Basilan Strait offshore. For dessert try a 'knickerbocker' – a localised version of *halo-halo*. Warning: travel here is considered risky. Check government advice before visiting.

INDONESIA

To eat in Indonesia is to savour the essence of the archipelago. The abundance of rice reflects the country's fertile landscape, the spices recall a time of trade and invasion, and the fiery chilli echoes the passion of the people. Chinese, Portuguese, Dutch colonists, and traders have all influenced the Indonesian table, and the cuisine, from Hindu Balinese to Muslim Acehnese, has been shaped by the nation's diverse landscape, people and culture.

WHAT TO EAT

Gado Gado
A Betawi (west Javanaese) original of steamed vegetables, potato, tofu and boiled egg with a peanut satay sauce.

Babi guling
Spit-roast suckling pig stuffed with chilli, turmeric, garlic and ginger.

Nasi Padang
Spicy Padang food from West Sumatra is among the most famous of Indonesian cuisines and beef *rendang* is the best-known dish.

Ayam Taliwang
The Sasak people of Lombok claim the spicy *ayam Taliwang* – roasted chicken served with a peanut, tomato, chilli and lime dip.

Coto Makassar
Sulawesi's contribution is *coto Makassar*, a piquant soup of beef innards, pepper, cumin and lemongrass.

PRICE RANGES
$ less than 50,000Rp
$$ 50,000–200,000Rp
$$$ 200,000Rp or more

Tipping: 10% in Bali.

KUNSTKRING PALEIS

JAKARTA | $$ | INDONESIAN
Jl Teuku Umar 1, Cikini; 021-390 0899; mains 68,000-488,000Rp

High tea or cocktails? You can have both, plus a divine Indonesian dinner at this alluring re-imagined Dutch colonial mansion, once Batavia's fine arts centre in Jakarta. The main Pangeran Diponegoro Room, with its wall-sized canvases, is where you'll take traditional tea service with an Indonesian twist or indulge in Betawi *rijsttafel* (Javan rice table).

WARUNG NGALAM

JAKARTA | $ | INDONESIAN
Jl KH Wahid Hasyim 106; 021-391 2483; mains 20,000-45,000Rp

A *warung* (Indonesian food stall) for a new age, this narrow, open-sided cafe with single seating in Jakarta's Jalan Jaksa area serves up delicious Indonesian dishes with a panoply of Asian influences. Patrons swoon for crispy duck, fried tofu, fish-head soup, homemade noodles and more.

HISTORIA

JAKARTA | $ | INDONESIAN
Jl Pintu Besar Utara 11, Kota; 021-690 4188; www.facebook.com/historiaJakarta; mains 40,000-51,000Rp

Served in chic, tiled warehouse environs with soaring ceilings, big art murals and a retro-industrial vibe in the heart of Jakarta's Kota area, Historia's dishes hail from around the archipelago. Try *bandeng goreng sambal* (grilled milkfish with steamed rice and Balinese sambal), *sate ayam* (grilled chicken satay with rice and peanut sauce) or *bakmie godog Jawa* (Javanese noodles with a spicy broth).

NUSA

JAKARTA | $$$ | INDONESIAN
Jl Kemang Raya 81; tel 021-719 3954; www.nusagastronomy.com; dishes 75,000-170,000Rp, 8-course set dinner menu 850,000Rp

Inside this grand old 1920s colonial house is one of Jakarta's swankiest restaurants. Dishes range from six-hour slow-braised organic local duck with pelawan mushroom to braised grass-fed Balinese beef served with chilli paste, all with nuanced flavours. The restaurant is halal in the Muslim tradition, so no alcohol is served.

PAVILIUN SUNDA

WEST JAVA | $$ | SUNDANESE
Jl Martadinata 97, Bandung; 022-426 7700; mains 40,000-100,000Rp

This classy restaurant is the place to try modern, well-presented Sundanese food, cuisine of the people of West Java. Popular dishes include fresh fish and karedok (salad of long beans and bean sprouts in a spicy sauce), soto Bandung (beef-and-vegetable soup with lemon grass) and ketupat tahu (pressed rice, bean sprouts and tofu with soy and peanut sauce). The fried or barbecued fish, which comes with a variety of interesting sides and sauces served on banana-leaf plates, is delicious. Decor is charming with dishes served at long, low tables.

OMAH SINTEN

EAST JAVA | $$ | INDONESIAN
Jl Diponegoro 34-54, Solo; 0271-641160; www.omahsinten.net; mains 25,000-75,000Rp

Opposite Solo's Mangkunegaran Palace, this is the place for home-style Solonese specialities such as *nasi golong* and *tahu goring* (fried tofu with a spicy sauce). The menu gives the history of the dishes and the atmosphere is satisfyingly formal, with live classical Javanese music attracting locals on an official night out.

SOTO BUJATMI

CENTRAL JAVA | $ | JAVANESE
Jl Wahid Hasyim 43, Kudus; 0291-446170; bowl of soto kudus 14,000Rp

This is the very best place to try the famed chicken soup of Kudus. Cooks stir up cauldrons of the brew over a log-fired oven and diners pack round simple tables decorated with jars of rice crackers. *Soto kudus* is served with optional extras, such as *sate* (satay) comprising entrails and cow-skin.

WHERE TO EAT...

FOOD MARKETS

Gianyar Night Market, East Bali
Clanging cooking pots and bright stall lights add festive clamour to Gianyar's delicious and wonderfully aromatic *pasar malam* (night market).

Mie Chino Pasar Santa, Jakarta
No-frills budget city market with just three things on the menu – meatballs, dumplings and tasty bowls of chicken and mushroom noodles.

Pasar Terapung Lok Baintan, Banjarmasin, Kalimantan
Take a dawn boat ride for breakfast of fruit and *sate* at Banjarmasin's traditional floating market on the Martapura River.

Jimbaran Fish Market, Bali
The fresh seafood at Bali's famous fish market is an early morning assault on the senses.

PATIO

EAST JAVA | $$$ | INDONESIAN
Plataran Borobudur Resort & Spa, Jl Dusun Kretek, Karangrejo, Borobudur; 0293-788888; www.plataranborobudur.com; mains 60,000-300,000Rp

For a magical hilltop setting enhanced by traditional music, this vintage restaurant, 2.5 miles (4km) west of the Borobudur temple complex, is hard to match. Eat in the colonial Patio dining room or out on the terrace with fine views of the monument. Local Javanese dishes such as *ayam bakar Jogja* (grilled spring chicken with traditional spices from the Yogyakarta region) are served with modern international flair.

KORINTJI HERITAGE

SUMATRA | $ | INDONESIAN
Jl Prof Dr Yakub Isman 1C, Sungai Penuh, Kerinci Valley; www.korintji.com; mains 15,000-65,000Rp

Set up as a social enterprise to empower locals, this cafe in Sungai Penuh is set inside an atmospheric bamboo building overlooking the town and Kerinci valley. Highlights include Danau Kerinci lobster and steaks, along with fine local, single-origin filter coffee.

PAGI SORE

SUMATRA | $ | INDONESIAN
Jl Pondok 143, Padang; 0751-32490; dishes from 9000Rp

This page: Dishes from Kunstkring Paleis.

As spiritual home to *nasi Padang*, the city of Padang offers plenty of places to sample the famous spicy cuisine, but it's unassuming Pagi Sore that is the real deal. In this simple *nasi Padang* house, choose from an array of spicy dishes such as beef *rendang*, take a plate of rice and pay for what you eat. Inexpensive and authentic.

COTA NUSANTARA

SULAWESI | $ | SOUP
Jl Nusantara 142, Makassar; 0822-5132 2220; soup 23,000Rp

The local Sulawesi beef soup of *coto Makassar* is found throughout Indonesia but this legendary hole-in-the-wall place near the Makassar dockyards is undoubtedly one of the best places in the country to sample it. The tiny bowl of piquant *kua* (broth) fills out to a meal once you help yourself to a few *ketupat* (rice steamed in palm leaves), and attendant staff will bring you more at a moment's notice.

OCEAN'S RESTO

KALIMANTAN | $$$ | SEAFOOD
Ruko Bandar, Balikpapan; 0542-739439; mains 60,000-300,000Rp

An entire reef's worth of fresh fish and crustaceans grace the menu at Balikpapan's finest seafood restaurant, all served in a bustling, breezy open-air waterfront space. Ocean's anchors a row of cafes along the waterfront of this cosmopolitan eastern Borneo city, and remains the most popular and the best.

'Our cuisine is crafted from locally harvested seafood and organic vegetables, light, delicious and suited to the tropical climate.'
Sardine

RESTO & CAFE RUMAH LAUT

PAPUA | $$ | INDONESIAN
Jl Koti, Jayapura; 0967-537673; mains 40,000-80,000Rp

Jayapura's best restaurant, built on stilts over the waters of Jayapura bay, is where locals come when they want to impress. The wide-ranging menu takes in Indonesian classics and lots of fish and seafood, while the decor features tribal Papuan motifs and large wooden tables designed for meal sharing.

PITUQ WAROENG

GILI ISLANDS | $$ | VEGAN
Jl Kelapa, Gili Trawangan; 0812 3677 5161; http://pituq.com; small plates 20,000-30,000Rp

Where else in the world will you find classic Indonesian fare reinterpreted as exquisite vegan tapas? Gather a group of friends (carnivores won't want to miss out), sit together at one of the low-rise tables and order like there is no tomorrow (proceeds go to a variety of projects to improve local living conditions). Try coconut and pumpkin patties with a sweet chilli sauce, tofu and potato baked in a banana leaf with local spices or aubergine and sambal – it's all good.

SARI RASA

FLORES | $ | INDONESIAN
Jl Ahmad Yani, Ende; 0812 3925 3699; mains 25,000-45,000Rp

This page: Sardine. Opposite page: Dish from Hujon Locale.

This sparkling-clean, bare-walled restaurant is filled with travellers out for a taste of local food, but who come back for Martin, the charismatic owner and self-appointed 'captain of the boat'. The ayam goreng (fried chicken) uses free-range village chickens, marinated, tenderised then fried. Empal is the Javanese answer to brisket – a hunk of tender, spiced fried beef.

BALI ASLI

EAST BALI | $$ | BALINESE

Jl Raya Gelumpang, Amlapura; 0822 3690 9215; www.baliasli.com.au; nasi campur (rice with a choice of side dishes) 165,000-228,000Rp

The green hills around Amlapura are some of east Bali's most beautiful and Australian chef Penelope Williams takes full advantage of the vistas at her elegant restaurant and Balinese cooking school. Produce sourced from the restaurant's own garden is used for meals that explore the vibrancy of Balinese and Indonesian flavours. This may be the best *nasi campur* you'll ever eat.

SARDINE

SOUTH BALI | $$ | SEAFOOD

Jl Petitenget 21, Kerobokan; 0811 397 811; www.sardinebali.com; mains from 200,000Rp

Seafood fresh from the famous Jimbaran market is the star at this elegant yet intimate, casual yet stylish restaurant. It's in a beautiful bamboo pavilion, with open-air tables overlooking a private sunflower garden, rice paddies and a lovely koi pond.

HUJON LOCALE

SOUTH BALI | $$ | INDONESIAN

Jl Sriwedari 5, Ubud; 0813 3972 0306; www.hujanlocale.com; mains 120,000-200,000Rp

Chef Will Meyrick is the culinary genius behind this Ubud outpost where the menu delivers traditional Indonesian cuisine with modern, creative flair and the results are uniformly delicious. Creations such as Northern Sumatran octopus *rendang* with star anise fennel and chopped turmeric leaf take their influence from across the archipelago. The setting within a chic colonial-style two-storey bungalow is casually stylish and cleverly flexible.

MOKSA

SOUTH BALI | $$ | VEGETARIAN
Gang Damai, Sayan, near Ubud; 0813-3977 4787; www.moksaubud.com; mains 40,000-80,000Rp

Based at its own permaculture farm near Ubud, Moksa shows that extraordinary meals can be created with vegetables prepared simply. Half the dishes are raw, half cooked; many are vegan. The setting is bucolic, but the kitchen is state of the art.

LOCAVORE

BALI | $$$ | FUSION
Jl Dewi Sita, Ubud; www.restaurantlocavore.com; 0361-977733; tasting menus 675,000-1,250,000Rp

Foodies book months in advance to sample the tasting menus at this temple to modern gastronomy. Flavours are fresh, bold and often unorthodox; presentation is exquisite. Tasting plates here are an unusual and exotic fusion of European and Asian while making the most of fresh local ingredients. Sample the food ethos in a simple setting in the charming (but busy) central Balinese village of Ubud or on a picnic at the nearby Locavore to Go.

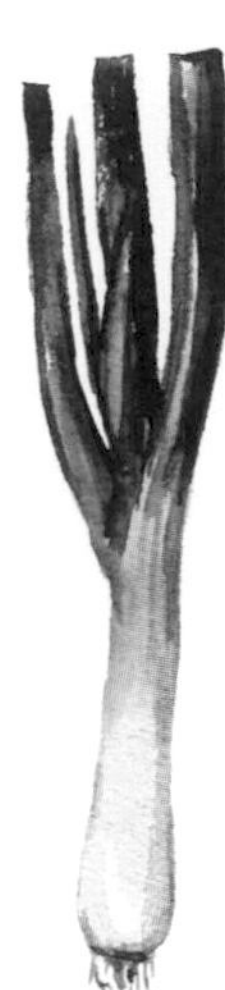

COURTESY HUJON LOCALE

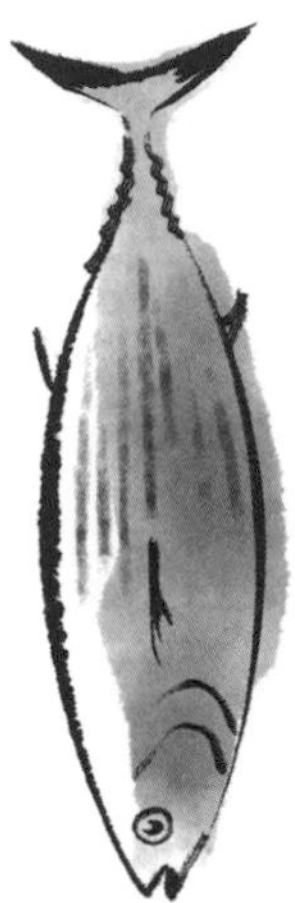

CILU BINTANG ESTATE

MALUKU | $$ | INDONESIAN

Jl Benteng Belgica, Bandaneira; www.cilubintang.com; 0813 3034 3377; mains 40,000-80,000Rp, buffet 100,000Rp

Bandaneira, the ramshackle capital of the remote Banda Islands, is home to this outstanding restaurant in the boutique Dutch-colonial hotel of the same name. During high season, or when there are enough guests, there's an superb evening buffet of spanking-fresh baked fish, soups liberally spiced with Banda nutmeg and cinnamon, curries, fritters, salads and more. But you can also order off a menu of mostly Indonesian and Bandanese 'Spice Island' classics, and bask in the elegant, airy colonial interior.

COCO BEACH

LOMBOK | $$ | INDONESIAN

off Jl Raya Senggigi, Senggigi; 0821 4468 3300; mains 55,000-80,000Rp

This wonderful beachside restaurant 2km north of Senggigi has a blissfully secluded setting off the main road, where dining takes place at individual thatch-covered tables. The nasi goreng and madras curry are locally renowned, and the seafood is the best in the area. There are also many choices for vegetarians. It has a full bar and blends its own authentic jamu tonics (herbal medicines).

DEPOT BAMBU KUNING

WEST TIMOR | $ | INDONESIAN

Jl Perintis Kemerdekaan 4, 0813 3910 9030; se'i babi portion/kg 20,000/170,000Rp

A popular place for authentic Kupang se'i babi. Choose from chopped up meat or ribs, both served with rice and a rich pork soup with red beans. Sate and a couple of veg dishes are also available. Check out the outdoor cooking area piled with kesambi leaves for smoking the meat.

TIMOR-LESTE

Timor-Leste's history means that both Portuguese and Indonesian culinary influences are present. A distinctively local style is emerging: think fresh organic ingredients, particularly fish, cooked in bamboo or on the grill, seasoned with local spices. Timorese coffee is also a standout.

WHAT TO EAT

Seafood skewers
Roadside stalls serve toothsome morsels of seafood on sticks. There's a particularly good scene on the beach in western Dili.

Fruit
Head to markets or kiosks for a dizzying array of delicious tropical fruit. Fresh coconut is a highlight.

Bakso
Indonesian-style meatball soup is a staple at cheap local restaurants.

Locally grown coffee
Timorese produces some brilliant beans from small-scale artisanal producers. You can increasingly find excellent espresso served in Dili's on-trend cafes.

PRICE RANGES
For a main course:
$ less than US$5
$$ US$5–10
$$$ US$10 or more

Tipping: Not mandatory; only tip if you feel the service deserves it.

RESTAURANTE DA MONTANHA

CENTRAL TIMOR-LESTE | $$ | INTERNATIONAL

Aileu; 7725 2527; www.facebook.com/projetomontanha; mains US$7-13

In the coffee town of Aileu, this restaurant of a development project is one of the best lunch stops around, offering a short but quality menu of comfort dishes like lasagne, steak and juicy fried chicken accompanied by delicious fresh-squeezed juices. Finish it off with local coffee and Brazilian fudge. Much of the produce comes from their organic garden and service is super-welcoming.

AGORA FOOD STUDIO

DILI | $$$ | MODERN TIMORESE

LELI Building, Kampung Alor; 7785 9912; www.timorlestefoodlab.com; mains US$11-15

Easily the capital Dili's most interesting restaurant, this sweet hideaway upstairs in an English school has a fabulous approach to food, sourcing traditional local ingredients to create seasonal fusion lunches that are packed with interesting flavours. All-day fare includes brunchy bowls with home-made yoghurt, stellar juices and barista-made coffee. The cheery chorus of welcome sets the scene for kind and helpful service. A standout.

DILICIOUS

DILI | $$ | TIMORESE

Rua Dom Boa Ventura; 7733 6512; www.facebook.com/DiliciousTimor; mains US$4-10

With an exceptionally friendly crew even for ultra-welcoming Timor-Leste, charismatic Cesar cooks up fresh and tasty Timorese morsels from his kitchen out front. Outside seating is shaded by vines, while the interior is attractively spacious. Specials revolve around grilled seafood and other goodies. Dishes can take a while to come out but it's good value and there's full bar service.

MALAYSIA

The delicious food you'll enjoy in Malaysia is a reflection of the cuisines of the country's Malay, Chinese and Indian communities. Zone in on the big cities – Kuala Lumpur, George Town, Melaka – for the best selection of restaurants. You'll often eat best with locals at street stalls and simple *kopitiam* (coffee shops), taking your pick from a tantalising range of hawker dishes.

WHAT TO EAT

Nasi lemak
The typical Malaysian breakfast is this dish of coconut milk rice served with a variety of accompaniments including fried crispy anchovies, toasted peanuts and cucumber slices.

Roti canai
These flaky Indian flat breads are served hot off the griddle to be dunked in soupy curries.

Laksa
This rice noodle dish is made in a variety of styles, including *asam laksa* made with a sour fish soup topped with slivered pineapple, cucumber and mint.

Ayam pong teh
A classic of Peranakan cuisine, this chicken and potato stew is flavoured with soy and *gula melaka* (palm sugar)

PRICE RANGES

For a main course:
$ less than RM15
$$ RM15–RM60
$$$ RM60 or more

Tipping: Not expected; restaurants in major cities may add 10%.

SITI FATIMAH

PULAU LANGKAWI | $ | MALAYSIAN
Jln Kampung Tok Senik, Kawasan Mata Air; 04-955 2754

This rustic self-service buffet is possibly Langkawi's most famous destination for Malay food – and it lives up to its reputation. Come mid-morning, dozens of rich curries, grilled fish, dips, stir-fries and other dishes are laid out. The flavours are strong and the prices low.

CHINA HOUSE

PENANG | $$ | INTERNATIONAL
153 & 155 Lr Pantai, George Town; 04-263 7299; www.chinahouse.com.my; mains RM25-35

You can't really say you've been to George Town unless you've stepped inside China House. This block-wide amalgamation of shophouses is home to a variety of dining, drinking and shopping options. It all starts splendidly with the buzzy bakery cafe, Kopi C, serving scrumptious baked goods, serious coffee and great light meals. Return in the evening to experience the elegant yet relaxed restaurant BTB.

GURNEY DRIVE HAWKER STALLS

PENANG | $ | HAWKER
Persiaran Gurney, Pulau Tikus; mains from RM4

COURTESY ISABEL

One of Penang's most famous hawker complexes sits amid modern high-rise buildings bordered by the sea. Tourists and locals rush in for both Muslim and Chinese-Malay dishes including laksa, rojak (a 'salad' of crispy fruits and vegetables in a thick, slightly sweet dressing), crushed-ice dessert cendol and many other dishes.

NAN GUANG

PENANG | $ | MALAYSIAN
67 Jln Balik Pulau, Balik Pulau; mains from RM5

Locals come to this no-frills *kopitiam* for delicious *laksa asam* – thick rice noodles in a tart, herbaceous fish-based broth – or *laksa siam*, in which the tartness is tempered with a dollop of coconut milk. Refreshing nutmeg juice is also available.

'Modernity and tradition go hand-in-hand at Nadodi. Our artisanal creations make creative use of exclusively sourced ingredients.'
Nadodi

TEKSEN

PENANG | $$ | CHINESE
18 Lr Carnarvon, George Town; 012-981 5117; www.facebook.com/TekSenRestaurant mains RM15-20

There's a reason this place is always packed: it's one of the tastiest, most consistent restaurants in town (and in a place like George Town, that's saying a lot). You almost can't go wrong here, but don't miss the favourites – the 'double-roasted pork with chilli padi' is obligatory and delicious – and be sure to ask about the daily specials.

WAI KEI CAFÉ

PENANG | $ | CHINESE
Lr Chulia, George Town; mains from RM7

This humble gem sits in the middle of the greatest concentration of travellers in George Town, yet is somehow almost exclusively patronised (in enthusiastic numbers) by locals. Come early for *char siew* (barbecued pork) and *siew yoke* (pork belly), probably among the best versions of these dishes in Asia.

SINGH CHAPATI

CAMERON HIGHLANDS | $ | INDIAN

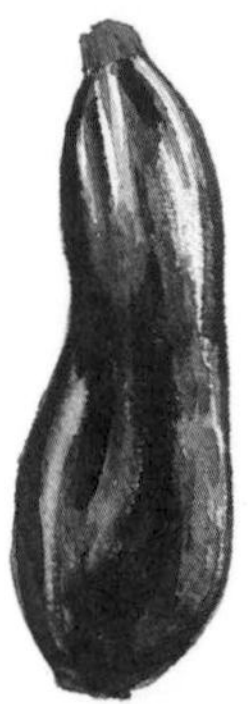

cnr Lg Perdah & Jln Besar, Tanah Rata; 017-578 6454; www.facebook.com/singhchapati; mains RM11-21

On a lofty perch behind Tanah Rata's main drag, Singh's is the sweetest Indian joint in town. Dig into fragrant biryanis, excellent veggie mains like butter paneer and smoky aubergine, and its famous chapati (flatbreads), and wash it down with mango lassi or masala tea. This no-frills restaurant benefits from a slightly secluded setting; try to bag a terrace table looking towards hills and mock-Tudor mansions.

RESTAURANT LOU WONG

IPOH | $$ | MALAYSIAN

49 Jln Yau Tet Shin; 05-254 4199; www.facebook.com/RestoranLouWong; mains from RM14

Ipoh's signature dish, *tauge ayam* (chicken bean sprouts), has been perfected at perennially popular Lou Wong. The restaurant is unadorned, with plastic seats spilling into the street, but the sole dish on offer is immensely satisfying: smooth poached chicken on soy-drenched cucumber, and crunchy bean sprouts sprinkled with pepper. Side dishes are either rice or noodles, and a bowl of chicken stock.

YAP KEE

KLANG | $ | MALAYSIAN

26 Jln Besar; mains from RM11.50

This spartan banana-leaf restaurant in an old shophouse, two blocks to the right as you leave the train station, usually has only a couple of choices available. But it's legendary in Klang: fish, crunchy fried chicken and expertly cooked vegetable curries laid onto banana leaves. No fanfare, just good food – a formula unchanged for more than 70 years.

ANNALAKSHMI VEGETARIAN RESTAURANT

KUALA LUMPUR | $ | INDIAN

Temple of Fine Arts, 116 Jln Berhala, Brickfields; 03-2274 0799; www.annalakshmi.com.my; lunch buffet adult/child RM25/21, dinner set meal RM21

The quality of the lunchtime buffet at this upmarket vegetarian restaurant is exceptional, with an extensive and constantly replenished array of freshly made salads, curries, biryanis, fried morsels, chutneys, raitas, pickles and breads. The buffet action continues for Friday and Saturday dinner; on other nights choose between the set meal or order à la carte.

CHŌ CHĂ FOODSTORE

KUALA LUMPUR | $$ | ASIAN

156 Jln Petaling, Chinatown; 03-2022 1100; www.chochafoodstore.com; mains RM20-60

Behind the raw concrete and timber facade of the old Mah Lian Hotel is this relaxed restaurant and teashop with a plant-filled courtyard and the original hotel tiles. Chocha's 'tea sommelier'

Previous spread: Dish from Isabel; Dish from Nadodi.

serves an extensive selection of speciality brews between 11am and 7pm, but it's the delicious modern Asian cooking (dishes include housemade flat pasta tossed in a pesto of local greens) using fresh farm-to-table ingredients that's the standout.

DEWAKAN

KUALA LUMPUR | $$$ | MALAYSIAN
Level 48 Naza Tower, 10 Persiaran KLCC; www.dewakan.my; tasting menu RM550

Darren Teoh heads a team of exciting young chefs at this innovative restaurant that relocated to central KL in late 2019. They get playful with their multi-course tasting menus showcasing local flavours and whimsical presentation, such as their black banana porridge, prawns in starfruit juice, and goat tartare. Book well in advance for this evening-long fine-dining experience.

ISABEL

KUALA LUMPUR | $$$ | SOUTHEAST ASIAN
21 Jln Mesui, Bukit Bintang; 03-2110 6366; www.isabel.com.my; small plates RM26-35, large plates RM58-158

Serving sophisticated twists on regional classics, this elegant restaurant offers a menu of small and large share plates inspired by Malaysian, Thai, Indonesian, Laotian and Vietnamese cuisines. There's an extensive cocktail menu, but few choices of wine by the glass. Vegetarians should steer clear, though, as there is little joy for them here.

'Each dish is made with ingredients sourced from Malaysia, carefully crafted to encourage deeper appreciation for the land and culture.'
Darren Teoh, chef at Dewakan

LAWANYA FOOD CORNER

KUALA LUMPUR | $ | INDIAN
1077/8 Lg Scott, Brickfields; 016-220 2117; meals from RM7

Don't be put off by the low-key appearance of this streetside joint with a few ramshackle tables under a sheet of corrugated iron. The same family has been preparing delicious curries here for more than 30 years, with a spread of meat and vegetarian dishes served from clay pots.

NADODI

KUALA LUMPUR | $$$ | SOUTH INDIAN
Lot 183, 1st fl, Jln Mayang, KLCC; 03-2181 4334; www.nadodikl.com; 9-/11-course menus from RM430/450

The recipes and ingredients of Tamil Nadu, Kerala and Sri Lanka are the foundation for the sensational tasting menus served at Nadodi (which means nomad). It's a sophisticated space and while 11 courses may sound like a lot, but the sizes of each beautifully presented plate are just right, allowing the chef's artistry to shine.

REBUNG

KUALA LUMPUR | $$ | MALAYSIAN
5th fl, 1 Jln Tanglin, Lake Gardens; 03-2276 3535; www.restoranrebungdatochefismail.com; buffet breakfast/lunch/dinner adult RM22/43/53

Occupying the top level of a multistorey car park overlooking the Botanical Garden, flamboyant celebrity chef Ismail's restaurant is one of KL's best. The seemingly endless buffet spread is splendid, with all kinds of dishes that you'd typically only be served in a Malay home. Don't miss the additional food stations outside for noodles, barbecued fish, banana fritters, *rojak* salad and desserts.

SEK YUEN

KUALA LUMPUR | $$ | CHINESE
313 Jln Pudu, Pudu; 03-9222 0903; mains RM15-80

In the same art deco pavilion for more than six decades, Sek Yuen is a Pudu institution. Some of the aged chefs toiling in the wood-fired kitchen have served three generations the same old-school Cantonese dishes. The *kau yoke* (pork belly), village chicken and crispy-skin roast duck are all classics.

YUN HOUSE

KUALA LUMPUR | $$$ | CANTONESE
Four Seasons Hotel KL, 145 Jln Ampang, KLCC; 03-2382 8888; www.fourseasons.com/kualalumpur; dim sum RM22-50, mains RM68-350

Superb dim sum (try the barbecue chicken buns, which melt in the mouth) are served at lunch in this upmarket restaurant, and an extensive array of perfectly executed Cantonese, Beijing and Szechuan dishes can be enjoyed at both lunch and dinner. The elegant dining room overlooks KLCC park; service is attentive.

NANCY'S KITCHEN

MELAKA | $ | MALAYSIAN
13 Jln KL 3/8, Taman Kota Laksamana; 06-283 6099; www.eatatnancyskit.com; mains from RM10

This page: China House. Opposite page: Laksa Sarawak from Madii's Restaurant.

COURTESY MADIL'S RESTAURANT

The Peranakan (Nonya) cuisine here has a dedicated following, but service can be a bit curt and a wait is inevitable at weekends. However, many consider it worth it for the juicy pork fried with bean curd or signature candlenut chicken dish – simmered in a nutty sauce, fragrant with lemongrass. Buy some *kuih* (sticky-rice sweets) on your way out.

KEE ANN FOOD STREET

MELAKA | $ | STREET FOOD

Jln Kee Ann; www.facebook.com/keeannfoodstreet; mains RM6-10.50

Forget about Melaka's touristy Jonker Street Market – if you are keen to sample the best street food in the city head to this strip near Little India, where stalls sell an extraordinary array of food, including satay, laksa, chicken rice, fried noodles and *otak-otak* (spicy fish paste grilled in banana leaves). Purchase your meal and eat at the communal tables.

NONYA 63

MELAKA | $$ | PERANAKAN

63 Jln Tun Tan Cheng Lock; 016-266 0338; www.facebook.com/nyonya63; mains RM10-90

The amiable chef at this upmarket Nonya eatery set in a handsome 19th-century house will come to your table and explain specialities such as the chicken dish *ayam pong teh* and

WHERE TO EAT...

HAWKER FOOD

Jalan Alor, Kuala Lumpur
Come sundown this KL street transforms into a continuous open-air restaurant, with hundreds of plastic tables and chairs and a bustling atmosphere. Don't miss the chicken wings from Wong Ah Whah.

Lorong Baru (New Lane) Hawker Stalls, Penang
George Town's favourite night-time street extravaganza. Prepare to battle for a spot if you're visiting on weekends. Oyster omelettes, noodles, grilled satay skewers... just about everything is available here.

A-Square Night Market, Kota Kinabalu
Part of KK's food revolution, this night market sells some kick-ass edible. Zone in on Punya Sadap offering indigenous Sabah dishes.

pork chilli *garam* (with a spicy Nonya paste) that feature on his menu. With his help you'll eat extraordinarily well here. Sit inside or outside.

MADAME BEE'S KITCHEN

KUALA TERENGGANU | $$ | CHINESE
177 Jln Kampung Cina; 012-988 7495; www.madam-bees-kitchen.business.site; mains RM12-20

In a delightful heritage building in the heart of Chinatown, Madame Bee turns excellent renditions of Peranakan dishes with local Terengganu influences. The award-winning chef's renowned dishes include *Terengganu laksa* made with a richly flavoured fish broth, and *mee Jawa* (sweet and sour yellow noodles) crammed with crunchy additions like yao char kuai (Chinese doughnuts) and peanuts.

LEPAU

KUCHING | $$ | MALAYSIAN
Persiaran Ban Hock; 012-884 5383; www.facebook.com/lepaurestaurant; mains RM15-25

Lepau translates as 'farm hut', and organic and free-range ingredients feature at this atmospheric restaurant showcasing the cuisine of Sarawak's indigenous Iban and Bidayuh people. The open kitchen encourages a breezy informality, as loyal Kuching locals and in-the-know visitors enjoy dishes such as *ayam pansuh* (chicken steamed in bamboo) and prawn *umai* (marinated raw seafood) accompanied by Bario rice. Booking is recommended.

MADLI'S RESTAURANT

MIRI | $ | MALAYSIAN
Lot 1088, ground fl, Block 9, Jln Merpati; 085-426615; www.facebook.com/madlisrestaurant; mains RM6-24

Specialising in lip-smackingly good chicken-fillet and Australian-beef satay this family business started off as a humble stall in the 1970s; read the history on the wall above the kitchen. Madli's is open on two sides for ventilation and is spotlessly clean. Satays start smoking after 6pm, the menu includes *nasi lemak* and *kampung* fried rice while *roti canai* (flaky flatbread) and Western breakfasts are served until noon.

AI XIN

SANDAKAN | $$ | VEGETARIAN
Bandar Indah; 089-232121; www.facebook.com/aixinveggie; mains RM16-29

Black sesame bean curd, braised shiitake mushrooms with yam, laksa with handmade noodles and tender steamed dumplings, bursting forth with crunchy, fresh vegetables from the restaurant's own organic farm, are just some of the treats on the menu here. Great care is taken both with presentation and flavour. Outstanding.

BRUNEI

Eating is the most popular pastime in Brunei Darussalam, and the dining scene reflects that. The tiny kingdom punches above its weight with its range of international restaurants, cosy coffee shops and vibrant night markets serving tasty local street food.

WHAT TO EAT

Ambuyat
A gelatinous, porridge-like mass made from the pith of the sago tree, which is ground to a powder and mixed with water. Ambuyat itself doesn't have a taste – it's the sauce that gives it its zing. It's served with cacah, a sambal belacan- and tamarind-based sweet-and-tart sauce.

Nasi katok
Rice, sambal (a fiery condiment) and a piece of fried chicken, usually served in a paper cone.

Kelupis
Glutinous rice cooked in coconut milk, wrapped in a nyirik leaf and steamed.

Bahulu
Simple round cakes made from eggs, flour and sugar.

PRICE RANGES

For a main course:
$ less than B$6
$$ B$6-B$16
$$$ B$16 or more

Tipping: Not expected.

ALTER EGO FUSION

BANDAR SERI BEGAWAN | $$ | FUSION
Lot 5788, Kampong Kiulap; 223 0388; www.facebook.com/alteregofoods; Mains B$10.50-23

It's hard to pin down Alter Ego, except to say that it's one of Bandar Seri Begawan's most creative offerings, located in an equally impressive space. Expect falafel, Mandarin short ribs, French onion soup and salted caramel eclairs.

PASAR MALAM GADONG

BANDAR SERI BEGAWAN | $ | MARKET
off Jln Pasar Gadong ; Dishes from B$1

Thanks to its authentic local snacks and dishes (grilled meats on skewers and rice topped with chicken and sambal inside a banana leaf), this is Brunei's most popular night market. It's geared towards take away customers, but there are picnic tables to eat at.

RACK & BREW

BANDAR SERI BEGAWAN | $$ | CAFE
Abdul Raak Complex, Gadong; 245 7886; www.facebook.com/rackandbrew; Mains B$9-18

'Coffee is always a good idea' announces a poster on the wall of this cheery cafe. Locals come here for the caffeine hit and the epic breakfasts, from soft-shell crab florentine and salmon avocado smash to French toast.

KAIZEN SUSHI

BANDAR SERI BEGAWAN | $$ | JAPANESE
Kompleks Yayasan Sultan Haji Hassanal Bolkiah, Jln McArthur; 222 6336; www.facebook.com/kaizensushibrunei/; Mains B$6-17

All clean lines and bamboo accents, the minimalist interior of this waterfront restaurant focuses your attention on the food. The menu is extensive, from the imaginative sushi rolls and sashimi sets to noodles, but everything, from the teriyaki skewers to tobiko roe popping on your tongue, bursts with flavour.

SINGAPORE

Singaporeans are obsessed with *makan* (food), from talking incessantly about their last meal, to feverishly photographing, critiquing and posting about it online. The nation's melting pot of cultures creates one of the world's most diverse culinary landscapes ranging from celebrated hawker centres and food courts serving knockout street food at wallet-friendly prices to a legion of top-notch, celebrity-chef nosheries.

BURNT ENDS

CHINATOWN | $$$ | BARBECUE
20 Teck Lim Rd; 6224 3933; https://burntends.com.sg; dishes S$8-45

Counter seats here offer a prime view of chef Dave Pynt and his 4-tonne, wood-fired ovens and custom grills. The affable Aussie cut his teeth under Spanish charcoal deity Victor Arguinzoniz (Asador Etxebarri), an education echoed in pulled pork shoulder in homemade brioche, and beef marmalade and pickles on chargrilled sourdough. The produce-driven, sharing-style menu changes daily, while the drinks list showcases smaller wineries and microbreweries.

A NOODLE STORY

CHINATOWN | $ | NOODLES
01-39 Amoy Street Food Centre, cnr Amoy & Telok Ayer Sts; 9027 6289; www.facebook.com/ANoodleStory; noodles S$8-15

SIMON PYNT, COURTESY BURNT ENDS

With a snaking line and proffered apology that 'we may sell out earlier than stipulated timing' on the facade, this one-dish-only hawker stall is a magnet for foodies. The object of desire is Singapore-style ramen created by two young chefs, Gwern Khoo and Ben Tham. It's Japanese ramen meets wanton mee (noodles): pure bliss in a bowl topped with a crispy potato-wrapped prawn.

WHAT TO EAT

Hainanese chicken rice
Steamed fowl and rice cooked in chicken stock, served with a clear soup, slices of cucumber and ginger, chilli and soy dips.

Char kway teow
Stir-fried noodles hardly get more luscious than this Hokkien Chinese dish made with cockles, Chinese sausage and dark sauces.

Thali Spicy
South Indian curries served with a large mound of rice, *rasam* (hot, sour soup) and a dessert.

Otak-otak
A typical Peranakan dish is this spicy fish and coconut milk sausage, wrapped and grilled in a banana leaf.

PRICE RANGES

Most restaurants add 10% service charge plus 7% for GST (indicated by ++ on menus). For a main course ++:
$ less than S$10
$$ S$10–30
$$$ S$30 or more

Tipping: Many add 10%, so tipping is discouraged.

AH CHIANG'S

CHINATOWN | $ | CHINESE
01-38, 65 Tiong Poh Rd; 6557 0084; www.facebook.com/ahchiangporridgesg; porridge S$5-6

Join gossiping uncles and Gen-Y hipsters for a little Cantonese soul food at Ah Chiang's. The star turn at this retro corner *kopitiam* (coffeeshop) is fragrant, charcoal-fired congee (a rice-based porridge) but don't pass up the raw sliced fish, delectably drizzled with sesame oil.

HAWKER CHAN HONG KONG SOYA SAUCE CHICKEN RICE & NOODLE

CHINATOWN | $ | HAWKER
02-126 Chinatown Complex, 335 Smith St; 6272 2000; www.liaofanhawkerchan.com; dishes S$2-4

With its shiny Michelin star, this humble hawker stall has been thrust into the culinary spotlight. The line forms hours before Mr Chan Hon Meng opens for business, and waiting times can reach two hours. Standout dishes are the tender soy sauce chicken and the caramelised pork *char siew* ordered with rice or perfectly cooked noodles. Worth the wait? You bet.

LUCHA LOCO

CHINATOWN | $$ | MEXICAN
15 Duxton Hill; 6226 3938; www.super-loco.com/luchaloco; tacos S$8-15, dishes S$11-38

'We sought to create the ultimate noodles dish and spent years of hard work and sweat learning from culinary masters in the best restaurants in the world.'
A Noodle Story

COURTESY ODETTE

On pumping Duxton Hill, Lucha Loco keeps the crowds purring with its flirtatious barkeeps, effortlessly cool vibe and finger-licking Mexican street food. Though we adore the ceviche, tostaditas (deep fried tortillas) and addictive DIY Loco guacamole, it's the tacos generously topped with fresh, beautiful produce that leave us loco.

COCONUT CLUB

CHINATOWN | $$ | MALAYSIAN
28 Ann Siang Hill; 6635 2999; www.thecoconutclub.sg; mains S$12.80

Not just any old *nasi lemak* joint, here they're nuts about coconuts and only a certain Malaysian West African (MAWA) hybrid will do. Chicken is super crispy, encrusted in a flavour-punching lemongrass, ginger and galangal coating. The *sambal* (sauce of fried chilli, onions and prawn paste) is on the mild side. Save room for the refreshing *cendol* dessert made up of green rice flour jelly, coconut milk and palm sugar syrup.

LIAN HE BEN JI CLAYPOT RICE

CHINATOWN | $$ | HAWKER

02-198/199 Chinatown Complex, 335 Smith St; 6227 2470; dishes S$2.50-5, claypot rice S$5-20

The most popular claypot rice stall in Chinatown Complex, and the only one cooking over charcoal stoves. Get the mixed claypot rice, which comes with Chinese sausage, pork and chicken. Pair it with deep-green vegetables with oyster sauce, sprinkled with fried shallots for crunch and extra sweetness. Expect to wait around 45 minutes, as each pot is cooked from scratch.

ODETTE

COLONIAL DISTRICT | $$$ | FRENCH

01-04 National Gallery Singapore, 1 St Andrew's Rd; 6385 0498; www.odetterestaurant.com; lunch from S$168, dinner from S$358

Cementing its place in the upper echelons of Singapore's saturated fine-dining scene, this modern French restaurant was awarded three Michelin stars in 2019. Chef Julien Royer expertly crafts his multi-course menus, guided by the seasons. The space is visually stunning, with a soft colour palette and floating aerial installation by local artist Dawn Ng. Book at least a month in advance.

NATIONAL KITCHEN BY VIOLET OON

COLONIAL DISTRICT | $$ | PERANAKAN

02-01 National Gallery Singapore, 1 St Andrew's Rd; 9834 9935; www.violetoon.com; dishes S$15-42

Chef Violet Oon is a national treasure, much loved for her faithful Peranakan dishes. Feast on made-from-scratch beauties like sweet, spicy kueh pie ti (pastry cups stuffed with prawns and turnip), dry laksa and beef rendang. True to its name, the restaurant also touches on Singapore's other culinary traditions, from Indian and Eurasian to Hainanese. Bookings two weeks in advance essential.

MAKANSUTRA GLUTTONS BAY

MARINA BAY | $ | HAWKER

01-15 Esplanade Mall, 8 Raffles Ave; www.makansutra.com; dishes from S$4.50

Selected by the locally respected Makansutra Food Guide, this row of alfresco hawker stalls is a great place to start your Singapore food odyssey. Get indecisive over classics like laksa, satay, barbecue stingray and carrot cake (opt for the black version). Its central, bayside location makes it a huge hit, so head in early or late to avoid the frustrating hunt for a table.

Previous spread: Dish from Burnt Ends; Mushroom tea from Odette.

JAAN

MARINA BAY | $$$ | EUROPEAN

Level 70, Swissôtel The Stamford, 2 Stamford Rd; 6837 3322; www.jaan.com.sg; lunch/dinner set menus from S$98/268

Seventy floors above the city, chic and intimate Jaan with just 40 seats is home to talented British chef Kirk Westaway. Since taking the reins, Westaway has dazzled diners with his artisanal cuisine and added a Michelin star to his accolades. Menu changes seasonally, flavours are revelatory and presentation utterly theatrical. Always book ahead.

IGGY'S

ORCHARD RD | $$$ | FUSION

Level 3, Hilton Hotel, 581 Orchard Rd; 6732 2234; www.iggys.com.sg; set lunch/dinner from S$105/250

Iggy's refined, sleek design promises something special, and with a large picture window drawing your eye to the magic happening in the kitchen, you can take a peek. Head chef Aitor Jeronimo Orive delivers with his ever-changing, highly seasonal, creative fusion dishes. Superlatives extend to the wine list, one of the city's finest.

GANDHI RESTAURANT

LITTLE INDIA | $ | SOUTH INDIAN

29-31 Chander Rd; 6299 5343; dishes S$2.50-6.50, set meals from S$4.50

It might be a canteen-style joint with erratic service and cheap decor, but who cares when the food is this good? Wash your hands by the sink at the back, and take a seat. A banana-leaf plate heaped with rice and condiments (set-meal thali) will appear, order extra items from the servers – chicken curry is a must – then tuck in.

LAGNAA BAREFOOT DINING

LITTLE INDIA | $$ | INDIAN

6 Upper Dickson Rd; 6296 1215; www.lagnaa.com; dishes S$8-22

You can choose your level of spice at friendly Lagnaa: level three denotes standard spiciness, level four significant spiciness, and anything above admirable bravery. Whatever you opt for, you're in for finger-licking-good homestyle cooking from both ends of Mother India. If you're indecisive, order chef Kaesavan's famous Threadfin fish curry.

CANDLENUT

DEMPSEY HILL | $$$ | PERANAKAN

Block 17A, Dempsey Rd; 1800 304 2288; www.comodempsey.sg; mains S$20-32

Singapore's first Peranakan restaurant to gain a Michelin star, Candlenut does not churn out any old Straits Chinese dishes; instead, chef Malcolm Lee elevates them to new culinary heights. Most dishes are amazing, such as wild-caught baby squid with ink, tamarind and chillis. If you can't choose, order the 'ah-ma-kase' menu and let the chef decide.

WHERE TO EAT...

CRAB

Mellben Seafood, Ang Mo Kio
A modern, hawker-style set-up at the bottom of a nondescript block. Signature dishes are claypot crab bee hoon (rice vermicelli noodles), butter crab and the ever-famous chilli crab.

Momma Kong's, Chinatown
While the compact menu features numerous finger-licking, MSG-free crab classics, opt for the phenomenal chilli crab, its kick and nongelatinous gravy unmatched in this town.

No Signboard Seafood, Geylang
Principally famous for its white-pepper crab, No Signboard also dishes up delightful lobster, abalone and less familiar dishes such as bullfrog.

THAILAND

WHAT TO EAT

Pàt tai
Thin rice noodles stir-fried with bean sprouts, tofu, egg and seasonings, traditionally served with lime halves, Chinese chives and a sliced banana flower.

Đôm yam
Lemongrass, kaffir lime leaf and lime juice give this soup its tang.

Gaang sôm
This sour/spicy soup gets its yellow hue from turmeric, a root commonly used in southern Thai cooking.

Gài tôrt hàht yài
The famous deep-fried chicken from the town of Hat Yai gets its rich flavour from a marinade of dried spices.

Durian
Known in Thai as *tú·ree·an*, the king of fruit is also Thailand's most infamous, due to its intense flavour and odour.

PRICE RANGES
For a main course:
$ less than 150B
$$ 150B–350B
$$$ 350B or more

Tipping: Leave loose change.

Thai food sits high on the world culinary stage but the regional variations of incendiary curries and the fine balance of sweet, sour, salt and spice found within the country will surprise and delight even the biggest fan. Whether it's a bowl of noodles from a streetside hawker stall or a degustation at a five-star Bangkok restaurant, prepare yourself for one of the most fun and diverse dining scenes on the planet.

SAAWAAN

BANGKOK | $$$ | INTERNATIONAL
39/19 Soi Suan Phlu, Lumphini; 02 679 3775; www.saawaan.com; set menu 2450B

Two exceptionally talented female chefs run Saawaan, one of the finest Thai restaurants in the world, right in the heart of Bangkok. The name meaning 'heaven,' this chic outfit presents a seven-course tasting menu themed on cooking methods, featuring dishes that are inherently Thai but are executed with the fancy, finesse and flair worthy of its Michelin star. Expect dishes conjured from sea urchins, wild betel leaves or rice paddy crabs, and wacky desserts.

KRUA APSORN

BANGKOK | $$ | THAI
Th Din So, Banglamphu; 021-2962 7771; www.kruaapsorn.com; mains 100-350B

This legendary Bangkok dining room is a favourite of members of the Thai royal family and restaurant critics alike. Just about all of the central and southern Thai dishes are tasty, but regulars never miss the chance to order the decadent

stir-fried crab with yellow pepper chilli or the tortilla-like fluffy crab omelette. Another (original) branch is on Th Samsen, where crab meat in curry powder remains a local favourite.

JAY FAI

BANGKOK | $$$ | SEAFOOD
327 Th Mahachai; 021-391 2483; mains 200-1000B

Wearing ski goggles and furiously cooking over a charcoal fire, Jay Fai is renowned for serving Bangkok's tastiest crab omelettes and *pàt kêe mow* (wide rice noodles fried with seafood and Thai herbs). The price is justified by copious fresh seafood and a frying style resulting in an almost oil-free finished dish. The downside is its popularity may require a wait.

GAA

BANGKOK | $$$ | INTERNATIONAL
68/4 Soi Langsuan; 091 419 2424; www.gaabkk.com; set menu 3200B

This uber-acclaimed Bangkok restaurant is run by Michelin-starred female chef Garima Arora, a protégé of former Bangkok chef Gaggan Anand who honed her craft at Copenhagen's famed Noma. Classic Indian and Thai dishes are the specialities here, upgraded with modern cooking techniques and presented in artful 10- to 12-course tasting menus. Wine pairing (if opted for) doubles the bill.

'We bring to you the flavours of India as we in the kitchen enjoy them the most.'
Gaa

COURTESY THIP SAMAI

THIP SAMAI

BANGKOK | $ | THAI
313 Th Mahachai, Banglamphu; mains 50-250B

This Bangkok institution reputedly serves the definitive version of *pàt tai* fried noodles. Every evening, scores of eager diners queue on the pavement for a table (the queue moves fast, so don't walk away in despair). Your patience is duly rewarded in the end with a delicious platter of the iconic dish.

BLUE RICE

KANCHANABURI | $$ | THAI
Mu 4, Ban Tamakham; 34512017; www.applenoikanchanaburi.com; mains from 135B

Masterful spice blends, a creative menu and peaceful river views make this one of the most irresistible restaurants in Kanchanaburi. The signature massaman curry is perfectly balanced, and Chef Apple puts a gourmet spin on Thai classics such as *yam sôm* oh (pomelo salad) and chicken-coconut soup with banana plant. The eponymous rice is stained with butterfly pea flower petals.

GINGER & KAFE @ THE HOUSE

CHIANG MAI | $$ | THAI
199 Th Moon Muang; 053 287681; www.thehousebygingercm.com; mains 160-390B

Dining at the restaurant in The House by Ginger boutique feels like eating in a posh Thai mansion, with antique furniture, comfy sofas and fine china. The Thai food is delicious and lavishly presented, with wonderful dishes such as Massaman curry with slow-beef in lime-coconut cream or stuffed squid with prawn in plum soup.

KHAO SOI LAM DUAN FAH HAM

CHIANG MAI | $ | THAI
352/22 Th Charoenrat/Th Faham; mains from 40B

North of the Th Ratanakosin bridge on the east bank, Th Faham is known as Chiang Mai's *kôw* soy (wheat-and-egg noodles in curry broth) ghetto. Khao Soi Lam Duan Fah Ham is the pick of the bunch, serving delicious bowls of *kôw* soy to eager crowds of locals and visitors alike.

LERT ROS

CHIANG MAI | $ | THAI
Soi 1, Th Ratchadamnoen; mains 30-160B

As you enter this local-style hole-in-the-wall, you'll pass the main course: delicious whole tilapia fish, grilled on coals and served with a fiery Isan-style dipping sauce. Eaten with sticky rice, this is one of the great meals of Chiang Mai. The menu also includes fermented pork grilled in banana leaves, curries and *sôm·đam* (spicy green papaya salad).

SAMUAY & SONS

UDON THANI | $$ | THAI
Th Phon Phisai; 86 309 6685; www.facebook.com/SamuayNsons; mains 79-280B

This small chef-driven, open-kitchen place in Thailand's northeastern regional capital of Udon Thani is the Isan (northeastern Thai region) version of a trendy Soho bistro. It does some Thai and Isan standards like Panang curry and om curry with algae, but sets itself apart with fusion dishes and modern twists on old recipes such as tapioca shrimp balls and coconut milk duck confit with mango jam.

LUNG EED

CHIANG RAI | $ | THAI
Th Watpranorn; mains 40-60B

One of Chiang Rai's most delicious dishes is the star at this simple, friendly

Previous spread: Dish from Saawaan; Thip Samai.

shophouse restaurant. Ignore the English-language menu on the wall and just order the sublime *lâhp gài*, a dish of minced chicken fried with local spices and topped with crispy deep-fried chicken skin, shallots and garlic.

LARP KHOM HUAY POO

MAE HONG SON PROVINCE | $ | THAI
Ban Huay Pu, Pai; 53699126

Escape the wheatgrass-and-tofu crowd at this unabashedly carnivorous local eatery in the traveller-friendly Northern Thailand town of Pai. The house special is *larp moo kua*, northern-style *lâhp* (minced pork fried with herbs and spices). Accompanied by sticky rice, bitter herbs and an ice-cold beer, it's one of the best meals in town and the soups and bamboo worms are fine, too.

KHAOMAO-KHAOFANG

MAE SOT | $$ | THAI
382 Rte 105; 2938185; www.khaomaokhaofang.com; mains 100-790B

Like dining in a gentrified jungle, Khaomao-Khaofang replaces chandeliers with hanging vines, and interior design with orchids and waterfalls. It's the most atmospheric place to eat in Mae Sot and the Northern Thai food is fine: try one of the several delicious *yam* (Thai-style spicy salads), spicy catfish or black pepper crab.

'We try to re-discover dishes that have almost been forgotten and we take great pride in cooking from scratch.'
Ginger & Kafe @ The House

KOTI

HUA HIN | $$ | CHINESE
61/1 Th Dechanuchit; 095 860 5364; mains 150-500B

This Thai-Chinese restaurant, opened in 1932, is a national culinary luminary. Thais adore the stir-fried oyster with flour and egg, while foreigners frequently aim for the *đôm yam gûng*. Everyone loves the *yam tá-lair* (spicy seafood salad) and classic green curry. Be prepared to wait for a table.

CHICKEN AND BEE

PRANBURI | $$$ | THAI
Sam Roi Yot; 092 054 5645; mains 100-1000B

Against the lush greenery of Khao Sam Roi Yot National Park, Chicken and Bee is an organic farm and open-air restaurant where you are sure to feel at home. Spicy seafood pasta, fresh-pressed juices with edible flowers and Thai curry are just a few highlights of their ever-changing nature-loving concept, all set in the peaceful gardens.

MUM AROI

PATTAYA | $$ | SEAFOOD
83/4 Soi 4, Th Naklua; 038 414802; mains 150-450B

This long-established beachfront restaurant, at the fishing-village end of Naklua, is regarded as one of Pattaya's best for seafood. Old fishing boats sit marooned offshore and crisp sea breezes envelop diners as they devour

fantastic Thai food. Try *sôm·đam þoo* (spicy papaya salad with crab) and *þlah mèuk nêung ma-now* (squid steamed in lime juice).

DINING ON THE ROCKS

KO SAMUI | $$$ | FUSION

Choeng Mon; 077 245678; www.sixsenses.com; set menu from 2800B

Ko Samui's ultimate fusion dining experience takes place on nine cantilevered verandas yawning over the gulf at Six Senses resort. After sunset (and wine), guests feel like they're dining on a barge set adrift on a starlit sea. Each dish on the set menu is the brainchild of cooks experimenting with taste, texture and temperature. A vegan menu can be found among the set menus.

TURM-ROM

KHON KAEN | $ | THAI

Th Chetakhon; 86 850 9779; mains 49-169B

This superb place combines one of the best kitchens in Khon Kaen with a covered garden to create the perfect place for a night out. The *þá·sá þlah chôrn* (hot and sour curry with snakehead fish) and *đam tùa mŏo gròrp* (spicy long-bean salad with fried pork) are especially good.

RICE PADDY

PHANG-NGA PROVINCE | $$$ | MULTICUISINE

Hat Pasai, Ko Yao Noi; 076 410 233; www.ricepaddy.website; mains 180-890B

COURTESY DINING ON THE ROCKS

This page: Dish from Dining on the Rocks. Opposite page: Chef from Suay.

Flash-fried *sôm·đam* (spicy green papaya salad), fantastic falafel and hummus, spicy, fruit-enhanced curries served in clay pots and fresh salads are some of the delicious dishes at this sweet German-owned Thai restaurant on a hilltop overlooking Ko Yao Noi. Enjoy island views as you dine.

SUAY

PHUKET | $$$ | FUSION

50/2 Th Takua Pa; 087 888 6990; www.suayrestaurant.com; mains 400-1000B

Fabulous fusion and fine wines, courtesy of top Phuket chef-owner Noi Tammasak, are the draw at this converted house just south of the Phuket's Old Town. Spicy aubergine salads, sweet-basil Shanghai noodles, braised-beef-cheek massaman and grilled-lemongrass lamb chops with papaya salsa are just some of the fusion highlights. Tables are dotted around the romantically lit house, garden and wraparound porch.

PAD THAI SHOP

PHUKET | $ | THAI

Th Patak East; mains 50-80B

This glorified roadside food shack makes absurdly good *kôw pàt þoo* (fried rice with crab), *pàt see·éw* (fried noodles), chicken stew and noodle soup. It also serves up some of the best pàt tai south of Bangkok: spicy and sweet, packed with tofu, egg and peanuts, and plated with spring onions, bean sprouts and lime. Don't miss the house-made chilli sauces.

KRUA TARA

PHUKET | $$ | SEAFOOD

82 Mu 5, Ao Nang; 75 661 166; mains 150-350B

This cavernous, tin-roofed delight on the beach at Phuket's Ao Nang comes highly recommended for its seafood selection. There's no pretension here, just the freshest fish, crab, clams, oysters, lobster, squid and prawns done dozens of ways. The snapper fried in red curry is a piquant Thai classic.

WHERE TO DRINK...

ROOFTOP BARS

Moon Bar, Bangkok
At 61 floors up, Moon Bar claims to be among the highest alfresco bars in the world.

Baba Nest, Phuket
Engulfed by beautiful Andaman and island views and bordered by glittering reflective pools, Baba Nest is a truly magical Phuket sunset-watching spot.

Vana Nava Sky, Hua Hin
Hua Hin's classiest cocktail joint opened in 2018, a 27th-floor stunner with marble floors and lattice iron framing high windows for a steampunk effect.

Brewski, Bangkok
This beer-centric Bangkok rooftop is a chilled-out spot to while away an evening 30 storeys above bustling Sukhumvit.

CAMBODIA

Cambodia has a great variety of national dishes, some drawing on the cuisines of neighbouring Thailand and Vietnam, but all with a unique Cambodian twist. Local specialities range from spring rolls and curry to the more adventurous: Cambodians find nothing strange in eating insects, algae, offal or fish bladders and will dine on a duck foetus and snack on spiders.

WHAT TO EAT

Banh chev
Rice pancake stuffed with herbs, bean sprouts and a meat or fish staple.

Bobor
Rice porridge, like congee in China, popular with dried fish and egg, or spiced up with chilli and black pepper.

Check chien
Deep-fried bananas; a popular street snack at any time of day.

Nam ben choc
Thin rice noodles served with a red chicken curry or fish-based broth.

Loat
Small white noodles that look like bean sprouts; they taste delicious fried with beef.

Kyteow
Rice-noodle soup that will keep you going all day.

PRICE RANGES
$ less than US$5
$$ US$5-10
$$$ US$15 or more

Tipping: 5–10%

BUNONG KITCHEN

MONDULKIRI PROVINCE | $ | CAMBODIAN
76 Krong, Sen Monorom; 097 7904244; mains US$3-4

Bunong Kitchen is a simple but charming training restaurant for Bunong people from the indigenous communities of Mondulkiri Province. Come here to try traditional soups such as *trav brang* (with jackfruit, pumpkin, long beans and eggplant) as well as locally sourced coffee and Bunong desserts including *skoo* (a boiled jungle root with honey and sugar).

MALIS

PHNOM PENH | $$ | CAMBODIAN
136 Norodom Blvd; 015 814 888; www.malis-restaurant.com; mains US$6-28

Phnom Penh's leading Khmer restaurant is a chic place to dine alfresco in a courtyard garden, resplendent with tropical plants. Chef Luu Meng and his team aim to revive traditional Khmer cooking and reinvent it for the modern day with dishes such as sour chicken lemongrass soup, pork and pumpkin stew, and kampot pepper brûlée. It's also popular for its Cambodian breakfasts (noodle soup, rice or congee).

ROMDENG

PHNOM PENH | $$ | CAMBODIAN
74 Street 174; 092 219565; www.romdeng-restaurant.org; mains US$5.50-8.50

Set in a gorgeous colonial villa with a small pool, Romdeng specialises in Cambodian country fare, including a famous baked-fish *amok*, two-toned pomelo salad and tiger-prawn curry. Sample deep-fried tarantulas or stir-fried tree ants with beef and spicy basil if you dare. It is staffed by former street youths and their teachers.

VIBE CAFÉ

PHNOM PENH| $$ | VEGAN

26A St 446; 061 764937; www.vibecafeasia.com; mains US$5-7.50

This three-storey air-conditioned cafe presents itself as Phnom Penh's first 100% vegan restaurant, creating superfood recipes in its laboratory-like kitchen. The signature Ritual Bowl is packed full of goodness, including quinoa, beetroot, hummus and a whole lot more. It also has innovative cleansing juices such as activated charcoal, coconut water, ginger, lemon and cayenne pepper. Detox!

FRIENDS

PHNOM PENH | $$ | FUSION
215 Street 13; 012 802072; www.tree-alliance.org; dishes US$6.25-7.50

The sunny yellow walls of this much-loved Phnom Penh institution form a cheery backdrop to a meal of tasty tapas dishes, a heavenly smoothie or a cocktail or two. The restaurant is part of the Tree Alliance group that offers former street children a head start in the hospitality industry.

LE BOUCHON

PHNOM PENH | $$ | EUROPEAN
82 Street 174; 077 881103; www.bouchon-wine-bar.business.site; mains US$7-29

Le Bouchon is part sophisticated restaurant, part elegant wine bar, located in a stunning colonial villa. The extensive menu features dishes like burgers, shepherd's pie and beef bourguignon, each with a suggested wine pairing. Don't miss the indulgent homemade desserts, plus some of the most potent cocktails in town.

'Cuisine Wat Damnak showcases unique Cambodian products and Khmer culinary heritage through degustation menus in a cosy traditional house.'
Joannès Rivière, chef and owner of Cuisine Wat Damnak

CUISINE WAT DAMNAK

SIEM REAP | $$$ | CAMBODIAN
Wat Dam Nak area; 077 347762; www.cuisinewatdamnak.com; 5/6-course set menu US$29/34

French chef Joannès Rivière's restaurant delivers the ultimate contemporary Khmer dining experience. Inspired by the use of herbs and vegetables from the family garden in traditional Cambodian cooking, the set menu highlights locally foraged ingredients and seasonal produce from nearby farms. The dining room is located in a traditional wooden house that oozes charm.

MAHOB

SIEM REAP | $$ | CAMBODIAN
137 Traing Village; 063-966986; www.mahobkhmer.com; dishes US$3.50-15

The Cambodian word for food is mahob, and at this restaurant it is delicious. Set in a traditional wooden house with contemporary styling, this place takes the same approach to cuisine as it does to decor, serving up dishes such as caramelised pork shank with ginger and black pepper, or wok-fried local beef with red tree ants.

MARUM

SIEM REAP | $$ | CAMBODIAN
Wat Polanka area; 017 363284; www.marum-restaurant.org; mains US$4-9.75

The delightful wooden house and spacious garden at Marum are just the start. Menu highlights include beef with red ants and chilli stir-fry, and mini crocodile burgers. Be sure to leave room for dessert: red sticky rice and sweet mango with pandan sauce, or chocolate and kampot pepper cake passion fruit syrup.

POU KITCHEN

SIEM REAP | $$ | CAMBODIAN
Phum Wat Damnak; 092 262688; www.poukitchen.com; mains US$3-6.50

Under the direction of chef Meng-ly, Pou Kitchen has taken off as one of the most popular and innovative Cambodian restaurants in Siem Reap. Choose from grilled beehive salad or chicken with red ant for starters, and move on to Phnom Kulen pork-belly sausage or spicy vegetable cake curry. Daily specials are prepared with fresh seasonal ingredients from a nearby organic farm.

SPOONS CAFÉ

SIEM REAP | $$ | CAMBODIAN
Bambu Road; 076 277 6667; www.spoonscambodia.org;mains US$6.25-12

Located in a bamboo building, this excellent contemporary-Cambodian restaurant supports local community EGBOK (Everything's Gonna Be OK), which offers education, training and employment opportunities in the hospitality sector. The menu includes fulsome flavours in dishes such as *trey saba* (whole mackerel) with coconut-turmeric rice, tiger-prawn curry and tuk kroeung, a pungent local fish-based broth.

SUGAR PALM

SIEM REAP | $$ | CAMBODIAN
Street 27; 012 818143; www.thesugarpalm.com; mains US$6-9

The high ceilings and contemporary, wooden-clad interior of the Sugar Palm is a beautiful space in which to sample the flavours of traditional Cambodian home cooking infused with aromatic herbs and spices, including delicious char kreung (curried lemongrass) dishes. Owner Kethana once showed celebrity chef Gordon Ramsay how to prepare *amok* (a baked fish dish).

CRAB MARKET

SOUTH COAST | $$ | MARKET
Kep, Kampot Province; 1kg crab from US$10

Eating at the crab market – a row of wooden waterfront restaurants by a

COURTESY TWENTY THREE BISTRO

This page: Twenty Three Bistro. Opposite page: Dish from Twenty Three Bistro.

COURTESY TWENTY THREE BISTRO

wet fish market – is a quintessential Kep experience. Crabs are kept in pens just off the pebbly beach. Fresh crabs fried with Kampot pepper are a taste sensation. There are lots of great places to choose from at the crab market, so keep an eye on where the Khmer crowd are eating.

TWENTY THREE BISTRO

SOUTH COAST | $$ | INTERNATIONAL
23 St 726, Kampot; 088 607 9731; www.facebook.com/23kampot; mains US$5-10

Looking for exquisitely prepared modern European cuisine made with locally-sourced seasonal produce? It's not clear how the owners manage it, but Twenty Three Bistro offers haute cuisine for bargain prices. Especially recommended is the smoked-mackerel pâté and the sea bass, which comes in a ravishing moat of pureed cauliflower, capers, brown butter and lime.

JAAN BAI

BATTAMBANG | $$ | FUSION
Street 2; 078 263144; www.facebook.com/jaanbaicct; mains US$4-10

Jaan Bai ('rice bowl' in Khmer) is Battambang's foodie highlight, with a sleekly minimalist interior offset by beautiful tilework. The menu is similarly bold: order a few of the small plates to experience the range of flavours, or go all out with the seven-plate tasting menu. Leave room for the coconut sorbet with salted honeycomb and lime syrup. Jaan Bai trains and employs vulnerable youth through the Cambodia Children's Trust.

WHERE TO EAT...

CAMBODIAN STREET FOOD

Road 60 Night Market, Siem Reap
A great place to sample local snacks, including the full range of deep-fried insects and barbecue dishes such as quail.

Jomno Street Food, Siem Reap
Twists on the classic *amok* (baked fish) include a crispy chicken *amok* salad and a vegan mushroom *amok*.

Naom Banchock Noodle Stalls, Banteay Srei District
Preah Dak village is renowned for its *naom banchok* stalls, serving homemade rice noodles with fish broth or chicken curry.

Sesame Noodle Bar, Phnom Penh
Cold noodles come heaped with egg and caramelised pork or grilled tofu at this Russian Market diner.

VIETNAM

Boasting a delicious cuisine of fresh, subtle flavours and intricate textures, Vietnam is one of the truly great eating destinations. Phenomenal meals can be found as much at tiny plastic tables perched on the side of a noisy road as in the luxurious surroundings of hip new urban eateries, while marked regional variations make exploring the map a tasty treat.

WHAT TO EAT

Pho
Vietnam's famed beef or chicken rice noodle soup. The best pho is found in the north, especially in Hanoi.

Banh Mi
Baguette sandwiches filled with delicacies such as paté, roast pork and pickled vegetables

Banh Cuon
Delicate savoury rice pancakes served with shrimp and fried onion

Che
A traditional dessert of preserved fruits, seeds and vegetable jelly served with crushed ice.

Nem Cuon/Goi Cuon
Fresh rice paper rolls filled with salad served with a tangy sauce

PRICE RANGES

$ less than 115,000d;
$$ 115,000-340,000
$$$ more than 340,000d

Tipping: Generally not expected; 5-10% in fancy restaurants.

SAIGONESE

PHU QUOC | $$ | FUSION

14 Đ Tran Hung Dao; 0938 059 650; meals 150,000-220,000d

The hippest, casual dining on Phu Quoc delights with fusion dishes lifted from designer cookbooks. The appetisers excel in *bao* (steamed buns filled with pulled beef and beetroot), and squid with avocado cream. Try the caramelised shrimp clay-pot and for dessert, popcorn banana cake. Manager Thao's experiences abroad show in the chic ambience; the biggest surprise is the reasonable bill for on-trend eats.

HILL STATION DELI & BOUTIQUE

SAPA | $$ | VIETNAMESE

7Đ Muong Hoa; www.thehillstation.com; meals from 125,000d

With cheese and charcuterie plates, pork terrine and local smoked trout, the Hill Station Deli & Boutique is a stylish addition to the Sapa dining scene. Factor in some of Sapa's best coffee and an interesting array of international beers and wines, and you've got the most diverse option in town. Also offers cooking classes with a skilled Hmong chef in a nearby indigenous village.

BASSAC RESTAURANT

MEKONG DELTA | $$$ | INTERNATIONAL

32 Đ Le Loi; Chau Doc; 0296-386 5010

Chau Doc's most sophisticated dining experience is at the Victoria Chau Doc Hotel where the menu veers between wonderful international dishes (roast rack of lamb, seared duck breast), dishes with a French accent (provençale tart, gratin dauphinoise) and beautifully presented Vietnamese dishes, such as grilled squid with green peppercorns. The apple pie with cinnamon ice cream makes for a sublime ending.

NEM NUONG THANH VAN

MEKONG DELTA | $ | VIETNAMESE
cnr Nam Ky Khoi Nghia & 30 Thang 4 Can Tho; 0292-382 7255; meals; 45,000d

The only dish this locally acclaimed spot does is the best *nem nuong* in town. Roll your own rice rolls using the ingredients provided: pork sausage, rice paper, green banana, star fruit (*carambola*), cucumber and a riot of fresh herbs, then dip into the peanut-and-something-else sauce, its secret jealously guarded. Simple and fantastic!

LAC CANH CHIM SAO

HANOI | $$ | VIETNAMESE
63-65 Ngo Hue; 024-3976 0633; www.chimsao.com; meals 45,000-120,000d

Sit at tables downstairs or grab a more traditional spot on the floor upstairs and discover excellent Vietnamese food, with some dishes inspired by the ethnic minorities of Vietnam's north. Definite standouts are the hearty and robust sausages, zingy and fresh salads, and duck with star fruit (carambola). Even simple dishes are outstanding. Come with a group to sample the full menu.

BLUE BUTTERFLY

HANOI | $$ | VIETNAMESE
69 P Ma May; 024-3926 3845; bluebutterflyrestaurant.com; meals 100,000-300,000d

Blue Butterfly floats above its weight with the lamp-lit dark-wood stylings of a heritage house and a good-value menu of Vietnamese classics. Staff offer knowledgeable suggestions and demonstrate how to tackle dishes such as *nem lui*, pork grilled on lemongrass skewers, wrapped in rice paper and dipped in peanut sauce. Set menus (from 350,000d) are available.

LA BADIANE

HANOI | $$$ | INTERNATIONAL
10 Nam Ngu; 024-3942 4509; www.labadiane-hanoi.com; meals from 280,000d

This stylish bistro is set in a restored, whitewashed French villa arrayed around a breezy central courtyard. French cuisine underpins the menu – La Badiane translates as 'star anise' – but Asian and Mediterranean flavours also feature. Menu highlights include sea-bass tagliatelle with smoked paprika, and prawn bisque with wasabi tomato bruschetta.

BUN CHA 34

HANOI | $ | VIETNAMESE
34 P Hang Than; 0948 361 971; meals 35,000d

Best *bun cha* in Vietnam? Many say 34 is up there. No presidents have eaten at the plastic tables, but you get perfectly moist chargrilled pork, zesty fresh herbs and delicious broth to dip everything in. The *nem* (seafood spring rolls) are great too. Aim for midday for patties straight off the coals.

WHERE TO EAT...

BANH MI

Banh Mi Hoi An, Hanoi
Open late and serves a fine grilled chicken, chili and lemongrass sandwich that doesn't skimp on the fillings.

Banh Mi Pho Hue, Hanoi
Hugely popular small shop with every single ingredient made in house. Great paté.

Banh Mi Phuong, Hoi An
Hoi An's most popular sandwich stall is worth waiting in line for.

Banh Mi Huynh Hoa, Ho Chi Minh City
A hole-in-the-wall sandwich shop that is hugely popular with locals for it's tasty pork rolls.

CHA CA THANH LONG

HANOI | $$ | VIETNAMESE
19-31 P Duong Thanh; 024-3824 5115; www.chacathanglong.com; mains 180,000d

Bring along your DIY cooking skills and grill your own succulent fish with a little shrimp paste and plenty of herbs. *Cha ca* (fish burger) is an iconic Hanoi dish heavy on turmeric and dill; while another nearby more-famous cha ca eatery gets all the tour-bus traffic, the food here is actually better.

MAISON DE TET DECOR

HANOI | $$ | CAFE
156 Tua Hoa, Nghi Tam, Tay Ho; 024-3823-9722

Sumptuous, healthy and organic (when possible) whole foods are presented with aplomb in one of Hanoi's loveliest settings, an expansive, airy villa overlooking West Lake.

QUAN BUI

HO CHI MINH CITY | $$ | VIETNAMESE
17a Đ Ngo Van Nam; 028-3829 1545; quani-bui.com; meals 69,000-169,000d

This slick restaurant in up-and-coming Đ Ngo Van Nam boasts stylish Indochinese decor and authentic Vietnamese cuisine. including hearty northern dishes, in contrast to the many places nearby offering Japanese flavours. Cocktails – from the associated bar across the lane – are among HCMC's best.

HUM LOUNGE & RESTAURANT

HO CHI MINH CITY | $$ | VIETNAMESE
2 Đ Thi Sach; 028-3823 8920; www.humvietnam.vn; meals 80,000-190,000d

Bringing the excellent Vietnamese-inspired vegetarian cuisine of the city's long-established Hum Vegetarian Cafe & Restaurant to a central garden location, the Hum Lounge is a welcome respite from the bustle of the city. Settle into the elegant and verdant space and enjoy dishes including papaya and banana flower salads, mushrooms steamed in coconut, and the subtle combination of braised tofu with star anise and cinnamon.

This page: Bun Bo Hua. Opposite page: Quan Bui.

COURTESY QUAN BUI

NHA HANG NGON

HO CHI MINH CITY | $$ | VIETNAMESE
160 Đ Pasteur; 028-3827 7131; meals 60,000-260,000d

Thronging with locals and foreigners, this is one of HCMC's most popular spots, with a large range of the very best street food in stylish surroundings across three levels. Set in a leafy garden ringed by food stalls, each cook serves up a specialised traditional dish, ensuring an authentic taste of Vietnamese, Thai, Japanese or Chinese cuisine.

CUC GACH QUAN

HO CHI MINH CITY | $$ | VIETNAMESE
10 Đ Dang Tat; 028-3848 0144; www.cucgachquan.com.vn/en; meals 85,000-210,000d

'Quan Bui uses only fresh, high quality ingredients just like we would serve at home. It's Vietnamese comfort food executed with love and passion.'
Quan Bui

It comes as little surprise to learn that the owner is an architect when you step into this cleverly renovated old villa. The decor is rustic and elegant at the same time, which is also true of the food. Despite its tucked-away location in the northernmost reaches of District 1, this is no secret hideaway: book ahead.

MAISON SAIGON MAROU

HO CHI MINH CITY | $ | CAFE
167-169 Đ Calmette; 028-8730 05010; www.maisonmarou.com; drinks & snacks from 90,000d

This stylish and colourful cafe is home base for Marou, Vietnam's first artisan chocolate producer. Watch Marou's skilled team tempering and moulding chocolate crafted from local fair-trade

cacao, and enjoy drinks and snacks also incorporating the stellar ingredients. Try the iced chocolate with cinnamon and chilli, and purchase Marou's excellent chocolate as gifts to take home.

GANH HAO

VUNG TAU | $$$ | SEAFOOD
3 Đ Tran Phu; 0254-355 0909; meals 140,000-450,000d

With tables by the ocean, this wonderful seafood restaurant boasts the perfect setting. Don't be put off by its size (Ganh Hao is huge and seats hundreds) as service is pretty efficient and you shouldn't have to wait too long for your meal. Try sublime crab (great with pepper sauce), clams, squid, prawn, fish claypot and seafood hotpots.

CO YEN

HAIPHONG | $ | VIETNAMESE
2 P Pham Ngu Lao; meals from 20,000d

This streetside stall sells one thing only, *banh da cua*, Haiphong's signature noodle dish, a combination of thick dark rice noodles in a clear broth with pork balls, shrimp and morning glory that is served for breakfast only. There's only a small sign; look for the vendor at the head of the tiny side street off P Pham Ngu Lao, just south of P Tran Phu.

NAM GIAO

HAIPHONG | $$ | VIETNAMESE
22 P Le Dai Hanh; meals from 100,000d

Haiphong's most atmospheric dining choice is hidden within this dilapidated colonial building. Rooms are an artful clutter of Asian art, old carved cabinets and antiques, while the small but well-executed menu includes an aromatic herbal sea bass wrapped in banana leaf and a succulent caramelised pork belly cooked in a clay pot.

HANH RESTAURANT

HUE | $ | VIETNAMESE
11 Pho Duc Chinh; 0905 520 512; meals 30,000-100,000d

Newbies to Hue specialities should start at this busy restaurant. Order the five-dish set menu (120,000d) for a speedy lesson of *banh khoai* (savoury prawn pancakes), *banh beo* (steamed rice cakes topped with shrimp and spring onions), and divine *nem lui* (grilled pork on lemongrass skewers) wrapped in rice paper and herbs. Ask the patient staff how to devour everything.

QUAN BUN BO HUE

HUE | $ | VIETNAMESE
17 Đ Ly Thuong Kiet; 23-4382-6460; meals from 35,000d

Excellent spot for a hearty bowl of *bun bo Hue*, the city's signature noodle dish combining tender beef, vermicelli and lemongrass. They sell out by early afternoon.

CARGO CLUB

HOI AN | $$ | INTERNATIONAL
107 Đ Nguyen Thai Hoc; 0235-391 1227; meals 70,000-160,000d

Remarkable cafe-restaurant, serving Vietnamese and Western food, with a terrific riverside location (the upper terrace has stunning views). A relaxing day here munching your way around the menu would be a day well spent. Breakfasts here are legendary and perfect fuel for a full day of sightseeing. The pastisserie and cakes are superb and the fine-dining dishes and cocktails also deliver.

SEA SHELL

HOI AN | $ | INTERNATIONAL
119 Đ Tran Cao Van; 094 298 337; meals 90,000D

Shaded by an impressive Banyan tree, Sea Shell is a flavour-packed offshoot of the much-loved Nu Eatery in Hoi An's Old Town that's a great place to enjoy a light meal. Try snacks like tempura-prawn rolls and turmeric-catfish wraps or the outstanding filled steamed buns. Mains dishes include spicy pork noodles with a refreshing calamari and apple salad.

'Sea Shell offers simple tasty food prepared from fresh local ingredients. Intimate and comfortable, it's like having a dinner party at your friend's house.'
Troy Ngo, Sea Shell

DONG VUI FOOD COURT

MUI NE | $ | FOOD HALL
246 Đ Nguyen Dinh Chieu; www.dongvuifoodcourt.com; meals 30,000-170,000d

This attractive open-air food court has loads of independently run cook stations offering everything from Punjabi cuisine to paella, German sausages and Thai curries – plus plenty of excellent Vietnamese options. Just grab a seat in one of the thatched huts and order what you fancy. There's also great craft beer on tap and live music some weekends.

LAC CANH

NHA TRANG | $$ | VIETNAMESE
44 Đ Nguyen Binh Khiem; 0258-382-1391

A unique experience, this scruffy, unadulterated barbecue place is where locals go to feast on meat (beef, richly marinated with spices, is the speciality, but there are other meats and seafood, too). It's DIY: you grill ingredients on your own charcoal burner. The place can get pretty smoky – try to get a table with good ventilation.

LAOS

Little known compared to that of its heavyweight neighbours, Laotian cuisine offers the chance to discover plenty of new flavours. In major towns there are good arrays of dining options ranging from buzzing street markets to gourmet bistros; in rural areas most meals consist of sticky rice and grilled meats. Favourite Laotian snacks include bugs, frogs and other critters.

WHAT TO EAT

Láhp
A delicious spicy salad made from minced beef, pork, duck, fish or chicken.

Đạm Màhk Hung
A salad of shredded green papaya mixed with garlic, lime juice, fish sauce, land crab or dried shrimp and chillies by the handful.

Fĕr
Laotian breakfast made of rice noodles served floating in a broth with meat and vegetables.

Kòw Þûn
Thin rice noodles generally eaten with a spicy curry-like broth or a clear pork broth.

Kòw Þeeak
Thick rice- and tapioca-flour noodles in a slightly viscous broth with crispy-fried pork belly or chicken.

PRICE RANGES

For a main course:
$ less than 40,000K
$$ 40,000–120,000K
$$$ 120,000K or more

Tipping: Not customary; 10% in posh restaurants.

DAAUW

HUAY XAI | $ | LAOTIAN
Th Chomkao; www.daauwvillagelaos.com; mains 20,000-50,000K

Head to this welcoming place to soak up sunset views on its chill-out terrace decked in low cushions and an open-pit fire, and choose from freshly prepared organic Hmong food, wood-fired pizza, plenty of vegetarian options, or whole barbecued Mekong fish or chicken. Linger for *laojitos* if there's a crowd, a mojito made with *lòw-lów* (rice wine).

PAUL_BRIGHTON/SHUTTERSTOCK ©

SOUPHAILIN RESTAURANT

UDOMXAI | $ | LAOTIAN
Highway 13; 081-211147; mains 20,000-50,000K

Don't be fooled by the modest bamboo exterior of this backstreet gem, as the tastiest Lao food in the city is served here. Friendly Souphailin creates culinary magic with her *mok phaa* (steamed fish in banana leaves), *láhp*, perfectly executed spring rolls, beef steak, fried noodles, and chicken and mushroom in banana leaf. Everything is fresh and seasonal.

BOUANG ASIAN EATERY

LUANG PRABANG | $$ | FUSION
Th Sisavangvong; 020-55632600; mains 35,000-65,000K

This attractive eatery on the main drag puts a smile on your face with its colourful chairs, funky light fixtures and mural-covered wall. The hand-written menu of exceptional (and affordable) 'Lao revision' food includes intriguing fusions like gnocchi green curry and cinnamon-pork stew. The plating is as playful as the vibe.

DYEN SABAI

LUANG PRABANG | $$ | LAOTIAN

Ban Phan Luang; 020-55104817; www.dyensabairestaurant.wordpress.com; mains 35,000-65,000K

One of Luang Prabang's top destinations for fabulous Lao food. The eggplant dip and fried Mekong riverweed are some of the tastiest dishes in town. Most seating is on recliner cushions in rustic open-sided pavilions.

KHAIPHAEN

LUANG PRABANG | $$ | LAOTIAN

Th Sisavang Vatthana; 030-5155221; www.tree-alliance.org; mains 30,000-55,000K

Khaiphaen is an inviting training restaurant run by NGO Friends International that boats an interesting Laotian menu with a creative twist. It includes buffalo carpaccio, five spices pork belly and a pea and apple eggplant curry. The shakes are also inventive. And do save space for the delicious desserts.

TAMARIND

LUANG PRABANG | $$ | LAOTIAN

'Khaiphaen is a warm and inviting vocational training restaurant dedicated to building bright futures for marginalized youth while serving creative local cuisine.'
JiHye, Khaiphaen Restaurant

MICK SHIPPEN/COURTESY DOI KA NOI

Th Kingkitsarat; 071-213128; www.tamarindlaos.com; set dinner 120,000-160,000K

On the banks of the Nam Khan, mint-green Tamarind has created its very own strain of 'Mod Lao' cuisine. The à la carte menu boasts delicious sampling platters with bamboo dip, stuffed lemongrass and *meuang* (DIY parcels of noodles, herbs, fish and chilli pastes, and vegetables). There's also buffalo *láhp* and Luang Prabang sausage.

CARPE DIEM

LUANG PRABANG | $$ | INTERNATIONAL

Tat Kuang Si; 020-98676741; www.carpediem.la; mains 45,000-175,000K

It's hard to envisage a more beautifully situated restaurant in all of Laos, as Carpe Diem is set in thatched pavilions dotted about the lower falls of Kuang Si south of Luang Prabang. Plan on lunch without the crowds and enjoy whiling away the best part of a day in their natural pools. The menu is heavily French accented with frog's legs, filet de boeuf and filet mignon while the house specialty is shrimp ravioli.

THAM MADA

VANG VIENG | $ | LAOTIAN
Sengasavang; mains 25,000-30,000K

The name here means 'normal', but there's lots that's unusual about this place. Chief among those is that the Korean owner is doing some of the best Thai-Lao food in town. Opt from a small menu that includes noodle soup, braised pork leg over rice, fried rice, and lighter dishes, all of which are prepared with care and very tasty.

COCO HOME BAR & RESTAURANT

NONG KHIAW | $$ | INTERNATIONAL
Main St; 020-23677818; mains 25,000-70,000K

This leafy riverside oasis has a great menu, with dishes like papaya salad, mango sticky rice, *mok phaa* (steamed fish in banana leaves) and duck in orange sauce. It's one of the best place in town to delight your taste buds either at tables in the lush garden or upstairs on the terrace.

DOI KA NOI

VIENTIANE | $$ | LAOTIAN
off Rue Sisangvone; 020-55898959; www.facebook.com/DoiKaNoi; mains 40,000-60,000K

With a menu that changes daily (check the restaurant's Facebook page at around 8.30am to see what's available), the dishes here range from Lao standards to regional specialities most of us have never heard of, with something to appeal both to newbies and grizzled foodies. The dining room has a charming old-school vibe with handsome food-related photos adorning the walls.

KA-TIB-KHAO

VIENTIANE | $$ | LAOTIAN
Rue Setthathirath; www.facebook.com/pg/katibkhao; mains 40,000-100,000K

Ka-Tib-Khao (Rice Basket) has a reassuringly short and delicious menu of dishes, many from the country's north. Think sheets of deep-fried Mekong River weed served with a spicy dip, lemongrass-stuffed pork and Luang Prabang-style herbal sausages, all served in a setting that manages to feel both sophisticated and traditional.

KHAMBANG LAO FOOD RESTAURANT

VIENTIANE | $$ | LAOTIAN
97/2 Rue Khounboulom; 021-217198; mains 20,000-90,000K

Previous spread: Láhp; Dish from Doi Ka Noi.

The slightly dreary, semi-open-air dining room couldn't be a bigger contrast with the tart, spicy, bold flavours served inside. This longstanding restaurant is the ideal introduction to Lao food via dishes such as *láhp* (spicy Lao-style salad of minced meat poultry or fish); roasted Mekong fish and stuffed frogs.

NEMNUENG SIHOM

VIENTIANE | $ | VIETNAMESE
Rue Hengboun | 021-213990 | mains 10,000-40,000K

A longstanding, bustling restaurant that offers a fun eating experience. It focuses on one product: *n em néuang* (Vietnamese barbecued pork meatballs) sold in 'sets' (*sut*) with *khào pûn* (thin, round rice noodles), fresh lettuce leaves, mint, basil, various sauces for dipping, sliced carambola (starfruit) and green banana – sort of a DIY spring roll.

PING KAI NAPONG

THA KHAEK | $$ | LAOTIAN
mains 39,000-89,000K

Right on the Mekong riverfront, Ping Kai Napong specialises in grilled chicken, but the menu is a virtual tour of Laotian cuisine, ranging from salads (the duck *láhp* is sublime) to soups, although the English-language translations may not always make total sense.

DAOLIN RESTAURANT

PAKSE | $ | LAOTIAN
Highway 13; mains 15,000-50,000K

Overlook the traffic noise – this popular restaurant has great food and service. It has some of the best Thai food in town and is a great introduction to Lao food, with set meals of sticky rice, steamed veggies, chilli sauce and fried fish/chicken/pork. Vegetarians can try Lao food that is usually meat-based, such as pumpkin soup (*om mahk éu*) and mushroom *gôy*.

NAKORN CAFE RESTAURANT

CHAMPASAK | $ | LAOTIAN
mains 20,000-53,000K

A pleasant melange of classy and casual, this riverside restaurant has a small mixed menu that covers duck *láhp* to chicken green curry to tuna sandwiches all of the highest quality. Wash it down with one of their imported Belgian beers.

CHEZ FRED ET LEA

SI PHAN DON | $ | INTERNATIONAL
Ban Khon, Don Khon; 020-22128882-187; www.facebook.com/ChezFredetLea; mains 20,000-50,000K

This cafe and 'salon de thé' serves organic coffees and teas, as well as top-quality Lao and Western cuisine that you won't find elsewhere on the island. There are no river views, but the Lao–French couple who runs the place makes up for it with inviting tunes and the freshest of ingredients.

WHERE TO EAT...

STREET FOOD

Ban Anou Night Market, Vientiane
An atmospheric open-air market in the capital dishing up tasty Lao food, from grilled meats to chilli-based dips representing a crash-course in the local cuisine.

Sepon Night Market, Sepon, Savannakhet
A small but high-quality night market serving bargain-priced Laotian favourites.

Luang Namtha Night Market, Northern Laos
Smoke-filled and tightly thronged with tribeswomen hawking freshly made broths, noodles and chicken on spits.

Phongsali Noodle Stalls, Northwestern Laos
Behind the Phongsali wet market, these noodle stands sell piping hot, deliciously fresh breakfast noodles.

MYANMAR

WHAT TO EAT

Mohinga
The landmark dish of Burmese cuisine, this fish and noodle soup is served for breakfast across the nation.

Hin
Less bold than Thai or Indian creations, Burmese-style curries are the default meal for millions of Myanmar citizens, and a roadhouse staple.

Lahpet Thoke
Pickled tea leaf salad appears as a side dish in teahouses all over Myanmar.

Balachaung
Myanmar's signature condiment is a dry, pungent combination of chillies, garlic and dried shrimp fried in oil.

PRICE RANGES

$ less than K6000; in Yangon less than K10,000
$$ K6000–15,000; in Yangon K15,000–25,000
$$$ K15,000 or more; in Yangon K25,000 or more

Tipping: Not expected, but 5–10% is welcome in restaurants.

Burmese cuisine might lack the stellar punch of Indian and Thai cooking, but its flavours have hidden depths, as you might expect from a nation at the threshold between Southeast Asia and the Indian subcontinent. From roadside teahouses serving pickled tea with *hin* (Burmese curry) and *t'ămin* (rice) to lavish Yangon restaurants concocting innovative modern fusions, Burmese cooking is unfamiliar, but undeniably exotic.

CHERRY HAKHA

HAKHA | $$ | BURMESE
Bo Gyoke Rd; mains K2500-15,000

There's no better exemplar of traditional Burmese food culture than this always-busy, atmospheric, wood-floored restaurant, crowded with families, couples and office mates holding meetings. The menu includes classic *mohinga*, roasted duck, a half-dozen crab dishes, grilled fish, spicy prawns and a squid hot plate. Fried rice and noodles are cheap sides to fill you up at lunchtime.

SANON

NYAUNG U | $$ | BURMESE
Pyu Saw Hit St; 09 45195 1950; www.facebook.com/sanonrestaurant; mains K4000-8700

Lap up delicious and exciting dishes surrounded by tropical plants in the open-sided dining room of this memorable restaurant. Step through the arched brick gate and you'll find inventive Burmese small plates that are meant for sharing: river-prawn and catfish curry, pan-seared squid stuffed with pork, and crispy watercress and onion pakora. It has delicious juices, too (try the mint and pomelo freeze).

BLACK BAMBOO

NYAUNG U | $$ | EUROPEAN
Off Yarkinthar Rd; 061-60782; dishes K3000-9000

Run by a French-Burmese couple, this lush garden-cafe and restaurant is a pure delight. It's a pleasant place to relax over creatively prepared and served Burmese, Thai and Western dishes, a powerful espresso or a delicious homemade ice cream (the best in Bagan). Service is friendly but leisurely so bring a book, order a drink and take your time.

MINGALABAR MYANMAR RESTAURANT

MANDALAY | $ | BURMESE
71st St, 28/29; 02-60480; www.mingalabarrestaurant.com; mains K2000-7900

This massive, two-storey, traveller-friendly favourite has a split personality. On one side is a traditional Burmese pick-and-pig-out kind of spot, on the other, a sit down restaurant where you can order by menu. Select your soup, small curry or salad, and have it served with a veritable forest of side dishes. Best visited in a group since there's no way a single eater can make a dent in things.

TAJ

PYIN OO LWIN | $$ | INDIAN
26 Nanda Rd; 09 78404 9880; www.facebook.com/TheTajPOL; mains K4600-9000

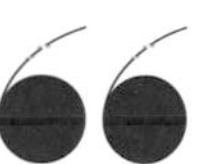

'We cook what we love. And we love a lot: flavours, colours, textures, spices, the abundant basket of the world.'
Seeds, Yangon

COURTESY SEEDS

Best by night, this standout lakeside eatery is much more reasonably priced than its extravagant look suggests. Served inside an elegant, barn-like dining hall, the curries, tikkas and baltis are superb and quite literally melt in the mouth. There are plenty of veggie options, a decent alcohol selection and the most attentive service in town.

LIN HTETT MYANMAR TRADITIONAL FOOD

INLE LAKE | $$ | BURMESE
Yone Gyi Rd, Nyaungshwe; 09 42832 6575; mains from K3500

This bright, clean and wholesome eatery is hands down the most appealing Burmese restaurant in Nyaungshwe, and one of the best curry houses in all Myanmar, where the service is as friendly as the food is delicious. Choose from a range of curries and

salads, all accompanied by soup, dips and rice. Staff can also arrange cooking classes for keen patrons.

JING HPAW THU

MYITKYINA | $ | BURMESE
Munkhrain Rd; 09 240 0518; dishes K2000-5000

If you roam to the far north of Myanmar, be sure to head out to this large, open-sided riverside restaurant on the outskirts of Myitkyina. The dining room catches waterborne breezes and is considered the top spot for real Kachin food. Specialties here include superb, tangy dried beef with a spicy dipping sauce, delectable fish dishes and chicken or pork served in a banana leaf.

SEEDS

YANGON | $$$ | INTERNATIONAL
63A U Tun Nyein St, Mayangone; 01-655 900; www.seedsyangon.com; mains US$38-48, set lunch/dinner from US$19/58

Swiss Michelin-star chef Felix Eppisser and his wife Lucia are the genial hosts at this superb fine-dining restaurant licking the shores of Inya Lake. The romantic lounge and stylish wicker pavilions look right onto the water and set menus of two or three courses of fine European-Asia fusion cooking (think seared prawns with vanilla and Kachin pepper) come with plenty of additional amuse-bouche. It's a very relaxed, chic atmosphere complemented by top-class service.

Previous spread: Dish from Rangoon Tea House; Preparing food at Seeds.

RANGOON TEA HOUSE

YANGON | $$ | BURMESE
77-79 Pansodan St, Kyauktada; 01-122 4534; https://en-gb.facebook.com/RangoonTeaHouse; snacks K2000-7800, mains K5000-17,000

This stylishly designed hipster teahouse is as popular with cashed-up locals as it is with travellers and expats – at peak meal times expect to wait for a table. Come to the high-ceilinged dining room for traditional Burmese cuisine, locally inspired cocktails, and curries and biryanis. All the usual teahouse snacks are available: tea-leaf salads, samosas, paratha (Indian-style bread), *bao* buns, you name it.

PANSODAN

YANGON | $$ | SOUTHEAST ASIAN
106 Pansodan St, Kyauktada; 09 44263 1066; www.thepansodan.com; mains K4500-58,000

Ticking all the right boxes for gourmet travellers, this restaurant gives a great first impression with its handsomely restored heritage setting and elegant, two-level dining room decorated in teak with gold-leaf detailing. Mirroring Myanmar's multicultural society, the expertly executed menu offers Burmese, Chinese and Indian dishes, ranging from the classic noodle dish *mohinga* to crispy chilli pomfret.

FEEL MYANMAR FOOD

YANGON | $ | BURMESE

124 Pyidaungsu Yeiktha St, Dagon; 01-511 6872; www.feelrestaurants.com; mains K1500-7000

This Yangon institution is a fine place to start discovering quality Burmese cuisine. At the front of the homey, informal dining room is a large counter of freshly made dishes on display – just go up and point out what you'd like. All the delicious meals come with soup, a plate of salad veggies and a small dessert. Outside, more stalls sell sweets, savoury snacks and other takeaways.

YANGON KITCHEN

NAY PYI TAW | $$$ | INTERNATIONAL

Kempinski Hotel, Shwe Pyi Taw Win Rd; 067-810 6061; www.kempinski.com/en/nay-pyi-taw/kempinski-hotel-nay-pyi-taw/dining/yangon-kitchen; mains K17,000-25,000

The acclaimed and highly exclusive gourmet restaurant inside the Kempinski Hotel is the place to come for succulent duck confit served with plum sauce on banana leaves, or delicate pan-fried sea bass. It's a refined, sophisticated space, and there's a fine multi-course Myanmar menu that's a tour de force of Burmese tastes.

TAJ KITCHEN

NAY PYI TAW | $$$ | THAI

Yana-Thing; 067-342 2282; mains K3000-8000

One of the capital's best restaurants not set in a hotel, Tai Kitchen whips up delicious chicken with Thai basil, whole steamed fish with lemon, Shan-style spare ribs and vegetable-filled rice cakes, among other Siamese hits. There's an attractive wood-filled interior and an outdoor deck for when the temperatures aren't too steamy.

SAN MA TAU MYANMAR RESTAURANT

HPA-AN | $ | BURMESE

1/290 Bo Gyoke St; 058-21802; mains from K2500

Set under striplights behind a row of giant cookpots, this local institution is one of the most appealing Burmese restaurants anywhere in the country. It serves a vast selection of rich curries, hearty soups and tart salads, accompanied by platters of fresh veggies and herbs, and an overwhelming 10 types of local-style dips to eat with them. It's easier to find now that there's a Roman-script sign.

DAW YEE

MAWLAMYINE | $ | BURMESE

U Ze Na Pagoda St; 09 42111 9556; mains from K3000

Although it looks humble from outside, Mawlamyine's down-home Daw Yee does some of the best Burmese food you'll find anywhere. Step under the corrugated canopy to find a tantalising selection of curries, including a deliciously fatty prawn stew, all on display for passing diners. To add fresh flavours, order one of the vegetable side dishes that change daily.

WHERE TO EAT...

LOCAL DELICACIES

Yellow Tofu, Khaung Daing
A speciality of the semi-submerged villages around Inle Lake, consumed with gusto at the roaming market that hopscotches around the lakeshore.

Shan kauq-sweh, Taunggyi
This Thai-influenced noodle soup is the dish to hunt down in hole-in-the-wall village restaurants in the tribal northeast.

Mandalay mondi, Mandalay
There are no prizes for guessing where to find this hearty dish of noodles topped with chicken curry, often subtly flavoured with pulse flour.

Rakhine mondi, Ngapali Beach
The Rakhine version of *mondi* (curry-topped noodles) is made with freshly caught seafood. Ngapali's beach strip is a great place to try it.

WHAT TO EAT

Bhorta
Bangladesh's signature dish: mashed vegetables, stewed in rich and spicy sauces, served as a side with almost everything.

Biryani
Steam-cooked rice and meat is the engine that drives the nation, served in pretty much every restaurant.

Bhuna khichuri
This braised, slow-cooked curry is a staple dish at local roadhouses and 'hotels' (cheap canteens).

Ilish mach
Bengal's favourite fish is served in myriad styles and sauces, but this curry with poppyseed and mustard sets the standard.

Mishti doi
Natural curd sweetened with palm sugar to finish a meal.

PRICE RANGES

For a main course:
$ less than Tk 150
$$ Tk 150–Tk 300
$$$ Tk 300 or more

Tipping: Small bills appreciated by restaurant staff.

BANGLADESH

Bangladesh takes the spice-infused cuisine of India and adds a unique Bengali twist...and an ocean's worth of seafood. 'Indian' restaurants outside India are often run by emigrés from Bangladesh, but the best place to sample Bengali food is at source, in humble village eateries and ritzy restaurants in Bangladesh's sprawling cities.

FAKRUDDIN

DHAKA | $ | BANGLADESHI
37 Bir Uttam AK Khandakar Rd, Gulshan Circle I; 01715-553330; www.fakruddin.com; mains Tk 120-200

It might sound like sticking our necks out, but we reckon this no-nonsense joint probably serves the best biryani in Dhaka, plateful by massive plateful. Or maybe it's not a gamble at all: this place is always packed by locals who know a good thing when they taste it. There's an English menu should you feel a need to go off-piste and order something other than biryani.

PREMIUM SWEETS

DHAKA | $ | SWEETS
Gulshan 2 Circle; 01759-115124; www.premiumsweets.ca; Sweets per kg from Tk 400

A Dhaka institution in its own right, this legendary store offers an amazing variety of traditional Bangladeshi sweetmeats, as well as a delicious mix of snacks and fast food. It has 14 showrooms scattered across the city, including this popular Gulshan 2 branch, where you can buy delicious *rasgulla* (cheese balls in rose syrup) and *mishti doi* (curd with palm sugar).

PANSHI RESTAURANT

SYLHET | $$ | BANGLADESHI
Jallarpar Rd; 01761-152939; www.en-gb.facebook.com/panshirestaurant; mains from Tk 200

At this iconic and wildly popular proletarian restaurant, the cooking is nothing short of culinary wizardry. Bringing every possible permutation of ingredients and flavours to your table, the alfresco eatery is perpetually thronged by locals, and you might have to share tables at peak hours. Skip the menu and simply ask the friendly waiters to surprise you – meaty mains come with a host of *bhorta* (mashed veg) and *bhaji* (fried fritter) dishes.

KUTUM BARI

SRIMANGAL | $$ | BANGLADESHI
Railway Station Rd; mains Tk 90-160

Split-level brick-walled seating, high windows and chic bamboo furnishings make this the coolest place to eat in Srimangal. It also serves up the best Bengali food – *bhorta* (mashed vegetable) preparations explode in the mouth with flavour, while the fish curries come in hearty portions and are finished in a diverse range of yummy gravies tempered with local spices.

MERMAID CAFÉ

COX'S BAZAR | $$$ | CAFÉ
01713-160029; www.facebook.com/mermaidcafe; mains from Tk 600

This sprawling, shaded, Goa-style beach shack on the seafront in Cox's Bazar serves such tasty food in such cool surroundings that you probably won't eat anywhere else once you've tried it. The fish dishes – prepared with fish straight from the bay – are sumptuous, but everything is top-notch, including the delicious desserts and fresh juices.

'Bringing every possible permutation of ingredients and flavours to your table, the alfresco eatery is perpetually thronged by locals'
Panshi Restaurant

COURTESY MERMAID CAFÉ

TOHZAH RESTAURANT

CHITTAGONG HILL TRACT | S$ | ADIVASI
Main Rd, Bandarban; 01552-386328; www.facebook.com/TohzahRestaurant-328132430697811; mains Tk 80-150

This low-key restaurant is the best place in Bandarban to sample tribal Marma cuisine. The main themes are a mountain of ginger and a volcano of chillies, plus the novelty of finding pork on offer in Muslim Bangladesh. If you're brave, you might even find lizard on the menu; those of a more hesitant disposition might prefer to opt for bamboo chicken.

BHUTAN

Dining in Bhutan depends on what you arrange as part of the obligatory organised tour, but there are some wonderful places to sample authentic local flavours. Rather than booking in for bland hotel buffets, ask your agent to tack on some upscale eateries in Thimphu and authentic Bhutanese canteens around the country, where you can feel the fiery force of Bhutanese home cooking.

BUKHARI RESTAURANT

PARO | $$$ | FUSION
Uma Paro Hotel, Paro Valley; 08-272813; www.comohotels.com/en/umaparo; set lunch/dinner US$66/102

The circular, timber-lined restaurant at the Uma Paro hotel is easily the best in the valley. The set dinner menu changes frequently and focuses on fresh, healthy and locally sourced food, with an international twist – at lunch, try the Wagyu burger with Bumthang 'Gouda' cheese. For a special occasion inquire about an expensive but magical private candlelit dinner in the lower courtyard.

SONAM TROPHEL RESTAURANT

PARO | $$ | BHUTANESE
Near Paro Chhu; 08-271287; mains Nu 180-300, set meals Nu 600

Downtown Sonam is a great stop for excellent home-style Bhutanese cooking, gently adapted to foreign tastes (so not quite as mouth-searingly spiced). The best bet is the set lunch (order in advance), which consists of seven delicious Bhutanese dishes, served at the table rather buffet-style. The *momos* (Tibetan dumplings), boneless chicken, ginger potatoes and *hentshey datse* (spinach and cheese) are a feast.

MY KIND OF PLACE

PARO | $$ | BHUTANESE
Near Paro Chhu; 77411784; www.facebook.com/My-Kind-of-Place-1586294645004888; mains from Nu 200, set meals from Nu 490

Stylish, clean and homey, this spacious 1st-floor restaurant has tasty Bhutanese dishes such as *hoentey* (buckwheat dumplings) and *ema datse* (chillies with cheese) with *bhaley* (Tibetan-style bread), plus some interesting Asian dishes too, including Indonesian-style chicken *rendang* and curry set meals with bok choy and garlic potatoes. The owner's personal touch elevates the place above the competition.

WHAT TO EAT

Ema datse
Chillies stewed with cheese is a Bhutanese institution; eat it toned-down for Western palates at hotels, or enjoy the incendiary local version at village canteens.

Momos
Tibetan dumplings, steamed or fried, are enjoyed enthusiastically all over Bhutan with hot chilli sauce.

Nakey
Fiddlehead fern fronds, stewed and served in a spicy cheese sauce – delicious, but only available for a few months each summer.

Ema kam
Not just a cooking ingredient, dried red chillies are deep fried and served on the side to add extra heat.

PRICE RANGES

$ less than Nu 250
$$ Nu 250–500
$$$ Nu 500 or more

Tipping: Not the norm but 5–10% is appreciated.

BRIOCHE CAFE

PARO | $ | CAFE

Near Paro Chhu; 17741231; cakes Nu 150-240

The espresso is rich and aromatic at this cute little cafe but the real draw is the wonderful range of pastries, from the signature apple pie to blueberry cake and seasonal tarts made with local fruit from the valley. Add a scoop of house-made *masala chai* ice cream to top things off. The owner is a pastry chef at the five-star Amankora, so knows exactly what she is doing.

TOU ZAIGA RESTAURANT

PARO | $$$ | BHUTANESE, INTERNATIONAL

Bondey; 77420979; www.bihtbhutan.org; set menu Nu 800

Trainee five-star chefs and aspiring waitstaff test their skills on lucky tourists at this restaurant run by the Bongde Institute of Hospitality and Tourism. The dishes fuse Western tastes with local seasonal organic produce, harvested from the Paro Valley. Ring the day before for a tailor-made three-course Bhutanese menu (ask if the locally-grown shiitake mushrooms are available), otherwise you'll get a less-ambitious Western set meal.

'Menus are based on seasonal, local produce sourced by Executive Chef Arsa Made, who delivers dishes with strong flavours and serious finesse.'
Bukhari, Paro

CLOUD 9

THIMPHU | $$$ | INTERNATIONAL

Chang Lam; 02-331417; www.facebook.com/Cloud9Thimphu; mains Nu 240-790

Despite the wonders of travel in Bhutan, it's easy to tire of hotel buffets, so make a beeline for this stylish restaurant, serving the best international menu in Thimphu. Visitors crowd in for sourdough pizzas with authentic Italian toppings, fat gourmet burgers with all the trimmings, deli sandwiches and delicious real gelato. You can't miss the ultra-modern silver-grey dining room, in a prime Chang Lam location, with a terrace overlooking Changlimithang Stadium (you can also enter from Clocktower Square).

7TH RESTAURANT

THIMPHU | $$$ | INDIAN, INTERNATIONAL

Druk Hotel, Wogzin Lam; 02-322966; www.drukhotels.com; mains Nu 220-580, buffet dinner Nu 840-1200

The elegant restaurant at the Hotel Druk elevates the hotel buffet to high art. Served in a moody, stone-floored dining room, lunch and dinner buffets roam from Europe to Bhutan and China, but it's the finely crafted Indian dishes that stand out above the pack. Swimming with flavours and spices, the Friday buffet is simply the best Indian meal in Bhutan, and you can also order Indian treats à la carte.

CLOVE BISTRO

THIMPHU | $$ | ASIAN

77737623; www.facebook.com/theclovebistrothimphu; mains Nu 250-320

There's a pan-Asian flavour at this inviting, upmarket bistro in the centre of Thimphu, serving dishes that draw influence from China, Japan, India and Southeast Asia. It's a calm, grown-up space for lunch or dinner, and the set meals with rice and side dishes (think honey-glazed chicken and raw papaya salad) are full of complex flavours and exotic ingredients, at reasonable prices.

BRUSNIKA RUSSIAN CAFE

THIMPHU | $$ | CAFE

Lhudrong Lam; 02-320888; www.facebook.com/brusnikarussianbakery; mains Nu 150-650

One of Thimphu's most welcoming spaces, Brusnika is run by a charming Russian-Bhutanese family and the calm, white dining room looks out over a small park towards Trashi Chho Dzong. It's a fine place to hole up with a book, and the menu runs to tasty pelmeni and blinis, soul-warming wild thyme tea and delicious home-baked crusty bread.

HAYATE RAMEN

THIMPHU | $$ | JAPANESE

Dungkhar Lam; 02-330240; www.facebook.com/BhutanRamen; mains Nu 155-350

It's ramen noodles all the way at this calm Japanese restaurant full of blond wood and bottles of condiments, upstairs off Dungkhar Lam. Bowls come topped with everything from roast pork to *ebi* (battered prawns), and you can finish off the dish with a suite of toppings, from roasted sesame seeds to *thingye* (Bhutanese pepper). Order an artisanal ale on the side to complete a fabulous meal.

SAN MARU

THIMPHU | $$$ | KOREAN

Norzin Lam; 02-334496; mains Nu 550-1200

A little slice of Seoul, transported to the centre of Thimphu, this graceful, wood-lined Korean restaurant serves excellent soups, hearty stews and, for groups of two or more, delicious beef *bulgogi*, barbecued at the table, with all the expected *banchan* (side dishes). The subtle flavours and fresh, healthy ingredients are a welcome treat after

P538-9: Rasgulla; Diah from Mermaid Café. This page: Momos. Opposite Page: Chillies.

KEITH LEVIT / DESIGN PICS/GETTY IMAGES ©

days of tray-warmed hotel buffets.

BABESA VILLAGE RESTAURANT

THIMPHU | $$$ | BHUTANESE

Thimphu-Babesa Expressway, Babesa; 02-351229; www facebook.com/Babesa-village-Restaurant-345727795636120; set menu Nu 600-700

About 6km south of Thimphu's centre, this charming restaurant offers traditional Bhutanese cuisine in a rammed-earth village home, one of four still standing incongruously next to the Thimphu–Babesa Expressway. The interior is decorated with antiques and the authentically spicy set menus include such local dishes as ribs with chilli, *lom* (dried turnip leaf) and *mengay*, optimistically described as 'Bhutanese pizza'. Extra dried chilli is provided for those with asbestos palates.

PEUNZHI DINER

PUNAKHA & KHURUTHANG | $$ | BHUTANESE

02-584145; Khuruthang; set lunch Nu 450

The 'Four Friends' is easily the best eating place in Khuruthang and is well known to guides, who are happy to bring groups here for proper Bhutanese home cooking, served in a homey and inviting dining room. The food is delicious and packs plenty of chilli punch, and there's welcoming air-con in summer. If you don't eat here, your guide will probably book lunch at one of the tourist hotels, so ask ahead of time.

WHERE TO DRINK...

CRAFT BEER

Bumthang Brewery, Jakar
A state-of-the-art microbrewery, specialising in Swiss-style unfiltered weiss beer; sample the curious Red Panda, with its subtle aftertaste of cloves.

Namgyal Artisanal Brewery, Paro Valley
Bhutan's premier microbrewery has a huge taproom where you can sample delicious Red Rice lager and Namgyal's hoppy IPA.

Ser Bhum Brewery, Hongtsho
The nation's first craft brewery, hidden down a bumpy 4WD track; after a tour, retreat to the sunny deck to sample lip-smacking Bhutan Glory amber ale and Dragon Stout.

NEPAL

There's more to Nepali cuisine than *daal bhaat* (lentil soup, rice and spiced vegetables), though you'll come to love this carb-rich feast on Nepal's trekking trails. At the end of a trek, the whole world's food is on offer in Kathmandu and Pokhara, from falafel, steaks and pizza to Thai curries, Tibetan momos (dumplings), Indian tandoori chicken and Nepali *thalis* (plate meals).

WHAT TO EAT

Daal bhaat tarkari
The engine that drives a million trekkers and sherpas: lentils, veg and rice, served in every trekking lodge across Nepal.

Momos
A much-loved Tibetan import, stuffed with buffalo meat, vegetables or cheese and served with a lip-tingling chilli dipping sauce. Found everywhere.

Chiura
Beaten, flattened rice, the default starch served across Nepal, but easiest to find in the Terai and outside of tourist towns.

Samsa
The Nepali samosa, these stuffed fried triangle-shaped pillows appear in roadside stalls and canteens across the Terai and Middle Hills.

PRICE RANGES
$ less than Rs 250
$$ Rs 250–500
$$$ Rs 500 or more

Tipping: Not expected but a 10% tip is appreciated.

CANDY'S PLACE

NEPALGANJ | $$ | INTERNATIONAL
Traveller's Village, Surkhet Rd; 081-550329; mains Rs 300-600

A stack of blueberry pancakes for breakfast? Real cheeseburgers with bacon? Oven-roasted chicken with stuffing – and tenderloin steak? Who would've thought you'd find American home cooking in Nepalganj?! And yet here you are, in the cosy six-table cafe atop the Traveller's Village. If you've OD'd on *daal bhaat*, this is heaven. Leave a space for their much-loved lemon meringue pie.

NANGLO WEST

TANSEN | $$ | NEPALI
Bhagwati Tole; 075-520184; www.nanglo.com.np; mains Rs 175-425, Newari set Rs 315-415

You can't visit Tansen without sampling the Nepali delights at this atmospheric oasis in the centre of the old town. In addition to a great Newari set *thali* with veg, chicken or mutton, they serve taste-bud tingling local dishes like *choela* (dried buffalo or duck meat with chilli and ginger), served with *chiura* (flattened rice) and spiced potatoes in curd. Out front you'll find Nanglo West's bakery with delicious buttery biscuits, cream cakes and pastries.

MOONDANCE RESTAURANT

POKHARA | $$ | INTERNATIONAL
Central Lakeside; 061-461835; www.moondancepokhara.com; mains Rs 240-1400

Much-loved Moondance is a Lakeside institution and deservedly so. Quality food, good service and a roaring open fire all contribute to the popularity of this tastefully decorated restaurant that has bookended a thousand treks around the Annapurna Range. The globe-trotting menu covers everything from salads, pizzas and imported steaks to excellent Indian and Thai curries. For dessert, the lemon meringue pie is legendary.

KRISHNA'S KITCHEN

POKHARA | $$$ | THAI
Khapaudi; 9846232501; www.facebook.com/krishnaskitchenandcottages; mains Rs 510-630

This superb Thai garden restaurant nestles at the north end of Phewa Tal, a rewarding detour from the bustle of downtown Pokhara. Homemade tofu, organic herbs and vegetables, and professional presentation mean this would be a great Thai restaurant anywhere in the world. To match the excellence of the food there are gourmet teas and a quality wine list. Walk, cycle or take a taxi to cover the 3km journey from Lakeside.

KC'S RESTAURANT

CHITWAN NATIONAL PARK | $$ | INTERNATIONAL
Gaida Chowk, Sauraha; 9855066483; mains Rs 350-550

A Sauraha classic, KC's is set in a cool, thatch-roofed bungalow with an open terrace overlooking a manicured garden, with a fire pit for winter dinners. The aproned chefs here look the part and the well-executed menu runs from Nepali and Indian curries to pizzas and pasta. We recommend the top-up-able thalis and authentic tandoori dishes, washed down with a lassi. Ever popular, this is a great place to meet people, including the friendly owner, who promises that Sherpa craft beer from Kathmandu will be on the menu soon.

'Our menu is inspired by the fresh, quality ingredients available to us, our al fresco dining area and the seasons.'
1905 Suites, Kathmandu

KITTIBOWORNPHATNON/SHUTTERSTOCK ©

FIRE & ICE PIZZERIA

KATHMANDU | $$$ | PIZZA
219 Sanchaya Kosh Bhawan, Tridevi Marg; 01-4250210; www.fireandicepizzeria.com; pizzas Rs 580-760

On the edge of Thamel, this excellent Italian place serves the best pizzas in Kathmandu (wholewheat crusts

available, as well as combo pizzas), alongside breakfasts, smoothies, *crespelle* (savoury crêpes) and good espresso, all to a cool soundtrack of Cuban son or Italian opera. The ingredients are top-notch, from the imported anchovies to the house-made tomato sauce. It's phenomenally popular so make a reservation and expect to share one of the tavern-style wooden tables.

KAISER CAFE

KATHMANDU | $$$ | AUSTRIAN
Garden of Dreams, Tridevi Marg; 01-4425341; www.kaisercafe.com; mains Rs 600-1650

This cafe-restaurant in the Garden of Dreams is run by Dwarika's Hotel so quality is high. More than anything else, the elegant neoclassical garden is one of the city's most romantic locations, especially at dusk. Fine Austrian-inspired dishes such as Wiener schnitzel and sweet Sachertorte are a nod to the country that financed and oversaw the garden's restoration. You'll have to pay the garden's admission fee to eat here.

THIRD EYE

KATHMANDU | $$$ | INDIAN
Chaksibari Marg; 01-4260160; www.thirdeye.com.np; mains Rs 500-650

Sensational Indian food can be hard to find in Kathmandu, so it's worth the splurge to eat this classy favourite in the back lanes of Thamel. Flavours are rich and authentic (tandoori dishes are especially good) and there's a grown-up, sit-down-dining mood, but spice levels are set at 'tourist' by default so let the suited waiters know if you'd like extra heat. Reserve a window seat at the sit-down section at the front or try the more informal section with low tables and cushions at the back; both are candlelit to create an intimate vibe.

1905 SUITES

KATHMANDU | $$$ | INTERNATIONAL
Naryanchaur; 01-4411348; www.1905suites.com; lunch mains Rs 600, dinner Rs 1000-1500

This classy restaurant is set in a charming former residence of a Rana court musician, with a gorgeous garden set off by a modernist glass pavilion. This is grown-up dining and the upscale menu ranges from tapas snacks and all-day breakfasts to home-grown salads and sophisticated dinner mains such as steaks and tempura prawns. It's also a wonderfully romantic place for a drink before or after dinner.

CHEZ CAROLINE

KATHMANDU | $$$ | FRENCH
Baber Mahal Revisited, Tanka Prasad Sadak; 01-4263070; www.chezcarolinenepal.com; mains Rs 600-1600

In the handsomely-restored Baber Mahal Revisited complex, an old Rana-era palace, Caroline's is a sophisticated outdoor bistro loved by expat foodies. Come if you crave French-influenced main courses such as wild-mushroom tart with walnut sauce, Roquefort salad,

Previous page: Daal bhaat tarkari.

and crêpes Suzette with passionfruit sorbet. They also serve fine quiches and pastries, daily specials and a lazy weekend brunch, with a wide range of desserts, teas and wines.

NEW ORLEANS CAFE

KATHMANDU | $$ | INTERNATIONAL

Thamel; 01-4700736; www.facebook.com/neworleanscafethamel; mains Rs 400-570

Hidden down an alley, just north of Kathmandu Guest House, New Orleans pulls in travellers in droves with an intimate candlelit vibe, a classy blues and jazz soundtrack and live music on Wednesdays and Saturdays. Set in a Newari courtyard, it's a fine spot for a romantic cocktail, but the food is also top class, and the menu ranges far and wide, from Thai curries to Creole jambalaya and oven-roasted veggies.

OLD HOUSE

KATHMANDU | $$$ | FRENCH

Lal Durbar Marg; 01-4250931; www.theoldhouse.com.np; mains Rs 800-1250

Easily missed but definitely worth hunting down, this graceful 200-year-old Rana residence is the place to come for wholesome, fresh-flavoured French-Nepali food in classy surroundings. Dishes range from light lunch salads to set five-course tasting menus with standout dishes including the lime trout, Mediterranean-style chicken leg with olives, bacon and wine sauce, and tempting desserts such as lime curd on almond cream. It's also a stylish place for a coffee in the peaceful garden or something stiffer in the patio bar.

NEWARI KITCHEN

PATAN | $$ | NEPALI

Gabahal Rd, Pulchowk; 01-5530570; 9810169601; www.newarikitchen.com.np; set meals Rs 170-520

This Patan favourite is a fine place to start exploring Newari food. Set meals offer an introduction to some of the most popular Nepali staples, or combine a *wo* (lentil) or *chatamari* (rice) pancake with the excellent *pancha kwa* (stew with bamboo shoots, potato and dried mushrooms). Patrons are mostly local Newaris, so you know the food is the real deal. If you really want to dive in face-first, try the *shapo mhicha* (bone marrow wrapped in tripe and deep fried).

WHERE TO EAT...

NEWARI FOOD

Bhojan Griha, Kathmandu
Enjoy fine traditional Nepali dining, sitting on cushions at low tables in a gorgeous 150-year-old mansion, once the home of royal priests. There are performances of traditional dance, but the food and setting are the big drawcards.

Thamel House, Paknajol Kathmandu
Set in a charming old Newari building, Thamel House offers elegant Newari-style dining in a calm courtyard or upstairs on the balcony, with entertainment from local dancers.

Krishnarpan Restaurant, Dwarika's Hotel, Kathmandu
This atmospheric, upscale hotel has an equally atmospheric restaurant, serving fine organic Nepali cuisine amidst ornate brickwork and carved timbers. Topping the menu is a 22-course banquet of Newari staples.

INDIA

Eating in India is a bolt of electricity delivered straight to the tastebuds: a carnival of flavours, colours and smells that transforms every meal into an intense, emotional experience. From the vegetarian goodness of a South Indian roadhouse breakfast to the intensity of sizzling kebabs straight from the tandoor in a lavish Mughlai restaurant, India simply offers the richest, spiciest, most complex cuisine on the planet.

WHAT TO EAT

Tandoori chicken
Best sampled fresh from the oven in Muslim-run restaurants in the Indian north.

Masala dosa
The fuel of the South, this stuffed rice and lentil-flour pancake is loved across the subcontinent.

Palak paneer
Two classic Indian flavours – spiced spinach and clean-on-the-palate cottage cheese – a staple of the northern plains.

Dhal
Spiced lentils take a remarkable variety of forms, from rich, buttery *dhal* fry in the Punjab to red lentil *masoor dhal* in the south.

Samosas
The nation's favourite portable snack, sold sizzling hot at bus stands, train stations and markets.

PRICE RANGES
$ less than Rs 250
$$ Rs 250–800
$$$ Rs 800 or more

Tipping: 10%

AGASHIYE

AHMEDABAD (AMDAVAD) | $$$ | GUJARATI
House of MG, Lal Darwaja; 079-25506946; www.houseofmg.com; set meal regular/deluxe 990/1200

On the rooftop terrace of House of MG, Ahmedabad's finest heritage hotel, Agashiye's daily-changing, all-veg menu begins with a traditional welcome drink before you embark on a cultural journey around the famously sweet, full flavoured and varied Gujarati thali. A multitude of diverse dishes are delivered to your plate before you finish with hand-churned ice cream.

COURTESY INDIAN ACCENT

NIRO'S

JAIPUR | $$$ | INDIAN
319 MI Rd; 0141-2374493; www.nirosindia.com; mains 400-580

Established in 1949, Niro's is a long-standing favourite on MI Rd that, like a good wine, only improves with age. Escape the chaos of the street by ducking into its cool, clean, mirror-ceilinged sanctum to savour veg and nonveg Rajasthani and north Indian cuisine with professional service. To get a feel for the menu, try the *lal maans* (mutton in red masala) or *gatta* curry (gram-flour dumplings in gravy).

INDIQUE

JODHPUR | $$$ | INDIAN
Pal Haveli Hotel, Gulab Sagar; 9672293328; www.palhaveli.com; mains 350-600

The candlelit rooftop restaurant at the Pal Haveli hotel is a dream-like place for a romantic dinner, with swoon-inducing views to the fort, clock tower and Umaid Bhawan. The food covers traditional tandoori, biryanis and North Indian curries, but Rajasthani dishes soar above other offerings – the *laal maas* (mutton curry) is a delight. Ask the bartender to knock you up a gin and tonic before dinner.

BUNDI VILAS

BUNDI | $$ | INDIAN
Balchand Para; 0747-2444614; www.bundivilas.com; set dinner 800

The most romantic restaurant in Bundi, this elegant hotel eatery welcomes visitors from other hotels. Dine in the sheltered, open-sided terrace, or on the rooftop with views of the fort. The kitchen cooks up a Rajasthani feast, and Bundi Vilas has its own farm on the outskirts of Bundi that supplies fresh fruit and vegetables. It's wise to book as spots are limited for the candlelit dinner experience beneath the floodlit palace.

AMBRAI

UDAIPUR | $$$ | NORTH INDIAN
Amet Haveli, Hanuman Ghat; 0294-2431085; www.amethaveliudaipur.com; mains 320-690

'Our signature Dal Bukhara (black lentils) is simmered over the slow coal fires of the tandoor overnight for 18 hours at a stretch.'
Bukhara, Delhi

Set at lakeshore level, looking across the water to the floodlit City Palace in one direction and towards Jagniwas island in the other, this is one highly romantic restaurant at night with candlelit, white-linen tables beneath spreading rayan trees. And the service and cuisine do justice to its fabulous position, with terrific tandoori dishes, intense curries and a well-stocked bar to complement the dining.

KESAR DA DHABA

AMRITSAR | $$ | PUNJABI
Shastri Market, Chowk Passian; 0183-2552103; www.kesardadhaba.com; dishes 75-250, thalis 195-295

Originally founded in Pakistan's Punjab province, this 100-year-old eatery relocated to Amritsar after Partition. Since then it has been serving up delicious paratha thalis and silver-leaf-topped *firni* (ground rice pudding) in small clay bowls, as well as arguably the best lassi in town from this hard-to-find old-city location. Just keep asking the way; everyone knows it.

BUKHARA

DELHI | $$$ | MUGHLAI
ITC Maurya, Sardar Patel Marg; 011-26112233; www.itchotels.in/dining/iconic-brands/bukhara.html; mains 1500-3000

One of Delhi's best (and most expensive) restaurants – regarded by some as the best in India – this hotel eatery with low seating and crazy-paving walls serves wow-factor Northwest Frontier–style cuisine, with silken kebabs and its famous Bukhara *dhal*, black lentils deliciously slow cooked for a day and night. Reservations are essential – don't expect to be able to get a table on the day.

KARIM'S

DELHI | $$ | MUGHLAI
Gali Kababyan; 011-23264981; www.karimhotels.com; mains 120-400

Down a whisper of an alleyway off a lane leading south from the Jama Masjid, Karim's has been delighting carnivores since 1913. Locals flock here for meaty Mughlai treats such as mutton *burrah* (marinated chops), delicious mutton Mughlai, and mutton-and-bread combo *nahari*, a breakfast favourite.

INDIAN ACCENT

DELHI | $$$ | INDIAN
Lodhi Hotel, Lodi Rd; 011-26925151; www.indianaccent.com/newdelhi; dishes 500-1750, tasting menu veg/nonveg 3600/3900

Inside the luxurious Lodhi hotel, Indian Accent lays on one of the capital's most stunning dining experiences. Chef Manish Mehrotra works his magic using seasonal ingredients married in surprising and beautifully creative combinations. The tasting menu is astoundingly good, with wow-factor combinations such as tandoori bacon prawns or paper dosa filled with wild mushrooms and water chestnuts. Dress smart and book well ahead.

'Chef Manish Mehrotra calls his cooking style 'inventive Indian' and 'Indian food with an international accent' or the other way around.'
Indian Accent, Dehli

ALCHI KITCHEN

ALCHI | $$ | LADAKHI
Monastery Rd; 9419438642; www.facebook.com/Alchi.Kitchen; mains 100-280

Alchi Kitchen offers a rare chance to taste traditional Ladakhi foods made with a modern twist. The striking, mod-trad open kitchen runs out flavoursome *skyu* (vegetable stew containing barley pasta, like Italian orecchiette) and *chutagi* (dumpling soup) but there are also saffron paneer momos, stuffed *khambir* (flatbreads) and *kushi pheymar*, a sweet confection of barley and apricot flour, cheese and sugar.

ADHOOS KITCHEN

SRINAGAR | $$$ | KASHMIRI
Adhoos Hotel, Residency Rd; 0194-2472593; www.ahdooshotel.com; mains from 425

This historic restaurant (a century old in 2018) is the classiest place in Srinagar to try meaty *wazwan* (the traditional Kashmiri multicourse meal), with stimulating dishes such as *methi maaz* (mutton with fenugreek) and *rista* (minced lamb meatballs in onion sauce), plus there are succulent kebabs from the tandoor. The service and decor are excellent and you can choose to eat indoors or out on the terrace.

ESPHAHAN

AGRA | $$$ | NORTH INDIAN
Taj East Gate Rd, Oberoi Amarvilas Hotel; 0562-2231515; www.oberoihotels.com/hotels-in-agra-amarvilas-resort/restaurants/esphahan; mains 1550-3500

There are only two sittings each evening at Agra's finest restaurant, so booking ahead is essential. Anything that comes out of the succulent North Indian tandoor is a showstopper (especially the *bharwan aloo*, a potato kebab stuffed with nuts, spices, mint and coriander). Melt-in-your-mouth dishes such as *aloobukhara maaz* (a Mughlai lamb kebab stuffed with prunes) redefine lamb as most know it. While you eat, a live *santoor* player plucks a romantic soundtrack.

DHARBHANGA

VARANASI | $$$ | INDIAN
Brijrama Palace Hotel, Munshi/Darbhanga Ghat; 9129414141; www.brijrama.com/dining/darbhanga; mains 750-1100, thalis 1750

Seriously some of the best Indian food we've ever had. The *palak chaman* (paneer in spinach and spices) is heaven in your mouth and the *aloo chaat* (fried pieces of parboiled potato mixed with chickpeas and chopped onions, and garnished with spices and chutney) is a gourmet street food revelation. For nonguests there's a minimum charge but it's a classy night out that's well worth it.

OUDHYANA

LUCKNOW | $$$ | MUGHLAI
Vivanta by Taj Hotel, Vipin Khand, Gomti Nagar; 0522-6711000; www.tajhotels.com/en-in/taj/taj-mahal-lucknow/restaurants/oudhyana-restaurant; mains 780-900

If you want to savour the flavours of the Nawabs, look no further than Oudhyana at the Vivanta, where Chef Nagendra Singh gives Lucknow's famous Awadh cuisine its royal due at this signature restaurant inside the city's top hotel. The flavours of everything Singh does, from the famous *galawat* and *kakori* kebabs to an entire menu of long-lost heritage dishes, unravel like an intricate gastronomic spy novel in your mouth.

TUNDAY KABABI

LUCKNOW | $ | NORTH INDIAN
Mughlai Naaz Cinema Rd, off Aminabad Rd; 0522-4307223; dishes 44-220

Tucked away just off the bustling main Aminabad chowk, this is the more accessible outlet of Lucknow's renowned, 100-year-old, impossible-to-find kebab shop in Chowk, where buffalo-meat kebabs fly out of the kitchen. Minced-mutton *galawati* kebabs are buttery soft and pack a spicy punch; eat them with silky paratha (Indian-style flaky bread made with ghee and cooked on a hotplate) or a *sheermal* (round bread flavoured with saffron).

WHERE TO EAT...

STREET FOOD

Chandni Chowk, Old Delhi
This Mughal-era bazaar is dotted with hole-in-the-wall canteens serving delicious parathas, *dahi balle* (lentil balls) and *jalebi* (syrupy fried dough).

SNDT to Cross Maiden Khau Gali, Mumbai
A Mumbai *khau gali* ('eat lane') packed with workers feasting on street treats such as *aloo tikki* (spiced potato patties) and *frankies* (spicy roti rolls).

Dacres Lane, Kolkata
Where Kolkata workers come to lunch, with dozens of stalls selling parathas, mutton stews, *bhajia* (fried fritters) and chicken curry and rice.

VV Puram Food Street, Bengaluru (Bangalore)
A carnival of flavours, from hot-from-the-*tawa* rotis to *idli* (rice cakes) and Mumbai-style *chaat* (Indian salad).

6 BALLYGUNGE PLACE

KOLKATA | $$ | BENGALI

6 Ballygunge Pl; 033-24603922; www.6ballygungeplace.in; mains 200-300

Housed in a superbly renovated mid-20th-century mansion, this top-notch restaurant serves some of the best Bengali fare in the capital of West Bengal. If you're confused about the ingredients, spices and gravies, skip the menu and hit the lunch buffet (a veritable banquet of fabulous vegetarian and nonvegetarian treats), and you'll be treated to a fantastic sampling of classic and contemporary Bengali cuisine.

CORNER COURTYARD

KOLKATA | $$$ | FUSION

92B Sarat Bose Rd; 9903990597; www.thecornercourtyard.com; mains 350-550, beers/cocktails 180/350

COURTESY UNDER THE MANGO TREE

P548: Dessert from Indian Accent. This page: Cocktail from Under the Mango Tree. Opposite page: Dish from Indian Accent.

This reincarnated Kolkata mansion from 1904 has had its walls artistically splattered with doorknobs, locks and old books, complementing its stylish distressed-look decor. The menu is creative, imaginative and designed to please discerning foodies, from classic Italian dishes such as margherita pizzas and spaghetti *aglio e olio* to Goan chicken curry from India's western shores, and aromatic sambal fish à la Singapore.

KEWPIES

KOLKATA | $$ | BENGALI

2 Elgin Lane; 033-24861600; thalis 425-800, mains 150-450

Kewpie's is a Kolkata gastronomic institution, and dining here feels like a lavish dinner party in a gently old-fashioned home. Reared to perfection by a speciality Bengali chef, this place serves impeccably traditional and authentic Bengali dishes made from the best local ingredients. Try the hilsa in mustard sauce or the 'steamer' (lamb and potato) curry and be amazed; the food (as well as the experience) is worth every rupee.

NIMTHO

GANGTOK | $$ | SIKKIMESE

MG Marg; www.facebook.com/nimthosikkim; 03592-205324; mains 120-200

Beautifully designed with adobe walls and a mock-up earthen stove, Nimtho gives Sikkimese food a tantalising gourmet twist. Sample a range of local

COURTESY INDIAN ACCENT

treats as part of a local thali, or go à la carte with traditional dishes including *shapta* (wok-fried beef slices), nettle soup, and delicious *ningro churpi* (fiddlehead fern cooked in local cheese). Finish the meal with a pot of *tongba* (warm millet beer).

CHOUKA

JORHAT | $$ | ASSAMESE

Mithapukuri; 9864010280; www.facebook.com/choukajorhat; mains 100-260

In a well-spaced dining room off MG Rd in downtown Jorhat, Chouka's menu is full of bamboo shoots, banana flowers, elephant apple, mustard greens, poultry in sesame-seed sauce, fish in *tenga* (sour) curry and items steamed in banana leaves. You'll be hard-pressed to find better Assamese cooking anywhere. The thalis, available for lunch and dinner, are superb samplers of owner-chef Dhruva Saikia's talent.

LUXMI KITCHEN

IMPHAL | $$ | ADIVASI

Jiribam Rd, Wahengbam Leikai; 0385-2455202; thalis 160

The last word in Manipuri lunch platters, ultra-popular Luxmi does a fabulous *chakluk* (thali) comprising more than a dozen local delicacies such as tangy fish stew, fried fish, leafy greens, *sinju* (a salad with cabbage, lotus stems and chillies), local *dhals, iromba* (fermented fish chutney) and *ngapi* (fermented shrimp paste). A meal here could well be one of the highlights of your Manipur trip.

WHERE TO EAT...

HIGH TEA

The Imperial, Delhi
A feast of cakes and pastries, high tea in the Atrium lounge at the Imperial is a Delhi institution, and a flashback to the final years of the British Raj.

The Taj Mahal Palace, Mumbai
Rising handsomely over Apollo Bunder, Mumbai's most famous hotel lays on a lavish spread of cakes, sandwiches and fine teas in the harbour-facing Sea Lounge.

Rambagh Palace, Jaipur
Feel like a prince in this opulent hotel, the former palace of millionaire maharaja Man Singh II; high tea is served in the Verandah Cafe.

THE BOMBAY CANTEEN

MUMBAI | $$$ | INDIAN
Process House, Kamala Mills, SB Marg; 022-49666666; www.thebombaycanteen.com; small plates 225-650, mains 450-975

In the swish Kamala Mills development, The Bombay Canteen is one of Mumbai's hottest restaurants, courtesy of Top Chef Masters winner Floyd Cardoz, and executive chef Thomas Zacharias, who spent time at New York's three-Michelin-star Le Bernardin. India-wide regional dishes and traditional flavours dominate – Kejriwal toast, Goan pulled-pork-vindaloo tacos, mustard chicken curry – each dish an explosion of texture and flavour.

BOHRI KITCHEN

MUMBAI | $$$ | BOHRI
Colaba; 9819447438; www.thebohrikitchen.com; set menu 1500

Served up in the family home of former Google employee Munaf Kapadia. this weekend-only pop-up dining experience showcases the spectacular home cooking of the Bohra Muslim community, who draw on influences from as far afield as Yemen and Gujarat. You must book ahead and pay a deposit – this is not a traditional restaurant! – and the address is revealed 24 hours in advance. Then settle in for a very special afternoon with the Kapadia family.

BASTIAN

MUMBAI | $$$ | SEAFOOD
B/1, New Kamal Bldg, Linking Rd, Bandra (W); 7045083714; www.bastianrestaurant.com; mains for 2 1100-3200

All the praise bestowed upon this trendy seafooder in the hip neighbourhood of Bandra is warranted. Canadian-Chinese chef Kelvin Cheung, has forged an East-meets-West gastronomic dream. Go with the market-fresh side menu: choose your catch (prawns, fish, mud crab or lobster) then pick from an insanely tempting list of impossibly tasty pan-Asian sauces.

TRISHNA

MUMBAI | $$$ | SEAFOOD
Ropewalk Ln, Kala Ghoda; 022-22703214; mains 460-1830

Behind a modest entrance on a quiet Kala Ghoda lane is this often-lauded, intimate South Indian seafood restaurant. It's not a trendy place – the decor is endearingly old school, the seating a little cramped and the menu overlong – but the cooking is superb. Just sample the quality of the Hyderabadi fish tikka, jumbo prawns with green-pepper sauce, and the outstanding king crab and lobster dishes.

GRAPEVINE

MAHABALESHWAR | $$$ | MULTICUISINE
Masjid Rd; 02168-261100; mains 170-950

Way too hip for Mahabaleshwar, this classy restaurant/wine bar is unmissable. Chef/owner Raio's culinary pedigree includes Taj Hotels and his creative takes on Parsi and fresh seafood are divine. The monstrous Mediterranean lamb burger (with feta and harissa mayo) and the soft-shell crab burger are worth the trip here alone, ditto the spicy tiger prawns, lamb shanks and lobster. Wrought-iron tables set up among stone walls lend a Mediterranean air.

MALAKA SPICE

PUNE | $$$ | ASIAN
Lane 5, North Main Rd, Koregaon Park; 7507011226; www.malakaspice.com; mains 340-710

Maharashtra's shining culinary moment is a fury of Southeast Asian fantasticness; trying to choose one dish among the delectable stir-fries, noodles and curries – all come in seafood, chicken, duck, mutton and vegetarian incarnations – is futile. Dine alfresco under colourful tree lights and relish the spicy and intricate flavour cavalcade from star chefs reared on a Slow Food, stay-local philosophy.

'Each dish and drink has a story to tell, promising you an exciting journey on a plate (and in a glass)!'
The Bombay Canteen, Mumbai

UNDER THE MANGO TREE

BHOPAL | $$$ | MUGHLAI
Jehan Numa Palace Hotel, 157 Shyamla Hills; 0755-2661100; www.jehannuma.com/palace-bhopal/dining/under-the-mango-tree-barbeque-grills.html; mains 400-750

The lavish Jehan Numa Palace's most refined restaurant specialises in barbecue kebabs and tandoor dishes (including vegetarian options). Almost everything on the menu is top-class, but the sampler platter of varied kebabs, from moist Northwest Frontier-style *chapli* kebabs to kofte-like *galouti* kebabs, may well be the best meal you have in Madhya Pradesh.

BLACK SHEEP BISTRO

PANAJI | $$$ | EUROPEAN
Swami Vivekanand Rd; 0832-2222901; www.blacksheepbistro.in; tapas 250-400, mains 350-600

Among the best of Panaji's burgeoning boutique restaurants, Black Sheep's impressive pale-yellow facade gives way to a sexy dark-wood bar and loungy dining room. The tapas dishes are light, fresh and expertly prepared in keeping with their farm-to-table philosophy. Salads, pasta, seafood and dishes like lamb *osso buco* grace the menu, while an internationally trained sommelier matches food to wine.

ZEEBOP BY THE SEA

BETALBATIM, MAJORDA & UTORDA | $$$ | SEAFOOD
Utorda Beach; 0832-2755333; www.zeeboprestaurantgoa.com; mains 200-500

The most famous beachfront restaurant north of Colva, Zeebop is renowned for its excellent seafood and party spirit. Stylish and award-winning Zeebop is set a little back from Utorda's main beach but still has a sandy floor, and the freshly caught fish – mackerel, kingfish, squid, tiger prawns, lobster, oysters, red snapper, sea bass, barracuda – is expertly prepared. It's a firm favourite with locals and is popular for weddings and parties so book ahead.

COURTESY BOMBAY CANTEEN

This page: Dish from The Bombay Canteen. Opposite page: Malabar House.

MAVALLI TIFFIN ROOMS

BENGALURU | $ | SOUTH INDIAN
14 Lalbagh Rd, Mavalli; 080-22220022; www.mavallitiffinrooms.com; snacks from 52, meals from 90

A legendary name in South Indian comfort food, this agreeably informal place has had Bengaluru eating out of its hand since 1924. Head up to the dining room, queue for a table, and then sit back and enjoy as waiters bring you delicious *idli* (fermented rice cakes) and *dosa*, capped by frothing filter coffee served in silverware. It's a definitive Bengaluru experience.

SODABOTTLE-OPENERWALA

BENGALURU | $$$ | PARSI
25/4 Lavelle Rd; 7022255299; www.sodabottleopenerwala.in; snacks from 55, meals 300-500

This terrific, growing Indian chain is gaining an excellent reputation for its brilliant comfort-food menu of Persian soups and Parsi specials like *salli boti* (mutton served with matchstick potatoes). The Bengaluru incarnation offers a kooky spin on a Bombay Irani cafe, with mismatched seating, clashing colours and quirky ornaments. Definitely order a rich, creamy and foamy Phateli coffee or Irani chai to finish your meal.

SHAH GHOUSE CAFE

HYDERABAD | $$ | HYDERABADI
Shah Ali Banda Rd; 040-24524506; mains 80-310

During Ramadan, foodie Hyderabadis rich and poor line up for Shah Ghouse's famous *haleem* (a rich, thick soup of pounded spiced wheat, with goat, chicken or beef, and lentils) but any time of year the mutton biryani is near-perfect. Don't expect romantic ambience: just delicious traditional food, served in a no-frills upstairs dining hall. Wash it down with a delicious lassi.

MALABAR HOUSE

KERALA | $$$ | INTERNATIONAL
Parade Ground Rd, Fort Cochin; 0484-2216666; www.malabarhouse.com; mains 450-800, tasting menus 2500

Set in an open-sided pavilion or at candlelit poolside tables, the outstanding restaurant at Malabar House is (almost) Bollywood-star glam. The ambitious East-meets-West menu creatively fuses local and European flavours – the signature dish is a stacked-high seafood platter, or try an elegant 'trilogy' of Indian curries.

VILLA MAYA

THIRUVANANTHAPURAM (TRIVANDRUM) | $$$ | KERALAN
120 Airport Rd, Injakkal; 0471-2578901; www.villamaya.in; mains 600-1600

Villa Maya is more an experience than a mere restaurant. Dining is either in the magnificent 18th-century Dutch-built mansion or in private curtained niches in the tranquil courtyard garden. The Keralan cuisine is expertly crafted, delicately spiced and beautifully presented. Seafood is a speciality,

COURTESY MALABAR HOUSE

though there are some tantalising vegetarian offerings too.

HOTEL SARAVANA BHAVAN

CHENNAI | $ | SOUTH INDIAN
70 North Mada St, Mylapore; 044-24611177; www.saravanabhavan.com; mains 125-250, thalis 125-155

Settle in for the ultimate all-veg South Indian thali at this uberpopular Chennai chain. Don't come for ambience or glamour, come for flavour! It's great for lunch and dinner thalis but also excellent for South Indian breakfasts (*idlis*, *vadas*, dosas and *uttapams*), filter coffee and veg offerings from across India. The air-conditioned hall provides a welcome cool environments.

PAKISTAN

Pakistani food draws on the same rich palette of spices as India, but ramps up the influences from Persia and Central Asia. Whether you fine dine in Islamabad or Karachi or feast on the streets in Lahore, menus are only superficially different from the meals served to Mughal emperors.

WHAT TO EAT

Nihari
A slow-cooked feast of mutton, ginger, onion and masala spices, brought to central Pakistan from the Mughal kitchens of Delhi and Hyderabad.

Aloo gosht
The nation's favourite lunch – a rich curry of meat and potatoes, served almost everywhere.

Dum Puhkt
A cooking style, not a dish, where meat and rice or vegetables are slow-cooked in an earthenware pot sealed with dough, a speciality of the central plains.

Pulao
Rice cooked with meat, stock and spices – this Central Asian speciality came to Pakistan's Northwest Frontier province via Afghanistan.

PRICE RANGES
For a main course:
$ less than Rs 400
$$ Rs 400–1300
$$$ Rs 1300 or more

Tipping: Not customary; small bills appreciated.

AL HAAJ BUNDOO KHAN

KARACHI | $ | PAKISTANI
MA Jinnah Rd; 315 230 6154; www.alhaajbundookhan.com; mains Rs 120-600

Open since before partition, Al Haaj Bundoo Khan is unashamedly old-fashioned, but it still serves the same drool-inducing parathas, kebabs and chicken tikka that pulled in the crowds before India and Pakistan were yoinked apart. Branches are scattered around the city, but the original MA Jinnah Rd branch has the most loyal following. Don't expect flashy flourishes, just hearty, homestyle Pakistani cooking at bargain prices.

KOLACHI

KARACHI | $$$ | PAKISTANI, INTERNATIONAL
Beach Ave; (0)21 111 111 001; www.facebook.com/KolachiSpiritofkarachi; mains Rs 500-1600

Sprawling over a cascade of wooden decks overlooking the Arabian Sea, Kolachi is undeniably the most atmospheric place to eat al fresco in Karachi. Sea breezes drive away the city fug, and the swoosh of the ocean provides a calm soundtrack while you gorge on sumptuously spiced boti kebabs, tandoori treats and a fine range of *handi-* and *karahi*-cooked masala dishes by the light of dangling lanterns.

SAKURA

KARACHI | $$$ | JAPANESE
Pearl Continental Hotel, Club Rd; (0)21 111 505 505; www.pchotels.com/pckarachi; mains Rs 575-4100

Live teppanyaki chefs, bamboo screens and imperial purple upholstery set the scene at the swish Japanese restaurant that gazes out over the city from the top of Karachi's top five-star hotel. Pakistani food is rich and delicious but heavy on oils and fats; you'll have no such problems with Sakura's delicate, light-on-the-palate seared salmon tataki and sushi and sashimi plates.

CAFE AYLANTO

LAHORE | $$$ | INTERNATIONAL
MM Alam Road, Gulberg III; 042-575 1886; www.facebook.com/Cafe.Aylanto; mains Rs 530-1535

When locals tire of lavish spices, they head to elegant Cafe Aylanto for a feast of modern European fare, from French escargot to steak with chanterelle mushrooms, minted lamb and prawn linguine. Served in a calm, grown-up dining room, or out under the stars on the terrace, this is cooking with class, for diners who know good flavours when they taste them.

HAVELI

LAHORE | $$$ | MUGHLAI
2170-A, Food St, Fort Rd; 321 465 1051; www.haveli.com.pk; mains Rs 845-1795

Fancy living like a Mughal? Housed in a towering *haveli*-style building on restaurant-crammed Fort Rd Food Street, Haveli looks out onto Aurangzeb's Badshahi Mosque through carved wooden windows. The menu, as you might expect, draws on the lavish traditions of the Mughal court – expect fine interpretations of classic Mughlai dishes such as mutton karahi, tandoori *jengha* (prawns) and boti kebabs.

'The fusion of indigenous flavors and aromas with culinary bequests from Arabia, Persia and Central Asia'
The Monal, Islamabad

THE MONAL

ISLAMABAD | $$$ | PAKISTANI
Pir Sohawa Road, Margalla Hills; +92 51 2898044 Ext 55; www.themonal.com; mains Rs 775-3595

Savvy Islamabad diners flee the city limits for the calm greenery of the Margalla Hills, where The Monal serves up fine Pakistani cooking on tiered terraces overlooking the twinkling city lights. The menu cherry-picks dishes from across Asia and Europe, but it's the Pakistani cooking that stands out – meaty gola, boti and kabuli kebabs, chicken and mutton tikka, best sampled in the form of huge, gut-busting platters and mixed grills.

DUMANI

GILGIT | $$ | MULTICUISINE
Gilgit Serena Hotel, Jutial; 5811 455894; www.serenahotels.com/serenagilgit/en/dining/default/dumani-restaurant.html; mains Rs 200-600

The wide, greenery cloaked facade of the Gilgit Serena Hotel hides the town's best restaurant, and the last chance for a lavish banquet spread before hitting the most dramatic and rugged section of the Karakoram Hwy. There's an à la carte menu, but most make a beeline for the buffet, which is piled high with full-flavoured Pakistani, Chinese and continental dishes.

SRI LANKA

Sri Lanka built its fortunes on tea and spices, and its cuisine is a map of medieval trade routes. Whether eating at local 'hotels' or lavish fine-dining restaurants, you'll taste the Indian influence everywhere, melded with local flavours in rich sauces, chutneys, marinated meats and pan-fried breads, and joined by subtle notes from Southeast Asia and the Middle East, and Europe, owing to Sri Lanka's colonial past.

WHAT TO EAT

Hoppers
A Sri Lankan staple, these bowl-shaped pancakes are dished up fresh from the pan and used to mop up spicy sauces.

Curry & Rice
The national dish comes in an amazing variety of forms, all delicious; sample it in restaurants and cafes, at roadside stalls, and even on trains.

Kotthu
Listen for click of chopping knives at restaurants serving this Sri Lankan treat of chopped *rotti* bread fried with spices and vegetables.

Pol Sambol
Meals everywhere gain extra pep from this fiery condiment of shredded coconut, lime juice, red onion and chilli.

PRICE RANGES
$ less than Rs 250
$$ Rs 250–800
$$$ Rs 800 or more

Tipping: 10%

HOTEL DE PILAWOOS

COLOMBO | $ | SRI LANKAN
417 Galle Rd; 077 741 7417; www.en-gb.facebook.com/Pilawoos; meals Rs 200-400

Just known as Pilawoos, this open-fronted purveyor of short eats is renowned for what may be the best *kotthu* (*rotti* sliced up with cheese and other fillings and fried) in town. Expect the mighty and the humble to drop by any time of day to grab some; take our advice and have the cheese version, and chase it with a fresh juice.

MINISTRY OF CRAB

COLOMBO | $$$ | SEAFOOD
Old Dutch Hospital, Col 1; 011-234 2722; www.ministryofcrab.com; mains Rs 2000-8000

Set beneath a soaring, timbered roof, this high-profile restaurant celebrates crawling crustaceans in a startling variety of ways, from Singaporean chilli crab to locally spiced crab curry and baked 2kg monsters – the garlic pepper preparation is sublime. Two owners are former captains of the Sri Lanka cricket team, while famous chef Dharshan Munidasa guides things in the kitchen.

NIHONBASHI HONTEN

COLOMBO | $$$ | JAPANESE
11 Galle Face Tce; 011-232 3847; www.nihonbashi.lk; mains from Rs 1200

Gird the expense account for an adventure at Colombo's best Japanese restaurant. The sushi, donburi and Kobe beef are as good as you can find anywhere in Asia. The interior is jewel-like, the food refined and the service superb. Don't miss the Yakitori Garden, where you can savour sake and cocktails surrounded by bamboo.

T-LOUNGE BY DILMAH

COLOMBO | $$ | CAFE
Dutch Sq, 18 Chatham St, Col 1; 011-244 7168; www.dilmaht-lounge.com; mains Rs 500-900

A spin-off from Sri Lanka's top tea producer, Dilmah, this gem of a cafe is in an annexe to the Old Dutch Hospital. The interior complements the restored colonial exterior: the walls are lined with books about Sri Lanka and tea, while the menu – as you might expect – is offers a tasting tour of Sri Lankan teas, plus crepes, sandwiches and desserts, and cocktails.

SANCTUARY AT TISSAWEWA

ANURADHAPURA | $$$ | INTERNATIONAL
off Old Puttalam Rd; 025-222 2299; www.tissawewa.com; mains Rs 800 1600

There is no more atmospheric place for a leisurely meal or drink than the veranda or dining room of this beautiful colonial hotel. Try the chilli-marinated grilled pork chops, a club sandwich or the four-course set dinner – rich in fusion flavours – followed by coffee, served in white embossed china cups. It's a feast, but no alcohol is served.

RIVIERA RESORT

BATTICALOA | $$ | SRI LANKAN
New Dutch Bar Rd, Kallady; 065-222 2164; www.riviera-online.com; meals Rs 350-1000

'Crabs are the stars of the show at Ministry of Crab, from 500g "small" crabs to 2kg "Crabzillas".'
Ministry of Crab, Colombo

Dining here evokes memories of colonial times, as smartly dressed waiters fix you up with a drink (ideally a gin and tonic) on the veranda, take your order and beckon you into the dining room (or onto the terrace), then set you up with all manner of flavoursome Sri Lankan dishes. The food is well worth the wait, with excellent lagoon crab, prawn and cashew curries and other seafood fresh from the bay.

SANA'S

UPPUVELI | $$$ | SRI LANKAN
Sarvodaya Rd; 077 700 4047; mains Rs 500-2000

A fine example of why the Sarvodaya Rd strip is becoming one of the most interesting eating neighbourhoods on the east coast. This restaurant is a two-level driftwood dream. The main menu is pocket friendly, but you can splurge on lobster and seafood mixed grills, plus all sorts of other seafood creations in richly spiced sauces.

CAFE CHILLI

ELLA | $$ | INTERNATIONAL
Main St; 077 180 4020; www.facebook.com/cafechillnescoffeeshop; meals Rs 500-800

Run by an engaging local team, this huge, stylish cafe-bar-restaurant goes from strength to strength. The upper deck is scattered with cushions and tables under a sculpted, wave-inspired wooden roof, and the food is a delight, from flavoursome local dishes such as *lamprais* (a Dutch-era dish of mixed

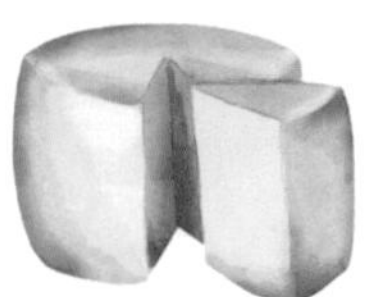

curries and rice wrapped in a banana leaf) to well-prepared Western imports and espresso coffee.

GRAND INDIAN

NUWARA ELIYA | $$$ | INDIAN
Grand Hotel Rd; 052-222 2881; www.thegrandhotelnuwaraeliya.com; mains Rs 600-1300

Far and away Nuwara Eliya's favourite restaurant, this upscale hotel restaurant at the graceful, colonial-era Grand is phenomenally popular. Diners often have to wait for a table – a surefire marker for quality food. The food here is the rich, delicious fare of northern India; to kick off, try the *palek* paneer (puréed spinach with fresh cheese) or perfectly spiced tandoori chicken.

COURTESY BEDSPACE KITCHEN

This page: Bedspace Kitchen. Opposite page: Dish from Bedspace Kitchen.

HILL CLUB

NUWARA EILYA | $$$ | BRITISH
29 Grand Hotel Rd; 052-222 2653; www.hillclubsrilanka.lk; set menu US$25

Dinner at the mock-Tudor Hill Club is an event in itself. The menu focuses on traditional English dishes such as roast beef with all the trimmings and rich puddings, and the whole thing is carried off with faded colonial panache. All diners must wear formal attire; ties and jackets are available at reception, and there's a temporary joining fee if you are not staying at the club.

CHURCH STREET SOCIAL

GALLE | $$$ | INTERNATIONAL
Fort Bazaar Hotel, 26 Church St; 077 363 8381; www.teardrop-hotels.com; meals Rs1200-3500

A classy retreat from Galle's steamy streets, this refined air-conditioned hotel restaurant is the perfect setting for a great meal, with the formality of its colonial dining rooms offset with hip lighting to eclectic effect. The menu is varied: light lunch sandwiches, wraps and burgers, sophisticated starters including fine tuna sashimi, and gourmet mains such as Moroccan lamb tagine and pork tenderloin.

BEDSPACE KITCHEN

UNAWATUNA | $$$ | INTERNATIONAL
Egodawatta Lane; 091-225 0156; www.bedspaceuna.com; mains Rs 900-1600

COURTESY BEDSPACE KITCHEN

One of the most progressive, enjoyable restaurants in the country, Bedspace Kitchen has it all right. Around 95% of their ingredients are sourced in Sri Lanka, most are organic and local, and food is served under an airy canopy. Stand-out dishes include black pork curry, a sublime sea platter, and coconut lemongrass soup; lunch is more casual. Book ahead as it's wildly, deservedly popular.

LORDS RESTAURANT

NEGOMBO | $$$ | FUSION

80B Porutota Rd, Ethukala; 077 285 3190; www.lordsrestaurant.net; dishes Rs 900-1500

By far Negombo's most creative eating experience, with dishes that fuse Western and Eastern flavours. Martin, the British owner, works on the floor and in the kitchen, making sure that everything is spot on. The Thai and Sri Lankan curries are strongly recommended, especially the prawn, coconut and arak curry, or you could always swing by for a mango and passionfruit mojito.

WHERE TO EAT...

SWEETS

Bombay Sweet Mahal, Colombo
Galle Rd's finest purveyor of sweet Indian treats such as *barfi* (milk fudge) and nut *musket* (semolina, nut and lemon sweets).

Rio Ice Cream, Jaffna
Jaffna's favourite stop for cold treats does a lively trade in pineapple and mango ice cream, *faluda* (rose milk with vermicelli) and syrup-topped sundaes.

Dairy King, Galle
No relation to the more famous Dairy Queen, this landmark Galle parlour serves delectable cashew, tea, ginger and passionfruit ice cream, and sticky, moreish cakes.

Cinnamon Lodge, Habarana
This swish Habarana Hotel is legendary for its sweet-toothed buffet, with a whole room devoted to desserts.

MALDIVES

Maldivian food draws on the rich bounty of the sea, and spices and cooking know-how carried on the waves from India and Sri Lanka. *Hedhikaa* (short eats) are best sampled in the teashops of the capital, Male, but Maldives' lavish resorts can rustle up a seafood feast fit for an emperor.

WHAT TO EAT

Hedhikaa
Maldive's deliciously spicy, fish-based 'short eats' are best enjoyed in the humble teashops dotted around Male and other inhabited islands.

Mas huni
The breakfast of Maldives, this medley of tuna , coconut, onion and chilli is munched cold with hot *roshi* bread. Find it in local cafes and in hotel buffets.

Garudia
A full-flavoured soup of dried, smokey fish, pepped up with lime and chilli and poured over rice – a popular lunch in local restaurants on inhabited islands.

Lobster
Local lobsters make it onto the menu in astonishingly extravagant preparations in the islands' top resorts.

PRICE RANGES
$ less than Rf100
$$ Rf100–250
$$$ Rf250 or more

Tipping: Not customary; service charge is normally added.

ITHAA UNDERSEA RESTAURANT

RANGALIFINOLHU & RANGALI ISLANDS, SOUTH ARI ATOLL | $$$ | MODERN EUROPEAN

Conrad Maldives; 668 0629; www.conradmaldives.com/dine/ithaa-undersea-restaurant; Set menu from US$390

Sure, the Conrad Maldives' signature restaurant is trading partly on its setting, but gosh, what a setting. The curving, glass-canopied dining room is literally under the sea, with fish swimming overhead in the 5m of brilliant blue ocean between you and the surface. You'll feel a bit like a James Bond supervillain as you dine on gastronomic treats such as lobster and snow crab with mango gel, and mustard-marinated Wagyu beef.

FRESH IN THE GARDEN

KUNFUNADHOO ISLAND, BAA ATOLL | $$$ | INTERNATIONAL

Soneva Fushi Resort; www.soneva.com/soneva-fushi/dining; 660 0304; mains from US$69

Castaway-style rope and timber walkways lead to dining tables perched above the tree canopy at Soneva Fushi's most atmospheric eatery. It's the Robinson Crusoe fantasy upgraded to high gastronomy, and the food – imaginative modern European, with subtle nods to Asia and the Middle East – is nothing short of spectacular. Come for such creative combinations as job fish served with organic pumpkin and endives.

BY THE SEA

LANKANFUSHI, NORTH MALE ATOLL | $$$ | JAPANESE

Gili Lankanfushi Resort; 664 0304; www.gili-lankanfushi.com/dine/by-the-sea; Mains US$30-125

The gourmet Japanese restaurant at the Gili Lankanfushi resort is effortlessly refined, and arguably the best spot in the islands to sample melt-on-the-tongue sushi and sashimi prepared with the fresh catch of the Indian Ocean. The setting is low key and intimate, beneath a leaf-lined canopy by the water, with a teppanyaki chef preparing dishes to order while you watch.

BARAABARU

KUDA HURAA, NORTH MALE ATOLL | $$$ | INDIAN

Four Seasons Resort Maldives at Kuda Huraa; 664 4888; www.fourseasons.com/maldiveskh/my_four_seasons/baraabaru; mains from US$20-100

Canopy-covered pavilions open directly on to the sea at the Four Seasons' landmark Indian restaurant, which draws inspiration from the sumptuous cooking of Kerala. Organic ingredients come fresh from farms in India, fulfilling the restaurant's commitment to authentic flavours. Standout dishes include Malabar *jhinga* (prawns marinated in coconut and turmeric) and pomfret wrapped in banana leaves.

FEELING KOI

HUVAFEN FUSHI, NORTH MALE ATOLL | $$$ | JAPANESE

Huvafen Fushi Resort; 664 4222; www.huvafenfushi.com/feeling-koi; mains from US$31-82

The wooden decks seem to melt into the ocean at Huvafen Fushi's best restaurant. The food is rather impressive too: Izakaya-style Japanese cooking with a hat tipped to Latin America, which translates to sumiso-marinated Maldivian tuna with morel mushrooms and Wagyu beef tacos. Flavours are fresh and layered, lingering on the palate long after the sun has dipped into the Indian Ocean.

'We're all about home-style authenticity, not fusion. That means fresh food, with as little fat and oil as possible.'

Baraabaru, Four Seasons Resort Maldives at Kuda Huraa

SALA THAI

MALE | $$$ | THAI

Buruneege; 334 5959; www.salafamilymaldives.com; mains Rf150-200

This smart and beautifully designed restaurant is generally held to be the best on the island, pulling in a crowd most nights of the week. The Thai menu is sumptuous and thoroughly authentic, with a huge choice of soups, noodles and curries full of sparkling Thai flavours of chilli, sweet basil and lemongrass. Eat al fresco on the charming walled terrace, or inside in a plush dining room.

DAWN CAFÉ

MALE | $ | MALDIVIAN

Haveeree Hingun; short eats from Rf10

One of the best teashops in Maldives' pint-sized capital, and due to its fish-market location it's phenomenally popular with fishermen and open around the clock. Come in the morning for a breakfast feast of excellent fish-themed *hedhikaa* (short eats), or swing by on Friday afternoon when people come in after going to the mosque, and plug into real Maldivian cooking.

OCEAN

NIA

AUSTRALIA

With climates as disparate as the cool reaches of Tasmania and the colourful tastes of tropics, plus world-famous vineyards and fresh, clean local produce, Australia is one of the world's great dining destinations. From the punchy flavours of indigenous bush tucker to effortlessly refined degustation menus, there is a continent of gastronomic delights packed into the Land Down Under.

WHAT TO EAT

Meat pies The ubiquitous Aussie pie now comes in gourmet versions with a side of mash or served food-truck style in a paper bag.

Vegemite Universally loved (pretty much), this umami-flavoured yeast extract is best dabbed on buttery toast; even better with some smashed avocado.

Kangaroo The national icon's lean, venison-like meat is revered in the country's top kitchens and many a local pub too.

Barramundi This delicious sea bass is best when just hauled from a Top End waterway.

Bowen mangoes Named for the Queensland town where they grow, these sunset-coloured beauties may be the sweetest, juiciest mangoes you'll ever eat.

PRICE RANGES

$ less than $20
$$ $20–40
$$$ $40 or more

Tipping: 5–10%

ARIMIA

MARGARET RIVER | $$ | WINERY

242 Quininup Rd, Wilyabrup; 08-9755 2528; www.arimia.com.au; tasting menu $90 per person

Down an unsealed road in dreamy, pastoral Margaret River you'll find this organic, biodynamic winery, with a restaurant serving excellent seasonal meals. Local delicacies such as Busselton octopus and foraged mushrooms are augmented by ingredients sourced from the property and matched to the chardonnay-, verdelho-, grenache- and syrah-based wines made here.

WILDFLOWER

CENTRAL PERTH | $$$ | MODERN AUSTRALIAN

State Bldgs, 1 Cathedral Ave; 08-6168 7855; www.wildflowerperth.com.au; tasting menus $145 per person

Filling a glass pavilion atop the restored State Buildings, Wildflower offers fine-dining menus inspired by the six seasons of the Noongar people of WA. There's a passionate focus on West Australian produce: dishes might include Rottnest Island scallops or kangaroo smoked over jarrah embers, as well as indigenous herbs and bush plants like lemon myrtle, native thyme and wattle seed.

LONG CHIM

CENTRAL PERTH | $$$ | THAI

State Bldgs, cnr St Georges Tce & Barrack St; 08-6168 7775; www.longchimperth.com; mains $28-40

David Thompson, guru of Thai street food, is the force behind this exceptional restaurant. Dishes like the Chiang Mai chicken larb (salad with fresh herbs, roasted rice and chilli) and sour, orange curry of fish definitely don't fight shy of challenging Western palates, while the spicy pork with rice cakes is the perfect appetiser.

BREAD IN COMMON

FREMANTLE | $$ | BISTRO, BAKERY
43 Pakenham St; 08-9336 1032; www.breadincommon.com.au; sharing plates $18-27

Follow the irresistible aroma to the in-house bakery before staying on for cheese and charcuterie platters, or larger, refined-yet-comforting dishes such as lamb ribs, cuttlefish and artichokes with borlotti beans. Shared tables and a chic warehouse ambience encourage conversation over WA wines and craft brews.

PEE WEE'S AT THE POINT

DARWIN | $$$ | AUSTRALIAN
Alec Fong Lim Dr, East Point; 08-8981 6868; www.peewees.com.au; mains $44-48

Arguably Darwin's premier kitchen, this place is indeed a treat. Enjoy double-roasted duckling with Kakadu plum or wild-caught barramundi in macadamia, herb and lemon-crust myrtle among tropical palms at East Point Reserve, right on the waterfront.

MARKSIE'S CAMP TUCKER

KATHERINE | $$ | AUSTRALIAN
363 Gorge Rd; 0427 112 806; www.marksiescamptucker.com.au; adults/children $65/30

Geoff Mark's (Marksie's) re-created stockman's camp, 7km from Katherine, is the setting for a night of fabulous food and storytelling. He prepares a three-course set menu that might include crocodile, wild-caught barramundi, camel, buffalo and/or kangaroo, all cooked over camp ovens and enlivened by native spices and hilarious bush yarns.

"'Our cuisine is very seasonal 'Our menus aim to reflect the produce, climate and multiculturalism of the Northern Territory'. *Lily Matthews, Pee Wee's at the Point*

AFRICOLA

CENTRAL ADELAIDE | $$ | AFRICAN
4 East Tce; 08-8223 3885; www.africola.com.au; mains $19-38

Adelaide's most hyped restaurant deserves the limelight: its generous, irreverent attitude has challenged fine-dining norms across the city. Expect plenty of colour and noise inside the lovely old bluestone building, and enjoy the likes of lamb-neck curry with whey pickles or salted cabbage with peanut achar (pickle) and green mango.

CENTRAL MARKET

CENTRAL ADELAIDE | $ | MARKET
44-60 Gouger St; 08-8203 7494; www.adelaidecentralmarket.com.au

Adelaide's Market is a barrage of smells, colours and the cries of stallholders selling fresh vegetables, breads, cheeses, seafood and gourmet produce.

ORANA

CENTRAL ADELAIDE | $$$ | MODERN AUSTRALIAN
Level 1, 285 Rundle St; 08-8232 3444; www.restaurantorana.com; tasting menus from $195 per person

Much-acclaimed Orana is a secretive beast, with minimal signage and access via a black staircase. Upstairs, rock-star chef Jock Zonfrillo's 10- and 16-course tasting menus await: expect intriguing plate such as cream of indigenous bunya nut with wild trout roe and long yam crisp, or crocodile soup with Australian botanicals.

D'ARENBERG CUBE

MCLAREN VALE | $$$ | FUSION

58 Osborn Rd; 08-8329 4888; www.darenberg.com.au/darenberg-cube-restaurant; tasting menu $210 per person

The vision of winemaker Chester Osborn, the d'Arenberg Cube is an eccentric, surprising place. Basically a multi-tiered, black-and-white Rubiks-style Cube, it houses a museum, wine tastings, and a fabulous restaurant with tasting menus highlighting the region's best produce.

FINO SEPPELTSFIELD

TANUNDA | $$$ | MODERN AUSTRALIAN

730 Seppeltsfield Rd, Seppeltsfield; 08-8562 8528; www.fino.net.au; set menus from $48 per person

One of Australia's best winery restaurants, Fino lives in the gorgeous 1851 Seppeltsfield estate. Food from the understated sharing menu highlights local ingredients – try the dry-aged rib eye with chard gratin, or the barramundi (Australian sea bass) with kohlrabi and snow peas.

PRAWN STAR

CAIRNS | $$ | SEAFOOD

E-Finger, Berth 31, Marlin Marina; 0456 421 172; www.facebook.com/prawnstarcairns; seafood $25-90

Peddling the freshest seafood from a dockside trawler, Prawn Star is tropical dining perfection. Clamber aboard and fill yourself with prawns, mud crabs, oysters and whatever else was caught that day, while taking in harbour views.

FLAMES OF THE FOREST

PORT DOUGLAS | $$$ | MODERN AUSTRALIAN

07-4099 3144; www.flamesoftheforest.com.au; dinner, drinks, show and transport from Port Douglas $224 per adult

Diners are escorted deep into the rainforest for a truly immersive night of theatre, culture and gourmet

Opening spread from left: Dishes from Subo; Sunda; Beef stew from Marksie's Camp Tucker; Dishes from Public Kitchen; Pork belly from Logan Brown. This page: Dish from Wildflower. Opposite page: d'Arenberg Cube.

OPENING SPREAD CREDITS: COURTESY SUBO, SUNDA, MARKSIE'S CAMP TUCKER, PUBLIC KITCHEN, LOGAN BROWN

COURTESY DARENBURG CUBE

cuisine. The seven-course banquet is accompanied by Australian wines, and Tuesday and Thursday dinners include an indigenous cultural experience.

URBANE

CENTRAL BRISBANE | $$$ | MODERN AUSTRALIAN

181 Mary St; 07-3229 2271; www.urbanerestaurant.com; set menus from $120 per person

Urbane's food bursts with intrigue and delight, from the pairing of ingredients to their presentation. Choose from two tasting menus – omnivore and herbivore – offered as five- or seven-course options, dive into the excellent wine list, and book ahead.

VAQUERO DINING

ALBION | $$ | AUSTRALIAN

344 Sandgate Rd; 07-3862 3606; www.vaquerodining.com.au; mains $26-34

Vaquero Dining has three obsessions: local produce, pickling and charcoal cooking. Expect beautifully executed dishes like wood-fired octopus with pickled white garlic and smoked-almond harissa, or smoked oysters with ocean trout and habanero-watermelon salad.

HAPPY BOY

FORTITUDE VALLEY | $ | CHINESE

East St; 0413 246 890; www.happyboy.com.au; mains $17-22

Fun, loud and always pumping, this place draws all types with its

WHERE TO EAT... PUB FOOD

Rose & Crown, Guildford WA
Serving since 1841, this pub offers top-shelf comestibles such as rabbit 'carbonara' and Feral Brewing's 'Perth Local'.

Napier Hotel, Melbourne VIC
A classic example of Melbourne's gregarious, Victorian-era pubs; drop in to meet the locals over a pot and some peppered kangaroo.

Duke of Clarence, Sydney NSW
The Sunday roast at this book-lined facsimile of an 18th-century English tavern will set you up for the week ahead.

New Sydney Hotel, Hobart TAS
This convivial, downtown-Hobart pub serves adventurous food like yakitori duck hearts and abalone schnitzel.

toothsome takes on big flavours from across China's regions. Dive into smashing dishes like twice-cooked dry-and-sticky beef rib, Chongqing chilli chicken, and smoky, burnt broccolini with black-bean butter.

SUMI OPEN KITCHEN

NOOSA | $$ | JAPANESE
4/19-21 Sunshine Beach Rd, Noosa Junction; 07-5447 3270; www.sumiopenkitchen.com.au; set menus from $60 per person

Intimate Sumi offers a set menu prepared before your eyes by owner/chef Giles Hohnen. From delicate *hiramasa* king fish with miso, daikon, shimeji mushrooms and fennel pickle to yellow-fin tuna with wasabi *tare* (dipping sauce), flavours are clean, nuanced and a testament to high-quality produce.

SPIRIT HOUSE

SUNSHINE COAST HINTERLAND | $$$ | ASIAN
20 Nindery Rd, Yandina; 07-5446 8994; www.spirithouse.com.au; banquets from $80 per person

Spirit House evokes the deep jungles of Southeast Asia with its moody tropical setting and sophisticated Thai-inspired menu. Savour anything from honey and clove-spiced chicken with cashew puree and green mango salad to Hervey Bay scallops with *nam phrik phao* (chilli paste) and turmeric and lime *kosho* (Japanese chilli condiment).

UNDERBAR

BALLARAT | $$$ | GASTRONOMY
3 Doveton St N; www.underbar.com.au; tasting menu $160 per person

This minimalist 16 seater only opens for a handful of services, and is booked out for months. Chef Derek Boath (formerly of New York's Michelin-starred Per Se) prepares weekly degustation menus comprising cutting-edge fare that's all locally sourced or foraged.

BRAE

BIRREGURRA | $$$ | AUSTRALIAN
4285 Cape Otway Rd; 03-5236 2226; www.braerestaurant.com; chef's menu $290 per person

Regional star Brae uses organic produce such as chesnok red garlic and superschmelz kohlrabi, grown on-site, to create delightful gastronomic concoctions. Enjoyed within an attractive farmhouse cottage, the eight-course tasting menu changes daily, reflects what traditionally grows in the area, and includes many indigenous ingredients.

IGNI

GEELONG | $$$ | AUSTRALIAN
Ryan Pl; 03-5222 2266; www.restaurantigni.com; tasting menu $150 per person

The set tasting menus here change on a whim, incorporating a mix of indigenous and European flavours from saltbush to oyster leaf, or marron to squab, using a wood-fired grill fuelled by ironbark and red gum.

CHIN CHIN

CENTRAL MELBOURNE | $$ | SOUTHEAST ASIAN

125 Flinders Lane; 03-8663 2000; www.chinchinrestaurant.com.au; mains $28-38

Showcasing the bold-flavoured, hawker-style food of Melbourne's huge southeast Asian communities, bustling Chin Chin is a local institution. Housed in a glammed-up warehouse (all marble, white tiles and neon) its salads, curries and stir fries are designed to share.

SUNDA

CENTRAL MELBOURNE | $$ | SOUTHEAST ASIAN

18 Punch Lane; 03-9654 8190; www.sunda.com.au; set menu $85 per person

This slick Southeast Asian kitchen churns out modern Indonesian, Vietnamese and Malaysian dishes spiked with native Australian ingredients such as Davidson's plum and marron (freshwater crayfish). Bar seats are best, while the off-menu roti with Vegemite curry is essential.

CUTLER & CO

FITZROY, COLLINGWOOD & ABBOTSFORD | $$$ | MODERN AUSTRALIAN

55-57 Gertrude St, Fitzroy; 03-9419 4888; www.cutlerandco.com.au; chef's selection menu $170 per person

Cutler & Co combines faultless service with joy-inducing dishes in one of Melbourne's top fine diners. Whether ordering à la carte or the degustation menu, expect clever, seasonal food using native ingredients such as finger limes and Hunter Valley partridge.

LUNE CROISSANTERIE

FITZROY, COLLINGWOOD & ABBOTSFORD | $ | BAKERY

119 Rose St, Fitzroy; 03-9419 2320; www.lunecroissanterie.com; pastries from $5.90

Be prepared to queue for Lune's unrivalled pastries, from innovative cruffins to plain croissants sometimes aclaimed the world's best. In the centre of this warehouse space is a glass, climate-controlled cube where the magic happens.

MINAMISHIMA

RICHMOND & EAST MELBOURNE | $$$ | JAPANESE

4 Lord St, Richmond; 03-9429 5180; www.minamishima.com.au; omakase menu $225 per person

The premier seats in perhaps Australia's best Japanese restaurant are at the bar, where sushi master Koichi Minamishima prepares seafood with surgical precision, serving it one piece at a time.

WHERE TO DRINK...

AUSSIE WINE AT THE CELLAR DOOR

Seppeltsfield, Barossa Valley SA
This handsome winery, planted in 1851 and famed for its port, also produces fine drops from vermentino, riesling, syrah, grenache and other grapes.

Stormflower Vineyard, Margaret River Region WA
Just nine hectares produce delicious, organic cabernet-shiraz, with the cellar door set in a colourful native garden.

Coombe, Great Ocean Rd VIC
Australian opera royalty Dame Nellie Melba once lived here; now there's an inviting cellar door, a great restaurant and Edna Walling-designed gardens.

MONA, Hobart TAS
Hobart's unique museum houses the cellar door for Moorilla, Tassie's oldest winery.

ATTICA

ST KILDA, ELWOOD & ELSTERNWICK | $$$ | MODERN AUSTRALIAN

74 Glen Eira Rd, Ripponlea; 03-9530 0111; www.attica.com.au; tasting menu $295 per person

One of only two Australian entries in San Pellegrino's list of the World's Top 120 Restaurants, Attica is where founding chef Ben Shewry gets wildly inventive with native ingredients like saltwater-crocodile ribs, emu liver and marron (freshwater crayfish).

PROVENANCE

BEECHWORTH | $$$ | MODERN AUSTRALIAN

86 Ford St; 03-5728 1786; www.theprovenance.com.au; tasting menu $150 per person

Housed in a handsome 1856 bank building, Provenance offers modern Australian fare with Japanese influences, such as seared kangaroo with fish sauce, egg-yolk dressing, pickled onion and cured mullet roe.

PARKER PIES

RUTHERGLEN | $ | BAKERY

86-88 Main St; 02-6032 9605; www.parkerpies.com.au; pies from $5

If you think pies can't be too special, this award-winning local institution might change your mind. Try the gourmet pastries – emu, venison, crocodile or the lovely Jolly Jumbuck (a lamb pastry with rosemary and mint).

LONG PADDOCK

LAKES DISTRICT | $$ | AUSTRALIAN

95 Main Rd, Lindenow; 03-5157 1638; www.longpaddock.com.au; mains $18-26

This esteemed restaurant in tiny Lindenow occupies a charming old bakery with its original wood-fired scotch oven. Expect treats such as raw King Dory from Lakes Entrance, Bruthen pork belly or more casual (but no less delicious) offerings of Maffra cheddar and leg-ham toasties or Gippsland beef pies.

LIMONE

GRIFFITH | $$$ | ITALIAN

482 Banna Ave; 02-6962 3777; www.limone.com.au; set menus from $60 per person

Limone offers two- and three-course menus of seasonal, local produce

This page: Dish from Limone. Opposite page: Aria.

transformed into regional Italian dishes with Australian flourishes such as kangaroo-tail ragu and bugs (small marine crustacea). The elegant dining room is largely constructed from recycled materials, and much of the food is grown on the restaurant's own Piccolo Family Farm.

CHARRED KITCHEN & BAR

ORANGE | $$$ | AUSTRALIAN
1-5 New St; 02-6363 1580; www.charred.com.au; set menus from $70 per person

Beautifully executed meals starring regional produce, an extensive, award-winning wine selection and impeccable service combine to create one of the region's best restaurants. Dishes cooked in the Lucifer wood oven, such as the Sichuan lamb rump, are the standouts.

'Melbourne dining like nowhere else: independent, embracing overlooked Australian ingredients and cuisines, committed to discovering the new.'
Kylie Staddon, Attica

WHEELERS

SAPPHIRE COAST | $$ | SEAFOOD
162 Arthur Kaine Dr, Pambula; 02-6495 6330; www.wheelersoysters.com.au; mains $30-36

At this oyster emporium and fine-dining restaurant the briny molluscs can be slurped casually from the takeaway or enjoyed with inventive garnishes (prosecco foam, wasabi aioli) in the dining room.

ARIA

SYDNEY | $$$ | MODERN AUSTRALIAN
1 Macquarie St, Circular Quay; 02-9240 2255; www.ariasydney.com.au; tasting menu $210 a head

Aria is a star in Sydney's fine-dining firmament, an award-winning combination of stellar cooking, Opera House views, stylish surrounds and faultless service. Dishes such as John Dory with white miso, cauliflower and surf clams bring a cosmopolitan sensibility to top-notch Australian ingredients.

QUAY

SYDNEY | $$$ | MODERN AUSTRALIAN
Level 3, Overseas Passenger Terminal, Circular Quay West; 02-9251 5600; www.quay.com.au; tasting menus from $240 a head

What many consider to be Sydney's best restaurant marries peerless views

with brilliant food. Chef Peter Gilmore never rests on his laurels, delivering exquisitely crafted, adventurous dishes such as smoked pork jowl with black-lipped abalone, shiitake mushrooms and fan-shell clams.

RESTAURANT HUBERT

SYDNEY | $$ | FRENCH

15 Bligh St, City Centre; 02-9232 0881; www.restauranthubert.com; banquets from $95 a head

The sexy, 1930s ambience at this downtown-Sydney favourite complements delicious French fare served in old-fashioned portions. Alongside traditional dishes such as terrine, black pudding or duck, you'll find more avant-garde creations such as roasted snails with funky Cantonese XO sauce.

SAINT PETER

SYDNEY | $$ | SEAFOOD

362 Oxford St, Paddington; 02-8937 2530; www.saintpeter.com.au; mains $40-48

Saint Peter's combination of precise service, impeccably sourced seafood and avant-garde dishes (perhaps a terrine of Albany bass-grouper head with beer mustard and pickles) makes this possibly Sydney's best fish restaurant.

PORTEÑO

SYDNEY | $$ | ARGENTINIAN

50 Holt St, Surry Hills; 02-8399 1440; www.porteno.com.au; mains $46-75

Where Surry Hills cool meets sizzling flesh, this acclaimed Argentine restaurant is famous for meats grilled on a *parilla* (grill) over a smouldering *asado* (fire pit). Other highlights include homemade chorizo and morcilla, plenty of lighter dishes and a tempting Argentine wine list.

BOURKE STREET BAKERY

SYDNEY | $ | BAKERY

633 Bourke St, Surry Hills; 02-9699 1011; www.bourkestreetbakery.com.au; baked treats from $5

Queuing outside this teensy bakery is an essential Surry Hills experience. It sells a tempting selection of pastries, cakes, bread and sandwiches, along with near-legendary sausage rolls.

GROUNDS OF ALEXANDRIA

SYDNEY | $$ | CAFÉ

2 Huntley St, Alexandria; 02-9699 2225; www.thegrounds.com.au; lunch mains $20-24

This extraordinary gustatory complex, housed in a former pie factory, sports futuristic coffee technology, tip-top baking and next-level café food such as the barramundi (Australian sea bass) sandwich with fried jalapeños, slaw and chipotle mayo. The

Next spread: Muse.

surrounding garden holds wandering chickens, Harry Trotter the waste-chewing pig and abundant greenery.

BEROWRA WATERS INN

HAWKESBURY RIVER | $$$ | MODERN AUSTRALIAN

Berowra Waters; 02-9456 1027; www.berowrawatersinn.com; tasting menus from $165 a head

Upstream from Berowa Waters township and only accessible by boat or seaplane, this Glenn Murcutt–designed restaurant is a real showstopper. The Inn makes sensational Mod Oz food to match dreamy river views – think local crab with miso, or beef with Pyengana cheddar from Tasmania.

SUBO

NEWCASTLE | $$S | MODERN AUSTRALIAN, VEGAN

551d Hunter St; 02-4023 4048; www.subo.com.au; set menus from $85 per person

This highly lauded restaurant serves exquisite food such as smoked mussels with taramosalata, fennel, apple and Chiu Chow chilli, or charcoal-grilled wagyu from the Hunter Valley with soy-cured egg yolk and mustard leaf. Vegetarian and vegan alternatives to the seasonal five-course menu are available.

THREE BLUE DUCKS AT THE FARM

BYRON BAY | $$ | CAFÉ

11 Ewingsdale Rd, Ewingsdale; 02-6684 7888; www.thefarmbyronbay.com.au; mains $28-37

This rustic café-restaurant forms the beating heart of The Farm. Breakfast features typical Byron healthy options, as well as a streaky bacon and egg roll, and slow-roasted brisket, while the lunch and dinner menus step things up to subtle sophistication.

FLEET

FAR NORTH COAST | $$$ | SEAFOOD

Shop 2/16 The Terrace, Brunswick Heads; 02-6685 1363; www.fleet-restaurant.com.au; tasting menu $100 per head

Fleet, one of Australia's most cultish dining destinations, seats just 14 guests for communal dining in its effortlessly stylish space. The menu sometimes includes foraged ingredients, and the series of small dishes that appear from the open kitchen are punchy in flavour and beautifully presented.

AUBERGINE

CANBERRA | $$$ | MODERN AUSTRALIAN

18 Barker St, Griffith; 02-6260 8666; www.aubergine.com.au; set menu $105 per person

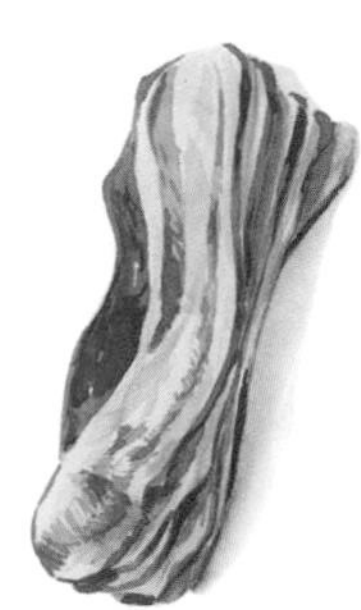

The innovative, seasonally-driven menu at Canberra's most esteemed restaurant offers plates such as Comté-cheese custard with fennel pollen, heirloom tomatoes and wakame (seaweed) oil and Eugowra quail with stuffed cabbage, baby turnips and parsley puree.

MUSE

CANBERRA | $$ | AUSTRALIAN
69 Canberra Ave, Kingston; 02-6178 0024; www.musecanberra.com.au; lunch mains $16-25

This restaurant-bookshop on the corner of the East Hotel effortlessly juggles its twin roles. Start with a drink from the Australian-only drinks list then move on to 'prologues' such as grilled chorizo with chimichurri (Argentinian herb sauce). Larger 'chapters' include Berkshire pork-cheek terrine and lime/yuzu-cured salmon gravlax.

THE AGRARIAN KITCHEN EATERY

HOBART & AROUND | $$$ | MODERN AUSTRALIAN
11a The Avenue, New Norfolk; 03-6262 0011; www.theagrariankitchen.com; chef's menu $80 per person

Occupying a cavernous former ward of the Willow Court psychiatric hospital, the Eatery is lined with jars of preserves, and uses produce from the adjacent community garden or the Agrarian Kitchen's garden. Expect the likes of wood-roasted Berksire pork belly and rich farmers' cheese dumplings.

'Our set menus change twice a season and are dictated by our commitment to quality, locality and seasonality.'
Suzie Vincent, Subo

TEMPLO

CENTRAL HOBART | $$ | ITALIAN
98 Patrick St, Hobart; 03-6234 7659; www.templo.com.au; chef's menu $70 per person

Unpretentious little Templo is a Hobart dining treasure. With only 20 seats, mostly on the communal table, and only three or four Italian-inspired mains to choose from, it's an exercise in selectivity and sharing (your personal space, and your food).

ALØFT

CENTRAL HOBART | $$$ | MODERN AUSTRALIAN
Brooke St Pier; 03-6223 1619; www.aloftrestaurant.com; banquet menus from $80 per person

Acclaimed Aløft occupies a scenic eyrie atop the floating Brooke St Pier. Menu hits include silken tofu with burnt onion and baby leeks, and charred octopus with *chimichurri* (Argentinian green-herb sauce) and egg yolk.

RETRO CAFE

SALAMANCA PLACE & BATTERY POINT | $ | CAFÉ
31 Salamanca Pl, Battery Point 03-6223 3073; mains $15-18

A classic Hobart cafe, funky Retro is ground zero for Saturday brunch among the market stalls. Masterful breakfasts, overstuffed bagels, imaginative salads and juicy burgers interweave with laughing staff, chilled-

COURTESY MUSE

out jazz and the whirr and bang of the coffee machine.

DOO-LISHUS

EAGLEHAWK NECK | $ | FISH & CHIPS

Blowhole Rd, Doo Town; 0437 469 412; www.tasmanregion.com.au/doo-lishus; meals $8-19

Sometimes rated as Tasmania's best fish and chips, this unexpected caravan at the Blowhole car park in Doo Town serves up the usual range of battered swimming things, plus good ice cream, fresh berry smoothies and interesting pies (eg curried-scallop, venison and rabbit).

FREYCINET MARINE FARM

COLES BAY & FREYCINET MARINE PARK | $$ | SEAFOOD

1784 Coles Bay Rd, Coles Bay 03-6257 0140; www.freycinetmarinefarm.com; plates $20-30, 12 oysters $22-25

Freycinet Marine Farm's oysters grow fat in the cold, clean waters around Coles Bay, while its cafe dishes up fish and chips, mussels, scallops and abalone. Sit on the deck, sip some chardonnay and dig into seafood as fresh as the Freycinet air.

WHAT TO EAT

Open-sea fish
Seafood is found in abundance. Tuna, bonito, wahoo, swordfish and marlin all feature prominently in traditional cuisine and are cooked (and served) in a bunch of different ways.

Land crab
Ukaeb is a definite must-try while in Palau. The oh-so-tender crab flesh is cooked in coconut milk, and may be topped with bread crumbs.

Meat
Pig and chicken are the main sources of meat proteins and are generally cooked simply, grilled or fried.

Taro
Taro roots are usually boiled and served as an accompaniment.

PRICE RANGES

For a main course:
$ less than US$10
$$ US$10–20
$$$ US$20 or more

Tipping: 10–15% if service charge is not included.

PALAU

Most visitors to Palau don't come for the food but it doesn't take long before they realise that the archipelago offers a great dining scene. Expect a mix of Palauan and Pacific Rim influences. If you love fusion food, you'll be in seventh heaven.

DROP OFF BAR & GRILL

MALAKAL ISLAND | $$ | SEAFOOD
Main St; tel 488 7505; www.facebook.com/DropOffPalau; mains US$10-20

The Drop Off has a great selection of fish delivered daily from the harbour, including blue marlin, yellowfin tuna and red snapper. It's also known for its knockout burgers, *kebabs* (skewers) and sashimi. The open-air terrace overlooking the marina is perfect for enjoying the cool, ocean breezes. Even if you aren't dining, it's a great place to pause for a drink and recharge the batteries.

THE TAJ

KOROR ISLAND | $$ | INDIAN
Main St, Downtown Koror; tel 488 2227; www.tajpalau.com; mains US$9-20

A highly-praised venue, the Taj serves authentic, richly flavoured korma, curry and tandoori dishes as well as a good selection of vegetarian options, all prepared with the best ingredients available and served by lovely sari-clad staff. Tandoori chicken is brought to your table impaled on what looks like a short sword. The bar here is also a supremely relaxed place to sip a tropical potion.

ELILAI SEASIDE DINING

KOROR ISLAND | $$$ | INTERNATIONAL
Main St, Koror; tel 488 8866; www.elilaipalau.com; mains US$15-40

Elilai has achieved a fantastic reputation thanks to its painstakingly constructed menu featuring Palauan and Asian dishes with a contemporary twist. Start with fabulous local crustaceans – the *ukaeb* (Palauan land crab) is succulent – then dig into a mangrove clam risotto, grilled tuna, or pork ribs, all beautifully presented. There are vegetarian options, too. The elegant decor, airy spaces, light music and outstanding sea views of Koror bay add to the appeal.

PAPUA NEW GUINEA

WHAT TO EAT

Mumu
Celebrations in PNG call for a pork and vegetable feast cooked in a *mumu* (ground oven).

Kaukau
If there's one root vegetable to rule them all in PNG, it's *kaukau* (sweet potato), with more than 400 species to choose from.

Sasak
These sweet dumplings are made by steaming sago and banana in banana leaves. Find them in coastal regions. Sago and banana are cooked with coconut milk in a similar dessert more commonly known as *dia*.

Chicken pot
This simple one-pot dish sees chicken cooked in a pot with chopped *kaukau*, green onions, corn, coconut milk, curry powder and salt.

PRICE RANGES
$ less than K20
$$ K20–40
$$$ K40 or more

Tipping: Not required.

While PNG may not excite the gourmet traveller, its food offerings have improved markedly in recent years, with crowd-pleasing international dishes complimented by local seafood and vegetables. And it wouldn't be a trip to PNG without visiting a *kai* – the nation's version of a greasy spoon.

VILLAGE CAFE

PORT MORESBY | $$ | MELANESIAN

Lot 28, Vaivai Ave, East Boroko; 675-323 8606; www.facebook.com/wellnessvillagekitchen2016; mains K20-70

For authentic PNG fare, it's difficult to go past the family-run Wellness Lodge's cafe. The menu changes daily pending the availability of local produce, but could include pork, lamb or beef cooked in a *mumu*, smoked fish, curry crab and creamed chicken, all served with local vegetables. Wash down your meal with a *kulau* (fresh young coconut water).

TASTY BITE INDIAN RESTAURANT

PORT MORESBY | $$ | INDIAN

ANG Haus, Hunter St; 675-321 2222; thali K15

This tiny place has a score of loyal expat fans, including a healthy contingent of resident Indians. Expect decent portions of northern Indian dishes from creamy chicken *pasanda* to rich lamb masala; Monday night is great-value all-you-can-gobble buffet night.

RAPALA

PORT MORESBY | $$$ | INTERNATIONAL

Cnr Douglas & Hunter Sts; 675-309 3000; www.crownhotel.com.pg; mains K62-85

One of Port Moresby's best restaurants is an elegant yet somewhat old-fashioned affair inside the Crown Hotel. The dishes are cutting-edge, though, with particularly tempting tasting plates – one-spoon bites of beef kibbeh, lobster tempura and seared scallops. The veal tenderloin is beautifully tender and the desserts are imaginative multi-part creations. Dress nicely.

VANILLA ROOM

EAST SEPIK PROVINCE | $$$ | INTERNATIONAL

Seaview Rd, Wewak; 675-456 2100; www.inwewak.com; mains from K$50

The In Wewak hotel's restaurant is hands down the best place to eat in the region, serving such culinary delights as seared yellow-fin tuna or chicken in green coconut curry. Look out for daily specials, including the terrific giant freshwater prawns from the Sepik. More exotic offerings include Australian scotch fillet and crocodile tail in green coconut curry.

SWEET SPOT

WESTERN HIGHLANDS PROVINCE | $$ | CAFE

Kuminga Rd, Mt Hagen; 675-7223 7430; www.facebook.com/hagencafeandrestaurant; mains K18-35

It's difficult to go past Mt Hagen's Kofi Kave for a brew, but this relative newcomer to the cafe scene of PNG's third-largest city boasts the town's best array of sweet treats along with a solid selection of international cafe dishes, with standout local trout.

EMMA'S RESTAURANT

EAST NEW BRITAIN PROVINCE | $$$ | INTERNATIONAL

Makau Esplanade, Kokopo; 675-982 5600; www.gazelleinterhotel.com; mains K45-75

Overlooking Blanch Bay, the Gazelle International's restaurant is top-notch. There are tropical seafood dishes: start with Peruvian ceviche and move onto grilled lobster or reef fish. Or try the chicken, steaks and an excellent Indian menu. The daily lunch special (four to five options) at K20 is great value.

PHOENIX RESTAURANT

EAST NEW BRITAIN PROVINCE | $$$ | INTERNATIONAL

Mango Ave, Rabaul; 675-982 1999; www.rabaulhotel.com.pg; mains K35-60

The Australian-run Rabaul Hotel has a great restaurant serving popular dishes reflective of PNG's social and cultural history (the Chinese chilli squid is particularly good). Purchased daily from the Rabaul Market, ingredients are always fresh, and vegetarians (and even vegans) can be catered for.

NUSA ISLAND RETREAT RESTAURANT

EAST IRELAND PROVINCE | $$$ | INTERNATIONAL

Nusa Lik Island; 675-723-18302; lunch mains K25-42

Non guests are welcome at the excellent restaurant attached to the Nusa Island Retreat, a short boat ride from Kaveing (call ahead to arrange transfers). It would be a shame to miss out on its dinner buffet (K88; by reservation), or you could tuck into a burger, red curry or Thai fishcake at lunchtime and then take a dip later on.

FEDERATED STATES OF MICRONESIA

While imported foods now play a big role in modern Micronesian cuisine, traditional recipes can still be sampled around the islands, each with its own unique regional speciality. Unlike more remote Pacific islands, tropical fruits are abundant. But fish is king.

WHAT TO EAT

Breadfruit
Known locally as *mahi*, breadfruit is a staple of Micronesian cuisine. Look out for *mahi um*, which sees breadfruit halves cooked over hot stones and coconut husks, then covered in taro leaves and steamed.

Chicken Micronesia
Chicken is marinated in soy, ginger and pineapple juice before being baked with pineapple, grated coconut and onions.

Pohnpeian pepper
Renowned for being the world's best pepper, this Pohnpei island crop is particularly rich and flavourful.

Kosraean soup
Typically served on Sundays in family homes on Kosrae, this hearty soup is made with tuna, coconut milk, with breadfruit, plantain or taro added.

PRICE RANGES
$ less than US$10
$$ US$10–$17
$$$ US$17 or more

Tipping: Leave loose change.

OCEANIA HOTEL RESTAURANT

YAP | $$ | INTERNATIONAL

718 Ocean Bvld, Colonia; 691-350 7707; www.oceaniayap.com; mains $11-20

A refreshing change from the standard international staples found on most Micronesian menus, this hotel restaurant morphs typical island produce into creative dishes such as grilled Cajun wahoo with local pineapple chilli, sizzling sweet and spicy octopus, and grilled Hawaiian teriyaki chicken breast.

JOY RESTAURANT

POHNPEI | $ | JAPANESE

Ohmine St, Kolonia; 691-320 2447; dishes US$6-9

This place is a lunch specialist and a perennial favourite at that, forever dishing up a menu of excellent Japanese food. Fresh fish is the speciality, though there are beef and chicken dishes, too.

BULLY'S

KOSRAE | $$ | INTERNATIONAL

Pacific Treelodge Resort; 691-370 7856; www.korasaetreelodge.com; daily special US$10

Reached via a raised walkway through the mangroves from the Pacific Treelodge Resort, Bully's is widely considered to be the best place to eat on the island. The menu includes a mix of local and international dishes, but the best deal is the daily special, which could be Kosraean soup one day, and coconut crab the next. The sashimi is also excellent.

WHAT TO EAT

Tuna sashimi
Served with fresh lime juice and soy sauce, this Marshallese take on sashimi can be found on just about every Majuro restaurant menu.

Pumpkin rice
Locally known as rice-banke, this simple preparation of diced pumpkins and rice, boiled together in water with the optional addition of coconut milk is typically served as a side.

Bwiro
Look for these banana-leaf parcels of sweetened, fermented breadfruit paste cooked in an underground oven at the market next to the Marshall Islands Resort in the capital Majuro.

Chukuchuk
These tasty balls of rice rolled in freshly grated coconut are a favourite snack across the islands.

PRICE RANGES
$ less than US$10
$$ $US10–$20
$$$ US$20 or more

Tipping: Leave loose change.

MARSHALL ISLANDS

First settled by Micronesians, named for a British explorer, and claimed by Spain, Germany, Japan, and the US before gaining independence in 1986, this remote cluster of coral atolls is quite the multicultural melting pot, with an eclectic cuisine to match.

ENRA

MAJURO | $$$ | INTERNATIONAL
Delap; www.facebook.com/marshallislandsresort; 692-625 2525; mains $15-30

Most people come to the Marshall Islands Resort's lagoon-view restaurant for the pizzas, but steaks, sushi, island fish dishes and other crowd-pleasers are also on offer. There's always a daily special, and regular themed cuisine nights include a teppanyaki barbecue and Sunday brunch.

DAR RESTAURANT

MAJURO | $ | MARSHALLESE
Uliga; 692-625 3174; dishes $7

Well-loved among locals for breakfast and lunch, DAR's speciality is Marshallese dishes such as fried fish with breadfruit or plantain and steamed breadfruit with boiled fish. Don't be surprised if your server sits at your table to discuss your options — it's a Marshallese custom.

TIDE TABLE

MAJURO | $$ | INTERNATIONAL
Uliga; 692-625 5131; www.hotelrobertreimers.com; mains $10-28

Operated by one of the pioneering Marshallese families, the Hotel Robert Reimers' restaurant is a popular meeting place for locals and expats. Fresh fish starters are the highlight of wide-ranging menu. Don't expect speedy service.

WON HAI SHIEN

MAJURO | $$ | CHINESE
Uliga; 692-625 6641; mains $10-12

The food is always fresh at Won Hai Shien – quite something when the Islands rely heavily on imports. Fish and vegetable dishes are standouts.

WHAT TO EAT

Yam
This starchy tuber is a Melanesian staple food. It can be prepared in numerous ways and can be served as an accompaniment to meat or fish dishes.

Tropical fruits
Market stalls are heaping with spectacular fresh tropical fruits, including banana, mango and papaya.

Meat
Pigs and chicken are the main sources of meat protein.

Seafood
It's hardly surprising that seafood features prominently across the archipelago. It's often cooked simply, grilled or fried. Honiara is a great place to indulge a sashimi craving, as a couple of restaurants serve authentic Japanese food.

PRICE RANGES
$ less than S$500
$$ S$500–1000
$$$ S$1000 or more

Tipping: Not expected.

SOLOMAN ISLANDS

While the Solomon Islands are not considered as a gourmet heaven, the culinary scene is steadily improving. Great seafood can be found on the coasts. The rest of the traditional diet consists largely of vegetables of the starchy variety. The best dining experiences are generally offered by hotel restaurants and resorts.

LIME LOUNGE

GUADALCANAL | $$ | CAFETERIA
Off Mendana Ave, Honiara; tel 23064; www.facebook.com/limeloungehoniara; mains S$40-100

Funky little Lime Lounge is a great place to decompress. There's everything from satisfying breakfasts to palate-pleasing salads, well-made sandwiches and yummy pastries. No view and no terrace, but the walls are adorned with paintings by local artists, which gives the place a splash of style.

THE BAMBOO BAR & CAFE

GUADALCANAL | $$ | CAFETERIA
King Solomon Hotel, Hibiscus Ave, Honiara; tel 21205; www.kingsolomonhotel.info; mains S$50-190

This cheerful place is perfect for a comforting breakfast, lunch or a snack attack any time. The straightforward menu features tasty dishes such as chicken curry, vegetarian omelette and focaccia. Healthy smoothies, great coffee and sweet treats are also on offer, and there's outdoor seating.

FATBOYS

WESTERN PROVINCE | $$$ | INTERNATIONAL
Mbabanga Island, Gizo; tel 7466252; www.solomonislandsfatboys.com.au; mains S$120-200

Dining on a pier that hovers over the turquoise waters of Vonavona Lagoon – it can't get more mellow than this. Choice is limited but the food, mostly fish dishes and salads, is fresh and tasty. Afterwards, swim in the sandy shallows that extend to Kennedy Island.

VANUATU

Vanuatu's tropical climate and fertile lands bless it with fresh seafood, succulent meats, organic tropical fruits and fresh-from-the-garden vegetables. Port Vila is by far the best place in Vanuatu for eating out, although there are also some good restaurants on Santo and a few on Tanna.

WHITE GRASS RESTAURANT

TANNA | $$ | PACIFIC

White Grass Ocean Resort; 30010; www.whitegrasstanna.com; 2600-3800VT

Inside the classy White Class Ocean Resort & Spa, this is undoubtedly West Tanna's fanciest restaurant. The blackboard menu changes daily, with local seafood and beef steak the highlights. The timber deck overlooks the ocean with fabulous sunset views.

MARKET MEAL BOOTHS

ESPIRITU SANTO | $ | MARKET

Luganville; mains 400VT

For an authentic, unforgettable dining experience in Santo, the market booths are hard to beat. Choose one of the tables next to the orange booths and a cheery woman will appear at the window, ready to take your order. Choose from chicken, fish or steak, piled with rice and vegetables, and watch it being cooked through the window.

L'HOUSTALET

EFATE | $$ | FRENCH

Captain Cook Ave, Port Vila; 22303; www.facebook.com/lhoustaletrestaurant; mains 900-2700VT

Still going strong after more than 40 years, L'Houstalet is famous for its offbeat French creations including stuffed flying fox, wild pigeon and garlic snails. Simpler fare such as pizza and pasta is also available. It's well worth a splurge for the rustic gastronomic atmosphere.

JILL'S CAFE

EFATE | $ | AMERICAN

Lini Hwy, Port Vila; 25125; mains 350-900VT

This American-style diner is always bustling with expats, tourists and locals, seeking out waffles, burgers, burritos, chilli cheese fries and yummy salads made of local ingredients. Try Jill's homemade earthquake chilli and famous Port Vila thick shakes.

WHAT TO EAT

Laplap
Vanuatu's national dish is made by grating manioc, taro roots or yams into a doughy paste that is soaked in coconut cream. Pieces of meat or fish are often added. Leaves from the *laplap* plant (similar to banana leaves) are wrapped around the doughy mix and then placed in a ground oven.

Nalot
This tasty dish is made from roasted taro, banana or breadfruit mixed with coconut cream.

Coconut
Coconut is used in five stages of ripeness. The third, when the flesh is firm but succulent, is the best for eating.

Roussette
Flying fox (or fruit bat) served *au vin* (in red wine) is a local speciality, found in restaurants on Port Vila.

PRICE RANGES

$ less than 1500VT
$$ 1500–3000VT
$$$ 3000VT or more

Tipping: Leave loose change.

FIJI

Fijian food has traditionally centered around staple ingredients such as seafood, coconut and cassava, but these days you can find everything from spicy Indian curries to convincingly authentic Italian on the main island, Viti Levu. Fresh, simply prepared seafood shines everywhere.

WHAT TO EAT

Lovo
The traditional Fijian banquet sees everything from whole chickens to legs of pork prepared in an underground oven. Lots of resorts offer a weekly *lovo* for guests.

Curry
With roughly half of Fiji's population claiming Indian ancestry, you'll be hard-pressed to find a restaurant menu without at least one curry dish.

Rourou
This traditional soup-like side dish is made from *dalo* (taro leaves) stewed in coconut milk.

Kava
Drinking this mildly narcotic liquid made from powdered kava (or *yaqona*) root is an essential part of Fijian life. When visiting villages, it's customary to present a kava root to the head of the village.

PRICE RANGES
$ less than F$15
$$ F$15–$25
$$$ F$25 or more

Tipping: Leave loose change.

NADINA AUTHENTIC FIJIAN RESTAURANT

DENARAU ISLAND | $$$ | FIJIAN
Denarau Marina; 679-675 0290; www.facebook.com/nadinarestaurant; mains F$30-55

This fantastic waterside restaurant specialises in Fijian cuisine, using homegrown and foraged ingredients. It's a great place to try kokoda (raw fish marinated in lemon juice and served in coconut milk) or opt for the divine fresh prawns with ota (a local bush fern) and chef-squeezed coconut cream.

TASTE FIJI

NADI | $$ | CAFE
Lot 1, Cawa Rd; 679-890 1197; www.tastefiji.com; mains F$15-29

Stylish, professionally run and with a cosmopolitan menu featuring dishes created from local produce, Taste Fiji has an excellent brunch menu featuring international favourites with Fijian flair (caramelised pork belly omelette, anyone?). The lunch offerings include substantial salads and hearty mains such as grilled local cherry perch with crispy ginger, spring onion, choy sum, oyster mushrooms, toasted sesame and soy chilli vinegar.

SITAR

NADI | $$ | INDIAN
Cnr Queens Rd & Wailoaloa Rdi; 679-672 7722; mains F$10-30

With a menu boasting flavoursome, flaming hot dishes from India, Fiji and Thailand, Sitar is a standout restaurant, even in a curry-mad town like Nadi. All the universal favourites are on the menu, or give goat or local seafood dishes a try. Good value banquets are available, as is a wide selection of vegetarian options. It's noisy, but in a fun way.

TATA'S

NADI | $ | INDIAN
Nadi Back Rd; mains $5-10

This rough-looking joint just down from the temple dishes up some of

BONCHAN/GETTY IMAGES ©

This page: Kokoda.

the most authentic and flavoursome curries on Viti Levu: just ask the droves of locals crowding the open-air deck. There's a menu, but for the best experience, let the friendly staff pick for you (though the 'Uncivilised Chicken' curry is worth seeking out).

BOATSHED RESTAURANT AND SUNSET BAR

VUDA POINT | $$ | INTERNATIONAL

Vuda Point Marina; www.vudamarina.com.fj; mains F$16-34

With indoor and outdoor seating, top views and cheery service, this is a popular spot with visiting yachties and those staying in this area north of Nadi. The varied menu features salads, pizzas, curries, seafood, and lush pastas (hello, lobster ravioli) alongside decadent Fijian dishes such as the seafood *kovu* (marinated in a coconut broth and steamed in banana leaf).

BEACH BAR & GRILL

CORAL COAST | $$ | BISTRO

Sunset Strip, Korotogo; 697-652 0877; mains F$18-37

This simple shack-style outfit is deservedly popular with those wanting to eat outside their Coral Coast resorts. Its impressive menu includes excellent local seafood dishes (try the herb-crusted mahi-mahi in coconut sauce) alongside a smattering of Thai, Indian and steak crowd-pleasers.

CRAB SCHACK FIJI

CORAL COAST | $$ | CRAB
Sunset Strip, Korotogo; 679-902 5979; mains F$23-65

Right next to the beach, this modern tin shack specialises in local mud crab (you can opt to have it cooked in chilli, garlic or Thai sauce), but also gets rave reviews for its mahi-mahi tacos. Served in a coconut, its prawn-skewer salad gets top points for presentation. Handily for drizzly days, the outdoor picnic table-style seating is covered.

HE-NI-UWA

CORAL COAST | $$ | FIJIAN
Queens Rd, Tagaqe; 679-932 9179; www.facebook.com/heniuwa.fj; mains F$22-120

Right on the beachfront, 15 minutes east of Sigatoka, this simple shack serves up some of the most authentic Fijian dishes on the island. Dive into heaped plates of prawn coconut curry, garlic buttered lobster, chicken chop suey and more. They also do a veggie dish.

OCEAN TERRACE RESTAURANT

CORAL COAST | $$$ | FIJIAN
Sunset Strip, Korotogo; 679-650 0476; www.bedarrafiji.com; mains $18-37

Boasting a breezy dining area overlooking the ocean, the Bedarra Inn's restaurant often lures guests from the snazzier nearby Outrigger. It's a great place to try Fijian dishes including pan-seared mahi-mahi, *ika vakalolo* (fish poached in coconut milk), Fijian curry, and a main-size kokoda.

GOVERNORS

SUVA | $$$ | INTERNATIONAL
Knolly St; 679-337 5050; www.governorsmuseumthemedrestaurantfiji.com; mains F$24-42

Housed in a converted colonial bungalow that was once home to Legendary Fijian chief Ratu Sir Laulu Sukuna, Governors is an atmospheric spot to sample Fijian classics such as prawn *palusami* (coconut cream cooked in taro leaves) and *kai* (freshwater clams) baked in coconut cream. The menu also features Asian and Italian dishes with a Fijian base (think: Thai fish curry with local reef fish and roti).

TASTE OF HIDDEN PARADISE RESTAURANT

SAVUSAVU | $ | INDIAN
Lesiaceva Rd; curries from F$8

This modest-looking joint is a strong contender for having the best curries in town, if not the entire island of Vanua Levu. There's a good selection, and all dishes are very flavourful, but do be prepared to wait, as they cook everything – slowly – from scratch. BYO.

WHERE TO DRINK...

COCKTAILS BY THE SEA

Malamala Beach Club, Malamala Island
Sip cocktails from coconut shells at the world's first beach club on its own island, just 25 minutes from Port Denarau.

Cloud 9
Swim, snorkel, sunbathe or just drink at this solar-powered floating bar off Port Denarau, named for Fiji's iconic surf break.

Sundowner Bar & Grill
Right on the beach, the Outrigger Fiji's bar is one of the most stylish spots on the Coral Coast to toast the sunset – perhaps with a passionfruit and lime mojito.

Beachcomber Island Resort
Beloved by backpackers, the sand-floor bar is a highlight of this party-ready resort, which has generous happy hours.

TUVALU

So remote is the dazzling cluster of palm-topped islets comprising Tuvalu that the Central Pacific nation's cuisine is largely based around its natural bounty: coconut and fish, with *pulaka* (swamp taro) providing an important source of carbohydrates. Most restaurants also sell cheap, filling Chinese-style dishes.

WHAT TO EAT

Palusami
Also referred to locally as 'Samoa', this regional favourite is made of pulaka leaves, coconut cream, lime juice, onions, and local spices, baked in foil parcels and served with *pulaka*.

Fresh fish
Served raw, fried, or steamed in a *lovo* (ground oven), fish is the lifeblood of Tuvalu.

Coconut tuna
This hearty local staple is made by simmering fresh-caught tuna in coconut cream with ingredients such as onions, ginger, garlic and chilies. It's served with rice.

Coconut and banana fritters
Prince William and the Duchess of Cambridge munched on these fried balls of goodness during their last official visit.

PRICE RANGES
$ less than AUD$10
$$ AUD$10–$15
$$$ AUD$15 or more

Tipping: Leave loose change.

FILAMONA HOTEL

FONGAFALE | $$ | INTERNATIONAL
Funafuti; 688-700 6034; www.filamona.com; mains around $12

On the block behind Tuvalu International Airport, the family-run Filamona Hotel is known for its home-cooked Tuvaluan dishes such as fish in coconut oil with taro, raw fish with breadfruit, fried fish with rice, and pork with plantain. If your visit doesn't coincide with a village feast, the hotel's friendly staff can arrange your very own traditional *lovo*.

FUNAFUTI LAGOON HOTEL RESTAURANT

FONGAFALE | $$ | INTERNATIONAL
Fongafale Rd Funafuti; 688-20500; www.funafutilagoonhotel.tv; mains around $12

Formerly the Vaiaku Lagi Hotel, this central hotel overlooking the lagoon prides itself on its seafood dishes, particularly sashimi. The short menu typically also includes sandwiches and generous servings of Pacific Chinese staples such as stir-fried pork with vegetables rice. Locals often drop by for a beer in the evenings, making it a good place to meet local characters.

3TS RESTAURANT

FONGAFALE | $$ | CHINESE
Fongafale Rd, Funafuti; dishes $7-12

Of the few eating options outside Tuvalu's hotels, this basic Chinese joint, about 100m south of the hospital, is the standout. The fish dishes are typically the freshest, but seafood options made with important ingredients (such as the spicy prawns) are tasty, too. Due to the limited availability of produce in Tuvalu, be prepared that some menu items might not be available. Expect huge servings.

WHAT TO EAT

Coffee

Not only does Tonga grow its own coffee, but it's organic and production supports families across the island. Look for the Tupu'anga Coffee label, or visit its cafe in Nuku'alofa.

Roasted suckling pig

Tongan celebrations call for a spit-roasted pig, prepared simply with a drenching of fresh coconut water to make the skin crisp up nicely.

Lo'i feke

Essentially octopus cooked in coconut cream, this classic Tongan dish is often served with a side of yam.

'Ota'ika

A favourite across the islands, Tongan ceviche uses more vegetables than other regional versions.

PRICE RANGES

$ less than T$15
$$ T$15–25
$$$ T$25 or more

Tipping: Leave loose change.

TONGA

Tonga is surrounded by the sea and Tongans will eat just about anything that comes out of it. Most resort restaurants serve some local dishes, but you'll find more variety (as well as street food classics such as ball-shaped doughnuts known as *keke 'isite*) in the capital Nuku'alofa.

FRIENDS CAFE

TONGATAPU | $$ | CAFE

Taufa'ahau Rd, Nuku'alofa; 676-22390; www.friendstonga.com; mains T$10-26

With a breezy charm, conversation, laughter and dependably good food, Friends is an irresistible social and culinary magnet for visitors to Tonga's capital and locals alike. Expect everything from all-day breakfasts and burgers to Tongan favourites like *'ota'ika*, garlic lobster, and coconut-and-lime-glazed pork chops.

CHEF ZERO

TONGATAPU | $$ | SEAFOOD

Tamakautonga Rd, Nuku'alofa; 676-771 3380; mains T$10-55

On the eastern fringe of the city, this no-frills restaurant also does burgers and pastas, but most locals come for the seafood, particularly the Polynesian-style lobster cooked with onion, garlic, tomato, coconut cream, lemon and dill (call ahead to ensure they have lobster on the day you wish to visit). It's not licensed to serve alcohol, but you can bring your own.

WATERFRONT RESTAURANT

TONGATAPU | $$$ | INTERNATIONAL

Vuna Rd, Nuku'alofa, 676-778 4759; www.waterfrontlodge-tonga.com; mains T$22-43

The breezy restaurant on the ground floor of Waterfront Lodge offers a more upmarket setting in which to try well-executed Tongan seafood dishes such as grilled mahi-mahi, seared tuna steak and *ota'ika* alongside steaks and Italian-style pastas. Angle for a terrace table.

MOM'S CAFÉ

TONGATAPU | $ | TONGAN

Laifone Rd, Nuku'alofa; mains T$6-20

Locals head to this simple shack for hearty portions of local staples such *lu sipi* (lamb cooked with taro leaves), *sapasui pulu* (beef chop suey) *kale moa* (chicken curry), fresh local fish with vegetables, and more.

SAMOA

Food is central to Samoan culture, with feasts marking every major life event. Influences from abroad have added a quirky dimension to the nation's culinary landscape, with the islands' star crop – coconut – playing a role in most dishes. Expect big servings everywhere.

AMOA RESTAURANT

SAVAI'I | $$$ | SAMOAN

North Coast Rd, Tuavivi; 685-53558; www.amoaresort.com; mains ST25-70

Unlike anywhere else you'll find on the island of Savai'I, the Amoa Resort's restaurant is a foodie destination unto itself. Fresh, locally sourced ingredients are used to create truly innovative takes on Samoan and Pacific classics, including *palusami* risotto balls, coconut-crusted chicken and *umu* roasted pork spaghetti.

PADDLES

UPOLU | $$$ | ITALIAN, SAMOAN

Beach Rd, Apia; 685-21819; mains ST25-60

Flavours from Samoa and Italy collide with aplomb at this terrace restaurant, where diners are welcomed like part of the Samoan-Italian *famiglia* behind it. Start with *oka* (like ceviche, with fresh tuna marinated in coconut milk) and some of the best calamari outside the Med, followed by homemade pasta marinara packed with local seafood.

SA'MOANA RESTAURANT

UPOLU | $$$ | SAMOAN, INTERNATIONAL

Salamumu Beach; 685-7672 843; www.samoanabeachbungalows.com; mains ST30-45

It's worth navigating the bumpy, unsealed road to Sa'Moana Beach Bungalows in the island's southwest, for this boutique resort's seaside restaurant is perhaps the best place on the island to ease yourself into Samoan cuisine. Think coconut-battered fish-and-chips, burgers with local fruit salsa, and bruschetta made with fresh raw local tuna. Or go full Samoan and order the coconut tuna bake.

FISH MARKET

UPOLO | $ | SEAFOOD

Off Beach Rd, Apia; fish-and-chips ST8

Battle local crowds for the best and most fresh fish-and-chips in town in an endearingly gritty, local-style setting.

WHAT TO EAT

To'ona'i
Attend Sunday mass for a chance to score an invite to this weekly tradition, which sees families gather after church for an *umu* (ground oven) feast of seafood, suckling pig, baked breadfruit, *palusami* (coconut cream wrapped in taro leaves), salads and curry dishes.

Keke 'isite
Sample these round, deep-fried doughnuts (also called *panikeke*) at street stalls.

Pani popo
Baked in a sweet coconut milk sauce, these brioche buns are a popular afternoon snack.

Palolo reefworm
On the seventh day after the full moon in October or November, locals head to worm-catching beaches to scoop up these prized blue delicacies.

PRICE RANGES

$ less than ST20
$$ ST20–35
$$$ ST35 or more

Tipping: Leave loose change.

KIRIBATI

Love seafood? Then you'll be at home in Kiribati. Like most remote Pacific island nations, the cuisine of this former British Protectorate revolves around the bounty of the sea, supplemented by the fruits of coconut, breadfruit, banana and pandanus trees, along with taro.

WHAT TO EAT

Seafood
Kiribati enjoys a more diverse banquet of local seafood than most of its neighbours, with prawns, crabs, lobster, octopus and even sandworms often on the menu.

Te waro
This dish of barbecued mantis shrimp (like a giant prawn) with rice and coconut is a local delicacy.

Pandanus
Locally known as screw pine, the nuts and leaves of the pandanus tree are used in many dishes including a dessert made by soaking boiled slices of pandanus nut in coconut cream.

Te botaki
Feasting plays a major role in the Kiribati lifestyle, with a typical *te botakai* usually including roast suckling pig and seafood.

PRICE RANGES
$ less than £10
$$ £10–40
$$$ £35 or more

Tipping: 10–15%

KOAKOA'S CORNER

TARAWA ATOLL | $$ | I-KIRIBATI
Bairiki; 686-7502 1423; mains $7-14

This cute, open-air thatched-roof place serves a good range of Pacific Chinese staples alongside local fish dishes such as sashimi, fish curry, and whole fried reef fish with coconut rice and *kangkong* (water spinach). It's also one of the very few places in Tarawa that serves breakfast.

CHATTERBOX CAFE

TARAWA ATOLL | $ | CAFE
Bikenibeu; 686-7402 8715; sandwiches $7

Doubling as a souvenir shop with locally made handicrafts and books about the island for sale, Chatterbox is known for brewing the best coffee in Tarawa. Smoothies, sandwiches, soups, and cakes are also on the menu. The air-con is a treat.

MARY'S MOTEL

TARAWA ATOLL | $ | INTERNATIONAL
Bairiki; 686-7502 2227; www.marysmoteltarawa.com; mains $7-12

One of Tarawa's most reliable hotel restaurants, Mary's serves up everything from burgers to Pacific Chinese favourites (the sizzling chicken is a good bet) with a smile. It's a good place to try sashimi, and when lobster is available, you won't regret ordering it.

COLORZ

TARAWA ATOLL | $$ | I-KIRIBATI
Bikenibeu; 686-7202 9733; www.imartkiribati.com; meals $12-15

Attached to the I-Mart supermarket are a bakery and this small oceanfront terrace restaurant serving a very short but solid menu of typical island dishes. Dinner options include fish-and-chips, a lime-infused fish burger, black pepper tuna steak, and chicken and chips. There's only one dish for lunch, which changes daily.

WHAT TO EAT

Hāngī
Experience a Māori 'barbecue', cooked in a pit over hot stones and served with *manaakitanga* (generous hospitality).

Seafood
Clean, cold oceans produce wonderful seafood, including *pāua* (abalone), crayfish and green-lipped mussels.

Lamb
With 27 million sheep nibbling its sweet grasses, lamb is NZ's favourite meat dish bar none.

Pavolva
Is it from New Zealand, Australia, or....Germany? The authorship of this fruity meringue confection is open to debate.

Southland Cheese Rolls
Slightly ironic Kiwi 'speciality': sliced white bread, filled with a cheese mixture, rolled and then grilled.

PRICE RANGES

For a main course:
$ less than $15
$$ $15–35
$$$ $35 or more

Tipping: 10%

NEW ZEALAND

New Zealand's food reputation has exploded like a rainbow-coloured gustatory firework in recent decades. A maritime country with over 15,000km of coastline, a mild climate, great agricultural diversity, a cosmopolitan, open-minded food culture and indigenous Māori flavours and cooking techniques for inspiration, Aotearoa is now a fantastic destination to fill your boots.

NERO RESTAURANT

PALMERSTON NORTH | $$$ | INTERNATIONAL

36 Amesbury St; 06-354 0312; www.nerorestaurant.co.nz; mains $42-45

Set in a refreshed 1918 Victorian with a manicured al fresco dining area, Nero is the peak of fine dining in Palmy. Carnivorous treats such as the 42-day whisky dry-aged scotch rib are outstanding, but lighter options such as pumpkin risotto and pan-seared fish are good too.

JOSH GRIGGS/COURTESY SIDART

OPUNAKE FISH, CHIPS AND MORE

SURF HIGHWAY 45 | $ | FISH & CHIPS

61 Tasman St, Opunake; 067618478; www.facebook.com/Opunakefishchipsandmore; fish $4-6.50

This is as good as fish and chips gets. Frying since the 1960s, its chips are hand cut, the range of fish includes fresh catch of the day, and the local owners are ready with a smile. Cheap, cheerful and nostalgic, it nonetheless offers gluten-free options.

SID AT THE FRENCH CAFÉ

AUCKLAND | $$$ | FRENCH

210 Symonds St, Eden Terrace; 09-377 1911; www.sidatthefrenchcafe.co.nz; tasting menu $140 per person

This legendary French restaurant has been rated one of Auckland's best for more than 20 years, and continues to excel. The cuisine is broadly French, but head chef Lesley Chandra sneaks tasty Asian and Pacific Rim touches into dishes such as spanner crab with pāua (abalone), horseradish and verjus.

GIAPO

AUCKLAND | $$ | ICE CREAM

12 Gore St, City Centre; 09-550 3677; www.giapo.com; ice cream $12-24

Queues outside this boutique ice-cream shop in the middle of winter attest to the magical confections sold within. Expect elaborate ice-cream 'art' topped with all manner of goodies: Giapo's creativity combines with gastronomic science to produce quite possibly the planet's best ice-cream extravaganzas.

AZABU

AUCKLAND | $$ | JAPANESE, PERUVIAN

26 Ponsonby Rd, Ponsonby; 09-320 5292; www.azabuponsonby.co.nz; omakase menus from $70 per person

Nikkei cuisine, an exciting blend of Japanese and Peruvian influences, is the focus at Azabu. Seated in a dramatic interior enlivened by striking images of Tokyo, you'll enjoy dishes such as tuna sashimi tostada, artichoke dumplings with mushroom puree, and snapper ceviche. Arrive early for a *margarita de verde* (with avocado, lime and jalapeño) at the attached bar, Roji.

COURTESY LOGAN BROWN

'Giapo is casual, vibrant, buzzy and hip. At its heart is the continuous revelation of what ice cream can be.'
Giapo

SIDART

AUCKLAND | $$$ | MODERN NZ

Three Lamps Plaza, 283 Ponsonby; 09-360 2122; www.sidart.co.nz; tasting menus from $120 per person

Sid Sahrawat, the guru of 'progressive Indian flavours', creates dishes unlike any other in Auckland. It's food as art and science that nonetheless fires taste buds and puts smiles on faces. Expect the unexpected: treatments such as kumara (sweet potato) roasted in gunpowder and served with lentil cream and green mango.

HELLO BEASTY

VIADUCT HARBOUR & WYNYARD QUARTER | $$ | ASIAN

95-97 Customs St W, Viaduct Harbour; 021-554 496; https://hellobeasty.nz; mains $24-36

Japanese, Korean and Chinese flavours collide with a sense of fun at this contemporary favourite. Secure a spot with ocean views, and fill your table with sharing plates of pan-fried nikiman pork buns, smokey Japanese-style tsukune (meatballs) and barbecued eggplant. New Zealand lamb and seafood is regularly featured and the thoughtful drinks list includes sake cocktails and spritzes.

TANTALUS ESTATE

WAIHEKE ISLAND | $$$ | MODERN NZ

70-72 Onetangi Rd; 09-372 2625; www.tantalus.co.nz; mains $38-44

This lovely winery restaurant channels an Iberian ambience, but offers a menu that freely roams the globe. Sit under chandeliers crafted from tree branches and enjoy dishes that complement their Rhone- and Bordeaux-style wines: beef tenderloin with chocolate, alliums and cranberries or spiced duck leg with black garlic, beetroot and blackberries.

GABLES

RUSSELL | $$ | CONTEMPORARY

19 The Strand; 09-403 7670; www.thegablesrestaurant.co.nz; mains $28-44

Serving an imaginative take on Kiwi classics (local rack of lamb sits on pumpkin/potato puree with goat's cheese, mint jelly and candied walnuts), the Gables occupies an 1847 building on the waterfront that uses whale vertebrae for foundations. Ask for a window table for maritime views and expect top-notch local produce, including Orongo Bay oysters and small-producer cheese.

DUNE

WHANGAREI DISTRICT | $$ | CAFÉ

40 Moir St, Mangawhai; 09-431 5695; www.facebook.com/thedunemangawhai; mains $25-35

In the heart of the village, far from the sand, Dune is half bar, half cafe – with sunny outdoor tables arrayed around both. The food – including a deliciously smoky brisket, wood-fired pizza and lots of yummy vegetable side dishes – makes good use of produce sourced from the owners' family farms.

CLAREVILLE BAKERY

THE WAIRARAPA | $ | BAKERY

3340 SH2, Clareville; 06-379 5333; www.theclarevillebakery.co.nz; mains $16-20

This brilliant bakery-cafe is famous for its sourdough bread, lamb-cutlet pie, and hot-beef Reuben sandwich – but everything displayed on the counter is borderline irresistible. There's garden seating, a play area for the kids and regular live-music evenings.

Previous spread: Dish from Sidart; Fried squid from Logan Brown.

LOGAN BROWN

WELLINGTON | $$$ | CONTEMPORARY
192 Cuba St, Te Aro; 04-830 2413; www.loganbrown.co.nz; chef's menu $105 per person

Mixing comfortably with Wellington's best restaurants, Logan Brown oozes class without being overly formal. Its 1920s banking-chamber dining room is a neoclassical stunner – a fitting complement to produce-driven modern NZ creations such as pāua (abalone) ravioli with coriander, lime and basil beurre blanc and Fiordland venison with cauliflower, poivrade (pepper sauce) and horseradish gremolata.

SHEPHERD

WELLINGTON | $$ | CONTEMPORARY
1/5 Eva St, Te Aro; 04-385 7274; www.shepherdrestaurant.co.nz; mains $29-36

This good Shepherd guides its trusting flock through fusion flavours, unusual produce and pickled accompaniments. Start with Cloudy Bay clams with Szechuan pork, kumara (sweet potato) and coriander, then progress to roast carrots with harissa, pumpkin seeds, tofu, pickled raisins and nigella seeds.

REFINERY

COROMANDEL PENINSULA | $ | CAFÉ
5 Willoughby St, Paeroa; 07-862 7678; www.the-refinery.co.nz; light meals $14-19

Get pleasantly lost in the Refinery, a spacious showcase of 1960s and 1970s Kiwiana style including a turntable where customers are encouraged to play the vinyl records. Good coffee and food (especially the grilled sandwiches – try the Cuban) are best enjoyed draped over the retro furniture within the heritage building.

HAYES COMMON

WAIKATO | $$ | CAFÉ
Cnr Plunket Tce & Jellicoe Dr, Hamilton East; 07-859 1041; www.hayescommon.co.nz; mains $32-36

Housed in a former garage, charmingly unpretentious Hayes Common offers breakfasts such as smoothie bowls and chilli-butter fried eggs, and lunches such as hoisin-spiced duck tortilla. Dinner options include spiced Merino lamb and thoughtful vegan options, complemented by a good wine list and local craft beers on tap.

SOUTHERN MEAT KITCHEN

LAKE TAUPO REGION | $$ | SOUTH AMERICAN
40 Tuwharetoa St, Taupo; 07-378 3582; www.smk.co.nz; mains $22-34

Taupo's foremost purveyor of dude food, SMK slow-cooks beef brisket, pulled pork and shredded chicken on an American wood-fire smoker. Laden plates also bear sides such as pit beans, mac'n'cheese, slaw and rice, but try to save room for jalapeño-and-cheddar cornbread with honey butter.

This page: Harry's Hawker House. Opposite page: Cocktail from Public Kitchen & Bar.

MACAU

BAY OF PLENTY | $$ | ASIAN
59 The Strand, Tauranga; 07-578 8717; www.dinemacau.co.nz; mains $19-30

Zingy pan-Asian flavours shine at Tauranga's top restaurant. Dishes, designed for sharing, include lamb-rib san choy bow (lettuce cups), tempura eggplant in Sichuan-spiced caramel, and moreish steamed buns with roasted pork belly. Stylish decor, Asian-inspired cocktails and a good craft-beer list complete the picture.

ELEPHANT HILL

HAWKE'S BAY | $$$ | MODERN NZ
86 Clifton Rd, Te Awanga; 06-872 6060; www.elephanthill.co.nz; mains $36-41

Outstanding even amongst this region's riches of winery-restaurants, Elephant Hill pairs its award-winning wines with wonderful, seasonal food. Huge picture windows provide unencumbered views of Cape Kidnappers and the plantings – pleasant visual fodder to accompany dishes such as gamefish with ponzu marshmallow, *goma-ae* (Japanese sesame-dressed greens) and sea grapes, or Hawkes Bay lamb rump with anchovy, garlic and silverbeet pie.

BISTRONOMY

NAPIER | $$$ | MODERN NZ
40 Hastings St; 06-834 4309; www.bistronomy.co.nz; chef's menus from $80 per person

Bistronomy is proof that some of NZ's best food can be enjoyed outside the biggest cities. The finely judged seasonal tasting menus, which could include Patangata beef tartare with lardo and hibiscus poached rhubarb or local fish with a smoky mousse and sea chicory, are highly recommended.

MISTER D

NAPIER | $$ | MODERN NZ
47 Tennyson St; 06-835 5022; www.misterd.co.nz; mains $29-34

This long, timber-floored room with its green-tiled bar is the pride of the Napier foodie scene. Hip and slick but not unaffordable, its quick-fire service delivers bone-marrow ravioli with salsa verde or fish cooked in a bag with Hohepa yoghurt and saffron butter to tables of demonstrably happy diners.

FOWLERS OYSTERS

CENTRAL SOUTHLAND | $$ | SEAFOOD
Ocean Beach Rd, Bluff; 03-212 8792;

COURTESY HARRY'S HAWKER HOUSE

COURTESY PUBLIC KITCHEN & BAR

www.facebook.com/fowlersoysters; half-dozen cooked $14.50, dozen raw from $24

Oyster-lovers must stop at Fowlers during the season for the best bivalves on the South Island. It's on the left-hand side as you head into Bluff, a town renowned for its oysters.

CHOP SHOP

ARROWTOWN | $$ | CAFÉ

7 Arrow Lane; 03-442; 1116; www.facebook.com/thechopshopfoodmerchants; mains $22-28

While the open kitchen and close-packed tables leave little space, this popular place is uniformly fabulous. Its food roams the globe (Levantine lamb shawarma, Mexican huevos rancheros, Korean bulgogi pork sliders) and the décor is interesting.

BESPOKE KITCHEN

QUEENSTOWN | $$ | CAFÉ

9 Isle St; 03-409 0552; www.bespokekitchen.co.nz; mains $20-23

Bespoke is the model of a smart Kiwi café: great counter food, beautiful cooked options (including vegan plates such as eggs 'benedict' with winter greens) outdoor seats with mountain views and, of course, great coffee. It was named NZ's cafe of 2015.

PUBLIC KITCHEN & BAR

QUEENSTOWN | $$ | MODERN NZ

Steamer Wharf, Beach St; 03-442 5969; www.publickitchen.co.nz; mains $26-38

Local is the law at this excellent lake-front eatery: Cardrona lamb, Fiordland venison, Geraldine pork, South Island fish. Plates of varying sizes allow

WHERE TO EAT...

JUST-CAUGHT SEAFOOD

Auckland Fish Market, Auckland NI
A 2019 upgrade brought food vendors to Auckland's premier retail fish market. Whatever's freshest from NZ's waters ends up here.

Te Matuku Seafood Market, Waiheke Island NI
Super-fresh scallops, clams, squid and fish sell alongside fancy deli goods at this market on Waiheke Island.

Coromandel Oyster Company, Coromandel NI
Take away squeaky-fresh oysters, mussels and clams or grab a table for flounder and chips or seafood chowder.

Oyster Cove, Bluff SI
Wrap-around windows with spectacular sea-views provide the ideal backdrop for sampling Bluff's famous oysters.

groups to mix-and-match, and meaty dishes such as braised beef cheeks with roasted cauliflower and raisins are particularly good.

BRACKEN

DUNEDIN | $$ | MODERN NZ
95 Filleul St; 03-477 9779; www.brackenrestaurant.co.nz; menus from $49 per person

Bracken's seasonal tasting menus offer pretty little plates graced with Scottish touches reflecting Dunedin's strong Caledonian heritage. While dishes such as Cullen Skink (smoked-fish soup) with smoked salmon and oat cakes are finely prepared, nothing's overly fussy, (very much like the old, classy-yet-informal wooden house Bracken occupies).

OTAGO FARMERS MARKET

DUNEDIN | $ | MARKET
Dunedin Railway Station; www.otagofarmersmarket.org.nz

This thriving market is all local, all edible (or drinkable) and mostly organic. Grab a freshly baked pastry and a flat white to sustain you while you browse fresh meat, seafood, veg and cheese.

FLEUR'S PLACE

MOERAKI | $$$ | SEAFOOD
Old Jetty, 169 Haven St; 03-439 4480; www.fleursplace.com; mains $22-45

This basic-looking fishing hut houses one of the South Island's best seafood restaurants. Its straightforward decor mirrors its unfussy handling of super-fresh seafood. Tuck into fresh shellfish, tender blue cod and other recently landed ocean bounty. There's a smokehouse onsite and you can even try titi (muttonbird) here.

RIVERSTONE KITCHEN

OAMARU | $$ | GASTRONOMY
1431 SH1, Waitaki Bridge; 03-431 3505; www.riverstonekitchen.co.nz; mains $36

A riverstone fireplace and polished concrete floors set the scene for a menu that's modern without being overworked. Award-winning chef Bevan Smith sources much of his produce from the extensive on-site kitchen gardens, adding locally sourced venison, pork, salmon, beef and wine.

5TH STREET

CHRISTCHURCH | $$$ | BISTRO
5 Elgin St, Sydenham; 03-365 9667; www.5thstreet.co.nz; mains $40-48

Global influences are splashed across the menu at this convivial bistro, serving food to share. The honey- and chipotle-fired chicken goes well with beers from Christchurch's Three Boys Brewery, while the pomegranate-glazed lamb shoulder partners with charred brassicas with almond dukkah, garlic hummus and feta. The cocktails are excellent too.

RIVERSIDE MARKET

CHRISTCHURCH | $$ | MARKET
96 Oxford Tce; www.riverside.nz; meals $10-20

Mandatory for visiting foodies, this multi-level market combines fresh produce stalls with abundant opportunities to eat and drink. Many of the city's most popular food trucks are represented, so great coffee, souvlaki, Argentinean barbecue, ramen, craft beer and more are close at hand.

EARL

CHRISTCHURCH | $$ | BISTRO
128 Lichfield St; 03-365 1147; www.earl.co.nz; mains $28-36

Earl's spacious dining room encourages groups to share plates of slow-cooked lamb with smoked yoghurt, taleggio *croquetas*, grilled octopus and *crudo* (raw) fish. The 'Eat like an Earl' option presents the chef's favourites, while the concise wine list highlights different local producers each week.

FAIRLIE BAKEHOUSE

SOUTH CANTERBURY | $ | BAKERY
74 Main St, Fairlie; 03-685 6063; www.liebers.co.nz; pies $5-8.50

Fairlie's best bakery turns out exceptional pies, including the legendary salmon and bacon and the 'ultimate steak pie' (with cheese and mushroom). On the sweet side, American doughnuts and raspberry cheesecake feature alongside Kiwi classics such as custard squares and cream buns.

WAIRAU RIVER

MARLBOROUGH REGION | $$ | INTERNATIONAL
11 Rapaura Rd, Rapaura; 03-572 9800; www.wairauriverwines.com; mains $22-30

This modish mud-brick cellar door and bistro has a wide veranda and beautiful gardens with plenty of shade. The adventurous menu features the likes of *togarashi* (Japanese spice mix) encrusted prawns with miso mayo, Marlborough mussel chowder, braised beef cheeks with *sambal* (Malaysian chilli paste) and hot-smoked salmon salad.

HARRY'S HAWKER HOUSE

NELSON REGION | $$ | ASIAN
296 Trafalgar St, Nelson; 03-539 0905; www.hawkerhouse.co.nz; mains $24-28

Order a fruity cocktail in a dim bar imbued with the glamour of old Shanghai before delving into creative dishes inspired by the street food of China and Southeast Asia. Beef-cheek rendang roti rolls and Thai-spiced salmon gravlax are just some of the many options to share.

WHERE TO EAT...

MODERN KIWI CUISINE

Oxford, Timaru SI
Stylish in its 1925 digs, this forward-looking restaurant treats South Island produce reverently.

Plato, Dunedin SI
Kooky décor belies the talent of a kitchen doing clever things to shellfish and other seasonal treats.

Odette's, Auckland NI
Odette's offbeat, relaxing dining room is the ideal setting for imaginative, market-fresh food.

Cable Bay, Waiheke Island NI
Sculptures, paintings and delightful views set the scene for exquisite food.

Huhu, Waitomo Caves NI
Slow-cooked lamb, smoked salmon and duck are just some of the delights elevated by Huhu's inventive treatment.

AFGHANISTAN

Its position at the confluence of four distinct cultural regions – Central Asia, the Middle East, Far East and Indian subcontinent – means Afghanistan's food has many influences. War has severely damaged the structures of society, but hospitality remains integral to local culture, particularly at meal times. Traditionally, food is served communally around low tables with large cushion seating. Rice, kebabs and nan are mainstays, and the country is known for its fruit crops such as grapes, melons and pomegranates. The national dish is *qabli pulao* – a steaming mountain of spiced rice, topped with almonds, raisins, grated carrots, and chicken or lamb.

BURKINA FASO

Burkinabé food is largely influenced by Senegalese and Ivoirian cuisines, though upmarket restaurants usually carry a French flavour. Locals head for basic *maquis*, which serve cheap meals and beer. Most dishes involve sauces – especially *arachide* (peanut) or *graine* (a hot sauce made with palm nuts) – served with a starch, usually rice. Grilled dishes of chicken, mutton, beef, guinea fowl, fish (especially Nile perch, known locally as capitaine) and agouti (a large rodent) are also commonplace menu items.

CENTRAL AFRICAN REPUBLIC

More than 75% of the population in CAR rely on subsistence farming, but in December 2018 the UN estimated that about a quarter of the population was at risk of famine. Cassava, koko (a little like grass), and bushmeat (particularly monkey, python and antelope) are all typical foods, usually complemented by a dash of *piment* (hot sauce).

CHAD

The food in Chad is typical of the Central African region: tiny street stalls dish up meals of rice, beans and soup or stew, while indoor restaurants offer omelettes, liver, salads, *brochettes* (kebabs), fish and *nachif* (minced meat in sauce).

LIBYA

Eating is a great social event in Libyan culture, though the food itself is not the most exciting in the region. Its cuisine shares many attributes with other North African nations: couscous is the national dish, while chickpeas and bread are also staples. *Shwarma* (strips of sliced meat in a pocket of bread) is a popular street snack. The country has a tradition of tea drinking (sweet, of course) and cooking meat and breads in sand pits.

MALI

Meal times in Mali are joyous, carb-loaded affairs, with most dishes revolving around one of the country's staple cereal grains (rice, millet or sorghum) accompanied by meat or fish in a sauce, often of edible leaves such as spinach or baobab. Food culture and typical dishes vary significantly between the north (arid, desert-like) and south (tropical).

MAURITANIA

The food culture of Mauritania is a tale of two halves. In the north, where the country borders Morocco and the Western Sahara, it is the desert cuisine of the Moors. There is very little agriculture in these arid parts, and most fruit and vegetables are imported. The cuisine of southern Mauritania, meanwhile, is essentially Senegalese and has more variety, spices and veg. Classic Mauritanian dishes include *mafé*, a groundnut-based stew, and *méchoui*, a traditional nomads' feast, where an entire lamb is roasted over a fire.

NIGER

Niger is a desert nation whose food culture stems from the nomadic Tuareg people. Dates, yoghurt, rice and mutton are standard Tuareg fare, while *riz sauce* (rice with sauce) is omnipresent in Niger's south. Standard restaurant dishes include grilled fish (particularly capitaine, or Nile perch), chicken, and beef brochettes. Couscous is also popular.

SOMALIA/SOMALILAND

The culinary traditions of Somalia, including the self-proclaimed Republic of Somaliland, are regional and varied thanks to influences from centuries of trade and colonisation. Perhaps most surprising is that pasta (called baasto locally as there's no 'p' in the Somali alphabet) is almost a de facto national dish – a legacy of Italy's colonisation of southern Somalia in the 1880s. Camels and goats provide most of the meat. Loxo, a spongy flat bread similar to Ethiopia's *injera*, is also a staple, either to mop up stews or for breakfast with a smear of butter and honey, dunked in tea.

SOUTH SUDAN

In 2019 it was reported than some seven million people are under threat of famine in South Sudan. The culinary repertoire is basic. Staples include pounded millet, *fuul* (stewed broad beans) and *ta'amiya*, known elsewhere as falafel. Rivers, including the Nile, and lakes also provide fresh fish such as perch and tilapia.

SYRIA

Syrian food culture is a rich and diverse facet of the national identity, but one that is sadly being threatened by a decade of unrelenting war. Much of its cuisine shares Levantine roots with its Arab neighbours, and typical dishes include kibbeh, tabbouleh, fattoush, hummus and falafel, while cooks prize lamb above all other meats. Kebabs and baklava are thought to be a legacy of the Ottoman Empire's influence in the region. Mezze is a common way to start a meal.

YEMEN

Set to become the world's poorest country if war continues, this Muslim nation teeters on the brink of suffering the world's worst famine. Historically, its food culture bears similarities to other countries of the Middle East, but is also influenced by nearby East Africa. The main meal of the day is lunch, and common dishes include *saltah* (a brown meat broth with fenugreek, herbs, tomatoes and chillies), and *mandi* (spiced rice with meat cooked in an underground pit).

BURUNDI

Although tiny, Burundi's access to huge Lake Tanganyika provides fish for the table and the country's volcanic soil gives fertile farming lands – agriculture covers around 80% of this central African country and crops include coffee, beans, corn and maize. As such, meals are loaded with fresh vegetables and fruits such as banana, cassava and sweet potato, usually boiled, stewed or roasted over wood fires. Stewed beans are a daily staple.

IRAQ

Iraq is the heartland of ancient Mesopotamia and some aspects of its food culture can be traced back 10,000 years. Its cuisine also shares dishes with its Levantine neighbours to the west and Persian influences from Iran. Lamb, tahini, honey, dates, yoghurt and rose water are all typical in Iraqi cuisine. Spiced biryani is a classic dish, as is *dolma* (grape leaves stuffed with rice or meat), kebab, and *masgoulf* (grilled skewers of fresh carp).

HAITI

In Haiti you can spend just a few gourdes on *fritay* (fried street food) or dine in posh Pétionville for US prices. The most typical food venue is a bar-resto (less formal than a proper restaurant), where you can gorge on a plateful of goat or chicken with plantains, salad and a beer, all for just a few dollars. Vegetables aren't common, but fresh fruit is plentiful. Excellent seafood is abundant along the coast.

VENEZUELA

Due to the dire economic situation in Venezuela, restaurants will seem cheap to foreigners but in many places there's a lack of fresh food. *Panaderías* (bakeries) are ubiquitous and popular for breakfast, selling sandwiches, pastries and yogurt, as well as delicious espresso. Venezuelan chocolate is some of the best in the world. Typical street snacks include empanadas and *arepa* (grilled corn pancakes stuffed with cheese, beef or other fillings), and the national dish is *pabellón criollo* – shredded beef, black beans, rice and plantains.

NAURU

Coconut, seafood and root vegetables are the traditional foods of Nauru, but this remote Micronesian island (the smallest island nation in the world) now has such poor soil that virtually nothing will grow here. Most of the foods available are tinned, processed and imported, except for what comes out of the Pacific waters.

INDEX

Lonely Planet's The Best Places To Eat In Every Country
May 2021
Published by Lonely Planet Global Limited
CRN 554153
www.lonelyplanet.com
10 9 8 7 6 5 4 3 2 1

Printed in Malaysia
ISBN 978 18386 9047 2

Publisher & VP Print: Piers Pickard
Commissioning Editor: Dora Ball
Designers: Brooke Ann, Catalina Aragón, Ania Bartoszek, Virginia Moreno, Kerry Rubenstein
Product Editor: Amy Lynch
Assistant Editors: Daniel Bolger, Claire Rourke
Contributors: Isabel Albiston, James Bainbridge, Mark Baker, Joe Bindloss, Greg Bloom, Jean-Bernard Carillet, Megan Eaves, Alex Egerton, Gemma Graham, Paul Harding, Jess Lee, Tom Masters, Lorna Parkes, Kevin Raub, Sarah Reid, Simon Richmond, Brendan Sainsbury, James Smart, Helena Smith, Polly Thomas, Anna Tyler, Brana Vladisavljevic, Tasmin Waby, Jenny Walker, Kerry Walker, Luke Waterson, Nicola Williams, Karla Zimmerman
Print Production: Nigel Longuet

Cover images: Lindsay Lauckner Gundlock; Ai Di Tsuke / EyeEm; JerSean Golatt; Jonathan Stokes; Justin Foulkes; Chip Kalback; River Thompson; Mark Weins; Alicia Taylor/Lonely Planet ©
Contents images: Alicia Taylor; JerSean Golatt; Lindsay Lauckner Gundlock; Chip Kalback; Ai Di Tsuke / EyeEm/Lonely Planet ©
Illustrations: Elena Pimonova; Daria Ustiugova; Myasnikova Natali; Lena Vetka; Marina Dormidontova; Natalia Hubbert; Gibanessa; Le Panda; Botanical Watercolor; Margarita L/Shutterstock ©

Lonely Planet Offices

Ireland
Digital Depot, Roe Lane (off Thomas St),
Digital Hub, Dublin 8,
D08 TCV4

USA
230 Franklin Rd, Building 2B
Franklin, Tennessee
37064

STAY IN TOUCH lonelyplanet.com/contact

Paper in this book is certified against the Forest Stewardship Council™ standards. FSC™ promotes environmentally responsible, socially beneficial and economically viable management of the world's forests.